A Civil W

A Contemporary Issues Reader

Elizabeth Cloninger Long

SACRAMENTO CITY COLLEGE

Longman

New York   San Francisco   Boston
London   Toronto   Sydney   Tokyo   Singapore   Madrid
Mexico City   Munich   Paris   Cape Town   Hong Kong   Montreal

To my most civil family

Mike
Annabelle
Annelise

Vice President/Editor-in-Chief: Joe Terry
Senior Acquisitions Editor: Steven Rigolosi
Marketing Manager: Melanie Craig
Supplements Editor: Donna Campion
Production Manager: Denise Phillip
Project Coordination, Text Design, and Electronic Page Makeup: WestWords, Inc.
Cover Design Manager: Wendy Ann Fredericks
Cover Designer: Kay Petronio
Cover Illustration: ©Lisa Gador/Getty Images, Inc./Artville LLC
Photo Researcher: WestWords, Inc.
Manufacturing Buyer: Al Dorsey
Printer and Binder: Hamilton Printers
Cover Printer: Coral Graphics

For permission to use copyrighted material, grateful acknowledgment is made to the copyright holders on pp. 518–521, which are hereby made part of this copyright page.

Library of Congress Cataloging-in-Publication Data

A civil word: a contemporary issues reader / by Elizabeth Cloninger Long.
    p. cm.
  Includes index.
  ISBN 0-321-08819-0
  1. Civil society. 2. Courtesy. 3. Etiquette. I. Long, Elizabeth Cloninger.

  JC337 .C57 2002
  300—dc21

                                                                    2001050532

Please visit our website at http://www.ablongman.com

ISBN 0-321-08819-0

1 2 3 4 5 6 7 8 9 10—HT—05 04 03 02

Brief Contents

Detailed Contents

Rhetorical Contents

Note: *Since pretty much everything in* A Civil Word *can be classified as an argument, the "argument" section of the rhetorical table of contents includes all but the most strictly modally defined essays (i.e., those essays that are almost purely cause and effect or definition or any other mode). Further, the placement of an essay under a particular heading indicates the presence of that mode, but does not mean that the entire essay is written in that mode. Hence, one essay may show up under two or three different headings, depending upon the number of modes employed.*

Description

Humor

Illustration and Example

Narrative

Process Analysis

Journalism[*]

*This is not a formal literary mode, but several of the readings come from newspapers and, as such, are written in a different style from those written for other audiences.

Preface

Civility, or the lack thereof, affects everyone. Every day the news reports incidents of injury due to people's inconsiderate words (sexual harassment, racial slurs), inconsiderate driving (road rage), inconsiderate displays by public figures (poor sportsmanship, negative campaigning), inconsiderate treatment of the environment (littering, water pollution) and others, all of which, before they become illegal, are simply examples of a failure to consider how one's behavior affects others. While saying that all conflicts can be solved by a quick skim of Emily Post is overly simple and unrealistic, recognizing that the connections between breaches in common courtesy and crime are close can help prevent minor aggravations from becoming major problems. The abundance of rudeness throughout different aspects of society raises many questions: What does civility entail? In what aspects of life does incivility manifest itself? Who is responsible for being civil? Where does civility end and the law begin? At what point is civility unnecessary or irrelevant? Does the definition of civility change with every generation? A contemporary issues-based reader with a slant toward civility, *A Civil Word* addresses these questions and more.

A second key reason for creating this text is that students care about civility more than we think they do. Whether they have been home-schooled or attended large, diverse public schools, students have encountered different types of behavior and have likely thought, at some level, about how people's actions—their bosses', their friends', their leaders'—affect them. In fact, civility issues are inherent in all of today's hottest and most controversial topics—from gender conflicts to diversity, from the environment to technology, and others. While mentioning "manners" seems likely to produce eye-rolling in students, they are the first ones to mention "that jerk who took my parking place" or the professional athlete who's been suspended yet again and, in turn, causes his team to suffer. Students are also the first to exonerate themselves from the charge of rudeness by offering "reasons" for their incivility: "She takes things too personally," "But he cut me off, so I had to speed up," "I might not act this way if you treated me with more respect." However, students may not have critically examined the impact their actions have on others or the effects of incivility on society as a whole. As students move toward careers and greater responsibilities in their personal lives, they need to understand how the impressions they make, through their words and actions, can have lasting consequences on their lives and on the lives of those around them.

Finally, considering others is part of good writing. One of the biggest challenges for students in the college composition classroom is to recognize that they are writing for an audience that extends beyond themselves and their classmates. Many students have difficulty separating what they know about a topic from what other people know and, thus, these students have gaps of information and explanation in their writing. Emphasizing that good writing is like good manners in that the writer must first consider another person, the reader, helps students see how ingrained civility is an advantage in writing as well as in life. *A Civil Word* gives teachers and students the opportunity to explore key issues affecting society in the new millenium while offering them the option of examining these issues in the light of civility.

Goals and Themes

While the overriding goal of *A Civil Word* is to raise students' consciousness about their own actions and the actions of those around them, the pedagogical goal is to sharpen students' critical thinking skills through synthesis of outside sources and analysis exercises. Additionally, the text encourages students to develop their own writing processes through the pre- and post-reading questions and group activities for every reading.

Content Overview/Organization

Source Book
- A Brief Guide to Reading Critically and Writing Well
- A Brief Guide to Writing Argument
- A Brief Guide to Evaluating Internet Sources

Overview: Defining Civility: Different Views
- Defines civility in different contexts
- Explores whether people are inherently civil or uncivil
- Raises the issue of whether we need behavior codes other than law

Chapter 1: Everyday Incivility
- Presents examples of "everyday" uncivil acts
- Questions whether incivility is becoming a greater problem
- Explores causes for contemporary incivility
- Explores ways to address incivility

Chapter 2: Incivility in Pop Culture
- Explores the role of civility in popular music, film, and television
- Examines the relationship between people's desires for entertainment and civility
- Asks whether incivility in popular culture in on the rise or on the wane

Chapter 3: Incivility in the Media

- Examines the ubiquitous nature of press coverage
- Weighs the individual's right to privacy against the public's right for news
- Explores possible licensing regulation for media members
- Questions whether media benefits outweigh media drawbacks

Chapter 4: Civility on Campus

- Examines the apparent rise in incivility on campus
- Questions who is responsible for classroom civility: teachers or students
- Explores possible causes for increased incivility
- Explores some educators' solutions for addressing campus incivility

Chapter 5: Civility and Technology

- Identifies electronic means of communication
- Explores benefits and drawbacks of different communication forms
- Explores the role of anonymity as a factor contributing to incivility
- Examines possible causes for and solutions to technology-oriented incivility

Chapter 6: Civility in the Workplace

- Identifies different types of work-related incivility
- Questions causes for workplace incivility
- Examines benefits of workplace civility
- Explores positive and negative effects of affirmative action

Chapter 7: Civility Toward the Environment

- Explores forms and consequences of environmental incivility
- Offers suggestions for civility toward animals and the environment
- Questions the point at which the environment and animals need protection from humans
- Examines the points at which the environment begins and ends serving humans

Chapter 8: Civility in Our Heroes

- Offers different, nontraditional descriptions of "heroes"
- Defines "hero" in different contexts
- Examines the role of the media in creating heroes and scapegoats
- Explores contemporary values contributing to, or confused with, heroism

Chapter 9: New Millenium Incivility: Are Manners a Generational Phenomenon?

- Identifies areas of contemporary civility and incivility
- Examines effects of younger generations on civility

- Questions the point at which incivility becomes cruelty
- Explores benefits of traditional etiquette and values

Chapter 10: Can Civility Go Too Far?
- Identifies contemporary areas where civility has negative consequences
- Questions the point at which civility becomes negative
- Examines effects of artificial civility

Features/Benefits

- **Flexible Assignments** provide opportunities for discussions of topics within a civility context but allow for discussions of the topics as distinct units unto themselves.
- **Chapter Summary Page** presents easy-to-read list of selected readings per chapter.
- **Guide to reading critically and writing well** provides overview to general writing skills.
- **Guide to argument** offers brief overview of elements of persuasion.
- **Internet evaluation section** provides guidelines for choosing and using online sources.
- **Multiple skill level, multicultural readings** allows students to experience easy-to-follow texts as well as more complex essays written by writers of all backgrounds.
- **Pre-reading critical thinking and writing exercises** allow students to consider a topic without the pressure of a formal assignment.
- **Vocabulary activities** as both pre- and post-reading activities enhance students' comprehension and sentence-variation skills.
- **Content, structure, and critical thinking questions** for every reading give students tools for greater comprehension and analysis.
- **Post-reading questions** encourage students to consider civility as a possible discussion topic but allow for other discussion possibilities as well.
- **Hands-on group activities** incorporate students' own experiences into their reading and writing while working collaboratively.
- **End-of-chapter synthesis questions** provide opportunities for students to integrate chapter readings into formal writing assignments.
- **List of relevant websites** for further study at beginning of each chapter allow students to pursue knowledge of a topic on their own.
- **Readings organized from least to most challenging** allow instructors to balance assignments according to level of difficulty.
- **Emphasis on textual analysis and integration of sources** help students to illustrate their ideas through outside sources.

Instructor's Manual for the Teachers: Integrating Civility in the Classroom (0-321-08820-4)

- Offers specific strategies for incorporating etiquette into the classroom through reading, writing, and critical thinking activities
- Provides activities as a means of creating a forum for discussing classroom incivility
- Provides guides for establishing a civil learning environment through syllabi and assignments
- Offers means for integrating civility into any, or all, lesson plans
- Includes a comprehension quiz for each reading in this text

Representative Tips and Activities in Instructor's Manual:

- Group activity guidelines
- Etiquette spectrum outlined via class and group discussion
- Etiquette lessons integrated into the curriculum
- Classroom management strategies
- Relevant, civility-oriented handouts
- Internet chat room civility exercise

The Teaching and Learning Package

In addition to the instructor's manual described earlier, a series of other skills-based supplements is available for both instructors and students. All of these supplements are available either free or at greatly reduced prices

For Additional Reading and Reference

The Dictionary Deal   Two dictionaries can be shrinkwrapped with *A Civil Word* at a nominal fee. *The New American Webster Handy College Dictionary* is a paperback reference text with more than 100,000 entries. *Merriam Webster's Collegiate Dictionary,* tenth edition, is a hardback reference with a citation file of more than 14.5 million examples of English words drawn from actual use. For more information on how to shrinkwrap a dictionary with your text, please contact your Longman sales representative.

Penguin Quality Paperback Titles   A series of Penguin paperbacks is available at a significant discount when shrinkwrapped with this text. Some titles available are Toni Morrison's *Beloved,* Julia Alvarez's *How the Garcia Girls Lost Their Accents,* Mark Twain's *Huckleberry Finn, Narrative of the Life of Frederick Douglass,* Harriet Beecher Stowe's *Uncle Tom's Cabin,* Dr. Martin Luther King, Jr.'s *Why We Can't Wait,* and plays by Shakespeare, Miller, and Albee. For a complete list of titles or more information, please contact your Longman sales consultant.

100 Things to Write About   This 100-page book contains 100 individual assignments for writing on a variety of topics and in a wide range of formats, from expressive to analytical. Ask your Longman sales representative for a sample copy. 0-673-98239-4

Newsweek Alliance Instructors may choose to shrinkwrap a 12-week subscription to *Newsweek* with any Longman text. The price of the subscription is 57 cents per issue (a total of $6.84 for the subscription). Available with the subscription is a free "Interactive Guide to *Newsweek*"—a workbook for students who are using the text. In addition, *Newsweek* provides a wide variety of instructor supplements free to teachers, including maps, Skills Builders, and weekly quizzes. For more information on the *Newsweek* program, please contact your Longman sales represetative.

Electronic and Online Offerings

≶NEW≷ **The Longman Writer's Warehouse** The innovative and exciting online supplement is the perfect accompaniment to any developmental writing course. Developed by developmental English instructors specially for developing writers, The Writer's Warehouse covers every part of the writing process. Also included are journaling capabilities, multimedia activities, diagnostic tests, an interactive handbook, and complete instructor's manual. The Writer's Warehouse requires no space on your school's server; rather, students complete and store their work on the Longman server, and are able to access it, revise it, and continue working at any time. For more details about how to shrinkwrap a free subscription to The Writer's Warehouse with this text, please consult your Longman sales representative. For a free guided tour of the site, visit **http://longmanwriterswarehouse.com.**

The Writer's ToolKit Plus This CD-ROM offers a wealth of tutorial, exercise, and reference material for writers. It is compatible with either a PC or a Macintosh platform, and is flexible enough to be used either occasionally for practice or regularly in class lab sessions. For information on how to bundle this CD-ROM FREE with your text, please contact your Longman sales representative.

The Longman English Pages Web Site Both students and instructors can visit our free content-rich Web site for aditional reading selections and writing exercises. From the Longman English pages, visitors can conduct a simulated Web search, learn how to write a resume and cover letter, or try their hand at poetry writing. Stop by and visit us at **http://ablongman.com/englishpages.**

The Longman Electronic Newsletter Twice a month during the spring and fall, instructors who have subscribed receive a free copy of the Longman Developmental English Newsletter in their e-mailbox. Written by experienced classroom instructors, the newsletter offers teaching tips, classroom activities, book reviews, and more. To subscribe, visit the Longman Developmental English Website at **http://www.ablongman.com/basicskills**, or send an e-mail to **Basic Skills@ablongman.com.**

For Instructors

≶NEW≷ **Electronic Test Bank for Writing** This electronic test bank features more than 5,000 questions in all areas of writing, from grammar to paragraphing, through essay writing, research, and documentation. With this easy-to-use CD-ROM, instructors simply choose questions from the electronic test bank, then print out the completed test for distribution. CD-ROM: 0-321-08117-X Print version: 0-321-08486-1

Competency Profile Test Bank, Second Edition   This series of 60 objective tests covers ten general areas of English competency, including fragments, comma splices and run-ons, pronouns, commas, and capitalization. Each test is available in remedial, standard, and advanced versions. Available as reproducible sheets or in computerized versions. Free to instructors. Paper version: 0-321-02224-6. Computerized IBM: 0-321-02633-0. Computerized Mac: 0-321-02632-2

Diagnostic and Editing Tests and Exercises, Fourth Edition   This collection of diagnostic tests helps instructors assess students' competence in Standard Written English for purpose of placement or to gauge progress. Available as reproducible sheets or in computerized versions, and free to instructors. Paper: 0-321-10022-0. CD-ROM: 0-321-10499-4

ESL Worksheets, Third Edition   These reproducible worksheets provide ESL students with extra practice in areas they find the most troublesome. A diagnostic test and post-test are provided, along with answer keys and suggested topics for writing. Free to adopters. 0-321-07765-2

Longman Editing Exercises   54 pages of paragraph editing exercises give students extra practice using grammar skills in the context of longer passages. Free when packaged with any Longman title. 0-205-31792-8

80 Practices   A collection of reproducible, ten-item exercises that provide additional practices for specific grammatical usage problems, such as comma splices, capitalization, and pronouns. Includes an answer key, and free to adopters. 0-673-53422-7

CLAST Test Package, Fourth Edition   These two 40-item objective tests evaluate students' readiness for the CLAST exams. Strategies for teaching CLAST preparedness are included. Free with any Longman English title. Reproducible sheets: 0-321-01950-4. Computerized IBM version: 0-321-01982-2. Computerized Mac version: 0-321-01983-0

TASP Test Package, Third Edition   These 12 practice pre-tests and post-tests assess the same reading and writing skills covered in the TASP examination. Free with any Longman English title. Reproducible sheets: 0-321-01959-8. Computerized IBM version: 0-321-01985-7. Computerized Mac version: 0-321-01984-9

***Teaching Online: Internet Research, Conversation, and Composition,* Second Edition**   Ideal for instructors who have never surfed the Net, this easy-to-follow guide offers basic definitions, numerous examples, and step-by-step information about finding and using Internet sources. Free to adopters. 0-321-01957-1

Teaching Writing to the Non-Native Speaker   This booklet examines the issues that arise when non-native speakers enter the developmental classroom. Free to instructors, it includes profiles of international and permanent ESL students, factors influencing second-language acquisition, and tips on managing a multicultural classroom. 0-673-97452-9

For Students

⟩NEW⟨ **The Longman Writer's Journal**   This journal for writers, free with *A Civil Word,* offers students a place to think, write, and react. For an examination copy, contact your Longman sales consultant. 0-321-08639-2

⟩NEW⟨ **The Longman Researcher's Journal**   This journal for writers and researchers, free with this text, helps students plan, schedule, write, and revise their research project. An all-in-one resource for first-time researchers, the journal guides students gently through the research process. 0-321-09530-8

***Researching Online,* Sixth Edition**   A perfect companion for a new age, this indispensable new supplement helps students navigate the Internet. Adapted from *Teaching Online,* the instructor's Internet guide, *Researching Online* speaks directly to students, giving them detailed, step-by-step instructions for performing electronic searches. Available free when shrinkwrapped with this text. 0-321-11733-6

Learning Together: An Introduction to Collaborative Theory   This brief guide to the fundamentals of collaborative learning teaches students how to work effectively in groups, how to revise with peer response, and how to co-author a paper or report. Shrinkwrapped free with any Longman Basic Skills text. 0-673-46848-8

***A Guide for Peer Response,* Second Edition**   This guide offers students forms for peer critiques, including general guidelines and specific forms for different stages in the writing process. Also appropriate for freshman-level course. Free to adopters. 0-321-01948-2

***Thinking Through the Test,* by D. J. Henry**   This special workbook, prepared specially for students in Florida, offers ample skill and practice exercises to help student prep for the Florida State Exit Exam. To shrinkwrap this workbook free with your textbook, please contact your Longman sales representative. Available in two versions: with and without answers. Also available: Two laminated grids (one for reading, one for writing) that can serve as handy references for students preparing for the Florida State Exit Exam.

Acknowlegments

I wish to acknowledge the contributions of my colleagues and reviewers who provided valuable advice and suggestions:

Alice Adams, Glendale Community College
Linda Black, St. Johns River Community College
Bruce Henderson, Fullerton College
Michael Hricik, Westmoreland City Community College
Patrick Hunter, California State University, Northridge
Laura Knight, Mercer County Community College
John Nicholson, Angelo State University

Diane Nowicki, Portland Community College
Ellen Olmstead, Bristol Community College
Velvet Pearson, Bakersfield College
Lynne Weller, John Wood Community College

The editorial staff of Longman Publishers deserves a special recognition and thanks for the guidance, support, and direction they have provided. In particular, I wish to thank Steven Rigolosi, Senior Acquisitions Editor, for his creative ideas and enthusiastic support of the text at every stage and Meegan Thompson for quickly following up on every special request. Further, I wish to thank Deborah Cloninger for her painstaking work on the permissions and Paul N. Cloninger, MD, for solid moral support. The librarians at Sacramento City College—Sandy Warmington, Pamela Posz, Nicole Wooley, and Maryanne Robinson, in particular—were also extremely helpful in searching online for sources, as was Kristin Romeis Ramsdell of CSU Hayward. Additionally, I wish to thank Pier Massimo Forni, Ph.D., of Johns Hopkins University both for his inspiration and his assistance in providing multiple sources for this text. Finally, thank you to the late Reverend Robert S. Romeis, Robin Ikegami, David J. Guy, and Janet Feil for their help in suggesting or lending readings or other materials over the course of the book's development.

Elizabeth Cloninger Long
Sacramento, California

Source Book

A Brief Guide to
Reading Critically and Writing Well

Without even realizing it, you have probably already practiced reading critically. Every time you question a writer's credibility or criticize her style, you are paying more attention to the text than if you simply read without comment. Critical reading is important not only because it demands that you take notice of what has been written, but also because it gives you tools by which to ingest and manage the information placed before you. The keys to understanding and remembering what you read require that you be involved in the reading process, actively seek meaning from the text, and respond as you read.

The question, then, is how do you read critically? The following is a list of steps designed to help you formulate a plan for attacking the readings in this book and in life. Follow every step, or skip the ones that don't seem to help you; your goal should be to craft a strategy to help you gain the most from every reading you undertake.

STEPS TO IMPROVE CRITICAL READING

1. Read All Titles, Beginnings, and Endings

Chances are, if a writer has taken the time to highlight part of his text by using a special title or heading, then that part of the text is important. Thus, you should take care to read it.

- Before reading the entire essay, skim the headings to catch the gist of the essay as well as to get a sense of the overall essay organization.
- Read the first and last paragraphs of the essay as well, since the main ideas of essays often appear in those sections.
- Consider, too, reading any biographical or bibliographical material in order to gain a sense of the context of the piece: when it was written, for whom it was written, why it was written.

2. Prewrite

Now that you have a sense of where the essay is headed, spend a few minutes (no more) responding to the information you have received so far, writing as quickly as you can any ideas or questions that come to mind. What do you expect from the essay? What conclusions do you think the author reaches? How relevant is the writer's message for you? This writing can occur in a notebook or in the margins of the essay itself, wherever your comments will benefit you most.

3. Ask Questions As You Read

Now that you are already thinking about the essay, plunge in and read it from start to finish, keeping your ideas and questions from prewriting in mind as you go. What is the writer's primary argument? How is the writer developing her points? Is she fulfilling your expectations of the essay? What does she need to do in order to be more persuasive? Keep these questions, and any answers to them, in mind as you read.

4. Ask Questions About This Reading As It Relates To Others

Since a big part of writing well involves synthesizing information for your reader, you should practice assimilating different ideas of your own as you read. Pay attention to ideas that you have heard or read before—in your life, in other classes, in other readings—and make notes in the margins (with a pencil or using sticky notes) as to the nature of the connections you discover.

5. Use Your Pencil (Or Sticky Notes) As You Read

Sometimes the best way to emphasize and remember a writer's important concepts is to underline or otherwise highlight key words, phrases, and ideas that stand out to you. Note sentences that you think best reveal the thesis, and identify examples that best illustrate the primary concepts of the reading. Also, write any questions that occur to you as you read in the margins of the essay, including words you are unfamiliar with or claims that you think need further support.

6. Reread and Rethink

Just as you will rewrite your own essays several times in order to clarify meaning, you should reread others' writings, too, in order to make sure the main ideas are clear to you. This second read need not be as in-depth as your first, but work on filling in any gaps from your first pass with information you glean the second time around.

7. Write After You Finish Reading

Just as you began your reading process by writing, so too should you end it. Summarize the main points of the essay, and ask yourself questions: Were your expectations of the essay fulfilled? Did the writer convince you of his point? What, if anything, made his case most convincing? Keep in mind that the strengths and weaknesses you note in others' writing can help you improve your own.

8. Talk It Over

Sometimes the best way to clarify questions or meaning is to discuss the reading with others. Talk with your classmates or friends about whether or not your impressions of the writer's argument are similar and whether those impressions were formed from the same examples and analysis in the essay. An easy way to begin this process is to share what you did or did not like or agree with in the piece and then move on to how you formed those opinions. The point is to gather as many different viewpoints as possible in order to revise or defend your own position.

WRITING CLEARLY

Probably the most important idea for students to remember about writing is that there are many ways to "get it right" when it comes to writing essays. Even if the way you choose to compose your essays isn't a way that anyone has ever tried before, that doesn't necessarily mean that your way won't work. In fact, even if you develop a set process for crafting your writing, that process may change as your writing becomes more sophisticated. The point, then, is to relax as much as possible when writing because you just may be in the process of developing a wonderful, effective writing strategy for yourself.

Relaxation is also an important concept to keep in mind as you write because it will help you get through the initial blank-page-syndrome, or Writer's Block. For many students, Writer's Block comes only because they feel pressured to produce something "perfect" their first time out, or perhaps they feel that they have nothing to say on a particular topic. Two writers in particular, Peter Elbow and Anne Lamott, address this idea of forgetting perfection in the early stages of writing and reveal how letting yourself write with permission to make changes later can ease the initial anxiety of writing an essay.

GETTING STARTED

Freewriting

Freewriting is the process by which you write as much as you can, as fast as you can, without stopping. Essentially, freewriting removes from your writing the roadblocks that inhibit the creative process; when freewriting you are only concerned with getting words and ideas down on paper, even if those ideas never come to fruition later in your essay. Peter Elbow writes in great detail about freewriting in the following essay.

Freewriting

Peter Elbow

Author of many articles and books on the topic of the writing process, Peter Elbow advocates "automatic writing," where the writer simply focuses on the act of writing and pays very little attention to content, diction, or other editorial concerns. In *Freewriting,* Elbow both argues for the efficacy of freewriting and offers suggestions to writers on how best to make use of this tool.

Pre-reading Questions

Write informally for five to ten minutes in response to the following questions:
What is the most difficult part about beginning a writing assignment? What strategies have you employed to combat this difficulty? How successful have you been?

Vocabulary Preview

Vocabulary Words:
- babbling
- prefers
- evaluated
- consciousness
- inhibited
- coherent
- ingrained
- reel
- compulsive
- vacuums

Look up the words above and use them in a paragraph on a topic of your choice. How difficult are these words to use? Write a few sentences evaluating the difficulty of using the words above.

1   The most effective way I know to improve your writing is to do freewriting exercises regularly. At least three times a week. They are sometimes called "automatic writing," "babbling," or "jabbering" exercises. The idea is simply to write for ten minutes (later on, perhaps fifteen or twenty). Don't stop for anything. Go quickly without rushing. Never stop to look back, to cross something out, to wonder how to spell something, to wonder what word or thought to use, or to think about what you are doing. If you can't think of a word or spelling, just use a squiggle or else write, "I can't think of it." Just put down something. The easiest thing is just to put down whatever is in your mind. If you get stuck it's fine to write "I can't think what to say, I can't think what to say" as many times as you want; or repeat the last word you wrote over and over again; or anything else. The only requirement is that you *never* stop.

2   What happens to a freewriting exercise is important. It must be a piece of writing which, even if someone else reads it, doesn't send any ripples back to you. It is like writing something and putting it in a bottle in the sea. The teacherless class helps your writing by providing maximum feedback. Freewritings help you by providing no feedback at all. When I assign one, I invite the writer to let me read it. But also tell him to

keep it if he prefers. I read it quickly and make no comments at all and I do not speak with him about it. The main thing is that a freewriting must never be evaluated in any way; in fact there must be no discussion or comment at all.

3   Here is an example of a fairly coherent exercise (sometimes they are very incoherent, which is fine):

> I think I'll write what's on my mind, but the only thing on my mind right now is what to write for ten minutes. I've never done this before and I'm not prepared in any way—the sky is cloudy today, how's that? Now I'm afraid I won't be able to think of what to write when I get to the end of the sentence—well, here I am at the end of the sentence—here I am again, again, again, again, at least I'm still writing—Now I ask is there some reason to be happy that I'm still writing—ah yes! Here comes the question again—What am I getting out of this? What point is there in it? It's almost obscene to always ask it but I seem to question everything that way and I was gonna say something else pertaining to that but I got so busy writing down the first part that I forgot what I was leading into. This is kind of fun oh don't stop writing—cars and trucks speeding by somewhere out the window, pens clattering across peoples' papers. The sky is still cloudy—is it symbolic that I should be mentioning it? Huh? I dunno. Maybe I should try colors, blue, red, dirty words—wait a minute—no can't do that, orange, yellow, arm tired, green pink violet magenta lavender red brown black green—now that I can't think of any more colors—just about done—relief? Maybe.

Freewriting may seem crazy but actually it makes simple sense. Think of the difference between speaking and writing. Writing has the advantage of permitting more editing. But that's its downfall too. Almost everybody interposes a massive and complicated series of editings between the time words start to be born into consciousness and when they finally come off the end of the pencil or typewriter onto the page. This is partly because schooling makes us obsessed with the "mistakes" we make in writing. Many people are constantly thinking about spelling and grammar as they try to write. I am always thinking about the awkwardness, wordiness, and general mushiness of my natural verbal product as I try to write down words.

4   But it's not just "mistakes" or "bad writing" we edit as we write. We also edit unacceptable thoughts and feelings, as we do in speaking. In writing there is more time to do it so the editing is heavier: when speaking, there's someone right there waiting for a reply and he'll get bored or think we're crazy if we don't come out with *something*. Most of the time in speaking, we settle for the catch-as-catch-can way in which the words tumble out. In writing, however, there's a chance to try to get them right. But the opportunity to get them right is a terrible burden: you can work for two hours trying to get a paragraph "right" and discover it's not right at all. And then give up.

5   Editing, *in itself,* is not the problem. Editing is usually necessary if we want to end up with something satisfactory. The problem is that editing goes on *at the same time* as producing. The editor is, as it were, constantly looking over the shoulder of the producer and constantly fiddling with what he's doing while he's in the middle of trying to

do it. No wonder the producer gets nervous, jumpy, inhibited, and finally can't be co-herent. It's an unnecessary burden to try to think of words and also worry at the same time whether they're the right words.

6   The main thing about freewriting is that it is *nonediting*. It is an exercise in bring-ing together the process of producing words and putting them down on the page. Prac-ticed regularly, it undoes the ingrained habit of editing at the same time you are trying to produce. It will make writing less blocked because words will come more easily. You will use up more paper, but chew up fewer pencils.

7   Next time you write, notice how often you stop yourself from writing down some-thing you were going to write down. Or else cross it out after it's written. "Naturally," you say, "it wasn't any good." But think for a moment about the occasions when you spoke well. Seldom was it because you first got the beginning just right. Usually it was a matter of a halting or even garbled beginning, but you kept going and your speech fi-nally became coherent and even powerful. There is a lesson here for writing: trying to get the beginning just right is a formula for failure—and probably a secret tactic to make yourself give up writing. Make some words, whatever they are, and then grab hold of that line and reel in as hard as you can. Afterwards you can throw away lousy beginnings and make new ones. This is the quickest way to get into good writing.

8   The habit of compulsive, premature editing doesn't just make writing hard. It also makes writing dead. Your voice is damped out by all the interruptions, changes, and hesitations between the consciousness and the page. In your natural way of pro-ducing words there is a sound, a texture, a rhythm—a voice—which is the main source of power in your writing. I don't know how it works, but this voice is the force that will make a reader listen to you, the energy that drives the meanings through his thick skull. Maybe you don't *like* your voice; maybe people have made fun of it. But it's the only voice you've got. It's your only source of power. You bet-ter get back into it, no matter what you think of it. If you keep writing in it, it may change into something you like better. But if you abandon it, you'll likely never have a voice and never be heard.

9   Freewritings are vacuums. Gradually you will begin to carry over into your regular writing some of the voice, force, and connectedness that creep into those vacuums.

POST-READING QUESTIONS

CONTENT

1. What does Elbow say is the "most effective way" to improve one's writing? How often does he suggest people practice this technique?
2. What is freewriting? Describe the process.
3. How does Elbow say freewriting helps the writer?
4. What does Elbow say is both an advantage and a disadvantage of writing, as opposed to speaking?
5. Under what circumstances, according to Elbow, is editing a problem? Explain.
6. Why does Elbow say one's "voice" is important?

STYLE AND STRUCTURE

7. What is Elbow's primary argument? Restate his main idea in your own words.

8. What examples does Elbow offer to illustrate his main idea? Of these, which are most effective? Why?

9. Who is Elbow's audience? To what extent is he writing for students? For teachers? Explain.

10. What conclusions can you draw about Elbow himself? Cite the text for support.

11. Is Elbow convincing? What could he have done, if anything, to make his message more persuasive?

CRITICAL THINKING AND ANALYSIS

DISCUSSION QUESTIONS

12. Have you tried freewriting before? Share your experiences with this type of writing.

13. What about freewriting seems like it could be helpful to you? What, if anything, seems like it might not help you? Explain and cite the text for support.

WRITING QUESTIONS

14. Elbow claims that "Many people are constantly thinking about spelling and grammar as they try to write." Is he right? Interview a few of your classmates about their writing processes and then write at least one well-developed paragraph in which you either agree or disagree with Elbow's assertion that people edit as they write.

15. Elbow states, "Maybe you don't *like* your voice . . . But it's the only voice you've got. It's your only source of power." Write a few paragraphs in which you describe a time when your voice has been your source of power. Be sure to use examples from your life in order to clarify your ideas.

VOCABULARY DEVELOPMENT

16. Elbow uses the term *freewriting* to label the uninhibited writing process he describes in his essay. Come up with at least two alternative titles for this process, and write a few sentences explaining how such terms are appropriate for *freewriting*.

GROUP ACTIVITIES

17. Freewrite as a group for five minutes. Then, without reading each other's writing, compare aspects of the writing such as length, penmanship, and variation of idea. How are your writings similar? Different? In what ways, if any, are these similarities or differences significant in terms of how they represent you as writers?

18. Have someone in the group choose a topic at random, and then freewrite about that topic for five minutes. Share your freewriting with the group and then use ideas from each person's freewriting to write one final, coherent paragraph on the topic suggested. How helpful were the ideas that resulted from people's freewriting? Could you each have come up with more ideas on your own? Discuss how freewriting did or did not help you come up with new ideas for this topic.

OTHER WAYS TO GET STARTED

Making an Outline

Despite the ease of freewriting for many students, others feel that it lacks a structure that they are comfortable with and, thus, these writers need another technique to help them begin the writing process. The most formal of these techniques, outlining, is an effective means of organizing your ideas if you already have a fair idea of what you want to say. Another advantage of outlining is that it helps you see any gaps in your support because your whole argument is laid out on paper before the actual writing begins. In general, outlines begin with the main point of the essay—or the thesis—and then include the supporting ideas and details throughout the rest of the outline. An example of this type of planning follows:

I.   GETTING STARTED

    A.   Freewriting (based on Peter Elbow's essay)

        1.1.   how to do it

        1.2.   benefits of freewriting

        1.3.   drawbacks of premature editing

    B.   Outlining

        1.1.   why some students need this technique

        1.2.   why it works

        1.3.   example of an outline

        1.4.   drawbacks of outlining

This outline is a very rough sketch of the material already covered in this section of the book, but it should give you an idea of the way outlining can help you map out your ideas before you sit down and begin to draft your essay. The idea behind outlining is to present all the information you have in a clear, organized pattern, one that you can easily transpose into an essay.

A drawback of outlining, however, is that many times students feel locked into their outlines and think they must have exactly the same number of support points or details for each item on their outlines, when in fact, some ideas do not lend themselves to as much development. If you choose to outline your essays, just be sure to stay flexible enough to allow yourself to spend more time on some ideas than on others, if you need to do so.

Clustering

Just as freewriting may be too unstructured for some students, outlining may be overly formulaic or restricting for others. Thus, some students search for a happy medium between the two. Clustering, a visual means of recording your ideas with some structure, provides a balance for students who need more structure than freewriting provides, but less structure than outlining requires.

Clustering involves beginning by writing down your main idea and then writing supporting ideas around that idea, using darts and circles to make the connection between ideas clear. For example:

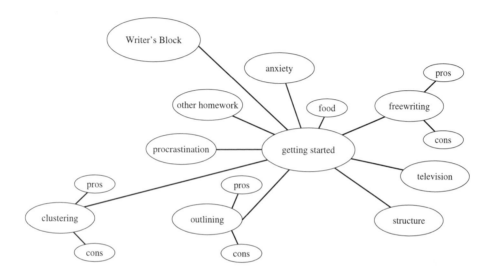

In the example above, most of the ideas stem from some aspect of beginning the writing process. However, the writer has other concerns or distractions as well: other homework, food, television, and procrastination all originate from the concept of getting started, but they offer little room for development if the topic is beginning the writing process. Thus, developing the other points—freewriting, clustering, outlining—gives the writer a greater opportunity for writing a coherent, well-supported essay.

An advantage of clustering is that it allows the writer to see all of the possibilities for development early in the writing process. This way, students do not get locked into one course of organization or development as easily as when they outline. However, clustering still requires that the student "let go" in the initial brainstorming phase, which can be difficult. Another downside to clustering is that, even in the freedom it allows writers in writing and connecting ideas before the drafting stage, sometimes students feel compelled to connect their ideas as they go, which can result in the stifling of some key concepts. The best way to decide which technique is right for you is to experiment with all three methods, paying attention to which one helps you most in beginning your writing process.

Drafting

After you have finished with your prewriting steps, you need to start working on crafting your thesis. Your thesis is the guiding principle of your essay, or your main idea, and it is the most important statement you will make in your writing. If your readers remember nothing else of your essay, they should be able to remember your thesis.

Some students feel intimidated by having to write a thesis statement and, thus, try too hard to write a sentence that they think a reader will want to read rather than focusing on writing what they, as the writers, believe. While writing an essay based on what you do not believe is possible, writing something you advocate is easier, and more often persuasive. For instance, if you have to write an essay on a political subject, but you really have no interest in world politics or even national politics, focus on something close to home: whether or not a proposition allowing cameras at intersections to catch speeders should be passed, or whether or not the local school budget should be expanded to support a gay student alliance. Make sure you have some interest in your topic, or every assignment you write will be drudgery. If you can find nothing at all to interest you, talk to your teacher or your classmates; they can assist you in brainstorming a subject to develop.

Once you have an idea of what you want to write, start drafting your essay. Don't worry about having your thesis set in stone at the outset; you can always revise it if you find contradictory research or change your mind about your point of view as you go. Do, however, write around a working thesis. This will give your essay shape and will allow you to see any holes in your argument as they develop.

Crafting a Thesis

Again, the most important part of any essay is its thesis, or main idea. Your job as a writer is, as for any assignment you undertake, to communicate a single idea clearly, powerfully, and thoroughly. If your thesis is strong, you will have an easier time connecting support points and examples to that thesis, making for a unified, coherent essay. If, on the other hand, your thesis is weak, you may end up poorly arguing two or three points, none of which will be convincing. Remember: everything you write in your essay should be born of and return to the thesis.

Many myths surround the creation of a good thesis, but keep in mind that a good thesis is simply one that manages to tie an essay together into one persuasive whole. Thesis statements can be different lengths, they can be placed at different points in an essay, and sometimes they can be left out altogether if the writer chooses to make an implicit, rather than an explicit, argument. The only hard-and-fast rule to crafting a thesis is that you believe in it; if you have no confidence in your argument, then neither will anyone else.

What follows are some simple guidelines that will help you craft your thesis. These guidelines are designed to help you write an explicit, or directly and specifically stated, thesis statement, but once you have mastered the art of writing good theses, then you can apply these same guidelines to the creation of implicit thesis statements, those not specifically stated, in your writing.

Let Your Thesis Evolve

Don't feel compelled to sit down, face a blank page or computer screen, and write a perfect, workable thesis on the first try. While you may be successful in your effort, you may also feel overwhelmed or frustrated at having to make such a big decision so early in your drafting process. Instead, follow the tips to get started, both on your essay and on your thesis, and see what ideas seem dominant even when you're just trying to get started. Chances are, the ideas that emerge as the strongest in your freewriting, outlining, or clustering will be those ideas that strike a chord in you and that you really want to explore. Distill your ideas down into a sentence or two and most likely the result of the distillation process will be a rough working thesis that you can use to start the drafting process.

Make Sure Your Thesis Is a Sentence

After you've come up with an idea that interests you, make sure this idea can take the form of a complete sentence. Even if your thesis is implicit, or not written out directly, the idea in your mind that controls your essay should be a sentence. Since a sentence is more likely to communicate a complete thought than part of a sentence, you need to make sure that your thesis is, indeed, a sentence. Writing "the need for tax reform" might tell some readers that you think tax reform is needed, but it also might send the message that you think tax reform is a waste of time. Most likely, it will leave your reader wondering what about the need for tax reform you want to write. On the other hand, if you write "The United States is in need of tax reform," your reader might still disagree with you, but at least he or she will be clear as to what you're arguing.

Make Sure Your Thesis Has Room for Development

This guideline is particularly important to follow because sometimes, even if we passionately believe in what we write, the idea we want to communicate doesn't lend itself to an entire essay. For instance, if you write "My dog's name is Rex," what are you going to talk about for the next few pages, or even paragraphs? Choose a topic that has many different directions and perspectives, such as trends in popular culture or politics, in order to give yourself room to expand your ideas. Something like, "Drunk driving penalties should be stiffer," gives you not only something to argue, but it also gives you different ways to develop your thesis:

- in terms of the damage caused by drunk driving
- in terms of the cost to tax payers
- in terms of the inconvenience to the driver him or herself

At any rate, you get to decide how you want to expand your ideas rather than being limited by a thesis that is too narrow.

Make Sure Your Thesis Has a Context, or Qualifier

Right after you've slaved crafting the perfect thesis that can lead you off into multiple directions, you now face a new task: narrow your thesis to make it manageable in the space you are allotted. Just as a thesis allows you to develop many different perspectives well, it can also be unmanageable if you can't decide which particular angle to follow.

An easy way to narrow your thesis is to include some sort of qualifying phrase or clause that lets your reader know the scope of your argument.

For instance, an overly
broad thesis might be: *"Drunk driving penalties should be stiffer."*

This sentence offers you almost too many different directions for development.

A better thesis would be: *"In order to lessen the number of drunk driving fatalities each year, drunk driving penalties need to be stiffer."*

Here, you are letting your reader know both *what* you're arguing—that the penalties need to be stiffer—and *why* you're arguing it—to decrease deaths.

Another option is: *"Although the penalties for drunk driving have become tougher over the past 20 years, they still are not tough enough."*

This lets your reader know, again, that you think tougher penalties are warranted, but also that your argument will cover the past rather than focus on potential future problems. Either way, the use of a qualifying phrase or clause can help you narrow your focus for your reader.

As you become a more experienced writer, you can abandon the explicit qualifier, just as you may jettison the explicit thesis altogether. But always be sure that you know, in your mind, just what your main argument is and how you plan to develop it.

Make Sure Your Thesis Is Arguable

Many students think that as long as they meet the word or page quota set by their teachers, then they have completed the assignment. On the contrary, just scrawling out words, if those words have no point, makes for difficult—and certainly not persuasive—writing. Just as you take care to limit your thesis to something you believe, so, too, be sure that your thesis can be argued.

A thesis that is tough to argue is: *"Michael's my best friend because he's nice."*

You have your argument—that Michael's your best friend—and your qualifier—that he's nice—but who can argue with you? At best, someone can argue with your qualifier and say Michael isn't nice, but no one can tell you that someone is or isn't your friend. Thus, your thesis isn't arguable, so there's not much point in writing something that gives your reader no chance to disagree with you. Remember that persuasion can only occur if your reader has the option not to agree with you; if you load your thesis with statements designed to give your reader no choice at all about your argument, you'll never know whether or not you're convincing.

Make Sure Your Thesis Has a Purpose

Perhaps the most important, yet often unstated, part of your thesis is its purpose. The purpose is the "why" for your essay, the reason you're writing it (other than that you have to because your teacher assigned it). You need to have a sense of why this thesis is worth developing because if there's no reason to develop it, there's no reason for your reader to read it, which makes persuasion difficult.

A thesis with a clear
purpose could be: *"We need tougher drunk driving laws because too many people are being killed by drunk drivers."*

In this case, the writer clearly wants to prevent more deaths.

A thesis with an implicit
purpose could be: *"Despite decreasing numbers of drunk driving fatalities in some states, we need tougher drunk driving laws."*

Since the two parts of the thesis seem to contrast with each other, the writer needs to make clear at some other point in the essay why this topic needs to be addressed. Even if the writer never explicitly says what his or her purpose is, the reader needs to get a sense at some point in the essay that this topic matters and why; otherwise, why should anyone bother reading it?

These guidelines are general and loose, and they overlap in many places. However, by making sure that you write a sentence that expresses an idea that you care about and can argue, you will be well on your way to writing a solid, workable thesis. There is no single way to write a good thesis, just as there is no one way to write a good essay, but the more you write, the closer you will be to coming up with your own guidelines for clear writing.

Now that you have some strategies for writing a thesis, you just need to organize your ideas around your working thesis. The following acronym is a strategy designed to help you make sure that you not only have enough support for your ideas, but also that your support is well-connected to the rest of your essay.

THE TBEAR ORGANIZATIONAL STRATEGY FOR IDEAS, PARAGRAPHS, AND ESSAYS

TBEAR stands for: "Thesis Echo," "Bridge to Examples," "Examples," "Analysis," and "Return to Thesis." This technique allows you to identify the elements in a point you are trying to develop, whether that point is made in a paragraph or over several pages, and to make sure that that point is relevant to your thesis.

THESIS ECHO

The "T," or Thesis Echo, is what keeps your reader on track from point to point throughout your essay. The Thesis Echo can be a repetition of key words in your thesis, or it can be an iteration of only the main concepts in your thesis. For instance, look at the following essay, which is a first draft of an assignment written in response to the topic: If you could change anything about your past education, what would you change, and why? The writer has identified his thesis in bold print.

STUDENT ESSAY: "Running Behind"

1   In my early years, I believed that an education was highly overrated. I found myself skipping my English class at least twice a week. An education was meant for teachers, lawyers, and presidents, and since I didn't desire to be any of those, I concluded school was a waste of time. After all, I already knew how to read and write, and like my father and his father before him, I was going to be a laborer. Working with my hands was something I was comfortable doing and I was determined to take the path of least resistance.

2   While I was still in high school, my father hurt his back and was forced to look for a less physical job. Without an education he was unable to find a decent-paying, less physical job. I never took into account the possibility of an injury and the impact it could have on one's career. The thought of this made me change my mind about school, but now high school was almost over. I was sure that I was too far behind to think about catching up. **If I could change anything about my education to this point, it would be to have paid attention in English class because not doing so put me behind now.**

3   One way not paying attention in English put me behind is that I didn't learn the basic reading skills necessary to excel in college. When I took my college assessment test, I found that I couldn't put a scrambled paragraph in order. Every sentence looked like it could go first. It was no surprise to me to see the results of the test. The placement center counselors told me that I should take a basic reading class along with a basic writing class. I didn't want my older brother to know that I wasn't at college level, so I didn't take any English my first semester. Instead, I took a history class. I soon found out that reading skills were also necessary in history class. I didn't understand the essay questions on the exams; therefore, I didn't answer them correctly and subsequently failed most of the tests. Although I didn't want to believe that skipping English early in my academic career hurt me, I couldn't deny that I was missing something that was keeping me from suc-

ceeding in school. I could only conclude that not paying attention in English class was the reason I failed history and was, since I still hadn't enrolled in any college English classes, behind in my education.

4   Another way not paying attention in English class put me behind was that I didn't learn the writing skills I needed to get a job with the state. The California Highway Patrol was accepting applications for several positions; however, the test was an essay about yourself. I sat in the testing room writing what I thought was an excellent essay, but whoever graded the test didn't agree, for I failed miserably. How could this be? I had used all the different kinds of punctuation marks that one could use. I had even broken up the essay into paragraphs. Just because I put commas in places that weren't necessary and broke up the paragraphs in the wrong places, that was no reason to fail me. Writing that essay showed a huge effort on my part, or maybe it showed that I was lacking writing skills. Again I had to wonder if my early attitude toward English was coming back to haunt me. I was finally waking up to the fact that I was falling further and further behind, in my life as well as in my education, and it was all because I hadn't paid attention in English class.

5   I was later reminded again of my poor writing skills by my Criminal Justice instructor. After not being accepted into the CHP, I decided to give school one more try. But I still didn't enroll in English. I figured I was smart enough to pick up the basics as I went, as long as I stayed away from history classes. So I enrolled in a Criminal Justice class, one that my friends assured me required very little writing (but enough, I reasoned, for me to get some practice). Sure enough, the teacher only gave us short essay quizzes. I thought I was safe because the answers only had to be a paragraph long, but that was long enough for the teacher to rip on my sentence structure and tell me I had gaps in my information. I finally realized that not only was I missing something, but I was missing English skills. If I couldn't read well enough for history and couldn't write well enough for

other classes, I figured I just wasn't ready for college. I had no doubt at that point that paying attention in English in class would have helped me write better and maybe pass that test.

6　　I began to take the English classes that were course requirements, the three most basic reading and writing courses the college had to offer. And because I finally realized that I blew it early in my education, I sat in the front row and paid attention to everything the teachers said. At long last, I'm one step away from taking a transfer-level course, and I even earned As and Bs along the way. Although it is going to take me much longer to graduate, I'm at least on the right track. I realize the importance of good English skills and how much easier things can be by doing them right the first time.

Most students choose the concepts of "not paying attention in English" and "behind" as being most significant in the student's writing. Therefore, those terms, or at least the concepts they represent, will serve as the student's "T" or Thesis Echo. Look in paragraphs three, four, and five, and note how they begin. Indeed, the writer has practically cut and pasted his thesis onto the beginning of each paragraph, repeating the terms "not paying attention" and "behind" several times. By echoing such key terms, the writer has ensured that the reader is absolutely on track and knows where the essay is going.

One downside to using a thesis echo that so closely mirrors the thesis is that the essay can sound redundant and boring. Two answers to this dilemma exist: first, echo the *concept* of the thesis rather than just the words. For instance, rather than saying "One way not paying attention in English caused me to fall behind," the student could say, "My failure to concentrate on what was going on in English led me to lag in my studies." The words, except for "English," are largely different from those in the thesis, but the concept of the thesis is the same, so the reader stays on track. Eventually, as your writing becomes more sophisticated, you can abandon an explicit Thesis Echo and make your reference to the thesis in other ways.

BRIDGE TO EXAMPLES

A second way to keep your reader from dozing throughout your essay while still keeping her on track is to introduce new material directly after you write your Thesis Echo. This new material is your "B" or Bridge to Examples, and it serves as the lure to your reader to continue on with your essay. You can easily combine the "T" and the "B" into a topic sentence that controls the direction of the paragraph, and this works very well to identify the focus of the paragraph. Once again, refer to the student essay. You probably notice that though the repetition of the thesis—the "One way not paying attention in English put me behind"—stays pretty much the same from paragraph to paragraph, the information that follows it does not.

This new information—in paragraph three, the "I didn't learn the basic reading skills necessary to excel in college" portion of the sentence—is the "B" or the Bridge to Examples. This statement tells your reader what to expect from the rest of the paragraph, particularly in terms of specific detail. And if you read on, you see that the writer does, indeed, recount how his failure to acquire basic reading skills led him to fall further behind in college, thus supporting his thesis. The Bridge to Examples works with the Thesis Echo to form a clear, if simple, topic sentence that both connects to the thesis and leads the reader into new detail.

EXAMPLES

Once you have let your reader know that you are still on track with your thesis but that you have some new information to share, you can present that new information. The "E" of TBEAR, or "Examples," is the element that presents facts, details, accounts of real events, or information from outside references that help you make your case. The "E" part of your essay should be indisputable; either the information you present is true or it isn't, but your own opinion should appear *through* the Examples, not instead of them.

For instance, the writer of the student essay tells in paragraph four of his struggles trying to get a job with the California Highway Patrol (CHP). He describes the exam he took and tells how he failed the exam. As he communicates these details, he does not deviate from the descriptions of his experience; he simply tells us what happened. These details are the proof of his thesis; they show us that not paying attention in English class caused him to fall behind, even if the writer himself does not tell us this directly at this point.

ANALYSIS

Because the significance of your Examples is not necessarily as clear in illustrating your thesis statement to a reader as it is to you, you need to explain their relevance within the context of the thesis. This explanation of how the Examples show that the thesis is true comes in the form of Analysis, or the "A" in TBEAR. Analysis is your chance to make your point through your Examples. You're essentially saying: "Here's my proof, and this is how it shows that my thesis is true." Good Analysis will explain what about certain parts of the Examples makes your case strong.

Again, in the student essay, read in paragraph four where the student explains his interpretation of his CHP test results. He writes, "Just because I put commas in places that weren't necessary and broke up the paragraphs in the wrong places, that was no reason to fail me. Writing that essay showed a huge effort on my part, or maybe it showed that I was lacking writing skills." These sentences are evaluating the Examples the writer has just offered, and they are strengthening his original argument—his thesis—that not paying attention in English has caused him to fall behind. The fact that this evaluation is the student's opinion—some people might think that his comma errors and poor paragraphing skills were, indeed, reason to fail him—and not fact makes it Analysis rather than Example. The student is furthering his argument by explaining how the Examples show that not paying attention in English put him behind.

RETURN TO THESIS

The "R" of the TBEAR strategy, or "Return to Examples," is probably the least important part of your writing. The "R" simply restates the thesis, much as the "T" or Thesis Echo did at the start of your point. If your Analysis is clear, then, you won't need to repeat your thesis again. For some students, however, having a little reminder at the end of a support point is helpful, but feel free to discard the "R" if you think your writing has become too repetitive.

In the student essay, look in paragraph four at the point where the student begins to connect his Analysis to the thesis. The student writes, "I was finally waking up to the fact that I was falling further and further behind, in my life, now, as well as in my education, and it was all because I hadn't paid attention in English class." Though the student is still evaluating—and, thus, still analyzing—his Example, he is weaving his thesis into his Analysis to remind the reader yet again of his main idea. Though the writer may seem to direct your attention to the CHP test and the student's results, he always returns to the idea that not paying attention in English caused him to be behind. This reiteration of "hadn't paid attention in English" and "behind" is the "R" or Return to Thesis, and this ensures that the writer keeps us on track with his message.

The student essay in this textbook is an example of fairly basic writing; this student wrote the essay at the beginning of a remedial English class, and by the end of the semester, he was writing clearly developed ideas that did not repeat the thesis word for word. But his writing clearly shows how the TBEAR elements work together throughout the course of an essay in order to communicate a single idea. The point is to understand the concepts in order to apply them to your own writing as you develop your own personal voice. Your teacher may not encourage you to write in the first person or use personal examples as the writer of the student essay has done, but just understanding how to weave your thesis throughout your writing and your facts will help you present a cogent, intelligent argument to your reader.

The TBEAR organizational strategy, while very helpful in structuring your ideas, can be overwhelming at first, so don't expect every piece of your writing to fit neatly into the TBEAR, or any other, mold. Instead, just concentrate on getting your ideas down on paper for a first draft and then follow writer Anne Lamott's lead, as she makes clear in the following essay, in revising your essays as they need it.

Shitty First Drafts

Anne Lamott

Using humor and sarcasm to combat her own prewriting anxiety, novelist Anne Lamott explores the realities of writing under pressure. Acknowledging that "not *one* [very great writer] sits down routinely feeling wildly enthusiastic and confident," Lamott identifies with beginning writers' worries and offers concrete strategies by which to counter writing-related stress.

Pre-reading Questions

Freewrite for five to ten minutes in response to the following questions:
What kinds of anxiety, if any, do you experience as you write? When you finish? Do these anxieties have to do with what you think of your writing or with what others think of your writing? What steps do you take to address these anxieties? Explain.

Vocabulary Preview

Vocabulary Words:	• uninitiated	• articulate	• emaciated
	• dewy	• stupefying	• discretion
	• rapturous	• incoherent	• hurtle
	• umbrage		

Look up the words above and use them in a paragraph to describe an object, person, or process of your choice. Pay attention to how exaggerated your language is as a result of using these words; then write a few sentences explaining how the vocabulary words do or do not make your own writing more exaggerated than it would normally be.

---

1   Now, practically even better news than that of short assignments is the idea of shitty first drafts. All good writers write them. This is how they end up with good second drafts and terrific third drafts. People tend to look at successful writers, writers who are getting their books published and maybe even doing well financially, and think that they sit down at their desks every morning feeling like a million dollars, feeling great about who they are and how much talent they have and what a great story they have to tell; that they take in a few deep breaths, push back their sleeves, roll their necks a few times to get all the cricks out, and dive in, typing fully formed passages as fast as a court reporter. But this is just the fantasy of the uninitiated. I know some very great writers, writers you love who write beautifully and have made a great deal of money, and not *one* of them sits down routinely feeling wildly enthusiastic and confident. Not one of them writes elegant first drafts. All right, one of them does, but we do not like her very much. We do not think that she has a rich inner life or that God likes

her or can even stand her. (Although when I mentioned this to my priest friend Tom, he said you can safely assume you've created God in your own image when it turns out that God hates all the same people you do.)

2   Very few writers really know what they are doing until they've done it. Nor do they go about their business feeling dewy and thrilled. They do not type a few stiff warm-up sentences and then find themselves bounding along like huskies across the snow. One writer I know tells me that he sits down every morning and says to himself nicely, "It's not like you don't have a choice, because you do—you can either type or kill yourself." We all often feel like we are pulling teeth, even those writers whose prose ends up being the most natural and fluid. The right words and sentences just do not come pouring out like ticker tape most of the time. Now, Muriel Spark is said to have felt that she was taking dictation from God every morning—sitting there, one supposes, plugged into a Dictaphone, typing away, humming. But this is a very hostile and aggressive position. One might hope for bad things to rain down on a person like this.

3   For me and most of the other writers I know, writing is not rapturous. In fact, the only way I can get anything written at all is to write really, really shitty first drafts.

4   The first draft is the child's draft, where you let it all pour out and then let it romp all over the place, knowing that no one is going to see it and that you can shape it later. You just let this childlike part of you channel whatever voices and visions come through and onto the page. If one of the characters wants to say, "Well, so what, Mr. Poopy Pants," you let her. No one is going to see it. If the kid wants to get into really sentimental, weepy, emotional territory, you let him. Just get it all down on paper, because there may be something great in those six crazy pages that you would never have gotten to by more rational, grown-up means. There may be something in the very last line of the very last paragraph on page six that you just love, that is so beautiful or wild that you now know what you're supposed to be writing about, more or less, or in what direction you might go—but there was no way to get to this without first getting through the first five and a half pages.

5   I used to write food reviews for *California* magazine before it folded. (My writing food reviews had nothing to do with the magazine folding, although every single review did cause a couple of canceled subscriptions. Some readers took umbrage at my comparing mounds of vegetable puree with various ex-presidents' brains.) These reviews always took two days to write. First I'd go to a restaurant several times with a few opinionated, articulate friends in tow. I'd sit there writing down everything anyone said that was at all interesting or funny. Then on the following Monday I'd sit down at my desk with my notes, and try to write the review. Even after I'd been doing this for years, panic would set in. I'd try to write a lead, but instead I'd write a couple of dreadful sentences, xx them out, try again, xx everything out, and then feel despair and worry settle on my chest like an x-ray apron. It's over, I'd think, calmly. I'm not going to be able to get the magic to work this time. I'm ruined. I'm through. I'm toast. Maybe, I'd think, I can get my old job back as a clerk-typist. But probably not. I'd get up and study my teeth in the mirror for a while. Then I'd stop, remember to breathe, make a few phone calls, hit the kitchen and chow down. Eventually I'd go back and sit down at my desk, and sigh for the next ten minutes. Finally I would pick

up my one-inch picture frame, stare into it as if for the answer, and every time the answer would come: all I had to do was to write a really shitty first draft of, say, the opening paragraph. And no one was going to see it.

6   So I'd start writing without reining myself in. It was almost just typing, just making my fingers move. And the writing would be *terrible.* I'd write a lead paragraph that was a whole page, even though the entire review could only be three pages long, and then I'd start writing up descriptions of the food, one dish as a time, bird by bird, and the critics would be sitting on my shoulders, commenting like cartoon characters. They'd be pretending to snore, or rolling their eyes at my overwrought descriptions, no matter how hard I tried to tone those descriptions down, no matter how conscious I was of what a friend said to me gently in my early days of restaurant reviewing. "Annie," she said, "it is just a piece of *chicken.* It is just a bit of *cake.*"

7   But because by then I had been writing for so long, I would eventually let myself trust the process—sort of, more or less. I'd write a first draft that was maybe twice as long as it should be, with a self-indulgent and boring beginning, stupefying descriptions of the meal, lots of quotes from my black-humored friends that made them sound more like the Manson girls than food lovers, and no ending to speak of. The whole thing would be so long and incoherent and hideous that for the rest of the day I'd obsess about getting creamed by a car before I could write a decent second draft. I'd worry that people would read what I'd written and believe that the accident had really been a suicide, that I had panicked because my talent was waning and my mind was shot.

8   The next day, though, I'd sit down, go through it all with a colored pen, take out everything I possibly could, find a new lead somewhere on the second page, figure out a kicky place to end it, and then write a second draft. It always turned out fine, sometimes even funny and weird and helpful. I'd go over it one more time and mail it in.

9   Then, a month later, when it was time for another review, the whole process would start again, complete with the fears that people would find my first draft before I could rewrite it.

10   Almost all good writing begins with terrible first efforts. You need to start somewhere. Start by getting something—anything—down on paper. A friend of mine says that the first draft is the down draft—you just get it down. The second draft is the up draft—you fix it up. You try to say what you have to say more accurately. And the third draft is the dental draft, where you check every tooth, to see if it's loose or cramped or decayed, or even, God help us, healthy.

11   What I've learned to do when I sit down to work on a shitty first draft is to quiet the voices in my head. First there's the vinegar-lipped Reader Lady, who says primly, "Well, *that's* not very interesting, is it?" And there's the emaciated German male who writes these Orwellian memos detailing your thought crimes. And there are your parents, agonizing over your lack of loyalty and discretion; and there's William Burroughs, dozing off or shooting up because he finds you as bold and articulate as a houseplant; and so on. And there are also the dogs: let's not forget the dogs, the dogs in their pen who will surely hurtle and snarl their way out if you ever *stop* writing, because writing is, for some of us, the latch that keeps the door of the pen closed, keeps those crazy ravenous dogs contained.

12   Quieting these voices is at least half the battle I fight daily. But this is better than it used to be. It used to be 87 percent. Left to its own devices, my mind spends much of its time having conversations with people who aren't there. I walk along defending myself to people, or exchanging repartee with them, or rationalizing my behavior, or seducing them with gossip, or pretending I'm on their TV talk show or whatever. I speed or run an aging yellow light or don't come to a full stop, and one nanosecond later am explaining to imaginary cops exactly why I had to do what I did, or insisting that I did not in fact do it.

13   I happened to mention this to a hypnotist I saw many years ago, and he looked at me very nicely. At first I thought he was feeling around on the floor for the silent alarm button, but then he gave me the following exercise, which I still use to this day.

14   Close your eyes and get quiet for a minute, until the chatter starts up. Then isolate one of the voices and imagine the person speaking as a mouse. Pick it up by the tail and drop it into a mason jar. Then isolate another voice, pick it up by the tail, drop it in the jar. And so on. Drop in any high-maintenance parental units, drop in any contractors, lawyers, colleagues, children, anyone who is whining in your head. Then put the lid on, and watch all these mouse people clawing at the glass, jabbering away, trying to make you feel like shit because you won't do what they want—won't give them more money, won't be more successful, won't see them more often. Then imagine that there is a volume-control button on the bottle. Turn it all the way up for a minute, and listen to the stream of angry, neglected, guilt-mongering voices. Then turn it all the way down and watch the frantic mice lunge at the glass, trying to get to you. Leave it down, and get back to your shitty first draft.

15   A writer friend of mine suggests opening the jar and shooting them all in the head. But I think he's a little angry, and I'm sure nothing like this would ever occur to you.

POST-READING QUESTIONS

CONTENT

1. Who, according to Lamott, writes *Shitty First Drafts?*
2. What myth does the notion of *Shitty First Drafts* dispel?
3. How does Lamott describe her first drafts? What do they contain?
4. How does Lamott feel about writing her first drafts?
5. What process does Lamott follow when writing her second drafts? Her third?
6. Why does Lamott say that writing without stopping is important?
7. What method does Lamott suggest for tuning out the negative voices in your head?

STYLE AND STRUCTURE

8. Does Lamott have a point? What is it?
9. What examples does Lamott offer to support her point? Of these, which are most compelling? Explain.
10. Who is Lamott's audience? How much do you feel part of her audience? Explain.

11. What is Lamott's attitude toward her subject? How serious is she?

12. What role does humor play in helping Lamott develop her ideas?

13. Is Lamott persuasive? Explain.

CRITICAL THINKING AND ANALYSIS

DISCUSSION QUESTIONS

14. How offensive is the title of Lamott's piece? To what extent does the title help or hurt Lamott's credibility?

15. Of all the suggestions Lamott offers, which seem most helpful to you? Least helpful? Explain.

WRITING ASSIGNMENTS

16. Lamott provides great detail describing her own writing process as well as describing other, fantasy-based writing processes. What is your writing process? In a few well-developed paragraphs, give an account of how you write and why you write that way. You may use examples from Lamott's text as a means for comparison, and be sure to cite your own experiences for support.

17. Lamott draws from her own experiences as a writer to offer advice to people on how to make their writing processes manageable. What advice can you offer? Write a few paragraphs to a writer less experienced than you, advising him or her on how to write well. Again, you may draw from Lamott's essay if you wish, but use examples from your own life to make your ideas clear.

18. What is the worst possible consequence you imagine facing as a result of your writing? Using humor if you wish, write a few paragraphs describing the results of writing less-than-perfect essays. Be sure to use examples from your own life or imagination in order to illustrate your ideas.

VOCABULARY DEVELOPMENT

19. Find two or three passages that you think best reveal Lamott's tone. Then, identify the words or expressions in those passages that you think most significantly contribute to Lamott's writing personality. Finally, write a few sentences analyzing how the passages you have identified are representative of Lamott's voice.

GROUP ACTIVITIES

20. Practice Lamott's "jar" activity as a group, isolating the "voices" she mentions and putting them in imaginary glass jars. Make notes of your own experience and share your results with your group. How effective is this technique in helping you to write? Explain.

21. Choose a paragraph that you think is representative of Lamott's humor, and write your own paragraph on another topic, imitating Lamott's style. How easy or difficult is her humor to re-create on your own? Discuss and share your results with the class.

REVISION

Now that you've finished your drafting, you're done. Right? If you're like many people, you'd prefer writing to be more like a Scantron test: you respond with your first instincts, answer the questions, and you're done. Unfortunately, as Anne Lamott points out in her essay, good writing most often results from writing, rewriting, and more rewriting, until the finished product is far more polished than the one you began with. On the bright side, while writing doesn't let you off the hook by letting you just scratch something out and be done, it does give you many chances to improve what you've done. Even if your first draft is practically chicken scratch, you have hope of improvement as long as you're willing to revise.

Revision, then, is the process of "re-seeing" or "re-looking-at" what you've already written. In revision, the writer steps back and tries to look objectively at what she's written. The best revision consists of numerous read-throughs on the part of the writer: each "pass" focuses on a different aspect of the essay until all the content-based concerns—organization, support, connections—are clear. Only after checking for the whole-essay issues should you focus on line-by-line concerns such as spelling, punctuation, and grammar because editing too soon will guarantee more editing later if you make changes to the "big picture" of your writing after you've proofread.

The following is a brief guide to revision, with some handy tips on what to look for in your own writing in order to make your point as clear as possible.

STEP-BY-STEP REVISION

Read your essay through one time for each focus area listed below. As you read your essay, concentrate only on one area at a time, taking breaks in between "passes" to clear your mind and help you re-focus your attention.

1. Check the Scope of Your Topic Before You Begin Writing

Check the length requirement for your assignment (if there is one) and make sure that you're not trying to do too much in your essay. Do some prewriting to see what sections of your topic will need more time and effort, and check to make sure that you have room to develop each section well. If the topic is so broad that you can't do justice to it, refer to your prewriting to determine what parts of the subject interest you the most, and then focus your essay accordingly.

2. Check For a Clear Purpose and Balance

Make sure your reader can tell what you're going to write about early in your essay. You don't need to put your thesis in any particular place, but if it's not in the first few paragraphs, make sure your opening comments definitely give your reader a sense that you do have a purpose and that you're moving toward that purpose.

After you've checked for a clear purpose in your opening paragraphs, make sure that the purpose is clear throughout your essay. Write your thesis on a 3x5" card and hold it next to each paragraph in isolation so that all you can read is the thesis and that paragraph. If the paragraph does not logically follow from your thesis, you need to revise one or the other. (And if no paragraph logically follows from the thesis, you probably need to change your thesis.)

Finally, make sure your topic is balanced. If you have multiple support points, check to see that each point gets approximately equal time in your essay. If one argument is your most important support point, it's fine to develop it a bit more, but if your essay is too lopsided and some points are thinly developed, then your reader might assume that certain points aren't important since they weren't explored fully.

3. Check For Clear Language For Your Reader

Think about who your audience is and what kind of vocabulary, sentence structure, and examples will most effectively persuade that audience. Remember that being clear is your job as a writer, so if you're in doubt as to whether or not your reader will follow you, revise the passage in question to be clear. If your reader is your teacher, you will probably need to pay more attention to using varied vocabulary and sentence types than if you are writing a draft for peer review. Either way, consider what your reader expects from you, and check your writing to ensure that you fulfill those expectations.

4. Check For a Logical Organizational Structure

Many essays have organizational patterns that originate from the topics themselves: compare/contrast essays develop point-by-point structures, for instance, while some cause and effect essays start with "cause" at the beginning of the essay and "effect" at the end. There is no one correct way to organize a particular topic or type of essay, but you should be sure that your essay is organized in some way. Consider checking for the TBEAR elements in each support point that you make to see that your connections to the thesis are clear; whatever elements are missing or underrepresented should be fleshed out in your final draft.

This is also the time to check if your support points are in a logical, effective order. Decide where certain points should go, and then move sections around, if necessary, in order to create a sense of progress and balance for your reader.

5. Check to Make Sure You Have Enough Information

This last pass is the time to look for gaps in your argument. Check your claims and assumptions, and be sure that you have support for whatever you're arguing. If necessary, consult outside references to strengthen your views, and then be sure to analyze those details within the context of your argument in order for their connection to your thesis to be clear.

EDITING

Now that you've moved around, filled in, and shored up different patches of your essay, you're ready to polish it. Editing is the most tedious part of the writing process, and the only way to get through it is to do it. Unfortunately, though you will become a better editor of your own work, you will probably always need to spend a fair amount of time fine-tuning your writing. So don't rush! The unnecessary comma you leave in place or the misspelled word you fail to change can seriously undermine your credibility as a writer and cause your reader to think you have little concern for your finished product or that you don't know any better than to make careless mistakes.

THREE MAIN STEPS CAN HELP YOU FIND SENTENCE-LEVEL ERRORS

1.   Read Your Essay Sentence By Sentence

Breaking your essay down one sentence at a time allows you to check for grammar errors. It lets you identify and correct run-on sentences, sentence fragments, or just plain confusing sentences. Make sure each sentence makes sense by itself first, and then read through your essay another time to see that each sentence leads logically into the next.

2.   Read Your Essay Word By Word

Slowing down and reading your essay word by word will allow you to find any grammar errors you may have missed when reading each sentence separately. You can check for subject-verb agreement, pronoun agreement, and switches in point of view (if you're writing using "I" or "you," for instance). Further, slowing down can help you listen to the voice of your writing and determine if you've repeated a word one too many times or have used too many multi-syllabic words when you could do with shorter ones.

3.   Read Your Essay Backwards

Plainly and simply, reading your essay backwards helps you find spelling errors. Your essay won't make sense that way, but you won't be able to anticipate—and thus skip—the upcoming words in a sentence. So, you won't be able to gloss over misspellings because you're in a hurry or because subconsciously you know what you mean to say and give yourself credit for having said it. This is the most painstaking of all the editing steps because you can't even distract yourself from editing by thinking about your scintillating content. However, it is because you must read every single word closely that this step is so effective.

Writing Argument

Depending upon your point of view, everything can be viewed as an argument. Just the simple act of pointing out a lovely flower, in fact, can be construed as being an argument. By pointing out that particular flower as opposed to any other flower, you are arguing that for the moment you're pointing it out, that that flower is somehow more significant than other flowers you could identify. Thus, without even meaning to, you probably "argue" your point of view much of the time, just by going through your normal daily routine.

Since this process of persuasion seems to emerge even when you do not try to offer your views, the question becomes, why bother to formally identify a statement or body of information as "argument," or why worry about crafting a particular message; why not just say what you think and move on? The problem in just offering your views without bothering to expound upon them lies in the fact that not all people think alike and, thus, not everyone can be convinced that your view is right for them. Your task, then, becomes to shape your argument in such a way as to lead others to think of your view as the "right" way, or at least one of the "right" ways, to address a topic.

KNOWING YOUR AUDIENCE

How, then, do you begin this process of crafting an argument? The first step is to know your audience. Since good writing is like good manners in that it requires you to consider someone else first, knowing your audience is key because you can only accurately and fairly consider your reader if you know your reader well enough to be familiar with his or her preferences. For instance, if you are writing an essay about the benefits of vegetarianism and your neighbor is a cattle rancher, you probably won't end up persuading your neighbor to give up meat. On the other hand, if your argument takes the form of recommending certain types of beef cuts over others as a matter of health, you might stand a reasonable chance of having your neighbor listen to you. The point is to know enough about your audience to be able to consider his or her knowledge and preferences, and then angle your writing accordingly.

THE COMPONENTS OF ARGUMENT

Once you've identified your audience, the next step is to break down the elements of argument into easily identifiable segments that Athenian philosopher Aristotle explained: ethos, pathos, and logos. These, in brief, are: appeal of the speaker, appeal to emotion, and appeal to logic.

ETHOS

Ethos is the appeal of the speaker, usually in terms of his or her ethics and credentials. If a speaker—or, in this case, a writer—is trying to convince an audience that his or her views are correct, that speaker must offer some credibility to support his or her ideas. For instance, a politician may claim that he is "one of you" or that he has special insight into a particular problem, say, in education, because he used to be a teacher. These sorts of qualifiers are appeals of *ethos,* appeals to what is "right" or "wrong" about the speaker and, thus what about the speaker makes him or her worth believing.

In your writing, you probably won't need to offer explicit statements of your credentials as an expert on a particular topic, but you will gain credibility with your audience if you are able to explain your connection to the subject at hand. Just as having a clear purpose is important for persuasion, so, too, is having a credible reason for exploring the topic.

Possible openings to an essay on the availability of free music through MP3 files online can be:

> *I've always craved the latest tunes.*

or,

> *People who want to hear the most contemporary music need to know about MP3 files.*

These types of statements tell your reader that you have an interest in and some knowledge about this area, thus giving yourself credibility on the subject and establishing your *ethos.*

Ethos alone may not be enough to persuade your audience of your views, but having no credibility with your audience is one sure way of sabotaging your efforts to be convincing.

PATHOS

Pathos is the appeal to emotion and is probably the most widely practiced appeal. Advertisers and politicians use emotional ploys in order to stir us—through hope, concern, or fear—to do what they want. For instance, ads for alcoholic beverages often show images of young, attractive people smiling and having a wonderful time. The implication is that the beverage is both the cause of the fun and a promise that a consumer who tries the beverage will have the same experience with the same attractive companions. We know intellectually that most likely a beverage won't radically alter our social lives, but the appeal to a sense of fun and inclusion convinces many people to at least try the product.

The appeal to *pathos* is not wrong, or even weak. The problem lies in people's dependence upon pathos as the primary means of persuasion. Some audiences are amenable to emotional appeals and will be convinced by pathos alone. A speaker addressing the families of gunshot victims needs only to mention violence and grief in order to convince those listeners that tougher gun laws are necessary. However, another speaker needs only to mention the Constitutional right to bear arms and the pride of being independent in order to convince a group of NRA members that gun control is no answer. Either way, the persuasion comes not from any logic or special credibility on the part of the speaker but from the emotions that the speaker is able to tap into, again by knowing the audience. If you know your audience is willing to hear your message, you can probably get away with indulging in a more emotional appeal than if your audience is undecided, but your best bet is to make emotion one tool, rather than your only tool, of persuasion.

LOGOS

Logos is the appeal to logic, and is the most solid foundation you can provide for your argument. Even if your audience doesn't respond to you as a "speaker" or writer, and even if your appeals to emotion don't inspire your audience, a logical appeal alone can still persuade. *Logos* primarily involves offering adequate evidence to support your claims.

The two most common forms of argument, which are often combined, are deductive and inductive reasoning. The deductive argument begins with a generalization, then follows with a specific example related to that generalization, and ends with a conclusion. The following example, offered by Aristotle himself, shows the relationship between the three statements:

All men are mortal.	(generalization)
Socrates is a man.	(specific example)
Socrates is mortal.	(conclusion)

The reasoning employed in deductive thinking links the most general statement to the most specific statement, thus making the conclusion inevitable. Essays that have sound deductive reasoning as their foundation stand much better chances of being persuasive than those that have weak logic.

The other commonly practiced form of logical argument is called inductive reasoning, and contrary to the practices of deductive reasoning, inductive reasoning begins with specific pieces of evidence and then follows with a general conclusion drawn from those pieces of evidence. An easy example of inductive reasoning is:

The sky is gray.	(specific detail)
The sidewalks are wet.	(specific detail)
People are carrying umbrellas.	(specific detail)
It is raining outside.	(general conclusion)

Inductive reasoning is particularly useful in the brainstorming process because often we have specific cases that seem not to connect, but through inductive logic we can infer a general conclusion from them which becomes the thesis.

Most likely, you will employ both types of argument in your writing, and this combination will make for the strongest argument overall. Just be aware of the thinking processes you use in order to structure your argument.

LOGICAL FALLACIES

Just as there are certain steps you want to take in order to ensure logical connections in your writing, there are also certain steps you want to avoid if you hope to be persuasive. Fallacies are incorrect or falsely reasoned facts and, left unchecked and uncorrected in your writing, they can seriously undermine your credibility as a writer and your powers of persuasion. Too many fallacies exist to cover fully in this brief overview, but the following is a list of the most common logical fallacies, or those most likely to appear in and harm your writing.

- **Faulty Sampling:** You already know that using evidence to support your claims is essential for persuasion; now just make sure that the evidence you offer is credible. For instance, if you write that 80% of Americans favor low-fat cooking, but your research included only 10 people who subscribe to *Cooking Light* magazine, you are not accurately representing all Americans; thus, your conclusion is not accurate.

- **Ad Hominem** (to the person): This reasoning shifts the focus of an argument onto the person making the argument. For instance, a speaker guilty of employing an *ad hominem* fallacy might spend more time discrediting his or her opponent than on dissuading the audience of the merits of capital punishment, or whatever his or her argument is.

- **Overgeneralization:** Overgeneralization implies that "many" or "most" of a particular group feel or think a certain way. Saying that "everybody" likes or dislikes something sets you up for failure because if just one person does not fit your description, then your whole statement is false. To avoid overgeneralizing, stay away from terms like *always, many, most, often, several, some, usually.*

- **Either/Or Fallacy:** This fallacy implies that only two options exist for a particular situation, thus oversimplifying the issue. For instance, saying that "Luc must choose between studying political science or dentistry for his career" fails to account for any other academic or career options available to him.

- **Stereotyping:** Stereotypes imply that just because a person is a member of a particular group, he or she has all the characteristics of that group. For instance, common stereotypes include: all people who wear glasses are intelligent, all convertible owners speed, and all Californians live near the beach. Using such statements can weaken, rather than strengthen, your argument.

- **False Cause:** This fallacy assumes that because one event precedes another, the first event causes the second. For instance, saying that "Every time I wash the windows, my two-year-old niece visits," implies that something about your washing causes your niece to appear, which is probably not the case.

- **Democratic Fallacy:** This fallacy assumes that just because many people think or act a certain way, then that thought or act is correct. Saying, for instance, that the Edsel was a great car because "thousands of Americans can't be wrong" is not enough to indicate that the car was worth buying.

These are just a few of the most common logical fallacies; unfortunately, many more exist! However, by embellishing your ideas with support from other sources, ensuring that the foundations of your argument are strong, and avoiding logical missteps, your task of persuasion becomes possible.

Note: Some people will never be convinced of any but their own points of view, regardless of the evidence stacked against them. While you can try all you wish to change the minds of these people, you will probably frustrate yourself; thus, don't be too discouraged by people who have already made up their minds. True persuasion occurs only in an open mind.

A Brief Guide to
Evaluating Internet Sources

Since the Internet has put multiple research sources literally at our fingertips—academic organizations' Websites, online databases, search engines—access to information has never been easier. In fact, we are able to learn more information more quickly about more topics than ever before. However, like anything else, for all these benefits we pay a price: sometimes the sources we find are not current or credible, in which case our research is compromised. How, then, do we determine what sources can help us without leading us astray? The following are some general guidelines by which to evaluate your Internet sources.

Test your sources according to each of the following four criteria in order to determine whether or not your source is credible:

WHAT TYPE OF SOURCE ARE YOU VIEWING?

Until very recently, a small number of online domain names made determining the type of source fairly straightforward:

"com" indicates a commercial, or for-profit, site; (Ex: www.amazon.com, the online bookseller)

"org" indicates some sort of organization, often cause-based; (Ex: www.npr.org, the Website for national public radio)

"gov" informs us that a site is sponsored and run by the government; (Ex: www.senate.gov, the Website for the United States Senate)

"mil" tells us we have reached a military site; (Ex: www.navy.mil, the Website for the United States Navy)

"net" identifies an Internet service provider (Ex: www.whitehouse.net)

"edu" connects us to educational sites, such as those of universities or other learning institutions (Ex: www.csus.edu, for the California State University at Sacramento)

a **"~"** informs us that an individual, rather than an organization, is responsible
or for the information we view; (Ex: www.dde.com/~Kjohnson/
"tilde" birdcare.htm)

Now, however, though examples of these domain names still exist in plenty, we soon will have many more to choose from, thus making the whole source evaluation process trickier. Look for the following in the near future:

"aero" indicates aviation groups

"biz" indicates a business

"coop"	identifies a cooperative such as a farm coop or credit union
"info"	anyone may use this domain name
"museum"	indicates a museum
"name"	to register a family name
"pro"	identifies a certified professional such as a certified public accountant or physician

Once you've determined the type of source you want to use, ask yourself three basic questions:

HOW CURRENT IS THE INFORMATION PROVIDED?

Information is only helpful if it's timely to the topic at hand. Look for a recent revision or posting date at the top or bottom of the WebPages. If the last site update was completed two years ago, for instance, chances are this site won't be much help. Another way to determine whether or not a site is current is to evaluate the links provided by that site, if any links are available. Current, functional links are a positive sign that the site has been recently tended; if, however, the links you click on are outdated or non-functional, then this site may not be as recent as you need.

WHAT IS THE PURPOSE OF THE WEBSITE?

Make sure you know what the slant or bias of the Website you're viewing is. For instance, is the site offering just a broad overview of the topic you're researching? If so, the information provided might not meet your in-depth needs. Make sure, too, that the site's purpose includes a broad enough population for your needs. If the information provided targets only children, for instance, you may need to look elsewhere. Finally, be aware that if the source has a particular bias, be aware of such a bias: http://forces.org, for instance, strongly advocates smokers' rights; if you seek to learn about the dangers of smoking, this site is probably not for you.

WHAT CREDENTIALS DOES THE SITE OFFER?

Make sure that the site offers some credible qualifications, such as affiliations with educational or professional organizations. While individuals may have much to offer on the topic you research, you will have an easier time verifying your information if it was posted by someone more knowledgeable than a middle school student.

While you may still find sources that don't always help you as much as you'd like, following these basic guidelines can help you find and evaluate the sources you do find.

Overview: Defining Civility

"... the idea that people are born naturally good but corrupted by civilization ... is a very sweet idea, but it bears no relation to human nature."

—Judith Martin

"Many feel that in our extremely competitive society civility is a luxury they can't afford."

—P.M. Forni

"... nature is often (by our standards) cruel ... and contains no moral messages ..."

—Stephen Jay Gould

Websites:

www.forbetterlife.com/

Website for the organization
For a Better Life, striving
through conscious civility to
create a kinder world.

www.washingtonpost.com/
wp-dyn/style/columns/
missmanners/

This *Washington Post* Website
allows viewers to read past
columns written by *Miss Manners,* Judith Martin.

"Recognizing for the first time both his godlikeness and his vulnerability, man lifted himself above the plane of a purely animal existence by freely choosing to become a morally responsible being, whose first rational duty is to be his human brother's keeper . . . ."

—Leon Kass
Am I My Brother's Keeper?

"For in reality this is a brutally impolite world where bad intentions frequently prevail, and nothing is going to change that . . . ."

—Verlyn Klinkenborg
We Are Still Only Human

"Think what a better world it would be if we all—the whole world—had cookies and milk about three o'clock every afternoon and then lay down with our blankies for a nap."

—Robert Fulghum

Introduction

Etiquette maven Elizabeth Post defines etiquette as "a code of behavior based on kindness, consideration, and respect," and many people agree that these virtues are well worth practicing daily. However, as the planet becomes more populated, and as we find new ways of being irritated by the same crowds which we help swell, we find that practicing these virtues becomes more difficult, particularly since the many cultures represented in the United States make the practice of "civility" multi-faceted and, thus, unclear. Consequently, while the need for some sort of order grows daily, the guidelines for civil behavior remain obscure.

Simply acknowledging the need for civility, however, is not enough. One of the fundamental concepts in determining the importance of civility lies in the question of whether or not human beings are inherently considerate of each other. "Miss Manners" writer Judith Martin claims that people are not "born good; that has to be learned," and essayist William Hazlitt goes so far as to say that those people who seem the most amiable are those whom we should trust least. The question of inborn human goodness is essential to address because, if we are born good, then civility should be easy, and being our "brother's keeper" is a pleasure; whereas, if we are not born good, then perhaps we are not so eager to rescue our foolish or reckless fellow humans, and civility takes a bit more thought and effort.

The overview in this textbook, "Defining Civility: Different Views" presents several writers' ideas on what comprises human nature and of how our changing social values affect our behavior. Do we need to concern ourselves with civility? If so, to what extent? If not, then at what point does the law step in to regulate our behavior? Are some people more likely to be civil or uncivil? These are some questions raised in this section, and writers exploring civility, then, will need to consider their own definitions of "etiquette" and "civility" in order to better determine what, for them, a working code of conduct should be.

All I Really Need to Know I Learned in Kindergarten

Robert Fulghum

Robert Fulghum describes himself as a philosopher, and over the course of his life he has held many jobs ranging from cowboy to IBM salesman. He has also published essays and written for the theater. In *All I Really Need to Know I Learned in Kindergarten,* Fulghum distills his personal "credo" down into several simple rules that apply to all aspects of life.

Pre-reading Questions

Freewrite for five to ten minutes in response to the following questions:
Make a list of any lessons or rules you learned as a young child that you think are still relevant today. Who taught you these rules? What about them made them relevant for you when you learned them? What makes them relevant for you now?

Vocabulary Preview

Vocabulary Words:
- credo
- cynical
- bland
- naïve
- idealism
- existential
- extrapolate

Look up the words above and use at least five of them in sentences related to a single topic of your choice.

---

1   Each spring, for many years, I have set myself the task of writing a personal statement of belief: a Credo. When I was younger, the statement ran for many pages, trying to cover every base, with no loose ends. It sounded like a Supreme Court brief, as if words could resolve all conflicts about the meaning of existence.

2   The Credo has grown shorter in recent years—sometimes cynical, sometimes comical, sometimes bland—but I keep working at it. Recently I set out to get the statement of personal belief, down to one page in simple terms, fully understanding the naïve idealism that implied.

3   The inspiration for brevity came to me at a gasoline station. I managed to fill an old car's tank with super-deluxe high-octane go-juice. My old hoopy couldn't handle it and got the willies—kept sputtering out at intersections and belching going downhill. I understood. My mind and my spirit get like that from time to time. Too much high-content information, and *I* get the existential willies—keep sputtering out at intersections where life choices must be made and I either know too much or not enough. The examined life is no picnic.

4   I realized then that I already know most of what's necessary to live a meaningful life—that it isn't all that complicated. *I know it.* And have known it for a long, long time. Living it—well, that's another matter, yes? Here's my Credo:

5   All I really need to know about how to live and what to do and how to be I learned in kindergarten. Wisdom was not at the top of the graduate-school mountain, but there in the sandpile at Sunday School. These are the things I learned:

Share everything.
Play fair.
Don't hit people.
Put things back where you found them.
Clean up your own mess.
Don't take things that aren't yours.
Say you're sorry when you hurt somebody.
Wash your hands before you eat.
Flush.
Warm cookies and cold milk are good for you.
Live a balanced life—learn some and think some and draw and paint and sing and dance and play and work every day some.
Take a nap every afternoon.
When you go out into the world, watch out for traffic, hold hands, and stick together.
Be aware of wonder. Remember the little seed in the Styrofoam cup: The roots go down and the plant goes up and nobody really knows how or why, but we are all like that.
Goldfish and hamsters and white mice and even the little seed in the Styrofoam cup—they all die. So do we.
And then remember the Dick-and-Jane books and the first word you learned—the biggest word of all—LOOK.

6   Everything you need to know is in there somewhere. The Golden Rule and love and basic sanitation. Ecology and politics and equality and sane living.

7   Take any one of those items and extrapolate it into sophisticated adult terms and apply it to your family life or your work or your government or your world and it holds true and clear and firm. Think what a better world it would be if we all—the whole world—had cookies and milk about three o'clock every afternoon and then lay down with our blankies for a nap. Or if all governments had as a basic policy to always put things back where they found them and clean up their own mess.

8   And it is still true, no matter how old you are—when you go out into the world, it is best to hold hands and stick together.

POST-READING QUESTIONS

CONTENT

1. What does Fulghum say his purpose is in writing his personal credo?
2. What changes has his credo undergone over the years?
3. What is the current form of his credo? How is this form significant?
4. What was the inspiration for his current credo?
5. What are at least three lessons Fulghum learned?

STYLE AND STRUCTURE

6. What is Fulghum's purpose in writing this essay? Restate his main idea in your own words.

7. Who is Fulghum's audience? How can you tell? To what extent are you part of his audience? Choose words and phrases that reveal his intended audience.

8. Fulghum uses "the sandpile at Sunday school" to illustrate one of his ideas. What other specific examples does Fulghum use? Why do you think he chooses these particular images to make his points?

9. What is Fulghum's tone in this essay? What about his essay makes you draw this conclusion?

CRITICAL THINKING AND ANALYSIS

DISCUSSION QUESTIONS

10. To what extent do you agree or disagree that "all [you] really need to know [you] learned in Kindergarten"?

11. What stage in your life do you think has taught you the most important lessons? Why? What are some of the lessons that this stage has taught you?

WRITING ASSIGNMENTS

12. To what extent does Fulghum's stating that he learned "all [he needs] to know" in Kindergarten imply that he has not learned since? How do you know that he has or has not learned important lessons since Kindergarten? Write a few paragraphs in response, citing text for support.

13. If you were writing a list of lessons to give to today's Kindergartners, what lessons would be on it? Explain (in a paragraph or two) why you would or would not include the lessons that Fulghum mentions on his list.

VOCABULARY DEVELOPMENT

14. Fulghum claims that his Kindergarten-learned lessons are most important, yet his language reveals an audience different from children. Choose at least five words or phrases that show who Fulghum's audience is, and explain in a few sentences how these terms do, indeed, reveal his target readers.

GROUP ACTIVITIES

15. Write two lists: one list of lessons you learned as a young child, and one list of lessons you have learned in adulthood, even young adulthood. Which lessons are more relevant to you now? Why? Share your results with the class in an effort to compile a single list that suits the entire class.

16. Scan the comics or watch some family-oriented television shows. Then, as a group discuss the messages that these media communicate. How in tune with contemporary culture is Fulghum?

Money for Morality

Mary Arguelles

A freelance writer whose articles have appeared in *New Mother, Baby Talk,* and *Reader's Digest,* Ms. Arguelles has also produced and hosted *Twigs,* a local parenting education program in Reading, Pennsylvania. Her essay first appeared in the *My Turn* section of *Newsweek* in 1991.

Pre-reading Questions

Freewrite for five to ten minutes in response to the following questions:
How do you define a "good deed"? What were the circumstances of your last "good deed"? Why did you do it? Did you expect a reward? Did you receive a reward? If so, did the reward fit your deed? If not, what would have seemed fair?

Vocabulary Preview

Vocabulary Words:	• mandatory	• collateral	• elicit
	• sufficient	• mercenary	• kowtowing
	• ubiquitous	• catapulted	

Look up the words above and then, as you read the essay, write a few sentences identifying the words you find most powerful in Arguelles' essay.

1   I recently read a newspaper article about an 8-year-old boy who found an envelope containing more than $600 and returned it to the bank whose name appeared on the envelope. The bank traced the money to its rightful owner and returned it to him. God's in his heaven and all's right with the world. Right? Wrong.

2   As a reward, the man who lost the money gave the boy $3. Not a lot, but a token of his appreciation nonetheless and not mandatory. After all, returning money should not be considered extraordinary. A simple "thank you" is adequate. But some of the teachers at the boy's school felt a reward was not only appropriate, but required. Outraged at the apparent stinginess of the person who lost the cash, these teachers took up a collection for the boy. About a week or so later, they presented the good Samaritan with $150 savings bond, explaining they felt his honesty should be recognized. Evidently the virtues of honesty and kindness have become commodities that, like everything else, have succumbed to inflation. I can't help but wonder what dollar amount these teachers would have deemed a sufficient reward. Certainly they didn't expect the individual who lost the money to give the child $150. Would $25 have been respectable? How about $10? Suppose that lost money had to cover mortgage, utilities and food for the week. In light of that, perhaps $3 was generous. A reward is a gift; any gift should at least be met with the presumption of genuine gratitude on the part of the giver.

3   What does this episode say about our society? It seems the role models our children look up to these days—in this case, teachers—are more confused and misguided about values than their young charges. A young boy, obviously well guided by his parents, finds money that does not belong to him and he returns it. He did the right thing. Yet doing the right thing seems to be insufficient motivation for action in our materialistic world. The legacy of the '80s has left us with the ubiquitous question: what's in it for me? The promise of the golden rule—that someone might do a good turn for you—has become worthless collateral for the social interactions of the mercenary and fast-paced '90s. It is in fact this fast pace that is, in part, a source of the problem. Modern communication has catapulted us into an instant world. Television makes history of events before any of us has even had a chance to absorb them in the first place. An ad for major-league baseball entices viewers with the reassurance that "the memories are waiting"; an event that has yet to occur has already been packaged as the past. With the world racing by us, we have no patience for a rain check on good deeds.

4   Misplaced virtues are rampant through our culture. I don't know how many times my 13-year-old son has told me about classmates who received $10 for each A they receive on their report cards—hinting that I should do the same for him should he ever receive an A (or maybe he was working on $5 for a B). Whenever he approaches me on this subject, I give him the same reply: "Doing well is its own reward. The A just confirms that." In other words, forget it! This is not to say that I would never praise my son for doing well in school. But my praise is not meant to reward or elicit future achievements, but rather to express my genuine delight in the satisfaction he feels at having done his best. Throwing $10 at that sends out the message that the feeling alone isn't good enough.

5   **Kowtowing to ice cream:** As a society, we seem to be losing a grip on our internal control—the ethical thermostat that guides our actions and feelings toward ourselves, others, and the world around us. Instead, we rely on external "stuff" as a measure of our worth. We pass this message to our children. We offer them money for honesty and good grades. Pizza is given as a reward for reading. In fact, in one national reading program, a pizza party awaits the entire class if each child reads a certain amount of books within a four month period. We call these incentives, telling ourselves that if we can just reel them in and get them hooked, then the built-in rewards will follow. I recently saw a television program where unmarried, teenaged mothers were featured as the participants in a parenting program that offers a $10 a week "incentive" if these young women don't get pregnant again. Isn't the daily struggle of being a single, teenaged mother enough of a deterrent? No, it isn't, because we as a society won't allow it to be. Nothing is permitted to succeed or fail on its own merits anymore.

6   I remember when I was pregnant with my son I read countless child-care books that offered the same advice: don't bribe your child with ice cream to get him to eat spinach: it makes the spinach look bad. While some may say spinach doesn't need any help looking bad, I submit it's from years of kowtowing to ice cream. Similarly, our moral taste buds have been dulled by an endless onslaught of artificial sweeteners. A steady diet of candy bars and banana splits makes an ordinary apple or orange seem sour. So too does an endless parade of incentives make us incapable of feeling a genuine sense of inner peace (or inner turmoil).

7   The simple virtues of honesty, kindness and integrity suffer from an image problem and are in desperate need of a makeover. One way to do this is by example. If my
son sees me feeling happy after I've helped out a friend, then he may do likewise. If
my daughter sees me spending a rainy afternoon curled up with a book instead of
spending money at the mall, she may get the message that there are some simple
pleasures that don't require a purchase. I fear that in our so-called upwardly mobile
world we are on a downward spiral toward moral bankruptcy. Like pre-World War II
Germany, where the basket holding the money was more valuable than the money itself, we too may render ourselves internally worthless while desperately clinging to a
shell of appearances.

POST-READING QUESTIONS

CONTENT

1. Arguelles writes that "the promise of the golden rule—that someone might
do a good turn for you—has become worthless collateral." What does she
mean by this? Do you agree with her assertion? Use the text to support your
response.

2. What are some examples of "misplaced virtues," according to Arguelles? Do
you agree that these examples illustrate a culture in crisis? Explain and give
examples.

3. What are some suggestions Arguelles offers us in order to reestablish the
"simple virtues of honesty, kindness, and integrity"? To what extent do you
think her suggestions will work? What suggestions can you offer?

4. Consider the comparison Arguelles makes between the teachers' reward to
the "good Samaritan" who returned the money and parents who offer their
children "$10 for each A." To what extent are these situations similar? Dif-
ferent? Explain how effective you find this comparison in terms of Arguelles' argument.

STYLE AND STRUCTURE

5. What is the focus of Arguelles' essay? Put her main idea into your own words.

6. Who is Arguelles' audience? How can you tell? What kinds of examples does
she use that hint as to the year this was written?

7. What effect do the images Arugelles uses—such as "our moral taste buds"
have been "dulled by artificial sweeteners"—have on your reading of the essay? Do they confuse you or help you understand her message? Explain.

8. What kind of tone does Arguelles adopt? What language in particular reveals
her tone? To what extent do you find her tone persuasive?

9. What kind of examples does Arguelles use in order to reveal a morality crisis
in our culture? To what extent is her evidence convincing? What types of examples would have convinced you more?

CRITICAL THINKING AND ANALYSIS

DISCUSSION QUESTIONS

10. To what extent did reading Arguelles' essay change your view toward the boy who received $3 for returning $600? Explain.

11. What do you think the title "Money for Morality" means? Do you agree with the message it sends? Why or why not?

WRITING ASSIGNMENTS

12. Arguelles argues that "misplaced virtues are running rampant through our culture." What virtues does she imply in her discussion of the 8-year old boy, the payment for grades, the national reading program, the parenting program, and other examples? What specific virtues does she praise in her essay? Write a few paragraphs summarizing the values Arguelles criticizes and praises, and then write one paragraph in which you argue that society's values, as presented by Arguelles, are or are not "misplaced." Be sure to cite the text for support.

13. What do you think of the practice of rewarding scholarly performance— getting As, for instance—with money? What do you think the positive and negative aspects of such rewards are? Write at least one well-developed paragraph in which you argue for or against the practice of rewarding scholarly performance. Use examples from the text and from your own experience in order to illustrate your ideas.

VOCABULARY DEVELOPMENT

14. Arguelles expresses different moods throughout her essay. Identify some of these moods and then choose a few words in order to best illustrate what those moods are.

GROUP ACTIVITIES

15. Consider Arguelles' criticism of the parents who offer monetary rewards to their children for good grades. Then, write a letter to one of those parents, offering your own system of motivation. You may use Arguelles' essay for support if you wish.

16. Divide your class into two parties, one that is for rewards in voluntary situations and one that is against such rewards. Hold a debate over whether or not rewards should be offered for good Samaritan acts. Which side has the stronger argument? Write a paragraph summarizing the results of the debate.

Manners Matter

Judith Martin

Widely known for her syndicated *Miss Manners* column, Judith Martin reigns as expert on contemporary etiquette. In *Manners Matter,* Martin contrasts the law with etiquette, stating that each performs necessary functions in society, though etiquette often addresses conflict before it escalates to the level where law must intercede.

Pre-reading Questions

Freewrite for five to ten minutes in response to the following questions:
Make a list of the manners you use daily. Your list may include such items as saying please or thank you, and it may include more active forms of behavior such as letting a driver enter your lane ahead of you. What determines when you employ manners? How important do you think manners are?

Vocabulary Preview

Vocabulary Words:
- etiquette
- repressive
- trivial
- pillage
- impulses
- provocations
- presiding

Look up the words above and, as you read Martin's essay, take note of at least three words—either on this list or not—that you find particularly effective. Be sure to write a few sentences explaining why you have chosen these words.

1   Society's condemnation of etiquette for being artificial and repressive stems from an idealistic if hopelessly naive belief in what we might call Original Innocence—the idea that people are born naturally good but corrupted by civilization. This is a very sweet idea, but it bears no relation to human nature. Yes, we're born adorable, or our parents would strangle us in our cribs. But we are not born good; that has to be learned. And if it is not learned, when we grow up and are not quite so cuddly, even our parents can't stand us. . . .

2   Administering etiquette, like administering law, is more than just knowing a set of rules. Even the most apparently trivial etiquette rules are dictated by principles of manners which are related to, and sometimes overlap with, moral principles. Respect and dignity, for example, are two big principles of manners from which a lot of etiquette rules are derived. This does not mean that you can simply deduce your rules of behavior from first principles. There are things you just have to know, like whether a man is supposed to show respect by taking his hat off as in church, or putting a hat on, as in a synagogue.

3   Moral people who understand these principles still figure that civility is not a top-priority virtue. First, they're going to fix the world, and then on the seventh day they're going to introduce civility. Deep in their hearts, they think etiquette is best applied to activities that don't really matter much, like eating or getting married.

4   But the absence of manners is a cause of some of our most serious social problems. For instance, our school systems have broken down from what is called lack of discipline. What does that mean? It means that such etiquette rules as sitting still, listening to others, taking turns, and not hitting others have not been taught. A great deal of crime begins with the short tempers people develop from being treated rudely all the time, and from perceived forms of disrespect. Getting "dissed," as it's called in the streets, is one of today's leading motivations for murder.

5   Nor will the business of government be done well, or sometimes done at all, by people who can't work together in civil, statesman-like ways. That is why we have all those highly artificial forms of speech for use in legislatures and courtrooms. Even in a courtroom where freedom of speech is being defended, there is no freedom to speak rudely. In legislatures we have phrases like "my distinguished colleague seems to be sadly mistaken"—because if we spoke freely and frankly, people would be punching each other out instead of airing arguments. We have a legal system that bars us from acting on natural human impulses to pillage, assault, and so forth. Whether we appreciate it or not, we also have an extra-legal system, called etiquette, that does many of the same things.

6   Law is supposed to address itself to the serious and dangerous impulses that endanger life, limb, and property. Etiquette addresses provocations that are minor but can grow serious if unchecked. Etiquette has some very handy conflict resolution systems—such as the apology, sending flowers in the morning, saying "I don't know what I was thinking"—that help settle things before they have to go through the legal system. But as we've seen in the past few decades, when people refuse to comply with etiquette the law has to step in. A classic example is smoking. We've had to use the law to explain such simple etiquette rules as: You don't blow smoke in other people's faces, and you don't blow insults into other people's faces pretending it's health advice. Sexual harassment is another example that had to be turned over to the law because those in a position of power refused to obey basic values as "Keep your hands to yourself."

7   It's a dangerous idea to keep asking the law to do etiquette's job. Not that I wouldn't love to have a squad of tough cops who would go around and roust people who don't answer invitations and write thank-you notes. But when we have to enlarge the scope of law to enforce manners, it really does threaten freedom. Even I think people should have a legal right to be obnoxious. I don't think they should exercise it. And I do think people should be prepared to take the consequences: If you stomp on the flag, some people will not want to listen to your opinions. If you disrupt and spoil activities for other people who want to participate, they're going to throw you out. Those are the mild little sanctions of etiquette, but they work.

8   Trying to live by law alone does not work. Every little nasty remark is labeled a slander and taken to court; meanness gets dressed up as "mental cruelty"; and everything

else that's annoying is declared a public health hazard. That's why we need the little extra-legal system over which I have the honor of presiding.

POST-READING QUESTIONS

CONTENT

1. Martin writes that society condemns etiquette for being "artificial and repressive." What do you think she means by this? To what extent do you agree or disagree with this idea? Be sure to give examples from your own experiences and observations in order to illustrate your ideas.

2. Martin cites respect and dignity as two moral principles from which etiquette is derived. What do you think Martin means by "moral principles"? What are some other moral principles that underlie etiquette? What are some rules of etiquette that stem from these principles? Be sure to give examples from your own life in order to support your response.

3. How does Martin differentiate between law and etiquette? Why does she feel we need both systems? Do you agree that we need both systems? Be sure to cite the text as well as your own experiences and observations in order to illustrate your ideas.

4. What assumptions about the nature of conflict does Martin make when she identifies "the apology, sending flowers in the morning, saying 'I don't know what I was thinking'" as tools of etiquette? Do you agree with this assumption? Explain.

5. Martin cites several issues—smoking, sexual harassment among them—that have had to result in laws in order for conflict resolution to occur. What are some other areas where the law has taken over where etiquette should have presided?

6. How does Martin define "etiquette"? What examples does she give to illustrate her definition?

STYLE AND STRUCTURE

7. What is Martin's argument? Write her main idea in your own words.

8. What kind of examples does Martin give to support her thesis? To what extent are these examples convincing? What other examples can you offer that would make Martin's essay even more persuasive?

9. Who is Martin's audience? How can you tell? Cite examples from the text in order to illustrate your ideas.

10. To what extent does Martin use exaggeration to make her point? How effective is it?

11. What is Martin's tone in this essay? How seriously does she take her topic? How can you tell? Be sure to cite the text in order to illustrate your response.

CRITICAL THINKING AND ANALYSIS

DISCUSSION QUESTIONS

12. To what extent do you agree or disagree with the idea that "we are not born good; that has to be learned"? Be sure to give examples from the text and from your own life in order to illustrate your ideas.

13. Where do you think etiquette and the law converge? At what point do they diverge?

WRITING ASSIGNMENTS

14. Using Martin's definition of etiquette as a starting point, write a few paragraphs defining that term. Use examples from at least three different areas of life to clarify your definition.

15. To what extent do you agree that some "minor provocations" that etiquette addresses "can grow serious" if unchecked? In a few well-developed paragraphs or a short essay, argue that "minor provocations" can or can not "grow serious" if unchecked. Cite examples from the text and your own experiences and observations in order to illustrate your ideas.

16. To what extent do you agree with the idea that "trying to live by law alone does not work"? Write at least one paragraph explaining how this statement is or is not true for you. Be sure to cite the essay and your own experiences for support.

VOCABULARY DEVELOPMENT

17. Choose one paragraph from Martin's essay and rewrite it twice: once for an audience of children, and once for another audience of your choosing. What words do you use in both versions? What words do you add for a particular version? Read your paragraphs to your classmates and have them try to determine who the audience for each revision is.

GROUP ACTIVITIES

18. Draw a spectrum upon which you plot various types of etiquette: using a particular fork at dinner, for example, and giving someone the right of way in traffic. Then, discuss why you plotted certain acts at certain points on the spectrum. How do you decide what kinds of etiquette are important?

19. Devise a scenario in which one person is rude to another, and have two people in your group act it out a few times, emphasizing who is at fault. For instance, have one person pay a compliment to another person of a different gender. At what point does this compliment become sexual harassment? Play the scene out several times in order to determine what, exactly, makes an action illegal as opposed to simply rude.

Nonmoral Nature

Stephen Jay Gould

Stephen Jay Gould is the Alexander Agassiz professor of zoology at Harvard University and has become well known for his ability to explain complex concepts to a general audience with exceptional clarity. In *Nonmoral Nature,* Gould explores the notion of "evil" in nature and suggests that the virtues and vices people seek to find in their own actions may not be found outside the human race.

Pre-reading Questions

Freewrite for five to ten minutes in response to the following questions:
List occurrences in nature that seem to you to be either "good" or "evil" or "right" or "wrong." Your list can include natural disasters or natural wonders, animal attacks or animal heroics, or any other event you consider to be found in nature. What about each item on your list rendered it good or evil in your mind? Do you think the concepts of right and wrong apply in nature? Why or why not?

Vocabulary Preview

Vocabulary Words:

• benevolent	• predation	• writhe
• pressing	• theologians	• commotion
• aggregate	• aberrant	• edible
• carnage	• anthropocentric	• forbearance
• parasite	• sentient	• extrapolated

As always, look up the words above, taking care to note their context in Gould's essay as you read. Are any of the words used differently from how you would have thought? Choose five words that you find most flexible in their use and explain what about those words is flexible.

1　　When the Right Honorable and Reverend Francis Henry, earl of Bridgewater,[1] died in February, 1829, he left £8,000 to support a series of books "on the power, wisdom and goodness of God, as manifested in the creation." William Buckland,[2] England's first official academic geologist and later dean of Westminster, was

---

[1]**Reverend Francis Henry, earl of Bridgewater (1756–1829)** He was the eighth and last earl of Bridgewater. He was also a naturalist and a Fellow at All Souls College, Oxford, before he became earl of Bridgewater in 1823. On his death, he left a fund to be used for the publication of the Bridgewater Treatises, essay discussions of the moral implications of scientific research and discoveries.

[2]**William Buckland (1784–1856)** An English clergyman and also a geologist. His essay "Geology and Mineralogy" was a Bridgewater Treatise in 1836.

invited to compose one of the nine Bridgewater Treatises. In it he discussed the most pressing problem of natural theology: If God is benevolent and the Creation displays his "power, wisdom and goodness," then why are we surrounded with pain, suffering, and apparently senseless cruelty in the animal world?

2   Buckland considered the depredation of "carnivorous races" as the primary challenge to an idealized world in which the lion might dwell with the lamb. He resolved the issue to his satisfaction by arguing that carnivores actually increase "the aggregate of animal enjoyment" and "diminish that of pain." The death of victims, after all, is swift and relatively painless, victims are spared the ravages of decrepitude and senility, and populations do not outrun their food supply to the greater sorrow of all. God knew what he was doing when he made lions. Buckland concluded in hardly concealed rapture:

> The appointment of death by the agency of carnivora, as the ordinary termination of animal existence, appears therefore in its main results to be a dispensation of benevolence; it deducts much from the aggregate amount of the pain of universal death; it abridges, and almost annihilates, throughout the brute creation, the misery of disease, and accidental injuries, and lingering decay; and imposes such salutary restraint upon excessive increase of numbers, that the supply of food maintains perpetually a due ratio to the demand. The result is, that the surface of the land and depths of the waters are ever crowded with myriads of animated beings, the pleasures of whose life are co-extensive with its duration; and which throughout the little day of existence that is allotted to them, fulfill with joy the functions for which they were created.

3   We may find a certain amusing charm in Buckland's vision today, but such arguments did begin to address "the problem of evil" for many of Buckland's contemporaries—how could a benevolent God create such a world of carnage and bloodshed? Yet these claims could not abolish the problem of evil entirely, for nature includes many phenomena far more horrible in our eyes than simple predation. I suspect that nothing evokes greater disgust in most of us than slow destruction of a host by an internal parasite—slow ingestion, bit by bit, from the inside. In no other way can I explain why *Alien,* an uninspired, grade-C, formula horror film, should have won such a following. That single scene of Mr. Alien, popping forth as a baby parasite from the body of a human host, was both sickening and stunning. Our nineteenth-century forebears maintained similar feelings. Their greatest challenge to the concept of a benevolent deity was not simple predation—for one can admire quick and efficient butcheries, especially since we strive to construct them ourselves—but slow death by parasitic ingestion. The classic case, treated at length by all the great naturalists, involved the so-called ichneumon fly. Buckland had sidestepped the major issue.

4   The ichneumon fly, which provoked such concern among natural theologians, was a composite creature representing the habits of an enormous tribe. The Ichneumonoidea are a group of wasps, not flies, that include more species than all the vertebrates combined (wasps, with ants and bees, constitute the order Hymenoptera; flies, with their two wings—wasps have four—form the order Diptera). In addition, many related wasps of similar habits were often cited for the same grisly details. Thus, the famous

story did not merely implicate a single aberrant species (perhaps a perverse leakage from Satan's realm), but perhaps hundreds of thousands of them—a large chunk of what could only be God's creation.

5   The ichneumons, like most wasps, generally live freely as adults but pass their larval life as parasites feeding on the bodies of other animals, almost invariably members of their own phylum, Arthropoda. The most common victims are caterpillars (butterfly and moth larvae), but some ichneumons prefer aphid and others attack spiders. Most hosts are parasitized as larvae, but some adults are attacked, and many tiny ichneumons inject their brood directly into the egg of their host.

6   The free-flying females locate an appropriate host and then convert it to a food factory for their own young. Parasitologists speak of ectoparasitism when the uninvited guest lives on the surface of its host, and endoparasitism when the parasite dwells within. Among endoparasitic ichneumons, adult females pierce the host with their ovipositor and deposit eggs within it. (The ovipositor, a thin tube extending backward from the wasp's rear end, may be many times as long as the body itself.) Usually, the host is not otherwise inconvenienced for the moment, at least until the eggs hatch and the ichneumon larvae begin their grim work of interior excavation. Among ectoparasites, however, many females lay their eggs directly upon the host's body. Since an active host would easily dislodge the egg, the ichneumon mother often simultaneously injects a toxin that paralyzes the caterpillar or other victim. The paralysis may be permanent, and the caterpillar lies, alive but immobile, with the agent of its future destruction secure on its belly. The egg hatches, the helpless caterpillar twitches, the wasp larva pierces and begins its grisly feast.

7   Since a dead and decaying caterpillar will do the wasp larva no good, it eats in a pattern that cannot help but recall, in our inappropriate, anthropocentric interpretation, the ancient English penalty for treason—drawing and quartering, with its explicit object of extracting as much torment as possible by keeping the victim alive and sentient. As the king's executioner drew out and burned his client's entrails, so does the ichneumon larva eat fat bodies and digestive organs first, keeping the caterpillar alive by preserving intact the essential heart and central nervous system. Finally, the larva completes its work and kills its victim, leaving behind the caterpillar's empty shell. Is it any wonder that ichneumons, not snakes or lions, stood as the paramount challenge to God's benevolence during the heyday of natural theology?

8   As I read through the nineteenth- and twentieth-century literature on ichneumons, nothing amused me more than the tension between an intellectual knowledge that wasps should not be described in human terms and a literary or emotional inability to avoid the familiar categories of epic and narrative, pain and destruction, victim and vanquisher. We seem to be caught in the mythic structures of our own cultural sagas, quite unable, even in our basic descriptions, to use any other language than the metaphors of battle and conquest. We cannot render this corner of natural history as anything but story, combining the themes of grim horror and fascination and usually ending not so much with pity for the caterpillar as with admiration for the efficiency of the ichneumon.

9   I detect two basic themes in most epic descriptions: the struggles of prey and the ruthless efficiency of parasites. Although we acknowledge that we witness little more than automatic instinct or physiological reaction, still we describe the defenses of hosts

as though they represented conscious struggles. Thus, aphids kick and caterpillars may wiggle violently as wasps attempt to insert their ovipositors. The pupa of the tortoise-shell butterfly (usually considered an inert creature silently awaiting its conversion from duckling to swan) may contort its abdominal region so sharply that attacking wasps are thrown into the air. The caterpillars of *Hapalia,* when attacked by the wasp *Apanteles machaeralis,* drop suddenly from their leaves and suspend themselves in the air by a silken thread. But the wasp may run down the thread and insert its eggs nonetheless. Some hosts can encapsulate the injected egg with blood cells that aggregate and harden, thus suffocating the parasite.

10   J. H. Fabre,[3] the great nineteenth-century French entomologist, who remains to this day the preeminently literate natural historian of insects, made a special study of parasitic wasps and wrote with an unabashed anthropocentrism about the struggles of paralyzed victims (see his books *Insect Life* and *The Wonders of Instinct*). He describes some imperfectly paralyzed caterpillars that struggle so violently every time a parasite approaches that the wasp larvae must feed with unusual caution. They attach themselves to a silken strand from the roof of their burrow and descend upon a safe and exposed part of the caterpillar:

> The grub is at dinner: head downwards, it is digging into the limp belly of one of the caterpillars. . . . At the least sign of danger in the heap of caterpillars, the larva retreats . . . and climbs back to the ceiling, where the swarming rabble cannot reach it. When peace is restored, it slides down [its silken cord] and returns to table, with its head over the viands and its rear upturned and ready to withdraw in case of need.

11   In another chapter, he describes the fate of a paralyzed cricket:

> One may see the cricket, bitten to the quick, vainly move its antennae and abdominal styles, open and close its empty jaws, and even move a foot, but the larva is safe and searches its vitals with impunity. What an awful nightmare for the paralyzed cricket!

12   Fabre even learned to feed some paralyzed victims by placing a syrup of sugar and water on their mouthparts—thus showing that they remained alive, sentient, and (by implication) grateful for any palliation of their inevitable fate. If Jesus, immobile and thirsting on the cross, received only vinegar from his tormentors, Fabre at least could make an ending bittersweet.

13   The second theme, ruthless efficiency of the parasites, leads to the opposite conclusion—grudging admiration for the victors. We learn of their skill in capturing dangerous hosts often many times larger than themselves. Caterpillars may be easy game, but the psammocharid wasps prefer spiders. They must insert their ovipositors in a safe and precise spot. Some leave a paralyzed spider in its own burrow. *Planiceps hirsutus,* for example, parasitizes a California trapdoor spider. It searches

---

[3]**Jean-Henri Fabre (1823–1915)** A French entomologist whose patient study of insects earned him the nickname "the Virgil of Insects." His writings are voluminous and, at times, elegant.

for spider tubes on sand dunes, then digs into nearby sand to disturb the spider's home and drive it out. When the spider emerges, the wasp attacks, paralyzes its victim, drags it back into its own tube, shuts and fastens the trapdoor, and deposits a single egg upon the spider's abdomen. Other psammocharids will drag a heavy spider back to a previously prepared cluster of clay or mud cells. Some amputate a spider's legs to make the passage easier. Others fly back over water, skimming a buoyant spider along the surface.

14   Some wasps must battle with other parasites over a host's body. *Rhyssella curvipes* can detect the larvae of wood wasps deep within alder wood and drill down to its potential victims with its sharply ridged ovipositor. *Pseudorhyssa alpestris,* a related parasite, cannot drill directly into wood since its slender ovipositor bears only rudimentary cutting ridges. It locates the holes made by *Rhyssella,* inserts its ovipositor, and lays an egg on the host (already conveniently paralyzed by *Rhyssella*), right next to the egg deposited by its relative. The two eggs hatch at about the same time, but the larva of *Psuedorhyssa* has a bigger head bearing much larger mandibles. *Psuedorhyssa* seizes the smaller *Rhyssella* larva, destroys it, and proceeds to feast upon a banquet already well prepared.

15   Other praises for the efficiency of mothers invoke the themes of early, quick, and often. Many ichneumons don't even wait for their hosts to develop into larvae, but parasitize the egg directly (larval wasps may then either drain the egg itself or enter the developing host larva). Others simply move fast. *Apanteles militaris* can deposit up to seventy-two eggs in a single second. Still others are doggedly persistent. *Aphidus gomezi* females produce up to 1,500 eggs and can parasitize as many as 600 aphids in a single working day. In a bizarre twist upon "often," some wasps indulge in polyembryony, a kind of iterated supertwinning. A single egg divides into cells that aggregate into as many as 500 individuals. Since some polyembryonic wasps parasitize caterpillars much larger than themselves and may lay up to six eggs in each, as many as 3,000 larvae may develop within, and feed upon, a single host. These wasps are endoparasites and do not paralyze their victims. The caterpillars writhe back and forth, not (one suspects) from pain, but merely in response to the commotion induced by thousands of wasp larvae feeding within.

16   The efficiency of mothers is matched by their larval offspring. I have already mentioned the pattern of eating less essential parts first, thus keeping the host alive and fresh to its final and merciful dispatch. After the larva digests every edible morsel of its victim (if only to prevent later fouling of its abode by decaying tissue), it may still use the outer shell of its host. One aphid parasite cuts a hole in the belly of its victim's shell, glues the skeleton to a leaf by sticky secretions from its salivary gland, and then spins a cocoon to pupate within the aphid's shell.

17   In using inappropriate anthropocentric language in this romp through the natural history of ichneumons, I have tried to emphasize just why these wasps become a preeiminent challenge to natural theology—the antiquated doctrine that attempted to infer God's essence from the products of his creation. I have used twentieth-century examples for the most part, but all themes were known and stressed by the great nineteenth-century natural theologians. How then did they square the habits of these

wasps with the goodness of God? How did they extract themselves from this dilemma of their own making?

18   The strategies were as varied as the practitioners; they shared only the theme of special pleading for an a priori doctrine[4]—they knew that God's benevolence was lurking somewhere behind all these tales of apparent horror. Charles Lyell[5] for example, in the first edition of his epochal *Principles of Geology* (1830–1833), decided that caterpillars posed such a threat to vegetation that any natural checks upon them could only reflect well upon a creating deity, for caterpillars would destroy human agriculture "did not Providence put causes in operation to keep them in due bounds."

19   The Reverend William Kirby,[6] rector of Barham and Britain's foremost entomologist, chose to ignore the plight of caterpillars and focused instead upon the virtue of mother love displayed by wasps in provisioning their young with such care.

> The great object of the female is to discover a proper nidus for her eggs. In search of this she is in constant motion. Is the caterpillar of a butterfly or moth the appropriate food for her young? You see her alight upon the plants where they are most usually to be met with, run quickly over them, carefully examining every leaf, and, having found the unfortunate object of her search, insert her sting into its flesh, and there deposit an egg. . . . The active Ichneumon braves every danger, and does not desist until her courage and address have insured subsistence for one of her future progeny.

20   Kirby found this solicitude all the more remarkable because the wasp will never see her child and enjoy the pleasures of parenthood. Yet her love compels her to danger nonetheless:

> A very large proportion of them are doomed to die before their young come into existence. But in these the passion is not extinguished. . . . When you witness the solicitude with which they provide for the security and sustenance of their future young, you can scarcely deny to them love for a progeny they are never destined to behold.

21   Kirby also put in a good word for the marauding larvae, praising them for their forbearance in eating selectively to keep their caterpillar prey alive. Would we all husband our resources with such care!

[4]**an a priori doctrine** *A priori* means beforehand, and Gould refers to those who approach a scientific situation with a preestablished view in mind. He is suggesting that such an approach prevents the kind of objectivity and fairness that scientific examination is supposed to produce.

[5]**Charles Lyell (1797–1875)** An English geologist who established the glacial layers of the Eocene (dawn of recent), Miocene (less recent), and Pliocene (more recent) epochs during his excavations of Tertiary period strata in Italy. He was influential in urging Darwin to publish his theories. His work is still respected.

[6]**The Reverend William Kirby (1759–1850)** An English specialist in insects. He was the author of a Bridgewater Treatise, *On the power, wisdom, and goodness of God, as manifested in the creation of animals, and in their history, habits, and instincts* (2 vols., 1835).

In this strange and apparently cruel operation one circumstance is truly remarkable. The larva of the Ichneumon, though every day, perhaps for months, it gnaws the inside of the caterpillar, and though at last it has devoured almost every part of it except the skin and intestines, carefully all this time it avoids injuring the vital organs, as if aware that its own existence depends on that of the insect upon which it preys! . . . What would be the impression which a similar instance amongst the race of quadrupeds would make upon us? If, for example, an animal . . . should be found to feed upon the inside of a dog, devouring only those parts not essential to life, while it cautiously left uninjured the heart, arteries, lungs, and intestines—should we not regard such an instance as a perfect prodigy, as an example of instinctive forbearance almost miraculous? [The last three quotes come from the 1856, and last pre-Darwinian, edition of Kirby and Spence's *Introduction to Entomology.*]

22   This tradition of attempting to read moral meaning from nature did not cease with the triumph of evolutionary theory after Darwin published *On the Origin of Species* in 1859—for evolution could be read as God's chosen method of peopling our planet, and ethical messages might still populate nature. Thus, St. George Mivart,[7] one of Darwin's most effective evolutionary critics and a devout Catholic, argued that "many amiable and excellent people" had been misled by the apparent suffering of animals for two reasons. First, however much it might hurt, "physical suffering and moral evil are simply incommensurable." Since beasts are not moral agents, their feelings cannot bear any ethical message. But secondly, lest our visceral sensitivities still be aroused, Mivart assures us that animals must feel little, if any, pain. Using a favorite racist argument of the time—that "primitive" people suffer far less than advanced and cultured people—Mivart extrapolated further down the ladder of life into a realm of very limited pain indeed: Physical suffering, he argued,

depends greatly upon the mental condition of the sufferer. Only during consciousness does it exist, and only in the most highly organized men does it reach its acme. The author has been assured that lower races of men appear less keenly sensitive to physical suffering than do more cultivated and refined human beings. Thus only in man can there really be any intense degree of suffering, because only in him is there that intellectual recollection of past moments and that anticipation of future ones, which constitutes in great part the bitterness of suffering. The momentary pang, the present pain, which beasts endure, though real enough, is yet, doubtless, not to be compared as to its intensity with the suffering which is produced in man through his high prerogative of self-consciousness [from *Genesis of Species,* 1871].

---

[7]**St. George Mivart (1827–1900)** English anatomist and biologist who examined the comparative anatomies of insect-eating and meat-eating animals. A convert to Roman Catholicism in 1844, he was unable to reconcile religious and evolutionary theories and was excommunicated from the Catholic Church in 1900.

23   It took Darwin himself to derail this ancient tradition—in that gentle way so characteristic of his radical intellectual approach to nearly everything. The ichneumons also troubled Darwin greatly and he wrote of them to Asa Gray[8] in 1860:

> I own that I cannot see as plainly as others do, and as I should wish to do, evidence of design and beneficence on all sides of us. There seems to me too much misery in the world. I cannot persuade myself that a beneficent and omnipotent God would have designedly created the Ichneumonidae with the express intention of their feeding within the living bodies of Caterpillars, or that a cat should play with mice.

24   Indeed, he had written with more persuasion to Joseph Hooker[9] in 1856: "What a book a devil's chaplain might write on the clumsy, wasteful, blundering, low, and horribly cruel works of nature!"

25   This honest admission—that nature is often (by our standards) cruel and that all previous attempts to find a lurking goodness behind everything represent just so much absurd special pleading—can lead in two directions. One might retain the principle that nature holds moral messages for humans, but reverse the usual perspective and claim that morality consists in understanding the ways of nature and doing the opposite. Thomas Henry Huxley[10] advanced this argument in his famous essay on *Evolution and Ethics* (1893):

> The practice of that which is ethically best—what we call goodness or virtue—involves a course of conduct which, in all respects, is opposed to that which leads to success in the cosmic struggle for existence. In place of ruthless self-assertion it demands self-restraint; in place of thrusting aside, or treading down, all competitors, it requires that the individual shall not merely respect, but shall help his fellows. . . . It repudiates the gladiatorial theory of existence. . . . Laws and moral precepts are directed to the end of curbing the cosmic process.

26   The other argument, more radical in Darwin's day but common now, holds that nature simply is as we find it. Our failure to discern the universal good we once expected does not record our lack of insight or ingenuity but merely demonstrates that nature

[8]**Asa Gray (1810–1888)** America's greatest botanist. His works, which are still considered important, are *Structural Botany* (1879; originally published in 1842 as *Botanical Text-Book*), *The Elements of Botany* (1836), *How Plants Grow* (1858), and *How Plants Behave* (1872). Gray was a serious critic of Darwin and wrote a great number of letters to him, but he was also a firm believer in Darwinian evolution. Since he was also a well-known member of an evangelical Protestant faith, he was effective in countering religious attacks on Darwin by showing that there is no conflict between Darwinism and religion.

[9]**Joseph Hooker (1817–1911)** English botanist who studied flowers in exotic locations such as Tasmania, the Antarctic, New Zealand, and India. He was, along with Charles Lyell, a friend of Darwin and one of those who urged him to publish *On the Origin of Species*. He was the director of London's Kew Gardens from 1865 to 1885.

[10]**Thomas Henry Huxley (1825–1895)** An English naturalist who, quite independent of organizations and formal support, became one of the most important scientists of his time. He searched for a theory of evolution that was based on a rigorous examination of the facts and found, in Darwin's work, the theory that he could finally respect. He was a strong champion of Darwin.

contains no moral messages framed in human terms. Morality is a subject for philosophers, theologians, students of the humanities, indeed for all thinking people. The answers will not be read passively from nature; they do not, and cannot, arise from the data of science. The factual state of the world does not teach us how we, with our powers for good and evil, should alter or preserve it in the most ethical manner.

27   Darwin himself tended toward this view, although he could not, as a man of his time, thoroughly abandon the idea that laws of nature might reflect some higher purpose. He clearly recognized that the specific manifestations of those laws—cats playing with mice, and ichneumon larvae eating caterpillars—could not embody ethical messages, but he somehow hoped that unknown higher laws might exist "with the details, whether good or bad, left to the working out of what we may call chance."

28   Since ichneumons are a detail, and since natural selection is a law regulating details, the answer to the ancient dilemma of why such cruelty (in our terms) exists in nature can only be that there isn't any answer—and that the framing of the question "in our terms" is thoroughly inappropriate in a natural world neither made for us nor ruled by us. It just plain happens. It is a strategy that works for ichneumons and that natural selection has programmed into their behavioral repertoire. Caterpillars are not suffering to teach us something; they have simply been outmaneuvered, for now, in the evolutionary game. Perhaps they will evolve a set of adequate defenses sometime in the future, thus sealing the fate of ichneumons. And perhaps, indeed probably, they will not.

29   Another Huxley, Thomas's grandson Julian,[11] spoke for this position, using as an example—yes, you guessed it—the ubiquitous ichneumons:

> Natural selection, in fact, though like the mills of God in grinding slowly and grinding small, has few other attributes that a civilized religion would call divine. . . . Its products are just as likely to be aesthetically, morally, or intellectually repulsive to us as they are to be attractive. We need only think of the ugliness of *Sacculina* or a bladderworm, the stupidity of a rhinoceros or a stegosaur, the horror of a female mantis devouring its mate or a brood of ichneumon flies slowly eating out a caterpillar.

It is amusing in this context, or rather ironic since it is too serious to be amusing, that modern creationists accuse evolutionists of preaching a specific ethical doctrine called secular humanism and thereby demand equal time for their unscientific and discredited views. If nature is non-moral, then evolution can not teach any ethical theory at all. The assumption that it can has abetted a panoply of social evils that ideologues falsely read into nature from their beliefs—eugenics and (misnamed) social Darwinism prominently among them. Not only did Darwin eschew any attempt to discover an antireligious ethic in nature, he also expressly stated his personal bewilderment about such deep issues as the problem of evil. Just a few sentences after invoking the ichneumons, and in words that express both the modesty of this splen-

---

[11]**Thomas's grandson Julian Huxley (1887–1975),** an English biologist and a brother of the novelist Aldous Huxley.

did man and the compatibility, through lack of contact, between science and true religion, Darwin wrote Asa Gray,

> I feel most deeply that the whole subject is too profound for the human intellect. A dog might as well speculate on the mind of Newton. Let each man hope and believe what he can.

POST-READING QUESTIONS

CONTENT

1. What creature does Gould say is the "greatest challenge to the concept of a benevolent deity" in nature? What about this particular creature identifies it, in Gould's eyes, as such a challenge?

2. What process does the ichneumon fly follow in providing for its young?

3. With what types of terms does Gould say humans describe parasitic survival? What two themes, thus, are present in such descriptions? Why does Gould think these themes are inappropriate for application to the natural world?

4. What are some arguments naturalists posed in order to illustrate the alleged "goodness" of nature?

5. What conclusion does Gould reach in response to the question of "why such cruelty . . . exists in nature"?

6. What does it mean to "anthropomorphize nature"? What are some effects of doing so in terms of how we view nature?

STYLE AND STRUCTURE

7. What is Gould's primary message? Put his main idea into your own words.

8. How does Gould illustrate humans' attempts to endow nature with human feelings? To what extent is he successful?

9. What are some techniques Gould employs to keep his reader on track? Cite at least two examples of how Gould organizes his ideas in order to promote coherence.

10. Who is Gould's audience? How do his vocabulary and sentence style reflect this audience?

11. Is Gould a credible writer? What techniques does he employ to establish his credibility? What suggestions can you make that would make him more credible to you?

CRITICAL THINKING AND ANALYSIS

DISCUSSION QUESTIONS

12. What does it say about humans that we attempt to reconcile parasitic survival strategies with the idea of a benevolent deity that created all beings?

13. What arguments can you offer that oppose the idea that nature is nonmoral?

WRITING ASSIGNMENTS

14. Gould describes natural theology as "the antiquated doctrine that attempted to infer God's essence from the products of his creation." Is this a reasonable description of natural theology as you understand it? What can a theology that bases its claims in an observation of nature claim about the essence of God? What kind of religion would support a theology that was based on the behavior of natural life, including ichneumons? Write at least a paragraph in response to each question above, using examples from your own experiences and from the text in order to illustrate your ideas.

15. How does Gould's idea of "nonmoral nature" compare to the idea of "Original Innocence" that Judith Martin raises in her essay? How do the two ideas differ? Compare and contrast these two ideas in a few well-developed paragraphs. Cite both texts for support.

16. According to Gould, Darwin ultimately could not "thoroughly abandon the idea that laws of nature might reflect some higher purpose." What are some examples in nature that might seem to reflect this "higher purpose"? To what extent does the behavior of the ichneumon contradict the concept of nature's higher purpose? Write a short essay in which you explain how the idea of a "higher purpose" is or is not present in nature, taking into consideration the ichneumon's actions. Use examples from your own experiences and from the text in order to illustrate your ideas.

VOCABULARY DEVELOPMENT

17. Stephen Jay Gould creates many personas in his writing: scientist, spiritual questioner, historian. Skim his essay and choose at least five words that best reveal him as each of the personas above. Then write a few sentences explaining how the words you choose help identify him each way.

GROUP ACTIVITIES

18. Share various "bug" stories with each other. What about a particular insect's actions either supports or refutes Gould's assertion? In what ways can the insect's actions be interpreted?

19. Animals are portrayed differently in fiction and entertainment, some being endowed with benevolent traits, while others are characterized as being evil. Why do you think animals are stereotyped the way they are? Brainstorm a list of animals that are personified one way or another, and discuss why you think animals gain the reputations they do.

SYNTHESIS QUESTIONS

1. Stephen Jay Gould writes that "nature is (by our standards) cruel," and Judith Martin asserts that "we are not born good," both emphasizing how civility is absent from much in nature. Write a paragraph or essay in which you argue

that nature is or is not "cruel." Be sure to cite the text of these and other essays and use your own experiences and observations in order to illustrate your ideas.

2. Robert Fulghum asserts that "all [he] needs to know [he] learned in Kindergarten," and Judith Martin cites several examples of incidents where breaches of basic consideration and respect—not keeping one's hands to one's self, for instance—bring about legal repercussions for the perpetrator. Consider these views and write a paragraph or essay in which you determine the age at which people become responsible for their acts. Contemplate, for instance, whether a six-year-old can be held accountable for shooting a classmate or whether an eleven-year-old can be held responsible for selling drugs to a younger acquaintance. Be sure to cite these essays and others and use your own experiences and observations in order to illustrate your ideas.

3. Citing from at least three of the writers in this chapter, write a well-developed paragraph or essay in which you define "etiquette." Be sure to use your own experiences and observations in order to illustrate your ideas.

4. Robert Fulghum makes a list of key lessons he learned in Kindergarten and carried through life. Review his list and then write a paragraph or essay in which you identify one or more lessons that you think are as important as Fulghum's. Be sure to use your own experiences and observations in order to illustrate your ideas.

5. Judith Martin points out how people often harm others by simply doing what they, themselves, want to do at the moment, and Mary Arguelles asserts that "doing the right thing seems to be insufficient motivation for action." Write a paragraph or essay in which you determine the point at which people's determination to serve themselves causes them to forfeit their right to be protected by another human being. Be sure to cite both of these texts and others, and use your own experiences and observations in order to illustrate your ideas.

6. Judith Martin writes that people have "a legal right to be obnoxious," but she claims "I don't think they should exercise it." Write a paragraph or essay in which you argue whether or not people have a legal or social right to be "obnoxious." Be sure to define what you mean by "obnoxious," and use examples from "Manners Matter" and from your own experiences and observations in crafting your argument.

7. Stephen Jay Gould argues that humans' ideas of morality do not exist in nature, while Robert Fulghum offers several rules by which to live our lives, implying, too, that "goodness" does not come naturally to humans. Write an essay in which you argue that we are or are not "good" by nature, using Gould's and Fulghum's essays to support your argument. You may also use some of your own rules as support, and be sure to cite both texts and your own experiences and observations in order to illustrate your ideas.

THERE AREN'T ENOUGH FRIENDLY PEOPLE TO FILL OUR CALL CENTER JOBS.

ALL WE CAN FIND ARE ANGRY PEOPLE WHO REFUSE TO PUT THEIR TELEPHONE HEADSET MICROPHONES NEAR THEIR MOUTHS.

NO, I'M SURE THE PROBLEM IS ON YOUR END.

DILBERT reprinted by permission of United Feature Syndicate, Inc.

WONDERFUL JOB, ELLY! WE LOVE WHAT YOU'VE DONE TO THE STORE!

GREAT HOBBY SECTION! FABULOUS WINDOWS!

NICE PLACE! CONGRAT-ULATIONS!

SNORT: I LIKED IT BETTER THE WAY IT WAS!

KNOW WHAT, EL— YOU'RE GONNA GET 5000 GREAT COMMENTS TODAY....BUT THAT'S THE ONE YOU'RE GOING TO REMEMBER.

© Lynn Johnston Productions Inc./ Dist. by United Features Syndicate, Inc.

"Everyone has to think to be polite; the first impulse is to be impolite."

— **Edgar Watson Howe**

"Aggressive driving is now the most common way of driving. It's not just a few crazies—it's a subculture of driving."

— **Sandra Ball-Rokeach**
co-director of the Media and
Injury Prevention Program at
the University of Southern California

"Imagine, as a consumer, how much more seriously your complaint would be taken if you were complaining from inside an armored vehicle capable of reducing the entire 'Customer Service' department to tiny smoking shards."

— **Dave Barry**
The Customer's Always Right

"This effort to deny women their biological identity, their individuality, their humanness, is such an important aspect of obscene language that one can only marvel at how seldom, in an era preoccupied with definitions of obscenity, this fact is brought to our attention."

— **Barbara Lawrence**

"At dark, shadowy intersections, I could cross in front of a car stopped at a traffic light and elicit the *thunk, thunk, thunk, thunk* of the driver— black, white, male, or female,—hammering down the door locks."

— **Brent Staples**

Chapter 1: Everyday Incivility

Readings:

Argument Pair:

Websites:

www.latimes.com

Website for the *Los Angeles Times,* where daily examples of civility and incivility are published in the paper's many different sections.

www.howzmydriving.com

This lighthearted site allows visitors to rate other drivers' roadway skills as well as checking their own driving abilities.

Introduction

So often, turning on the radio, opening a newspaper, or even leaving the house ends up being an exercise in frustration. We hear of traffic slowdowns and read of the latest types of abuse, and we experience road rage and the nosiness of telemarketers on a daily basis.

Not surprisingly, many of us adopt defensive strategies to combat those who offend us. From the impolite driver, we jealously guard our places in traffic, and to the telemarketer, we offer curt responses to initial questions before hanging up without hearing the whole "pitch." And when we see someone irritating or threatening, it is all too easy to side-step that person in order to avoid what, surely, will be an unpleasant encounter. In taking all of these steps, we feel justified, validated, certain in our desire and ability to preserve our own health, wealth, and well-being.

But have we ever stopped to consider the people on the receiving end of our defense? Is the raging roadster rude or inattentive? And could the telemarketer simply be trying to earn an honest living? Finally, when we cross the street to avoid a stranger, how aware is he that we do not want to meet him? Incivility, while usually easy to detect in others, often becomes invisible in ourselves, particularly when we feel that some aspect of our lives is jeopardized. Yet often this incivility, while wearing away our tolerance with every set of high beams reflected in our rear view mirrors, goes both ways and lies within our control.

How responsible we are for other people's feelings, their reactions to us, even if they have "started it," is one aspect of polite behavior often lost in the heat of retaliation. Just how far we should go to entertain thoughts of patience before indulging in vengeance is one issue this chapter addresses.

The Ways We Lie

Stephanie Ericsson

Author of *Companion Through Darkness: Dialogues on Grief* and *Companion into Dawn: Inner Dialogues on Loving*, Stephanie Ericsson addresses the ways we attempt to fool ourselves and others with dishonesty as well as the consequences of such acts. Her essay was first compiled from notes from *Companion into Dawn* in 1997.

Pre-reading Questions

Freewrite for five to ten minutes in response to the following questions:
What is your definition of a lie? What kinds of lies, if any, do you tell regularly? What are your usual reasons for telling lies? How harmful do you think society considers lying to be? How harmful do you consider lying to be?

Vocabulary Preview

Vocabulary Words:

- minimize
- keels
- travails
- penance

- misdemeanors
- facades
- blatant
- precedent

- indignantly
- sleight
- gamut
- reticent

Look up the words above and then use each in a sentence, varying the structure of the sentences you write.

---

1   The bank called today and I told them my deposit was in the mail, even though I hadn't written a check yet. It'd been a rough day. The baby I'm pregnant with decided to do aerobics on my lungs for two hours, our three-year-old daughter painted the living-room couch with lipstick, the IRS put me on hold for an hour, and I was late to a business meeting because I was tired.

2   I told my client the traffic had been bad. When my partner came home, his haggard face told me his day hadn't gone any better than mine, so when he asked, "How was your day?" I said, "Oh, fine," knowing that one more straw might break his back. A friend called and wanted to take me to lunch. I said I was busy. Four lies in the course of a day, none of which I felt the least bit guilty about.

3   We lie. We all do. We exaggerate, we minimize, we avoid confrontation, we spare people's feelings, we conveniently forget, we keep secrets, we justify lying to the big-guy institutions. Like most people, I indulge myself in small falsehoods and still think of myself as a honest person. Sure I lie, but it doesn't hurt anything. Or does it?

4   I once tried going a whole week without telling a lie, and it was paralyzing. I discovered that telling the truth all the time is nearly impossible. It means living with some serious consequences: The bank charges me $60 in overdraft fees, my partner

keels over when I tell him about my travails, my client fires me for telling her I didn't feel like being on time, and my friend takes it personally when I say I am not hungry. There must be some merit to lying.

5   But if I justify lying, what makes me different from slick politicians or the corporate robbers who raided the S & L industry? Saying it's okay to lie one way and not the other is hedging. I cannot seem to escape the voice deep inside me that tells me: When someone lies, someone loses.

6   What far-reaching consequences will I, or others, pay as a result of my lie? Will someone's trust be destroyed? Will someone else pay *my* penance because I ducked out? We must consider the *meaning of our actions.* Deception, lies, capital crimes, and misdemeanors all carry meanings. *Webster's* definition of a *lie* is specific: *1: a false statement or action especially made with the intent to deceive; 2: anything that gives or is meant to give a false impression.*

7   A definition like this implies that there are many, many ways to tell a lie. Here are just a few.

8   **The White Lie:** The white lie assumes that the truth will cause more damage than a simple, harmless untruth. Telling a friend he looks great when he looks like hell can be based on a decision that the friend needs a compliment more than a frank opinion. But, in effect, it is the liar deciding what is best for the lied to. Ultimately, it is a vote of no confidence. It is an act of subtle arrogance for anyone to decide what is best for someone else.

9   Yet not all circumstances are quite so cut-and-dried. Take, for instance, the sergeant in Vietnam who knew one of his men was killed in action but listed him as missing so that the man's family would receive indefinite compensation instead of the lump-sum pittance the military gives widows and children. His intent was honorable. Yet for twenty years this family kept their hopes alive, unable to move on to a new life.

10   **Facades:** We all put up facades to one degree or another. When I put on a suit to go to see a client, I feel as though I am putting on another face, obeying the expectation that serious businesspeople wear suits rather than sweatpants. But I'm a writer. Normally, I get up, get the kid off to school, and sit at my computer in my pajamas until four in the afternoon. When I answer the phone, the caller thinks I'm wearing a suit (though the UPS man knows better).

11   But facades can be dangerous because they are used to seduce others into an illusion. For instance, I recently realized that a former friend was a liar. He presented himself with all the right looks and right words and offered lots of new consciousness theories, fabulous books to read, and fascinating insights. Then I did some business with him, and the time came to pay me. He turned out to be all talk and no walk. I heard a plethora of reasonable excuses, including in-depth descriptions of the big break around the corner. In six months of work, I saw less than a hundred bucks. When I confronted him, he raised both eyebrows and tried to convince me that I'd heard him wrong, that he'd made no commitment to me. A simple investigation into his past revealed a crowded graveyard of disenchanted former friends.

12   **Ignoring the Plain Facts:** In the '60s, the Catholic Church in Massachusetts began hearing complaints that Father James Porter was sexually molesting children. Rather than relieving him of his duties, the ecclesiastical authorities simply moved him

from one parish to another between 1960 and 1967, actually providing him with a fresh supply of unsuspecting families and innocent children to abuse. After treatment in 1967 for pedophilia, he went back to work, this time in Minnesota. The new diocese was aware of Father Porter's obsession with children, but they needed priests and recklessly believed treatment had cured him. More children were abused until he was relieved of his duties a year later. By his own admission, Porter may have abused as many as a hundred children.

13   Ignoring the facts may not in and of itself be a form of lying, but consider the context of the situation. If a lie is a false action done with the intent to deceive, then the Catholic Church's conscious covering for Porter created irreparable consequences. The church became a coperpetrator with Porter.

14   **Deflecting:** I've discovered that I can keep anyone from seeing the true me by being selectively blatant. I set a precedent of being up-front about intimate issues, but I never bring up the things I truly want to hide; I just let people assume I'm revealing everything. It's an effective way of hiding.

15   Any good liar knows that the way to perpetuate an untruth is to deflect attention from it. When Clarence Thomas exploded with accusations that the Senate hearings were a "high-tech lynching," he simply switched the focus from a highly charged subject to a radioactive subject. Rather than defending himself, he took the offensive and accused the country of racism. It was a brilliant maneuver. Racism is now politically incorrect in official circles—unlike sexual harassment, which still rewards those who can get away with it.

16   Some of the most skillful deflectors are passive-aggressive people who, when accused of inappropriate behavior, refuse to respond to the accusations. This you-don't-exist stance infuriates the accuser, who, understandably, screams something obscene out of frustration. The trap is sprung and the act of deflection successful, because now the passive-aggressive person can indignantly say, "Who can talk to someone as unreasonable as you?" The real issue is forgotten and the sins of the original victim become the focus. Feeling guilty of name-calling, the victim is fully tamed and crawls into a hole, ashamed. I have watched this fighting technique work thousands of times in disputes between men and women, and what I've learned is that the real culprit is not necessarily the one who swears the loudest.

17   **Omission:** Omission involves telling most of the truth minus one or two key facts whose absence changes the story completely. You break a pair of glasses that are guaranteed under normal use and get a new pair, without mentioning that the first pair broke during a rowdy game of basketball. Who hasn't tried something like that? But what about the omission of information that could make a difference in how a person lives his or her life?

18   For instance, one day I found out that rabbinical legends tell of another woman in the Garden of Eden before Eve. I was stunned. The omission of the Sumerian goddess Lilith from Genesis—as well as her demonization by ancient misogynists as an embodiment of female evil—felt like spiritual robbery. I felt like I'd just found out my mother was really my stepmother. To take seriously the tradition that Adam was created out of the same mud as his equal counterpart, Lilith, redefines all of Judeo-Christian history.

19   Some renegade Catholic feminists introduced me to a view of Lilith that has been suppressed during the many centuries when this strong goddess was seen only as a spirit of evil. Lilith was a proud Goddess who defied Adam's need to control her, attempted negotiations, and when this failed, said adios and left the Garden of Eden.

20   This omission of Lilith from the Bible was a patriarchal strategy to keep women weak. Omitting the strong-women archetype of Lilith from Western religions and starting the story with Eve the Rib helped keep Christian and Jewish women believing they were the lesser sex for thousands of years.

21   **Stereotypes and Clichés:** Stereotype and cliché serve a purpose as a form of shorthand. Our need for vast amounts of information in nano-seconds has made the stereotype vital to modern communication. Unfortunately, it often shuts down original thinking, giving those hungry for the truth a candy bar of misinformation instead of a balanced meal. The stereotype explains a situation with just enough truth to seem unquestionable. All the "isms"—racism, sexism, ageism, et al.—are founded on and fueled by the stereotype and the cliché, which are lies of exaggeration, omission, and ignorance. They are always dangerous. They take a single tree and make it a landscape. They destroy curiosity. They close minds and separate people. The single mother on welfare is assumed to be cheating. Any black male could tell you how much of his identity is obliterated daily by stereotypes. Fat people, ugly people, beautiful people, old people, large-breasted women, short men, the mentally ill, and the homeless all could tell you how much more they are like us than we want to think. I once admitted to a group of people that I had a mouth like a truck driver. Much to my surprise, a man stood up and said, "I'm a truck driver, and I never cuss." Needless to say, I was humbled.

22   **Groupthink:** Irving Janis, in *Victims of Group Think,* defines this sort of lie as a psychological phenomenon within decision-making groups in which loyalty to the group has become more important than any other value, with the result that dissent and the appraisal of alternatives are suppressed. If you've ever worked on a committee or in a corporation, you've encountered groupthink. It requires a combination of other forms of lying—ignorance of facts, selective memory, omission, and denial, to name a few.

23   The textbook example of groupthink came on December 7, 1941. From as early as the fall of 1941, the warnings came in, one after another, that Japan was preparing for a massive military operation. The Navy command in Hawaii assumed Pearl Harbor was invulnerable—the Japanese weren't stupid enough to attack the United States' most important base. On the other hand, racist stereotypes said the Japanese weren't smart enough to invent a torpedo effective in less than 60 feet of water (the fleet was docked in 30 feet); after all, U.S. technology hadn't been able to do it.

24   On Friday, December 5, normal weekend leave was granted to all the commanders at Pearl Harbor, even though the Japanese consulate in Hawaii was busy burning papers. Within the tight, good-ole-boy cohesiveness of the U.S. command in Hawaii, the myth of invulnerability stayed well entrenched. No one in the group considered the alternatives. The rest is history.

25   **Out-and-Out Lies:** Of all the ways to lie, I like this one the best, probably because I get tired of trying to figure out the real meanings behind things. At least I can trust the bald-faced lie. I once asked my five-year-old nephew, "Who broke the fence?" (I had seen him do it.) He answered, "The murderers." Who could argue?

26   At least when this sort of lie is told it can be easily confronted. As the person who is lied to, I know where I stand. The bald-faced lie doesn't toy with my perceptions—it argues with them. It doesn't try to refashion reality, it tries to refute it. *Read my lips . . .* No sleight of hand. No guessing. If this were the only form of lying, there would be no such thing as floating anxiety or the adult-children of alcoholics movement.

27   **Dismissal:** Dismissal is perhaps the slipperiest of all lies. Dismissing feelings, perceptions, or even the raw facts of a situation ranks as a kind of lie that can do as much damage to a person as any other kind of lie.

28   The roots of many mental disorders can be traced back to the dismissal of reality. Imagine that a person is told from the time she is a tot that her perceptions are inaccurate: *"Mommie, I'm scared."* "No you're not, darling." *"I don't like that man next door, he makes me feel icky."* "Johnny, that's a terrible thing to say, of course you like him. You go over there right now and be nice to him."

29   I've often mused over the idea that madness is actually a sane reaction to an insane world. Psychologist R. D. Laing supports this hypothesis in *Sanity, Madness & The Family,* an account of his investigation into the families of schizophrenics. The common thread that ran through all of the families he studied was a deliberate, staunch dismissal of the patient's perceptions from a very early age. Each of the patients started out with an accurate grasp of reality, which, through meticulous and methodical dismissal, was demolished until the only reality the patient could trust was catatonia.

30   Dismissal runs the gamut. Mild dismissal can be quite handy for forgiving the foibles of others in our day-to-day lives. Toddlers who have just learned to manipulate their parents' attention sometimes are dismissed out of necessity. Absolute attention from the parents would require so much energy that no one would get to eat dinner. But we must be careful and attentive about how far we take our "necessary" dismissals. Dismissal is a dangerous tool, because it's nothing less than a lie.

31   **Delusion:** I could write a book on this one. Delusion, a cousin of dismissal, is the tendency to see excuses as facts. It's a powerful lying tool because it filters out information that contradicts what we want to believe. Alcoholics who believe the problems in their lives are legitimate reasons for drinking rather than results of the drinking offer the classic example of deluded thinking. Delusion uses the mind's ability to see things in myriad ways to support what it wants to be the truth.

32   But delusion is also a survival mechanism we all use. If we were to fully contemplate the consequences of our stockpiles of nuclear weapons or global warming, we could hardly function on a day-to-day level. We don't want to incorporate that much reality into our lives because to do so would be paralyzing.

33   Delusion works as an adhesive to keep the status quo intact. It shamelessly employs dismissal, omission, and amnesia, among other sorts of lies. Its most cunning defense is that it cannot see itself.

34   These are only a few of the ways we lie. Or are lied to. As I said earlier, it's not easy to entirely eliminate lies in our daily lives. No matter how pious we may try to be, we will still embellish, hedge, and omit to lubricate the daily machinery of living. But there is a world of difference between telling functional lies and living a lie. Martin Buber once said, "The lie is the spirit committing treason against itself." Our acceptance

of lies becomes a cultural cancer that eventually shrouds and reorders reality until moral garbage becomes as invisible to us as water is to a fish.

35   How much do we tolerate before we become sick and tired of being sick and tired? When will we stand up and declare our *right* to trust? When do we stop accepting that the real truth is in the fine print? Whose lips do we read this year when we vote for president? When will we stop being so reticent about making judgments? When do we stop turning over our personal power and responsibility to liars?

36   Maybe if I don't tell the bank the check's in the mail I'll be less tolerant of the lies told me every day. A country song I once heard said it all for me: "You've got to stand for something or you'll fall for anything."

POST-READING QUESTIONS

CONTENT

1. What does Ericsson mean when she says, "when someone lies, someone loses"? To what extent do you agree with her?

2. Why does Ericsson say we lie? What other reasons can you think of?

3. What does Ericsson say is the lie she likes best? Why does she "like" this one the most?

4. How does Ericsson differentiate between "telling functional lies and living a lie"? Give examples from your own experiences and observations in order to illustrate this concept.

5. In what ways does Ericsson say stereotypes and clichés are forms of lying? To what extent do you agree with her?

STYLE AND STRUCTURE

6. What is the focus of Ericsson's essay? Restate her main idea in your own words.

7. How well do Ericsson's examples illustrate her main idea? Do you agree with her? Explain.

8. What can you tell about Ericsson's audience? In what ways do her vocabulary and examples target her audience?

9. What purpose does Ericsson's anecdote at the beginning of the essay serve?

10. What effect do Ericsson's questions in her next-to-last paragraph have on her essay? To what extent do you think the questions strengthen or weaken her essay? Explain.

CRITICAL THINKING AND ANALYSIS

DISCUSSION QUESTIONS

11. Rank the lies Ericsson lists in terms of most or least harmful both according to what Ericsson thinks and according to what you think. Then, explain how some lies are more harmful than others, citing the text for support.

12. List some other types of lies that Ericsson does not mention and explain how the lies you list are more or less harmful than the ones Ericsson describes. Be sure to use examples from your own experiences and observations in order to illustrate your ideas.

WRITING ASSIGNMENTS

13. In two to three paragraphs, assume the opposite stance from Ericsson and argue that lying is necessary, even beneficial. You may use some of Ericsson's own examples to support your argument, but be sure to use your own experiences and observations, too.

14. At what point do you think children should be told the truth, regardless of its brutality or unpleasantness? Explain in a well-developed paragraph or short essay, offering examples from your life and from Ericsson's essay for support.

15. If, as Ericsson states, lying to someone is "an act of subtle arrogance for anyone to decide what is best for someone else," to what extent can lying ever be considered an act of civility? Write a few well-developed paragraphs arguing that lying can or cannot be a form of civility. Be sure to cite the text and your own life in responding to this question.

VOCABULARY DEVELOPMENT

16. Write a list of all the different terms you can think of for "lying," and then skim Ericsson's essay to find how many of your terms are there and how many new expressions you learn. Then, look up these expressions for lying, paying attention to each word's original meaning. Write a sentence or two explaining which expressions have changed the most.

GROUP ACTIVITIES

17. Brainstorm your own examples for each type of lie Ericsson mentions. Then, draw a visual representation of the lies you find most offensive. For instance, make a graph or chart to show how harmful certain lies are, or sketch the reaction of a victim of one of the lies. Present your results to other groups, explaining how you came to your conclusion.

18. Choose at least three situations where being completely honest is particularly difficult, and then discuss whether or not lies in those situations are ever appropriate. For instance, what do you say to the parents of a baby that you do not find adorable? Present your findings to the class in an open forum setting.

Four-Letter Words Can Hurt You

Barbara Lawrence

In her essay *Four-Letter Words Can Hurt You,* first printed in *The New York Times* in 1973, teacher Barbara Lawrence explores possible reasons for profanity's offensiveness. She raises the issue of obscene words' offensiveness to women, in particular, and she presents an etymological context for some of the most common sexual profanities.

Pre-reading Questions

Freewrite for five to ten minutes in response to the following questions:
How do you react to profanity? Do you think it is more offensive to certain groups of people than others? If so, which groups do you think are most offended by profanity? Why do you think profanity is, or can be, offensive? Why do you think people use profanity?

Vocabulary Preview

Vocabulary Words:

- taboos
- etymological
- crotchet
- sadistic

- mutilating
- antecedent
- procreative

- denigrating
- aesthetically
- pejoratives

Look up the words above and write a few sentences explaining how they are effective or ineffective in communicating a point about offensive language.

---

1   Why should any words be called obscene? Don't they all describe natural human functions? Am I trying to tell them, my students demand, that the "strong, earthy, gut-honest"—or, if they are fans of Norman Mailer,[1] the "rich, liberating, existential"—language they use to describe sexual activity isn't preferable to "phony-sounding, middle-class words like 'intercourse' and 'copulate'?" "Copy You Late!" they say with fancy inflections and gagging grimaces. "Now, what is *that* supposed to mean?"

2   Well, what is it supposed to mean? And why indeed should one group of words describing human functions and human organs be acceptable in ordinary conversation and another, describing presumably the same organs and functions, be tabooed—so much so, in fact, that some of these words still cannot appear in print in many parts of the English-speaking world?

3   The argument that these taboos exist only because of "sexual hangups" (middle-class, middle-age, feminist), or even that they are a result of class oppression (the contempt of the Norman conquerors for the language of their Anglo-Saxon serfs), ignores a much more likely explanation, it seems to me, and that is the sources and functions of the words themselves.

---

[1]Norman Mailer: An American writer.

4   The best known of the tabooed sexual verbs, for example, comes from the German *ficken,* meaning "to strike"; combined, according to Partridge's etymological dictionary *Origins,* with the Latin sexual verb *futuere;* associated in turn with the Latin *fustis,* "a staff or cudgel"; the Celtic *buc,* "a point, hence to pierce"; the Irish *bot,* "the male member"; the Latin *battuere,* "to beat" the Gaelic *batair,* "a cudgeller"; the Early Irish *bualaim,* "I strike"; and so forth. It is one of what etymologists sometimes call "the sadistic group of words for the man's part in copulation."

5   The brutality of this word, then, and its equivalents ("screw," "bang," etc.), is not an illusion of the middle class or a crotchet of Women's Liberation. In their origins and imagery these words carry undeniably painful, if not sadistic implications, the object of which is almost always female. Consider, for example, what a "screw" actually does to the wood it penetrates; what a painful, even mutilating, activity this kind of analogy suggests. "Screw" is particularly interesting in this context, since the noun, according to Partridge, comes from words meaning "groove," "nut," "ditch," "breeding sow," "scrofula" and "swelling," while the verb, besides its explicit imagery, has antecedent associations to "write on," "scratch," "scarify," and so forth—a revealing fusion of a mechanical or painful action with an obviously denigrated object.

6   Not all obscene words, of course, are as implicitly sadistic or denigrating to women as these, but all that I know seem to serve a similar purpose: to reduce the human organism (especially the female organism) and human functions (especially sexual and procreative) to their least organic, most mechanical dimension; to substitute a trivializing or deforming resemblance for the complex human reality of what is being described.

7   Tabooed male descriptives, when they are not openly denigrating to women, often serve to divorce a male organ or function from any significant interaction with the female. Take the word "testes," for example, suggesting "witnesses" (from the Latin *testis*) to the sexual and procreative strengths of the male organ; and the obscene counterpart of this word, which suggests little more than a mechanical shape. Or compare almost any of the "rich," "liberating" sexual verbs, so fashionable today among male writers, with that much-derided Latin word "copulate" ("to bind or join together") or even that Anglo-Saxon phrase (which seems to have had no trouble surviving the Norman Conquest) "make love."

8   How arrogantly self-involved the tabooed words seem in comparison to either of the other terms, and how contemptuous of the female partner. Understandably so, of course, if she is only a "skirt," a "broad", a "chick," a "pussycat" or a "piece." If she is, in other words, no more than her skirt, or what her skirt conceals; no more than a breeder, or the broadest part of her; no more than a piece of a human being or a "piece of tail."

9   The most severely tabooed of all the female descriptives, incidentally, are those like a "piece of tail," which suggest (either explicitly or through antecedents) that there is no significant difference between the female channel through which we are all conceived and born and the anal outlet common to both sexes—a distinction that pornographers have always enjoyed obscuring.

10   This effort to deny women their biological identity, their individuality, their humanness, is such an important aspect of obscene language that one can only marvel at how seldom, in an era preoccupied with definitions of obscenity, this fact is

brought to our attention. One problem, of course, is that many of the people in the best position to do this (critics, teachers, writers) are so reluctant today to admit that they are angered or shocked by obscenity. Bored, maybe, unimpressed, aesthetically displeased, but—no matter how brutal or denigrating the material—never angered, never shocked.

11   And yet how eloquently angered, how piously shocked many of these same people become if denigrating language is used about any minority group other than women; if the obscenities are racial or ethnic, that is, rather than sexual. Words like "coon," "kike," "spic," "wop," after all, deform identity, deny individuality and humanness in almost exactly the same way that sexual vulgarisms and obscenities do.

12   No one that I know, least of all my students, would fail to question the values of a society whose literature and entertainment rested heavily on racial or ethnic pejoratives. Are the values of a society whose literature and entertainment rest as heavily as ours on sexual pejoratives any less questionable?   [1973]

POST-READING QUESTIONS

CONTENT

1. What reasons does Lawrence claim others use in support of profanity? What reason does Lawrence herself offer for why profanity should not be used?

2. What reasons does Lawrence give for why the "best known of the tabooed sexual verbs" is offensive? To whom does she say it is most offensive?

3. What "similar purpose" does Lawrence say other swear words serve?

4. What does Lawrence mean when she says that "tabooed male descriptives . . . often serve to divorce a male organ or function from any significant interaction with the female"?

5. How does Lawrence claim women are denied "their biological identity, their individuality, their humanness" through profanity?

6. How does Lawrence claim sexual obscenities are similar to ethnic slurs?

STYLE AND STRUCTURE

7. What is Lawrence's focus? Rewrite her main idea in your own words.

8. How does Lawrence establish her credibility in this article? Why should her readers believe her?

9. Who is Lawrence's audience? Does she target one gender more than another? How can you tell?

10. Why does Lawrence begin her essay by quoting her students and relating their responses to profanity?

11. What effect does Lawrence's use of questions have on your interpretation of the essay? Do her questions help you focus or distract you? Explain.

CRITICAL THINKING AND ANALYSIS

DISCUSSION QUESTIONS

12. Why do you think the etymology of obscene words is, or could be, significant?

13. To what extent do you think profanity is a social issue? Should it be more of a social issue than it is? Explain.

14. Which gender do you think is more easily offended by profanity? Why?

WRITING ASSIGNMENTS

15. How much greater or less of a societal problem is profanity since Lawrence's article was written in 1973? Write a well-developed paragraph arguing your point, and ask people who remember that time if you don't remember it yourself in order to support your point.

16. Do you think sexual slurs or ethnic slurs are more offensive? To whom? Why? Write at least a paragraph explaining why you think some slurs are more offensive than others, citing the text and your own experience for support.

17. What factors do you think contribute to people using profanity? What, if anything, can people do to solve the profanity dilemma? Write a few paragraphs or short essay outlining the causes for profanity and the solution to the problem of obscene language. Be sure to use your own experiences as well as examples from the essay in order to strengthen your ideas.

18. To what extent do you think obscenities mirror a deeper type of incivility? Explain in a brief essay, citing Lawrence's essay and your own experiences for support.

19. When, if ever, is profanity acceptable? What kinds of profanity are, do you think, more acceptable than others? In a few well-developed paragraphs, explain when and what kinds of profanity are acceptable and give examples from the text and your life.

VOCABULARY DEVELOPMENT

20. Make three lists of offensive words: mildly offensive, offensive, and very offensive. (You need not write the actual words for the "very offensive" category; just write the first letter or so to indicate what the word is.) Then, use a dictionary to look up three of the words on each list. How similar are the dictionary definitions to the common meanings of the words? Write a short paragraph drawing a conclusion about the relationship between a word's root meaning and its offensiveness.

GROUP ACTIVITIES

21. Perform your normal entertainment-oriented activities such as watching television, reading a contemporary periodical, or listening to popular music before

coming to class. Then, in small groups, list the areas in which profanity manifests itself and talk about how necessary, if at all, profanity is in entertainment.

22. Lawrence identifies obscenities originated from men and directed at women. As a group, discuss whether or not you think it is possible for men to be as harmed by profanity as women, and why.

Black Men and Public Space

Brent Staples

Brent Staples is an Editorial writer for *The New York Times*. He received his Ph.D. in psychology from the University of Chicago, taught briefly, then worked for several magazines and newspapers before moving to New York. In his essay, Staples explores the reasons why people feel threatened by African-American men, how people's reactions to him make him feel, and how he himself has taken steps to dissipate his own frustration at having his presence misinterpreted by strangers.

Pre-reading Questions

Freewrite for five to ten minutes in response to the following questions:
Have you ever crossed the street to avoid passing someone "threatening" as you walked? Have you ever had someone cross the street or employ other tactics to avoid you? How did that person's actions make you feel? Explain. Under what circumstances, if any, do you think obviously avoiding someone is OK? Explain.

Vocabulary Preview

Vocabulary Words:

• affluent	• taut	• bravado
• uninflammatory	• bandolier	• cursory
• wayfarers	• perpetrators	• berth
• pedestrians	• retrospect	• congenial

Look up the words above and write a short paragraph on a topic of your choice using at least five of them.

---

1   My first victim was a woman—white, well dressed, probably in her early twenties. I came upon her late one evening on a deserted street in Hyde Park, a relatively affluent neighborhood in an otherwise mean, impoverished section of Chicago. As I swung onto the avenue behind her, there seemed to be a discreet, uninflammatory distance between us. Not so. She cast back a worried glance. To her, the youngish black man—a broad six feet two inches with a beard and billowing hair, both hands shoved into the pockets of a bulky military jacket—seemed menacingly close. After a few more quick glimpses, she picked up her pace and was soon running in earnest. Within seconds she disappeared into a cross street.

2   That was more than a decade ago, I was twenty-two years old, a graduate student newly arrived at the University of Chicago. It was in the echo of that terrified woman's footfalls that I first began to know the unwieldy inheritance I'd come into—the ability to alter public space in ugly ways. It was clear that she thought of herself the quarry of a mugger, a rapist, or worst. Suffering a bout of insomnia, however, I was stalking sleep, not defenseless wayfarers. As a softy who is scarcely able to take a knife to a raw

chicken—let alone one to a person's throat—I was surprised, embarrassed, and dis-mayed all at once. Her flight made me feel like an accomplice in tyranny. It also made it clear that I was indistinguishable from the muggers who occasionally seeped into the area from the surrounding ghetto. That first encounter, and those that followed, signi-fied that a vast, unnerving gulf lay between nighttime pedestrians—particularly woman—and me. And I soon gathered that being perceived as dangerous is a hazard in itself. I only needed to turn a corner into a dicey situation, or crowd some frightened, armed person in a foyer somewhere, or make an errant move after being pulled over by a policeman. Where fear and weapons meet—and they often do in urban America— there is always the possibility of death.

3   In that first year, my first year away from my hometown, I was to become thor-oughly familiar with the language of fear. At dark, shadowy intersections, I could cross in front of a car stopped at a traffic light and elicit the *thunk, thunk, thunk, thunk* of the driver—black, white, male, or female—hammering down the door locks. On less trav-eled streets after dark, I grew accustomed to but never comfortable with people cross-ing to the other side of the street rather then pass me. Then there were the standard un-pleasantries with policemen, doormen, bouncers, cabdrivers, and others whose business it is to screen out troublesome individuals *before* there is any nastiness.

4   I moved to New York nearly two years ago and I have remained an avid night walker. In central Manhattan, the near-constant crowd cover minimizes tense one-on-one street encounters. Elsewhere—in SoHo, for example, where sidewalks are narrow and tightly spaced buildings shut out the sky—things can get very taut indeed.

5   After dark, on the warrenlike streets of Brooklyn where I live, I often see women who fear the worst from me. They seem to have set their faces on neutral, and with their purse straps strung across their chests bandolier-style, they forge ahead as though bracing themselves against being tackled. I understand, of course, that the danger they perceive is not a hallucination. Woman are particularly vulnerable to street violence, and young black males are drastically overrepresented among the perpetrators of that violence. Yet these truths are no solace against the kind of alienation that comes of be-ing ever the suspect, a fearsome entity whom pedestrians avoid making eye contact.

6   It is not altogether clear to me how I reached the ripe old age of twenty-two with-out being conscious of the lethality nighttime pedestrians attributed to me. Perhaps it was because in Chester, Pennsylvania, the small, angry industrial town where I came of age in the 1960s, I was scarcely noticeable against a backdrop of gang warfare, street knifings, and murders. I grew up one of the good boys, had perhaps a half-dozen fist-fights. In retrospect, my shyness of combat has clear sources.

7   As a boy, I saw countless tough guys locked away; I have since buried several, too. They were babies, really—a teenage cousin, a brother of twenty-two, a childhood friend in his mid-twenties—all gone down in episodes of bravado played out in the streets. I came to doubt the virtues of intimidation early on. I chose, perhaps uncon-sciously, to remain a shadow—timid, but a survivor.

8   The fearsomeness mistakenly attributed to me in public places often has a perilous flavor. The most frightening of these confusions occurred in the late 1970s and early 1980s, when I worked as a journalist in Chicago. One day, rushing into the office of a magazine I was writing for with a deadline story in hand, I was mistaken for a burglar.

The office manager called security and, with an ad hoc posse, pursued me through the labyrinthine halls, nearly to my editor's door. I had no way of proving who I was. I could only move briskly toward the company of someone who knew me.

9   Another time I was on assignment for a local paper and killing time before an interview. I entered a jewelry store on the city's affluent Near North Side. The proprietor excused herself and returned with an enormous red Doberman pinscher straining at the end of a leash. She stood, the dog extended toward me, silent to my questions, her eyes bulging nearly out of her head. I took a cursory look around, nodded, and bade her good night.

10   Relatively speaking, however, I never fared as badly as another black male journalist. He went to nearby Waukegan, Illinois, a couple of summers ago to work on a story about a murderer who was born there. Mistaking the reporter for the killer, police officers hauled him from his car at gunpoint and but for his press credentials would probably have tried to book him. Such episodes are not uncommon. Black men trade tales like this all the time.

11   Over the years, I learned to smother the rage I felt at so often being taken for a criminal. Not to do so would surely have led to madness. I now take precautions to make myself less threatening. I move about with care, particularly late in the evening. I give a wide berth to nervous people on subway platforms during the wee hours, particularly when I have exchanged business clothes for jeans. If I happen to be entering a building behind some people who appear skittish, I may walk by, letting them clear the lobby before I return, so as not to seem to be following them. I have been calm and extremely congenial on those rare occasions when I've been pulled over by the police.

12   And on late-evening constitutionals I employ what has proved to be an excellent tension-reducing measure: I whistle melodies from Beethoven and Vivaldi and the more popular classical composers. Even steely New Yorkers hunching toward nighttime destinations seem to relax, and occasionally they even join in the tune. Virtually everybody seems to sense that a mugger wouldn't be warbling bright, sunny selections from Vivaldi's *Four Seasons*. It is my equivalent of a cowbell that hikers wear when they know they are in bear country.

POST-READING QUESTIONS

CONTENT

1. In what ways is the young woman Staples describes early in his essay his "first victim"?

2. Why does Staples say people alter their behavior when he is around? What do you think of their reasoning? Explain.

3. What are some examples of how Staples has been treated that shows how people perceive him? How fair do you think this perception is? Explain.

4. How does Staples alter his own behavior in order to put people at ease? Why does he say he does this?

STYLE AND STRUCTURE

5. What point is Staples trying to make in his essay? Write his main idea in your own words.

6. What examples does Staples use in order to illustrate his main idea? To what extent do these examples convince you that Staples' point is valid?

7. Who is Staples' audience? To what extent are African-Americans included in his audience? Cite the text in order to illustrate your idea.

8. What purpose does Staples' opening sentence serve?

9. What is Staples' tone? How does it change throughout the essay?

10. What role, if any, does humor play in Staples' essay?

CRITICAL THINKING AND ANALYSIS

DISCUSSION QUESTIONS

11. List any examples of what you consider to be uncivil behavior in Staples' essay. At whom are the uncivil acts directed? What about these actions shows that they are uncivil?

12. Whom do you identify with more in the essay: Staples himself or his "victims"? Why?

13. What other groups, if any, have the power to "alter public space in ugly ways"? How so?

WRITING ASSIGNMENTS

14. How responsible is Staples for other people's reactions to him? Write a well-developed paragraph in which you argue the extent to which you think Staples should alter his behavior to make other people feel comfortable and why. Be sure to cite Staples' essay and your own experiences in order to support your ideas.

15. Write a few paragraphs or short essay in which you explain whether or not you think people should take steps to make themselves feel comfortable, even at the expense of someone's feelings. What if the person who makes people feel uncomfortable is not a stranger? Explain and give examples from your life and from Staples' essay.

16. This essay was first published in 1987. Do you think what Staples calls black males' ability to "alter public space in ugly ways" has become more or less pronounced since then? Explain in a few paragraphs, citing your observations for support.

VOCABULARY DEVELOPMENT

17. Staples describes numerous situations where he knows he is perceived as being threatening. Re-read his essay and choose at least five words that best reveal the threat that Staples says he poses to others.

GROUP ACTIVITIES

18. As a group, perform an online search for information on one African-American man who has been controversially accused of wrongdoing over the past ten years. Some examples are: Rodney King, O.J. Simpson, Latrell Sprewell, Amadou Madillo. Compare descriptions of these men as you find them in mainstream articles to sources targeting African-Americans. What is the difference in the tone and descriptions in the articles?

19. For one day, pay attention to how people "alter public space" around you or other people that you notice. For whom do people "alter" their space for most? Why? Bring your results to class and write a short paragraph drawing a conclusion about what causes people to alter their personal space.

My Mother's English

Amy Tan

Author of *The Joy Luck Club, The Kitchen God's Wife,* and *The Bonesetter's Daughter,* Amy Tan raises the issue of civility toward those who do not speak English as fluently as others. Tan explores the potential power, or impotence, people possess as a result of their perceived language mastery, and reveals how her mother's English speaking skills often causes her to be treated with less respect than she deserves.

Pre-reading Questions

Freewrite for five to ten minutes in response to the following questions:
What kind of speaking skills do you possess? Make a list of the different ways you speak to different groups such as friends, family, coworkers, teachers. How does your speech differ from one group to another? How do people's reactions to you change depending upon your speech?

Vocabulary Preview

Vocabulary Words:		
• aspect	• transcribed	• empirical
• wrought	• imagery	• regrettable
• nominalized	• fractured	• insular
• self-conscious		

Write sentences using the words above, before you look those words up. Then, look up the words and revise your sentences for clarity and to avoid faulty diction.

1   As you know, I am a writer and by that definition I am someone who has always loved language. I think that is first and foremost with almost every writer I know. I'm fascinated by language in daily life. I spend a great deal of time thinking about the power of language—the way it can evoke an emotion, a visual image, a complex idea or a simple truth. As a writer, language is the tool of my trade and I use them all, all the Englishes I grew up with.

2   A few months back, I was made keenly aware of the Englishes I do use. I was giving a talk to a large group of people, the same talk I had given many times before and also with notes. And the nature of the talk was about my writing, my life, and my book, *The Joy Luck Club.* The talk was going along well enough until I remembered one major difference that made the whole thing seem wrong. My mother was in the room, and it was perhaps the first time she had heard me give a lengthy speech, using a kind of English I had never used with her. I was saying things like "the intersection of memory and imagination," and "there is an aspect of my fiction that relates to this and thus." A speech filled with carefully wrought grammatical sentences, burdened

to me it seemed with nominalized forms, past perfect tenses, conditional phrases, all the forms of standard English that I had learned in school and through books, a form of English I did not use at home or with my mother.

3   Shortly after that I was walking down the street with my mother and my husband and I became self-conscious of the English I was using, the English that I do use with her. We were talking about the price of new and used furniture and I heard myself saying to her, "Not waste money that way." My husband was with me as well, and he didn't notice any switch in my English. And then I realized why: because over the twenty years that we've been together he's often used that English with me and I've used that with him. It is sort of the English that is our language of intimacy, the English that relates to family talk, the English that I grew up with.

4   I'd like to give you some idea what my family talk sounds like and I'll do that by quoting what my mother said during a recent conversation which I videotaped and then transcribed. During this conversation, my mother was talking about a political gangster who had the same last name as her family, Du, and how the gangster in his early years wanted to be adopted by her family which was by comparison very rich. Later the gangster became more rich, more powerful than my mother's family and one day showed up at my mother's wedding to pay his respects. And here's what she said about that, in part, "Du You Sung having business like food stand, like off the street kind; he's Du like Du Zong but not Tsung-ming Island people. The local people call him Du, from the river east side. He belong to that side, local people. That man want to ask Du Zong father take him in become like own family. Du Zong father look down on him but don't take seriously until that man becoming big like, become a Mafia. Now important person, very hard inviting him. Chinese way: come only to show respect, don't stay for dinner. Respect for making big celebration; he shows up. Means gives lots of respect, Chinese custom. Chinese social life that way—if too important, won't have to stay too long. He come to my wedding; I didn't see it I heard it. I gone to boy's side. They have YMCA dinner; Chinese age I was nineteen."

5   You should know that my mother's expressive command of English belies how much she actually understands. She reads the *Forbes Report,* listens to *Wall Street Week,* converses daily with her stockbroker, reads all of Shirley MacLaines's books with ease, all kinds of things I can't begin to understand. Yet some of my friends tell me that they understand 50 percent of what my mother says. Some say maybe they understand maybe 80 percent. Some say they understand almost nothing at all. As a case in point, a television station recently interviewed my mother and I didn't see this program when it was first aired, but my mother did. She was telling me what happened. She said that everything she said, which was in English, was subtitled in English, as if she had been speaking in pure Chinese. She was understandably puzzled and upset. Recently a friend gave me that tape and I saw that same interview and I watched. And sure enough—subtitles—and I was puzzled because listening to that tape it seemed to me that my mother's English sounded perfectly clear and perfectly natural. Of course, I realize that my mother's English is what I grew up with. It is literally my mother tongue, not Chinese, not standard English, but my mother's English which I later found out is almost a direct translation of Chinese.

6   Her language as I hear it is vivid and direct, full of observation and imagery. That was the language that helped shape the way that I saw things, expressed things, made

sense of the world. Lately I've been giving more thought to the kind of English that my mother speaks. Like others I have described it to people as broken or fractured English, but I wince when I say that. It has always bothered me that I can think of no other way to describe it than broken, as it if were damaged or needed to be fixed, that it lacked a certain wholeness or soundness to it. I've heard other terms used, "Limited English" for example. But they seem just as bad, as if everything is limited including people's perceptions of the Limited English speaker.

7   I know this for a fact, because when I was growing up my mother's limited English limited my perception of her. I was ashamed of her English. I believed that her English reflected the quality of what she had to say. That is, because she expressed it imperfectly, her thoughts were imperfect as well. And I had plenty of empirical evidence to support me: The fact that people in department stores, at banks, at supermarkets, at restaurants did not take her as seriously, did not give her good service, pretended not to understand her, or even acted as if they did not hear her.

8   My mother has long realized the limitations of her English as well. When I was fifteen she used to have me call people on the phone to pretend I was she. In this guise, I was forced to ask for information or oftentimes to complain and yell at people that had been rude to her. One time it was a call to her stockbroker in New York. She had cashed out her small portfolio and it just so happened that we were going to New York the next week, our very first trip outside of California. I had to get on the phone and say in my adolescent voice, which was not very convincing, "This is Mrs. Tan." And my mother was in the back whispering loudly, "Why don't he send me check already? Two weeks late. So made he lie to me, losing me money." Then I said in perfect English, "Yes, I'm getting rather concerned. You had agreed to send the check two weeks ago, but it hasn't arrived." And she began to talk more loudly, "What you want—I come to New York, tell him front of his boss you cheating me?" And I was trying to calm her down, making her be quiet, while telling this stockbroker, "I can't tolerate any more excuses. If I don't receive the check immediately I'm going to have to speak to your manager when I arrive in New York." And sure enough the following week, there we were in front of this astonished stockbroker. And there I was, red-faced and quiet, and my mother the real Mrs. Tan was shouting at his boss in her impeccable broken English.

9   We used a similar routine a few months ago for a situation that was actually far less humorous. My mother had gone to the hospital for an appointment to find out about a benign brain tumor a CAT scan had revealed a month ago. And she had spoken very good English she said—her best English, no mistakes. Still she said the hospital had not apologized when they said they had lost the CAT scan and she had come for nothing. She said that they did not seem to have any sympathy when she told them she was anxious to know the exact diagnosis since her husband and son had both died of brain tumors. She said they would not give her any more information until the next time; she would have to make another appointment for that, so she said she would not leave until the doctor called her daughter. She wouldn't budge, and when the doctor finally called her daughter, me, who spoke in perfect English, lo-and-behold, we had assurances the CAT scan would be found, they promised a conference call on Monday, and apologies were given for any suffering my mother had gone through for a most regrettable mistake. By the way, apart from the distress of that episode, my mother is fine.

10   But it has continued to disturb me how much my mother's English still limits people's perceptions of her. I think my mother's English almost had an effect on limiting my
possibilities as well. Sociologists and linguists will probably tell you that a person's developing language skills are more influenced by peers. But I do think the language spoken
by the family, especially immigrant families, which are more insular, plays a large role in
shaping the language of the child. . . . [While this may be true, I always wanted, however,] to capture what language ability tests can never reveal—her intent, her passion, her
imagery, the rhythms of her speech, and the nature of her thoughts. Apart from what any
critic had to say about my writing, I knew I had succeeded where it counted when my
mother finished reading my first book and gave me her verdict. "So easy to read."

POST-READING QUESTIONS

CONTENT

1. What does Tan mean when she mentions "all the Englishes I grew up with"?
2. Why does Tan feel self-conscious, after giving her speech, when she walks with her mother and husband?
3. Why doesn't Tan like the terms "broken English" or "limited English"? What does she say they imply about the speaker?
4. How is Tan's mother treated by the hospital staff? By her stockbroker? What is her mother's response to such treatment?
5. Is Tan's mother capable of understanding the medical and financial professionals she deals with? How do you know?
6. What does Tan mean when she describes her mother's language as "impeccable broken English"?

STYLE AND STRUCTURE

7. What is Tan's focus in her essay? Write her main idea in your own words.
8. What examples does Tan use to show the differences between the "Englishes" she refers to? Are these examples effective? Cite the text to support your response.
9. What function does Tan's opening paragraph serve? How does it lay the foundation for her discussion of her mother's language?
10. Who is Tan writing this for? What assumptions can you make about her audience?

CRITICAL THINKING AND ANALYSIS

DISCUSSION QUESTIONS

11. How responsible is Tan's mother for the way she is treated? Do you think she could or should do anything in order to be taken more seriously?

12. How accurate do you think Tan's portrayal of the professionals her mother deals with is? Do you think employees are more or less likely to treat non-native English speakers poorly? Explain.

WRITING ASSIGNMENTS

13. How powerful have you found language to be? Write a few paragraphs arguing how powerful you think language is. Give some examples from your own experience that show how people's language, yours or someone you have come in contact with, can affect their influence over others.

14. What steps do you think people can take to better their English skills? Write a letter to people new to this country, explaining how they can best improve their language facility. You can cite Tan's essay if you wish, and use examples from your own experience and observations in order to illustrate your ideas.

15. How much should people try to understand others who have limited language skills? In a few well-developed paragraphs, explain listeners' responsibility to understanding non-native English speakers and give examples from Tan's essay and from your own experiences.

VOCABULARY DEVELOPMENT

16. What types of expressions cause us not to understand people? Examine Tan's mother's comments, and write a short paragraph explaining what about her language is most difficult for you to understand.

GROUP ACTIVITIES

17. Make a list of your own languages—either different forms of English or any other languages you speak—and evaluate the situations in which you use each one. Which forms are the most versatile? The most limiting? Why? Share your results with the class in an open forum setting.

18. As a group, visit online chat rooms targeting different audiences. How do people speak in a women-oriented chat room versus a teen chat room, for instance? How does the level of language skill vary? Discuss your results with other groups in order to broaden your conclusions about how language facility labels people.

The American Uncivil Wars

How crude, rude, and obnoxious behavior has replaced good manners and why that hurts our politics and culture

John Marks

Founder and President of Search for Common Ground, a Washington-based nonprofit organization seeking societal conflict resolution in the United States and abroad, John Marks takes a look at people's behavior in "The American Uncivil Wars." Marks classifies and evaluates the degree of societal incivility, and he identifies several key areas in society where people's actions often seem to be degenerating, relating explanations and possible solutions for these types of behavior.

Pre-reading Questions

Freewrite for five to ten minutes in response to the following questions:
Make a list of the times you feel someone has been impolite or insensitive to you over the past week. Do you think that your list is longer now than it would have been a year ago? Five years ago? Explain. What forms does incivility in your life most commonly take?

Vocabulary Preview

Vocabulary Words:
- zealot
- decorum
- erodes
- flouting
- ideologies
- scrupulous
- altercation
- provocative
- crusade
- paragon
- intransigent

Look up the words above and use at least five of them in a short paragraph on incivility.

1   On the first warm day of spring in Montgomery, Ala., Michael Walcott takes his guitar down to Loveless Elementary School and wages war on incivility. Speak clearly, he tells the sixth graders of Loveless; do not use profanity or chew gum in class or answer the phone in an unpleasant voice; but do show respect for the aged, say "thank you" and "please" and, most of all, treat others the way you want to be treated. Then Walcott plugs his guitar into a pair of giant amps and sweetens the struggle to save civilization with a little soul music. "All the world over, it's easy to see;/People everywhere need a little courtesy," he sings in an original composition set to a 1960s pop tune. "Shout it from the mountain so everyone can see,/Courtesy can bring har-mo-ny." After finishing the song, Walcott asks the sixth graders, "Would you behave more courteously in school if I promise to come back and play a concert for you"? "No!" they exclaim in unison.

2   Walcott's song is an anthem out of season, a lonely plea for the virtue of respect in a time when schools use metal detectors to keep out guns and knives, when universities insist on speech and behavior codes to stem the tide of hatred and disrespect, when legal cases become shouting matches, when the Internet is littered with raunch and menace, when political campaigns resemble food fights, when trash talk and head butts are the idiom of sports, and when popular culture tops itself from week to week with displays of violence, sex, foul language and puerile confession. At best, it is a bad time to be a zealot for decorum; at worst, anarchy lurks just around the corner.

3   **Condition Critical**. Walcott is not the only citizen alarmed at this prospect. As a new poll conducted in February by U.S. News and Bozell Worldwide reveals, a vast majority of Americans feel their country has reached an ill-mannered watershed. Nine out of 10 Americans think incivility is a serious problem, and nearly half think it is extremely serious. Seventy-eight percent say the problem has worsened in the past 10 years, and their concern goes beyond annoyance at rudeness. Respondents see in incivility evidence of a profound social breakdown. More than 90 percent of those polled believe it contributes to the increase of violence in the country; 85 percent believe it divides the national community, and the same number see it eroding healthy values like respect for others.

4   Talk to Americans and a picture emerges of a nation addicted to the pleasures of an unruly society—its emphasis on individual expression, its flouting of convention and its free vent of emotions—but shocked at the effects of this unruliness and increasingly willing to take action against it. Americans feel embattled in their personal and professional lives by a rising tide of nastiness. And in an era when ideologies of race, gender, class and religion divide the country, says Martin Marty, a philosopher of religions who has written on the subject, it is a nastiness the country can ill afford, because it amounts to a kind of social deafness. "You cannot have a complex society in which you do not hear the other party, the antagonist," explains Marty. "If you're just doing a monologue, or just hanging out with your crowd, it's impossible to sustain a society, and if there is to be any justice, it has to come through a conversation of different interests and different wills. Incivility says, 'I'm right, you have no hearing; I'm going to do the talking; I'm going to shout you down.'"

5   Ironically, definition presents a first obstacle to solving the problem. The word civility is derived from the Latin civis, or citizen, and is also foreshadowed in the word civitas, or the art of government. It can mean, among other things, good breeding, politeness, consideration or courtesy but may also refer to a "polite act or utterance," according to Webster's. But postmodernism makes hash of such definitions. When few people can agree on a common set of behaviors or values, civility can be seen as both a code word for right-wing Christian values and a stalking horse for left-wing multiculturalism, the former an antiabortion agenda, the latter a pro-diversity platform. But in the best of worlds, as Marty suggests, civility should be nonpartisan. It should be the glue holding dialogue together. "The alternative to civility is first incivility," he states, "and then war."

6   That message is dire, but it seems to be taking root. Convinced that the country's coarseness has gone far enough, people of different economic backgrounds, ethnicities, sexes and ideological persuasions, along with institutions as varied as schools, state bar

associations, churches and businesses, have begun to take the first tentative steps to reverse the trend. They have their work cut out for them.

SCHOOLS

7 From one end of the country to the other, parents and teachers complain of the lack of civility among children and the disrespect they show their elders. The problem cuts across all class and racial lines. In the recent survey of educators by the American Association of School Administrators, the teaching of the golden rule—treat others as you want to be treated—was found to be an urgent necessity.

8 "No Rules," reads a decal on the back window of a car parked at Robert E. Lee High School in Montgomery, student population of 1,758, where, a handful of seniors agree, it is far too late to learn respect for one another. At the school's entrance, a statue of Lee, the Confederate general and quintessential Southern gentleman, presides over a teenage brawl that might be a microcosm of the nation as a whole. At this racially mixed school in a middle-class neighborhood, getting by means getting mean. Students generally don't open doors or speak to people they don't know. In the hallways, it's shove or be shoved. "If you're standing in the hallway, and someone's coming, if they want to come your way, you better move," explains Cindy Roy, a senior. "Because if you don't, they're just going to take you down and keep on going."

9 Underlying this attitude toward rudeness, unspoken but universally acknowledged, is a nervousness about violence. Rumor has it that some girls carry knives in their hair and some boys have guns. Recent metal detector tests have not turned up ample evidence of such weapons, says guidance counselor Carole Mackin, but students at Robert E. Lee remain cautious just the same.

10 Five minutes a day at Robert E. Lee is devoted to character education, a program popular around the country and put into place last year by the Alabama Legislature. As students gather in their homerooms in the morning, someone reads a poem or story or an edifying thought over the intercom, an effort that has about as much attention-grabbing power as a sermon at a rock concert. Seniors say character education is widely regarded as a joke. By and large, no one listens, and teachers don't have much say in the matter. They get only as much respect as they show to the students, and that is precious little in some classes. State Rep. Bill Fuller, who helped to push through the legislation, now believes high school is too late to teach values like respect and courtesy. He says the work has to begin much earlier—at home, for instance, or elementary school. And that is where Walcott concentrates the efforts he has launched under the auspices of the American Foundation for Courtesy, Inc. The Guyanese native wonders at the breakdown of manners here, and one aspect of his schooling seems particularly lacking in his adopted country now. "The teacher always remained in charge and was always respected," he remembers. "Even if you didn't have respect for the person, you still had respect for the office. I believe America could learn something from that."

LAW

11 One area in which this kind of respect for institutions has eroded dramatically in recent years is the law. Outside of their profession, lawyers have become symbols of everything crass and dishonorable in American public life; within it, they have become increasingly

combative and uncivil toward each other. One survey of lawyers and judges by federal court officials in the upper Midwest found that 41 percent believe the lack of civility is a problem and, of those, a large majority think problems exist when lawyers deal with each other. The respondents blamed economic competition among law firms, the rise of "Rambo" litigators who battle opponents ruthlessly, lying, cheating and threats of malpractice from angry clients for their colleagues' unmannerly behavior. Of course, it is also true that while Americans revile lawyers, they have a hand in this mess because they have turned virtually every kind of unhappiness into a legal claim.

12   Since the late 1980s, state bar associations around the country have attempted to clean up their acts, asking lawyers to treat clients, judges and each other with "courtesy, candor, cooperation and scrupulous observance," as the Texas Lawyer's Creed reads. "There were more than a few stories about physical altercations in depositions, between lawyers, sometimes involving clients, more than a few stories about lawyers on the verge of physical altercation in courthouse hallways," says Texas Supreme Court Justice Nathan Hecht. "We felt like we needed to do something to turn down the fire." The value of those codes is now being debated at the national level. Next month, a panel at the American Bar Association Center for Professional Responsibility will look at the impact and value of the codes. There has been nothing but improvement in Texas, says Justice Hecht, but any deep-seated change in behavior will take at least half a generation.

POLITICS

13   But even good manners can go only so far. Many believe the real issue is to develop a more profound sense of respect to undergird those manners—the kind of respect necessary to make political processes work. For many Americans, government is one of those institutions most lacking in civility—as campaigns are dominated by negative and sometimes misleading ads and a favorite tactic is demonizing opponents.

14   Historically, Americans have alternated cycles of ugly behavior with those of admirable decorum. George Washington was famous for his manners, displaying them both at the personal level to show respect to individuals and at the political level to demonstrate respect before the law. On at least one occasion, says Richard Brookhiser, author of a recent biography on Washington, he combined both to momentous effect. In 1797, John Adams was inaugurated as second president of the United States, and on the dais next to him were Vice President Thomas Jefferson and retiring president Washington. "When the new president finished and left," writes Brookhiser, "Washington motioned to Jefferson to go next. The two Virginians had known each other since 1769, when Washington had been 37 years old and Jefferson only 26. From long habit and lingering respect, Jefferson now held back. But Washington gestured again, in a manner not to be ignored. The younger man was now vice president and must go first."

15   Vestiges of that decorum still exist and allow the government to get on with its business. Despite its current reputation for divisiveness, says freshman Rep. Jesse Jackson Jr., a Democrat known for his good manners, the House of Representatives might even serve as a model for civility in other avenues of American life. "Whether you agree with what Newt Gingrich and his crowd are doing, whether you agree on the Democratic side if our leadership is doing the right thing or not, the decorum of the House

keeps it from breaking into an all-out fight," says Jackson, "and if the same level of civility existed in other levels of society, there would probably be a lot less violence, a lot less hostility. Can you imagine if gangs were saying, 'Will the gentleman who represents everyone who lives south of 63rd Street please give me just a moment to make a point?' as opposed to saying, 'Let's shoot everyone who lives south of 63rd Street.'"

POPULAR CULTURE

16   Provocative behavior has been big in the entertainment business at least since Elvis Presley shook his pelvis on national television back in the 1950s. But even there, times seem to be changing, as the crudities of Sharon Stone kickbox with the niceties of Jane Austen. For the past decade, since the unexpected box office success of *A Room With a View* in 1986 and culminating last year in the appearance of three widely acclaimed movies based on Austen novels, moviegoers have flocked to see stories set in eras when manners and restraint played a dominant role in society. In terms of both receipts and critical praise, these films have buried more sensational fare like the overhyped striptease extravaganza Showgirls and the grotesquely violent *Copycat,* a sign that audiences may be as willing to sit through decorous parlor chat as through nude scenes and mutilation.

17   But the popularity of civility in the popular culture may have less to do with opposition to violence, sex and bad language, says Bill Maher, host of a popular talk show called "Politically Incorrect," than with the indignities of public confession. "There is a daily monument to the breakdown of civilization every day in all these talk shows," Maher insists. "I call them galk shows. What's uncivil to me is this idea that the worse thing you could be is not famous." On the other hand, Maher himself admits he is the last person in the world to start a manners crusade. While part of his show is dedicated to civil conversations between people with different views of the world—"a sophisticated cocktail party," as Maher describes it—another essential element is provocation, the attempt, for instance, to get creative obscenities by the censor. "It's just fun," explains Maher. "It feels good, so I do it."

18   As harmless as they may seem, Maher's words reveal a central paradox about America's approach to its own bad behavior. On the one hand, we do not like to see children talking rudely to parents, students disrespecting teachers or politicians dragging each other through the mud. Nevertheless, we tend to applaud rebels, those who speak and behave honestly, if not properly. We like our rough-hewn cowboys who walk into the saloon loaded with integrity but short on cultivation. And we especially enjoy the spectacle of a good fight, as the competitiveness of national sports and politics, the violence in movies and the aggressiveness of pop music from rock-and-roll to rap make clear.

19   That's because a certain kind of incivility is key to being American, believes seasoned talk show host Sally Jesse Raphael, whose top-rated program has been a frequent target of criticism and a showcase for all kinds of behavior, from the angelic to the rude to the psychotic. She argues that it is difficult for Americans to make up their minds about what actually constitutes bad behavior. Raphael believes, for instance that her talk show is a paragon of civil discourse, because it promotes a cleareyed view of people and the country. "If we reflect any kind of degradation of

the moral fiber of the country, it's a reflection of what is," she explains in her own defense, "and I think we represent that with honesty and compassion, and when you do that, you're not lowering the level of civility. You're presenting what I consider to be the present state of affairs."

20   In the end, whether American culture is uncivil or not may be less relevant than how it is received by the rest of us. The U.S. News/Bozell poll suggests that people are worried about the impact of a coarsening culture on others; they seem confident in their own ability to withstand the mean-spirited tide. For instance, one senior at Robert E. Lee, Tamika Crittenden, refuses to hold rap stars, athletes and other celebrities responsible for her behavior. Crittenden grew up among three generations of family: parents, grandparents and great-grandparents. All three passed on their beliefs about manners and good behavior, and those beliefs form the basis of how Crittenden treats other people, she says, not what Charles Barkley, Tupac Shakur and Beavis and Butt-head do. If nothing else, Crittenden has survived high school with those beliefs firmly in place.

ETIQUETTE

21   If the content of civility is respect, then its form might be manners, say those like Marjabelle Young Stewart, who specializes in trying to improve them. Saying "please" and "thank you," opening doors for others and allowing an elderly person to have your seat on the bus may seem like little things, but they amount to a physical recognition of the dignity of the other person, says Stewart. Surprisingly, etiquette seems to be making a comeback, as books like Executive Etiquette, Multicultural Manners, Do As I Say (gay etiquette) and old standards like the Miss Manners guide proliferate on shelves. Stewart herself is a popular evangelist. For the first time since the 1960s her schedule is now booked years in advance. One client is Associated Employers, an Illinois-based employers' association representing 196 companies and around 60,000 employees in the Quad Cities region. Five years ago, AE invited Steward to give a lecture on table manners. The event was so popular that it has become an annual event.

22   At AT&T offices in New Jersey, after years of more casual dress and behavior inspired by cultural trends of the 1960s and 1970s, manners have become a priority, too. Executives at the company have received training from Stewart in recent years, as have executives at Merrill Lynch. "Manners are the new status accessory," Stewart tells her students, "pricier than a Rolex, more portable than a Day-Timer, and shinier than handmade shoes. Polished graces can get you where you're going faster then a speeding BMW."

23   There are those, however, who argue that civility can be overrated. As civil-society advocate Amitai Etzioni points out, even if people treat each other with respect across the table, they must still resolve differences that go far beyond civil discourse and behavior. Matters of sexual and racial equality, unemployment, health care, religious belief and hatred may remain intransigent, as they have in the past, no matter how respectful people are to one another.

24   But back in Montgomery, Walcott believes civility does affect the larger questions. "Incivility makes a bad situation worse," he says. "I believe that two groups who hate one another and may not know why they hate one another, may very well find out that their hatred and suspicion were unfounded when they realize how human each can be to the other." So, with music, T-shirts, guitars and tokens, Walcott does what he can

to spread the word. Still, on a bad day, he says, with a weary glint in his eyes, he feels like Don Quixote tilting at windmills, and most of the time, the windmills do not even say "thank you."

POST-READING QUESTIONS

CONTENT

1. What areas in society does Marks identify as being representative of a slide in good manners? What are some other areas he might have included?
2. What is the term "civility" derived from? How is this root significant?
3. How is the term "civility" interpreted by different groups, according to the article? Which definition do you agree with most? Explain.
4. What are some causes of incivility, according to Marks? Do you agree? Explain and cite examples from the text.
5. What are some ways people have attempted to address the problem of incivility? How effective are these methods as they are presented in the text?
6. How large a role, if any, does violence play in the absence of school civility? Does the threat of violence lead people to be more or less civil? Explain.
7. What role do talk shows play in promoting, or downplaying, the importance of civility? Cite examples from the text and from your own life.

STYLE AND STRUCTURE

8. What is Marks' main point in this essay? Restate his idea in your own words.
9. How effective are Marks' examples in supporting his main idea? Which examples are most effective? Why?
10. Who is Marks' audience? How might the date that this essay was written be significant?
11. What purpose do the various headings—"Schools," "Law," "Politics," among others—serve? Do they help you follow Marks' argument, or do they detract from it?
12. What are some words or phrases you find particularly effective in communicating Marks' point? Explain.
13. What is the tone of the essay? What examples and/or words help determine this tone?

CRITICAL THINKING AND ANALYSIS

DISCUSSION QUESTIONS

14. In what ways is the title significant?
15. To what extent do you agree with Martin Marty's statement that "The alternative to civility is first incivility and then war"? Explain and give examples from the essay and from your own life.

16. Marks writes that many people think that civility will only take root if we develop "the kind of respect necessary to make political processes work." How great a factor are manners in the political sphere? How great an influence do you think politicians have on the way we act on a daily basis?

WRITING ASSIGNMENTS

17. If, as the seniors at Robert E. Lee High School in Montgomery, Alabama are correct in claiming that high school is "far too late to learn respect for one another," at what point do you think people need to start learning respect? Why? Write a well-developed paragraph in which you argue that civility needs to be taught beginning at a specific time in a person's life. Be sure to cite Marks' essay and experiences from your own life in responding to this question.

18. Do you agree that as Americans we "tend to applaud rebels, those who speak and behave honestly, if not properly"? In a few paragraphs, support your response with examples from society and your own life.

19. Teacher Michael Walcott states that "incivility makes a bad situation worse." To what extent do you agree or disagree with him? Write a few paragraphs or short essay in which you explain how incivility does or does not worsen situations and give examples from the text and your life.

VOCABULARY DEVELOPMENT

20. Advocates of etiquette have been criticized for being artificial in their manners and speech. Write a quick note to a friend, and then revise the note, using the most formal courtesy-oriented language you can think of (feel free to consult an etiquette book, if you wish). Bring your paragraphs to class and discuss how the language of the notes does or does not change their tone or meaning.

GROUP ACTIVITIES

21. For one day, make a conscious effort to be more civil than usual: say "please" and "thank you" whenever appropriate, and go out of your way to treat people with courtesy, even going so far as to let someone cut ahead of you in line. Then, as a group, discuss the results: did your behavior have any noticeable effect on others? Were some kinds of courtesy more effective than others? Is being polite more trouble than it's worth? Share your results with the class.

22. Again, for one day, be a "civility detective." Observe the ways people treat each other—in class, on the road, in stores, in the media—and watch the reactions that various types of behavior receive. Then, as a group, write a paragraph explaining the causes and effects of everyday civility upon people's actions.

Argument Pair: Is *Road Rage* a New Phenomenon?

Road Rage, Jason Vest, Warren Cohen, and Mike Tharp
Road Rage: Just the Same Old Risky Driving

To read the newspapers—with their accounts of people's outrage at bad manners on the road—one might conclude that "road rage," or the condition of losing one's self-control while driving, is an entirely new societal affliction. Indeed, Jason Vest, Warren Cohen, and Mike Tharp cite researchers who claim there is "a growing trend of simple aggressive behavior" on our roadways. Writers of *Road Rage: Just the Same Old Risky Driving,* however, claim that recent attention to driving-related unpleasantness is just the same story told for generations, but with a contemporary spin. The extent to which our driving has become worse—not to mention our manners on the road—is the central issue these writers explore.

Writing Assignments Based on *Road Rage* and *Road Rage: Just the Same Old Risky Driving*

1. In both *Road Rage* articles, the writers argue that aggressive driving presents risks for people on the road. Write an essay or paragraph in which you explain which type of driving is most risky: tailgating, speeding, racing, running red-lights, driving overly slowly, or any other type of risky driving that you can imagine. Be sure to describe how this type of driving is risky and explain what about the driving is riskier than other types of driving.

2. Both *Road Rage* articles point out how dangerous risky driving can be, but the writers of the articles disagree upon whether or not Road Rage presents new risks. Write an essay or paragraph in which you argue whether or not aggressive driving is a new phenomenon. Be sure to cite both texts and draw from your own life in order to support your argument.

Road Rage

Tailgating, giving the finger, outright violence—Americans grow more likely to take out their frustrations on other drivers

Jason Vest, Warren Cohen, and Mike Tharp

First published in *U.S. News and World Report* in June of 1997, "Road Rage" explores the apparent rise in aggressive driving and explains why this phenomenon has occurred. Authors Jason Vest, Warren Cohen, and Mike Tharp argue that overcrowded thoroughfares and drivers' anonymity, among others, are key causes in road rage.

Pre-reading Questions

Freewrite for five to ten minutes in response to the following questions:
What does the term "road rage" mean to you? Describe a time when you have encountered road rage, either in yourself as a driver or in another driver. Do you think road rage is getting worse? Explain. What do you think causes road rage?

Vocabulary Preview

Vocabulary Words:
- ludicrous
- albeit
- temerity
- initiated
- unduly
- context
- exemplary
- anecdotal
- errant

Without using a dictionary, define the words above. Then, check your definitions in a dictionary. How close were you? Write a sentence or two explaining how on-target you were with your original definitions.

1   Some of the incidents are so ludicrous you can't help but laugh—albeit nervously. There was the case in Salt Lake City, where 75-year-old J.C. King—peeved that 41-year-old Larry Remm Jr. honked at him for blocking traffic—followed Remm when he pulled off the road, hurled his prescription bottle at him, and then, in a display of geriatric resolve, smashed Remm's knees with his '92 Mercury. In tiny Potomac, Md., Robin Ficker—an attorney and ex-state legislator—knocked the glasses off a pregnant woman after she had the temerity to ask him why he bumped her Jeep with his.

2   Other incidents lack even the element of black humor. In Colorado Springs, 55-year-old Vern Smalley persuaded a 17-year-old boy who had been tailgating him to pull over; Smalley decided that, rather than merely scold the lad, he would shoot him. (And he did. Fatally—after the youth had threatened him.) And last year, on Virginia's George Washington Parkway, a dispute over a lane change was settled with a high-speed duel that ended when both drivers lost control and crossed the center lane, killing two innocent motorists.

3   Anyone who spent the Memorial Day weekend on the road probably won't be too surprised to learn the results of a major study to be released this week by the American Automobile Association: The rate of "aggressive driving" incidents—defined as events in which an angry or impatient driver tries to kill or injure another driver after a traffic dispute—has risen by 51 percent since 1990. In those cases studied, 37 percent of offenders used firearms against other drivers, an additional 28 percent used other weapons, and 35 percent used their cars.

4   Fear of (and participation in) aggressive driving has grown so much that in a poll last year residents of Maryland, Washington D.C., and Virginia listed it as a bigger concern than drunk driving. The Maryland highway department is running a campaign called "The End of the Road for Aggressive Drivers," which, among other things, flashes anti-road-rage messages on electronic billboards on the interstates. Delaware, Pennsylvania, and New Jersey have initiated special highway patrols targeting aggres-

sive drivers. A small but busy community of therapists and scholars has arisen to study the phenomenon and counsel drivers on how to cope. And several members of Congress are now trying to figure out ways to legislate away road rage.

5   Lest one get unduly alarmed, it helps to put the AAA study's numbers in context: Approximately 250,000 people have been killed in traffic since 1990. While the U.S. Department of Transportation estimates that two thirds of fatalities are at least partially caused by aggressive driving, the AAA study found only 218 that could be directly attributable to enraged drivers. Of the more than 20 million motorists injured, the survey identified 12,610 injuries attributable to aggressive driving. While the study is the first American attempt to quantify aggressive driving, it is not rigorously scientific. The authors drew on reports from 30 newspapers—supplemented by insurance claims and police reports from 16 cities—involving 10,037 occurrences. Moreover, the overall trendlines for car accidents have continued downward for several decades, thanks in part to increases in the drinking age and improvements in car technology like high-mounted brake lights.

6   But researchers believe there is a growing trend of simple aggressive behavior—road rage—in which a driver reacts angrily to other drivers. Cutting them off, tailgating, giving the finger, waving a fist—experts believe these forms of nonviolent fury are increasing. "Aggressive driving is now the most common way of driving," says Sandra Ball-Rokeach, who codirects the Media and Injury Prevention Program at the University of Southern California. "It's not just a few crazies—it's a subculture of driving." In focus groups set up by her organization, two thirds of drivers said they reacted to frustrating situations aggressively. Almost half admitted to deliberately braking suddenly, pulling close to the other car, or taking some other potentially dangerous step. Another third said they retaliated with a hostile gesture. Drivers show great creativity in devising hostile responses. Doug Erber of Los Angeles keeps his windshield-wiper-fluid tank full. If someone tailgates, he turns on the wipers, sending fluid over his roof onto the car behind him. "It works better than hitting the brakes," he says, "and you can act totally innocent."

MAD MAX

7   While the AAA authors note there is a profile of the lethally inclined aggressive driver—"relatively young, poorly educated males who have criminal records, histories of violence, and drug or alcohol problems"—road-rage scholars (and regular drivers) believe other groups are equally represented in the less violent forms of aggressive driving. To some, it's tempting to look at this as a psychologically mysterious Jekyll-and-Hyde phenomenon; for others, it's simply attributable to "jerk drivers." In reality, there's a confluence of emotional and demographic factors that changes the average citizen from mere motorist to Mad Max.

8   First, it isn't just your imagination that traffic is getting worse. Since 1987, the number of miles of roads has increased just 1 percent while the miles driven have shot up by 35 percent. According to a recent Federal Highway Administration study of 50 metropolitan areas, almost 70 percent of urban freeways today—as opposed to 55 percent in 1983—are clogged during rush hour. The study notes that congestion is likely to spread to currently unspoiled locations. Forty percent of the currently gridlock-free

Milwaukee County highway system, for example, is predicted to be jammed up more than five hours a day by the year 2000. A study by the Texas Transportation Institute last year found that commuters in one third of the largest cities spent well over 40 hours a year in traffic jams.

9   Part of the problem is that jobs have shifted from cities to suburbs. Communities designed as residential suburbs with narrow roads have grown into "edge cities," with bustling commercial traffic. Suburb-to-suburb commutes now account for 44 percent of all metropolitan traffic versus 20 percent for suburb-to-downtown travel. Demographer and *Edge City* author Joel Garreau says workers breaking for lunch are essentially causing a third rush hour. He notes that in Tysons Corner, Va., it takes an average of four traffic signal cycles to get through a typical intersection at lunchtime. And because most mass transit systems are of a spoke-and-hub-design, centering on cities and branching out to suburbs, they're not really useful in getting from point A to point B in an edge city or from one edge city to another. Not surprisingly, fewer people are relying on mass transit and more on cars. In 1969, 82.7 percent drove to work; in 1990, 91.4 percent did. Despite the fact that the Washington D.C., area has an exemplary commuter subway system, it accounts for only 2 percent of all trips made.

10   Demographic changes have helped put more drivers on the road. Until the 1970s, the percentage of women driving was relatively low, and many families had only one car. But women entered the work force and bought cars, something developers and highway planners hadn't foreseen. From 1969 to 1990 the number of women licensed to drive increased 84 percent. Between 1970 and 1987, the number of cars on the road more than doubled. In the past decade, the number of cars grew faster (17 percent) than the number of people (10 percent). Even carpooling is down despite HOV lanes and other preferential devices. The cumulative effect, says University of Hawaii traffic psychology professor Leon James, is a sort of sensory overload. "There are simply more cars—and more behaviors—to deal with," says James.

11   As if the United States couldn't produce enough home-grown lousy drivers, it seems to be importing them as well. Experts believe that many immigrants come from countries that have bad roads and aggressive styles. It's not just drivers from Third World countries, though. British drivers are considered among the safest in Europe, yet recent surveys show that nearly 90 percent of British motorists have experienced threats or abuse from other drivers. Of Brits who drive for a living, about 21 percent report having been run off the road. In Australia, one study estimates that about half of all traffic accidents there may be due to road rage. "There are different cultures of driving all over the world—quite clearly, if we mix new cultures in the melting pot, what we get is a culture clash on the roadway," says John Palmer, a professor in the Health Education and Safety Department at Minnesota's St. Cloud State University.

12   The peak moment for aggressive driving comes not during impenetrable gridlock but just before, when traffic density is high but cars are still moving briskly. That's when cutting someone off or forcing someone out of a lane can make the difference (or so it seems) between being on time and being late, according to Palmer. Unfortunately, roads are getting more congested just as Americans feel even more pressed for time. "People get on a time line for their car trips," says Palmer. "When they perceive that

someone is impeding their progress or invading their agenda, they respond with what they consider to be 'instructive' behavior, which might be as simple as flashing their lights to something more combative."

SUBURBAN ASSAULT VEHICLES

13 This, uh, "instruction" has become more common, Palmer and others speculate, in part because of modern automotive design. With hyperadjustable seats, soundproof interiors, CD players, and cellular phones, cars are virtually comfortable enough to live in. Students of traffic can't help but wonder if the popularity of pickup trucks and sport utility vehicles has contributed to the problem. Sales have approximately doubled since 1990. These big metal shells loom over everything else, fueling feelings of power and drawing out a driver's more primal instincts. "A lot of the anecdotal evidence about aggressive driving incidents tends to involve people driving sport utility vehicles," says Julie Rochman of the Insurance Institute for Highway Safety. "When people get these larger, heavier vehicles, they feel more invulnerable." While Chrysler spokesman Chris Preuss discounts the notion of suburban assault vehicles being behind the aggressive-driving phenomenon, he does say women feel more secure in the jumbo-size vehicles.

14 In much of life, people feel they don't have full control of their destiny. But a car—unlike, say, a career or a spouse—responds reliably to one's wish. In automobiles, we have an increased (but false) sense of invincibility. Other drivers become dehumanized, mere appendages to a competing machine. "You have the illusion you're alone and master, dislocated from other drivers," says Hawaii's James.

15 Los Angeles psychologist Arnold Nerenberg describes how one of his recent patients got into an angry road confrontation with another motorist. "They pulled off the road and started running toward each other to fight, but then they recognized each other as neighbors," he says. "When it's just somebody else in a car, it's more two-dimensional; the other person's identity boils down to, 'You're someone who did something bad to me.'"

16 How can aggressive driving be minimized? Some believe that better driver's education might help. Driver's ed was a high school staple by the 1950s, thanks to federal highway dollars given to states. But a 1978 government study in De Kalb County, Ga., found no reduction in crashes or traffic violations by students who took a driver's ed course compared with those who didn't. Rather than use these results to design better driver's ed programs, the feds essentially gave up on them and diverted money to seat belt and anti-drunk-driving programs. Today, only 40 percent of new drivers complete a formal training course, which may be one reason 20 percent to 35 percent of applicants fail their initial driving test.

THE INNER DRIVER

17 But governments are looking anew at the value of driver's education. In April, Michigan passed sweeping rules that grant levels of privilege depending on one's age and driving record. States with similar systems, like California, Maryland, and Oregon, have seen teen accident rates drop. Those who lose their licenses often have to return to traffic school. But some states have generous standards for these schools. To wit:

18   California's theme schools. There, errant drivers can attend the "Humor's My Name, Traffic's My Game," school, in which a mock jury led by a stand-up comic decides who the worst drivers are; the "Traffic School for Chocoholics," which plies errant drivers with chocolate and ice cream; and the gay and lesbian "Pink Triangle Traffic School."

19   But the real key to reducing road rage lies deep within each of us. Professor James of the University of Hawaii suggests that instead of emphasizing defensive driving—which implies that the other driver is the enemy—we should focus on "supportive driving" or "driving with the aloha spirit." Of course that's hard to do if a) someone has just cut you off at 60 mph or b) you live in Los Angeles instead of Hawaii. Nerenberg, the Los Angeles psychologist, has published an 18-page booklet called "Overcoming Road Rage: The 10-Step Compassion Program." He recommends examining what sets off road rage and to "visualize overcoming it." Other tips: Imagine you might be seeing that person at a party soon. And remember that other drivers "are people with feelings. Let us not humiliate them with our aggression." In the chapter titled, "Peace," he suggests, "Take a deep breath and just let it go." And if that doesn't work, the windshield-wiper trick is pretty clever.

POST-READING QUESTIONS

CONTENT

1. What, according to the authors, is "aggressive driving"?
2. What examples of road rage do the authors give?
3. What are some causes of road rage, according to the article?
4. What role does anonymity play in road rage? Why?
5. What are some ways aggressive driving can be minimized, according to the article?

STYLE AND STRUCTURE

6. What is the point of the article? Write the main idea of the essay in your own words.
7. How do the writers support their main idea? What evidence do they offer? Is this evidence convincing? Why or why not?
8. Who is the audience for this essay? To what extent are you part of the audience? Explain.
9. What purpose do the opening examples serve? Would the essay be more persuasive without them? Explain.

CRITICAL THINKING AND ANALYSIS

DISCUSSION QUESTIONS

10. The writers claim that road rage may come from "Jekyll-Hyde" behavior or from "jerk drivers." Which of these two claims do you think best explains the road rage phenomenon? Why?

11. What effect do you think the type of car someone drives has on that person's driving? Be careful to avoid stereotypes and to illustrate your response with specific examples from your own experience and observations.

WRITING ASSIGNMENTS

12. What effect do you think driver's education courses, or the lack of them, has had on the driving population? Explain in a few paragraphs, citing your experience for support.

13. To what extent do you agree or disagree with the authors' notion that drivers "become dehumanized" in their vehicles? What effect, if any, does this dehumanization have on people's driving? In a short essay, argue that people do or do not become "dehumanized" in their vehicles, and explain the effects of this dehumanization. Be sure to cite the essay and your own experience and observations for support.

VOCABULARY DEVELOPMENT

14. Choose one paragraph from the essay and rewrite it so that it targets another audience. What changes did you make? Share your paragraph with other students and see if they can guess your audience, and discuss how certain changes—such as vocabulary or examples—more significantly affected the way you communicate than others.

GROUP ACTIVITIES FOR BOTH *ROAD RAGE* AND *ROAD RAGE: JUST THE SAME OLD RISKY DRIVING*

15. Keep notes of all traffic incidents you hear or read about, either in the news or in the newspaper, and bring your notes to class. Discuss the causes and effects of the incidents, and write a brief paragraph drawing some conclusion about the connection between road rage and traffic accidents.

16. Brainstorm a list of all the times you have experienced road rage, either your own or someone else's. Discuss the causes of the road rage incidents, and write a short paragraph explaining how road rage occurs.

Road Rage: Just the Same Old Risky Driving

In *Road Rage: Just the Same Old Risky Driving*, the writer argues that road rage is not a new phenomenon but one that is recycled every decade or so. Citing examples of impolite driving from early in car history, the author illustrates how aggressive driving has been present for nearly as long as cars themselves.

Pre-reading Questions

Freewrite for five to ten minutes in response to the following questions:
What does the term "road rage" mean to you? Describe a time when you have encountered road rage, either in yourself as a driver or in another driver. Do you think road rage is getting worse? Explain. What do you think causes road rage?

Vocabulary Preview

Vocabulary Words:
- dubbed
- bemoaned
- antiquated
- prose
- hostile
- proliferation
- defunct
- cascades

Look up the words above, using at least five of them in sentences of varying structure.

1   The perception is a driver who snaps and goes charging-down the crowded roads of the 1990s, taking risks with the lives of all who get in the way. But road rage isn't a recent phenomenon. And it doesn't have to be this extreme to present a safety problem. Aggressive driving, dubbed "road rage," has been around about as long as cars. It's just that we seem to pay attention to it in cycles, rediscovering it as a highway safety issue every decade or two.

2   Back in 1915, Engleman's Autocraft noted that "some automobilists abuse their rights and heedlessly run over the rights of others." And from a 1937 textbook: "Control the desire to beat or get ahead of the other fellow. . . . A good driver never permits himself to become angry. Anger frustrates good judgment."

3   By 1951 the message hadn't changed much. A traffic manual listed the "thoughtless and inconsiderate actions that so often contribute to accidents failure to give signals, cutting in and not giving enough room to other vehicles, not keeping a safe distance from other vehicles."

4   A 1954 magazine bemoaned the driver "who cannot tolerate being held up by a long line of traffic. . . . He pulls out of line and tries passing on the right or on the wrong side of the road. He runs through red lights or jumps the gun before the light has turned green . . . cuts in and out, races, and gets ahead of everybody else."

5   Except for some antiquated prose, these reports could have been written last week. And there's some more. "Highway Massacre," a 1978 Wall Street Journal report, called

attention to the "guns, knives, fists, and cars [that have] become drivers' weapons on packed roads in the West."

6   The same year, a Los Angeles police psychologist told The Chicago Tribune that "People are beginning to lose control. . . . They get frustrated at the stack-ups on our freeways, they get angry at other inconsiderate drivers, and their tolerance level overflows. They explode. Their car becomes a weapon, and they strike out." Even the *National Enquirer* got into the act, warning in 1979's "Car Wars" that "angry motorists are using tons of speeding metal as deadly weapons."

7   Same in the 1990s. More recent news coverage is strikingly similar. A Washington Times article, also headlined "Car Wars," says "the weapon of choice has six cylinders" and claims a 51% increase in violent highway incidents since 1990.

8   There's no objective evidence to support the notion that highway hostility is increasing. "There always have been hostile drivers," Insurance Institute for Highway Safety President Brian O'Neill points out. "Certain egregious examples generate media coverage which, in turn, tends to lead to additional reports of such incidents." High-profile media attention isn't the only focus on aggressive driving. Congress has held hearings. There's been a proliferation of programs aimed at the problem.

9   If the phenomenon of aggressive driving gets rediscovered over and over, so does speculation about its possible causes. Everything is cited from summer heat, an increase in traffic congestion, and the stepped-up pace of urban life to an overall increase in violence and a general break-down in manners. "Experts place much of the blame on TV commercials and programs that stress macho themes and on self-awareness courses that emphasize individual assertion over concern for others," a source told The Los Angeles Times in 1978. A decade later, another Times source said continuing immigration is a problem because it brings "motorists from the screech and-batter school of driving." Even the now defunct 55 mph national speed limit has been cited as a cause: "One driver is out in the speed lane doing exactly 55 and a faster driver wants to pass. The guy going 55 gets righteous and this is when the 'car war' begins."

10   Whatever the causes, aggressive driving is a continuing problem that's often viewed as a new one. In 1997, three out of four people surveyed by Gallup said people were driving more aggressively than they had been five years before. No one admitted to being personally at fault. (See, also, "The Other Guy's Fault," CR, September 1997.) This is a common reaction," O'Neill says. "Almost everyone believes he or she is a good driver, but they also believe there are lots of bad drivers. The belief that problems are caused by other drivers is one reason it's hard to change driver behavior through education."

11   Road congestion, often mentioned as a contributor to aggressive driving, also seems to be longstanding. The 1951 traffic manual points out that "since 1910, the number of motor vehicles has increased by over 2,000 percent, but new road construction for the same period has been less than 3 percent. This, in a nutshell, is the problem!" In 1988, The Los Angeles Times was making the same point: "There are more than 6 million vehicles in Los Angeles County. That's about . . . 10,000 vehicles for every mile of freeway." More recently, U.S. News & World Report put road rage on its cover and claimed much the same thing: "It isn't your imagination that traffic is getting

worse. Since 1987, the number of miles of roads has increased just 1 percent while the miles driven have shot up 35 percent."

12   So the problem isn't new, the causes aren't new, and "the consequences can be as deadly now as in previous decades," says Allan F. Williams, Institute senior vice president. "At the same time, we must take care not to seize on ineffective measures just to do something. The goal is to be effective."

13   Last year, the National Highway Traffic Safety Administration awarded grant money for special enforcement in the Washington, D.C. area. Police in nearby Fairfax County, Virginia, got a state grant to increase the ticketing of drivers who speed, run traffic controls, tailgate, change lanes improperly, fail to signal, or who drive on the shoulder. Maryland State Police announced they, too, are targeting aggressive drivers. Programs like these are useful because they not only ticket more violators but also raise public awareness. Still, limited programs aren't the whole solution. It takes ongoing enforcement against the most common kinds of aggressive driving. Targeting everyday aggressors: "Media coverage focuses on outlandish examples of aggressive driving including motorists who run others off the road or pull guns. It makes for good newspaper copy, but, thankfully, it's rare," Williams says. "Much more common is the aggressive practice of deliberately entering an intersection after—sometimes several seconds after—the light has turned red."

14   While this "everyday" kind of aggression doesn't attract the same attention, it does contribute substantially to urban crashes. Williams notes that red-light runners "are responsible for an estimated 260,000 crashes each year, of which approximately 750 are fatal." On a national basis, fatal crashes at traffic signals increased 19% during 1992–96, and red-light-running crashes increased 15%—both far outpacing the 6% increase in all other fatal crashes during the same period.

15   Apprehending violators one by one through traditional enforcement isn't realistic, given the extent of red-light running, but technology can help. Several cities use cameras to ticket and deter violators. In cities in both California and Virginia, this led to big decreases in violations.

16   Similarly, photo radar is effective against speeders. Pictures are taken of speeding vehicles, and tickets are mailed to violators. Signs typically warn drivers about camera locations but don't indicate which cameras are active at any given time. Studies in Norway showed such enforcement reduced injury crashes by 20% on rural roads, and a subsequent study in British Columbia showed significant reductions in speeding vehicles. Cameras also are effective on urban roads, according to a London study in which researchers report "highly significant" decreases of 9% in all crashes and 56% in fatal crashes "as a direct outcome of the cameras."

17   The continuous application of proven enforcement techniques like these "can substantially reduce a range of traffic violations generally referred to as aggressive driving," Williams concludes. O'Neill echoes this, saying "the solution to this and most other driver problems is, in theory, simple. If all motorists obeyed all traffic laws, aggressive driving would disappear. But unfortunately, motorists routinely ignore many traffic laws, and this cascades into extreme behavior by a few."

18   Despite recent media attention rediscovering aggressive drivers, this has been a problem in one form or another for most of this century.

POST-READING QUESTIONS

CONTENT

1. What evidence does the article give for the notion that road rage is not a new phenomenon?
2. Why, according to the article, do people think road rage is new?
3. How have the causes of road range changed over the years, according to the essay?
4. Why is driver behavior difficult to change?
5. What are some steps that some states are taking to address road rage? How effective are these steps?
6. What role does the media play in contributing to road rage?

STYLE AND STRUCTURE

7. How does the brief length of this article affect its persuasiveness? Would it be more or less persuasive if it were longer? Why?
8. What is the primary argument of the essay? Restate the main point in your own words.
9. Is the evidence for the writer's main point convincing? Why or why not?
10. Who is the audience for this article? Is the audience the same as for "Road Rage"? Explain.

CRITICAL THINKING AND ANALYSIS

DISCUSSION QUESTIONS

11. What, to you, is risky driving? What factors—such as weather, time of day, disposition of the driver—determine how "risky" someone's driving is? Explain.
12. In what ways do you think the methods listed in the article to control aggressive driving are effective? Explain.

WRITING ASSIGNMENTS

13. What role does civility, or etiquette, play on the road? How effective are current traffic laws and law enforcement in curtailing aggressive driving? Write a few well-developed paragraphs explaining the role that civility plays on the road. Be sure to give examples from your own experience and observations to support your claims.
14. To what extent do you agree or disagree that road rage is "just the same old risky driving"? Write at least two paragraphs arguing that road rage is nor is not a new phenomenon, citing the article and your own experiences and observations for support.

VOCABULARY DEVELOPMENT

15. *Road Rage* has had numerous names over the years, and the article mentions several. Write down all the ways that *Road Rage* is described in the essay, and then write a few sentences explaining why you think some of the descriptions are more accurate than others.

GROUP ACTIVITIES FOR BOTH *ROAD RAGE* AND *ROAD RAGE: JUST THE SAME OLD RISKY DRIVING*

16. Keep notes of all traffic incidents you hear or read about, either in the news or in the newspaper, and bring your notes to class. Discuss the causes and effects of the incidents, and write a brief paragraph drawing some conclusion about the connection between road rage and traffic accidents.

17. Brainstorm a list of all the times you have experienced road rage, either your own or someone else's. Discuss the causes of the road rage incidents, and write a short paragraph explaining how road rage occurs.

SYNTHESIS QUESTIONS

1. Brent Staples writes that, as a black male, he has the power to "alter public space in ugly ways." Write an essay or paragraph in which you discuss whether or not people have a right to be rude if they perceive themselves to be at risk. Be sure to cite Staples' essay and your own experiences in order to illustrate your ideas.

2. Amy Tan's mother, because of her imperfect English usage, is treated unkindly by strangers, and Tan reports that her mother yells at a stockbroker who has not honored her wishes promptly. Write an essay or paragraph in which you argue whether or not people have the right to be rude if they are irritated by someone first. Use examples from at least two essays in this chapter as well as examples from your own life in order to support your points.

3. Amy Tan writes that her mother's English "limits people's perceptions of her," while Brent Staples writes that he has been "perceived as dangerous" by strangers. Write an essay or paragraph in which you discuss the ways people are labeled as a result of external characteristics. Be sure to cite both essays and your own life for support.

4. Brent Staples reveals that he has been falsely presumed dangerous by strangers, and Amy Tan's mother, while very intelligent, is not always treated with great respect by people who do not know her. Between these two groups—people perceived, for whatever reason, as dangerous, and limited English speakers—whom do you sympathize with more? Why? Citing both essays and your own experiences, write a paragraph or essay in which you explain why one group should work harder to get along with the other.

5. Judith Martin in *Manners Matter* (Overview) states that without etiquette "every little nasty remark is labeled a slander and taken to court," while John Marks

writes in *The American Uncivil Wars* that "Americans . . . have turned virtually every kind of unhappiness into a legal claim." Explore this idea of people using the law to enforce kindness in a paragraph or essay, citing these two texts and using examples from your own experiences and observations in order to illustrate your ideas.

6. Barbara Lawrence and Amy Tan point out how other people's offensiveness—via profanity and blatant disrespect—can hurt people, yet Brent Staples takes steps to make people feel more comfortable around him despite the fact that he has done nothing to make people feel uncomfortable. Choose an everyday situation where one person feels uncomfortable around another and argue that one side is responsible for ensuring the comfort of both parties. Write at least a paragraph in responding to this question and cite these three writers for support.

7. John Marks writes that Americans tend "to applaud rebels," but Brent Staples tries to be less noticeable in order to put people at ease. Write an essay or paragraph in which you discuss whether or not it is possible to be both a considerate person and a rebel. You will need to define both of these terms in order to make your meaning clear, and you should cite both texts, among others, in order to best illustrate your ideas.

8. If, as John Marks writes, people "tend to applaud rebels" in society, then at what point does a "rebel" move from someone who wins public approval to someone who loses it? What role does civility play in the "rebel's" portrayal? Write an essay or paragraph in which you discuss the point at which "rebelliousness" becomes negative rather than positive. Cite at least two writers from this chapter, and use your own experiences for support.

9. Stephanie Ericsson writes, "when someone lies, someone loses," but Barbara Lawrence points out how harmful obscenities can be. What is an angry person to say? Write an essay or paragraph in which you explain what someone should do if his/her only honest response to someone comes in the form of profanity. Be sure to cite both writers and your own life in order to illustrate your ideas.

Incivility in Pop Culture

Reprinted with special permission of King Features Syndicate.

"The First Amendment was designed to protect offensive speech, because nobody ever tries to ban the other kind."

— **Mike Godwin**
staff counsel, EFF

"The bar of incivility is being constantly lowered."

— **Anita Creamer**
on the game show The Weakest Link

"...Don Bell has been tried, convicted, and now executed by the media."

— Roger Carter

private investigator on suicide victim
Donald Bell
who was accused of manslaughter

"...Good Girls seem to be all over the place, winning again."

— Sandra Tsing Loh

"...the more expensive forms of popular culture offer their customers the foulest language."

— Lisa de Morales
A Coarse Study in Trash Talk

Websites:

www.ksu.edu/humec/tele.htm
This site offers reprints of several articles (some with good bibliographies) addressing the impact of television violence.

www.tvrundown.com
This site provides articles (for a fee) addressing current trends in television as well as information on employment and education issues in television.

teenmusic.about.com/library/blgames.htm
An interactive site providing games designed to further music knowledge, this Website allows users to test their knowledge of contemporary artists.

Introduction

In "real life," Americans seem to value fairness and civility: schools still teach children to take turns and to follow the Golden Rule; politicians gain points in the polls when their debates are civil but lose points when their campaigns become too negative; and companies emphasizing excellent customer service bring in large profits. Clearly, we have been sending the message that we value a higher standard of behavior in all areas of life.

When we turn on the television or pop in a movie, however, our standards seem to drop. Programs with high instances of profanity and multiple instances of unkindness dominate the airwaves, and musicians who address hate-laden topics via violent lyrics sell millions of albums. Further, movies that present vulgar language and themes prove to be highly profitable ventures.

The question is, then, at what point do we no longer desire a higher standard of behavior? According to polls and ratings, the use of profanity, sex, and violence in our entertainment all but guarantees success with the public. Sure, we value family life and kind acts, but not when we want to laugh. Since the late 1980s, television, music, and movie popularity have largely hinged on the "gross" factor; if lewd or unkind behavior is present, then so are we. Obvious uncivil acts such as profanity and assaults are not the only form of entertainment we value. Seeing minority groups underrepresented and women stereotyped are just two of the ways civility has been left out of primetime programming, yet from the continued patterns of underrepresentation we can infer that, really, people do not mind the status quo.

This chapter seeks to address whether or not the trend of grossness has peaked or has begun to wane, and it explores what, exactly, is uncivil behavior within the context of popular culture.

Profits by the Gross

Entertainer seeking a bigger bottom line just need to aim lower

Robert La Franco

Writer Robert La Franco addresses the issue of vulgarity's popularity in his article, *Profits by the Gross.* In it, he reveals how movies, television programs, and radio celebrities have grown immensely popular, seemingly through the use of profane language and crude situations. What La Franco finds particularly disturbing, however, is how producers of such "gross" entertainment are making huge profits, thus validating their decisions to lower the standards of behavior in their features.

Pre-reading Questions

Freewrite for five to ten minutes in response to the following questions:
What are your favorite current movies and/or television shows? Make a list of your favorites and rank them according to which are more "G-rated." What factor, if any, do coarse language and base situations (dealing with bodily functions, for instance) play in determining which shows and movies you prefer? Why?

Vocabulary Preview

Vocabulary Words:	• scatological	• degradation	• hijinks
	• infuriates	• caustic	• revenue

Look up the words above and use them in a paragraph on a topic of your choosing.

---

1   Hollywood wants the youth market—and why not? Currently there are 37 million U.S. consumers between 14 and 24; and millions more think like them. And, according to Roper Starch Worldwide, the annual spending power of Americans between 19 and 29 is more than $100 billion.

2   What's the newest way to get their attention and their dollars? Be rude like Comedy Central's animated hit South Park, gross like Twentieth Century Fox's summer blockbuster There's Something About Mary and lewd like shock jock Howard Stern and talk-TV's Jerry Springer.

3   Watch 17-year-old Princeton freshman Giselle Woo and her 15-year-old cousin Azella Perryman as they sing along with South Park's scatological opening theme. They know every word by heart. In schools and offices the show's plotlines have become underground water cooler chat. And while the show's popularity may infuriate parents and bosses, it only inspires advertisers and programmers to even greater degradation.

4   South Park is unquestionably gross. Witness talking feces, a boy who dies every episode, three grammar school buddies who rant about lesbians (one of whom pukes all over his classmates at the very mention of love) and their favorite TV stars, who do nothing but fart on each other.

5   Perfect. Ratings at Comedy Central have climbed over 30% since the controversial show first aired last summer. It has added 7 million new subscribers to the network, and on one evening last season even beat out network competition among viewers 18 to 49. Merchandise sales from the show have hit about $100 million. As a result, creators Trey Parker and Matt Stone scored a $15 million movie and TV development deal, and a 1998 income estimated at about $8 million.

6   There's Something About Mary, a story about a young man's obsession with his long-lost high school dream date, is loaded with yuckiness.

7   In one scene an ambulance carts away comic actor Ben Stiller, in the role of Mary's suitor, after he injures his private parts zipping his prom tuxedo pants. In another, a stray fishing hook rips into his cheek while he flirts with her. Young audiences rolled in the aisles with laughter, boosting ticket sales for the R-rated summer comedy to $110 million. Walt Disney's family-fare Mulan will barely beat it with $120 million.

8   Howard Stern, the infamous number-one-rated morning radio jock, now also appears on both cable and broadcast television, putting him on the tube every evening. His nightly E! broadcast is the cable channel's highest rated nighttime series. The rude-and-crude factor will bring the caustic Stern an estimated $17 million this year.

9   Jerry Springer's ugly hijinks feed the popularity of down-and-dirty fare. His slugfest-filled shows now outrate Oprah's touchy-feely talk sessions and generate some $150 million in annual ad revenue.

10   Expect more outrageous plots and programming, not less. By the year 2000 there will be 5 million more kids to entertain in this country, and South Park will be yesterday's gross-out.

POST-READING QUESTIONS

CONTENT

1. According to La Franco, why does Hollywood want the youth market?

2. By what means does La Franco say Hollywood can capture this market?

3. What does La Franco mean when he says that "gross" shows have become "underground water cooler chat"? Do you agree? Explain.

4. What examples of "gross" entertainment does La Franco offer?

STYLE AND STRUCTURE

5. What is La Franco's main idea? Use your own words to restate his main point.

6. Who is La Franco's audience? To what extent are you part of his audience? How can you tell?

7. What examples does La Franco give to show that "gross" sells? How effective are these examples?

8. Does the brief nature of the article hurt La Franco's credibility? Why or why not?

CRITICAL THINKING AND ANALYSIS

DISCUSSION QUESTIONS

9. To what extent do you think that being "rude," "gross," and "lewd" are effective means for entertainers to get people's "attention and their dollars"? Explain.

10. How "gross" are the examples that La Franco offers? Do you think he has a point, or is he being oversensitive? Explain.

WRITING ASSIGNMENTS

11. La Franco writes that "while [South Park's] popularity may infuriate parents and bosses, it only inspires advertisers and programmers to even greater degradation." Is he right? Write a few paragraphs discussing whether or not the current popularity of "gross" shows leads to the production of more such shows. Give examples from current television programming to illustrate your ideas.

12. What trends in entertainment do you notice in terms of the "gross" factor? To what extent are television, movies, and music becoming more gross? Write at least one well-developed paragraph showing how programming is or is not becoming more "gross." Cite your own observations in responding to this question.

VOCABULARY DEVELOPMENT

13. What words does La Franco use to communicate the "gross" concept? What other ways can you think to communicate a "gross" idea without resorting to crude language? Brainstorm a list of alternatives for off-color expressions.

GROUP ACTIVITIES

14. How funny can clean humor be? Write a skit in which nothing "gross" occurs but which is, nonetheless, funny. What subject matter do you choose? How successful are you? Share your skits and your opinions with the class.

15. Why is "gross" humor funny? As a group, write a paragraph explaining the appeal of "gross" humor. Or, if you do not find "gross" humor funny, write a paragraph arguing that lewd humor is not entertaining.

TV Talk Shows: Freak Parades

Charles Oliver

First published in *Reason* in 1995, *TV Talk Shows: Freak Parades* explores the reasons for daytime television's popularity. Charles Oliver compares the talk shows to carnival side shows, citing many of the same types of attractions on television today as were included in circus tents, and he explains how women are the primary audience for the "dark spectacle" that such shows as Ricki Lake, Oprah, and Jerry Springer provide.

Pre-reading Questions

Freewrite for five to ten minutes in response to the following questions:
What television talk shows, if any, have you watched? What is your impression of these shows? Are some more informative, entertaining, or offensive than others? How so? Explain.

Vocabulary Preview

Vocabulary Words:
- rickety
- spectacle
- vicarious
- exploitative
- enticed
- voyeurism
- averted
- boisterous
- squabbling
- preened
- jaded

Look up the words above. Then, add your own connotative meanings to at least five of the words. What images do these words bring to mind, even without their formal definitions?

1   Bearded ladies. Siamese twins. Men and women who weigh more than 300 pounds each. Tattooed men. These are just a few of the guests to grace the stages of daytime talk shows in recent months. If those examples remind you of a carnival sideshow, there's a reason.

2   In the 19th century and for the first few decades of this century, carnivals crisscrossed the United States, providing entertainment to people in small towns. Carnivals catered to the dark side of man's need for spectacle by allowing people to escape temporarily from their dull everyday lives into a world that was dark, sleazy, and seemly dangerous. Of course, the danger wasn't real, and the ultimate lure of the carnival was that you could safely return from its world to your everyday life.

3   Television and regional amusement parks took their toll on the carnival. Today, the few carnivals in existence are generally sad collections of rickety rides and rigged games. But man's need for dark spectacle hasn't gone away, and a new generation of entrepreneurs has found a way to allow people to experience the vicarious thrill of the dark, the sleazy, and the tawdry—all without leaving the safety of their homes.

4   The gateways to this dark world are daytime talk shows. Phil Donahue created the mold for this genre, and Oprah Winfrey carried it to perhaps its greatest success. Both their shows are essentially women's magazines on the air, alternating celebrity profiles,

services-oriented features, discussion of political issues, and more exploitative episodes. Both mix the tawdry with the serious. Donahue was the man who gave us daytime debates between presidential candidates, and he was also the man who wore a skirt on a show devoted to cross dressing.

5   However, a new generation of hosts has emerged that trades almost exclusively in the sleaze their audiences demand: Geraldo, Montel, Ricki, Jerry. Their names may not be familiar to you, but they have millions of viewers. *Oprah* alone is watched by 7 million households each day. Each has managed to recreate the carnival in a contemporary setting.

6   One of the main attractions of the old carnivals were the "hoochie coochie" dancers. Men would eagerly wait in line, enticed by the talker's promise that these women would "take it off, roll it up, and throw it right at you." This was the origin of modern striptease. Today, the heirs of Little Egypt are a staple on daytime television. In fact, they are so common that producers really have to try to come up with new angles. Male strippers, female strippers, old strippers, grossly overweight strippers, amateur strippers— these are just a few of the variations that I saw on daytime talk shows in just one four-week period. Of course, these people didn't just talk about their profession; they inevitably demonstrated it. While the television viewer could see the naughty bits only in digitized distortions, the live audience for these shows were treated to an eyeful.

7   However, most of the strippers on these shows are attractive young women. Given that the audience for daytime talk is also women, this seems like a strange choice of guests. I can only assume that at least some of the women who watch these shows are intrigued by the profession and wonder what it would be like to be a stripper. By presenting these women strippers—indeed, by actually taking their cameras into clubs for performances—talk shows give those women viewers the chance to live out their fantasies vicariously without risking any of the dangers involved. Based upon the comments offered, female audience members generally seem to sympathize with the strippers who appear on these shows, usually defending them against those brought on to attack the profession.

8   Of course, at times the subject of stripping is simply an excuse for these shows to engage in emotional voyeurism. A perfect example was an episode of *Jerry Springer* dealing with strippers and family members who disapproved of how they earned their money. Naturally, the strippers couldn't just talk to their parents and siblings: they had to demonstrate their art to them. So while the assembled families and the studio audience watched, the girls stripped naked.

9   On one side of a split television screen, the home audience saw a lovely young girl strip down to her distorted birthday suit. On the other side, her family, some of them crying, averted their eyes and tried to ignore the hooting and catcalls of the audience.

10   It was tacky; it was sleazy. It was the perfect daytime moment. Whoever thought of it is a veritable P.T. Barnum of the airwaves. At once, this sordid mess provides the viewer with the voyeuristic thrill of seeing a family conflict that one really shouldn't observe, the vicarious thrill of stripping before an audience, and, ultimately, the confirmation that a dull, "normal" lifestyle is superior to that of the women on the show.

11   An important part of carnivals was the freak show, an assortment of real and contrived physical oddities: pinheads, fat people, bearded ladies. While the carnival talkers

would try to entice people into the sideshow tents with come-ons about the scientific oddities inside, the real lure of these attractions wasn't intellectual curiosity. It was terror and pity. The customer could observe these people and think to himself that no matter how bad his life seemed at times, it could be much, much worse.

12   Daytime talk shows have their own version of the freak show. Indeed, on her now-defunct show, Joan Rivers had actual sideshow freaks. These were politically correct "made" freaks (people who purposefully altered their bodies), not natural ones. The guest who drew the biggest reaction from the audience was a man who lifted heavy weights attached to earrings that pierced various parts of his body. (I've actually seen this guy perform, and I can say that the audience didn't see his most impressive piece of lifting. But there was no way that it could have been shown on television, at least not without some serious digitizing of the screen.)

13   More often, talk shows will feature people with physical conditions similar to those who were attractions in sideshows. I've seen various shows do episodes on women with facial hair, and the lives of the very large are always a popular topic. One episode of *Jerry Springer* featured greeting card models who weigh more than 300 pounds. In typical fashion these women were not dressed as they presumably would be in everyday life, but in revealing lingerie. So much the better for gawking, I guess.

14   Again, the host will set up one of these shows with some remarks about understanding these people, and to their credit, many of the guests on these programs do try to maintain their dignity. The greeting card models seemed a happy, boisterous lot of people. But more often guests are asked to tell tales of discrimination and broken hearts. It's easy to conclude that they were invited on the show so that the audience could feel sorry for them and feel superior to them.

15   And speaking of feeling superior, how could anyone help but laugh at and feel better than the endless parade of squabbling friends and relatives who pass through these shows? Judging from the looks of guests on some of these shows, you'd think that the producers comb every trailer park and housing project in the nation looking for them. In fact, most are solicited through telephone numbers given during the show: "Are you a white transsexual stripper whose family disapproves of your Latino boyfriend? Call 1-800-IMA FREK."

16   The guests then are invited on the show, where they battle it out for the amusement of the audience. A typical example was a show hosted by Ricki Lake on the topic of promiscuity. Ricki began by introducing Shannon, a girl who claimed her best friend Keisha sleeps around too much. Amid much whooping from the audience, Shannon detailed her friend's rather colorful sex life: "It ain't like she getting paid."

17   Then Keisha came out and accused Shannon of being the one who sleeps around too much. They spent an entire segment arguing. After the break Ricki introduces a mutual friend of the two and asked the question everyone in the audience now wanted to know: "Which one is the real slut?" A dramatic pause. The emphatic answer: "Both of them." The audience erupts.

18   Conflict is a key element on the new breed of talk shows. Physical fights seem to break out on Ricki Lake's show more frequently than at hockey games. These conflicts are not always mere arguments between friends or family members. Often, there are clear-cut

good guys whom the audience is supposed to cheer and bad guys whom the audience boos. These episodes resemble the low-brow morality plays of professional wrestling.

19   Pro wrestling, in fact, had its origins in the carnival. Sometimes the resemblance to pro wrestling is quite pronounced. Daytime talk shows have a fascination with the Ku Klux Klan. It seems a week doesn't go by without one show bringing on members of the Klan to discuss their views on race relations, welfare, abortion, or child rearing. Usually there'll be representatives from some civil rights organization present to offer an opposing view.

20   The Klansmen look every inch the pro wrestling "heel." They are invariable overweight and have poor skin and a bad haircut. Watching them sitting there in their Klan robes, shouting racial slurs at their opponents as the audience curses them, I always expect these people to pull out a set of brass knuckles and clobber the "babyface" while the host has his back turned.

21   More often, though, the villains on talk shows are a little more subtle. The audience seems to value family quite a bit because the most common types of villains on these shows are people who pose a threat to the family: child-deserting wives, cheating husbands, and abusive parents.

22   One typical show was an episode of *Jenny Jones* where women who date only married men faced off with women whose husbands had left them for other women. The women who dated married men certainly made no attempt to win the audience over. They came in dressed in short skirts or low-cut dresses. They preened; they strutted; they insulted the other guests and the audience members; they bragged about their sexual prowess. "Nature Boy" Buddy Rogers himself could not have worked the crowd better.

23   Why do such people even show up for these shows? It can't be for the money, since guests receive no more than a plane ticket and a night in a nice hotel. After watching countless shows, I've come to the conclusion that these people really think there is nothing wrong with what they do, and they usually seem quite surprised that the audience isn't on their side.

24   Is the public's appetite for this sleaze unlimited? Probably not. After all, the carnival came around but once a year. With close to two dozen daytime talk shows competing for viewers, people are bound to grow jaded. Last year, Oprah Winfrey, who already had one of the less sleazy shows, began a policy of toning down the tawdry elements. Even her sensational admission to using crack cocaine during the 1980s came in the middle of an "inspirational" program on recovering addicts. The show, which was already the top-rated daytime program, saw its ratings climb. But for those with a taste for the dark side of life, there'll always be a Ricki Lake or a Gordon Elliott.

POST-READING QUESTIONS

CONTENT

1. Why, according to Oliver, are people fascinated by sideshows? Do you agree? Explain.

2. What does Oliver identify as the modern equivalent to "hoochie coochie" dancers? Why does he say people are still fascinated by this type of entertainment?

3. What does the viewer derive from seeing the talk shows, according to Oliver? What motivates people to watch such "oddities"?

4. What role does the feeling of superiority play in determining whether people watch these shows? Do you agree? Explain.

5. Why, according to Oliver, is conflict "a key element on the new breed of talk shows"?

STYLE AND STRUCTURE

6. What is Oliver's point in writing this? Restate his main idea in your own words.

7. Who is Oliver's audience? Does his audience include people who watch television talk shows? How can you tell?

8. What is Oliver's attitude toward his topic? Choose several examples from the text that best illustrate his tone.

9. What function do Oliver's opening examples serve in his essay? Are they effective? Explain.

10. How apt is Oliver's comparison of television talk shows to women's magazines? Give examples of both types of entertainment for support.

CRITICAL THINKING AND ANALYSIS

DISCUSSION QUESTIONS

11. Do you agree that, as Oliver says, "people are bound to grow jaded" by the type of talk shows he writes about? Explain.

12. Why do you think, according to Oliver, "the audience seems to value family quite a bit"? What examples from the text support this notion?

WRITING ASSIGNMENTS

13. Do you think television talk shows promote the uncivil, often sordid, behavior they spotlight, or do they simply reflect people's fascination with this type of behavior? In a few paragraphs or short essay, argue that these shows do or do not promote uncivil behavior and give examples from your own life.

14. To what extent is class a factor in Oliver's essay? How can you tell? Write a paragraph in which you discuss the role of class in terms of people's involvement on television talk shows. Cite the text, as well as your own ideas, for support.

15. Oliver claims that people who appear on daytime talk shows "really think there is nothing wrong with what they do . . . " Watch at least 30 minutes of a television talk show and explain in a well-developed paragraph whether or not you agree with Oliver's assertion.

VOCABULARY DEVELOPMENT

16. Charles Oliver has a strong bias throughout his essay. Choose words and expressions that reveal his bias, and write a few sentences explaining how his bias does or does not help him be persuasive.

GROUP ACTIVITIES

17. Without watching daytime television talk shows, write your own skit of a show and present it to the class. How do people on your show act? How interested is the rest of the class? What is the connection, if any, between the two? Jot down your conclusions and share them with the class.

18. Watch at least 30 minutes of some daytime talk show, and pay attention to how people—including the audience—treat each other. How accurate are Oliver's assertions? How do people treat each other? Share your findings with those of other groups in an attempt to discern how correct Oliver is in his argument.

Signs of Intelligent Life on TV

Susan Douglas

Seeking escapism in primetime television drama, Susan Douglas writes about three programs that, while they mark decided progress in their depiction of women and minorities in professional roles, still portray their lead males as the most sympathetic characters. Douglas criticizes television even as she admits to watching it, and she raises the question of whose point of view needs to be presented in order for on-screen equality to occur.

Pre-reading Questions

Freewrite for five to ten minutes in response to the following questions:
What television shows do you watch? Who are the heroes, or at least the main characters, on these shows? Are men and women treated equally? Are different races equally represented? Which shows do you think best represent different genders, races, and cultures? Why?

Vocabulary Preview

Vocabulary Words:
- pundits
- diurnal
- resonates
- simultaneous
- hybrid
- masquerade
- recurring
- infuriates
- devoted
- contrary
- patriarchy

Look up the words above in a dictionary. Then, find at least five of these words in the text of Douglas' essay and substitute their definitions (groups of words rather than one word) for the word itself. What effect do these substitutions have on the sentences?

1   When the hospital show *ER* became a surprise hit, the pundits who had declared dramatic television "dead" were shocked. But one group wasn't surprised at all.

2   Those of us with jobs, kids, older parents to tend to, backed-up toilets, dog barf on the rug, and friends/partners/husbands we'd like to say more than "hi" to during any diurnal cycle don't have much time to watch television. And when we do—usually after 9:38 P.M.—we have in recent years been forced to choose between Diane Sawyer interviewing Charles Manson or Connie Chung chasing after Tonya [Harding] and Nancy [Kerrigan]. People like me, who felt that watching the newsmagazines was like exposing yourself to ideological smallpox, were starved for some good escapist drama that takes you somewhere else yet resonates with real life and has ongoing characters you care about.

3   When *NYPD Blue* premiered in the fall of 1993 with the tough-but-sensitive John Kelly, and featuring strong, accomplished women, great lighting, bongo drums in the sound track, and male nudity, millions sighed with relief. When *ER* hit the air, we made it one of the tube's highest rated shows. Tagging farther behind, but still cause for hope, is another hospital drama, *Chicago Hope.*

4   All three shows acknowledge the importance of the adult female audience by featuring women as ongoing characters who work for a living and by focusing on contemporary problems in heterosexual relationships (no, we haven't yet achieved everyday homosexual couples on TV). More to the point, hound-dog-eyed, emotionally wounded yet eager-to-talk-it-through guys are center stage. So what are we getting when we kick back and submerge ourselves in these dramas? And what do they have to say about the ongoing project of feminism?

5   For those of you who don't watch these shows regularly, here's a brief précis: *NYPD Blue* is a cop show set in New York City and has producer Steven Bochco's signature style—lots of shaky, hand-held camera work, fast-paced editing (supported by the driving, phallic backbeat in the sound track), and multiple, intersecting plots about various crimes and the personal lives of those who work in the precinct. Last season there were more women in the show; and last season there was John Kelly.

6   This year, the show is more masculinized. Watching Bobby Simone, played by Jimmy Smits, earn his right to replace Kelly was like witnessing a territorial peeing contest between weimaraners. Bobby had to be as sensitive and emotionally ravaged as Johnny, so in an act of New Age male one-upmanship, the scriptwriters made him a widower who had lost his wife to breast cancer. But Bobby had to be one tough customer too, so soon after we learn of his wife's death, we see him throwing some punks up against a fence, warning them that he will be their personal terminator unless they stop dealing drugs.

7   *ER* has the same kind of simultaneous, intersecting story lines, served up with fast-tracking cameras that sprint down hospital corridors and swirl around operating tables like hawks on speed. And there are the same bongo drums and other percussive sounds when patients are rushed in for treatment. *Chicago Hope* is *ER* on Valium: stationary cameras, slower pace, R&B instead of drumbeats. It's also *ER* on helium or ether, kind of a *Northern Exposure* goes to the hospital, with more offbeat plots and characters, like a patient who eats his hair or a kid whose ear has fallen off.

8   Whenever I like a show a lot—meaning I am there week in and week out—I figure I have once again embraced a media offering with my best and worst interests at heart. Dramatic TV shows, which seek a big chunk of the middle- and upper-income folks between 18 and 49, need to suck in those women whose lives have been transformed by the women's movement (especially women who work outside the home and have disposable income) while keeping the guys from grabbing the remote. What we get out of these twin desires is a blend of feminism and antifeminism in the plots and in the female characters. And for the male characters we have an updated hybrid of masculinity that crossbreeds decisiveness, technical expertise, and the ability to throw a punch or a basketball, with a soft spot for children and a willingness to cry.

9   On the surface, these shows seem good for women. We see female cops, lawyers, doctors, and administrators, who are smart, efficient, and successful. But in too many ways, the women take a backseat to the boys. In *NYPD Blue,* for example, we rarely see the women actually doing their jobs. The overall message in the three shows is that, yes, women can be as competent as men, but their entrance into the workforce has wrecked the family and made women so independent and hard-hearted that dealing with them and understanding them is impossible. Despite this, they're still the weaker sex.

10   In *ER* it is Carol Hathaway (Julianna Margulies), the charge nurse, who tried to commit suicide. It is Dr. Susan Lewis (Sherry Stringfield) who is taken in by an imposter who claims to be a hospital administrator. Dr. Lewis is also the only resident who has trouble standing up to white, male authority figures: she is unable to operate while the head cardiologist watches her. In *Chicago Hope,* a psychiatrist prevails upon a female nurse to dress up like Dorothy (ruby slippers, pigtails, and all) because a patient refusing surgery is a *Wizard of Oz* junkie. Even though she points out that no male doctor would be asked to do anything like it, the shrink insists she continue the masquerade because the patient's life is at stake. Here's the crucial guilt-shifting we've all come to know and love—this patient's illness is somehow more her responsibility than anyone else's. Her humiliation is necessary to save him.

11   The Ariel Syndrome—Ariel was the name of Walt Disney's little mermaid, who traded her voice for a pair of legs so that she could be with a human prince she'd seen from afar for all of ten seconds—grips many of the women, who have recurring voice problems. Watch out for female characters who "don't want to talk about it," who can't say no, who don't speak up. They make it even harder for the women who do speak their minds, who are, of course, depicted as "bitches."

12   One major "bitch" is the wife of *ER*'s Dr. Mark Greene (Anthony Edwards). He's a doctor who's barely ever home, she's a lawyer who lands a great job two hours away, and they have a seven-year-old. Those of us constantly negotiating about who will pick up the kids or stay late at work can relate to this. The problem is that *ER* is about *his* efforts to juggle, *his* dreams and ambitions. We know this guy, we like him, we know he's a great doctor who adores his wife and child. Her, we don't know, and there's no comparable female doctor to show the woman's side of this equation. As a result, when conflicts emerge, the audience is primed to want her to compromise (which she's already done, so he can stay at the job he loves). When she insists he quit his job and relocate, she sounds like a spoiled child more wedded to a rigid quid pro quo than to flexibility, love, the family. It's the conservative view of what feminism has turned women into—unfeeling, demanding blocks of granite.

13   One of the major themes of all three shows is that heterosexual relationships are a national disaster area. And it's the women's fault. Take *NYPD Blue.* Yes, there's the fantasy relationship between Andy Sipowicz (Dennis Franz) and Sylvia Costas (Sharon Lawrence), in which an accomplished woman helps a foul-mouthed, brutality-prone cop with really bad shirts get in touch with his feelings and learn the pleasures of coed showering. While this affair has become the emotional anchor of the show, it is also the lone survivor in the ongoing gender wars.

14   It looks like splitsville for most of the show's other couples. Greg Medavoy (Gordon Clapp) infuriates Donna Abandando (Gail O'Grady) by his behavior, which includes following her to see whom she's having lunch with. She's absolutely right. But after the shots of Greg looking at her longingly across the office (again, we're inside his head, not hers), the audience is encouraged to think that she should give the guy a break. By contrast, her explanations of why she's so angry and what she wants have all the depth and emotional warmth of a Morse code message tapped out by an iguana. Of course Greg doesn't understand. She won't help him.

15   In this world, female friendships are nonexistent or venomous. And there is still worse ideological sludge gumming up these shows. Asian and Latina women are rarely seen, and African American women are also generally absent except as prostitutes, bad welfare moms, and unidentified nurses. In the *ER* emergency room, the black women who are the conscience and much-needed drill sergeants of the show don't get top billing, and are rarely addressed by name. There is also an overabundance of bad mothers of all races: adoptive ones who desert their kids, abusive ones who burn their kids, and hooker ones (ipso facto bad). Since the major female characters—all upper-middle class—don't have kids, we don't see their struggles to manage motherhood and work. And we certainly don't see less privileged moms (the real majority in the U.S.), like the nurses or office workers, deal with these struggles on a lot less money.

16   One of the worst things these shows do, under a veneer of liberalism and feminism, is justify the new conservatism in the U.S. The suspects brought in for questioning on *NYPD Blue* are frequently threatened and sometimes beaten, but it's O.K. because they all turn out to be guilty, anyway. Legal representation for these witnesses is an unspeakable evil because it hides the truth. After a steady diet of this, one might assume the Fourth Amendment, which prohibits unreasonable search and seizure, is hardly worth preserving.

17   So why are so many women devoted to these shows? First off, the women we do see are more successful, gutsy, more fully realized than most female TV characters. But as for me, I'm a sucker for the men. I want to believe, despite all the hideous evidence to the contrary, that some men have been humanized by the women's movement, that they have become more nurturing, sensitive, and emotionally responsible. I want to believe that patriarchy is being altered by feminism. Since I get zero evidence of this on the nightly news, I want a few hours a week when I can escape into this fantasy.

18   Of course, we pay a price for this fantasy. TV depicts "real men" being feminized for the better and women masculinized for the worse. The message from the guys is, "We became the kind of men you feminists said that you wanted, and now you can't appreciate us because you've forgotten how to be a 'real' woman." It's a bizarre twist on the real world, where many women have changed, but too many men have not. Nevertheless, in TV land feminism continues to hoist itself with its own petard. Big surprise.

POST-READING QUESTIONS

CONTENT

1. What three television dramas does Douglas use as a context for her discussion? In what ways do you find these programs apt choices for her argument? Explain.

2. What challenge does Douglas say dramatic TV must meet? To what extent does she think dramatic TV is successful in its quest to meet this challenge? Explain.

3. What is the "Ariel Syndrome," and how does Douglas say it is significant in terms of dramatic TV?

4. How, according to Douglas, are viewing audiences primed to sympathize with male, rather than female, characters on television?

5. In what ways does Douglas say the primetime dramas "justify the new conservatism in the U.S."?

6. What overt message about gender roles does Douglas say these television shows promote? What is the hidden message?

STYLE AND STRUCTURE

7. What does Douglas say is her purpose in writing this? Restate her main idea in your own words.

8. How does Douglas identify her audience? Is her audience the same as that of the television prime-time dramas? How can you tell? Cite the text to show who each audience is.

9. How seriously does Douglas take her subject? Choose examples from the text that best reveal Douglas' attitude toward dramatic TV.

10. What examples does Douglas use in order to illustrate her main idea? How convincing are these examples? Explain.

11. What does the title of the essay lead you to expect? Does the essay fulfill your expectations? Explain.

CRITICAL THINKING AND ANALYSIS

DISCUSSION QUESTIONS

12. Do you agree with Douglas that "in too many ways, women [in these shows] take a backseat to the boys"? Explain and give examples.

13. Of all the negative messages that Douglas claims primetime drama communicates, which do you find the most offensive? Why?

WRITING ASSIGNMENTS

14. Douglas claims that "TV depicts 'real men' being feminized for the better and women masculinized for the worse." Is she right? Write a few paragraphs or short essay in which you either agree or disagree with Douglas' assertion. Support your response with examples from the text and from your own television viewing experiences.

15. Based on your own television viewing and upon your reading of the essay, do the positive messages sent by primetime dramas, particularly those concerning women and minority characters, outweigh the negative messages? Explain in a well-developed paragraph, providing plenty of examples from contemporary television programs.

16. Watch at least one episode of a popular television drama and discuss in a paragraph or two whether or not Douglas' messages apply as much as she claims they do. Be sure to cite both Douglas' essay and the program you watch in order to illustrate your ideas.

VOCABULARY DEVELOPMENT

17. Choose three sentences from Douglas' essay that speak to you at some level, and rewrite them, changing the structure and vocabulary. What effect do your changes have on the meaning of the sentence?

GROUP ACTIVITIES

18. Watch one hour of a primetime television drama, and pay attention to the roles men and women play on the show. Then, in small groups, discuss whether or not Douglas is on target in her assertions. Cite the programs for support.

19. Create your own television drama, developing men and women characters into "real" people. Write down your descriptions of the main characters, and create dialogue for them in one short scene. How different is your creation from what you see on television? Share your "program" with the class.

The Return of Doris Day

Sandra Tsing Loh

A journalist with a B.S. in physics from Cal Tech, Sandra Tsing Loh has authored *Growing Old in Van Nuys* and is an actor as well as a writer. Claiming that "Bad Girls" went out with the eighties and that "Good Girls" are in, Loh cites several examples from popular culture in order to illustrate how the appeal of Doris Day is experiencing a resurgence.

Pre-reading Questions

Freewrite for five to ten minutes in response to the following questions:
Who, if anyone, on television or in movies do you consider to be a genuinely nice person? What about that person makes you think so? What role, if any, does a famous person's perceived niceness or rudeness play in determining that person's popularity, particularly for women?

Vocabulary Preview

Vocabulary Words:
- heyday
- platonic
- treatise
- demure
- akimbo
- archetypes
- quintessential
- symbiosis
- vixen
- gamboled

Without looking up the words above, use at least five of them in a short paragraph on some aspect of popular culture. Then, use a dictionary to learn the formal definition of each word, revising your paragraph accordingly to improve clarity and avoid faulty usage.

1   The seventies and eighties were tough times for us Good Girls. As polite people, we like to do what's expected of us. Unfortunately, what was expected, in our sexual heyday, was for Girls to be . . . anything but Good.

2   In junior high, I dutifully grappled with whatever icky senior boy that Spin the Bottle sent me. By college, my sisters and I had graduated to smoking pot and swimming nude in the Sierras, sleeping with men on the first date (or before—you're welcome!), and developing evasive "mumble vaguely and give back rubs" routines if forced into a threesome.

3   We were lost, I tell you. Lost. But not anymore. Recently I was faced with a Nude Hot Tub Situation. It was a tame one by eighties standards. The tub was vast, the night was dark, and my companions were three platonic male friends—thirtysomethings like me stooped with worry, hardly a threat.

4   "C'mon!" I heard that inner coach urging me. It was the voice born in 1975, when everyone in my junior high had Chemin de Fer jeans and Candie's sandals. *Don't be a drag,* it said. *Take off your clothes and jump in!*

5   But then, for the first time, I heard another voice. Clear as a bell, it was the soaring soprano of Mary Martin in *South Pacific,* or perhaps Shirley Jones in *Oklahoma!* It sang:

> I've got a guy!
> A really great guy!
> He makes me as high
> As an elephant's eye!

6   Or something to that effect. It was like a light bulb going on. Suddenly I felt right with my world—fresh, natural, confident, all the panty-shield adjectives. It was so simple, so clear. The wandering days of these breasts were over.

7   "If you'd known me in my twenties," I lectured my hot tub companions, as though sharing an amazing story from ancient lore, "you would have seen my boobs and seen them often!" I'm in the water now, but demurely covered in my white cotton T-shirt from Victoria's Secret. (A white cotton T-shirt is typical of what we women actually *buy* there.) "But no more." I lift a teacherly finger. "Today, I feel much more liberated keeping my shirt on. I don't have to prove anything anymore. I can turn the world on with a smile!" I hear myself excitedly half-singing, flashing on Mary Tyler Moore.

8   My treatise is cut short by the arrival of two 24-year-old modern dancers who rip off towels and flash their naked pink everything. The men's attention snaps away with the zing of taut bungee cords. But I don't feel bad. I know it's only I, Goody Two Shoes, who feels that wonderful glowing specialness inside.

Good Girls: A Cleaned and Buffed Thumbnail History

9   Were our moms actually right way back when? Maybe so. Because like it or not, these days Good Girls are back in. Demure behavior is suddenly clever, fashionable, even attractive.

10   Who *is* the nineties Good Girl? She is: (a) spunky; (b) virginal; (c) busy with purposeful activity. But not obsessively so. Her hormones are in balance. Brave chin up, she works within society's rules, finds much to celebrate in her immediate surroundings, makes the best of her lot. Good Girls don't challenge the status quo.

11   Good Girls have been around a long time in Western culture. The star of the very first novel in English? A Good Girl! We find her in Samuel Richardson's 1740 opus, *Pamela*. In it, Pamela's resistance to sex charges five-hundred-plus pages of narrative tension; it's so effective a gambit that Good Girls (typically poor but beautiful governesses) become the very foundation of the eighteenth- and nineteenth-century novel.

12   It is in twentieth-century America, however, that we start to see the rowdy Good Girl. She does more than keep her knees crossed. In fact, if so moved, she may even spread her legs boldly akimbo! (If only to punctuate a funny singalong.)

13   The forties and fifties brought the U.S. Good Girl her two most sacred boons: World War II, and Rodgers & Hammerstein. The former yielded new busy-but-virginal archetypes like Rosie the Riveter, the Andrews Sisters, and the Chipper Navy Nurse. The latter fleshed out the canon via the Fiesty Governess of the past (Anna in *The King and I*), the Chipper Navy Nurse of the semipresent (Nellie Forbush in *South Pacific*), even the boldly innovative Frisky Nun of the future (Julie Andrews in *The Sound of Music*). Indeed, Frisky Nun proved so popular she'd soon hop mediums and become TV's *The Flying Nun* (comical ex-Gidget Sally Field). Even *The Mary Tyler Moore Show*—a milestone in the modern Good Girl's progress—almost had Moore playing a

version of Frisky Nun. Laugh no more at winged hats: in the past, Frisky Nun was a female star's emancipated alternative!

14   The quintessential Good Girl of midcentury American—indeed the mother of all modern Good Girls—was Doris Day. We mean, of course, Nubile Doris Day, in her guise as pert, urban, apartment-dwelling career girl (*Pillow Talk*), as opposite to harangued suburban housewife (*Please Don't Eat the Daisies*). Never mind that Doris typically chucked her career at the end of the film for Rock Hudson; what mattered was that while Doris *was* a Good Girl, she was hardly a nun—in fact, she was quite sexy in her spunky purposefulness.

15   It was too bad that Doris stayed mainly in the movies, for the most perfect form for the American Good Girl remains the musical. Here emerges a unique symbiosis: on one hand, the musical needs the Good Girl's soprano, her can-do optimism, the soaring love songs only she can inspire. On the other, not to put too fine a point on it, the Good Girl needs the musical. The musical could *create* Good Girls where there once were none. Example: where, outside the musical, do you find the rarest of beings—the ethnic Good Girl? Sure, ethnic girls can have hearts o' gold, but in the real world they—can we say it?—tend to be a bit sassy. Happily, the musical has the miraculous power to freshen, sanitize, uplift even ethnicities who might feel too irked with society to be Good. We see Jewish Good Girls: Tevye's daughters in *Fiddler on the Roof*. (Imagine "Matchmaker, Matchmaker" done in dialogue on a hot afternoon in Queens—another tale entirely.) It also gave us Yentl. Hm. *West Side Story* produces Latina Good Girl Maria (Natalie Wood, but we quibble). *Flower Drum Song* yields that mousy Asian Good Girl whose name no one can remember (not Nancy Kwan, the other one). *The Wiz* even gives us a black Good Girl: Diana Ross (who was never that Good again).

16   As we move into the late seventies, however, even white Good Girls are hard to come by. There's a general Fall of the Musical (we could discuss Andrew Lloyd Webber, but why?)—and Fall of Filmic Good Girls. We lose our bright, dependable, ponytailed stars—our June Allysons, Shirley Joneses, Julie Andrewses. We collapse into the nude/seminude group therapy "line" musicals: *Oh! Calcutta!*, *Pippin*, the exhaustingly confessional *A Chorus Line*. By 1977, we have, God forbid, Liza Minnelli trying to play an ex-WAC in *New York New York*. Liza Minnelli? The eyelashes alone would have scared Our Boys.

17   And you know why we saw this fall, this demise, this dismal sinking? Because national hope is failing. No one whistles a happy tune. We're moving into bad times for optimism. Bad times for patriotism. Bad times for Good Girls. Forrest Gump drifts out of touch with Jenny . . . and America itself becomes very *dark*.

The Enduring Power of Good Girls

18   If Good Girls are back in the nineties, what does this imply? That we've come full circle? Forgiven Mom and Dad? We're in love with a wonderful guy? More deeply, does the Good Girl's resurgence signal an uplift in national character, a kind of neo-fifties patriotism, a return to what we might call, without irony, American values?

19   We have no idea—Good Girls are notoriously poor at political analysis. All we know is, we look around and Good Girls seem to be all over the place, winning again.

20   Look how they flourish, in the very bosom of our society! Good Girls are our great: morning-show hosts (Katie Couric now, Jane Pauley before); figure skaters (Nancy Kerrigan vanquishing Tonya Harding now, Dorothy Hamill vanquishing all those foreigners before); country singers (Reba, Tammy & Co. now; Dolly Parton before); middle-of-the-road pop stars (Whitney Houston, Paula Abdul now; Linda Ronstadt before); goyische straight gals to nervous Jewish comics (Sally to Harry, Helen Hunt to Paul Reiser now; Diane Keaton to Woody Allen before); Peter Pans (Sandy Duncan now-ish, Mary Martin way before); androgynous gals (Ellen DeGeneres now, Nancy Drew's pal boyish George before); astronauts (Sally Ride); Australians (Olivia Newton-John); MTV newspersons (Tabitha Soren); princesses (Di).

21   Can a video vixen be Good? Absolutely. Look at ex-Aerosmith girl and rising star Alicia Silverstone. You thought she was Drew Barrymore, but she's not. In Amy Heckerling's surprise summer hit *Clueless* (loosely based on Jane Austen's *Emma!*), Silverstone played Cher, a fashion-obsessed virgin ("You see how picky I am about my shoes, and *they* only go on my feet!"). Alicia the person is very spunky, clean, convincingly virginal, attends Shakespeare camp, takes tap-dancing lessons, and loves animals!

22   Good Girl accessories are in. Look what Hillary Clinton did for the headband—an astounding semiotic statement. Look how she reinvented cookie baking. Too-thin Nancy Reagan in her let-them-eat-cake Adolfo suit is over. Today, posing as a Good Girl—as clever Hillary does—seems powerfully subversive.

23   Look how even yesterday's swampy girls are cleaning up. Jane Seymour bounced back from whatever seamy B-stuff she was doing to triumph today as Dr. Quinn, Medicine Woman. Consider post-Donald Ivana, her pertness and brave industry recalling the Czech girl skier of yore. Even Sharon Stone seems downright nice. She makes an effort to dress "up" for press briefings and is so polite, modest, funny! (She showed us her home in *In Style*—the essence of nice! Is a *Redbook* cover in her future?)

24   And why not? Being a Good Girl pays off. Look how well Meg Ryan/Sandra Bullock films are doing. These girls don't titillate by getting naked. Why? They can turn the world on with a smile!

25   Even the musical is coming back! Via Disney, we have Belle and the Little Mermaid, even Princess Jasmine and Pocahontas. Look how ethnic! Maybe there *is* a place called Hope.

The Nastiest Truth of All

26   But what is the bottom-line appeal of the Good Girl? Why do we urban nineties women want to *be* her? It's not as uncalculated as one might think. The Good Girl's draw is that she is the opposite of Bad. And Bad is something we no longer want to be.

27   You remember Bad Girl—she who reigned in the go-go eighties. Bad Girl is very Bad. Ow. She needs a spanking, she wants it, but beware of giving it to her because ironically it is you (or, more likely, Michael Douglas) who will suffer afterward.

28   Good Girl's opposite, Bad Girl, has out-of-control hormones. Bad Girl comes from a wildly dysfunctional family; her past makes her do strange, erratic things. Bad Girl tells us something is terribly wrong with society. Bad Girl challenges the status quo. Bad Girl uses sex for everything but love and babies: it's power, self-expression, psychosis, hate, revolt, revenge.

29   What we have in Bad Girl is Power Slut. Like Madonna in, well, ninety percent of
her oeuvre. Joan Collins in *Dynasty*. Glenn Close in *Fatal Attraction*. Sharon Stone in
Basic Instinct. Demi Moore in *Disclosure*. (Sure those last few are technically nineties,
but anything written by Joe Eszterhas is really quite eighties, no?)

30   Good feminists we, we have saluted Bad Girl/Power Slut's right to exist, to demol-
ish, to flourish in her dark way. But the nagging question remains: Is this a good behavior model for us? Is Bad Girl's life healthy, happy, productive? Does she get enough
love? Even more creepily we ask: Is she aging well?

31   Because the fact is, even we—once-nubile twentysomething gals who gamboled
defiantly topless in the mountain streams of yore—feel ourselves gently softening with
age each day. The drama in the bathroom no longer centers around the scale. Forget
that—we've gained and lost the same fifteen pounds so often that the cycle has become
like an old pal, natural as our monthly period. But our skin! Each new wrinkle tells us
there's no going back. No wonder our obsessions have become all Oil of Olay, Clin-
ique moisturizer, antiwrinkle cream!

    And while we hate to be unsupportive of our Badder sisters, we can't help noticing
that, well, Bad Girlhood seems so bad *for* you. Look at Heidi Fleiss—drawn and
witchy and actually too thin at 29. Partying, prostitution, cocaine, and, heck, the eight-
32 ies don't wear well on a gal. And look at spooky seventysomething *Cosmo* girl Helen
Gurley Brown, a.k.a. "the Crypt Keeper in capri pants," as she is known to AM-radio
wag Peter Tilden.

33   Even the indestructible Madonna is looking a bit exhausted. Sure she's a zillion-
aire and superpowerful and has been on top forever. Her *Sex* book broke every boundary, sold tons. But it must be tough, we secretly think, for Madonna to greet her 5,012th
weekend with only those girly dancing boys with the weird hair for company. Sean is
off having babies with Robin Wright (a Good Girl, if oddly skinny). Geez: Madonna's
going to be 40 soon. If she keeps hanging onto Bad Girl, soon she'll be Old Crone girl.
Can we women age with dignity? By what strategy will we engineer fabulous forties,
fifties, sixties, and beyond? (My God—a healthy woman of 65 today can expect to live
to 83! Almost half our life will be spent being 50 or older!)

34   As we drift past our midthirties, we begin to question the idea of relentlessly pushing the boundaries of society, psychology, and biology. Will we end up like tart-talking
Roseanne? We used to love her. We still do, but it's 1995 now and we are confused.
She had a hit show, but still she felt the need for plastic surgery, butt tattoos, Tom
Arnold tattoos, a Tom Arnold divorce, she hates her family, belched the anthem, lit her
farts (or could if she'd wanted), married her bodyguard and has had a new baby, like,
surgically implanted . . . where? Is this feminism? Help!

35   We will not go like that. (Anyway, we can't afford to.) We women are survivors,
and we are battening down our hatches . . . for the future.

The Good Girl Manifesto

36 Herewith, then, a declaration of our principles:

    1. We're no longer promiscuous. Diseases suck. And so do noncommittal men our
       age (often spoiled for commitment by all that free sex we gave them in the six-
       ties, seventies, and eighties). There's really no point. We can do it ourselves.

2. We're tailing down on booze and drugs. Eight glasses of water a day—better for the skin.

3. We're trying not to be anorexic. That seems very eighties. Then again, we don't want to be fat. As a result, we're just a wee bit bulimic. Sorry! We know this is not good.

4. We're *trying* to envision a future without plastic surgery. We try to keep happy, confident, glowing, nonlifted, fortysomething earth mothers Meryl/Cybill/Susan foremost in our minds. (See Nivea wrinkle cream ad: a blond mom in white feels good about her face, baby splashing in the background.)

5. We're trying to love our parents again. Their mortality weighs heavily upon us. When a parent dies, we peruse the photo album, weep while contemplating their jauntily hopeful forties hats, the huge families they came from. We feel suddenly lonely.

6. Were the forties and fifties really so bad? Gee, we feel nostalgic. We yearn for old love songs and old movies. At least our filmic Good Girl heroines do. (See Meg Ryan in *Sleepless in Seattle,* Marisa Tomei in *Only You.*) Although I must tell you: if I hear Harry Conick Jr. singing "It Had to Be You" again on the soundtrack of one more light romantic comedy, I will kill someone.

7. We're drawn to stuff that seems traditional, even if it isn't. Laura Ashley sheets. Coach bags. *Martha Stewart Living.*

8. We're back to white cotton underpants. (And as Victoria's Secret tells us, cotton is sexy again!)

9. We love our pets—our very own Disney familiars. (If we are starring in a movie, we can be expected to talk to our cat or dog in a very cute way. Starlets who need their tawdry images to be cleaned up can be expected to join PETA.)

10. We believe in true love, but we don't expect to find it in Rock Hudson. That's a dream of the past. Urban Lotharios *never* settle down—we've learned that, unlike Doris, we can't domesticate them through interior design.

37   That's why we're looking for love in all new places. Maybe we find it via a much younger man (a third of today's women already do). Maybe we find it by falling in love again with the family (like Sandra Bullock does in *While You Were Sleeping*). Maybe we find it in our children, postdivorce.

38   Consider that the template for the female sitcom today is not single newsgal Mary Tyler Moore, but single mom Murphy Brown, divorced mom Brett Butler, divorced mom Cybill. Exhusbands are reduced to comic characters sticking their heads in the door, like Howard the neighbor in the old *Bob Newhart Show*. In these days, when conception's becoming increasingly immaculate, maybe we have a baby without a guy.

39   Or maybe, hell, we find love for a few beautiful days with a fiftysomething shaman/photographer called Robert Kincaid with a washboard stomach. Maybe we never see him again after that. But today's Good Girl is tough and prudent—a little bit of love and she says, uncomplainingly, "I'm fine. I'm full. I have plenty."

40   Then goes outside and, into the air, high above her head, throws not her bra . . . but her hat.

POST-READING QUESTIONS

CONTENT

1. Why does Loh say that the seventies and eighties were "tough times for . . . Good Girls"?

2. How does Loh define "Good Girls" in the nineties? Does her definition still make sense today? Explain.

3. What is the relationship between "Good Girls" and musicals?

4. Who does Loh claim were "Good Girls" in the nineties? Do you agree that these women are "Good" in the way that Loh defines it? Explain.

5. How does Loh define "Bad Girl"? Why does she say that women no longer want to be like her? Do you agree?

6. Of the ten principles Loh offers as part of the "Good Girl Manifesto," which two or three make the most sense to you as being "Good" acts? Why?

STYLE AND STRUCTURE

7. Why does Loh begin her essay with a "Nude Hot Tub Situation"? What effect does her capitalization of the type of situation she describes have on your reading of the situation?

8. What is Loh's main idea? Rewrite her point in your own words.

9. Is Loh writing her essay for one gender more than another? How can you tell? Cite the text for support.

10. What purpose does Loh's "Thumbnail History" of "Good Girls" serve? Would her essay be as convincing without it? Explain.

11. What evidence does Loh offer that "Good Girls" are experiencing a resurgence? Are her examples persuasive? Why or why not?

12. What role does humor play in Loh's essay? Does humor help or hurt her case? Choose examples of words and phrases that illustrate your point.

CRITICAL THINKING AND ANALYSIS

DISCUSSION QUESTIONS

13. What do you think Loh's primary reason is for wanting to be "Good"? Cite the text for support.

14. Do you agree that the "Good Girl" became popular again in the nineties? If so, why? If not, why not?

WRITING ASSIGNMENTS

15. How long do you think "Good Girls" will have appeal? Write a well-developed paragraph in which you argue that the popularity of "Good Girls" is either tem-

porary or permanent. Be sure to explain and give examples from Loh's essay and from your own observations.

16. What characteristic—appearance, behavior, or any other you can think of— plays the greatest role in determining whether or not a woman is a "Good Girl"? Write an essay in which you define what a "Good Girl" is, and give examples from popular culture to illustrate your ideas.

17. How widely represented are "Good Girls" in advertising? How closely do you think advertisers stick to Loh's definition of "Good" in their representations of women? Why? Write a few paragraphs or short essay in which you argue that "Good Girls" do or do not make up a significant portion of advertising images. Cite examples from popular culture in order to illustrate your ideas.

VOCABULARY DEVELOPMENT

18. Loh creates a distinct tone throughout her essay using both specific vocabulary— words and phrases—and examples. Find at least three expressions that clearly reveal Loh's voice, and write a few sentences explaining how those expressions best communicate Loh's tone.

GROUP ACTIVITIES

19. Brainstorm a list of contemporary television programs and movies that have women as their stars. Then, analyze women's role in those productions. How true are Loh's assertions for today? Is the "Good Girl" still present? Is her popularity growing or waning, and if so, to what extent? Share your results with the class in an open forum setting.

20. Review current popular magazines for articles and advertisements featuring women, and discuss what you think a "Good Girl" is. Then, write your own advertisement featuring your idea of a contemporary "Good Girl." Make sure that your audience can figure out from your ad just what your idea of a "Good Girl" is. Share your ad with other groups in order to broaden your ideas of a "Good Girl."

Argument Pair: What's the Answer to Ending Violent and Misogynistic Themes in Gangsta' Rap?

Bum Rap, Michael Eric Dyson

Bad Sistas, Tricia Rose

With accounts of violence against women in the media seemingly daily, people are quick to point fingers at various aspects of popular culture in order to identify a scapegoat and—through the elimination of that scapegoat—a solution to such violence. Both Michael Eric Dyson and Tricia Rose agree that male rappers' depiction of women is, at best, unflattering, yet these two writers disagree on the solution to ending misogyny in rap. Dyson suggests attacking the societal ills from which rap music has sprung, while Rose urges women to shoulder the burden and rap themselves into a better place with their own music.

Writing Assignments for *Bum Rap* and *Bad Sistas*

1. Michael Eric Dyson argues that "Censorship of gangsta' rap cannot begin to solve the problems of poor black youth," and Tricia Rose writes that female rappers' strategy to combat the misogyny in male rappers' music often "can be subverted and its power diminished." What is the best way to contain offensive music? Write an essay in which you argue for a particular way to solve the dilemma of offending people through gangsta' rap. Be sure to cite both Dyson's and Rose's essays, and use examples from your own experiences in order to illustrate your ideas.

2. Tricia Rose claims that, in order for women to be taken seriously in their complaints against negative male treatment, they must develop "sustained, strong female voices that stake claim to public space generally." Michael Eric Dyson, however, while acknowledging the "vicious misogyny" of gangsta' rap, claims that societal ills must be cured before musical themes will improve. Write a paragraph or essay in which you argue that Rose or Dyson is correct. Be sure to use examples from both essays as well as your own experience in order to support your claims.

Bum Rap

Michael Eric Dyson

Director of the Institute of African-American Research and professor of Communication Studies at the University of North Carolina at Chapel Hill, Michael Eric Dyson has authored numerous books including, *Reflecting Black: African-American Cultural Criticism* (1993) and has won the Award of Excellence from the National Association of Black Journalists in 1992.

Dyson acknowledges the sexist and violent themes in gangsta' rap, but he claims that such ideas only reflect reality and, thus, should not be censored, as he suggests in this essay which was first published in 1995 as a part of *From God to Gangsta' Rap: Notes on Black Culture.*

Pre-reading Questions

Freewrite for five to ten minutes in response to the following questions:
How familiar are you with rap music? What is your overall impression of this kind of music? Upon what is your impression based? How seriously do you take any messages of violence in the songs? Do you think rap music, particularly songs that communicate violent or mysoginistic ideas, is a reflection of social ills or a contributing factor to them? Explain.

Vocabulary Preview

Vocabulary Words:
- aesthetic
- torturous
- elegies
- aggrandizing
- malevolence
- beleaguered
- beset
- metaphoric
- bourgeois
- castigate
- precipitated
- ecclesiastical

Look up the words above, noting which words seem most or least familiar to you. Then, as you read Dyson's essay, take note of which words' meanings would have been clear to you from their context. Write a few sentences explaining how significant the context of at least five words in this essay is.

1   As a 35-year-old father of a 16-year-old son (yes, I was a teen father), and as a professor and ordained Baptist minister who grew up in Detroit's treacherous inner city, I am disturbed by some elements of gangsta' rap. But I'm even more anguished by the way many black leaders have scapegoated its artists. How can we avoid the pitfall of unfairly attacking black youth for problems that bewitched our culture long before they came on the scene? First, we should understand what forces drove the emergence of rap. Second, we should acknowledge that gangsta' rap crudely exposes harmful beliefs and practices that are often maintained with deceptive civility in many black communities.

2   If the 15-year evolution of hip-hop teaches us anything, its that history is made in unexpected ways by unexpected people with unexpected results. Rap is now safe from the perils of quick extinction predicted at its humble start. But its cesarian birth in the bitter belly of the seventies proved to be a Rosetta stone of black popular culture.

3   Afros, platforms, blunts, funk music and carnal eruptions define a "back-in-the-day" hip-hop aesthetic. But in reality, the severe seventies busted the economic boom of the sixties. The fallout was felt in restructured automobile industries and collapsed steel-mills. It was extended in exported employment to foreign markets. Closer to home, there was the depletion of social services to reverse the material ruin of black

life. Later, public spaces for black recreation were gutted by Reaganomics or violently transformed by lethal drug economies.

4   Hip-hop was born in these bleak conditions. Hip-hoppers joined pleasure and rage while turning the details of their difficult lives into craft and capital. This is the world hip-hop would come to "represent": privileged persons speaking for less visible or vocal peers. At their best, rappers shape the torturous twists of urban fate into lyrical elegies. They represent lives swallowed by too little love or opportunity. They represent themselves and their peers with aggrandizing anthems that boast of their ingenuity and luck in surviving. The art of "representin'" that is much ballyhooed in hip-hop is the witness of those left to tell the afflicted's story.

5   As rap expands its vision and influence, its unfavorable origins and its relentless quest to represent black youth are both a consolation and challenge to hip-hoppers. They remind rappers that history is not merely the stuff of imperial dreams from above. It isn't just the sanitizing myths of those with political power. Representing history is within reach of those who seize the opportunity to speak for themselves, to represent their own interests at all costs.

6   Even rap's largest controversies are about representation. Hip-hop's attitudes toward women and gays continually jolt in the unvarnished malevolence they reveal. But the sharp responses to rap's misogyny and homophobia signify its importance in battles over the cultural representation of other beleaguered groups. This is particularly true of gangsta' rap.

7   While gangsta' rap takes the heat for a range of social maladies from urban violence to sexual misconduct, the roots of our racial misery remain buried beneath moralizing discourse that is confused and sometimes dishonest.

8   There's no doubt that gangsta' rap is often sexist and that it reflects a vicious misogyny that has seized our nation with frightening intensity. For black women who are already beset by attacks from outside their communities, to feel the thrust of musical daggers to their dignity from within is doubly wounding. How painful it must be for black women, many of whom have fought valiantly for black pride, to hear the dissonant chord of disdain carried in the angry epithet "bitch."

9   But gangsta' rap often reaches higher than its ugliest, lowest common denominator. At its best, this music draws attention to complex dimensions of ghetto life ignored by many Americans. Of all the genres of hip-hop—from socially conscious rap to black nationalist expressions, from pop to hardcore—gangsta' rap has most aggressively narrated the pains and possibilities, the fantasies and fears, of poor black urban youth. Situated in the surreally violent climes of postindustrial Los Angeles and its bordering cities, gangsta' rap draws its metaphoric capital in part from the mix of myth and murder that gave the Western frontier a dangerous appeal a century ago.

10   Gangsta' rap is largely an indictment of bourgeois black cultural and political institutions by young people who do not find conventional methods of addressing personal and social calamity useful. When the leaders of those institutions, national and local alike, castigate the excessive and romanticized violence of this music without trying to understand what precipitated its rise in the first place, they drive a greater wedge between themselves and the youth they so desperately want to help.

11   The recent attempts by black figures like C. Delores Tucker and Dionne Warwick, as well as national and local lawmakers, to have the sale of gangsta' rap censored, even

outlawed, are surely misguided. When I testified before the U.S. Senate's Subcommittee on Juvenile Justice, as well as the Pennsylvania House of Representatives, I tried to make this point while acknowledging the need to responsibly confront gangsta' rap's problems. Censorship of gangsta' rap cannot begin to solve the problems of poor black youth; nor will it effectively curtail their consumption of music that is already circulated through dubbed tapes and without the benefit of significant air-play.

12   A crucial distinction needs to be made between censorship of gangsta' rap and edifying expressions of civic responsibility and community conscientiousness. The former seeks to prevent vulgar music from being sold that offends the moral sensibilities of particular groups by suppressing the First Amendment. The latter, however, is the admittedly more difficult but rewarding task of opposing—through protest and pamphleteering, through community activism and consciousness raising—the expression of misogynistic and sexist sentiments in rap lyrics and hip-hop culture. But we can't stop there.

13   If blacks really want to strike at the heart of sexism and misogyny in our communities, shouldn't we take a closer look at one crucial source of these blights? The central institution of black culture, the black church, which has given hope and inspiration to millions of blacks, has also given us an embarrassing legacy of sexism and misogyny.

14   Despite the great good it has achieved through a heroic tradition of emancipatory leadership, the black church continues to practice and justify *ecclesiastical apartheid.* More than 70 percent of black church members are female, yet they are generally excluded from the church's central station of power, the pulpit. And rarely are the few ordained female ministers elected to be pastors.

15   Yet black leaders, many of them ministers, excoriate rappers for their verbal sexual misconduct. It is difficult indeed to listen to civil rights veterans deplore the hostile depiction of women in gangsta' rap without mentioning the sexism of the movements for racial liberation of the 1960s. And of course the problem persists in many civil rights organizations today.

16   Sad, too, is the silence of most black leaders in the face of the vicious abuse of gay men and lesbians in gangsta' rap. "Fags," and "dykes" are prominent in the genre's vocabulary of rage, and black leaders' failure to make this an issue only reinforces the inferior, invisible status of gay men and lesbians in black cultural institutions, including the black church.

17   Gangsta' rap's greatest sin, in the eyes of many critics, is that it tells the truth about practices and beliefs that rappers hold in common with the black elite. This music has embarrassed black bourgeois culture and exposed its polite sexism and its disregard for gay men and lesbians. We should not continue to blame it for ills that existed long before hip-hop uttered its first syllable.

POST-READING QUESTIONS

CONTENT

1. What reasons does Dyson give for why rap music should not be blamed for social ills?

2. What role does "representin'" play in rap music? How is this role significant, according to Dyson?

3. What, according to Dyson, was the original purpose of rap music? How has its purpose changed?

4. Why does Dyson say gangsta' rap should not be judged solely on the basis of its sexist themes?

5. How does Dyson say that institutional leaders "drive a greater wedge between themselves and the youth they so desperately want to help"? Do you agree? Explain.

6. What role does Dyson say the black church plays in promoting misogyny?

7. What does Dyson say is gangsta' rap's "greatest sin, in the eyes of many critics"? Why?

STYLE AND STRUCTURE

8. What is Dyson's primary argument? What are some secondary arguments he presents? How do these points work together?

9. Who is Dyson's audience? Is his audience more directed at men or women? At African-Americans or European-Americans? How can you tell?

10. What function does the metaphor of the Rosetta stone serve?

11. How does Dyson identify with the black youth he writes about? Does the connection he make serve to strengthen or weaken his credibility? Why?

12. What does the expression "ecclesiastical apartheid" mean? What purpose does this expression serve in Dyson's essay?

CRITICAL THINKING AND ANALYSIS

DISCUSSION QUESTIONS

13. Since this article has been written, numerous other gangsta' rappers have emerged that include successful athletes and non-African-American artists. If these rappers do not come from the traditionally negative backgrounds of the original rappers, to what extent should their music be celebrated or censored? What would Dyson say? Explain, citing examples from contemporary rappers.

14. How can you explain the popularity of misogynistic themes in rap music? What role, if any, can women play in solving the problems presented in gangsta' rap?

15. To what extent do you agree or disagree with Dyson's comparison of gansta' rap's themes to the Western frontier? How similar or dissimilar are these two images? Explain.

WRITING ASSIGNMENTS

16. If gangsta' rap stems from the rappers' notion of underprivileged lives, then are the rappers' attacks on women and law enforcement uncivil, or are they

justified responses to oppression? In a few well-developed paragraphs, explain and give examples.

17. What suggestions can you offer for how the public can "avoid the pitfalls of unfairly attacking black youth for problems" in existence before rap music's introduction? Write a short essay in which you explain ways by which people can avoid blaming victims, in this case African-American youth, for problems in society. Be sure to cite Dyson's essay and your own experience and observations in order to illustrate your ideas.

18. To what extent do you agree that "Censorship of gangsta' rap cannot begin to solve the problems of poor black youth"? Write at least one paragraph in which you argue that censoring rap can or cannot help solve the problems of the youth Dyson targets in his essay. Give examples from the text and from your own life.

VOCABULARY DEVELOPMENT

19. Michael Eric Dyson balances academic writing with slang in order to communicate his ideas. Choose at least three examples of both types of writing—formal and informal—and write a few sentences explaining how both kinds of language are appropriate or effective in Dyson's essay.

20. Dyson uses vivid language to illustrate his ideas throughout his essay. Choose four or five examples of language that you find particularly effective, and write a few sentences explaining why the expressions you choose stand out for you. Be sure to look up any words that are unfamiliar to you.

GROUP ACTIVITIES

21. Write a letter to someone not from the United States, arguing that rap music should or should not be censored. Be sure to explain the First Amendment and anything specifically American to your reader, and cite Dyson's essay in order for your points to be clear.

22. Conduct a survey on your school campus in order to learn people's feelings about censorship of rap music. Bring your results to class and share them in an open forum discussion in order to determine if Dyson's views are credible.

Bad Sistas

Tricia Rose

Although male rappers are often blamed for misrepresenting women in their songs, women can be just as guilty of stereotyping themselves in their own raps, says writer Tricia Rose. Women rappers, while they do portray women as having the upper hand in sexual relationships with men, still depict women in many of the same roles as men do. In this essay, first published in *Black Noise: Rap Music and Black Culture in Comtemporary America* (1994), Rose poses the question of whether rapping about situations that have nothing to do with sex would go furthest toward accurately representing women in rap music.

Pre-reading Questions

Freewrite for five to ten minutes in response to the following questions:
How familiar are you with rap music? What is your overall impression of this kind of music? Upon what is your impression based? How seriously do you take any messages of violence in the songs? Do you think rap music, particularly songs that communicate violent or mysoginistic ideas, is a reflection of social ills or a contributing factor to them? Explain.

Vocabulary Preview

Vocabulary Words:	• caustic	• predatory	• wrath
	• patriarchal	• disingenuous	• dialogic
	• parameters	• implicitly	• chastises
	• undermines	• paradigm	

Look up the words above and write sentences using at least five of the words, making sure to vary the structure and length of your sentences.

COURTING DISASTER

1 Raps written by women that specifically concern male-female relationships almost always confront the tension between trust and savvy; between vulnerability and control. Some raps celebrate their sisters for "getting over" on men, rather than touting self-reliance and honesty. For example, in Icey Jaye's "It's a Girl Thang," she explains how she and her friends find ways to spend as much of their dates' money as possible and mocks the men who fall for their tricks. Similarly, in the video for Salt 'N' Pepa's "Independent" Salt accepts several expensive gifts from a string of dates who hope to win her affection with diamond necklaces and rings. In raps such as these, women are taking advantage of the logic of heterosexual courtship in which men coax women into submission with trinkets and promises for financial security. Nikki D's "Up the Ante for the Panty" and B.W.P.'s "We Want Money" are more graphic examples of a similar philosophy. However, for the most part, when they choose to rap about male-female relations, women rappers challenge the depictions of

women in many male raps as gold diggers and address the fears many women share regarding male dishonesty and infidelity.

2   MC Lyte and Salt 'N' Pepa have reputations for biting raps that criticize men who manipulate and abuse women. Their lyrics tell the story of men taking advantage of women, cheating on them, taking their money, and leaving them for other unsuspecting female victims. These raps are not mournful ballads about the trials and tribulations of being a heterosexual woman. Similar to women's blues, they are caustic, witty, and aggressive warnings directed at men and at other women who might be seduced by them in the future. By offering a woman's interpretation of the terms of heterosexual courtship, these women's raps cast a new light on male-female sexual power relations and depict women as resistant, aggressive participants. Yet, even the raps that explore and revise women's role in the courtship process often retain the larger patriarchal parameters of heterosexual courtship.

3   Salt 'N' Pepa's single "Tramp" is strong advice, almost boot camp, for single black women. "Tramp" is not, as Salt 'N' Pepa warn, a "simple rhyme," but a parable about courtship rituals between men and women:

> Homegirls attention you must pay to what I say
> Don't take this as a simple rhyme
> Cause this type of thing happens all the time
> Now what would you do if a stranger said "Hi"
> Would you dis him or would you reply?
> If you'd answer, there is a chance
> That you'd become a victim of circumstance
> Am I right fellas? tell the truth
> Or else I'll have to show and prove
> You are what you are I am what I am
> It just so happens that most men are TRAMPS.[1]

In the absence of any response to "Am I right fellas?" (any number of sampled male replies easily could have been woven in here), Salt 'N' Pepa "show and prove" the trampings of several men who "undress you with their eyeballs," "think you're a dummy, on the first date, had the nerve to tell me he loves me" and of men who always have sex on the mind. Salt 'N' Pepa's parable defines promiscuous *males* as tramps, and thereby inverts the common belief that male sexual promiscuity is a status symbol. This reversal undermines the degrading "woman as tramp" image by stigmatizing male promiscuity. Salt 'N' Pepa suggest that women who respond to sexual advances made by these men are victims of circumstance. In this case, it is predatory, disingenuous men who are the tramps.

4   The music video for "Tramps" is a comic rendering of a series of social club scenes that highlight tramps on the make, mouth freshener in hand, testing their lines on the nearest woman. Dressed in the then-latest hip hop street gear, Salt 'N' Pepa perform the song on television, on a monitor perched above the bar. Because they appear on the television screen, they seem to be surveying and critiquing the club action, but the club members cannot see them. There are people dancing and talking together

---

[1]Salt 'N' Pepa, "Tramp," *Hot, Cool & Vicious* (Next Plateau Records, 1986).

(including likable men who are coded as "nontramps"), who seem unaware of the television monitor. Salt 'N' Pepa are also shown in the club, dressed in very stylish, sexy outfits. Salt 'N' Pepa act as decoys, talking and flirting with the tramps to flesh out the dramatization of tramps on the prowl. They make several knowing gestures at the camera to reassure the viewer that they are unswayed by the tramps' efforts.

5   The tramps and their victims interact only with body language. The club scenes have no dialogue; we hear only Salt 'N' Pepa lyrics over the musical tracks for "Tramp," which serve respectively as the video's narrative and the club's dance music. Viewing much of the club action from Salt 'N' Pepa's authoritative position—through the television monitor—we can safely observe the playful but cautionary dramatization of heterosexual courtship. One tramp who is rapping to a woman, postures and struts, appearing to ask something like the stock pick-up line: "what is your zodiac sign, baby?" When she shows disgust and leaves her seat, he repeats the same body motions and gestures on the next woman who happens to sit down. Near the end of the video, a frustrated "wife" enters the club and drags one of the tramps home, smacking him in the head with her pocketbook. Salt 'N' Pepa are standing next to the wife's tramp in the club, shaking their heads as if to say "what a shame." Simultaneously, they are pointing and laughing at the husband from the television monitor. At the end of the video, a still frame of each man is stamped "tramp," and Salt 'N' Pepa revel in having identified and exposed them. They then leave the club together, without men, seemingly enjoying their skill at exposing the real intentions of these tramps.

6   Salt 'N' Pepa are "schooling" women about the sexual politics of the club scene, by engaging in and critiquing the drama of heterosexual courtship. The privileged viewer is a woman who is directly addressed in the lyrics and presumably can empathize fully with the visual depiction and interpretation of the scenes. The video's resolution can be interpreted as a warning to both men and women. Women: Don't fall for these men either by talking to them in the clubs or believing the lies they'll tell you when they come home. Men: You will get caught eventually, and you'll be embarrassed. Another message suggested by the video for "Tramp" is that women can go to these clubs, successfully play along with "the game" as long as the power of female sexuality and the terms of male desire are understood and negotiated.

7   However, "Tramp" does not interrogate "the game" itself. "Tramp" implicitly accepts the larger dynamics and power relationships between men and women. Although the tramps are embarrassed and momentarily contained at the end of the video, in no way can it be suggested that these tramps will stop hustling women and cheating on their wives. More important, what of women's desire? Not only is it presumed that men will continue their dishonest behavior, but women's desire for an idealized monogamous heterosexual relationship is implicitly confirmed as an unrealized (but not unrealizable?) goal. In their quest for an honest man, should not the sobering fact that "most men are tramps" be considered a point of departure for rejecting the current courtship ritual altogether?

8   Salt 'N' Pepa leave the club together, seemingly pleased by their freedom and by their ability to manipulate men into pursuing them "to no end." But the wife drags her husband home—she is not shocked but rather frustrated by what appears to be frequent dishonest behavior. What conclusion is to be drawn from this lesson? Do not trust tramps, separate the wheat from the tramps, and continue in your quest for an honest, monogamous man. "Tramp" is courtship advice for women who choose to participate

in the current configuration of heterosexual courtship, it does not offer an alternative paradigm for such courtship, and in some ways it works inside of the very courtship rules that it highlights and criticizes. At best, "Tramp" is an implicit critique of the club scene as a setting for meeting potential mates as well as of the institution of marriage that permits significant power imbalances clearly weighted in favor of men.

9   MC Lyte has a far less comedic response to Sam, a boyfriend whom she catches trying to pick up women. MC Lyte's underground hit "Paper Thin" is one of the most scathingly powerful raps about male dishonesty and infidelity and the tensions between trust and vulnerability in heterosexual relations. Lyte has been burned by Sam, but she has turned her experience into a black woman's anthem that sustains an uncomfortable balance between brutal cynicism and honest vulnerability:

> When you say you love me it doesn't matter
> It goes into my head as just chit chatter
> You may think it's egotistical or just very free
> But what you say, I take none of it seriously . . . .
>
> I'm not the kind of girl to try to play a man out
> They take the money and then they break the hell out.
> No that's not my strategy, not the game I play
> I admit I play a game, but it's not done that way.
> Truly when I get involved I give it my heart
>
> I mean my mind, my soul, my body, I mean every part.
> But if it doesn't work out—yo, it just doesn't.
> It wasn't meant to be, you know it just wasn't
> So, I treat all of you like I treat all of them.
> What you say to me is just paper thin.[2]

10   Lyte's public acknowledgment that Sam's expressions of love were paper thin is not a source of embarrassment for her but a means of empowerment. She plays a brutal game of the dozens on Sam while wearing her past commitment to him as a badge of honor and sign of character. Lyte presents commitment, vulnerability, and sensitivity as assets, not indicators of female weakness. In "Paper Thin," emotional and sexual commitment are not romantic, Victorian concepts tied to honorable but dependent women; they are a part of her strategy, part of the game she plays in heterosexual courtship.

11   "Paper Thin's" high-energy video contains many elements present in hip hop. The video opens with Lyte, dressed in a sweatsuit, chunk jewelry, and sneakers, abandoning her new Jetta hastily because she wants to take the subway to clear her head. A few members of her male posse, shocked at her desire to leave her Jetta on the street for the subway, follow along behind her, down the steps to the subway tracks. (Her sudden decision to leave her new car for the subway and her male posse's surprised reaction seem to establish that Lyte rarely rides the subway anymore.) Lyte enters a subway car with an introspective and distracted expression. Once in the subway car, her DJ K-Rock, doubling as the conductor, announces that the train will be held in the station because

[2]MC Lyte, "Paper Thin," *Lyte as a Rock* (First Priority Records, 1988).

of crossed signals. While they wait, Milk Boy (her female but very masculine-looking bodyguard) spots Sam at the other end of the car, rapping heavily to two stylish women, and draws Lyte's attention to him. Lyte, momentarily surprised, begins her rhyme as she stalks toward Sam. Sam's attempts to escape fail; he is left to face MC Lyte's wrath. Eventually, she throws him off the train to the chorus of Ray Charles's R&B classic, "Hit the Road Jack," and locks Sam out of the subway station and out of the action. The subway car is filled with young black teenagers, typical working New Yorkers and street people, many of whom join Lyte in signifying on Sam while they groove on K-Rock's music. MC Lyte's powerful voice and no-nonsense image dominate Sam. The taut, driving music, which is punctuated by sampled guitar and drum sections and an Earth Wind and Fire horn section, complement Lyte's hard, expressive rapping style.

12   It is important that "Paper Thin" is set in public and on the subway, the quintessential mode of urban transportation. Lyte is drawn to the subway and seems comfortable there. She is also comfortable with the subway riders in her video; they are her community. During musical breaks between raps, we see passengers grooving to her music and responding to the drama. By setting her confrontation with Sam in the subway, in front of their peers, Lyte moves a private problem between lovers into the public arena and effectively dominates both spaces.

13   When her DJ, the musical and mechanical conductor, announces that crossed signals are holding the train in the station, it frames the video in a moment of communication crisis. The notion of crossed signals represents the inability of Sam and Lyte to communicate with one another, an inability that is primarily the function of the fact that they communicate on different frequencies. Sam thinks he can read Lyte's mind to see what she is thinking and then feed her all the right lines. But what he says carries no weight, no meaning. His discourse is light, it's paper thin. Lyte, who understands courtship as a game, confesses to being a player, yet expresses how she feels directly and in simple language. What she says has integrity, weight, and substance.

14   After throwing Sam from the train, she nods her head toward a young man standing against the subway door, and he follows her off the train. She will not allow her experiences with Sam to paralyze her but instead continues to participate on revised terms. As she and her new male friend walk down the street, she raps the final stanza for "Paper Thin" that sets down the new courtship ground rules:

> So, now I take precautions when choosing my mate
> I do not touch until the third or fourth date
> Then maybe we'll kiss on the fifth or sixth time that we meet
> Cause a date without a kiss is so incomplete
> And then maybe, I'll let you play with my feet
> You can suck the big toe and play with the middle
> It's so simple unlike a riddle . . .

15   Lyte has taken control of the process, She has selected her latest companion; he has not pursued her. This is an important move, because it allows her to set the tone of the interaction and subsequently articulates the new ground rules that will protect her from repeating the mistakes she made in her relationship with Sam. Yet, a central revi-

sion to her courtship terms involves withholding sexual affection, a familiar strategy in courtship rituals for women that implicitly affirms the process of male pursuit as it forestalls it. Nonetheless, Lyte seems prepared for whatever takes place. Her analysis of courtship seems to acknowledge that there are dishonest men and that she is not interested in negotiating on their terms. Lyte affirms her courtship rules as she identifies and critiques the terms of men such as Sam. In "Paper Thin" she has announced that her desire will govern her behavior and *his* ("you can suck my big toe and then play with the middle") and remains committed to her principles at the same time.

16   As "products of an ongoing historical conversation," "Paper Thin" and "Tramp" are explicitly dialogic texts that draw on the language and terms imbedded in long-standing struggles over the parameters of heterosexual courtship. These raps are also dialogic in their use of black collective memory via black music. Salt 'N' Pepa's "Tramp" draws its horns and parts of its rhythm section from the 1967 soul song of the same name performed by Otis Redding and Carla Thomas. Otis's and Carla's "Tramp" set a dialogue in which Carla expresses her frustration over Otis's failure in their relationship while he makes excuses and attempts to avoid her accusations.[3] Salt 'N' Pepa's musical quotation of Otis's and Carla's "Tramp" set a multilayered dialogue in motion. The musical style of Salt 'N' Pepa's "Tramp" carries the blues bar confessional mode of many rhythm and blues songs updated with rap's beats and breaks. Salt 'N' Pepa are testifying to Carla's problems via the music, at the same time providing their contemporary audience with a collective reference to black musical predecessors and the history of black female heterosexual struggles.

17   Lyte's direct address to Sam ("when you say you love it doesn't matter") is her half of a heated conversation in which Sam is silenced by her, but nonetheless present. Lyte's announcement that she "admits playing a game but it's not done that way" makes it clear that she understands the power relationships that dictate their interaction. Lyte encourages herself and by extension black women to be fearless and self-possessed ("sucker you missed, I know who I am") in the face of significant emotional losses. Her game, her strategy, have a critical sexual difference that lays the groundwork for a black female-centered communal voice that revises and expands the terms of female power in heterosexual courtship.

18   The dialogic and resistive aspects in "Tramps" and "Paper Thin" are also present in the body of other women rappers' work. Many female rappers address the frustration heterosexual women experience in their desire for intimacy with and commitment from men. The chorus in Neneh Cherry's "Buffalo Stance" tells men not to mess with her, and that money men can't buy her love because it's affection that she's lookin' for; "Say That Then" from West Coast female rappers Oaktown 3-5-7, give no slack to "Finger popping, hip hoppin' wanna be bed rockin'" men; Monie Love's "It's a Shame" is a pep talk for a woman breaking up with a man who apparently needs to be kicked to the curb; Ice Cream Tee's "All Wrong" chastises women who allow men to abuse them; Monie

---

[3]See Atlantic Records, *Rhythm and Blues Collection 1966–1969,* vol. 6. In the linear notes for this collection, Robert Pruter refers to "Tramp" as a dialogue between Carla and Otis, in which Carla's "invectives" are insufficiently countered by Otis. It should be pointed out that the Otis and Carla "Tramp" is a remake of (an answer to?) Lowell and Fulsom's version made popular in 1966.

Love's "Just Don't Give a Damn" is a confident and harsh rejection of an emotionally and physically abusive man; and MC Lyte's "I Cram to Understand U," "Please Understand," and "I'm Not Havin' It" are companion pieces to "Paper Thin."

19   This strategy, in which women square off with men, can be subverted and its power diminished. As Laura Berlant suggests, this mode of confrontational communication can be contained or renamed as the "female complaint." In other words, direct and legitimate criticism is reduced to "bitching" or complaining as a way of containing dissent. Berlant warns that the "female complaint . . . as a mode of expression is an admission and recognition both of privilege and powerlessness . . . circumscribed by a knowledge of woman's inevitable delegitimation within the patriarchal public sphere." Berlant argues that resistance to sexual oppression must take place "in the patriarchal public sphere, the place where significant or momentous exchanges of power are perceived to take place," but that the female complaint is devalued, marginalized, and ineffective in this sphere. Berlant offers an interpretation of "Roxanne's Revenge," an early and popular rap record by black female rapper Roxanne Shante, as an example of the pitfalls of the "female complaint." Attempts were made to contain and humiliate Roxanne on a compilation record that included several other related answer records. Berlant says that "Roxanne's Revenge" is vulnerable to "hystericization by a readily available phallic discourse (which) is immanent in the very genre of her expression."[4]

20   Berlant is making an important point about the vulnerability of women's voices to devaluation. No doubt women's angry responses have long been made to appear hysterical and irrational or whiny and childlike. I am not sure, though, that we can equate attempts to render women's voices as "complaint" with the voices themselves. To do so may place too much value on the attempts to contain women. "Roxanne's Revenge" gave voice to a young girl's response to real-life street confrontations with men. She entered into black male-dominated public space and drew a great deal of attention away from the UTFO song to which she responded. More importantly, "Roxanne's Revenge" has retained weight and significance in hip hop since 1985 when it was released. This has not been the case for UTFO, the UTFO song, or any of the fabricated responses on the compilation record. Much of the status of the original UTFO song "Roxanne Roxanne" is a result of the power of Roxanne Shante's answer record. What Berlant illustrates is the ways in which Roxanne's "female complaint" needed to be labeled as such and then contained precisely because it was threatening. It did not go unnoticed, because it was a compelling voice in the public domain that captured the attention of male and female hip hop fans. The compilation record is clearly an attempt at containing her voice, but it was in my estimation an unsuccessful attempt. Furthermore, such attempts at circumscription will continue to take place when partial, yet effective, attacks are made, whether in the form of the female complaint or not. Nonetheless, Berlant's larger argument, which calls for substantial female public sphere presence and contestation, is crucial. These public sphere contests must involve more than responses to sexist male speech; they must also entail the development of sustained, strong female voices that stake claim to public space generally.

[4]Laura Berlant, "The Female Complaint," *Social Text,* Fall, 237–59, 1988.

POST-READING QUESTIONS

CONTENT

1. What does Rose say are common themes in women's raps? What types of examples does Rose offer in order to illustrate the themes she mentions?

2. In what ways does Rose say female rappers actually perpetuate the stereotypes they hope to subvert?

3. What is Rose's interpretation of Salt 'N' Pepa's "Tramp" video? Do you agree with her interpretation? What are some other ways to interpret the video?

4. What is Rose's interpretations of MC Lyte's video "Paper Thin"? In what other ways can you interpret the video, even if you have not seen it?

5. How does Rose explain that "female complaint" is "devalued, marginalized, and ineffective in [the patriarchal public sphere]"? What does she mean?

STYLE AND STRUTURE

6. What is Rose's point? Restate her main idea in your own words.

7. How similar or dissimilar is Rose's tone to the female rappers she spotlights? In what ways does Rose establish credibility? Cite examples from the text.

8. Who is Rose's audience? Are they people who listen to women rappers? How can you tell?

9. How effective are Rose's examples in illustrating her ideas? Explain.

10. How convincing do you find Rose's analysis of women's rap videos? Why?

CRITICAL THINKING AND ANALYSIS

DISCUSSION QUESTIONS

11. How effective do you think women rappers' attacks on male mistreatment are? If so, how is their protest effective? If not, what would serve as a stronger protest? Explain.

12. Do you agree that the "female complaint" is often ineffective in expressing women's views? Explain.

WRITING ASSIGNMENTS

13. Since this essay was published in 1994, what other female rappers have voiced unhappiness with men's treatment? Has men's characterization of women improved? Write a paragraph or two in which you discuss whether or not women's depiction in raps has become more or less flattering. Be sure to cite Rose's essay and examples from popular music to support your views.

14. How civil or uncivil are women rappers compared to men? Even if male rappers' depiction of women is unflattering, do you think women's protests are justified? Write a short essay in which you agree or disagree with the idea that

women's protests against male rappers are justified. Be sure to cite examples from contemporary music in order to illustrate your ideas.

15. How persuasive are entertainers of any sort who portray a group of people a certain way? Using examples from music, television, and cinema, write two to three well-developed paragraphs in response to this question.

VOCABULARY DEVELOPMENT

16. Choose at least six words from Rose's essay that evoke a strong reaction from you. Then, use those words in a paragraph arguing EITHER that women are justified in their frustration with men as depicted in female rappers' music, OR that men are innocent of the charges that many female rappers bring against them.

GROUP ACTIVITIES

17. Since the subjects of Rose's essay produced their music in the late 1980s, many new female vocalists have made their marks. As a group, discuss the direction women rapper's music seems to have gone in the last 15 years. Does Rose's essay still have merit today? If so, why? If not, what about music has changed and, thus, made Rose's argument outdated? Explain.

18. Brainstorm a list of popular vocalists, male and female, and then make notes as to the subject matter of each one. Do you notice a trend, according to the gender of the performer? Is one gender more civil, or less offensive, than the other? Write a short paragraph explaining your conclusions, and share your results with the class.

SYNTHESIS QUESTIONS

1. According to Tricia Rose and Michael Eric Dyson, many rappers' lyrics include apparent defamation of women, even making reference to violence against women. Yet writer Robert La Franco makes the point that being "rude," "gross," and "lewd" is highly profitable. Citing at least three writers from this chapter, write a paragraph or essay in which you discuss why you think violent and/or vulgar themes are so successful.

2. Both Tricia Rose and Michael Eric Dyson acknowledge the presence of misogynistic themes in gangsta' rap, and both offer examples or explanations of how rap is anti-woman. Should women buy into the criticism and change? Write a paragraph or essay in which you explain how seriously these themes should be taken by women. Be sure to cite contemporary rappers and rappers from the recent past, as well as from both readings and your own experiences, in order to illustrate your points.

3. Susan Douglas claims that viewers' empathy lies with whatever character's point of view television producers reveal regardless of how empathetic other characters might be, while Robert La Franco cites statistics revealing that entertainers who use profanity are making huge profits. Write an essay in which you

argue when, if ever, profanity is acceptable in entertainment. Consider whether or not profits justify the use of obscenities or whether the state of a character's mind (if she's angry, for instance) validates the use of such language. Be sure to cite both essays and your own experience and observations for support.

4. Tricia Rose and Susan Douglas in *Bad Sistas* and *Signs of Intelligent Life on TV,* respectively, comment on how elements of popular culture effectively reinforce traditional gender roles even as those elements seem to have a feminist slant. Write a paragraph or essay in which you argue that popular culture does or does not perpetuate gender-oriented behavior. Use examples from both readings and from your own life in order to illustrate your ideas.

5. Susan Douglas claims that even though television now shows women in positions of authority in its programs, the overall message these shows send is that "[women's] entrance into the workforce has wrecked the family and made women so independent and hard-hearted that dealing with them and understanding them is impossible." Sandra Tsing Loh, however, writes that "Good Girls" who are "busy with purposeful activity . . . flourish, in the very bosom of our society," and she offers examples of many successful "Good Girls" in the media. How do audiences want to see women—or men, or minorities, or any other group—portrayed? Write an essay or paragraph in which you argue that the most successful programs characterize women, or any group of characters you choose, a certain way. Be sure to cite current television programs for support, as well as both readings, and you may use examples from movies and videos as well.

6. Charles Oliver claims that people watch daytime talk shows in order to feel superior to the subjects of the programs, yet Susan Douglas writes that she feels disappointment in not finding more women to identify with. Citing at least two writers from this chapter, write an essay or paragraph in which you discuss whether or not characters on television or in movies should be "inferior" to their viewers or role models for them in order for television to have the greatest entertainment value.

7. Many television shows, movies, and songs are offensive to particular groups of people, yet these same forms of entertainment are wildly popular. Write a paragraph or essay in which you discuss whether entertainers should try not to offend people. Cite at least three writers from this chapter and your own life for support.

8. Susan Douglas writes of the "ideological sludge gumming up" television programs, and Charles Oliver claims that daytime talk shows focus on "dark, sleazy, and seemingly dangerous" topics. However, the major networks now offer some shows where civility is present. Write an essay or paragraph in which you discuss whether or not television is becoming more or less civil in the programs it offers, taking care to use examples from both readings and contemporary television shows.

9. What does the popularity of vulgarity say about society? Citing at least three readings from this chapter and using examples from your own life, write a paragraph or essay in which you discuss the significance of the viewing public's love for crude language and situations.

THE BORN LOSER reprinted by permission of Newspaper Enterprise Association, Inc.

". . . the immediacy and intimacy of the media have somehow confused the issue of heroism, blurring the traditional criteria by which we measure our heroes and allowing mere exposure— that is, "fame"—to precede, and occasionally preempt, "worthiness" as a qualification for heroism.**"**

— Jean Picker Firstenberg

"I think the media is so prevalent in society today it's no longer an industry that comments on what's happened but an industry that contributes to and influences what's happening.**"**

— David E. Kelley
television producer

"Journalists sometimes are the First Amendment's worst enemy."

— **Paul McMasters**
The Freedom Forum's First Amendment Ombudsman

"Movies have lent the most perishable qualities, such as youth, beauty and comedy, a millennial shelf life."

— **Paul Rudnick**

"... TV and film are probably the best place for gays and lesbians— and other groups affected by bias and discrimination—to be."

— **Patrick McCormick**

Chapter 3: Incivility in the Media

Readings:

Argument Pair:

Websites:

www.nytimes.com

Website for the *New York Times,* where daily examples of civility and incivility are published in the paper's many different sections.

www.loc.gov

The Library of Congress offers the full text of pending legislation, including issues related to freedom of speech and privacy rights.

www.cnn.com

CNN Interactive provides on-line access to current news stories as well as links to news-oriented chat groups.

Introduction

For all Americans' talk about valuing privacy and solid morals, we sure do flock to watch the unfortunate: we slow down to get a good look at the burning crash on the freeway, we point and speak in hushed tones about the poor little boy in the wheelchair, and we love, with great concern and pity of course, to see the poor souls on television who have just been arrested, or evicted, or victimized in some way.

And the media is onto us. We need just flip to any major network, and we'll be treated to real-life tales of serial killers, school shooters, failed parents, and abused children—all in the name of "news." The question arises, then: are we so fascinated by tragedy that the media simply follows our desires and feeds us what we wish, or have we become brainwashed by all the "true" misfortune that we see on a daily basis? And what of the victims we view with intense interest? Are they pleased by the attention they receive, or do they wish we all would close our eyes and turn off our television sets in order to let them grieve in peace?

Chapter 3 seeks to explore the balance between communicating the truth to the public and sheltering the victims of public tragedy. Further, the readings will probe the issue of privacy: who has a right to it and who has a right to invade it. Finally, Chapter 3 asks where, if at all, the law should step in and restrict media access and what the consequences of such restrictions should be.

On Heroes and the Media

Jean Picker Firstenberg

Director and CEO of the American Film Institute, Jean Picker Firstenberg helped establish the institute's eight-acre campus in Los Feliz and has assembled an impressive and influential board of trustees. With the media playing a huge role in our lives—dictating the information we get, when we get it, and how much of it we get—it is no wonder, claims Firstenberg, that our views of heroes are slanted toward fame and away from traditionally heroic values.

Pre-reading Questions

Who, if anyone, do you consider a hero? How have you learned about this person in order to label him/her a "hero"? What role, if any, do you think the media plays in determining who is or is not a hero? Explain.

Vocabulary Preview

Vocabulary Words:
- bards
- incarnation
- recurrent
- wrought
- venal
- frailties
- personified
- preempt
- laurels
- boons

Look up the words above, and then use each word in a sentence of its own, making sure you vary the structure of each sentence you write.

1   Storytellers, bards, and dramatists have always shared with us the legends of our heroes. And in this era of the moving image, filmmakers have become the prime chroniclers of the twentieth-century experience. As a result, the images of film and television have had enormous impact on the evolution of the modern hero.

2   Our earliest heroes were god figures from mythology, later half-divine and half-man (or half-animal); then heroes became men, which is to say "persons"—like you and me. Or perhaps not quite like you and me, because, as the great scholar Joseph Campbell tells us in his book *The Hero With a Thousands Faces,* in every incarnation, and age, certain recurrent characteristics have defined the hero and set him apart from ordinary men.

3   "The hero ventures forth from the world of common day," Campbell says, "into a region of supernatural wonder; fabulous forces are there encountered and a decisive victory is won; the hero comes back from this mysterious journey with the power to bestow boons on his fellow man."

4   With minor variations, this classic heroic adventure has been related in myths, folk legends, and fairy tales for thousands of years. It is only in the last two hundred years that we've modified the formula to downplay its "supernatural" and "fabulous" elements

and recast our heroes to reflect the changes that modernization has wrought. Clearly, the nature of a hero changes with, and mirrors, the values of the times.

5   In the forties and fifties, Americans still embraced heroes who were "larger than life." John Wayne, Gary Cooper, Jimmy Stewart, and Henry Fonda obeyed most of the traditional heroic rules: overcoming "evil"—rustlers, venal politicians, and other forms of corruption—in order to create a new order, as Campbell would have it.

6   But by the midfifties, and for the next fifteen to twenty years, huge advances in technology and increased sophistication in the audiences shouldered these supermen aside in favor of what has been called the "antihero"—an ordinary man with recognizable frailties. Dustin Hoffman in *The Graduate,* Paul Newman in *Hud* and *Cool Hand Luke,* Alan Arkin in *Catch-22,* Al Pacino in *Dog Day Afternoon,* and Woody Allen in all his films personified a modern hero whose biggest victory was frequently the mere fact of his survival in a mechanized world that often seemed unhealthy for children and other living things.

7   By the late seventies, the war in Vietnam and the Watergate affair had taken their toll on the American spirit, leaving a need for the old-school heroes again—larger-than-life types like Rocky and even those with supernatural qualities like Luke Skywalker and Superman.

8   Recently, however, the immediacy and intimacy of the media have somehow confused the issue of heroism, blurring the traditional criteria by which we measure our heroes and allowing mere exposure—that is, "fame"—to precede, and occasionally preempt, "worthiness" as a qualification for heroism.

9   It was also during the late seventies that television-news coverage, assisted by the new satellite technology, began to bring "instant news" into our living rooms. Before that, Walter Cronkite, with his thoughtful objectivity and measured delivery, had been the most trusted man in America—Dante's Virgil guiding us through the confusion and chaos of the day's events. Now we often find ourselves abandoned, watching the news along with the commentator as it unfolds. The laurels for broadcast journalism often seem to be going to the first, as opposed to the "best," coverage.

10   And paralleling the trend in movies and fictional television, the emphasis in news began to shift away from analysis and toward action: We could watch a hostage crisis unfold right on the runway, see crash victims hoisted from an icy river, watch firemen spray water on a burning hotel. News began to resemble drama, except that with drama, the hero is readily identified, and in reality, he often is not.

11   Have we in fact begun to create heroes in order to make reality more dramatic? . . . Debates over Sen. Gary Hart, Jim and Tammy Bakker, and Lt. Col. Oliver North should have made abundantly clear to us that we need to take a long, hard look at the role the media has begun to play in creating/evaluating/rejecting/destroying/contemporary heroes.

12   Are we now confusing fiction with fact and imbuing people who simply have wide media exposure with the heroic ideals that fictional figures represent? Against what criteria are we measuring their "victories" and what "boons have they bestowed on [their] fellow men"? These are disturbing thoughts, but ones that we should all begin to consider. If we don't know where reality ends and fiction begins, I think we need to be concerned with our visual literacy.

POST-READING QUESTIONS

CONTENT

1. Who does Firstenberg say our first heroes were? How have they evolved from their original inception?
2. What characteristics define a hero, according to Firstenberg?
3. Who are some heroes of America's past? To what extent do you consider these people heroes? Explain.
4. What is an "antihero"? Who are some "antiheroes" in America's past?
5. How does Firstenberg say the media has "confused the issue of heroism"? What do you think?
6. How has the emphasis in the news shifted? What effect has this shift had on the determination of heroes?

STYLE AND STRUCTURE

7. What is Firstenberg's primary argument? Rewrite her main idea in your own words.
8. What examples does Firstenberg offer to support her main idea? How convincing are these?
9. Who is the audience? How can you tell?
10. What is Firstenberg's tone? Cite the text for support.
11. Is Firstenberg convincing? What about the essay does or does not persuade you of Firstenberg's main idea? Explain.

CRITICAL THINKING AND ANALYSIS

DISCUSSION QUESTIONS

12. Who are some people that you think have been identified as heroes, or villains, largely because of media attention rather than because of their deeds? Cite recent events for support.
13. Do you think heroes are more, or less, prevalent than they were ten years ago? Twenty? Why?

WRITING ASSIGNMENTS

14. Firstenberg writes that "the images of film and television have had enormous impact on the evolution of the modern hero." What do you think? Write a few paragraphs in which you discuss the extent of the effect that film and television have had on the development of heroes. Cite the text and your own experiences and observations in order to illustrate your ideas.

15. Do you agree that the media "have somehow confused the issue of heroism . . . allowing mere exposure . . . to precede, and occasionally preempt, 'worthiness' as a qualification for heroism"? Write a few paragraphs or short essay in which you argue that fame, rather than merit, determines a hero today. Cite the text and your own observations for support.

16. Firstenberg asks, "Have we in fact begun to create heroes in order to make reality more dramatic?" Write a well-developed paragraph in response to this question, citing the essay and your own examples for support.

VOCABULARY DEVELOPMENT

17. Using at least five words from Firstenberg's essay, write your own definition of "hero" in a few sentences. You do not need to cite the Vocabulary Preview list, but you may if you wish.

GROUP ACTIVITIES

18. Have each member of your group bring at least one popular magazine to class. Then, as a group, examine the pictures in each publication. What can you conclude about the ways "ideal" men and women are portrayed? Based on your analysis of advertisements and photographs, write a paragraph in which you argue that "ideal" men and women are portrayed in a certain way.

19. Create a visual representation of a "hero." You may draw a picture, make a mosaic from magazines, or use any sort of artistic presentation that you choose. Present your representation to the class in order to see if they can guess your feelings about heroes based on your art.

Kelley's Shows Give Media a Fair Trial

Brian Lowry

Brian Lowry earned a degree in Communication Studies from the University of California at Los Angeles and has since written two books: *The Truth is Out There: The Official Guide to the X-Files* and *Trust No One: The Official Third Season Guide to the X-Files.* Currently, Lowry is a reporter for the *Los Angeles Times,* covering the television industry and writing a weekly column analyzing industry trends. In *Kelley's Shows Give Media a Fair Trial,* Lowry reveals how, despite much public criticism of the media, producer David E. Kelley delves into the issues surrounding freedom of speech and privacy.

Pre-reading Questions

Freewrite for five to ten minutes in response to the following questions:
How responsible, if at all, do you think television is for promoting violent or otherwise un-pleasant behavior? Are some types of programs more culpable than others in encouraging a low standard of behavior? To what extent do you think television programs fairly represent the issues they cover? Explain and give examples.

Vocabulary Preview

Vocabulary Words:
- emanate
- predicated
- detractors
- advocacy

- garnering
- complicity
- befitting
- zealotry

- purveyors
- culpability

Look up the words above and, as you do, make notes as to the words' connotative, or sub-liminal, meanings. What tone do these words lead you to expect from the text? Write a few sentences predicting the tone of the article based upon the vocabulary words; then check to see if you're correct after you've done the reading.

1 Television often finds itself under siege by critics who insist its handling of sex, violence and language causes ills ranging from real-life violence and a coars-ening of society to gout and the heartbreak of psoriasis.

2 Seldom, however, does discussion of these issues emanate from television itself, as it has with notable persistence on "The Practice" and "Ally McBeal," both series cre-ated by producer David E. Kelley.

3 Historically, TV executives and producers have exhibited a knee-jerk reflex when someone tries to blame television for bad behavior, using a defense predicated either on the 1st Amendment or of the "Guns kill people, TV doesn't kill people" variety.

4 This instinct to circle the wagons is not without some justification. While many of the industry's most vocal detractors in political, academic and advocacy circles fervently

believe television is a negative force, some clearly gravitate to bashing Hollywood as safe, fertile terrain, serving interests that can include fund-raising or simply garnering attention.

5   Another study regarding TV and sex, in fact, will be released today by the Kaiser Family Foundation. Highlighting the distrust that colors this debate, a similar 1996 analysis was greeted with derision by industry officials when researchers concluded three-quarters of prime-time programs broadcast at 8 p.m. contained significant sexual content—a figure arrived at by counting "flirting" and "kissing" among acts that constituted sexual behavior.

6   If this were true, my formative years, and probably those of many others, were a lot more fun than we previously realized.

7   In this guarded climate, where every appalling act of teenage violence seems to elicit cries from someone about the media's complicity, it's disarming to see media responsibility dissected so thoughtfully within Kelley's series.

8   Each show approaches the topic in ways befitting its tone, exploring whether broadcasting can be taken to task legally for, in essence, polluting the cultural environment. Consider the following plot lines:

9   On "Ally McBeal," a woman sued a Howard Stern-type shock jock for creating a hostile workplace environment with his misogynistic radio routine.

10   On "The Practice," a TV executive was put on trial for contributing to a Dr. Kevorkian-esque assisted suicide by making clear he would air the segment during sweeps.

11   In two weeks, "The Practice" will focus on a case involving a TV report about cockroaches in a restaurant, raising faint echoes of the lawsuit the Food Lion chain filed against ABC News over its hidden-camera investigation.

12   Another episode depicted a judge agonizing over what to do with a 13-year-old boy who shot his mother, citing television and movies among the culprits she wanted to blame for "brainwashing children with violence, all disgustingly denying any accountability."

13   Kelley said he has returned to this theme less as a cause than to mine its dramatic potential.

14   "I think the media is so prevalent in society today it's no longer an industry that comments on what's happened but an industry that contributes to and influences what's happening," he said.

15   Yet Kelley's mere willingness to provocatively tackle such media-related conflict underscores how television virtually ignores these topics elsewhere.

16   Granted, TV and media companies are common prime-time settings and usually portrayed in a less-than-flattering light, from "The Mary Tyler Moore Show's" clownish anchorman Ted Baxter to the self-absorbed characters seen currently on NBC's "Lateline" or "NewsRadio."

17   These are broad caricatures, however, which don't address the real or imagined concerns many Americans harbor about the media's impact on society. Broadcast news in particular does a surprisingly shallow job examining these stories, which become increasingly important with each new media merger or frenzied chase of a major news story.

18   As testimony to Kelley's writing skills, which generally inspire awe among his peers, "The Practice" has managed to bring out the complexity of such matters while still providing captivating drama.

19   Most notably, Kelley's point of entry in looking at the media contemplates not whether the 1st Amendment shields news people or producers from engaging in free expression, but the role self-restraint plays in that process, and where each new televised breach in civility might eventually lead.

20   Although he supported "60 Minutes'" recent handling of a segment showing an assisted suicide, Kelley said, "As I watched it, I just couldn't help but think, 'What if it were not "60 Minutes"?'" It wasn't much of a leap, he noted, to imagine a less principled news program encouraging dangerous zealotry in the headlong pursuit of ratings.

21   In a related vein, Kelley has stated he doesn't think the label "artist" affords someone license, as he put it, "to do anything I damn well please." This seems to contrast with the standard response to critics from many in the so-called creative community, which is that as long as there is a ready audience for distasteful stuff they have the right to serve them the video equivalent of junk food.

22   True enough, but that skirts the real issue—namely, whether a portion of the public's appetite for vulgar material absolves the purveyors of culpability if an innocent bystander gets hurt along the way.

23   It's a question the media must ponder, especially those responsible for the muck that pops up on TV—from late-night slasher movies on pay channels to specials like Fox's "When Animals Attack" and "Shocking Moments: Caught on Tape," which make the excesses foreshadowed in the 1976 film "Network" seem almost quaint.

24   With media now all but inescapable, will these folks fret about boundaries and responsibility, or just their shareholders? Perhaps they need to be armed with Kelley's compass, which, he said, begins with considering how he'll feel when his own children see his work 15 or 20 years from now.

25   "I never want to say I put something on because I thought it would get a great {rating}," Kelley said. "There's got to be something more to it than that."

26   And with that, ladies and gentlemen, the prosecution rests . . . for now.

POST-READING QUESTIONS

CONTENT

1. Why does television find itself "under siege," according to Lowry?
2. What support is there for the idea that television does send messages promoting sex and violence?
3. How are David E. Kelley's programs different from those commonly attacked by the media and the public?
4. How does Kelley characterize the media?
5. What does Kelley's "point of entry in looking at the media" address? What does this mean?
6. What is Kelley's attitude toward the First Amendment in terms of the media?

STYLE AND STRUCTURE

7. What is Lowry's primary argument? Restate his main idea in your own words.

8. Does Lowry agree or disagree with Kelley's stance on the media? How can you tell?

9. What examples does Lowry use in order to illustrate his ideas? Of these, which are most effective? Explain.

10. Who is Lowry's audience? How can you tell?

11. What is Lowry's tone? Cite the text for support.

12. Is Lowry convincing? Explain.

CRITICAL THINKING AND ANALYSIS

DISCUSSION QUESTIONS

13. To what extent do you think the First Amendment should cover inflammatory or potentially harmful material on television?

14. What television programs, if any, do you think go too far in their quest for ratings or "real" stories? Why? Explain and give examples.

WRITING ASSIGNMENTS

15. According to David E. Kelley, "the media . . . is no longer an industry that comments on what's happened but an industry that contributes to and influences what's happening." What do you think? In a few paragraphs, explain what you think the media's primary identity is. Cite the text and contemporary television programs for support.

16. Just because the media has the constitutional right to express offensive ideas, should it? Write a few well-developed paragraphs or short essay in which you argue that the media should or should not temper its views to protect people. Cite Lowry's article and your own experiences for support.

17. Lowry paraphrases members of the creative community who claim that "as long as there is a ready audience for distasteful stuff, they have the right to serve them the video equivalent of junk food." What do you think? Write at least one well-developed paragraph in which you discuss whether or not some people's desire for tasteless material is enough to justify offering such material to the public. Cite the text and your own opinions and observations for support.

VOCABULARY DEVELOPMENT

18. How is the media portrayed in Lowry's article? Choose at least five words or expressions, either from the Vocabulary Preview or from elsewhere in the text, and write a few sentences explaining what you think Lowry's attitude toward the media is.

GROUP ACTIVITIES

19. Before coming to class, watch any television program that somehow deals with controversial material. Then, in small groups, discuss how valuable the program was in terms of the information it imparted or the issues it raised. To what extent do you think the media should restrict itself from covering potentially upsetting issues? Use your viewing experience for support.

20. Draw a spectrum along which you rank television programs in terms of offensiveness or potential harm. Your spectrum should show at what point, if any, certain material should not be broadcast. Feel free to make more than one graph if you think different audiences or different programs need to be considered according to different criteria. Share your results with the class.

Marilyn Monroe
She sauntered through life as the most delectable sex symbol of the century and became its most enduring pop confection

Paul Rudnick

Author of *The Most Fabulous Story Ever Told,* Paul Rudnick also writes for stage and screen, which explains his interest in his topic for this essay. Rudnick explores Marilyn Monroe's ongoing popularity, forty years after her death, and explains why she remains quintessentially American. Though troubled and often difficult to work with, Rudnick reports, Marilyn Monroe remains an icon of superficial womanhood.

Pre-reading Questions

Freewrite for five to ten minutes in response to the following questions:
What do you know about Marilyn Monroe? How have you come by this knowledge? Based upon what you know, what is your opinion of her? Do you consider her a hero? How significant has the media been in creating, or perpetuating, Monroe's popularity? Explain.

Vocabulary Preview

Vocabulary Words:	• trysts	• seminal	• imperiled
	• lurid	• pixilated	• turgid
	• mesmerized	• burbles	• evanescent
	• alchemy	• savant	

Without using a dictionary, define the words above as you read, paying attention to how they are used in Rudnick's essay. Then, do use a dictionary to learn the meanings of the words. How close were your definitions? Write a few sentences explaining how accurate, or inaccurate, you were in defining the terms above. Note: if not knowing the dictionary definition of a word prevents you from understanding a significant portion of the essay, feel free to look that word up as you read.

---

1   How much deconstruction can one blond bear? Just about everyone has had a go at Marylin Monroe. There have been more than 300 biographies, learned essays by Steinem and Kael, countless documentaries, drag queens, tattoos, Warhol silk screens and porcelain collector's dolls. Marilyn has gone from actress to icon to licensed brand name; only Elvis and James Dean have rivaled her in market share. At this point, she seems almost beyond comment, like Coca-Cola or Levi's. How did a woman who died a suicide at 36, after starring in only a handful of movies, become such an epic commodity?

2   Much has been made of Marilyn's desperate personal history, the litany of abusive foster homes and the predatory Hollywood scum that accompanied her wriggle to star-

dom. Her heavily flashbulbed marriages included bouts with baseball great Joe DiMaggio and literary champ Arthur Miller, and her off duty trysts involved Sinatra and the rumor of multiple Kennedys. The unauthorized tell-alls burst with miscarriages, abortions, rest cures and frenzied press conferences announcing her desire to be left alone. Her death has been variously attributed to an accidental overdose, political necessity and a Mob hit. Her yummily lurid bio has provided fodder for everything from a failed Broadway musical to Jackie Susann's trash classics to a fictionalized portrait in Miller's play *After the Fall*. Marilyn's media-drenched image as a tragic dumb blond has become an American archetype, along with the Marlboro Man and the Harley-straddling wild one. Yet biographical trauma, even when packed with celebrities, cannot account for Marilyn's enduring stature as a goddess and postage stamp. Jacqueline Onassis will be remembered for her timeline, for her participation in events and marriages that mesmerized the planet. Marilyn seems far less factual, more Cinderella or Circe than mortal.

3   There have been other megablonds of varying skills, a pinup parade of Jean Harlow, Carole Lombard, Jayne Mansfield, Mamie Van Doren and Madonna—but why does Marilyn still seem to have patented the peroxide that they've passed along? Marilyn may represent some unique alchemy of sex, talent and Technicolor. She is pure movies. I recently watched her as Lorelei Lee in her musical smash, Gentlemen Prefer Blondes. The film is an ideal mating of star and role, as Marilyn deliriously embodies author Anita Loos' seminal, shame-free gold digger. Lorelei's honey-voiced, pixilated charm may be best expressed by her line, regarding one of her sugar daddies, "Sometimes Mr. Esmond finds it very difficult to say no to me." Whenever Lorelei appears onscreen, undulating in second-skin, cleavage-proud knitwear or the sheerest orange chiffon, all heads turn, salivate and explode. Who but Marilyn could so effortlessly justify such luscious insanity? She is the absolute triumph of political incorrectness. When she swivels aboard a cruise ship in clinging jersey and a floor-length leopard-skin scarf and matching muff, she handily offends feminists, animal-rights activists and good Christians everywhere, and she wins, because shimmering, jewel-encrusted, heedless movie stardom defeats all common morality. Her wit completes her cosmic victory, particularly in her facial expression of painful, soul-wrenching yearning when gazing upon a diamond tiara, a trinket she initially attempts to wear around her neck. Discovering the item's true function, she burbles. "I always love finding new places to wear diamonds!" Movies can offer a very specific bliss, the gorgeousness of a perfectly lighted fairy tale. Watching Marilyn operate her lips and eyebrows while breathlessly seducing an elderly millionaire is like experiencing the invention of ice cream.

4   Marilyn wasn't quite an actress, in any repertory manner, and she was reportedly an increasing nightmare to work with, recklessly spoiled and unsure, barely able to complete even the briefest scene between breakdowns. Only in the movies can such impossible behavior, and such peculiar, erratic gifts, create eternal magic—only the camera has the mechanical patience to capture the maddening glory of a celluloid savant like Monroe. At her best, playing warmhearted floozies in Some Like It Hot and Bus Stop, she's like a slightly bruised moonbeam, something fragile and funny and imperiled. I don't think audiences ever particularly identify with Marilyn. They may love

her or fear for her, but mostly they simply marvel at her existence, at the delicious un-
likeliness of such platinum innocence. She's the bad girl and good girl combined: she's
sharp and sexy yet incapable of meanness, a dewy Venus rising from the motel sheets,
a hopelessly irresistible home wrecker. Monroe longed to be taken seriously as an
artist, but her work in more turgid vehicles, like The Misfits, was neither original nor
very interesting. She needs the tickle of cashmere to enchant for the ages.

5   Movies have lent the most perishable qualities, such as youth, beauty and comedy, a millennial shelf life. Until the cameras rolled, stars of the past could only be
remembered, not experienced. Had she been born earlier, Marilyn might have existed as only a legendary rumor, a Helen of Troy or Tinker Bell. But thanks to
Blockbuster, every generation now has immediate access to the evanescent perfection of Marilyn bumping and cooing her way through that chorine's anthem, Diamonds Are a Girl's Best Friend, in Gentlemen Prefer Blondes. Only movie stars
have the chance to live possibly forever, and maybe that's why they're all so crazy.
Madonna remade Diamonds in the video of her hit Material Girl, mimicking Marilyn's
hot-pink gown and hot-number choreography, and the sly homage seemed fitting: a
blond tribute, a legacy of greedy flirtation. Madonna is too marvelously sane ever to
become Marilyn. Madonna's detailed appreciation of fleeting style and the history
of sensuality is part of her own arsenal, making her a star and a fan in one. Madonna
wisely and affectionately honors the brazen spark in Marilyn, the giddy candy-box
allure, and not the easy heartbreak.

6   Marilyn's tabloid appeal is infinite but ultimately beside the point. Whatever
destroyed her—be it Hollywood economics or rabid sexism or her own tormented
psyche—pales beside the delight she continues to provide. At her peak, Marilyn was
very much like Coca-Cola or Levi's—she was something wonderfully and irrepressibly American.

> BORN Norma Jean Baker on June 1, 1927, in Los Angeles
> 1946 Changes name to Marilyn Monroe
> 1949 Nude calendar shots
> 1950 Launches career with role in All About Eve
> 1953 Gentlemen Prefer Blondes
> 1954 Weds Joe DiMaggio
> 1956 Marries Arthur Miller
> 1959 Some Like It Hot
> 1962 Dies Aug. 5, a suicide

DEATH AS A CAREER MOVE

James Dean

7   Dean starred in only one movie before his death in 1955. But with the release of Rebel
Without a Cause one month after his fatal car accident, Dean became a movie superstar. Teenagers thronged to see the film, and Dean was nominated for an Oscar. By July
1956, the dead actor was receiving 7,000 fan letters a month.

Valentino

8 Rudolf Valentino was the century's original heartthrob. After his death in 1926, at age 31, thousands of women came close to rioting at his funeral. And on each anniversary of his death, a mysterious black-clad woman left a wreath near his grave. Two biopics and a mention in the 1985 Bangles hit Manic Monday revived his legend for later generations.

Kurt Cobain

9 "It's better to burn out than to fade away," Cobain wrote in his suicide note, quoting Neil Young. His end captivated troubled teens. In 1997 two French girls committed dual suicide while watching a Nirvana video and playing the band's CDs. This year sales of Nevermind reached 10 million; Rolling Stone anointed Cobain Artist of the Decade.

Jim Morrison

10 The Doors' front man often spoke of faking his own death and coming back as "Mr. Mojo Risin'." At 27 he was found dead of an apparent heart attack in Paris. But no autopsy was done, and fans soon claimed the death was staged. Morrison's grave site became a favorite destination for teen carousers—Europe's most popular open-air nightclub.

Hank Williams Sr.

11 After his debut at the Grand Ole Opry in 1949, Williams became one of the best-selling stars in country music. He died at 30 on New Year's Day, 1953, after one of his customary drinking binges. Williams had three consecutive posthumous No. 1 hits, including Your Cheatin' Heart; hundreds of singers have since covered his songs.

Selena

12 She was the Madonna of Tejano music, a role model for scores of young Mexican Americans. In 1995, at 23, she was killed by the former head of her fan club. Within two years her life story was made into a reverent $23 million movie. After her death her family continued to promote Selena hair salons, clothing lines, even a Selena Doll.

POST-READING QUESTIONS

CONTENT

1. What are the ways that Rudnick describes Marilyn Monroe in the opening paragraphs of his essay? Who else has fame that rivals Monroe's, according to Rudnick?

2. What does Rudnick mean when he describes Monroe as "the absolute triumph of political correctness"?

3. What is Monroe's appeal, as Rudnick presents it in his essay? What do you think?

4. What about Monroe is the "bad girl and good girl combined"? How appealing do you think this combination is? Explain.

5. What, according to Rudnick, makes Monroe's ongoing fame possible?

6. What do the people in the "Death as a Career Move" section have in common? How "heroic" do you find any of these people? Explain.

STYLE AND STRUCTURE

7. What is Rudnick's main idea? Restate his purpose for writing this essay in your own words.

8. What examples does Rudnick use to support his main idea? Of these, which do you find most compelling? Explain.

9. Who is Rudnick's audience? To what extent are you a part of his audience? Cite the text to reveal his target readers.

10. How seriously does Rudnick take his subject? Cite the text to find examples of Rudnick's attitude toward Marilyn Monroe.

11. What effect does comparing Monroe to other famous people have on how you interpret Rudnick's argument? Would his essay be more convincing if he did not compare Monroe to anyone? Explain.

CRITICAL THINKING AND ANALYSIS

DISCUSSION QUESTIONS

12. If Marilyn Monroe were alive today, how popular would she be? Discuss, using other famous entertainers as illustrations of your ideas.

13. What role do you think the media has played in perpetuating Marilyn Monroe's popularity? What do you think her ongoing popularity says about the values of Americans?

WRITING ASSIGNMENTS

14. Why do you think Marilyn Monroe has remained a sex symbol, even forty years after her death? Write a few paragraphs explaining what about Monroe causes her to remain appealing to people long after she has died. Cite the articles and examples from popular culture in order to illustrate your ideas.

15. Rudnick describes Monroe as a star, a sex symbol, an icon, and an archetype, among others. Do these labels indicate heroism? Write at least one well-developed paragraph in which you describe the difference between a star or an icon and a hero. Be sure to quote Rudnick and use your own observations in order to support your main idea.

16. Rudnick writes that "At her peak, Marilyn was . . . something wonderfully and irrepressibly American." What about Monroe was "American"? And in what ways were these "American" qualities "wonderful"? Write a few paragraphs or short essay arguing that Monroe was, or was not, representative of American values and priorities, taking care to make your opinions of American val-

ues clear. Be sure to cite Rudnick's essay and your own experiences in order to strengthen and clarify your ideas.

VOCABULARY DEVELOPMENT

17. Rudnick describes Monroe several times throughout the course of his essay. Choose at least five words or expressions that stand out to you as being particularly vivid; then, write a few sentences defending your choices.

GROUP ACTIVITIES

18. To what extent did the media "create" Marilyn Monroe? Using your knowledge of Marilyn Monroe, make a list of the qualities that you think were genuinely Monroe's—things she could not change such as her face, or her eye color—as opposed to qualities the media emphasized or endowed her with—sex appeal, empty-headed sweetness, for instance. Do any of them overlap? Discuss popular entertainers and other famous people in order to determine whether or not celebrities can, or should, stay true to themselves if they want to be famous.

19. Has anyone taken Monroe's place in American culture? Who, if anyone, reigns as the contemporary Marilyn Monroe? Who comes close? Skim contemporary magazines and web sites in order to respond to this question.

Along for the Ride
Reality journalism and the right to privacy

Julie Johnson

Now the U.S. media relations practice leader and a senior managing director at Hill & Knowlton, Inc., in New York, Julie Johnson has covered the White House, Congress, the Supreme Court, and the Justice Department for the *Baltimore Sun,* the *New York Times, Time Magazine,* and *ABC News.* In *Along for the Ride,* Johnson contrasts the benefits of media ride-alongs with law enforcement—up-to-the-minute coverage, "real" stories—with the drawbacks—the invasion of individuals' privacy—in an effort to determine how much access the media should be given by law.

Pre-reading Questions

Freewrite for five to ten minutes in response to the following questions:
If a person is under arrest, does the public have a right to know everything about that person via the media? At what point, if any, do journalists not have the right to report a story? What do you think should be done once a person's privacy has been unfairly invaded by the press? Explain.

Vocabulary Preview

Vocabulary Words:
- implicated
- journalistic
- commonplace
- intrusion

- liable
- immunity
- potency
- sanctioned

- roughshod
- succinctly

Look up the words above and use them in no more than three sentences on any topic you choose. How difficult was fitting these words into a set number of sentences? Write a few sentences explaining how some words were more or less difficult to use.

---

1   Bad boys, bad boys, what ya gonna do? What ya gonna do when they come for you?[1]

2   Around 8:30 P.M. on March 5, 1992, four special agents of the U.S. Secret Service led a CBS News television crew from the prime-time magazine Street Stories into the New York apartment of a man wanted for credit card fraud. The suspect, Babatunde Ayeni, wasn't there. His wife and their preschool-age son, who were not implicated in the warrant, were at home alone. Mrs. Tawa Ayeni was wearing a dressing gown when agents and the camera crew entered her apartment. When she held a magazine in front

---

[1]Theme song for the Fox television series Cops. Inner Circle, "Bad Boys, on Bad Boys," Big Beat/Atlantic Records, 1993.

of her son's face to prevent the crew from videotaping him, Special Agent James Mottola grabbed the magazine, threw it on the floor, and told her to "shut up" (Ayeni v. Mottola 1994). Then agents instructed the camera crew to videotape Mrs. Ayeni's face as agents questioned her. The CBS crew also taped the apartment search, including the agents' review of "books, photographs, financial statements and personal letters" (Ayeni v. CBS, Inc. 1994).

3   One month later, just after dawn on April 16, 1992, Charles and Geraldine Wilson were lying awake in bed, listening to the still spring morning in a suburb of Washington D.C. Then they heard loud and persistent banging on their front door. When Charles Wilson reached his living room, he encountered a half dozen U.S. Marshals and Montgomery County, Maryland sheriff's deputies with their weapons drawn. Recording each detail of the scene inside the house was veteran Washington Post reporter Paul Valentine and his photographer both of whom entered the Wilson home with police. Wilson stood in his underwear, in plain view of officers and the Post staffers. Officers said they were searching for the Wilson's adult son, Dominic, who did not live in his parents' home. Dominic, a clean-shaven twenty-seven-year-old, weighed 185 pounds. Charles Wilson weighed 220 pounds. Yet upon seeing the undressed, forty-seven-year-old African-American man—with a beard so gray that it was almost completely white—sheriff's deputies ordered him to lie down on the floor. Though he looked nothing like the suspect they claimed to seek, U.S. Marshals then began "questioning" Wilson, alternatively cursing at him and threatening to arrest him if his son Dominic was found in the house.[2] He wasn't.

4   Each story represents a journalistic practice that has become commonplace. The two events also vividly display the pitfalls of "reality"[3] or "reality-based"[4] journalism, in which reporters and camera crews ride along for a firsthand look at law enforcement. Specifically, reality journalism describes broadcast news and entertainment programming that relies on actual footage of law enforcement officers, firefighters, and emergency medical technicians responding to calls on the job. Reality-based programming uses actors to reenact incidents based on actual events without benefit of original on-scene videotape.

5   In either case, dramatic footage and graphic stories are the payoff. But such coverage can come at a cost that should make journalists worry. At what point does access—granted not by the resident but bartered on the back of a law enforcement officer's shield—demand payment in the form of a wrongful damages suit? Independence in storytelling and the First Amendment protections that journalists have fought hard to fortify are both at risk. The press cannot expect courts to indefinitely uphold reporters' right to refuse to turn over notebooks, videotape outtakes, and sources when they are no longer acting independently but rather as publicists for law enforcement.

[2]Richard K. Willard, David H. Coburn, James S. Felt, Arthur B. Spitzer, and Richard Seligman, Petition for Writ of Certiorari, Wilson v. Layne, filed July 7, 1998.

[3]Linda Shrieves, "New Show Fuels Reality TV: 'Firefighters' Stars Everyday Heroes," Orlando Sentinel, Jan. 21, 1993: E1.

[4]Thomas Mills, "Wake up to Reality: Actors Profit from the Rapid Growth of Reality-Based TV Shows," Back Stage, Feb. 18–24, 1994: p.1.

6   That idea startles Valentine, who worked as a reporter at the Washington Post for thirty-three years. Valentine, who retired last spring, defends the right of the press to observe the "behavior of the police" but concedes that he is troubled by the fact that ride-alongs could carry a heavy price. Speaking in a telephone interview, Valentine said, "I wouldn't want to be viewed as an instrument or agent of the government. When I'm performing my job as a reporter, I want to feel and know I am independent and not in any way acting under the color of the state."[5]

7   But law enforcement dictated which case, what time, and what home Valentine entered when he found himself in the Wilsons' living room. Valentine's objective was to obtain background for a story about a joint federal and local law enforcement task force dubbed Operation Gunsmoke. The operation targeted prison escapees, bail jumpers, and individuals violating probation or parole.

8   Dominic Wilson, who was suspected of violating probation, was not captured in the raid. But his father, Charles, was captured on film, lying on his living room floor, clearly subdued by police. Geraldine Wilson, who came into the room wearing a nightgown and pleading with police to free her husband, was also photographed. Ultimately, the newspaper chose not to publish the photographs.

9   Later the couple located their son and compelled him to surrender to authorities. He did. Then the Wilsons filed a lawsuit, asserting that U.S. Marshals and sheriff's deputies violated their constitutional rights by bringing the Post reporter and photographer into their home, without permission, while executing a search warrant for Dominic Wilson.

10   That suit—Wilson v. Layne—reached the U.S. Supreme Court last fall. The Court ruled unanimously on May 24 that police violate "the right of residential privacy at the core of the Fourth Amendment," when they bring members of the news media into private homes during the execution of a warrant.[6]

11   Justices, during the March 24 oral argument, openly expressed skepticism about the value of media ride-alongs which bring reporters into private homes.[7] Observed Justice Sandra Day O'Connor about the entry by the Washington Post into the Wilson Home: "This was an amazing intrusion." She added, "There is a very weighty interest on the part of homeowners to have privacy in their home."[8] Justice David Souter posed a similar question. Asked Souter: "Why do you have to take photographers into someone's house? You can have a news conference when it's over."[9]

12   Richard Willard, a lawyer for the Wilsons, said: "We're not challenging in the Supreme Court the legitimacy of the entry into the home. We're saying it's unconstitutional to bring the journalists inside the home."[10] The Wilsons' lawsuit argued that officers should be held personally liable for allowing news media to enter homes on raids and arrests. Federal courts are split over that question. The Wilsons' appeal stemmed

---

[5]Paul Valentine, interview, Feb. 12, 1999.

[6]Linda Greenhouse, "Police Violate Privacy in Home Raids with Journalists," New York Times, May 25, 1999: p. A25.

[7]Joan Biskupic, "Justices Question TV's Use on Raids," Washington Post, Mar. 25, 1999: p. A2.

[8]Tony Mauro, "High Court Frowns on News Media 'Ride-alongs'," USA Today, March 25, 1999: p. 13A.

[9]Linda Greenhouse, "Justices Question the Presence of News Crews at Police Searches and Arrests," New York Times, March 25, 1999: p. A28.

[10]Richard Willard, interview, Dec. 8, 1998.

from a lower court ruling that held that law enforcement authorities were immune from prosecution because they had not exceeded the scope of the arrest warrant simply by bringing reporters along.

13   However, the U.S. Supreme Court, in granting the Wilsons' petition, combined their case with a separate lawsuit from Montana. There, the Ninth Circuit Court of Appeals took the opposite view and ruled that ranchers Paul and Emma Berger could sue the U.S. Fish and Wildlife Service for allowing CNN to wire agents with hidden microphones and cameras to videotape a federal raid of the Bergers' seventy-five-thousand-acre ranch. Federal agents were investigating whether the Bergers had been illegally using pesticides to protect livestock at the expense of federally protected endangered species of wildlife. At trial, Paul Berger was acquitted of charges that he violated federal laws to protect eagles. He was, however, found guilty of a misdemeanor charge that he improperly used a pesticide. After the trial, CNN used edited segments of the search footage in a story about government initiatives to protect endangered species.

14   Lawyers for the sheriff's deputies and U.S. Marshals in Wilson argued that police should not be held liable, thus granting law enforcement qualified immunity from prosecution, because the officers "were simply implementing the terms of a facially valid policy" issued by the U.S. Justice Department.

15   That defense—that the officers were just following policy—relied on a U.S. Marshals Service media ride-along advisory guide. It stated, "Keeping the public adequately informed of what the service does can be viewed as a duty in its own right, and we depend on the news media to accomplish that." The guide booklet urged officers to establish ground rules with the press in advance of the actual ride-along. Those ground rules, noted the guide, "must be realistic but balanced—remember, the media will want good action footage, not just a mop-up scene" (Wilson v. Layne 1998: Appendix A). By an eight to one majority the Court ruled that the officers in these cases were entitled to qualified immunity because the practice of media ride-alongs was not "clearly established" as unconstitutional in 1992 and 1993.

16   More than two dozen news organizations joined together to file a "friend of the court" brief in the Wilson case.[11] In the brief, four major television news networks, the Washington Post, the New York Times, and the Los Angeles Times among others asserted that the reporting that comes from media ride-alongs "has contributed meaningfully to public scrutiny of official conduct."[12]

17   The American Civil Liberties Union takes issue with that argument. "This isn't an instance where the press is covering news; the press are only there at the invitation and desire of the police," says Arthur Spitzer, an attorney for the ACLU, which helped prepare the Wilsons' case before the court. "Having the media as watchdogs of the police is a very important part of what the media do and is something that the ACLU wishes the media did more of. But . . . the Washington Post can't bust into my house and cover a story, and they can't do it behind the police."[13]

[11]Lee Levine, James E. Grossberg and Jay Ward Brown, Brief Amici Curiae of ABC Inc., et al. in Support of Petitioners in No. 97-1927 and Respondents in No. 98-83.

[12]Brief Amici Curiae of ABC, Inc., p. 4.

[13]Arthur Spitzer, interview, Dec. 7, 1998.

18   When the Ayeni case came to trial in New York, the Justice Department policy that allowed media ride-alongs was ruled to be in violation of the Fourth Amendment. The Fourth Amendment provides "the right of the people to be secure in their persons, houses, papers, and effects, against unreasonable searches and seizures."[14] Its central purpose is control of the police (Bond 1997:825,830). Courts routinely recognize that the Fourth Amendment's greatest potency is within an individual's home (Lunday 1997: 278,302). It was upon these principles that the Second Circuit rested in ruling against the U.S. Secret Service. Said the court, "A private home is not a soundstage for law enforcement theatricals" (Ayeni v. Mottola 1994).

19   CBS never broadcast the Ayeni search footage. Initially, the network argued that it was entitled to the same qualified immunity as law enforcement because the crews were present with government permission. The court disagreed. Later, the network reached a confidential settlement with the Ayenis and was not party to the case when it reached the Second Circuit on appeal.

20   After the Ayeni case, but before the search occurred in the Wilsons' Maryland home, the Justice Department amended its media ride-along policies and prohibited press accompaniment inside private homes while federal agents execute search warrants.[15] In this era of reality journalism, it is often forgotten that the U.S. Supreme Court has never explicitly granted First Amendment-protected access to the scenes of news events (Branzburg v. Hayes 1972:684). Justice Byron White, writing for the Court in 1972, stated that "newsmen have no constitutional right of access to the scenes of crime or disaster when the general public is excluded." Added White, "The First Amendment does not reach so far as to override the interest of the public in ensuring that . . . [the] reporter is invading the rights of . . . citizens" (Branzburg v. Hayes 1972:691–92).

21   The last two decades have seen an increasing number of cases in which news organizations, acting alongside law enforcement, are being sued by individuals who neither asked for press presence nor sanctioned media entry onto their property or into their homes (Gonzalez 1997:935). Plaintiffs have included a suicidal teenager who placed a call to 911. When police arrived at her home, they brought along a television camera crew covering a "day in the life" of police officers.[16] Similarly, a heart attack victim's wife sued NBC when a producer at one of its local affiliates entered the woman's apartment with paramedics who had been called to administer CPR to her husband. Attempts to revive the dying man were broadcast on the local news (Miller v. National Broadcasting Co. 1986). Courts are split over the appropriate rule of law.

22   And it's a tough call, even for the Post's Valentine, who has "done dozens of ride-alongs" with local law enforcement officers, although only one in which he entered a private home while police executed a search warrant. "My mind is not made up on this issue. I can see two different strands of thought. One is that the property

---

[14]U.S. Constitution, Amendment IV.

[15]An FBI law enforcement bulletin was issued after the Second Circuit's decision in Ayeni under the title "News Cameras." DOJ Alert, Oct. 3, 1994: p. 1–11.

[16]David Kidwell, "Girl Sues TV Show for Airing Rescue Call," Miami Herald, Jan. 23, 1994: B6.

owner has the right to exclude people who have no legal right to be there. A reporter following along on a ride-along may fall into that category. I just don't know. On the other hand, reporters are not just there as voyeurs watching someone being taken into custody. We are also observing the behavior of police, and that's an important function in journalism."[17]

23 Other journalists, and journalism scholars with experience in this area, are equally divided. "I'm mixed on it," says Gary Fields, a national correspondent for USA Today who covers law enforcement. Fields's first experience with police was as a seventeen-year-old honors student in Rapides Parish, Louisiana, when a sheriff's deputy "had me stretched out over the hood of a car as a murder suspect." Fields adds, "I came into police reporting with a healthy dose of skepticism." Even so, as a reporter for the Shreveport (La.) Times, Fields went on his share of media ride-alongs with police. "The ride-alongs were helpful in getting a better understanding of what cops do." But Fields sees a tension between being a " good aggressive reporter" and going into an individual's home. "When I'm on my own covering a story, I have to knock on the door and say, 'Can I talk to you?' If you tell me no, I can't break into the house. Does that change or should it change because [the reporter] is hooked up in a ride-along?"[18]

24 Shannon Martin, an assistant professor of journalism at Rutgers University, says no. Martin, a former reporter for the Louisville Courier-Journal, rode along with the Louisville vice squad earlier in her career. She says it is important to note that reporters "don't have the same privileges [as police]. They're not law enforcement." Adds Martin, "The Fourth Amendment is about law enforcement behavior, and everybody ought to be one step further back after that."[19]

25 Dean Tom Goldstein of the Columbia University Graduate School of Journalism says that the cases decided by the Supreme Court focused on "the intersection of a constellation of tricky issues and competing interests." But Goldstein comes down on the side of the press, abiding by a standard of "openness." "The overriding interest is the public's ability to know how its law enforcement officers behave. You have to hope that the press would be responsible," says Goldstein.[20]

26 Oftentimes, that "hope" offers little consolation to individuals who believe that the press has run roughshod over the right to privacy—defined more than a century ago by Samuel Warren and Louis Brandeis as "the right to be let alone" (Warren and Brandeis 1890:193,195). More recently, a federal district court in Pennsylvania put it even more succinctly: "A search warrant is simply not a press pass" (Hagler v. Philadelphia Newspaper 1996).

27 The Wilson case raised questions about whether police should be held liable for damages when they allow press access inside private homes. Added Willard, the Wilson's lawyer, "We think a simple rule requiring that consent first be obtained before law enforcement officials bring the media into an area protected by the

[17]Valentine, interview.

[18]Gary Fields, interview, Dec. 8, 1998.

[19]Shannon Martin, interview, Dec. 7, 1998.

[20]Dean Tom Goldstein, interview, Dec. 9, 1998.

Fourth Amendment . . . There are many ways for law enforcement officials to publicize their efforts and many ways for the media to report on those efforts without barging into homes without the occupants' consent."[21] Underlying this question however, is a related inquiry that should be even more troubling for reporters: Should the press be held liable for violating individual privacy rights when they are covering law enforcement operations?

28   The question of reporter liability, particularly in an era of "lowest common denominator journalism" (Denniston 1998: 1255, 1257) could be next. Still pending before the Court is the related question of whether journalists can be punished financially, too.

REFERENCES

Ayeni v. CBS, Inc. 1994. 848 F. Supp. 362(E.D.N.Y.).

Ayeni v. Mottola. 1994.35 F. 3d 680. Second Circuit.

Bond, David E. 1997. "Police Liability for the Media 'Ride-Along.'"

Boston University Law Review 77(Oct.): 825–872.

Branzburg v. Hayes. 1972. 408 U.S. 665.

Denniston, Lyle. 1998. "From George Carlin to Matt Drudge: The Constitutional Implications of Bringing the Paparazzi to America." American University Law Review 47(5): 1255–1271.

Gonzalez, Eduardo W. 1997. "'Get That Camera Out of My Face!' An Examination of the Viability of Suing 'Tabloid Television' for Invasion of Privacy." University of Miami Law Review 51(Apr.): 935–953.

Hagler v. Philadelphia Newspapers. 1996. No. 96–2154. Media Law Reporter 24 (July 10): 23322336.

Lunday, Kevin E. 1997. "Permitting Media Participation in Federal Searches: Exploring the Consequences for the United States Following Ayeni v. Mottola and a Framework for Analysis." George Washington Law Review 65 (Jan.): 278–308.

Miller v. National Broadcasting Co. 1986. California Court of Appeals for the Third District. 187: 1463–1493.

Warren, Samuel D., and Louis D. Brandeis. 1890. "The Right to Privacy." Harvard Law Review 4(Dec. 15): 193–220.

Wilson v. Layne. 1998.98–83 U.S.

POST-READING QUESTIONS

CONTENT

1. What do the two opening incidents have in common?

2. What is the media's motivation for riding along with law enforcement and filming their activities?

---

[21]Richard K. Willard, David H. Coburn, James S. Felt, Richard Seligman, Steven Shapiro, Arthur B. Spitzer and Dwight H. Sillivan, Reply Brief for Petitioners, pp. 17–19.

3. How has the Supreme Court ruled in *Wilson v. Lane?* What are the implications of this ruling?

4. Were law enforcement officers punished for allowing the press to accompany them and film their activities? Why or why not?

5. Who else has sued news people for invasion of privacy? What were the results of those cases?

6. What do the media claim is one benefit of having law enforcement's activities on film? What do you think?

STYLE AND STRUCTURE

7. Does Johnson have a primary argument? What is it?

8. What other issues does Johnson also address in her article? What relationship to her main idea do these sub-arguments have?

9. What examples does Johnson use to support her points? To what extent are these examples effective?

10. Who is Johnson's audience? Cite the text in order to illustrate the types of readers Johnson targets.

11. To what extent does Johnson think that the press should have the same rights as law enforcement in terms of entering an individual's home? Cite the text for support.

12. Is Johnson convincing? Explain.

CRITICAL THINKING AND ANALYSIS

DISCUSSION QUESTIONS

13. What are your feelings about television programs that show "real" law enforcement officers making "real" searches and/or arrests? Upon what do you base these feelings?

14. At what point, if any, do you think the media should not be allowed to record people being arrested or otherwise disciplined by law enforcement? What factors, such as citizens' age and location, factor into your decision?

WRITING ASSIGNMENTS

15. Johnson raises the question: "At what point does access [to residents' homes by the media] demand payment in the form of a wrongful damages suit?" What do you think? Write a well-developed paragraph or two in which you discuss the point at which residents have a legal right to financial restitution as a result of being "invaded" by the media. Cite the article and your own observations for support.

16. In many cases, law enforcement officers have been caught on tape treating people poorly, either through physical or verbal abuse or through the threat of abuse. Does the press have a greater right to record law enforcement's

wrong-doings than it does to record private citizens'? Write a few paragraphs or short essay in which you explain whether or not the police or other law enforcement officials have the same right to privacy by the media as private citizens do. Be sure to cite the text and your own experiences and observations in order to illustrate your ideas.

17. The press claims, "the public has a right to know" about the issues it covers. At what point does the individual's right to privacy outweigh the public's right to know about an issue? Write a few paragraphs or short essay in which you define the point at which, if ever, the individual's rights override the public's. Be sure to use examples from the text and from your own observations for support.

VOCABULARY DEVELOPMENT

18. Analyzing Johnson's language and examples in particular, write a few sentences drawing a conclusion about the type of publication Johnson is writing for. Consider how her words and illustrations differ from those you might see in a daily local newspaper.

GROUP ACTIVITIES

19. As a group, discuss the point at which you think the media should not pursue a story in order to respect an individual's or group's privacy. Then, write a letter to the editor of your local newspaper or television station defining the terms under which you think the media should limit its coverage. Share your letter with the class.

20. Before coming to class, watch some "reality-based" television show in which law enforcement plays a role. Put yourself in the position of the people being filmed, and then think about how you, as a viewer, react to the information you see. Then, as a group, decide whose rights are more important: the rights of the people being filmed or the rights of the viewer. Share your results with other groups.

Argument Pair: Do the Media Do More Harm Than Good?

Out of the Closet and Into Your Livingroom, Patrick McCormick

The Diana Aftermath, Jacqueline Sharkey and Lara M. White

With so many television channels now available to us through cable and satellite programming, it's no wonder that we receive news of incidents and people we might otherwise have no knowledge of. Everyday people can become heroes in a day if the news coverage is timely, and people who commit crimes in private suddenly become known to us through primetime broadcasts. While we may take this influx of information for granted, we need to examine the consequences of such exposure. For instance, is the national raising of money via newscasts for a child who's lost her parents worth the intrusion an accidental celebrity suffers as a result of his fame? Weighing the good that the media can do, as presented by Patrick McCormick, against the media's potential harm, as argued by Jacqueline Sharkey and Lara M. White, is a key concept to consider for this unit.

Writing Assignments Based on *Out of the Closet and Into Your Livingroom* and *The Diana Aftermath*

1. Jacqueline Sharkey and Lara M. White quote Paul McMasters, The Freedom Forum's First Amendment Ombudsman, who claims that "Journalists sometimes are the First Amendment's worst enemy" while Patrick McCormick lauds the media for "[getting] us used to seeing and watching people we might not normally meet or attend to." How positive is the media overall? Write a few paragraphs or short essay in which you discuss whether or not the drawbacks to intense media coverage outweigh the benefits. Cite both essays and your own experiences and observations for support.

2. The writers of *Out of the Closet and Into Your Livingroom* and *The Diana Aftermath* make mention of issues where media attention can have both positive and negative effects. For instance, Patrick McCormick tells of how television and film "[offer] role models . . . for young men and women who are gay or lesbian," even though entertainment media has traditionally portrayed homosexuals as being "either pathetic or despicable." Sharkey and White, additionally, cite CNN Editor-at-large Ed Turner who claims that the media coverage of Diana's death provided "millions of Americans to share their grief" in a time when "there aren't that many shared experiences that occur . . . ." but that the public still blamed photojournalists for "being responsible for killing Diana." In a few well-developed paragraphs, choose what you consider to be a significant issue related to the media—telling the truth, invading people's privacy, giving people common experience—and discuss how this issue can have both a positive and a negative side. Be sure to quote both texts and cite your own experiences for support.

Out of the Closet and Into Your Livingroom

Patrick McCormick

Author of *Character, Choices, and Community* (with Russell B. Conners), a textbook about Christian ethics, Patrick McCormick is an assistant professor of ethics at Gonzaga University. He is also a columnist for *U.S. Catholic,* where this selection first appeared in April 1998. In *Out of the Closet and Into Your Livingroom,* McCormick raises the issue of whether or not increased public exposure to gays and lesbians through television and film has a positive effect in terms of homosexuals' general acceptance by the public.

Pre-reading Questions

Freewrite for five to ten minutes in response to the following questions:
How have you seen gays and lesbians portrayed on television? To what extent are these portrayals positive or negative? How, if at all, has television programming changed in terms of depicting homosexual characters? Explain.

Vocabulary Preview

Vocabulary Words:	• dissipate	• despicable	• commonplace
	• ballyhooed	• outlandishly	• foibled
	• lesbians	• homophobia	
	• recurring	• debunking	

Look up the words above and use them in no more than three sentences on some topic related to homosexuality or the media. Which words are the most emotionally loaded? Pay attention to what words are most difficult to fit into a discussion of a particular subject and why.

---

1   For most of the 20th century, movies and television have cast gay and lesbian characters as deviant bad guys. But as attitudes in the larger public change, so has Hollywood's portrayal of gays.

2   It's been just about a year since Ellen DeGeneres and the character she plays on her ABC sitcom came out of the closet. Time enough for all the media hype around this "sweeps week" event to dissipate, and for those of us curled up on our couches to wonder if the much ballyhooed episode was one giant leap for gays and lesbians everywhere— or just one small step for ABC/Disney's ratings.

3   On the plus side, gay couples can now adopt children in New Jersey, the U.S. bishops voted in November to recommend that parents everywhere should love and nurture their homosexual children, and Bill Clinton recently attended a formal dinner for gays and lesbians. But it would be hard to hang all the credit or blame on DeGeneres. After all, by the time she came out of the closet—on *Prime Time Live, Oprah,* and the cover of *Time*—there were already close to two dozen recurring gay characters on TV, in-

cluding, among others, lesbian and/or gay couples on *Roseanne, Mad About You, NYPD Blue,* and *Friends.* And don't forget the assorted homosexuals on *Spin City, Frasier,* and *The Simpsons.*

4   Of course, it wasn't always this way. Not so very long ago gays and lesbians were invisible on television, and when they showed up in films they tended to be cast as either guilt-ridden deviants or pathological sadists. In *Suddenly Last Summer* (1959), Montgomery Clift played a tortured lover of boys who is brutally murdered for his guilty passion, while in *Advise and Consent* (1962) and *The Children's Hour* (1962), rumors of homosexual love drove both Don Murray's and Shirley McLaine's characters to suicide.

5   Meanwhile, in dozens of Roman epics and World War II dramas, the most sadistic of Caligulas or Gestapo agents were inevitably portrayed as full-lipped and tubercular dandies with an appetite for "the love that dare not speak its name." To be really mean in Hollywood, it seems, it helped to be homosexual.

6   Even today these tired stereotypes continue to be trotted out with some regularity. Most recently Albert Finney gave us a reprise of the homosexual as a desperately lonely deviant in *A Man of No Importance* (1994), and he is joined by the killers in *Looking for Mr. Goodbar* (1977), *Cruising* (1980), *Basic Instinct* (1992), and *The Silence of the Lambs* (1991), as well as by the foppish evil Prince Edward in Mel Gibson's *Braveheart* (1994). This is evidence enough that sadistic gays continue to play well in tinsel town. As Rob Epstein's 1995 documentary *The Celluloid Closet* and David Johnson's *The Lavender Lens: 100 Years of Celluloid Queens* (1996) both argue, when they haven't been invisible, homosexuals have usually been treated either as pathetic or despicable.

7   Yet in the past several years significant strides have been made, both in Hollywood and on TV. And while cruel and silly stereotypes still endure, a rich variety of gay and lesbian characters have begun to surface on both the small and big screens, at first in small cameos and later in major, often complex, and interesting parts.

LOVE IN A TIME OF PLAGUE

8   One fresh set of gay roles that began to appear in the mid-'80s concerned young men and women coming to grips with AIDS. The screen showed ordinary, compassionate, and frightened people trying to make sense of their experience of love, secrecy, and death in the midst of the growing plague.

9   As many of us began to hear about or attend the all-too-early funerals of friends, relatives, and—occasionally—clergy who had died of AIDS, the stories of these personal losses began to surface in films and TV movies like *An Early Frost* (1985), *Our Sons* (1991), and *The Gloaming* (1997). Usually they starred mothers played by the likes of Gena Rowlands, Julie Andrews, and Glenn Close—and handsome, decent, and dying sons like Aidan Quinn and Hugh Grant (whose character behaved much better as a homosexual than his character did as a straight man in *Four Weddings and a Funeral*).

10 Often enough these stories were about reconciliation, about forgiving parents and friends who couldn't abide the central character's orientation, about letting go of old hurts and trying to accept one another for who we really are. They are also tales of

courage and fidelity, of lovers accompanying each other through the long processes of illness and death, and about coming to grips with grief and abandonment. *Philadelphia* (1993) and *Love! Valor! Compassion!* (1997) are two of my favorite movies that deal with some of these issues.

OUT OF THE BIRDCAGE

11 But not all the roles have been for the Aidan Quinn and Tom Hanks types. Some fresh opportunities are to be found in madcap comedies that have turned old homosexual stereotypes inside out by going way, way over the top.

12   In movies such as *The Adventures of Priscilla, Queen of the Desert* (1994), *To Wong Foo, Thanks for Everything! Julie Newmar* (1995), and *The Birdcage* (Mike Nichols' and Elaine May's 1996 remake of *La Cage aux Folles*), actors like Nathan Lane and Robin Williams, as well as Patrick Swayze and Wesley Snipes, got to play outlandishly funny and deeply sympathetic characters in whom there was clearly no perverse or unnatural moral disorder. In these movies the joke was not on the gays but the straights, or at least those straights whose uptight homophobia kept them from recognizing the humanity of men who wear—and look terrific in—dresses.

PERFECTLY GAY?

13 Most recently there's been something of a surge in what might be called "drop-dead perfect" gay characters. These are men and women who aren't merely just as nice, attractive, and moral as their heterosexual neighbors, but who are indeed a whole lot better.

14   I first noticed this trend in *Four Weddings and a Funeral* (1994) where the gay couple in the story proves to be eminently more stable, mature, and poetic than any of the gaggle of rather silly straights running from bedroom to bedroom in search of true love. So too are the lesbian couples in *Fried Green Tomatoes* (1991) and *Antonia's Line* (1995), who are just smarter and nicer than the folks around them. Indeed, the "straight" gene pool in both of these films seems terribly shallow and polluted.

15   Certainly the clearest examples of this new phenomenon are Tom Selleck and Kevin Kline in *In and Out* (1997) and Rupert Everett as Julia Roberts' editor and friend in *My Best Friend's Wedding* (1997). Cary Grant and Fred Astaire together never have more charm and grace than these guys, nor Henry Fonda and Gregory Peck more integrity.

THE CURRENT MOVEMENT

16 And just what are we to make of all this increased coverage of gays and lesbians on television and at the movies? What are we to think about the presence of dozens of gay and lesbian characters on cable and the networks, about the mainstreaming of homosexual roles in movies playing at the local cineplex rather than the art theater downtown?

17   Does the increased presence of gays and lesbians in our visual mass entertainment translate into progress and increased understanding, or are they simply being added as local color?

18   On the downside I sometimes wonder if any group, particularly one identified by its sexuality, is likely to get either fair play or intelligent treatment from a medium designed for visual stereotyping.

19   After all, look at the way primetime TV portrays heterosexuals on shows like *Married with Children, Spin City, Men Behaving Badly, Cybil, Seinfield,* and *Frasier.* Amidst this assortment of silly, shallow, and pathetically oversexed cartoon characters, it would certainly be tough to find either an intelligent presentation of the meaning and challenges of adult sexuality—or role models for adolescents seeking guidance or inspiration in healthy relationship matters. (OK, *Mad About You* does a nice, funny job, but it's clearly the exception that proves the rule.)

20   And in a medium that loves to fill its afternoon programming with carnival sideshows populated by pathetic folks willing to show their sexual dysfunction to the gaping audience, can we really expect serious reflection or conversation about the morality or experience of homosexuality?

THE POWER OF TV

21   And yet, in another sense, TV and film are probably the best place for gays and lesbians—and other groups affected by bias and discrimination—to be. Although these visual mediums usually lack any subtlety or capacity to engage us in serious reflection, it can often slip its messages past our defenses and get us used to seeing and watching people we might not normally meet or attend to. TV and movies can bring gays and lesbians into the living rooms of our imagination and get them walking around inside our heads—debunking other images created by ignorance and bias.

22   It's true that homophobia and gay-bashing won't be stopped by putting more gays on TV, or even by giving them good roles and interesting characters to play, but it's also true that Bill Cosby's friendly, intelligent, and witty presence in hundreds of millions of American households over the past 30 years has done more than a little good for the cause of racial harmony in America.

23   It's also true that the growing presence of gays and lesbians on TV and in films offers role models—mostly silly, but sometimes helpful—for young men and women who are gay or lesbian and who need to know they have a place among us.

24   So the growth of roles, particularly sympathetic ones, for homosexual characters over the past dozen years or so has for the most part been good news for gays and straights alike. And even though Ellen's coming out of the closet last April was hardly the start, or even the height of this progress, this overhyped media event may turn out to have been important precisely because the character DeGeneres plays is so ordinary, so commonplace.

25   Neither tortured nor despicable, Ellen is also not particularly brave, gracious—or in my opinion—riotously funny. Instead, she is just an ordinarily neurotic and humorous sitcom character whose personality isn't more pathetic than Drew Carey's or Cybil's. And for that very reason she may indeed represent some small but real step in our society's gradual recognition of the humanity of gays and lesbians.

26   Even more than the brave men and women struggling with AIDS, or the suave, debonair folks in some recent films, Ellen represents homosexuals as being just as ordinary as the rest of us—revealing them as just as normal, decent, neurotic, foibled, and funny as straight people. She lets us know not only that gays and lesbians aren't demons and perverts, but also that they don't need to be Jackie Robinsons or Madame Curies.

27   Gays and lesbians are simply the folks sitting next to us in the bleachers or doctor's waiting room. And that's not a mean achievement.

POST-READING QUESTIONS

CONTENT

1. According to McCormick, what strides have gays and lesbians made in terms of public acceptance?
2. How have homosexual people been traditionally portrayed in the media? How has this portrayal changed?
3. How do homosexual characters in film compare to their heterosexual counterparts, in terms of character and personality?
4. To what extent has television followed film in updating its portrayals of gays and lesbians?
5. Why is Ellen DeGeneres' sitcom character's "coming out" important in terms of gays' and lesbians' progress in the media?

STYLE AND STRUCTURE

6. What is McCormick's primary argument? How is the placement of this message significant?
7. What examples does McCormick offer in support of his main idea? Does he offer enough support? Explain.
8. Who is McCormick's audience? To what extent are you part of his audience? Explain and give examples.
9. What is McCormick's attitude toward his topic? Cite the text for support.
10. Is McCormick convincing? Explain.

CRITICAL THINKING AND ANALYSIS

DISCUSSION QUESTIONS

11. How important is a television or film character's sexual orientation in terms of your identifying with him/her? Must a character have the same sexual orientation as you in order for you to want to watch him/her? Explain.
12. How, if at all, has your attitude toward gays and lesbians in film and on television changed? What accounts for this change or lack of change? Explain.

WRITING ASSIGNMENTS

13. Since 1998 when this article was first published, how much headway do you think gays and lesbians have made in terms of their portrayal in film and on television? Write a few paragraphs or short essay in which you discuss whether or not homosexual characters have made positive strides in the media, citing the text and your own observations for support.
14. McCormick cites traditional portrayals of gays as being "either pathetic or despicable," while pointing out that contemporary portrayals of gay characters

have been "a whole lot better" than their heterosexual counterparts. How do you think gay characters fare in comparison with their heterosexual co-stars? Write a few paragraphs in which you explain how gays are portrayed as being better or worse than heterosexuals on television and in film. Use examples from the essay and your own observations to illustrate your ideas.

15. McCormick claims that "homophobia and gay-bashing won't be stopped by putting more gays on TV . . ." What do you think? Write at least one well-developed paragraph arguing that having more gay and lesbian characters on television will or will not help break down prejudice against homosexual people. Cite the text and your own life for support.

VOCABULARY DEVELOPMENT

16. What role do language and example play in helping McCormick communicate his feelings about gays and lesbians? Find at least three examples of words or illustrations that reveal McCormick's attitude toward homosexuals.

GROUP ACTIVITIES

17. Ask a gay or lesbian friend to read McCormick's article. What is his/her take on the piece? Share your results with the class.

18. Before coming to class, watch a contemporary television program that includes gay or lesbian characters, taking notes on how such characters are portrayed. Then, as a group, draw a conclusion about homosexuals' depiction on television and write a brief paragraph outlining your views. Share your results with other groups.

The Diana Aftermath

Media excesses fueled public outrage and triggered calls for restrictions on news-gathering. Will another round of criticism set the stage for reform?

Jacqueline Sharkey and Lara M. White

First published in the *American Journalism Review*, *The Diana Aftermath* raises questions about just how far the media should go in order to inform the public, and who should pay the price if someone gets hurt in the pursuit of news. Jacqueline Sharkey and Lara M. White overview proposed legislation that would require journalists to become licensed, and they address issues of free speech and privacy within the context of the media.

Pre-reading Questions

Freewrite for five to ten minutes in response to the following questions:
What do you consider to be the news media's primary purpose? What responsibilities does meeting this purpose include? How successful do you think the news media is in terms of achieving its purpose and upholding its responsibilities? Explain.

Vocabulary Preview

Vocabulary Words:

- exploitative
- confluence
- commemorative
- participatory
- animosity

- paparazzi
- titillate
- defensible
- Faustian
- paradox

- injunction
- superseding
- trump
- travesty
- malfeasance

Look up the words above and use at least eight of them in sentences of varying length, structure, and difficulty. Then, write a few sentences explaining how some words were more difficult to place in context than others.

---

1   THE EARL SPENCER'S VOICE TREMBLED SLIGHTLY AS HE read a statement the day his sister, Princess Diana, died in an automobile accident. Initial press reports said the accident occurred as news photographers chased the car through the streets of Paris after midnight on August 31.

2   "I always believed the press would kill her in the end. But not even I could imagine that they would take such a direct hand in her death as seems to be the case," Spencer said.

3   "It would appear that every proprietor and editor of every publication that has paid for intrusive and exploitative photographs of her, encouraging greedy and ruthless individuals to risk everything in pursuit of Diana's image, has blood on his hands today."

4   New York Times columnist A.M. Rosenthal agreed. "Someday," Rosenthal wrote, "I believe, the words of Earl Spencer will hang in the private offices of publishers, network chiefs, and print and electronic editors worthy of any respect or trust."

5   The public, and some members of the press, denounced the photopraphers—and journalists in general—as "barracuda," "jackals," "piranha" and "vultures" feeding off celebrities.

6   Barbara Cochran, president of the Radio-Television News Directors Association, says it was impossible to "ignore how angry the public was" immediately after Diana's death.

7   "Numerous news directors have said to me that their photographers would be yelled at on the street," she says. Some passers-by accused photojournalists of "being responsible for killing Diana."

8   Following Diana's death other issues involving the press emerged because of the public's lingering anger toward the news media. This hostility symbolizes what Nieman Foundation Curator Bill Kovach calls "an enormous disconnect" between the American people and the press that has "profound implications" for journalists' legal protections and privileges.

9   In addition, economic and technological developments made Diana's image such a marketing force that broadcast network news operations devoted more time in one week to her fatal accident than to any news event since the 1991 coup attempt against Soviet leader Mikhail Gorbachev, according to The Tyndall Weekly, a newsletter that monitors broadcast network news.

10   In the weeks since Diana's death, this confluence of controversies has led the American media to re-examine fundamental questions about their role, responsibilities and relationship to the American people.

11   It is ironic that this soul-searching began as U.S. journalism organizations were already launching initiatives to explore what Sandra Mims Rowe, president of the American Society of Newspaper Editors, calls "the damaging erosion of our credibility with the public."

12   One impetus for these initiatives has been a series of public opinion polls during the last 10 years that indicates many Americans have doubts about the news media's priorities and the ways in which they exercise their First Amendment rights.

13   A 1996 poll by the Center for Media and Public Affairs found that 80 percent of those surveyed thought the press ignored people's privacy; 52 percent thought the news media abused their press freedoms. More than 95 percent of respondents to an informal USA Today online survey thought the princess had been unfairly hounded by the news media, which confounded some journalists, given Diana's skill at using the press.

14   The day after the princess died, University of Southern California law professor and CNBC legal analyst Erwin Chemerinsky predicted that public outrage "will lead to attempts to restrict paparazzi in the United States and elsewhere."

15   During the next two weeks, French and British officials called for such laws, and a U.S. congressman introduced a bill to make some invasions of privacy a federal crime. California state lawmakers drafted legislation to create a "zone of privacy" in public places, change state defamation law and establish a commission to examine paparazzi behavior.

16   These initial reactions could have troubling long term ramifications for the U.S. press.

17   Technology and corporate values are increasingly influencing the priorities of U.S. news media, which are competing in a global information marketplace, say some media analysts. The fact that Diana's death received more network news coverage than the landing of U.S. troops in Somalia is a clear sign of this.

18   Proposed federal and state laws indicate that privacy rights are becoming more important than press rights to legislatures and the public. These measures are part of a growing movement by legislators and courts to control newsgathering practices in the name of privacy.

19   The increasing intrusiveness of some photographers has led to renewed debate about licensing journalists.

20   Reaction to the press—and calls for additional regulations in the wake of Diana's death—shows that public support for the First Amendment can be very fragile. This support for limiting press freedom makes it imperative that journalists understand the dynamic that exists between the American people and the press, and reevaluate their responsibilities to the public.

21   SOME JOURNALISTS AND PRESS ANALYSTS believe coverage of Diana's life and death reflect how entertainment values have replaced traditional news values in many U.S. newsrooms.

22   Print media found coverage of Diana so profitable, both before and after her death, that Newsweek media critic Jonathan Alter wrote, "Lady Di launched at least a thousand covers, and hundreds of millions of newspaper and magazine sales."

23   When Diana died, magazines such as Time and Newsweek scrambled to redo their covers and devote dozens of pages to stories about the princess. As reporters started to question what Time contributor Martha Smilgis called the "media gush" about Diana, Time, Newsweek, People and TV Guide all published special commemorative editions.

24   Time's first issue about Diana's death had newsstand sales of about 850,000–650,000 more than normal. The commemorative edition sold about 1.2 million copies. They are the two largest sellers in the history of the magazine, according to Managing Editor Walter Isaacson.

25   Newspaper sales also rose. USA Today's total circulation for the week after Diana's death was several hundred thousand above normal. The Washington Post sold more than 20,000 additional copies of its Sunday editions the day Diana died and the day after her funeral.

26   Television news ratings also increased. CNN reported "a dramatic surge in viewership," and the highest ratings ever for its Sunday night newsmagazine, "Impact," which aired the night Diana died. More than 15 million people watched the August 31 "60 Minutes" devoted to the princess, according to Nielsen Media Research.

27   Television coverage of Diana's funeral was watched in more than 26 million households, Nielsen estimates. The week of September 15—two weeks after Diana died—broadcast networks devoted more time to the princess and the British monarchy than any other story, according to The Tyndall Weekly.

28   "We overdosed on Diana," says Steve Geimann, immediate past president of the Society of Professional Journalists.

29   Jeff Cohen, an attorney who is executive director of Fairness & Accuracy In Reporting (FAIR), agrees. He notes with irony that in a country that revolted against the British crown to form a democratic union, many people "can give you chapter and verse now on the in-fighting amongst British royalty," but "can't identify their representative to the U.S. Congress."

30   "They're getting facts that are utterly meaningless to them acting as informed citizens in a participatory democracy," Cohen says.

31   Some journalists, however, think the coverage was appropriate. Jeff Pager, executive producer of the "CBS Evening News," says Diana's death had "huge political overtones," revealing the British people's animosity toward the monarchy, and involving top British and French officials in discussions of the accident investigation.

32   Maxwell E.P. King, editor and executive vice president of the Philadelphia Inquirer, who is stepping down in January, says the coverage "represented an important public catharsis about all sorts of different issues—about women and their place in society, about how the famous and their fans interact."

33   CNN Editor-at-Large Ed Turner points out that Diana's funeral enabled millions of Americans to share their grief, and "there aren't that many shared experiences that occur these days."

34   In the early days of TV, "the nation sort of went through the same news stories together," Turner says, but technology has been "fracturing the viewing audience" by providing "a diversity of not only sources, but alternatives to news."

35   Critics, he says, don't take this diversity into account. Turner points out that CNN, unlike the broadcast networks, provides news 24 hours a day and has given the public extensive coverage of events in Russia, the Middle East and Bosnia. "You think that's numbers? Wrong! It's a killer" for ratings, says Turner. "If at times we are excessive, in other ways, well, we paid our dues. . . . We're not tabloid all the time."

36   But several incidents during the coverage of Diana's death show how difficult it can sometimes be to distinguish between the so-called tabloid and mainstream media.

37   Newsweek, Time and other publications used photographs of Diana that some readers and journalists found intrusive, while captions talked about the pictures capturing intimate moments. Isaacson defends his magazine, saying Time used valid news photographs taken in public places, and rejected pictures by "stalking paparazzi invading people's privacy."

38   In the meantime, National Enquirer Editor Steve Coz made a televised plea for news organizations to refuse to publish pictures of the injured princess and her dead companion. "We have refused to buy these pictures," Coz said, "and we're asking that the rest of the world press join us in shunning these photos."

39   Dana Kennedy, an Entertainment Weekly reporter, called Coz's comments "the worst hypocrisy," especially since the National Enquirer's cover the previous week had a headline that said, "Di Goes Sex-Mad—'I Can't Get Enough!'"

40   However, journalists thought other news media also were hypocritical. Time columnist Margaret Carlson decried the practice of "tabloid-laundering, which is we take what the tabloids do and write about it, and that way get what we wouldn't write about originally into the magazine. And then we run pictures of the pictures to show how terrible the pictures are."

41   Newsweek seemed to do just that with two Alter stories. On September 8, his full page spread about the media's celebrity obsession included a color picture of one cover of the British tabloid The Sun, published before Diana's death. The cover included a now famous photo of Diana, her swimsuit straps slipped down her arms, on a boat with her companion, Emad Mohamed "Dodi" al-Fayed. The headline: "Dodi's to Di For, World Picture Exclusive."

42   The next week, his article about Diana and the news media—in which the princess is quoted as calling paparazzi photography "face rape"—was accompanied by a blurry full page picture of the princess, visibly upset, putting her hand in front of the camera lens.

43   Newsweek Managing Editor Mark Whitaker defends the pictures, saying, "You have to look at the context in which photographs are being used. When the subject of a legitimate news story is the paparazzi phenomenon, and you're running these pictures in a way that's used to illustrate . . . that news story, and not just to titillate people with exclusive photographs that have never been seen that you pay a lot of money for, then I think that that is still a defensible and legitimate use of the photographs."

44   Alter believes the photos "are not a good example of tabloid laundering," because the motivation is to "illustrate a serious article," not a gossip-oriented feature.

45   But some readers were irate about the use of pictures they considered invasive. "I would never have expected to find such photos in your publication," wrote Allison Seale of Los Angeles to Newsweek. "Shame on you and shame on us all."

46   One reason the line between tabloid and mainstream media is fading is that the press is under mounting pressure to provide entertainment-oriented news, says long-time journalist Ben Bagdikian, author of "The Media Monopoly."

47   Stockholders in major media corporations expect high profits, and entertainment products deliver them, he says. This puts news subsidiaries "under terrible pressure" to deliver reports that will boost the bottom line.

48   "The value system of commercial television and of entertainment companies has made dangerous intrusions into the integrity of real news," says Bagdikian.

49   King says this has not happened with Knight-Ridder, which he says has "a very, very good level of awareness of news values." But he acknowledges that "some so-called news companies," which he declined to name, "don't reflect the most serious values."

50   U.S. News & World Report Editor James Fallows believes corporate pressures are forcing more news organizations to produce entertainment-oriented reports, and says this is a "Faustian bargain."

51   "In the short run it raises your audience, "Fallows says, but "in the long run it threatens to destroy your business, because if the only way you make journalism interesting is by making it entertainment, in the long run people will just go to entertainment, pure and simple, and skip the journalistic overlay."

52   Meanwhile, despite the high ratings and circulation figures for stories about Diana, a Wall Street Journal/NBC News poll of more than 2,000 people in mid-September showed 56 percent of respondents thought there had been too much coverage of Princess Diana's death.

53   Some news executives say such polls reveal a paradox about the public's relationship with the press. People respond to certain types of coverage, then criticize the press

for providing it. However, other polls show the American people want the news media to provide them with information that is not only interesting, but important to their lives, regardless of ratings.

54   So does one lawmaker who proposed legislation to restrict the press following Diana's death. If journalism is simply a "profit-seeking, market oriented enterprise," then the controversy about the news media's involvement with Diana "becomes a much bigger issue than who chased who into a tunnel," says California State Sen. Tom Hayden. It's about whether entertainment has "taken root in the very heart of journalism" and become a "substitute for information."

55   The public's reation to coverage of Diana's life and death, Hayden says, is "one of those moments along the way when we need to take an accounting."

56   Hayden is one of several lawmakers who, in the weeks after Diana died, drafted laws to limit access to public figures. On Capitol Hill, Rep. Sonny Bono (R-Calif.) introduced a bill that could result in jail sentences and fines for anyone who "persistently" follows a person who "has a reasonable expectation of privacy and has taken reasonable steps to insure that privacy," for the purpose of obtaining "a visual image, sound recording, or other physical impression of the victim for profit in or affecting interstate or foreign commerce."

57   In California, State Senate Majority Leader Charles Calderon has prepared draft legislation for a "Personal Privacy Act" that provides broad definitions for terms such as "intrusion" and would change the civil defamation law.

58   Hayden is drafting a "Paparazzi Harassment Act" that would enable courts to fine journalists engaging in behavior that was "threatening, intimidating, harassing, or causes alarm, harm or the potential of harm to any person who is the subject of media interest." Such behavior could be penalized even if it is unintentional.

59   Publishers who know or have reason to know of such behavior also would be liable. Pursuit of a story "of meaningful public interest" would be a recognized legal defense, says Hayden.

60   The draft legislation also calls for creating a Commission of Inquiry into Paparazzi Behavior to evaluate the impact of new technology, such as long-range telephoto lenses, on privacy and trespass laws; to study "the growth, behavior, structure, funding and ethics of the paparazzi and tabloid journalism"; and to explore ways to "preserve and enhance freedom of the press while curbing abusive practices that threaten legitimate privacy and safety rights."

61   Miami Herald Executive Editor Douglas C. Clifton thinks these laws could be passed, "given the state everyone seems to be in" following Diana's death. He is concerned that "political figures will use this as an opportunity to further restrict press coverage of public events."

62   Some journalists and attorneys are optimistic that such legislation won't be enacted because it is unconstitutional and unnecessary.

63   "There are enough laws on the books already to protect the privacy of public figures," says Cohen of FAIR. These include criminal laws dealing with assault, stalking and trespass, and civil remedies.

64   Hayden believes such laws are "insufficient." He compares these arguments to those used by opponents of sexual harassment laws, which he helped draft in California.

"We heard all these same arguments—that women didn't need a specific sexual harassment statute, there was existing law," he says. But specific legislation was needed to deal with the unique circumstances surrounding date rape and domestic violence. Now, Hayden believes, special laws also need to be written to address the paparazzi's invasion of privacy.

65   Attorney Martin London disagrees. He argued in a New York Times op-ed piece that in 1973 he and other attorneys helped Jacqueline Kennedy Onassis get an injunction preventing photographer Ron Galella from approaching her or her children by asking a judge to apply principles in existing law "to the singular phenomenon of paparazzi." The injunction was tailored specifically to Onassis' situation. London urged other public figures to look to the court rather than the legislature for relief.

66   Some journalists believe the proposed laws would not stop the paparazzi. "Extremist photographers," says David R. Lutman, president of the National Press Photographers Association, believe "chancing arrest for breaking a minor law" is worth the risk, because they can make hundreds of thousands of dollars for a single picture. Lutman worries that the law will be used to stop other news photographers from pursuing legitimate stories.

67   Media analysts and attorneys also are concerned that the bills being considered by Congress and California lawmakers are the latest indication that privacy rights are superseding press rights.

68   "It seems more and more in our society that we want the right to be left alone to trump the right to know," says Paul McMasters, The Freedom Forum's First Amendment ombudsman. "If that happens, democracy is in real danger."

69   The proposed laws are the latest in a series of moves by legislatures and the courts to cite privacy as a reason for restricting newsgathering-techniques. Some states restricted access to drivers' license information after a stalker obtained actress Rebecca Schaeffer's address from the California motor vehicles department and killed her in 1989. The federal government passed a similar law in 1994. (See The Press and the Law, page 50, and "License Revoked," November 1995.)

70   Some news outlets originally supported the drivers' license laws, not realizing these measures don't protect people from stalkers, says Jane Kirtley, executive director of the Reporters Committee for Freedom of the Press, but do provide governments with a rationale for declaring public records off-limits.

71   The courts also have moved to limit newsgathering. A federal judge in Pennsylvania granted an injunction last year prohibiting an "Inside Edition" team from following executives of a large health maintenance organization. The team was preparing a story on the large compensation packages paid to HMO executives.

72   The judge ruled that "the right to gather the news is not absolute," and that a jury would probably agree the team was not trying to obtain information for journalistic purposes, but for "entertaining background for their TV expose."

73   Although "Inside Edition" frequently is referred to as a "tabloid" television show, it has won several journalism awards from groups such as Investigative Reporters & Editors.

74   The Freedom Forum's McMasters is "very troubled" by the "trend for the public to want judges and now legislatures to take on a new job of being editors and reporters."

If the trend continues, he says, "it will be a travesty for the public" because "when you put shackles on newsgathering operations, it's across the board. It doesn't just apply in one place, Because a law that perhaps is meant to help a future Princess Diana will be used and abused by an elected official to restrict the kind of coverage that might expose corruption or malfeasance."

75   Some media analysts worry that these initiatives could erode journalists' privileges as well as protections.

76   Kovach of the Nieman Foundation expects that "rules and regulations that keep the press out, that restrict the press access both to institutions and to people in certain circumstances, are going to get a hell of a lot tighter."

77   Another development that jolted news organizations and their attorneys was the serious discussion of whether journalists—especially photographers—should be licensed.

78   Security consultant Gavin de Becker wrote in USA Today that "a person who chooses to earn money as a paparazzo should be required to obtain a permit, just like any street vendor. Permits could then be revoked for violations of the law. Paparazzi want to call this a profession, so let's regulate it."

79   According to California State Sen. Diane Watson, the legislature is "looking at" licensing professional photographers.

80   "That is completely out of bounds in a country that values a free press," says RTNDA President Cochran. She points out that the licensing system used by the British crown to stifle the press in the 1700s was one reason the First Amendment was written.

81   But some mainstream journalists have unwittingly helped fuel the licensing debate by struggling to distinguish themselves from colleagues who work for the so-called "tabloid" press. USA Today White House Bureau Chief Susan Page told CNN's Frank Sesno that she didn't think "the paparazzi who pursued this car are part of the press, frankly."

82   Katharine Graham of the Washington Post Co. wrote in an essay published in the Post and Newsweek, "One point we all have to keep clear is that the paparazzi are different from the news media. The problem the paparazzi present will not be solved by abridging press freedom."

83   But pushing the distinction too hard is not without peril, says CNN executive Ed Turner. "This characterizing as 'legitimate' or 'not legitimate' seems to me to be a dangerous sort of road to travel" because such statements imply that restrictions on "irresponsible" journalists might be acceptable.

84   Many members of the public already believe restrictions on the press are acceptable. A survey last year by the Center for Media and Public Affairs showed 53 percent of the 3,000, respondents support licensing, and 70 percent favored court-imposed fines for inaccurate or biased reporting.

85   Some of these attitudes might result from ignorance. A 1997 Freedom Forum poll showed that 85 percent of respondents could not name press freedom as one of the five First Amendment freedoms.

86   But others arise from anger and resentment. That poll, and others during the past five years, show that a majority of Americans believe that special interests, such as corporate media owners and advertisers, as well as pressures for profits, improperly influence the way news is gathered and presented.

87   People's perception that the news media don't "seem to be serving their needs very well" is often correct, says Washington Post Ombudsman Geneva Overholser. "The trouble is that newspapers have become so profitable—profitable beyond any normal retailers' dreams—that the pressure on corporate executives to run them with an emphasis on the short term as opposed to the long term is just enormous."

88   This means "the debate is between enormous profit expectations . . . and the community's need to know, which requires real investment."

89   Advertisers contribute to the problem. They used to be interested in newspapers' mass market appeal, but now "think it's altruistic to service a wide readership," says Overholser. Advertisers want to attract wealthy, well-educated readers, so they want to place ads in sections where subjects aren't too controversial and have strong human interest components, she says.

90   Broadcast, cable and satellite media face similar pressures, which increase as they become subsidiaries in multinational conglomerates, some media analysts say These corporations believe that "the marketplace sets the standard" for what is important, Kovach says.

91   Executives look at a picture of Princess Diana and ask, "'What's the picture worth to us economically?'" says Kovach. "That has nothing to do with the journalistic value of it. It has to do with the uses they can put it to."

92   "All of those trends take journalism closer to entertainment values and further away from what I think are the values that justify the protection the First Amendment offers a free press."

93   Some news executives say not all corporations view information this way. Time magazine Managing Editor Isaacson says there "absolutely" is a wall between Time Warner's news and entertainment divisions. In the two years since he has been in his job, the magazine has done "fewer pure entertainment covers than were done in the '70s," Isaacson says.

94   The press has a moral obligation to balance profits and public benefits, because it is the only business given explicit constitutional protection, says Lutman of the National Press Photographers Association. "It isn't necessarily our responsibility to give people what they want, it's to give them what they need." Those who put profitability ahead of public service, he says, "are betraying our profession."

95   When the public senses this betrayal, its support for the media's First Amendment protections and privileges begins to decline, SPJ's Geimann points out. This sets up a climate in which legislatures, judges and juries feel justified in placing limits on the press.

96   "We the press depend on the public support for all the rights and liberties that are built into the Constitution and the Bill of Rights," he says. "When the public support disappears, our rights and liberties disappear."

97   McMasters believes journalists must address the situation quickly, because "the global nature of news today presents some unique challenges to the First Amendment."

98   As the American people gain access to news around the world via satellite television feeds and the Internet, they are questioning whether the restrictive laws of countries such as France and England do in fact lead to a more responsible press, he says.

99   This is why "freedom of the press in the United States depends as much on how we fulfill our responsibilities as they do on how we exercise our rights." says McMasters.

100   Journalism organizations initiated several projects during the past year to focus attention on the media's responsibilities and to look for ways to restore public confidence in the press.

101   The American Society of Newspaper Editors recently began a three-year project to examine how to increase the print media's credibility. The Society of Professional Journalists updated its code of ethics, adding a section on accountability, and is sponsoring ethics workshops at news organizations and professional conferences. The National Press Photographers Association plans to emphasize privacy issues during workshops and seminars.

102   CBS newsman Mike Wallace is leading a drive to establish a national news council that would consider complaints about the media (see "Going Public," April). The Freedom Forum recently announced a major initiative to improve press fairness and freedom. The Nieman Foundation and the Project for Excellence in Journalism, funded by the Pew Charitable Trusts, have helped organize the Committee of Concerned Journalists, which hopes to clarify the purposes and principles that should guide the news media.

103   Several new programs involve public participation. The ASNE Journalism Credibility Project includes research partnerships with eight newspapers that will study credibility issues in their communities and implement solutions. The Freedom Forum's Free Press/Fair Press project will include town meetings and discussions with business leaders and minority groups.

104   The Committee of Concerned Journalists will hold public meetings as part of a "period of national reflection about journalism," says Nieman Curator Kovach, the committee chairman. The meetings will deal with issues such as "the meaning of news" at a time "when serious journalistic organizations drift toward opinion, infotainment and sensation," according to the committee's Statement of Concern. Any journalist can join the committee by signing its statement.

105   Doug Clifton of the Miami Herald believes that during such a period of reflection, a journalist should think about the First Amendment in terms of what it means to the American people. "They don't see us as defenders of their First Amendment freedom; they see us as protectors of a special legislation that permits us to make a profit," Clifton says.

106   McMasters has been surprised at how many journalists have "a real ignorance of what the First Amendment stands for," and how many do not understand the ethical responsibilities that come with the rights the press enjoys.

107   "Journalists," he says, "sometimes are the First Amendment's worst enemy."

POST-READING QUESTIONS

CONTENT

1. Whom does the Earl Spencer blame for Princess Diana's death?
2. How did the public react to Princess Diana's death? Whom did they blame?

3. How did the press respond to Princess Diana's death?

4. What effect did Diana's death have on the profit margins of major newspapers and magazines?

5. What does CNN Editor-at-Large Ed Turner claim is a benefit of widespread coverage of Diana's death and funeral?

6. What is "tabloid laundering"? How is this practice viewed by the media itself?

7. What types of laws are being proposed in relation to the media? Who is in favor of such laws? Against them?

8. What factors contribute to news media becoming more like entertainment media?

9. What role does the First Amendment play in determining what the media reports?

10. What are some of the implications of limiting the press in its quest for news?

STYLE AND STRUCTURE

11. Do the writers have a primary message? What is it?

12. What are the writers' sub-arguments? How do these secondary arguments help develop the overall message?

13. What types of examples do the writers use to develop their ideas? How effective are the examples? Explain.

14. What conclusions can you draw about the audience for this article? Cite the text for support.

15. Are Starkey and White convincing? Explain.

CRITICAL THINKING AND ANALYSIS

DISCUSSION QUESTIONS

16. How far do you think reporters should go to get a story? How far is too far?

17. What was your reaction when Princess Diana died? How responsible did you hold the press for her death?

WRITING ASSIGNMENTS

18. According to Jeff Cohen, executive director of Fairness and Accuracy In Reporting, American citizens are "getting facts that are utterly meaningless to them [and are then] acting as informed citizens in a participatory democracy." Is he right? Write at least three well-developed paragraphs in which you explain whether or not Americans are "informed citizens" as a result of the media. Cite the text and your own life for support.

19. *Newsweek* Managing Editor Mark Whitaker defends publishing controversial photographs, saying if "you're running these pictures in a way that's

used to illustrate . . . that news story . . . then I think that that is still a defensible and legitimate use of the photographs." What do you think? Write a few paragraphs or short essay in which you discuss the circumstances, if any, under which publishing controversial photographs is "indefensible" or inappropriate. Use examples from the article and your own observations for support.

20. Sharkey and White write of several proposed laws designed to limit the media in its pursuit of news stories. Do you think paparazzi should be punished for aggressively seeking photographs for a story, even if the harm they do is unintentional? Write a few paragraphs or short essay in which you argue that paparazzi should or should not be punished for taking pictures of subjects that do not wish to be photographed. Cite the text and your own life in order to illustrate your ideas.

VOCABULARY DEVELOPMENT

21. Sharkey and White report several views toward the media and paparazzi, in particular. Choose at least three descriptions of members of the media, and then write sentences explaining how those descriptions reveal a specific tone toward the media being described.

GROUP ACTIVITIES

22. Bring in magazines or tabloids that cover recent events, and analyze the photographs in them to determine whether or not you think the pictures in questions constitute an invasion of privacy. What determines, for you, whether or not photographs are invasive? Share your results with the class.

23. Before coming to class, watch part of some news program such as "Inside Edition" or "Extra." Pay attention to the nature of the stories covered, whether or not they are more news- or entertainment-oriented. Do the programs offered indicate a focus toward truth or toward ratings? Share your findings with your group and discuss the implications of the programming for the public.

SYNTHESIS QUESTIONS

1. Jean Picker Firstenberg writes, "the images of film and television have had enormous impact on the evolution of the modern hero," while Paul Rudnick claims that "Only movie stars have the chance to live possibly forever . . ." through the continual re-running of their films. What effect has the media had in creating, or perpetuating, stardom? Write a few paragraphs or short essay in which you discuss the role of the media in determining people's lasting influence. Be sure to cite both essays and the movies and television in order to illustrate your ideas.

2. Jean Picker Firstenberg writes, "the immediacy and intimacy of the media have somehow confused the issue of heroism, . . . allowing mere exposure—that is "fame"—to precede, and occasionally preempt, "worthiness" as a qualification for heroism." Is she right? Citing at least two writers from this chapter, write at least one well-developed paragraph defining "hero" according to what values you think the media emphasizes. Feel free to use examples from contemporary entertainment, politics, and sports in order to illustrate your ideas.

3. Paul Rudnick writes, "Movies have lent the most perishable qualities, such as youth, beauty and comedy, a millennial shelf life." However, Jacqueline Sharkey and Lara M. White cite people who feel that the media were responsible for Princess Diana's death. Choose two qualities that you think are representative of the media's best and worst aspects and write a few paragraphs or short essay explaining whether the positive aspect of the media that you identify outweighs the negative aspect. Use examples from these two readings as well as from your own experiences and observations in order to make your ideas clear.

4. Brian Lowry claims that "Television often finds itself under siege by critics who insist its handling of sex, violence and language causes ills ranging from real-life violence and a coarsening of society to gout and the heartbreak of psoriasis." Patrick McCormick, however, writes that television "can often slip . . . messages past our defenses and get us used to seeing and watching people we might not normally meet or attend to." How great is the media's impact upon society? In a few well-developed paragraphs or short essay, discuss how significant the media's impact upon society is, citing both readings and your own life for support.

5. Brian Lowry raises the issue of "whether a portion of the public's appetite for vulgar material absolves the purveyors of culpability if an innocent bystander gets hurt along the way," while Julie Johnson details lawsuits against the media for invasion of privacy issues. How responsible is the media if someone gets hurt in its pursuit of a story? Write a few paragraphs arguing that the media is or is not responsible for the harm to "an innocent bystander" if the harm comes in the pursuit of news. Cite at least three essays from this chapter and your own observations in order to make your points clear.

6. Patrick McCormick claims that television and movies can "[debunk] other images created by ignorance and bias," and Jacqueline Sharkey and Lara M. White quote CNN Editor-at-Large Ed Turner, who says that television provides an opportunity for viewers to "share" an experience via the broadcast. What other positive effects can television and the movies have for people? Write a few paragraphs or short essay in which you explain how the media can have positive effects on people's lives. Be sure to cite both readings and your own life in order to illustrate your ideas.

7. Julie Johnson cites journalists who claim that media ride-alongs with law enforcement both help the public to better understand what law enforcement does and also help to monitor law enforcement. Yet Sharkey and White write about the possibility of reporters and photographs needing to be licensed to practice their profession. At what point should the law intervene to limit the media's access to private citizens' lives or property? Write at least three well-developed paragraphs in which you discuss the role the law should play in granting or limiting the media's freedom to pursue a story. Be sure to cite these essays and your own observations in order to clarify your points.

Reprinted with special permission of King Features Syndicate.

FOXTROT © 2001 Bill Amend. Reprinted with permission of UNIVERSAL PRESS SYNDICATE. All rights reserved.

❝In youth we learn, in age we understand.❞

— Marie von Ebner-Eschenbach

"If we were a people much given to revealing secrets, we might raise monuments and sacrifice to the memories of our poets, but slavery cured us of that weakness."

— **Maya Angelou**
Graduation

"We all do no end of feeling, and we mistake it for thinking."

— **Mark Twain**
Corn-Pone Opinions

"Contrary to all the nattering about political correctness, the social atmosphere on many campuses is macho and exclusionary and determinedly anti-intellectual."

— **Anna Quindlen**

Chapter 4: Civility on Campus

Readings:

Argument Pair:

Websites:

www.psu.edu/ur.civility/

This site offers goals, policies, and programs of Penn State to curb incivility through racism, homophobia, and sexism on its campus.

www.sunysb.edu/stuaff/scd/archives/civility.html

Offering features on new-student experiences on campus, this site also includes a good bibliography on the topic of campus-oriented civility.

Introduction

A cross the country, many schools are facing brutal battles to educate and protect their students. From increasing enrollment to decreasing graduation rates, schools find themselves beleaguered by new challenges. Among these, safety on campus is foremost, for educators feel that if students cannot be protected, they cannot be taught. However, violence at school is not the only conflict educators face.

Many teachers, while trying to create a safe learning environment for their students, face disruptions from the very population they try to teach. Instructors claim that a breakdown of respect in all areas of society has permeated the walls of academia, and they are left attempting to pass on knowledge even as they struggle to maintain control of their classes. Teachers explain that any respect for authority has been questioned or diluted at the hands of the media, and students feel free to question or criticize teachers whose methods they dislike. Thus, the authority that—for professors—was once a given is now one more challenge to meet before the real teaching begins.

Finally, even as teachers complain that students offer little respect for them, students themselves face mounting pressure to earn a degree. While education has long been important for acquiring a profession such as law, medicine, or education, only lately—with the disappearance of many assembly-line positions and with the population ever growing—has education begun to mean the difference between minimum wage and maximum opportunities in the workplace. Thus, more students scramble for the schools, classes, and degrees they need in order to make a place for themselves among those employed. Competition is fierce, and some students have found that their best chance of advancing their careers is through dishonest means. Academic fraud, school violence, and classroom respect are some of the areas this chapter explores, each of these underscored by an absence of civility in education.

Freedom

Joyce M. Jarrett

Assistant Provost at Hampton University, Joyce M. Jarrett has written several creative works, all of which, she states, stem from her experience as an African-American in the United States. In *Freedom,* Jarrett addresses the issue of taking responsibility for one's education, even in the face of great obstacles.

Pre-reading Questions

Freewrite for five to ten minutes in response to the following questions:
Have you ever felt uncomfortable in an academic setting? What caused you to feel uncomfortable? What did you do as a result of your discomfort? How much responsibility for a student's comfort should a teacher take? The student him or herself? Explain.

Vocabulary Preview

Vocabulary Words:	• desegregation	• denigrating	• emancipation
	• saunter	• futile	
	• crave	• irate	

Look up the words above and, as you read Jarrett's essay, write two-to-five sentences explaining how these words help Jarrett communicate a particular tone.

"Born free, as free as the wind blows, as free as the grass grows, born free to follow your heart." (Don Black)

1   My first illusion of freedom came in 1966, many years following the Supreme Court's decision on school desegregation. Of course to a fifteen-year-old girl, isolated, caged like a rodent in the poverty-stricken plains of the Magnolia State,[1] Brown vs. the Board of Education had no meaning. Though many must have thought that my decision to attend the all-white city high school that fall, along with 49 other blacks, was made in protest or had evolved from a sense of commitment for the betterment of my people, nothing could have been further from the truth. Like a rat finding a new passageway, I was propelled to my new liberty more out of curiosity than out of a sense of mission.

2   On the first day of school, I was escorted by hordes of national guardsmen. Like a funeral procession, the steady stream of official-looking cars followed me to the campus. Some patrolmen were parked near campus gates, while others, with guns strapped to their sides, stood near building entrances. Though many of my escorts had

---

[1]Magnolia State (1) Mississippi.

given me smiles of support, still I was not prepared for what I encountered upon entering *my* new school.

3   There, I had to break through lines of irate white protestors, spraying obscenities at me while carrying their denigrating signs: "KKK Forever," read one; "Back to Africa," said another. And as I dashed toward the school door, blinded with fear, I nearly collided with another sign that screamed "Nigger Go Home."

4   Once inside the fortress, I was ushered by school administrators and plain-clothes police to and from my respective classes. The anger and fear that I had felt outside of those walls were numbed by the surprisingly uneventful classroom experiences—until I went to geometry, my last scheduled class for that day.

5   As I sauntered into the classroom and took a seat, there was a flurry of activity. When everyone had settled, I sat in the center of the class, surrounded by empty desks—on each side, and in front and back.

6   "We have a nigger in the class," someone shouted.

7   "Let's get quiet and make the best of it," Mr. Moore smugly replied. Then he proceeded with the course orientation.

8   Near the end of the class, I mustered up enough courage to ask a question, so, nervously, I raised my hand. Keeping silent, Mr. Moore stared, and stared, and stared at me until my arm grew heavy and began to tremble. My heart sank, and my picture of freedom shattered in infinite pieces as he said, "I see that there are no questions. Class dismissed."

9   I have always blamed myself for that crushing moment. Why did I allow myself to be overlooked? Why did I not feel free? That painful, dehumanizing incident within itself did not provide any answers, though it signaled the beginning of my search. And finally, through years of disappointments, I discovered the truth—the truth that had evaded me during those high school years.

10   Freedom is not a gift, but a right. Officials did not, could not, award "freedom." It had to be something that I wanted, craved, demanded. The Supreme Court had liberated me of many external restrictions, but I had failed to liberate myself. In some instances internal constraints can be more binding than the overt ones. It is impossible to enslave one who has liberated oneself and futile to pry off the external chains of an internally bound person. Only when there is emancipation of both body and soul are any of us truly *free* to follow our hearts.

POST-READINGS QUESTIONS

CONTENT

1. Why does Jarrett say she chose to attend an all-white high school?
2. Based on her descriptions of her first day of school, what conclusions can you draw about Jarrett's experience at her new school?
3. What "moment" does Jarrett say she blames herself for? Why does she say this?
4. What does Jarrett mean when she says that "Freedom is not a gift, but a right"?
5. What does Jarrett mean when she says that she "failed to liberate [herself]"?

STYLE AND STRUCTURE

6. Jarrett writes of her "first illusion of freedom" in the first paragraph. To what extent does her essay reveal how her perception of freedom changed as a result of her experiences in high school?

7. Who is Jarrett's audience? In what ways does Jarrett connect with her audience while still communicating the painful racism she experienced?

8. What is Jarrett's overall message? Restate her main idea in your own words.

9. How does Jarrett reconcile the two conflicting messages of the "emancipation of both body and soul" and feeling her "freedom [shatter] in infinite pieces"?

10. What is Jarrett's tone? To what extent is her tone appropriate for her subject matter? Choose several words or phrases that exemplify her tone.

CRITICAL THINKING AND ANALYSIS

DISCUSSION QUESTIONS

11. Of the unkind acts Jarrett experienced on her first day at her new high school, which was the worst? Why?

12. Why do you think Jarrett allowed herself to be overlooked in her geometry class? Do you think that her situation would have improved if she had spoken out? Explain.

WRITING ASSIGNMENTS

13. Do you agree that "In some instances internal constraints can be more binding than the overt ones"? Explain and give examples from the text and your own experiences.

14. Jarrett was motivated to start her "search" as a result of her experience in geometry class. What do you think causes other people to take action in terms of improving their lives? Explain and give examples.

VOCABULARY DEVELOPMENT

15. Explain the difference between the denotation and the connotation of meaningful words in this essay. How does the word "caged," for example, construe Jarrett's place in life before she entered her new high school?

GROUP ACTIVITIES

16. In small groups, look up the court case *Brown vs. the Board of Education.* What was the purpose of this decision? How great a difference did it make? Present your findings to the class and compare them with other groups.

17. Brainstorm why people in Jarrett's situation, and others, respond to incivility with silence rather than with action. What causes people to become paralyzed in the face of rudeness? Explain.

Musings in the Wake of Columbine

Mary Anne Raywid and Libby Oshiyama

Mary Anne Raywid is professor emerita at Hofstra University and a member of the Graduate Affiliate Faculty at the University of Hawaii, and Libby Oshiyama is an international education consultant who resides in Hawaii. Addressing the topics of school violence and student alienation, Raywid and Oshiyama seek to explain the tragedy at Columbine High School in terms of community, noting that adolescence is the time when isolation is often the most difficult to deal with, and they suggest that more adult supervision at school could prevent future violence.

Pre-reading Questions

Freewrite for five to ten minutes in response to the following questions:
What, if anything, do you know of the Columbine shootings of 1999? How did that situation affect you? Why? Do you think violence in schools, particularly high school, is a problem? Why? How does your own high school experience compare to what you know of Columbine in terms of day-to-day conflict? Were people generally kind, unkind, or indifferent to their fellow students?

Vocabulary Preview

Vocabulary Words:		
• seductive	• logistical	• commonality
• deliberately	• clique	• suffice
• inadvertently	• comportment	• paradoxical
• anonymity	• customary	• equitable
• aberrations	• benign	• hewn
• apportioned	• empathy	• multifaceted

As always, look up ten of the words above; then, write at least three sentences using at least two of the words per sentence.

1   There have been multiple attempts to figure out the reasons for the Columbine High School tragedy. The availability of guns has been widely blamed, as has the violence depicted in films and videos. Some analysts have turned their sights on parental failure. Others have looked to deep-seated personality problems within the young assassins, while still others have focused on the seductive power of hate groups. There is probably some truth in most of these explanations, plus others, with the choice among them being largely a matter of individual perspective.

2   "The truth" lends itself to many interpretations. We know that if we look to psychologists for explanations of human behavior, we characteristically get different answers from what sociologists would offer and different answers from what anthropologists

would offer. Educators venture answers, too. But unless they are going to content them-selves with mere hand wringing, they must look to explanations that schools can do something about. Otherwise they are simply placing the problem beyond their control.

3   Actually, there is a good bit of knowledge suggesting directions that schools can take in order to avoid more tragedies like Columbine. It is also knowledge about which we can be fairly confident. In this article we will be reflecting on the broad strategies that strike us as most promising. They pertain to school size and organization, as well as to what we teach—both deliberately and inadvertently.

4   There is overwhelming evidence that violence is much less likely to occur in small schools than in large ones. In fact, not surprisingly, students behave better generally in schools where they are known. It is in large schools, where alienation often goes hand in hand with anonymity, that the danger comes. As James Garbarino of Cornell Univer-sity, one of the nation's top scholars on juvenile delinquency, has put it, "If I could do one single thing [to stop the scourge of violence among juveniles], it would be to en-sure that teenagers are not in high schools bigger than 400 to 500 students."[1]

5   As suggested by all the standard indicators—truancy, dropout rates, involvement rates, graffiti, vandalism, violence—youngsters in small schools rarely display the anger at the institution and the people in it that was so blatant at Columbine and is evi-dent in many high schools elsewhere as well.

6   The evidence regarding school size and risk comes not only from individual school studies but also from research syntheses—analyses of relevant studies undertaken across the country. Here are claims from three such syntheses:

7   Larger school size is related to . . . higher levels of disorder and violence, student alienation, and teacher dissatisfaction.[2]

8   Student social behavior—as measured by truancy, discipline problems, violence, theft, substance abuse, and gang participation—is more positive in small schools.[3]

9   Research has consistently found that students at small schools are less alienated than students in large schools—and this positive effect is especially strong for students labeled "at risk."[4]

10   Behavior problems are so much greater in larger schools . . . that any possible virtue of larger size is canceled out by the difficulties of maintaining an orderly learn-ing environment.[5]

11   The reason why size is important is because the first lesson Columbine seems to urge for schools is the need to make them genuinely user-friendly places for all students—places where everyone is welcomed into a genuine community and each student is known well by at least one adult staff member who assumes responsibility for his or her positive growth and success. The student assassins of Columbine, by contrast,

[1]Quoted in Robert M. Gladden, "The Small School Movement: A Review of the Literature," in Michelle Fine and Janis I. Somerville, eds., Small Schools, Big Imaginations (Chicago: Cross City Campaign for Urban School Reform, May 1998), p. 116.

[2]Ibid., p. 113.

[3]Kathleen Cushman, "Why Small Schools Are Essential," Horace, January 1997, p. 3.

[4]Gladden, p. 114.

[5]Kathleen Cotton, "Affective and Social Benefits of Small-Scale Schooling," ERIC Digest, Clearinghouse on Rural Education and Small Schools, Charleston, W.Va., December 1996.

were outcasts who banded together after repeated acts of rejection and humiliation by two high-status campus groups, the "jocks" and the "preps."[6] And although they and others paraded around the campus in identifiable dress (black trench coats), gave one another Nazi salutes, and submitted assignments that should have spelled danger (videos on killing, poetry about death, violence-filled essays), no single faculty member was in a position to put the picture together, and evidently none felt a personal responsibility to address these particular aberrations. Indeed, with no one responsible for seeing and acting on the whole picture with regard to these boys, the multiple signs of trouble couldn't even be tallied. And the principal could report that he had actually never heard of the "trench coat mafia" in his school.[7]

12   The situation is not atypical of comprehensive high schools of nearly 2,000 youngsters. In such schools, many students remain virtually anonymous for their entire stay. Others are singled out by their peers for harassment and humiliation, which teachers typically find beyond their province—if they become aware of it at all. It is a mistake to assume that teachers in such schools don't care or that they are indifferent to students. We are reaping the results of the way we have organized schools and divided up staff responsibilities. We have apportioned things so that teachers' primary responsibility is not for youngsters but for content and grade levels. (Only the guidance counselors could be thought to be more responsible for individuals than for content—but they too must focus primarily on accomplishing specific duties, like programming and college admissions, and with such large numbers of students that it is ludicrous to think they have time to find out what's on an individual youngster's mind.) No matter what we choose to focus on in articulating school organization— content or something else—it means that other things become less visible and may be obscured. Sometimes they are things that are centrally related to the kinds of human beings we are creating.

13   Yet there are schools today in which students are the focus and these human requirements are being met. Such schools are largely to be found in cities—which have been far more alert to potential crises than have suburbs and rural areas. But obviously, one of the clearest lessons of suburban Columbine High School is that violence is not confined to the inner city or to disadvantaged youngsters. Indeed, both at Columbine and at other schools in which multiple killings have occurred, the assassins have come from middle-class families.

14   The first requirement for making schools into communities where all youngsters are known is the one with which we began, the obvious need to make them smaller. You simply can't have much by way of genuine community in a school of several thousand. There are just too many logistical obstacles for community to emerge in schools of such scale. And so subcommunities of various sorts develop there instead—cliques, including the jocks and the nerds. In most high schools, the cliques, plus the gangs formed outside school, are left to fulfill the human need—peaking at adolescence—for close ties and peer recognition. Our failure to acknowledge and respond to this need in school organizational design is strange: we know the "herding" instinct is strongest

[6]Bruce Shapiro, "The Guns of Littleton," The Nation, 17 May 1999, p. 4.

[7]David Von Drehlem "A Model School for Some, Cliques and Taunts for Others." Washington Post National Weekly Edition, 3 May 1999, pp. 7–8.

during adolescence. Never before or afterward does it seem more important to people. Yet most schools just leave fulfillment of that instinct to chance. Columbine suggests that if we fail to acknowledge and deliberately nurture human connection in schools, youngsters will find it for themselves. And it will not always be the kind of connection and connecting that we would want for the young.

15   There is another strange feature about the way we have organized high schools. We are quite aware that adolescents are not adults—and that adolescence can be the most difficult and painful stage of growing up. Yet we defer little if at all to the immaturity of the school's "clients," placing them in the most unpleasant and demanding circumstances they may ever have to encounter: they are moved every 45 minutes all day long and are expected to shift attention and mental gears at the ringing of a bell. They can find themselves in seven or eight entirely different groupings during the day, with seven or eight different bosses (teachers—who may not know one another, either). And rules regarding their dress, speech, and comportment may be rigid in an effort to exert control over the nameless faces. As the principal of one famous high school has put it, "If God knew what high schools were going to be like, He'd have made kids differently."

16   What do high schools need to be instead? Small enough so that people can know one another. Small enough so that individuals are missed when they are absent. Small enough so that the participation of all students is needed. Small enough to permit considerable overlap in the rosters from one class to another. Small enough so that the full faculty can sit around a table together and discuss serious questions. Small enough to permit the flexibility essential to institutional responsiveness—to the special needs of individuals and to the diverse ways teachers want to teach. (In large schools, instruction must always bow to the schedule, which controls everyone's time impartially. Small schools can simply suspend customary arrangements for a day or rewrite the weekly schedule as the need arises.)

17   As we analyze and reanalyze the tragedy at Columbine High School, many people identify it as a series of events crying out for education in tolerance. They seem both right and wrong. Certainly they are correct in the notion that youngsters must be taught how to relate to others—to groups as well as to individuals. The famous line from a song in South Pacific, "You have to be taught to hate and fear," may be half right. But you also have to be taught to appreciate. Thus positive lessons on how to see and treat others must be included in formal education. But to the extent that aims determine our strategy for reaching them, it might be well to examine whether "tolerance" is really sufficient. Tolerance, after all, is the parallel in human affairs of the laws we have established to bring "justice" to the public sector. They are parallel in that both are intended to apply not primarily to friends but to strangers.

18   Toward individuals for whom we lack the personal feelings we have for friends, tolerance is supposed to be the broad general attitude. And it is an attitude of neutrality or benign indifference: you live your way, and I'll live mine. We are really just beginning to sense that it is not enough. There is much to recommend it as legal policy, but there seems less to be said for it as a general principle of living to be taught the young. There are other approaches that would probably have a lot more psychological validity. In the first place, it would help if schools modeled respect for individuals—that is, if all coming in contact with the school—students, parents, visitors—were consistently treated with courtesy and in such a fashion that their dignity remained intact. This is a

broader demand than we often construe it. It shows a lack of respect, for instance, says former resident principal at the U.S. Department of Education, Paul Schwarz, for school officials to fail to learn the names of students enrolled in a given school. It shows a lack of respect for schools to repeatedly assign youngsters to groups widely recognized to consist of "dummies" or "losers." It telegraphs another sort of lack of respect when lavatory doors can't be closed or locked—or when there is no toilet paper.

19   Somewhat more directly, youngsters must be taught about and held responsible for respecting their classmates. This is a matter first just of physical respect. Although we may think of this point as too obvious to deserve mention, a survey of one college class revealed that every single student in the class had been physically threatened by others in high school![8] But what is also necessary is respect for the individual's persona. It would be surprising if the ridiculing and the repeated rejections of the Columbine boys who became assassins were unrelated to their rage. But the kind of respect indicated will probably have to go well beyond the tolerance that schools typically state as their official position.

20   We need to deliberately cultivate in schools the qualities associated with acceptance, such as empathy and compassion. This is not to say that we want youngsters to find acceptable any behavior that a schoolmate exhibits. But it is reasonable to ask them to accept that even behaviors we might abhor are motivated by the same needs that motivate our own behavior—and that the needs, if not the manner in which we fulfill them, define the commonality among human beings.

21   Again, these traits must be both modeled by staff members and deliberately cultivated among students. The major ways of cultivating them are, first, through the personal relationships that constitute school communities, but also through what is taught—certainly in the humanities. Literature can instruct eloquently in kinship, empathy, and compassion, as can people's history, to cite just two examples. Over the years, schools have tended to focus on making youngsters more informed, more rigorously trained, more skilled. Perhaps we had better begin focusing on also making them more humane. The tragedy at Columbine would certainly recommend it.

22   As is the case with respect, there are other ways than the curriculum in which schools teach tolerance or acceptance—or their opposites. Just as it is possible for institutions to operate in ways that make them, in effect, racist or ethnically biased, sexist or homophobic, they can also operate in ways that make plain their rejection of such stances. Some small schools guard against negative institutional bias—and against the stinging comments youngsters can deliver to their peers—by deliberately generating bonds among students. Other schools content themselves with having strictly enforced rules against malicious statements. (At one small high school, for instance, one of the very few rules to which there can be no exceptions is "No dissing"—no slurs, no taunts, no jabs.) And at another institution, the discovery of humiliating graffiti on a wall of the school prompted a three-stage response: first, indignation; then a student-led march through the campus; and then the establishment of "Acceptance Month."[9]

[8]Barbara Kantrowitz and Pat Wingert, "Beyond Littleton: How Well Do You Know Your Kid?" *Newsweek*, 10 May 1999, pp. 36–40.
[9]"A Response to Hate." *Franklin and Marshall*, Spring 1999, p. 7.

23   In addition to teaching respect and tolerance or acceptance, high schools must figure out ways to meet another adolescent need: young people need contact and interaction with adults—and we seem to have forgotten how central such contact is to the purposes of education. A goodly part of what we are trying to do in educating, after all, is to sell youngsters the adult world—to initiate them into its perspectives and cultivate appreciation for what it values. But we've been trying to do so on an absolute minimum of personal contact. And as sociologist James Coleman pointed out, while so-called disadvantaged youngsters may be deprived of this "social capital" because their parents lack it, middle-class and affluent youngsters are often just as deprived of it because their parents don't spend the time to share it with them.[10]

24   In high schools we try to dole out this precious capital in packages called "courses." And we do so in ways that reduce interaction demands on adults: one teacher is expected to lay it out for 30 students at a time, with minimal or no out-of-class interaction with most of them. But youngsters need to talk to adults, and education might work a lot more effectively for many more of them if we built more interaction into the equation. You simply can't manage it when a teacher is responsible for 150 students. This hardly suffices for knowledge transmission, let alone individualized instruction. Small schools manage to build in interaction in a number of ways—for example, with the advisories described below; in assessment procedures wherein a group of adults confer with a student over his or her work; in mentorship programs that strive to generate long-term, significant connections between one adult and one youngster; and in joint-inquiry projects that cast students and teachers as co-researchers.[11]

25   Even socially adept adolescents are often lonely. They need adults who will talk and listen to them. Moreover, they need to feel that they are being taken seriously by an adult. Today's circumstances honor well adolescents' desire to establish distance between themselves and those adults to whom they've always been closest. It fails the paradoxical need, however, to interact with other adults, to test ideas on them, to see what earns the approval of a respected adult confidante and what doesn't fly.

26   So how can we accommodate all of these needs and imperatives? What must we do to shift the sights of comprehensive high schools so that concerns such as these—the teaching of acceptance and respect, the provision of cross-generational interaction— can become prominent in their organization and programs? Some changes will certainly be required. First, we would have to set out to make high schools much smaller. Enrollments would not exceed 700 or 800 if we were serious. It wouldn't have to mean new buildings. But it would have to mean reorganization to the extent of breaking down an existing high school of 3,000 into perhaps five or six separate autonomous schools, each with its own faculty and students and its own separate program. It's not impossible, and in fact it is being done in a number of cities. But it takes some venturesome and courageous leadership to redefine school organization this way.

[10]James S. Coleman and Thomas Hoffer, *Public and Private High Schools: The Impact of Communities* (New York: Basic Books, 1987).

[11]See, for example, Mary Anne Raywid, "Central Park East Secondary School: The Anatomy of Success," *Journal of Education for Students Placed at Risk*, April 1999, pp. 131–51; and idem. "A School That Really Works: Urban Academy," *Journal of Negro Education*, Winter 1994, pp. 93–110.

27   But small is not enough. It is possible to cut high schools down to enrollments of 400 or 500 and then try to operate mini-comprehensive high schools! To avoid this, schools must be reorganized to display alternative priorities and virtues. If the school is to be arranged to make the positive development of each youngster paramount, quite a reshuffling of roles and responsibilities will be necessary.

28   The second requirement for making schools into communities is to find some equitable way to assemble students (and teachers) into groups in which genuine community can be launched and sustained. Routine assignment practices won't work because they don't produce groupings in which people have enough in common to generate community. We've tried age grouping in schools and ability grouping. Neither of these has yielded enough commonality for community, and ability grouping has proved highly inequitable as well. So why not try interests as the basis for grouping? Why not let teachers who share an interest—in the arts, or in the sea, or in sports, or in critical thinking—band together to offer a program that will attract students with similar interests? It doesn't mean that the school will teach only the content connected with the arts or the sea or with sports or thinking. Every youngster needs and should have a full curriculum. But it does mean that the sea or sports will provide the context in which as much of the rest of the curriculum as possible is presented.

29   This way, what calls the group into being—on the part of teachers as well as students—is a shared interest or concern. This interest becomes the nucleus around which a school community can be based. It's not enough to ground a community, but it's a start—as well as an acknowledgment of the obvious truth that a real community is unlikely to emerge from just any collection of human beings that chance brings together. For instance, teachers who disagree fundamentally on what education is about and what its top priorities should be cannot arrive at a very viable professional community. Youngsters who share few common interests or concerns aren't very likely to bond into a community of learners. To fail to acknowledge this (as we schoolpeople often do) is to close one's eyes to the way the world is.

30   The third requirement for making schools into communities is the recognition that it takes deliberate effort. It won't just happen by itself, even in a small school. In addition to encouraging common and generally shared pursuits, effective small schools accomplish this goal by organizing carefully hewn cooperative learning activities, community-building activities involving self-disclosure, and—especially for severely alienated students—collective problem-solving events.

31   A concern to establish community also requires seeing students quite differently. Teachers cannot be content with dealing with their students as one-dimensional, exclusively academic creatures. They must be concerned with them as multifaceted human beings. They must commit to aiding development of multiple sorts—cognitive, social, emotional, moral, as well as academic—and this requires close-up knowledge of individuals. There are a number of approaches that can be used to stimulate the sharing among students that community must involve. For instance, students might remain with a single group for most of their classes and perhaps for several years. Arrangements are needed to generate close ties with at least one adult and one group of peers. In many schools, the practice chosen consists of advisory groups of perhaps 12 to 15 youngsters who may meet daily with the same advisor over a period of several years.

There may also be out-of-school, weekend advisory activities, such as visits to college campuses. The advisor is charged with becoming a source of assistance and advice, an advocate, an adult friend, and a liaison between home and school.

32   Successful small schools conceive of and pursue community in a variety of ways. One principal summarizes his school's philosophy as "There are no strangers here."[12] Another educator casts the ideal climate in terms of the "four R's": mutual respect among all the school's constituents, reciprocity among students and between them and adults, responsibility to self and the greater community, and a reverence for place and its connections.[13] And as still others see it, establishing school community is a matter of deliberately fostering interdependence and interconnectedness among and between faculty members and students.[14] But despite the different ways of expressing it, what lies at the core for all is a "personalization" that large schools, and even some small ones, lack an awareness of, and willingness to acknowledge and work with, human beings in full dimension, not just as students perceived in cohorts or batches to be processed (e.g., sophomores, the second-period German 2 class, gifted and talented, hyperactive). Shifting to this perspective is not easy. But unless and until we do, we may well be headed for more tragedy and heartbreak. Until we make schools engaging learning communities whose members value those communities and feel welcome within them, we are right to think that the next Columbine could happen anywhere.

POST-READING QUESTIONS

CONTENT

1. Why do Raywid and Oshiyama claim that violence is more likely to occur in large schools? What do you think?

2. How does a school's organization affect students and, in turn, their behavior? Explain.

3. What is the "herding instinct," and how is it relevant to the issue of school violence?

4. How do the writers define "tolerance"? Do you agree that tolerance as they define it is not enough to solve the problem of school violence? Explain.

5. What kinds of disrespect do the writers say schools themselves are guilty of? Do you agree? Give examples to support your ideas.

6. Why, according to Raywid and Oshiyama, should students be taught respect, compassion, and empathy toward their peers? What do you think?

7. Why is contact with adults important for student development in school?

[12]Paul Schwarz, "New Models of Educational Leadership," speech presented at the Outreach College, University of Honolulu, 30 July 1998.

[13]Libby Oshiyama, "A Response to Columbine: What We Must Do," speech presented to the Rotary Club of Honolulu, 3 May 1999.

[14]Gregory A. Smith, ed., Public Schools that Work: Creating Community (New York: Routledge, 1993).

8. What solutions do the writers offer to lessen violence on campus? Which of these do you think would work best? Explain.

9. What is the role of the community as Raywid and Oshiyama define it in terms of schools?

STYLE AND STRUCTURE

10. What is the tone of the article? What words and ideas, in particular, set this tone?

11. What assumptions do the writers make about high school students? Do you think the writers are correct in these assumptions? Explain.

12. What message are the writers primarily communicating? Are they convincing? Why or why not?

13. What examples do you think best represent the problem that Raywid and Oshiyama are exploring? What types of examples would have helped the writers present their point better?

14. Who are Raywid and Oshiyama writing for? To what extent does their language include or exclude you? Explain and give examples.

15. Do the writers do justice to the topic of school violence, or do they make it seem more or less serious than it is? Explain.

CRITICAL THINKING AND ANALYSIS

DISCUSSION QUESTIONS

16. How big a problem is violence in schools today? Explain and give examples.

17. To what extent do you think increased adult contact at school could lessen on-campus violence? Explain.

WRITING ASSIGNMENTS

18. How significant a role do "rejection and humiliation" play in causing campus violence? Write at least a paragraph explaining how great "rejection and humiliation" are in causing campus violence, citing the text and giving examples from your experience and observations.

19. The writers claim "positive lessons on how to see and treat others must be included in formal education" in order to prevent school violence. At what point in their education, if ever, do you think students need to be taught compassion and respect, and by whom? Write a few paragraphs in response to this question.

20. The writers claim that, "if we fail to acknowledge and deliberately nurture human connection in schools, youngsters will find it for themselves." Are they right? Write a few paragraphs in which you discuss the importance of human connection to high school-aged youth, citing the essay and your own life for support.

21. Raywid and Oshiyama write "these traits [empathy and compassion] must be both modeled by staff members" in high school in order for students to treat fellow students accordingly. Write a paragraph or two in which you explain whether or not staff role models make a significant difference in terms of how students treat each other. Cite the text and your life for support.

VOCABULARY DEVELOPMENT

22. As you did in question 10, examine the tone of the article, this time emphasizing the words you looked up for the Vocabulary Preview. In a short paragraph, explain how several of the words in the Preview help communicate, or detract from, the tone you identified in question 10.

GROUP ACTIVITIES

23. Poll your classmates to find out how violent their high schools were. Taking into account school size, socio-economic make-up, and location, draw conclusions about what causes school violence. Present your findings to the class in an open-forum setting.

24. Dividing the class into two groups, debate the issue of whether greater school supervision and discipline would decrease violence on campus.

Aria: A Memoir of Bilingual Education

Richard Rodriguez

Richard Rodriguez received his B.A. from Stanford and graduate degrees from Columbia and the University of California at Berkeley. He is currently an educational consultant and a free-lance writer whose work has appeared in *Harper's, Saturday Review, American Scholar,* and *The New York Times.* Born to Mexican immigrants, Rodriguez recalls how, despite bilingual education advocates' good intentions to make non-native English speakers feel comfortable in school by speaking their "home" language, they actually hinder their charges' progress in becoming Americans.

Pre-reading Questions

Freewrite for five to ten minutes in response to the following questions:
What language(s) do you speak? Do you speak exactly the same way with all groups you know—friends, family, colleagues, employers, teachers? How does your language change from group to group? Why do you think it changes? Explain and give examples of the different types of language you use with each group.

Vocabulary Preview

Vocabulary Words:		
• intimidated	• incongruity	• decadent
• consoling	• accentuated	• disconcerting
• guttural	• eccentrically	• devoid
• feigned	• bemused	• glibly
• cloistered	• effusive	• idioms
• diffident	• assimilated	• obliterated

Look up at least ten of the words above and write a paragraph explaining the type of message you expect from the essay and how these words foster that expectation.

1   I remember, to start with, that day in Sacramento, in a California now nearly thirty years past, when I first entered a classroom—able to understand about fifty stray English words. The third of four children, I had been preceded by my older brother and sister to a neighborhood Roman Catholic school. But neither of them had revealed very much about their classroom experiences. They left each morning and returned each afternoon, always together, speaking Spanish as they climbed the five steps to the porch. And their mysterious books, wrapped in brown shopping-bag paper, remained on the table next to the door, closed firmly behind them.

2   An accident of geography sent me to a school where all my classmates were white and many were the children of doctors and lawyers and business executives. On that first day of school, my classmates must certainly have been uneasy to find themselves

apart from their families, in the first institution of their lives. But I was astonished. I was fated to be the "problem student" in class.

3   The nun said, in a friendly but oddly impersonal voice: "Boys and girls, this is Richard Rodriguez." (I heard her sound it out: *Rich-heard Road-ree-guess.*) It was the first time I had heard anyone say my name in English. "Richard," the nun repeated more slowly, writing my name down in her book. Quickly I turned to see my mother's face dissolve in a watery blur behind the pebbled-glass door.

4   Now, many years later, I hear of something called "bilingual education"—a scheme proposed in the late 1960s by Hispanic-American social activists, later endorsed by a congressional vote. It is a program that seeks to permit non-English-speaking children (many from lower-class homes) to use their "family language" as the language of school. Such, at least, is the aim its supporters announce. I hear them, and am forced to say no: It is not possible for a child, any child, ever to use his family's language in school. Not to understand this is to misunderstand the public uses of schooling and to trivialize the nature of intimate life.

5   Memory teaches me what I know of these matters. The boy reminds the adult. I was a bilingual child, but of a certain kind: "socially disadvantaged," the son of working-class parents, both Mexican immigrants.

6   In the early years of my boyhood, my parents coped very well in America. My father had steady work. My mother managed at home. They were nobody's victims. When we moved to a house many blocks from the Mexican-American section of town, they were not intimidated by those two or three neighbors who initially tried to make us unwelcome. ("Keep your brats away from my sidewalk!") But despite all they achieved, or perhaps because they had so much to achieve, they lacked any deep feeling of ease, of belonging in public. They regarded the people at work or in crowds as being very distant from us. Those were the others, *los gringos.* That term was interchangeable in their speech with another, even more telling: *los americanos.*

7   I grew up in a house where the only regular guests were my relations. On a certain day, enormous families of relatives would visit us, and there would be so many people that the noise and the bodies would spill out to the backyard and onto the front porch. Then for weeks no one would come. (If the doorbell rang, it was usually a salesman.) Our house stood apart—gaudy yellow in a row of white bungalows. We were the people with the noisy dog, the people who raised chickens. We were the foreigners on the block. A few neighbors would smile and wave at us. We waved back. But until I was seven years old, I did not know the name of the old couple living next door or the names of the kids living across the street.

8   In public, my father and mother spoke a hesitant, accented, and not always grammatical English. And then they would have to strain, their bodies tense, to catch the sense of what was rapidly said by *los gringos.* At home, they returned to Spanish. The language of their Mexican past sounded in counterpoint to the English spoken in public. The words would come quickly, with ease. Conveyed through those sounds was the pleasing, soothing, consoling reminder that one was at home.

9   During those years when I was first learning to speak, my mother and father addressed me only in Spanish; in Spanish I learned to reply. By contrast, English (*inglés*) was the language I came to associate with gringos, rarely heard in the house. I learned

my first words of English overhearing my parents speaking to strangers. At six years of age, I knew just enough words for my mother to trust me on errands to stores one block away—but no more.

10   I was then a listening child, careful to hear the very different sounds of Spanish and English. Wide-eyed with hearing, I'd listen to sounds more than to words. First, there were English (gringo) sounds. So many words still were unknown to me that when the butcher or the lady at the drugstore said something, exotic polysyllabic sounds would bloom in the midst of their sentences. Often the speech of people in public seemed to me very loud, booming with confidence. The man behind the counter would literally ask, "What can I do for you?" But by being so firm and clear, the sound of his voice said that he was a gringo; he belonged in public society. There were also the high, nasal notes of middle-class American speech—which I rarely am conscious of hearing today because I hear them so often, but could not stop hearing when I was a boy. Crowds at Safeway or at bus stops were noisy with the birdlike sounds of *los gringos.* I'd move away from them all—all the chirping chatter above me.

11   My own sounds I was unable to hear, but I knew that I spoke English poorly. My words could not extend to form complete thoughts. And the words I did speak I didn't know well enough to make distinct sounds. (Listeners would usually lower their heads to hear better what I was trying to say.) But it was one thing for *me* to speak English with difficulty; it was more troubling to hear my parents speaking in public: their high-whining vowels and guttural consonants; their sentences that got stuck with "eh" and "ah" sounds; the confused syntax; the hesitant rhythm of sounds so different from the way gringos spoke. I'd notice, moreover, that my parents' voices were softer than those of the gringos we would meet.

12   I am tempted to say now that none of this mattered. (In adulthood I am embarrassed by childhood fears.) And, in a way, it didn't matter very much that my parents could not speak English with ease. Their linguistic difficulties had no serious consequences. My mother and father made themselves understood at the county hospital clinic and at government offices. And yet, in another way, it mattered very much. It was unsettling to hear my parents struggle with English. Hearing them, I'd grow nervous, and my clutching trust in their protection and power would be weakened.

13   There were many times like the night at a brightly lit gasoline station (a blaring white memory) when I stood uneasily hearing my father talk to a teenage attendant. I do not remember what they were saying, but I cannot forget the sounds my father made as he spoke. At one point his words slid together to form one long word—sounds as confused as the threads of blue and green oil in the puddle next to my shoes. His voice rushed through what he had left to say. Toward the end, he reached falsetto notes, appealing to his listener's understanding. I looked away at the lights of passing automobiles. I tried not to hear any more. But I heard only too well the attendant's reply, his calm, easy tones. Shortly afterward, headed for home, I shivered when my father put his hand on my shoulder. The very first chance that I got, I evaded his grasp and ran on ahead into the dark, skipping with feigned boyish exuberance.

14   But then there was Spanish: *español,* the language rarely heard away from the house; *español,* the language which seemed to me therefore a private language, my family's language. To hear its sounds was to feel myself specially recognized as one of

the family, apart from *los otros.* ["the others"]. A simple remark, an inconsequential comment could convey that assurance. My parents would say something to me and I would feel embraced by the sounds of their words. Those sounds said: *I am speaking with ease in Spanish. I am addressing you in words I never use with* los gringos. *I recognize you as someone special, close, like no one outside. You belong with us. In the family. Ricardo.*

15   At the age of six, well past the time when most middle-class children no longer notice the difference between sounds uttered at home and words spoken in public, I had a different experience. I lived in a world compounded of sounds. I was a child longer than most. I lived in a magical world, surrounded by sounds both pleasing and fearful. I shared with my family a language enchantingly private—different from that used in the city around us.

16   Just opening or closing the screen door behind me was an important experience. I'd rarely leave home all alone or without feeling reluctance. Walking down the sidewalk, under the canopy of tall trees, I'd warily notice the (suddenly) silent neighborhood kids who stood warily watching me. Nervously, I'd arrive at the grocery store to hear there the sounds of the gringo, reminding me that in this so-big world I was a foreigner. But if leaving home was never routine, neither was coming back. Walking toward our house, climbing the steps from the sidewalk, in summer when the front door was open, I'd hear voices beyond the screen door talking in Spanish. For a second or two I'd stay, linger there listening. Smiling, I'd hear my mother call out, saying in Spanish, "Is that you, Richard?" Those were her words, but all the while her sounds would assure me: *You are home now. Come closer inside. With us. "Sí,"* I'd reply.

17   Once more inside the house, I would resume my place in the family. The sounds would grow harder to hear. Once more at home, I would grow less conscious of them. It required, however, no more than the blurt of the doorbell to alert me all over again to listen to sounds. The house would turn instantly quiet while my mother went to the door. I'd hear her hard English sounds. I'd wait to hear her voice turn to soft-sounding Spanish, which assured me, as surely as did the clicking tongue of the lock on the door, that the stranger was gone.

18   Plainly it is not healthy to hear such sounds so often. It is not healthy to distinguish public from private sounds so easily. I remained cloistered by sounds, timid and shy in public, too dependent on the voices at home. And yet I was a very happy child when I was at home. I remember many nights when my father would come back from work, and I'd hear him call out to my mother in Spanish, sounding relieved. In Spanish, his voice would sound the light and free notes that he never could manage in English. Some nights I'd jump up just hearing his voice. My brother and I would come running into the room where he was with our mother. Our laughing (so deep was the pleasure!) became screaming. Like others who feel the pain of public alienation, we transformed the knowledge of our public separateness into a consoling reminder of our intimacy. Excited, our voices joined in a celebration of sounds. *We are speaking now the way we never speak out in public—we are together,* the sounds told me. Some nights no one seemed willing to loosen the hold that sounds had on us. At dinner we invented new words that sounded Spanish, but made sense only to us. We pieced together new words by taking, say, an English verb and giving it Spanish endings. My

mother's instructions at bedtime would be lacquered with mock-urgent tones. Or a word like *sí,* sounded in several notes, would convey added measures of feeling. Tongues lingered around the edges of words, especially fat vowels. And we happily sounded that military drum roll, the twirling roar of the Spanish *r.* Family language, my family's sounds: the voices of my parents and sisters and brother. Their voices insisting: *You belong here. We are family members. Related. Special to one another. Listen!* Voices singing and sighing, rising and straining, then surging, teeming with pleasure which burst syllables into fragments of laughter. At times it seemed there was steady quiet only when, from another room, the rustling whispers of my parents faded and I edged closer to sleep.

19   Supporters of bilingual education imply today that students like me miss a great deal by not being taught in their family's language. What they seem not to recognize is that, as a socially disadvantaged child, I regarded Spanish as a private language. It was a ghetto language that deepened and strengthened my feeling of public separateness. What I needed to learn in school was that I had the right, and the obligation, to speak the public language. The odd truth is that my first-grade classmates could have become bilingual, in the conventional sense of the word, more easily than I. Had they been taught early (as upper middle-class children often are taught) a "second language" like Spanish or French, they could have regarded it simply as another public language. In my case, such bilingualism could not have been so quickly achieved. What I did not believe was that I could speak a single public language.

20   Without question, it would have pleased me to have heard my teachers address me in Spanish when I entered the classroom. I would have felt much less afraid. I would have imagined that my instructors were somehow "related" to me; I would indeed have heard their Spanish as my family's language. I would have trusted them and responded with ease. But I would have delayed—postponed for how long?—having to learn the language of public society. I would have evaded—and for how long?—learning the great lesson of school: that I had a public identity.

21   Fortunately, my teachers were unsentimental about their responsibility. What they understood was that I needed to speak public English. So their voices would search me out, asking me questions. Each time I heard them I'd look up in surprise to see a nun's face frowning at me. I'd mumble, not really meaning to answer. The nun would persist. "Richard, stand up. Don't look at the floor. Speak up. Speak to the entire class, not just to me!" But I couldn't believe English could be my language to use. (In part, I did not want to believe it.) I continued to mumble. I resisted the teacher's demands. (Did I somehow suspect that once I learned this public language my family life would be changed?) Silent, waiting for the bell to sound, I remained dazed, diffident, afraid.

22   Because I wrongly imagined that English was intrinsically a public language and Spanish was intrinsically private, I easily noted the difference between classroom language and the language of home. At school, words were directed to a general audience of listeners. ("Boys and girls . . .") Words were meaningfully ordered. And the point was not self-expression alone, but to make oneself understood by many others. The teacher quizzed: "Boys and girls, why do we use that word in this sentence? Could we think of a better word to use there? Would the sentence change its meaning if the words

were differently arranged? Isn't there a better way of saying much the same thing?" (I couldn't say. I wouldn't try to say.)

23   Three months passed. Five. A half year. Unsmiling, ever watchful, my teachers noted my silence. They began to connect my behavior with the slow progress my brother and sisters were making. Until, one Saturday morning, three nuns arrived at the house to talk to our parents. Stiffly they sat on the blue living-room sofa. From the doorway of another room, spying on the visitors, I noted the incongruity, the clash of two worlds, the faces and voices of school intruding upon the familiar setting of home. I overheard one voice gently wondering, "Do your children speak only Spanish at home, Mrs. Rodriguez?" While another voice added, "That Richard especially seems so timid and shy."

24   *That Rich-heard!*

25   With great tact, the visitors continued, "Is it possible for you and your husband to encourage your children to practice their English when they are home?" Of course my parents complied. What would they not do for their children's well-being? And how could they question the Church's authority which those women represented? In an instant they agreed to give up the language (the sounds) which had revealed and accentuated our family's closeness. The moment after the visitors left, the change was observed. *"Ahora* ['now'], speak to us only *en inglés* ['in English']," my father and mother told us.

26   At first, it seemed a kind of game. After dinner each night, the family gathered together to practice "our" English. It was still then *inglés,* a language foreign to us, so we felt drawn to it as strangers. Laughing, we would try to define words we could not pronounce. We played with strange English sounds, often overanglicizing our pronunciations. And we filled the smiling gaps of our sentences with familiar Spanish sounds. But that was cheating, somebody shouted, and everyone laughed.

27   In school, meanwhile, like my brothers and sisters, I was required to attend a daily tutoring session. I needed a full year of this special work. I also needed my teachers to keep my attention from straying in class by calling out, *"Rich-heard!"*—their English voices slowly loosening the ties to my other name, with its three notes, *Ri-car-do.* Most of all, I needed to hear my mother and father speak to me in a moment of seriousness in "broken"—suddenly heartbreaking—English. This scene was inevitable. One Saturday morning I entered the kitchen where my parents were talking, but I did not realize that they were talking in Spanish until, the moment they saw me, their voices changed and they began speaking English. The gringo sounds they uttered startled me. Pushed me away. In that moment of trivial misunderstanding and profound insight, I felt my throat twisted by unsounded grief. I simply turned and left the room. But I had no place to escape to where I could grieve in Spanish. My brother and sisters were speaking English in another part of the house.

28   Again and again in the days following, as I grew increasingly angry, I was obliged to hear my mother and father encouraging me: "Speak to us *en inglés.*" Only then did I determine to learn classroom English. Thus, sometime afterward it happened: one day in school, I raised my hand to volunteer an answer to a question. I spoke out in a loud voice and I did not think it remarkable when the entire class understood. That day I moved very far from being the disadvantaged child I had been only days earlier. Taken hold at last was the belief, the calming assurance, that I *belonged* in public.

29   Shortly after, I stopped hearing the high, troubling sounds of *los gringos*. A more and more confident speaker of English, I didn't listen to how strangers sounded when they talked to me. With so many English-speaking people around me, I no longer heard American accents. Conversations quickened. Listening to persons whose voices sounded eccentrically pitched, I might note their sounds for a few seconds, but then I'd concentrate on what they were saying. Now when I heard someone's tone of voice—angry or questioning or sarcastic or happy or sad—I didn't distinguish it from the words it expressed. Sound and word were thus tightly wedded. At the end of each day I was often bemused, and always relieved, to realize how "soundless," though crowded with words, my day in public had been. An eight-year-old boy, I finally came to accept what had been technically true since my birth: I was an American citizen.

30   But diminished by then was the special feeling of closeness at home. Gone was the desperate, urgent, intense feeling of being at home among those with whom I felt intimate. Our family remained a loving family, but one greatly changed. We were no longer so close, no longer bound tightly together by the knowledge of our separateness from *los gringos*. Neither my older brother nor my sisters rushed home after school any more. Nor did I. When I arrived home, often there would be neighborhood kids in the house. Or the house would be empty of sounds.

31   Following the dramatic Americanization of their children, even my parents grew more publicly confident—especially my mother. First she learned the names of all the people on the block. Then she decided we needed to have a telephone in our house. My father, for his part, continued to use the word gringo, but it was no longer charged with bitterness or distrust. Stripped of any emotional content, the word simply became a name for those Americans not of Hispanic descent. Hearing him, sometimes, I wasn't sure if he was pronouncing the Spanish word *gringo,* or saying gringo in English.

32   There was a new silence at home. As we children learned more and more English, we shared fewer and fewer words with our parents. Sentences needed to be spoken slowly when one of us addressed our mother or father. Often the parent wouldn't understand. The child would need to repeat himself. Still the parent misunderstood. The young voice, frustrated, would end up saying, "Never mind"—the subject was closed. Dinners would be noisy with the clinking of knives and forks against dishes. My mother would smile softly between her remarks; my father, at the other end of the table, would chew and chew his food while he stared over the heads of his children.

33   My mother! My father! After English became my primary language, I no longer knew what words to use in addressing my parents. The old Spanish words (those tender accents of sound) I had earlier used—*mamá* and *papá*—I couldn't use any more. They would have been all-too-painful reminders of how much had changed in my life. On the other hand, the words I heard neighborhood kids call their parents seemed equally unsatisfactory. "Mother" and "father," "ma," "papa," "pa," "dad," "pop" (how I hated the all-American sound of that last word)—all these I felt were unsuitable terms of address for *my* parents. As a result, I never used them at home. Whenever I'd speak to my parents, I would try to get their attention by looking at them. In public conversations, I'd refer to them as my "parents" or my "mother" and "father."

34   My mother and father, for their part, responded differently, as their children spoke to them less. My mother grew restless, seemed troubled and anxious at the scarceness of words exchanged in the house. She would question me about my day when I came

home from school. She smiled at my small talk. She pried at the edges of my sentences to get me to say something more. ("What . . . ?") She'd join conversations she over-heard, but her intrusions often stopped her children's talking. By contrast, my father seemed to grow reconciled to the new quiet. Though his English somewhat improved, he tended more and more to retire into silence. At dinner he spoke very little. One night his children and even his wife helplessly giggled at his garbled English pronunciation of the Catholic "Grace Before Meals." Thereafter he made his wife recite the prayer at the start of each meal, even on formal occasions when there were guests in the house.

35   Hers became the public voice of the family. On official business it was she, not my father, who would usually talk to strangers on the phone or in stores. We children grew so accustomed to his silence that years later we would routinely refer to his "shyness." (My mother often tried to explain: both of his parents died when he was eight. He was raised by an uncle who treated him as little more than a menial servant. He was never encouraged to speak. He grew up alone—a man of few words.) But I realized my father was not shy whenever I'd watch him speaking Spanish with relatives. Using Spanish, he was quickly effusive. Especially when talking with other men, his voice would spark, flicker, flare alive with varied sounds. In Spanish he expressed ideas and feel-ings he rarely revealed when speaking English. With firm Spanish sounds he conveyed a confidence and authority that English would never allow him.

36   The silence at home, however, was not simply the result of fewer words passing be-tween parents and children. More profound for me was the silence created by my inatten-tion to sounds. At about the time I no longer bothered to listen with care to the sounds of English in public, I grew careless about listening to the sounds made by the family when they spoke. Most of the time I would hear someone speaking at home and didn't distinguish his sounds from the words people uttered in public. I didn't even pay much attention to my parents' accented and ungrammatical speech—at least not at home. Only when I was with them in public would I become alert to their accents. But even then their sounds caused me less and less concern. For I was growing increasingly confident of my own public identity.

37   I would have been happier about my public success had I not recalled sometimes, what it had been like earlier, when my family conveyed its intimacy through a set of con-veniently private sounds. Sometimes in public, hearing a stranger, I'd hark back to my lost past. A Mexican farm worker approached me one day downtown. He wanted directions to some place. *"Hijito* ['little boy, little son'], . . ." he said. And his voice stirred old longings. Another time I was standing beside my mother in the visiting room of a Carmelite convent, before the dense screen which rendered the nuns shadowy figures. I heard several of them speaking Spanish in their busy, singsong, overlapping voices, assuring my mother that, yes, yes, we were remembered, all our family was remembered, in their prayers. Those voices echoed faraway family sounds. Another day a dark-faced old woman touched my shoulder lightly to steady herself as she boarded a bus. She murmured something to me I couldn't quite comprehend. Her Spanish voice came near, like the face of a never-before-seen relative in the instant before I was kissed. That voice, like so many of the Spanish voices I'd hear in public, recalled the golden age of my childhood.

38   Bilingual educators say today that children lose a degree of "individuality" by be-coming assimilated into public society. (Bilingual schooling is a program popularized in the seventies, that decade when middle-class "ethnics" began to resist the process of

assimilation—the "American melting pot.") But the bilingualists oversimplify when they scorn the value and necessity of assimilation. They do not seem to realize that a person is individualized in two ways. So they do not realize that, while one suffers a diminished sense of *private* individuality by being assimilated into public society, such assimilation makes possible the achievement of *public* individuality.

39   Simplistically again, the bilingualists insist that a student should be reminded of his difference from others in mass society, of his "heritage." But they equate mere separateness with individuality. The fact is that only in private—with intimates—is separateness from the crowd a prerequisite for individuality; an intimate "tells" me that I am unique, unlike all others, apart from the crowd. In public, by contrast, full individuality is achieved, paradoxically, by those who are able to consider themselves members of the crowd. Thus it happened for me. Only when I was able to think of myself as an American, no longer an alien in gringo society, could I seek the rights and opportunities necessary for full public individuality. The social and political advantages I enjoy as a man began on the day I came to believe that my name is indeed *Rich-heard Road-ree-guess.* It is true that my public society today is often impersonal; in fact, my public society is usually mass society. But despite the anonymity of the crowd, and despite the fact that the individuality I achieve in public is often tenuous—because it depends on my being one in a crowd—I celebrate the day I acquired my new name. Those middle-class ethnics who scorn assimilation seem to me filled with decadent self-pity, obsessed by the burden of public life. Dangerously, they romanticize public separateness and trivialize the dilemma of those who are truly socially disadvantaged.

40   If I rehearse here the changes in my private life after my Americanization, it is finally to emphasize a public gain. The loss implies the gain. The house I returned to each afternoon was quiet. Intimate sounds no longer greeted me at the door. Inside there were other noises. The telephone rang. Neighborhood kids ran past the door of the bedroom where I was reading my schoolbooks—covered with brown shopping-bag paper. Once I learned the public language, it would never again be easy for me to hear intimate family voices. More and more of my day was spent hearing words, not sounds. But that may only be a way of saying that on the day I raised my hand in class and spoke loudly to an entire roomful of faces, my childhood started to end.

41   I grew up the victim of a disconcerting confusion. As I became fluent in English, I could no longer speak Spanish with confidence. I continued to understand spoken Spanish, and in high school I learned how to read and write Spanish. But for many years I could not pronounce it. A powerful guilt blocked my spoken words; an essential glue was missing whenever I would try to connect words to form sentences. I would be unable to break a barrier of sound, to speak freely. I would speak, or try to speak, Spanish, and I would manage to utter halting, hiccuping sounds which betrayed my unease. (Even today I speak Spanish very slowly, at best.)

42   When relatives and Spanish-speaking friends of my parents came to the house, my brother and sisters would usually manage to say a few words before being excused. I never managed so gracefully. Each time I'd hear myself addressed in Spanish, I couldn't respond with any success. I'd know the words I wanted to say, but I couldn't say them. I would try to speak, but everything I said seemed to me horribly anglicized. My mouth

wouldn't form the sounds right. My jaw would tremble. After a phrase or two, I'd stutter, cough up a warm, silvery sound, and stop.

43   My listeners were surprised to hear me. They'd lower their heads to grasp better what I was trying to say. They would repeat their questions in gentle, affectionate voices. But then I would answer in English. No, no, they would say, we want you to speak to us in Spanish *("en español").* But I couldn't do it. Then they would call me *pocho.* Sometimes playfully, teasing, using the tender diminutive—*mi pochito.* Sometimes not so playfully but mockingly, *pocho.* (A Spanish dictionary defines that word as an adjective meaning "colorless" or "bland." But I heard it as a noun, naming a Mexican-American who, in becoming an American, forgets his native society.) *"¡Pocho!"* my mother's best friend muttered, shaking her head. And my mother laughed, somewhere behind me. She said that her children didn't want to practice "our Spanish" after they started going to school. My mother's smiling voice made me suspect that the lady who faced me was not really angry at me. But searching her face, I couldn't find the hint of a smile.

44   Embarrassed, my parents would often need to explain their children's inability to speak fluent Spanish during those years. My mother encountered the wrath of her brother, her only brother, when he came up from Mexico one summer with his family and saw his nieces and nephews for the very first time. After listening to me, he looked away and said what a disgrace it was that my siblings and I couldn't speak Spanish, *"su propria idioma."* ("their own language"). He made that remark to my mother, but I noticed that he stared at my father.

45   One other visitor from those years I clearly remember: a long-time friend of my father from San Francisco who came to stay with us for several days in late August. He took great interest in me after he realized that I couldn't answer his questions in Spanish. He would grab me, as I started to leave the kitchen. He would ask me something. Usually he wouldn't bother to wait for my mumbled response. Knowingly, he'd murmur, *"¿Ay pocho, pocho, dónde vas?"* ("Pocho, where are you going?"). And he would press his thumbs into the upper part of my arms, making me squirm with pain. Dumbly I'd stand there, waiting for his wife to notice us and call him off with a benign smile. I'd giggle, hoping to deflate the tension between us, pretending that I hadn't seen the glittering scorn in his glance.

46   I recount such incidents only because they suggest the fierce power that Spanish had over many people I met at home, how strongly Spanish was associated with closeness. Most of the people who called me a *pocho* could have spoken English to me, but many wouldn't. They seemed to think that Spanish was the only language we could use among ourselves, that Spanish alone permitted our association. (Such persons are always vulnerable to the ghetto merchant and the politician who have learned the value of speaking their clients' "family language" so as to gain immediate trust.) For my part, I felt that by learning English I had somehow committed a sin of betrayal. But betrayal against whom? Not exactly against the visitors to the house. Rather, I felt I had betrayed my immediate family. I knew that my parents had encouraged me to learn English. I knew that I had turned to English with angry reluctance. But once I spoke English with ease, I came to feel guilty. I sensed that I had broken the spell of intimacy which had once held the family so close together. It was this original sin against my family that I recalled whenever anyone addressed me in Spanish and I responded, confounded.

47   Yet even during those years of guilt, I was coming to grasp certain consoling truths about language and intimacy—truths that I learned gradually. Once, I remember playing with a friend in the backyard when my grandmother appeared at the window. Her face was stern with suspicion when she saw the boy (the *gringo* boy) I was with. She called out to me in Spanish, sounding the whistle of her ancient breath. My companion looked up and watched her intently as she lowered the window and moved (still visible) behind the light curtain, watching us both. He wanted to know what she had said. I started to tell him, to translate her Spanish words into English. The problem was, however, that though I knew how to translate exactly what she had told me, I realized that any translation would distort the deepest meaning of her message; it had been directed only to me. This message of intimacy could never be translated because it did not lie in the actual words she had used but passed through them. So any translation would have seemed wrong; the words would have been stripped of an essential meaning. Finally I decided not to tell my friend anything—just that I didn't hear all she had said.

48   This insight was unfolded in time. As I made more and more friends outside my house, I began to recognize intimate messages spoken in English in a close friend's confidential tone or secretive whisper. Even more remarkable were those instances when, apparently for no special reason, I'd become conscious of the fact that my companion was speaking *only to me*. I'd marvel then, just hearing his voice. It was a stunning event to be able to break through the barrier of public silence, to be able to hear the voice of the other, to realize that it was directed just to me. After such moments of intimacy outside the house, I began to trust what I heard intimately conveyed through my family's English. Voices at home at last punctured sad confusion. I'd hear myself addressed as an intimate—in English. Such moments were never as raucous with sound as in past times, when we had used our "private" Spanish. (Our English-sounding house was never to be as noisy as our Spanish-sounding house had been.) Intimate moments were usually moments of soft sound. My mother would be ironing in the dining room while I did my homework nearby. She would look over at me, smile, and her voice sounded to tell me that I was her son. *Richard.*

49   Intimacy thus continued at home; intimacy was not stilled by English. Though there were fewer occasions for it—a change in my life that I would never forget—there were also times when I sensed the deep truth about language and intimacy: *Intimacy is not created by a particular language; it is created by intimates.* Thus the great change in my life was not linguistic but social. If, after becoming a successful student, I no longer heard intimate voices as often as I had earlier, it was not because I spoke English instead of Spanish. It was because I spoke public language for most of my day. I moved easily at last, a citizen in a crowded city of words.

50   As a man I spend most of my day in public, in a world largely devoid of speech sounds. So I am quickly attracted by the glamorous quality of certain alien voices. I still am gripped with excitement when someone passes me on the street, speaking in Spanish. I have not moved beyond the range of the nostalgic pull of those sounds. And there is something very compelling about the sounds of lower-class blacks. Of all the accented versions of English that I hear in public, I hear theirs most intently. The Japanese tourist stops me downtown to ask me a question and I inch my way past his accent to concentrate on what he is saying. The eastern European immigrant in the

neighborhood delicatessen speaks to me and, again, I do not pay much attention to his sounds, nor to the Texas accent of one of my neighbors or the Chicago accent of the woman who lives in the apartment below me. But when the ghetto black teenagers get on the city bus, I hear them. Their sounds in my society are the sounds of the outsider. Their voices annoy me for being so loud—so self-sufficient and unconcerned by my presence, but for the same reason they are glamorous: a romantic gesture against public acceptance. And as I listen to their shouted laughter, I realize my own quietness. I feel envious of them—envious of their brazen intimacy.

51   I warn myself away from such envy, however. Overhearing those teenagers, I think of the black political activists who lately have argued in favor of using black English in public schools—an argument that varies only slightly from that of foreign-language bilinguists. I have heard "radical" linguists make the point that black English is a complex and intricate version of English. And I do not doubt it. But neither do I think that black English should be a language of public instruction. What makes it inappropriate in classrooms is not something in the language itself but, rather, what lower-class speakers make of it. Just as Spanish would have been a dangerous language for me to have used at the start of my education, so black English would be a dangerous language to use in the schooling of teenagers for whom it reinforces feelings of public separateness.

52   This seems to me an obvious point to make, and yet it must be said. In recent years there have been many attempts to make the language of the alien a public language. "Bilingual education, two ways to understand . . ." television and radio commercials glibly announce. Proponents of bilingual education are careful to say that above all they want every student to acquire a good education. Their argument goes something like this: Children permitted to use their family language will not be so alienated and will be better able to match the progress of English-speaking students in the crucial first months of schooling. Increasingly confident of their ability, such children will be more inclined to apply themselves to their studies in the future. But then the bilingualists also claim another very different goal. They say that children who use their family language in school will retain a sense of their ethnic heritage and their family ties. Thus the supporters of bilingual education want it both ways. They propose bilingual schooling as a way of helping students acquire the classroom skills crucial for public success. But they likewise insist that bilingual instruction will give students a sense of their identity apart from the English-speaking public.

53   Behind this scheme gleams a bright promise for the alien child: one can become a public person while still remaining a private person. Who would not want to believe such an appealing idea? Who can be surprised that the scheme has the support of so many middle-class ethnic Americans? If the barrio or ghetto child can retain his separateness even while being publicly educated, then it is almost possible to believe that no private cost need be paid for public success. This is the consolation offered by any of the number of current bilingual programs. Consider, for example, the bilingual voter's ballot. In some American cities one can cast a ballot printed in several languages. Such a document implies that it is possible for one to exercise that most public of rights—the right to vote—while still keeping oneself apart, unassimilated in public life.

54   It is not enough to say that such schemes are foolish and certainly doomed. Middle-class supporters of public bilingualism toy with the confusion of those Americans who cannot speak standard English as well as they do. Moreover, bilingual enthusiasts sin

against intimacy. A Hispanic-American tells me, "I will never give up my family language," and he clutches a group of words as though they were the source of his family ties. He credits to language what he should credit to family members. This is a convenient mistake, for as long as he holds on to certain familiar words, he can ignore how much else has actually changed in his life.

55 It has happened before. In earlier decades, persons ambitious for social mobility, and newly successful, similarly seized upon certain "family words." Workingmen attempting to gain political power, for example, took to calling one another "brother." The word as they used it, however, could never resemble the word (the sound) "brother" exchanged by two people in intimate greeting. The context of its public delivery made it at best a metaphor; with repetition it was only a vague echo of the intimate sound. Context forced the change. Context could not be overruled. Context will always protect the realm of the intimate from public misuse. Today middle-class white Americans continue to prove the importance of context as they try to ignore it. They seize upon idioms of the black ghetto, but their attempt to appropriate such expressions invariably changes the meaning. As it becomes a public expression, the ghetto idiom loses its sound, its message of public separateness and strident intimacy. With public repetition it becomes a series of words, increasingly lifeless.

56 The mystery of intimate utterance remains. The communication of intimacy passes through the word and enlivens its sound, but it cannot be held by the word. It cannot be retained or ever quoted because it is too fluid. It depends not on words but on persons.

57 My grandmother! She stood among my other relations mocking me when I no longer spoke Spanish. *Pocho,* she said. But then it made no difference. She'd laugh, and our relationship continued because language was never its source. She was a woman in her eighties during the first decade of my life—a mysterious woman to me, my only living grandparent, a woman of Mexico in a long black dress that reached down to her shoes. She was the one relative of mine who spoke no word of English. She had no interest in gringo society and remained completely aloof from the public. She was protected by her daughters, protected even by me when we went to Safeway together and I needed to act as her translator. An eccentric woman. Hard. Soft.

58 When my family visited my aunt's house in San Francisco, my grandmother would search for me among my many cousins. When she found me, she'd chase them away. Pinching her granddaughters, she would warn them away from me. Then she'd take me to her room, where she had prepared for my coming. There would be a chair next to the bed, a dusty jellied candy nearby, and a copy of *Life en Español* for me to examine. "There," she'd say. And I'd sit content, a boy of eight. *Pocho,* her favorite. I'd sift through the pictures of earthquake-destroyed Latin-American cities and blonde-wigged Mexican movie stars. And all the while I'd listen to the sound of my grandmother's voice. She'd pace around the room, telling me stories of her life. Her past. They were stories so familiar that I couldn't remember when I'd heard them for the first time. I'd look up sometimes to listen. Other times she'd look over at me, but she never expected a response. Sometimes I'd smile or nod. (I understood exactly what she was saying.) But it never seemed to matter to her one way or the other. It was enough that I was there. The words she spoke were almost irrelevant to that fact. We were content. And the great mystery remained: intimate utterance.

59   I learn nothing about language and intimacy listening to those social activists who propose using one's family language in public life. I learn much more simply by listening to songs on a radio, or hearing a great voice at the opera, or overhearing the woman downstairs at an open window singing to herself. Singers celebrate the human voice. Their lyrics are words, but, animated by voice, those words are subsumed into sounds. (This suggests a central truth about language: all words are capable of becoming sounds as we fill them with the "music" of our life.) With excitement I hear the words yielding their enormous power to sound, even though their meaning is never totally obliterated. In most songs, the drama or tension results from the way that the singer moves between words (sense) and notes (song). At one moment the song simply "says" something; at another moment the voice stretches out the words and moves to the realm of pure sound. Most songs are about love: lost love, celebrations of loving, pleas. By simply being occasions when sounds soar through words, however, songs put me in mind of the most intimate moments of life.

60   Finally, among all types of music, I find songs created by lyric poets most compelling. On no other public occasion is sound so important for me. Written poems on a page seem at first glance a mere collection of words. And yet, without musical accompaniment, the poet leads me to hear the sounds of the words that I read. As song, a poem moves between the levels of sound and sense, never limited to one realm or the other. As a public artifact, the poem can never offer truly intimate sound, but it helps me to recall the intimate times of my life. As I read in my room, I grow deeply conscious of being alone, sounding my voice in search of another. The poem serves, then, as a memory device; it forces remembrance. And it refreshes; it reminds me of the possibility of escaping public words, the possibility that awaits me in intimate meetings.

61   The child reminds the adult: to seek intimate sounds is to seek the company of intimates. I do not expect to hear those sounds in public. I would dishonor those I have loved, and those I love now, to claim anything else. I would dishonor our intimacy by holding on to a particular language and calling it my family language. Intimacy cannot be trapped within words; it passes through words. It passes. Intimates leave the room. Doors close. Faces move away from the window. Time passes, and voices recede into the dark. Death finally quiets the voice. There is no way to deny it, no way to stand in the crowd claiming to utter one's family language.

62   The last time I saw my grandmother I was nine years old. I can tell you some of the things she said to me as I stood by her bed, but I cannot quote the message of intimacy she conveyed with her voice. She laughed, holding my hand. Her voice illumined disjointed memories as it passed them again. She remembered her husband—his green eyes, his magic name of Narcissio, his early death. She remembered the farm in Mexico, the eucalyptus trees nearby (their scent, she remembered, like incense). She remembered the family cow, the bell around its neck heard miles away. A dog. She remembered working as a seamstress, how she'd leave her daughters and son for long hours to go into Guadalajara to work. And how my mother would come running toward her in the sun—in her bright yellow dress—on her return. "MMMMAAAAMMMMÁÁÁÁ," the old lady mimicked her daughter (my mother) to her daughter's son. She laughed. There was the snap of a cough. An aunt came into the room and told me it was time I should leave. "You can

see her tomorrow," she promised. So I kissed my grandmother's cracked face. And the last thing I saw was her thin, oddly youthful thigh, as my aunt rearranged the sheet on the bed.

63   At the funeral parlor a few days after, I remember kneeling with my relatives during the rosary. Among their voices I traced, then lost, the sounds of individual aunts in the surge of the common prayer. And I heard at that moment what since I have heard very often—the sound the women in my family make when they are praying in sadness. When I went up to look at my grandmother, I saw her through the haze of a veil draped over the open lid of the casket. Her face looked calm—but distant and unyielding to love. It was not the face I remembered seeing most often. It was the face she made in public when the clerk at Safeway asked her some question and I would need to respond. It was her public face that the mortician had designed with his dubious art.

POST-READINGS QUESTIONS

CONTENT

1. Why does Rodriguez identify himself as the "problem student" in his elementary school class?

2. Why does Rodriguez say he cannot support bilingual education?

3. How does Rodriguez describe his parents' use of English and Spanish? What emotions accompany each description?

4. What finally induces Rodriguez to learn English? How does learning English affect him at school?

5. Why does Rodriguez emphasize the "sounds" of language rather than the words?

6. What does Rodriguez say is "the great lesson of school"? Do you agree?

7. What effect does Rodriguez's mastery of English have on his family life? Explain.

8. What does Rodriguez say is necessary for one to gain a "full public identity"? Do you agree?

9. Why does Rodriguez write that Spanish "would have been a dangerous language for me to have used at the start of my education"?

10. What does Rodriguez mean when he says that bilingual activists "want it both ways"?

STYLE AND STRUCTURE

11. What is Rodriguez's purpose in writing this? Rewrite his main idea in your own words.

12. What is the effect of Rodriguez's writing that his parents "were nobody's victims"? How is this distinction important within the context of his argument? Explain.

13. What is the tone of this essay? Choose several words and/or expressions that you think best convey the tone.

14. What types of examples does Rodriguez use in order to illustrate his ideas? Which ones do you find most effective? Why?

15. What purpose does Rodriguez's closing description of his grandmother serve?

16. What role does style play in Rodriguez's communication in "Aria"? Would his essay be convincing if it were written in the style of a newspaper article? Why or why not?

CRITICAL THINKING AND ANALYSIS

DISCUSSION QUESTIONS

17. Do you agree with Rodriguez that "It is not possible for a child, any child, ever to use his family's language in school"? Explain and give examples.

18. Rodriguez writes that his parents lacked "any deep feeling of ease, of belonging in public." What do you think comprises this feeling of belonging? Explain and give examples from your own experiences.

19. What do you think the most important aspect of one's "family language" is? Must a "family language" be a recognizable language, such as Spanish? What is the family language for people who speak only English?

WRITING ASSIGNMENTS

20. Rodriguez feels that the trade-off between losing his fluency in Spanish is worth the benefits of developing a public identity. What do you think? Write a paragraph or two discussing whether one's home language or one's public sense of self is most important.

21. Rodriguez expresses the differences between his family life and his public life, and he presents these two worlds as being often in conflict. Do you agree that these two spheres are necessarily separate? Write at least two paragraphs in answering this question, and draw from your own family and school experiences.

22. Do you think feeling equally comfortable in public and in private is possible? If so, are different identities necessary to do so? Explain in a paragraph or two.

23. To what extent do you think one's feeling of comfort and one's civility are connected? Do you think comfort at the start of one's education, as through bilingual education, would make a difference in classroom civility? Explain.

VOCABULARY DEVELOPMENT

24. What is an "aria"? How does understanding this term deepen your comprehension of the essay?

25. Choose at least five words you did not look up in the Vocabulary Preview and use them in a paragraph on the topic of bilingual education. Next, look up the words and check your word usage to see that your vocabulary choices make sense. If not, revise your paragraph in order to improve the sense of your message and to eliminate incorrect usage.

GROUP ACTIVITIES

26. Choose a simple sentence (such as "You are late") and say it out loud three times, each time emphasizing a different word. What effect does the stress on different words have on the overall meaning of the sentence? Explain.

27. Using the sentence from the exercise above, vary the volume and tone you use as you say the sentence. What factor(s) do you find make the greatest difference in changing the sentence's meaning? Present your discoveries to the class.

28. Make a list of the different "languages" you use and discuss why you use each one when you do. How different are the expressions found in each "language"? Why?

29. Make a glossary of all the words that are "intimate" or particular to your English class. What about these words makes them appropriate for English class but less so for others?

Of Academic Fraud and the Education Crisis: Confessions and Revelations From an Ivy League Whore

Iain Steinberg

Many of us have had some experience with people who choose not to be completely honest in their academic endeavors, and with the advent of the Internet, cheating has never been easier. Iain Steinberg, now seeking to pursue a career in screenwriting, writes of his experience as a professional homework writer and ventures to explain the causes for his former employment and some of the long-term effects of assisting cheaters.

Pre-reading Questions

Have you ever cheated in school or know someone who did? What form did this cheating take? What were the results of the academic dishonesty? Why do you think people cheat? What do you think the penalties for cheaters should be, if any?

Vocabulary Preview

Vocabulary Words:
- parasitic
- stringent
- adulation
- viable
- unilaterally

- degenerative
- curtailed
- plethora
- pandemic
- panderer

- extortionist
- endemic
- systemic
- alleviate
- oblivious

Look up at least ten of the following words and write a paragraph explaining why you think these words are particularly effective or ineffective as you find them in the text.

1   There are no chartreuse silk suits hanging in my closet, just a few pairs of jeans, some shirts, some books, and the odd skeleton. My past is my prison. My present, a holding cell. As for my future, there are those like Texas Republican state Sen. Teel Bivins of Armadillo, who would prefer that this exposé confession be written from behind bars. Still others hail my experiences as the finest expressions of academic entrepreneurship of the twentieth century. You decide.

2   The path to higher learning can be approached from many directions as long as a pupil's emotional and psychological state of readiness is regularly accounted for. To Jean-Jacques Rousseau, considered the grandfather of modern-day educational theory, schooling had to be customized this way lest it lose sight of the individual student.

3   Rousseau's prizewinning discourse The Origin and Foundation of Inequality Among Mankind (1755) expounded on his belief that science, art, and the social institutions of the eighteenth century were corrupting humanity. This colossal truth is

profoundly more realized in the jungles of postmodernity, however, as technology, like a parasitic infestation, forges itself deeper into the soil of human experience, invariably imposing mutations at the root level.

4   At the forefront of this now constantly mutating New World script, students, our youth, meander through postsecondary studies semiconscious; the have-nots, like disoriented lab rats in a maze, the more affluent, like tycoons buying their academic workloads the way most of us purchase lunch. On this most alarming allegation, I can offer firsthand testimonial evidence, but first some necessary background.

5   Nine years ago, disillusioned by the substandard offerings of universities, I took my formal leave, with the compunction to never give up on learning, just institutions. I had attended a private high school where academic demands were stringent and the academic environment, competitive. With thirteen courses and an average of eleven exams per semester, four of which were languages, I had become accustomed to the pressures of the academic trek. For me, university was a demotion, snapping me back from high school graduate to grade nine so fast I got cerebral whiplash.

FREELANCE WRITING BUSINESS

6   So I left. Marooned out in the real world, unable to find paid work, I eventually took it upon myself to create a home-based freelance writing business. One newspaper ad later, I unwittingly stumbled upon a niche industry that seemed intent on crowning me its whore.

7   Although university students were not the targets of my generic twenty-five-dollar newspaper ad, I fielded dozens of phone calls from characters desperate enough to promise me a variety of human organs in exchange for taking over their academic workloads. Cash-strapped and physically healthy, I opted for the money instead. And so it all began.

8   Caught off guard by the storm of student assignments flooding in, suddenly inundated in a sea of cerebral candy and dollar signs, I was too overwhelmed to be overwhelmed with the implications of what I was doing. In my first "semester" as an academic whore, I worked for thirty-three undergraduate students, producing over sixty-five unique, custom-tailored papers in over fifteen disciplines. Every day brought with it yet another deadline and more money! And this was just the beginning.

9   Without realizing it, I was fast becoming the smartest kid on the block, fanatically learning across the disciplines in a way that would not have been afforded me as a student with a single or even double major. Plowing forward in this dubious career, I remained naively oblivious to the sociopathic stigma that would follow me for years to come.

10   As someone who was getting paid to read, write, and learn, I considered myself extremely privileged. Next to my contemporaries, many of whom were drowning in a sea of academic debt, I was a hero of sorts, though I sought no adulation. I knew my unconventional learning path was not for everyone and so never advocated or promoted it as a viable university alternative. In fact, I routinely found myself counseling the disenfranchised segment of my student clientele, always emphasizing the need for them to stay in school.

11   Word of mouth ensured that local demand continued to soar. As in any service industry, a satisfied customer is a repeat customer. And so they came in what seemed like a never-ending procession: future teachers, lawyers, psychologists, social workers, journalists, nurses, business majors, stoned zombies, wearing down my carpeting as fast as they were my nerves and patience.

12   In the winter of 1995, I sought escape from these local nudniks online, slowly wading into the already saturated U.S. term paper market, not quite sure what to expect. With a few online ads and the help of some friends at several *Ivy* League universities, Americans quickly began to dominate my academic harem, shelling out upward of forty dollars per page for my services. Supply and demand would ultimately determine my price structure: The busier I got, the more expensive my services became.

13   Many sleepless nights were spent mulling over the implications of what I was doing, especially as I began to see my local clientele graduate to assume their professional roles as teachers, journalists, social workers, and psychologists. Unlike Mary Shelley's Dr. Frankenstein, I had unleashed not one but a whole assembly line of inept creatures into the mainstream to wreak whatever havoc they would. Was I prepared to deal with the consequences? Did it even matter?

14   Either way, the long-term effects to society were as frightening as they were immeasurable. And whether I wanted to admit it to myself or not, my new business was part of the problem. Were one-man businesses like mine unilaterally responsible for this corruption, as the academic establishment of administrative scapegoaters would have the public believe? Or were we symptoms of a much larger, degenerative, systemic ailment?

15   The university landscape of today is foreign terrain even to graduates of just ten years past. Many of the once indelible foundations of higher learning have been gnawed away, gradually rendered impotent, soon perhaps even obsolete. Libraries, books, teachers, and the classroom itself—all are facing extinction because of what promises to be a century of rampant technological change.

16   In the not-too-distant future, scientists envision humanity's direct interface with artificial intelligence. Some form of cyber-genetic bridge will allow for neuron-speed downloads of whole libraries directly into one's cerebral cortex, overnight, perhaps while asleep. Such a technological milestone would virtually do away with universities altogether, much the same way the Internet is rewriting the rules of university life today.

17   For now, personal computers and the World Wide Web have given the student access to global cornucopias of knowledge, before and otherwise unavailable. Whole databases of information—accessible, clickable, and downloadable—all for one's learning or cheating convenience.

A DISAPPEARING LINE

18   Therein lies the first problem: The line between cheating and learning has been blurred, in part by our technocracy's growing dependence and infatuation with the World Wide Web. Many university students today don't consider it cheating to download a term paper off the Internet, change some words and a few bibliographical sources, and hand it in as their own. The Internet is, after all, a recognized research tool, not a societal subversion. In fact, it can be both.

19   Internet-based research and term paper mills are a booming industry that have been spewed out of the World Wide Web's womb like a series of unwanted, bastard children. And they continue to multiply like vermin on Viagra, despite increased legislation and national attention. Calls to exterminate these online varmints invariably wind up confronting the First Amendment before dying a fizzled death.

20   Since 1995, sixteen states have made it illegal to sell academic research and term papers. The legislatures of Massachusetts and Texas have laws imposing fines of up to five hundred dollars on students caught committing academic fraud. This is on top of existent university penalties, which almost always guarantee the culprit's expulsion. As yet, neither state can produce any raw data on whether term paper fraud has actually been curtailed.

21   While politicians and bureaucrats have been making laws that lull the public into believing the crisis of academic fraud is contained, incidents of university cheating continue to rise. Sites that masquerade as legitimate college resources have been proliferating exponentially, deeply entrenching themselves in the information highway. Five years ago, there were fewer than one hundred of these sites. Today, an innocent "Term Paper" search string on Yahoo reveals only the surface of this mammoth iceberg, yielding well over one million hits!

22   The plethora of online services targeted at today's downtrodden, brain-dead student is enough to perturb even the most stable minded. At the bottom of this food chain, hundreds of databases big and small offer downloadable university research. Not surprisingly, these polluted communal cesspools are a breeding ground for inaccuracy and error. Students should avoid these like the plague, and yet they remain among the Web's most-trafficked sites.

23   www.schoolsucks.com, www.essaydepot.com, and www.houseofcheat.com are several of the most popular sites accessed by online student denizens. Although they were considered beyond containment just a few years back, today's enforcement technology may well have caught up with these five-and-dime term paper mudholes.

24   The latest in Web development is the increased availability of search-engine technology. Many sites are now equipped with a site-search feature as well as a Web engine. This permits the student-surfer to enter a search string into a queue while the engine scans the Web, returning possible matches. Finding an online term paper on any given subject is easier than ever for both student and professor alike.

25   Programs like plagiarism.org, developed by John Barrie, a Berkeley graduate student, have already nabbed dozens of university plagiarizers but only those foolish enough to hand in papers downloaded directly off the Net. The online service employs proprietary plagiarism-detection algorithms to compare work against the thousands of papers posted on the Web. The technology is limited, and anyone clever enough to edit and update an existing online paper will likely get away with academic fraud.

26   Still, many are not even that savvy: The majority of those caught committing academic plagiarism to date have submitted term papers printed directly off their browsers. In still more cases, the term paper mill's logo was printed at the bottom of every page! Imagine the reaction of a college professor turning to the cover page of a student's report to read: "The Increased Rise of Extreme Nationalism in Eastern Europe: Post-Soviet Era (term paper courtesy of www.schoolsucks.com)."

27   As search-engine technology becomes better honed and professors begin to take advantage of it, say good-bye to the drudges of online term paper databases and prepare to enter the spa of "cybercheatdom"—the custom-tailored site.

28   The online ocean is already dotted with hundreds of these sites. Luring their lazy student prey with promises of unique, custom research are ex-university professors, international writing companies, and ex-students, operating out of mildew-ridden basements and marble-towered office buildings alike. Their tsunami-sized putsch onto the World Wide Web has shown no signs of ebbing. These sharks are hungry, and they're circling.

29   Catching these behemoths will require a lot more than the helpful hand of technology. How can legislators, professors, or administrators rightfully tell if a submitted piece of academic work was personally written or professionally subcontracted? With class sizes growing and more teacher assistants correcting assignments, the task of monitoring this type of academic fraud seems well beyond the system's ability. Ultimately, one would need a net the size of the Internet itself to catch all these entrepreneurial predators, and for every one caught, ten will rise to take its place. University cheating has become big business.

30   Further complicating matters is the internal wrangling of many educational bureaucracies, now run more like corporations than institutions of higher learning. With international companies such as Coca-Cola sponsoring universities and their sport teams, administration has become big business, often forcing education to take a backseat. What happens when professors, coaches, and administrators allow and promote cheating among their star athletes, many of whom, it turns out, are completely illiterate?

31   In the spring of 1998, a tutor at the University of Minnesota confessed to having written some four hundred term papers for many of the college's high-profile basketball stars. Her revelations sent the academic world into a frenzied public relations tailspin. The incident, played down as an aberration by university administrators, served to illustrate the complexity and pervasiveness of academic fraud at universities today. Students are only a small part of a much bigger problem.

AN UNDERMINED BUREAUCRACY

32   Whatever their political or ideological association, all seem to agree that education is in crisis. While politicians scramble to contain the tempest of academic fraud, administrators debate classroom management minutiae, virtually ignoring the pandemic before them. Is the Establishment's relative inaction due to ignorance or a form of acknowledged self-defeat? The educational and political bureaucracies recognize how dwarfed and utterly powerless they are in facing off with the resource-rich student underground and its most prized information resource, the Internet.

33   So, if the solution to this educational crisis isn't going to come from technology and laws continually prove ineffective, the answer must be found at the heart of the university experience itself. What aspects of formal university education can be adapted to better fit the diverse needs of today's savvy, information-saturated learner? Can the university experience itself be modified, perhaps even custom-tailored to an individual's personal needs? This Rousseauian design will have to become a lot more prevalent if institutional academia is to survive through the twenty-first century.

34   A quick glimpse into my cracked academic mirror reveals but one fragment of the problem: If I were to return to university in pursuit of an education degree, for example, I would invariably be required to begin this slackly sojourn with such sources as Introduction to Education 101. Though I have written and researched several master's theses in educational psychology as well as hundreds of other undergraduate assignments within the discipline, the system would expect me to sit through umpteen hours of redundant, pedantic introductory lectures and courses. This would be mentally torturous at best and would require leaving my brain at home for the first two years of university. The individual disciplines at the university level must be prepared to offer equivalency-placement testing so that degree learning can be custom-tailored to an individual's time frame, taking into account his intellectual and life experience background.

35   In my seven-year stint as an "academic whore," I have been privy to the student voice. I have heard all the student excuses, and the complaints raised against university professors and the faceless bureaucratic institutions that tenure them without any regard for their teaching ability. I believe the scripts of excuses I have heard are especially relevant to the discussion, because they reveal what brought students to my doorstep in the first place.

ACADEMIC EXCUSES

36   Without further ado, and respecting everyone's anonymity, of course, I present my parade of lost academics:

37   "I completely forgot about the assignment until today. . . . Oh yeah, and it was due yesterday, can you do it?"

38   Although I did work for students who often found themselves in this type of bind, the majority of my clientele were upscale high-achievers, who held down 3.8 grade-point averages. In fact, the most common line I heard was more of a war-torn plea:

39   "I'm so exhausted, and I have three other assignments due next Monday. I don't have the time to devote to them all. If I give you an extra $500, can you please squeeze me in?"

40   Then there were the regulars. Clients with whom I had biweekly engagements paid me well and thus received the bulk of my time and attention. Often juggling the workloads of several such student-dependents simultaneously, I often topped off my week with output levels of twenty-five thousand words or more.

41   One regular, Elyssa, went on to pursue postgraduate work, thanks in large part to my academic omnipresence. In fact, I wrote her master's thesis! Afraid of her own shadow, she never went anywhere without her mother. The pair would make the thirty-minute drive to my office three or four times a week, regularly picking up and dropping off slews of assignments and research material. Like many of my regular clients, Elyssa performed well academically but was completely unable to express herself, both verbally and in writing. Interestingly, Mommy, not daughter, was writing all the checks, paying me upon pickup and delivery of each and every assignment.

42   Elyssa's mom was not the only parent to commission my services. Over the years, dozens of predominantly affluent parents engaged me on behalf of their bored or academically challenged children. Often I dealt exclusively with parents as their children were away at out-of-town universities. The parent script of excuses was the most predictable, no doubt because I heard it repeated so often:

43   "Nowadays, the kids need all the help they can get.... Teachers are crazy.... Half the courses my kid wanted he couldn't even get into.... You spend good money for what ...?"

44   The parents I dealt with were good, caring people who only wanted the best for their children. Ironically, just a few decades ago, "the best" inferred getting a university education. In today's competitive job market, however, a university transcript is standard issue. Without the 3.8 grade-point average, many of the choice jobs are simply unavailable. With their child's whole future riding on these few quick years of postsecondary education, it's surprising that more parents haven't been recruited into the cheating contingent. From my perspective, it certainly seemed that everyone was involved, including university staff and administration.

SERVICING THE JOCKS

45 After tackling one running back's workload for an entire semester, I was expecting a full-court press of phone inquiries from other college jocks to follow. Instead, I received a single phone call from Coach Jenkins, who invited me to the campus to conference. After an hour-long meeting, I was "awarded" the unofficial title of team tutor and promised a steady wave of assignments all semester in return for big bucks. Naturally, I had to keep quiet about the arrangement that ultimately transformed me into Coach Jenkins' personal fast-food service window:

46   "Yeah, so I got six English assignments for ya, two political science essays, I got a take-home exam in sociology, two ten-question-and-answer assignments—I think one is history, the other is anthropology or something. I gotta buncha psychology crap here. So when can you pick it all up?"

47   Several times I jokingly asked him if he "wanted fries with that," genuinely taken aback by his nonchalance as he dumped countless assignments on my plate for what turned out to be a two-year, all-you-can-eat academic buffet. His insatiable demands on my time never seemed to be met. After two years' worth of twelve-hour workdays, fearing complete burnout, I told the coach I had had enough. Coach Jenkins, however, was not prepared to release his "star writer" that easily. It was only after I threatened to expose his ring of fraud that he let me walk away unencumbered and unscathed. A panderer, now an extortionist in the student underground, I certainly felt like I was getting full exposure to the cancerous underbelly of university life.

48   Rounding out my parade of patrons was the unending line of education students, drawn to my doorstep like drone ants to their queen. No other discipline was as represented in my portfolio of academic experience as education. Ironic, isn't it? Future teachers paying me to do work that would ultimately put them in charge of classrooms! This startling irony points to an array of fundamental problems at the core of educational scholarship today.

49   Teachers are the most underpaid, underappreciated contributors to society. As a result, the field often attracts two breeds of student: the dedicated scholar and the totally vacant. Both types graced my doorstep, though I must admit to doing more academic work for more dimwits in education than any other discipline. Many of these "graduates" are now teaching in the field. Look for them at an elementary or high school near you!

FACULTY FRAUD

50   The problems of plagiarism and academic fraud are not limited to students. In 1992, a professor at Concordia University in Montreal went on a shooting rampage, killing four fellow professors. The attack was not random. The murderer's courtroom testimony, fraught with allegations of theft, copyright infringement, and research fraud, prompted the university to commission an independent investigation into its own inner workings.

51   Exposed was the popular research culture that assigns grants exclusively to the tenured professor, inevitably creating huge interdepartmental rifts. Exposed was the vicious competition for research grant money, without which many professors say they couldn't afford to live. Exposed was the reality that the engineering department at Concordia routinely published papers that were coauthored by eight people when in fact only one or two were actively involved. Were all these problems endemic to this one particular university, or were they representative of a much larger, more corrupt research culture?

52   Research integrity becomes an issue when it is difficult to discern the primary authors and contributors of the research. With responsibility shared among so many, the most logical question to arise is who is responsible for the actual research and writing of the work? If this most basic question becomes blurred by a new research ethic dictating that researchers assign credit where none is due (to colleagues with whom they wish to gain favor, for instance), the public and the whole academic culture suffer.

53   Academic researchers routinely publish studies that are hailed as breakthroughs one moment, only to be totally discredited the next. Four years ago, researchers at the University of Montreal announced that they were on the threshold of a cure for breast cancer. The international media got hold of the story and ran it with jubilant fervor. Forced into a corner by the heat of the international spotlight, the Montreal research team was forced to concede that the announcement was made to assure continuous flow of government grant money. They were not on the brink of a cure but of bankruptcy.

54   More often, research is being bankrolled by corporate money so that results can be manipulated to fit a company's agenda. Phillip Morris was a contributor of research capital in a study that, not surprisingly, demonstrated that nicotine was nonaddictive. Big money not only commissions and finances these studies, it determines their outcomes before any research is even undertaken. As a result, study findings regularly contradict themselves, making it near impossible to discern empirical scientific result from special interest.

SYSTEMIC PROBLEMS

55   The problems in education are systemic, beginning at the primary level and continuing beyond the postsecondary stage. Arriving at university unable to read or write, dumbfounded by the inner workings of a library card catalog, many are legitimately overwhelmed. In several of my first-year college classes, professors took the entire class down to the library so students could familiarize themselves with the mechanics of library research procedures. We were being shown how to use a library! The first time this happened, I spent the period looking for the "Candid Camera," convinced we were being filmed for an upcoming episode. How could one be at a university without having previously used a library?

56   You don't need a diploma on your wall to see the ominous writing: The public school system is not doing its job in readying students for the academic challenges of university life and workload. Here once again, an outmoded, strained infrastructure is chiefly to blame: Broken-down, asbestos-poisoned schools, schools without libraries, outdated textbooks, uncertified teachers, violence, classroom overcrowding—these are just a few of the more pressing challenges facing public education today. Twenty years of national and state budget slashing has created rips in the educational fabric through which many students have been allowed to fall. Often, it was my doorstep they crashed-landed on.

57   With public school class sizes now averaging around thirty students, and the classroom populace more socioeconomically and linguistically diverse than ever, teachers are finding it increasingly difficult to design lesson plans that are all-inclusive. More often than not, they wind up teaching to about half the class at best, with one-quarter falling progressively behind and the other quarter struggling to stay awake. Breaking out of the standard teacher-centered classroom mold is the first step that public school teachers can make to alleviate this classroom imbalance.

58   Cooperative or small group-based learning environments repeatedly proved to increase overall performance and participation among students. Mixed-age and performance-group situations also bestow greater responsibility on the individual learner, fostering an environment that promotes student self-regulated learning. Teaching new and existent teachers alternative strategies and methods as well as innovative classroom-management designs would result in a more adaptive, responsive, problem-solving role model. This improved facilitator would likely be capable of teaching more than 50 percent of the class at a time, ensuring that more students reached university in a state of academic preparedness.

59   As it becomes increasingly difficult to earn a decent living without a university diploma, more and more otherwise nonacademically inclined students pour into the halls of higher learning in search of something, they know not what. More often than not, however, higher learning is not taking place there, unless one considers learning how to beat the system to be a form of higher learning.

60   The majority of my clientele confided to me that they were studying education because no other three- or four-year program resulted in immediate job placement after graduation. Many more admitted that they were in the field because they had no sense of direction, singular calling, or passion. Just the right combination of attributes for the type of public school teacher we all want teaching our children!

61   I find it sad and even a little maddening. Knowing there are teachers so void of passion, direction, and, thanks to me, formal academic background molding young minds . . . into what? They may very well have their diplomas and transcripts, but it is I who hold their educations hostage. These are the skeletons trapped in my closet, forever taunting me, begging for their freedom. How do I let them out, get credit for what I have done, and avoid incarceration? Sounds like a job for Superman!

COMING CLEAN

62   Last year, after seven years of "informal" study in over thirty disciplines, with thousands of pages researched and written from hundreds of books and thousands of academic periodicals, I felt it was finally time to set my skeletons free and come clean. It was time to take all

that I had learned over the years and enter the mainstream. Mainstream society would have none of that, however, repeatedly proving unready for this whore's official premiere.

63   Years of self-employment in a field as risqué and shunned as this have handicapped my efforts at societal reemergence. Despite my years of informal study, I am still viewed as a mere high school graduate with some university under my belt—insufficient criteria for an entry-level position nowadays. Today's employers place inordinate emphasis on transcripts, marks, and GPAs, more so than they do on the people holding them. Many are oblivious to the fact that marks, transcripts, and even diplomas can be bought as easily as an online term paper.

64   I know beyond doubt that my freelance education was comprehensive, if not superior to the one I would have received as a formally enrolled student, spending $10,000 a year on tuition. Ironically, the students I helped to graduate are now secure in their $25,000–$40,000 annual income brackets while I repeatedly get passed over for jobs scrubbing toilets or cutting deli meats at the local grocer. After a full year of wretched pavement-pounding unemployment, depleted and near bankrupt, I was about ready to consider a career in the circus when a familiar epiphany came over me.

65   This January, one year after retiring the whore to the back of my now-crowded closet, the term paper king was born, out of financial necessity, not spite. I have no subversive agenda to undermine society, although society has repeatedly given me the short end. I would much prefer working on the legitimate side of the fence but, to do so, the system insists I spend at least $25,000 for what I consider an inferior product. Until university becomes more adaptive and responsive to the individual needs of learners, the system will likely continue to produce incompetents, while people such as myself are held back by the likes of a piece of paper.

66   As my own boss, deciding what to learn, when and how to approach it, and finally getting paid to do it all in my pajamas, perhaps I have been spoiled. Why then should I have to settle for a minimum-wage job at some deli counter when I can get good money learning on behalf of those less inclined? It seems the perfect arrangement until one ponders the long-term societal consequences.

67   On the eve of my fateful decision to reenter the world of the student underground, I received the omen I was hoping would never come: a phone call from one of the societal consequences—my longest standing client, Elyssa. Having graduated from a master's program in educational psychology a little over a year ago, why would she now be calling? Could she be going for her Ph.D. in education? No, Elyssa was looking for work and had a serious, albeit mind-numbing question to ask:

68   "Now that I have my master's degree, what sorts of jobs are for me?"

I haven't been able to accept a single assignment since.

SOURCES AND ADDITIONAL READING

Additional Reading: Joe Chidley, "Tales Out of School: Cheating Has Long Been a Great Temptation and the Internet Makes It Easier Than Ever," MacLean's, 24 Nov. 1997.

John Hickman, "Cybercheats: Term Paper Shopping Online," New Republic, 23 Mar. 1998.

Jon Marcus, "Tuitions Continue to Spiral," Associated Press, 9 Sept. 1994.

Neil Postman, The End of Education: Redefining the Value of School, Knopf, New York, 1996.

Karen Seidman, "High-Tech Helps Cheaters Prosper," Montreal Gazette.

Margaret Wang and Stephen Peverly, "The Self-Instructive Process in Classroom Learning Contexts," Contemporary Educational Psychology 11 (1986).

Abigail Witherspoon, "This Pen for Hire: On Grinding Out Papers for College Students," Harper's, June 1995.

M. Wolfe, "Dr. Fabrikant's Solution," Saturday Night, July–Aug. 1994.

POST-READING QUESTIONS

CONTENT

1. What caused the author to begin completing other people's assignments for a fee?

2. To what does Steinberg attribute his success as a professional homework writer?

3. What are the existing penalties for academic fraud in some states?

4. What are some steps people have taken to stop internet-assisted plagiarism?

5. According to Steinberg, what aspects of academia allow cheating to continue?

6. What does Steinberg say are some of the excuses people give when hiring him? How reasonable do you think they are?

7. Who else, besides students, has committed forms of academic fraud? What role do these people's frauds play in perpetuating academic dishonesty?

8. From what discipline does Steinberg claim the majority of his clients came? What are the implications of these people's cheating?

9. What ultimately caused the author to stop helping people cheat?

STYLE AND STRUCTURE

10. What is the writer's primary argument? Restate his main idea in your own words.

11. What are some of the writer's supporting arguments? How do these sub-points work together to communicate the main idea of the essay?

12. What types of examples does Steinberg use in order to illustrate his ideas? Are these examples convincing? Explain.

13. What function does the "You decide" sentence in the introduction serve?

14. Who is Steinberg's audience? Between business people, educators, and students, who do you think he would most easily persuade? Why?

15. What purpose does the use of the word "whore" in the title and throughout the essay serve? Why do you think Steinberg uses what, to many, is considered an offensive term?

CRITICAL THINKING AND ANALYSIS

DISCUSSION QUESTIONS

16. Whose problem is academic fraud? Who should ultimately be responsible for addressing this issue? Why?

17. How prevalent do you think academic fraud is? Cite examples from your own experience here, and ask your teacher for examples, in order to support your views.

18. Steinberg writes that "cooperative or small-group-based learning environments have repeatedly proved to increase overall performance." At what point do you think "cooperative" learning becomes cheating?

WRITING ASSIGNMENTS

19. Steinberg lists several factors that he says contribute to poor education: poor facilities, overcrowding, violence, to name a few. Write a short essay (three to five paragraphs) in which you argue that one or two factors are most responsible for a weak academic system. Be sure to cite the essay and your own experiences and observations in order to illustrate your ideas.

20. How should cheaters be dealt with? Write a few paragraphs explaining what you think the penalties for cheating should be. Be sure to differentiate between different levels and different types of cheating (crib notes versus hiring someone to write your master's thesis, for instance) if you think such a distinction is significant.

21. Steinberg lists many excuses people gave when they hired him, some more honorable, perhaps, than others. Write a short essay in which you argue whether or not there is ever a good excuse to cheat. Be sure to cite the reading and your own experience in order to illustrate your ideas.

22. Steinberg lists numerous excuses people offered him when they retained his services to do their school work. Write a short essay to one of your teachers presenting your best excuse for why you did not complete your work as assigned. (Feel free to use humor for this assignment.)

23. Who does cheating ultimately harm? Write three to five paragraphs in which you explain how far-reaching the effects of academic dishonesty can be.

VOCABULARY DEVELOPMENT

24. Choose at least five words, from the Vocabulary Preview or from the entire essay, and explain how you think these words are particularly apt in an essay about academia. What about the words makes them effective?

GROUP ACTIVITIES

25. In small groups, visit some of the online websites available for purchasing term papers. Examine the cost and the benefits of these sites, and report back to your class just how easy, or difficult, online cheating can be.

26. As a group, research some of the penalties for cheating on your own and other campuses. What policies seem most strict? Most effective? Why? Based on your research, write your own "academic dishonesty" policy, making very clear what the penalties for cheating in school are.

27. Brainstorm excuses for failure to complete academic work, having one person record your ideas. Then decide which excuses, if any, are most likely to be convincing and why. Share your ideas with the class and get your teacher's feedback to determine whether you are correct in the conclusions you draw.

Argument Pair: Where Do the Greatest School Problems Lie: In the Classroom or Out?

Insubordination and Intimidation Signal the End of Decorum in Many Classrooms, Alison Schneider

Welcome to Animal House, Anna Quindlen

Few educators disagree that discipline, or the lack of it, is an issue in the classroom. Indeed, Alison Schneider recounts horror stories of teachers experiencing extreme frustration by students' treatment of them. Anna Quindlen expresses concern over students' actions as well, but she questions the priorities set by the learning institutions themselves in contributing to student disrespect on campus. How great the problem of student disrespect toward faculty is, and what measures we should take to address it, are two issues raised by these writers.

Writing Assignments for *Insubordination and Intimidation Signal the End of Decorum in Many Classrooms* and *Welcome to Animal House*

1. Alison Schneider writes that "Part of the problem [of disrespect in the classroom] . . . is a crisis of authority in this country that leaves no one above question," and Anna Quindlen writes that at some schools "a basketball coach can be infinitely more important than the school's president." What causes people in academia to earn respect? Write a paragraph or essay in which you evaluate what authority figures on campus—teachers, counselors, coaches, administrators—are treated with respect by students and why. Be sure to cite these two essays as well as your own experiences and observations in order to illustrate your ideas.

2. Anna Quindlen writes that students respond "really badly" to "any attempt to curtail" their social activities, and Alison Schneider claims that more and more classes are "totally out of control" due to student behavior. How much should students be able to shape their academic experience? Write a well-developed paragraph or essay in which you argue that students should, or should not, have input as far as their academic and social activities on campus are concerned. Be sure to cite these essays, others from the chapter, and your own experiences and observations in order to best illustrate your ideas.

Insubordination and Intimidation Signal the End of Decorum in Classrooms

Alison Schneider

Though students have long been accused of exhibiting less than perfect manners, Alison Schneider claims, classroom behavior seems to be taking a nosedive. In her article for *The Chronicle of Higher Education,* Schneider explores the causes and effects of student insubordination as well as the teacher's role in setting the tone for an amicable class, and she compares student actions today with those of students in earlier generations.

Pre-reading Questions

Freewrite for five to ten minutes in response to the following questions:
What changes, if any, has student behavior undergone over the last five years? The last fifteen years? What do you think has caused these changes? What role do you think the teacher's behavior plays in determining the students' behavior? Explain.

Vocabulary Preview

Vocabulary Words:

- decorum
- affronts
- consternation
- apathetic

- demoralizing
- contempt
- egregious
- impunity

- beleaguered
- tete-a-tete
- overbearing

Use a dictionary to define each of the words above and, as you read the essay, write a few sentences explaining how each word helps to communicate Schneider's message or detracts from it.

1   It's every professor's nightmare: losing control of the class. And if anecdotal evidence counts for anything, it's happening more and more.

2   Professors are complaining that their courses are being hijacked by "classroom terrorists." Among the milder affronts: Students are arriving late and leaving early, napping in the back of the room, carrying on running conversations, reading the newspaper, even bringing portable televisions into class.

3   The hard-core infractions range from insubordination to outright intimidation. When a chemistry professor at Virginia Tech asked his class how to solve an equation, a student in the back of the room shouted, "Who gives a s—?" When a scholar at Utah State University refused to change a grade, a student screamed at her, "Well, you goddamned bitch, I'm going to the department head, and he'll straighten you out!" That professor may have gotten off easy; a historian at Washington State University was challenged to a fight when a student disliked the grade he'd received. Other professors have been stalked by angry students, and a few physically attacked.

'TEACHING AND CROWD CONTROL'

4   Some scholars argue that academe has never been above a good slugfest. But close encounters of the uncivil kind are leaving many professors stunned, even shaken. How, they ask, did the decorous world of academe disintegrate into a free-for-all?

5   Peter Sacks, the pseudonym of a journalist-turned-professor, ponders that question in *Generation X Goes to College* (Open Court, 1996), which he wrote after teaching droves of apathetic students who were more interested in chatting on their cell phones than listening to lectures.

6   His book struck a chord. Scholars have started publishing articles on the problem; universities are offering workshops. Last fall, the cover story of the newsletter of the National Teaching and Learning Forum was devoted to "Teaching and Crowd Control."

7   Undergraduate insolence grew so bad recently at Virginia Tech that the Faculty Senate formed a "Climate Committee" to look into the situation. A case in point: The head of the Senate, Skip Fuhrman, returned to his office last year after giving a sociology exam and found a message on his answering machine: "You fat f— with yellow teeth! You hump!" a student bellowed. The cause of her consternation: She couldn't resell her textbook.

8   Most students aren't ill-mannered brats, professors say, but it takes only a few bad apples to spoil the pie. "Even a small proportion of rowdy and uncontrollable students ruins the whole atmosphere," Says Henry H. Bauer, a professor of chemistry and science studies at Virginia Tech. "It's very difficult to concentrate if there's a buzz of conversation and giggles of laughter. It's very demoralizing."

9   "The problem is much worse than it was," says his colleague Jack A. Cranford, an associate professor of zoology and ecology, and chairman of the Climate Committee. "I think the incidence of this in the last 10 years has doubled, if not tripled, in terms of the amount and the severity. Things were much more respectful when I entered the professoriate."

ASSIGNING BLAME

10   The questions remains, Why? Many of the explanations being bandied about have the touchy-feely pop-psychology tone of the *Oprah* show, "Latch-key children," "media violence," "substance abuse," people say. Parents are setting poor examples. High schools are falling down on the job. Religious groups aren't as involved as they should be.

11   "If you haven't civilized young people by the time they get to college, I don't think you're going to civilize them at all," says Stephen L. Carter, a professor at Yale Law School, whose book *Civility: Manners, Morals, and the Etiquette of Democracy* will be published in April by Basic-Books. Does he agree that students today possess a diminished sense of decorum? "Yes, I do," he responds politely.

12   Part of the problem, scholars explain, is a crisis of authority in this country that leaves no one above question. "Television and politics have defrocked the social lives of adults and made everything look hypocritical," says Paul A. Trout, an associate professor of English at Montana State University, who has written about classroom conflict. "Kids develop a certain contempt for adults as a result. They come in questioning: 'Why is this an A? Why is this a B? Why am I reading this?' They're suspicious of all the rules established by adults."

13   At Montana State, the problem grew serious enough that in 1995, the university created a task force to look into disruptive classroom behavior, especially in large lectures. That's where the problem is most egregious, professors say. Not only is it easy to act up if you're 60 rows back in a cavernous lecture hall; it's reason to act out, explains Mary Deane Sorcinelli, associate provost for faculty development at the University of Massachusetts at Amherst and director of its Center for Teaching. "I can see it from the student's perspective," she says. "What's the point? I'm sitting here with 300 students. This isn't civil to me."

14   The fact that these large lectures are often required courses pours gasoline on the fire. Students who choose to take a course show up interested in the subject matter. But students who have to take a course often come with a chip on their shoulder.

A FOCUS ON MARKETABILITY

15   Learning for learning's sake, scholars maintain, has flown out the window. Today's students are more interested in finding a job than in debating the fine points of Foucault. Anything that won't enhance their marketability is ripe for disrespect.

16   On top of that, students are paying money—often big money—for a degree, and in the minds of many students, that puts them in the driver's seat. "Consumerism is taking over college campuses," says Kathy K. Franklin, an assistant professor of higher education at the University of Arkansas at Little Rock. "I'm hearing more students saying, 'After all, I pay your salary, and since I pay your salary, I should be able to tell you when I want to come to class and when my paper should be due.' Students live in a Wal-Mart society, where it's convenience that counts."

17   That said, Ms. Franklin thinks the brouhaha over bad manners is overblown. She's been researching the history of undergraduate life for years and says that students have been making mischief ever since universities opened their doors. In the 13th century, professors at the University of Bologna were so terrorized by their students—who beat them up if they didn't like their grades—that they formed guilds to protect themselves.

18   In the United States, in the 1820s, there was the "Bread and Butter" rebellion at Yale University. Students, distressed by demanding classes, started throwing food at professors in the dining hall and beaning them with plates and silverware that they tossed out of windows. They also took a fancy to cannonballs, which they rolled—in the dead of night—through the dormitories, where their professors were sleeping.

19   "Historically, what's happening today isn't unusual," Ms. Franklin says. "Are students today different from students 10 years ago? Probably, because of demographic changes, consumerism, K-to-12 experiences. But is this a new trend? No."

SLAPS ON THE WRIST

20   Professors haven't changed much, either, she adds. They were griping about student incivility hundreds of years ago, too. What's different, she notes, is that today's academics receive less respect than the generation of scholars who trained them. Because their predecessors were held in higher esteem, the cheekier conduct of today's students seems particularly insulting. It probably wouldn't have fazed Yale professors in the 1820s, she says.

21   Chana Kai Lee, an assistant professor of history at Indiana University, finds that argument hard to buy. Last October, a student who had been misbehaving for weeks during her U.S.-history lectures jumped out of his seat, leaped over a row of chairs, tripped, and headed out the door, she says. He returned with some campus newspapers, which he shared with two seatmates. The three students spent the rest of the period reading the papers, passing around a game of tic-tac-toe, and loudly gabbing. Ms. Lee repeatedly asked them to settle down, but they ignored her. When she tried to talk to them after class, she says, one of them grabbed his genitals and pumped his hand up and down.

22   Another student in the course kept telling Ms. Lee's supervisors that she was missing from class, even though, Ms. Lee says, she was there. Then came the harassing phone calls, the first of which contained obscene, racist language. An insulting anonymous letter soon followed.

23   Ms. Lee filed grievances against the four students. The result: four slaps on the wrist, she says. None of the students were suspended or expelled. Three received warnings, she says, and the one who was accused of making the obscene gesture—and who subsequently dropped her class—was found not guilty of that offense, although he admitted that he did cause the other disruptions.

24   Richard McKraig, dean of students at Indiana, says privacy concerns prohibit the university from commenting on disciplinary proceedings. But, he adds, "just because a student is not suspended or expelled does not mean that a serious sanction wasn't given. The incident was taken seriously, and the sanctions that were given, we think, were appropriate."

25   Ms. Lee disagrees: "Students have become more disruptive because they know they can be that way with relative impunity. I would never have thought that anything could happen in the classroom that would make me mentally unprepared to return there. But I've been thoroughly demoralized. This has been the biggest battle of my career."

26   She's not fighting it alone. Since her debacle, she has learned of other lapses in campus decorum, and some 30 faculty members have rallied around her, forming the Committee for a Respectful Learning Environment.

27   Indiana had taken steps in the past to deal with the problem. Last year, the university published guidelines on dealing with disruptive students. And administrators have urged professors to add civility clauses to their syllabi, describing appropriate classroom behavior.

28   But such steps, professors complain are little more than a Band-Aid on a bleeding wound. Ms. Lee included a civility clause in her syllabus—which, she points out, the four undergraduates studiously ignored, even when she repeatedly invoked it.

29   Susanne J. Warma, an associate professor of art history at Utah State University, has the same complaint. Her syllabus pointedly asks students to refrain from "idle chatter and giggling. The students who sit near you are not interested in your romantic lives, how out-of-touch you think your parents are, how stupid you think your teachers are."

30   The effect: not much. Ms. Warma walked out of one class after spending 10 minutes fruitlessly trying to shut her students up.

ESTABLISHING CLEAR RULES

31   So what's a beleaguered professor to do? For starters, they should use day one to lay down the law—what they can live with and what they can't, says Ms. Sorcinelli, of the University of Massachusetts. As associate provost, she's dealt with classroom misbehavior since the early '90s, when a professor fled from one late-afternoon class because a group of students showed up drunk. Since then, she's run workshops and written a how-to chapter on coping with surly students for the *Handbook of College Teaching* (Greenwood Press, 1994).

32   Try to connect with students, Ms. Sorcinelli advises. Learn their names, have them fill out questionnaires, come to class early and work the aisles, stay late to encourage students to talk with you.

33   If students are yammering, she says, make eye contact, stop the lecture until they quiet down, direct a question to the person sitting next to the offender, or walk over to where the student is sitting ("the Oprah Winfrey design"). If all else fails, have a *tête-à-*

tête after class on the do's and don'ts of classroom etiquette. Above all, she warns, avoid a public blowup. Bring in the department head or the dean if necessary.

34 And remember, say conduct coaches, that the problem might be you. "As we talk about incivility among the student body, we should also talk about incivility among the teaching body," says P.M. Forni, a professor of Italian at the Johns Hopkins University and co-director of the Hopkins Civility Project, a constellation of academic activities focusing on manners and mores. "Teachers can be overbearing. They can adopt behavior that can mortify students. They can exhibit a purported intellectual superiority, belittle students, use sarcasm in a way that's hurtful."

35 Showing up late for class, arriving unprepared, turning a blind eye to rudeness, or using profanity encourages students to do the same, says Gerald Amada, co-director of the mental-health program at the City College of San Francisco and author of *Coping with the Disruptive College Student* (College Administration Publications, 1994). "Everything we do in a class conveys something about ourselves and our moral values. If we're teaching brilliantly, but in the classroom uncivil behavior occurs and we ignore it, then we're also teaching something else—that those behaviors are permissible. By default, we encourage the behavior."

36 But what, professors wonder, should they do when their gender or race is at the root of student rudeness? Male students are far more likely to try to run roughshod over female professors—especially those working in male-dominated disciplines like chemistry, physics, and math, scholars say.

RACIAL STEREOTYPES

37 But race is a real clincher, Ms. Lee says. "Students could not only see me as the permissive mammy, who could be controlled, or the stereotypical sinister black bitch, who needed to be challenged at every turn." She lacked the "cultural currency" to command their respect, she says. "When I resisted, my students felt authorized to resist me even more."

38 These days, she's finding it tough to resist at all. After five weeks in the classroom this semester, she decided to take a leave of absence. "I kept having these moments when I would think about what happened and would start to feel afraid and angry. What if this crazy madness happens again?"

39 Ms. Warma, of Utah State, is also thinking of leaving the classroom. "If you go in and do your job and every day the behavior tells you the job is not worth doing, it's very discouraging. No one is doing it for the fabulous salary."

40 What's really disheartening, professors say, is the lack of support they get from the administration when the problems arise. In Colonial days, college presidents would flog unruly students. Now administrators cower at the idea of kicking hellions out of class. The specter of a lawsuit, Mr. Amada says, makes universities fearful to take a stand against incivility.

41 Many professors themselves are afraid to come forward. "It doesn't take much for your colleagues to wonder if you're competent," Ms. Lee says.

42 Despite the difficulties, not everyone is pessimistic. Guilia Sissa, the head of the classics department at Johns Hopkins and co-director of the Civility Project there, saw a student head for the door during a lecture. Where was he going? To watch a basketball

game, he replied. On the spot, she discussed the appropriateness of his behavior with him, and he sat back down. He also took two more classes with her. One of them was a course she taught with Mr. Forni. It's title: "Civility, Manners, and Politeness."

POST-READING QUESTIONS

CONTENT

1. What are some types of student behavior that Schneider claims professors complain about? How serious are these? Explain.
2. What are some causes of uncivil classroom behavior, according to Schneider? Which causes seem most relevant to you? Why?
3. What role does Schneider say class size plays in determining student behavior?
4. What role does consumerism play in terms of how students view their education? How does this attitude, in turn, affect students' behavior?
5. According to the article, to what extent is classroom incivility a new problem?
6. What steps are some teachers taking in order to combat incivility in the classroom?
7. What role do teachers' actions play in determining how students act? Explain.

STYLE AND STRUCTURE

8. Who is the audience here? How can you tell?
9. Between teachers and students, what side does the writer take? Choose examples from the text to support your view.
10. What is Schneider's primary message? Restate her main idea in your own words.
11. What points does Schneider need to establish in order for her argument to be convincing? How successfully does she do this?
12. What types of examples does Schneider rely on for support? Are these examples convincing? Explain.

CRITICAL THINKING AND ANALYSIS

DISCUSSION QUESTIONS

13. Schneider writes that a "crisis of authority" leaves "no one above question." To what extent do you think this type of attitude has affected students' classroom demeanor? Explain.
14. How often do you think classroom incivility is the teacher's fault? Explain and give examples.
15. What are some solutions to impolite class behavior that you can offer?

WRITING ASSIGNMENTS

16. Do you agree with Schneider that "every professor's nightmare" of "losing control of the class" is "happening more and more"? Explain and give examples.

17. Writer and Yale Law School professor Stephen Carter says that "If you haven't civilized young people by the time they get to college, I don't think you're going to civilize them at all." Is he right? Explain.

18. Ms. Sorcinelli, of the University of Massachusetts, states that professors should "lay down the law" for students on the first day of class. What effect do you think this approach has on student behavior? Explain.

VOCABULARY DEVELOPMENT

19. Choose at least three of the words listed in the Vocabulary Preview and use them to write one-to-three sentences arguing against Schneider's main idea. Do you find the words more, or less, powerful when you use them to oppose Schneider's argument? Why?

GROUP ACTIVITIES

20. Present two skits to your class: one in which the teacher is rude to a student, and one in which the student is rude to the teacher. Make sure your depiction of "rudeness" falls within the guidelines of everyday, rather than extreme, incivility. Discuss which situation you feel to be more common and brainstorm suggestions to counter the rudeness without contributing to it.

21. Compare the course information sheets for all of your classes and discuss which behavior policies seem most effective for ensuring a positive learning experience. Then, as a group, write your own statement of classroom policy and present it to the class in an open forum style.

Welcome to Animal House

Anna Quindlen

Writing after the University of Indiana fired its long-term basketball coach Bobby Knight, Anna Quindlen raises the issue of whether or not campuses have made progress in terms of sensitivity to women and minority students. She questions the motivation behind many seemingly harmful student activities and argues that academics, particularly at schools with large athletic programs, take a back seat to sports.

Pre-reading Questions

What types of school-related experiences do you participate in, outside the classroom? How important do you think social activities are in terms of your college experience? At what point do you think non-academic activities should be limited by the school you attend? In what ways do you think they can be limited? Explain.

Vocabulary Preview

Vocabulary Words:	• zenith	• hyperannuated	• nattering
	• nadir	• ethos	• in loco parentis
	• keening	• boorish	• salutary

Write a paragraph using at least five of the words above without looking them up first. Then, use a dictionary to determine how appropriate your usage of those words is, and revise your paragraph based on the words' definitions in order to clarify meaning and eliminate faulty usage.

1   The student occupation of buildings at Columbia University in 1968 remains the zenith or the nadir of all campus protests, depending on your politics. Richard Nixon (he was on the nadir side) warned in its wake that it was "the first major skirmish in a revolutionary struggle to seize the universities of the country."

2   If Mr. Nixon were alive today, perhaps he would be surprised to learn that the revolutionary struggle is now in defense of beer, basketball and bad behavior.

3   College students have settled in to campuses across America, with their backpacks, their laptops and their some-assembly-required bookshelves, and as certain as carbohydrates in the food-service menu, sooner or later there will be keening about how the poor kids are awash in a welter of political correctness. "Menstruation and Medea: Fear of the Female in the Classics," or "From the Slave Cabins to the Recording Studio: Black in a White Economy"—it's so easy to lampoon on the lament that campus life is infused with hyperannuated regard for the sensibilities of minority students and women. There is a sadly out-of-date white Anglo-Saxon term for this point of view. It is balderdash.

4   The real prevailing ethos on many campuses is quite the opposite. Take the uprisings this semester at Indiana University. These demonstrations were inspired not by the economic disparity between rich and poor or by corporate imperialism, but by the firing of a man who coaches basketball. Space here is limited, so it is not possible to describe all the boorish behavior for which the Indiana coach, Bobby Knight, has become known over the years. He's thrown furniture, assaulted players, verbally abused both school officials and referees, cursed at opponents and won a lot of games.

5   Obviously, Mr. Knight's personal style made a huge impact on campus, since students responded to his long-overdue dismissal by setting fires, toppling light poles and so menacing the president of the university that he and his wife fled their home and moved into a hotel. "History was in the making, and I was not going to miss this for the world, and certainly not for homework," one dopey student, whose parents should stop payment on his tuition immediately, wrote of the riot.

6   This reaction was not totally unexpected. A professor of English, Murray Sperber, who has been critical of Knight in print and on television, was on leave last year from the university, in part because of letters like the one with the Star of David repeatedly scribbled on it, or the voice-mail message "If you don't shut up, I'll shut you up." In his book "Beer and Circus: How Big-Time College Sports Is Crippling Undergraduate Education," Professor Sperber says that at schools like Indiana with prominent and successful sports programs, athletics overshadow scholarship, leading to a culture in which students spend more time partying than studying, in which a basketball coach can be infinitely more important than the school's president.

7   But the "Animal House" effect in higher education is not confined to big state schools with monster sports teams. MIT, one of the finest science schools in the world, recently agreed to pay almost $5 million to the family of a student who died of acute alcohol poisoning during a fraternity-pledge event. Any number of colleges have identified the fraternity culture of long nights and endless kegs as a source of problems ranging from vandalism to date rape, but students respond badly to any attempt to curtail the Greek system. Really badly. When she was president of Denison, Michele Tolela Myers decided that the fraternities at the Ohio school should be nonresidential to cut down on the boozing and bad behavior.

8   "Frat boys put dead animals outside the front door of our house, someone threw a billiard ball through our living room window," recalled Myers, who is now president of Sarah Lawrence. And it was clear that the students had learned at the knee of like-minded adults. Myers got name-calling hate mail from alums: "the bitch, the Jew, she should go back East where she belongs." So much for P.C.

9   Contrary to all the nattering about political correctness, the social atmosphere on many campuses is macho and exclusionary and determinedly anti-intellectual. It's an atmosphere in which much of the social life revolves around drinking. It's an atmosphere in which date rape is rampant. One study says that six or seven out of every 50 college women have been victims of acquaintance rape within a single year. It may be provocative to suggest that the new civility codes and sexual-assault policies on certain campuses are a product of oversensitivity about issues of race and gender. But it's more accurate to say that they are long-overdue responses to problems of speech and behavior that have been ignored for years.

10   The Columbia protests marked the beginning of the end of in loco parentis, the no-tion that the administration stood in for parents in terms of setting limits and making rules. But Myers's experience indicates that if officials are willing to take a strong stand against individuals and organizations that poison a community—and are willing to put up with a distressing amount of personal abuse and enforce real-world legal statutes—the end result will be salutary. She recalls that Denison had its best applicant pool of her tenure after the fraternity decision because it was no longer seen by parents and college counselors as an unreconstructed party school.

11   Americans of my parents' generation were horrified by what happened at Co-lumbia in 1968: the files destroyed, the dean held hostage. But if the actions were questionable, the impulse had meaning: opposition to the war in Vietnam, to the university's research contracts with the Pentagon and its plan to co-opt a park in Harlem to build a gym. Three decades later, and we have campus uprisings dedi-cated to the preservation of a winning season at all cost. Left wing on campus? Don't be fooled. In lots of places, it's not a political stance. It's a position on the hockey team.

POST-READING QUESTIONS

CONTENT

1. What issues or causes does Quindlen say students demonstrate for? How have these causes changed from the 1968 protest Quindlen describes? How is this change significant?

2. What attitude does Quindlen say the public takes about political correctness? Is she right? Explain.

3. What does Quindlen say Bobby Knight is known for? What does she say Indi-ana University's reaction to his dismissal is a sign of?

4. What is the current relationship between academics and athletics on campus, according to Quindlen's article? Is she right? Explain and give examples.

5. How does Quindlen describe the social atmosphere on many campuses? Do you agree?

STYLE AND STRUCTURE

6. What point is Quindlen making? Rewrite her primary argument in your own words.

7. What examples does Quindlen use to support her ideas? Are these examples sufficient? Explain.

8. Who is Quindlen's audience? To what extent are you, a student, part of her au-dience? Choose examples and expressions from the essay that best reveal the target audience.

9. What is the tone of the article? Choose words and phrases that best communi-cate the tone.

10. How convincing is Quindlen? What points do you find particularly effective or ineffective? Explain.

11. Why does Quindlen mention, at the end of her list of Bobby Knight's uncivil actions, that he "won a lot of games"?

CRITICAL THINKING AND ANALYSIS

DISCUSSION QUESTIONS

12. How prevalent is the "party" and "win at any cost" attitude on your campus? What factors contribute to or detract from the presence of this attitude?

13. Are people's priorities any less academically oriented than they were ten years ago? Fifteen? Upon what do you base your conclusion?

14. How seriously should schools take the political correctness movement? In what areas of school—classroom, social events, student government—should policies regarding political correctness be implemented?

WRITING ASSIGNMENTS

15. Quindlen quotes Indiana University's Professor Murray Sperber who writes that "at schools . . . with prominent and successful sports programs, athletics overshadow scholarship." Write three to five paragraphs in which you agree or disagree with Sperber's assertion. Be sure to use examples from your own experience and observations in order to illustrate your ideas.

16. Do you agree that "the social atmosphere on many campuses is . . . exclusionary and determinedly anti-intellectual"? Explain your response in a few paragraphs, citing the reading and your own experiences.

VOCABULARY DEVELOPMENT

17. Look up whatever words you did not look up for the Vocabulary Preview and use them in sentences related to the topic of Quindlen's article.

GROUP ACTIVITIES

18. Make a list of all campus-related terms (club or courses titles, student newspaper articles, for instance) that you think reflect the political correctness movement, and discuss which terms seem appropriate and which terms go overboard. What, as a group, do you notice about the types of groups labeled with politically correct language? Present your findings to the class and compare them with others' conclusions.

19. Choose a paragraph from any essay in this chapter and rewrite it twice, once using extremely politically correct language and once using slang (be sure to identify the audience the slang targets). Which version do you think is most appropriate for your peer group? For your academic group? Why? Exchange versions with other groups to compare your "P.C." expressions and slang with theirs.

SYNTHESIS QUESTIONS

1. Joyce Jarrett writes of being negatively labeled by another student on her first day in geometry class, and she speaks of "That painful, dehumanizing incident" when her teacher overlooked her. However, Alison Schneider writes that teachers are being "hijacked by 'classroom terrorists.'" In a well-developed paragraph or essay, argue that teachers or students have more challenges to face in the classroom as a result of uncivil behavior directed toward them. Be sure to cite both essays and other readings from this chapter in order to support your points.

2. Alison Schneider writes of student incivility toward teachers while Mary Anne Raywid and Libby Oshiyama claim that students are the victims of incivility from each other and that teachers do not do enough to stop their unkind actions. Further, Iain Steinberg writes that students, faculty, and professionals all practice forms of unfair behavior through the ways they complete their work and assign credit for it. Who should be most responsible for halting uncivil or unfair behavior? Write a few paragraphs or an essay in which you explain which one of these three bodies—students, teachers, or professionals—should bear the burden of being civil and fair; then explain why this is so. If you think that all three groups are responsible, explain why you believe this and to what extent each group is responsible.

3. Richard Rodriguez claims that "one suffers a diminished sense of private individuality by being assimilated into public society" while Mary Anne Raywid and Libby Oshiyama write that the "herding instinct" is strongest during adolescence and must be nurtured. Write an essay in which you argue whether or not it is possible for students to maintain their "private individuality" and simultaneously follow their "herding instinct" during high school. Be sure to mention any conditions that make this reconciliation of opposite ideas possible, and use your own experiences and observations in order to illustrate your ideas.

4. Joyce Jarrett writes that she felt "dehumanized" at the treatment of her teacher and classmates, and Mary Anne Raywid and Libby Oshiyama assert that the "student assassins of Columbine . . . were outcasts who banded together after repeated acts of rejection and humiliation . . ." How big a problem do you think unkindness is in high school? Write an essay in which you discuss the extent of unkindness in high schools. Cite both articles and your own experiences in order to support your ideas.

5. Anna Quindlen claims that athletics overshadow academics at many institutions of higher learning, and Iain Steinberg claims that some of his clients were "dedicated scholars" who simply had too much to do. How important is education today? Write a few paragraphs or short essay in which you argue whether or not education for its own sake is a lower priority for students than it was ten years ago (you may broaden or narrow this scope, if you like). Be sure to cite both articles and others from this chapter, and use your own experiences in education in order to make your points convincing.

6. Joyce Jarrett reveals how white students at her new high school sat apart from her in class, and Mary Anne Raywid and Libby Oshiyama claim that the "jocks" and "preps" of Columbine High School performed acts of unkindness that signaled "rejection and humiliation" of the student shooters. Write a well-developed paragraph or an essay in which you discuss how aware people are that their actions, particularly during adolescence, affect others. Be sure to use examples from the articles and from your own school experiences in order to illustrate your ideas.

7. Mary Anne Raywid and Libby Oshiyama recount how the Columbine shooters focused their attention on "jocks," who were among the popular students at their school. Further, Anna Quindlen writes that at schools with successful sports programs "athletics overshadow scholarship" and create "a culture in which students spend more time partying than studying." How important are school sports? Write an essay in which you argue that sports do or do not have a strong influence on a school's academics. Be sure to cite your own experiences as well as articles from this chapter in order to illustrate your ideas.

8. Richard Rodriguez writes that if his teachers had spoken Spanish, the language his family spoke, he would have felt more comfortable at school, and Mary Anne Raywid and Libby Oshiyama argue that students need to feel a sense of connection and community at school. Write a paragraph or essay in which you offer suggestions as to how to make students feel at ease on campus.

"Nobody knows if you're a dog on the Internet."

— Anonymous

". . . computers make our worst educational nightmares come true."

— David Gelerntner
Unplugged

"We shall encounter virtual sex and cyberspace marriage, computer psychotherapists, robot insects, and researchers who are trying to build artificial two-year-olds. . . . Indeed, in much of this, it is our children who are leading the way, and adults who are anxiously trailing behind."

— Sherry Turkle
Identity in the Age of the Internet

"The Internet seems to be laced with truth serum."

— **Marshall Jung**
Romancing the Net

"The goal of all inanimate objects is to resist man and ultimately to defeat him . . ."

— **Russell Baker**

Chapter 5: Civility and Technology

Readings:

Argument Pair:

Websites:

www.epic.org/free_speech/censorship

This site provides links to current Internet censorship legislation and to other groups concerned about freedom on speech online.

www.whitehouse.gov

The website for the White House offers access to an on-line archive of press releases and other documents issued by the White House, including many related to the Internet

Introduction

Here at the beginning of the twenty-first century, we have many more ways to communicate with each other than we had 100 years ago. In addition to face-to-face communication and the postal service, we now employ telephones, cellular telephones, pagers, voice mail, Internet chat rooms, email, Internet "Instant Messaging," and other technologically-oriented means of contacting other people. We also have a seemingly infinite amount of information available at our fingertips through the Internet's vast resources. People's names, addresses, and phone numbers are a click of the mouse away, and full-text documents await our retrieval through online databases. Research has never been so speedy and so multi-faceted.

However, this ease of information acquisition breeds the desire for privacy in the same people who eagerly seek information about others; we want to learn all we can about and communicate with people when we choose, yet we want to reserve our right to solitude and anonymity when the mood strikes. We also want to be assured that we are safe online, that our identities, credit card numbers, and personal information will remain intact if we decide to visit a dot-com website. Thus, some people take steps to protect themselves from unwanted intrusion; they screen calls, lie about their identities online, and ignore email in an effort to maintain personal privacy in the common space of the electronic age.

More and more, technology is showing itself to be two-sided: for every benefit we derive from our light-speed communications, we face new forms of unpleasantness or even danger. Thus, the question arises: what role does civility play in technology? Do the same manners generated and agreed upon for dinner table conversation and polite correspondence apply to email and electronic pages? What are the new rules, and who decides them? What are the causes of some of the irritating, even dishonest, actions people display online, and what are the effects of those same behaviors? This chapter addresses these questions and others, seeking to define civility in an electronic context. As writers, then, we need to consider our experiences with technology in order to determine what we mean by civility within the bounds of technology and how important civility is in the midst of so much innovation.

The Plot Against People

Russell Baker

A two-time Pulitzer prize winner for his *New York Times* column and his autobiographical novel *Growing Up,* Russell Baker is known for his wit and humor in addressing topics familiar to many. In *The Plot Against People,* Baker discusses the challenge humanity struggles daily to meet: dealing successfully with inanimate objects designed to help us. Through his own humor, Baker shows us how to circumvent the frustrations of mechanical progress via laughter.

Pre-reading Questions

Freewrite for five to ten minutes in response to the following questions:
Have you ever lost your temper with an inanimate object? What happened to make you lose your temper? Why do you think people become angry with things that cannot move or think or speak? What solutions, if any, can you offer to people who lose their tempers with inanimate objects?

Vocabulary Preview

Vocabulary Words:		
• cunning	• virtually	• baffled
• plausible	• invariably	• aspire
• locomotion	• constitutes	
• burrow	• conciliatory	

Look up the words above and, as you read, write a few sentences explaining how these words are or are not effective in helping Baker communicate his ideas.

1   Inanimate objects are classified scientifically into three major categories—those that break down, those that get lost, and those that don't work.

2   The goal of all inanimate objects is to resist man and ultimately to defeat him, and the three major classifications are based on the method each object uses to achieve its purpose. As a general rule, any object capable of breaking down at the moment when it is most needed will do so. The automobile is typical of the category.

3   With the cunning peculiar to its breed, the automobile never breaks down while entering a filling station which has a large staff of idle mechanics. It waits until it reaches a downtown intersection in the middle of the rush hour, or until it is fully loaded with family and luggage on the Ohio Turnpike. Thus it creates maximum inconvenience, frustration, and irritability, thereby reducing its owner's lifespan.

4   Washing machines, garbage disposals, lawn mowers, furnaces, TV sets, tape recorders, slide projectors—all are in league with the automobile to take their turn at breaking down whenever life threatens to flow smoothly for their enemies.

5   Many inanimate objects, of course, find it extremely difficult to break down. Pliers, for example, and gloves and keys are almost totally incapable of breaking down. Therefore, they have had to evolve a different technique for resisting man.

6   They get lost. Science has still not solved the mystery of how they do it, and no man has ever caught one of them in the act. The most plausible theory is that they have developed a secret method of locomotion which they are able to conceal from human eyes.

7   It is not uncommon for a pair of pliers to climb all the way from the cellar to the attic in its single-minded determination to raise its owner's blood pressure. Keys have been known to burrow three feet under mattresses. Women's purses, despite their great weight, frequently travel through six or seven rooms to find hiding space under a couch.

8   Scientists have been struck by the fact that things that break down virtually never get lost, while things that get lost hardly ever break down. A furnace, for example, will invariably break down at the depth of the first winter cold wave, but it will never get lost. A woman's purse hardly ever breaks down; it almost invariably chooses to get lost.

9   Some persons believe this constitutes evidence that inanimate objects are not entirely hostile to man. After all, they point out, a furnace could infuriate a man even more thoroughly by getting lost than by breaking down, just as a glove could upset him far more by breaking down than by getting lost.

10   Not everyone agrees, however, that this indicates a conciliatory attitude. Many say it merely proves that furnaces, gloves and pliers are incredibly stupid.

11   The third class of objects—those that don't work—is the most curious of all. These include such objects as barometers, car clocks, cigarette lighters, flashlights and toy-train locomotives. It is inaccurate, of course, to say that they *never* work. They work once, usually for the first few hours after being brought home, and then quit. Thereafter, they never work again.

12   In fact, it is widely assumed that they are built for the purpose of not working. Some people have reached advanced ages without ever seeing some of these objects—barometers, for example—in working order.

13   Science is utterly baffled by the entire category. There are many theories about it. The most interesting holds that the things that don't work have attained the highest state possible for an inanimate object, the state to which things that break down and things that get lost can still only aspire.

14   They have truly defeated man by conditioning him never to expect anything of them. When his cigarette lighter won't light or his flashlight fails to illuminate, it does not raise his blood pressure. Objects that don't work have given man the only peace he receives from inanimate society.

POST-READING QUESTIONS

CONTENT

1. How does Baker classify inanimate objects?

2. What does Baker say is "the goal of all inanimate objects"? What about Baker's reasoning communicates that he does not mean for his reader to take him seriously?

3. What proof does Baker offer for the idea that inanimate objects are "not entirely hostile to man"?

4. Why does Baker say objects that don't work comprise "the most curious [class] of all"?

5. What has given humans "the only peace . . . from inanimate society"? Why?

STYLE AND STRUCTURE

6. Does Baker have a serious point? What is it?

7. What audience is Baker addressing? What clues does he give you as to when this article was written, and for whom?

8. What examples does Baker give? How effective are these examples in illustrating his main idea? Explain.

9. What is the tone of this essay? Choose some words or phrases that you think best reveal the tone.

10. Is Baker convincing, even though he uses humor? Why?

CRITICAL THINKING AND ANALYSIS

DISCUSSION QUESTIONS

11. Do you agree with Baker that inanimate objects can be frustrating? Discuss your experiences with inanimate objects in order to draw a conclusion to answer this question.

12. Since this essay's publication in 1968, what other categories of inanimate objects might you add that Baker does not include?

WRITING ASSIGNMENTS

13. Imitating Baker's tone as best you can, write a short essay classifying inanimate objects in your life. You do not need to use Baker's classifications, but you can if you wish. Be sure to provide examples from your own life.

14. Write a few paragraphs arguing that one object in particular is the most frustrating of all inanimate objects. Be sure to use examples from your own experiences in order to illustrate your ideas.

VOCABULARY DEVELOPMENT

15. What role does language play in determining humor? Choose several expressions that you find funny in Baker's essay, and write a few sentences explaining why these particular terms are humorous.

GROUP ACTIVITIES

16. Make a list of all the objects that members of your group use at school that can be frustrating in some way. What do you notice about the objects that serve as the greatest source of frustration? Compare your findings to other groups.

17. Assume the point of view of an inanimate object that is plotting against humans, and write a few paragraphs explaining how this object will achieve its goals. If possible, draw diagrams in order to provide visual aids for the plan. Present your findings to the class.

Anywhere but Here: More Connected but More Alone

Anne Taylor Fleming

Writer and television commentator Anne Taylor Fleming is also the author of *Motherhood Deferred.* In *Anywhere but Here: More Connected but More Alone,* she claims that cell phones have "blurred the line between the public sphere and the private." She offers several explanations for this change in behavior and questions whether or not our attempts at increased connection with others instead isolate us more.

Pre-reading Questions

Freewrite for five to ten minutes in response to the following questions:
What are the different ways you communicate with other people? Of these, which is the most personal? What do you think of people who hold personal conversations on their cell phones in public?

Vocabulary Preview

Vocabulary Words:		
• profound	• banquette	• tethered
• implications	• wangle	• titillating
• decorum	• idyllic	• fodder
• blanch	• coifed	• grist

Without looking up the words above, write a few related sentences using at least five of the words. Then, use a dictionary to learn the formal definitions of all the words, and rewrite your sentences, if necessary, to clarify meaning and avoid faulty usage.

1   Cellular telephones are so ever-present now that we somehow no longer bother about them or register the profound changes they have wrought in our culture and our behavior. After all, we've all had telephones forever. The cell phone is just a ready-to-trot wireless version, a gadget of the utmost convenience. So what's the big deal? The big deal is that the cellular phone has completely changed the way we behave in public and, even more, completely blurred the line between the public sphere and the private without us even realizing it, with wide-reaching implications for how we treat each other—and ourselves. The technology got ahead of any etiquette, any sense we might have had of public decorum, so that we no longer blanch when we overhear people confiding in, yelling at, or cooing in the ear of someone else through their cell phones.

2   We've become a nation of compulsive communicators, nonstop babblers airing our most private thoughts in the most public of places—an airport lounge, a restaurant banquette, a city street. We're now all part of each other's audiences. It's as if we live

in a virtual-reality TV talk show, a rolling 12-step public marathon, with complete strangers spewing out intimacies or fighting right in front of us, needful of validation of our attention. It's as if nothing is real anymore unless it happens in public with an audience, and the cellular phone is the perfect little gizmo to make this possible. You don't have to wangle your way onto Jerry or Oprah, or any of the other confessional TV shows. All you need is a public place and a cellular telephone, and you can be center stage, living one of your life's little or big dramas out loud for all the rest of us to overhear. Look at me, the caller says. I'm somebody. I can't even wait to get back to the office or to a pay phone.

> I have to make this call right now. I am needed. I am important. Just listen. My friends love me. My kids need me. My boss can't breathe without me.
> I matter.

3   In fairness, this isn't just an American addiction. Many of us have had the experience of being in a hillside town in Tuscany or an idyllic, isolated resort and being privy to the same techno-din. In fact, when I was last in Europe, the cellular-phone epidemic seemed even worse than here—all manner of coifed matrons and hip Eurokids strolling down the street barking into their portable phones over the roar of motorbikes.

4   What's wrong with all of us? Why the desperate need to be vocally tethered to someone else at all times? Can we not stand the downtime, the silence of our own company? Even children are wired up, toting their own phones and beepers, overscheduled to the max—this play date, that soccer game—so that they, too, will learn to be strangers to themselves, unused to stillness, unaware that there is, or should be, a demarcation between public and private. Only in private do we take the measure of our own gifts and failings—no doubt why we avoid it so. Only in private—away from the crowd and the audience—do we do original and creative work and plumb the depths of our consciences. Only in private do we experience the truest and deepest emotions, be they agony or ecstasy.

5   The rest is posturing: Life as a spectator sport, precisely what we've turned sex into. The accent is no longer on the act itself but on the postcoital play-by-play. Like the tabloid TV shows, the postmodern sitcom is often little else but a titillating talkathon in which groups of friends sit around and dissect their sexual encounters for each other. They cannibalize their meaningful experiences and turn them into cheap anecdotes to be served up on a platter to the rest of their clique. Cell phones have sped up that process. Jump out of bed and jump on the phone. Guess what I did; guess what he did. These phones have changed the very nature of gossip; they've made it quicker, crueler, more pervasive and instantaneous. There is no time to edit, pull back, savor. Everything is fodder, fair game, grist for the cell-phone mill.

6   All to say that we seem to have given up on privacy altogether— on the very idea of its virtues. It's as if the entire twentieth century has been about this technologically abetted trend away from privacy, so that we now arrive at a point where nothing is off-limits for public confiding, and where you cannot or need not be alone anywhere. In a car, in a forest, you're reachable and so is your circle of friends. (Friends are the families of the '90s.) You're not alone as long as you have your phone tucked in your purse or pocket, your cellular hedge against loneliness.

7   No doubt, that's what the phones are ultimately about: loneliness and a frantic attempt to evade it. But the irony is that they make it worse. Think of it: You're walking down a throbbing city street, noise and people all around, human pageantry, but you're busy chatting with a friend or arguing with a spouse via your speed dial. You're cocooned, disconnected from the things and people around you, experiencing that weird nonintimate-intimacy, that weird public-privacy that characterizes so many of our modern interactions, be they via the cellular phone or the Internet. It's not unusual these days to see two people having lunch, forks in hand, talking not to each other but to someone else via their respective cell phones. Clearly we're more hooked up than ever and, on some level, more lonesome. Why else all the manic phoning, the need to be reachable by somebody, anybody, anywhere and everywhere?

8   There's a little grandiosity in it, too, a sense of self-importance conferred by a ringing phone. Excuse me, somebody needs me right now, this minute. But are any of us that important? Sure, we all have deadlines, personal and professional, but barely a one of us is so vital to some enterprise that the call has to be made this second, in public, no matter where you are or what the circumstances. That's just self-congratulatory folderol. Kids, too, can wait. They don't have to be phoned or fetched at a given instant. After all, we did all get along before we had these things. They provide a false sense of urgency, of faux drama, of life lived to the fullest.

9   By any measure, cell phones waste more time than they save, like many of our other so-called "timesaving devices." They embroil us in endless, unnecessary chatter that only serves to abbreviate our already overstimulated attention spans.

10   Yes, there are true emergencies—on the road, in an accident, in a faltering democracy where a coup is imminent. Then a cellular phone can be a lifeline. But that's not what most people are using them for on a daily basis. They're using them to ward off the stillness, the demons, the specter of loneliness. Millions of people around the globe, walking down a jam-packed city street or sunbathing on a beach or lying in bed with a lover, reaching for their cell phones at this very moment, connecting up while simultaneously disconnecting from the time and place and pleasure at hand.

11   It's a loud, lonesome tableau that speaks to the profound revolution these simple, hand-held devices have brought about in all our lives.

POST-READING QUESTIONS

CONTENT

1. What are some reasons Fleming gives for people's seeming need for constant connection, via cell phone, with others? Do you agree that people do need constant connection?

2. How does Fleming describe public cell phone conversations? To what does she compare them?

3. Fleming states that there "should be . . . a demarcation between public and private" life. What reasons does she give for feeling this way? What are some benefits of "stillness" or privacy, according to Fleming?

4. What does Fleming say must occur before people feel like their lives are "real"? Do you agree with her?

5. What effect(s) does Fleming claim cell phones have had on people's private lives?

STYLE AND STRUCTURE

6. How does Fleming reconcile the two seemingly opposite concepts in the title?

7. What is Fleming's primary argument? Rewrite her idea in your own words.

8. What examples does Fleming use to illustrate her main idea? How effective are her examples?

9. What is Fleming's tone? Choose words and expressions that identify her tone and explain how her tone does or does not cause Fleming to be convincing.

10. Is Fleming persuasive? Explain.

CRITICAL THINKING AND ANALYSIS

DISCUSSION QUESTIONS

11. In what ways, if any, do you think people are "more connected but more alone"?

12. What other elements of technology do you think have affected our behavior? Explain, using examples, how specific aspects of technology have had positive or negative influences on people's behavior.

WRITING ASSIGNMENTS

13. Fleming writes that the cellular phone, "has completely changed the way we behave in public . . ." Describe some ways that you have observed the cell phone to have changed people's public behavior and explain why you think the cell phone has had this effect.

14. Fleming claims that the cell phone has made gossip "quicker, crueler, more pervasive and instantaneous." In what ways, if any, do you think the cell phone has affected the nature of gossip? What reasons can you give to account for this effect? Write a few paragraphs explaining how cell phones have affected the nature of gossip.

15. To what extent do you think public cell phone conversations constitute uncivil behavior? Write at least three well-developed paragraphs in responding to this question, and be sure to cite your own experiences for support.

VOCABULARY DEVELOPMENT

16. Of the words listed in the Vocabulary Preview, which have you heard the most? Choose at least five of the words in the Preview that you think are more commonly used, and write a few sentences explaining why you think those words are used more than others in the list.

GROUP ACTIVITIES

17. Role-play using a group member's cellular phone—if no one has a phone, then use a prop. Have two people be engaged in conversation when the phone rings. How does the person receiving the call react? How does the call affect the conversation? How is the caller treated? Repeat the situation two or three times in order for everyone to participate and then discuss how the call made each member of the situation feel.

18. Survey members of your family or your friends as to who takes priority when a call comes during a face-to-face conversation, the caller or the person at hand. Then, bring your results to class, and in small groups, share your results and draw a conclusion about how technology has affected people's behavior and priorities. Share your results with the class in an open-forum situation.

The Telephone

Anwar F. Accawi

Born and raised in Magdaluna, the very small Lebanese village in the hills above the city of Sidon, Anwar Accawi was educated in the United States and began writing stories about his adolescence in the old country in order to share his early life with his children. "The Telephone" explores the effects of technology on old-world ways of living and, in turn, raises the questions of whether humans need connection through technology, whether technology improves quality of life, and whether the desire for connection begets technology or vice versa.

Pre-reading Questions

Freewrite for five to ten minutes in response to the following questions:
How often do you use a telephone daily? How much time on the phone do you spend as opposed to how much time you spend in face-to-face conversation? What effect does the phone have on your ability to connect with other people? Under what circumstances, if any, does the phone have a negative effect on your life?

Vocabulary Preview

Vocabulary Words:
- tampered
- toiled
- pestilences
- milestones
- protruding
- shunned
- utmost
- homey

Look up the words above and, examining the words within the context of the essay, write a few sentences explaining how they are or are not effective in helping the writer communicate his tone.

1   When I was growing up in Magdaluna, a small Lebanese village in the terraced, rocky mountains east of Sidon, time didn't mean much to anybody, except maybe to those who were dying, or those waiting to appear in court because they had tampered with the boundary markers on their land. In those days, there was no real need for a calendar or a watch to keep track of the hours, days, months, and years. We knew what to do and when to do it, just as the Iraqi geese knew when to fly north, driven by the hot wind that blew in from the desert, and the ewes knew when to give birth to wet lambs that stood on long, shaky legs in the chilly March wind and baaed hesitantly, because they were small and cold and did not know where they were or what to do now that they were here. The only timepiece we had need of then was the sun. It rose and set, and the seasons rolled by, and we sowed seed and harvested and ate and played and married our cousins and had babies who got whooping cough and chickenpox—and those

children who survived grew up and married *their* cousins and had babies who got whooping cough and chickenpox. We lived and loved and toiled and died without ever needing to know what year it was, or even the time of day.

2 It wasn't that we had no system for keeping track of time and of the important events in our lives. But ours was a natural—or, rather, a divine—calendar, because it was framed by acts of God. Allah himself set down the milestones with earthquakes and droughts and floods and locusts and pestilences. Simple as our calendar was, it worked just fine for us.

3 Take, for example, the birth date of Teta Im Khalil, the oldest woman in Magdaluna and all the surrounding villages. When I first met her, we had just returned home from Syria at the end of the Big War and were living with Grandma Mariam. Im Khalil came by to welcome my father home and to take a long, myopic look at his foreign-born wife, my mother. Im Khalil was so old that the skin of her cheeks looked like my father's grimy tobacco pouch, and when I kissed her (because Grandma insisted that I show her old friend affection), it was like kissing a soft suede glove that had been soaked with sweat and then left in a dark closet for a season. Im Khalil's face got me to wondering how old one had to be to look and taste the way she did. So, as soon as she had hobbled off on her cane, I asked Grandma, "How old is Teta Im Khalil?"

4 Grandma had to think for a moment; then she said, "I've been told that Teta was born shortly after the big snow that caused the roof on the mayor's house to cave in."

5 "And when was that?" I asked.

6 "Oh, about the time we had the big earthquake that cracked the wall in the east room."

7 Well, that was enough for me. You couldn't be more accurate than that, now, could you? Satisfied with her answer, I went back to playing with a ball made from an old sock stuffed with other, much older socks.

8 And that's the way it was in our little village for as far back as anybody could remember: people were born so many years before or after an earthquake or a flood; they got married or died so many years before or after a long drought or a big snow or some other disaster. One of the most unusual of these dates was when Antoinette the seamstress and Saeed the barber (and tooth puller) got married. That was the year of the whirlwind during which fish and oranges fell from the sky. Incredible as it may sound, the story of the fish and oranges was true, because men—respectable men, like Abu George the blacksmith and Abu Assad the mule skinner, men who would not lie even to save their own souls—told and retold that story until it was incorporated into Magdaluna's calendar, just like the year of the black moon and the year of the locusts before it. My father, too, confirmed the story for me. He told me that he had been a small boy himself when it had rained fish and oranges from heaven. He'd gotten up one morning after a stormy night and walked out into the yard to find fish as long as his forearm still flopping here and there among the wet navel oranges.

9 The year of the fish-bearing twister, however, was not the last remarkable year. Many others followed in which strange and wonderful things happened: milestones added by the hand of Allah to Magdaluna's calendar. There was, for instance, the year of the drought, when the heavens were shut for months and the spring from which the entire village got its drinking water slowed to a trickle. The spring was about a mile

from the village, in a ravine that opened at one end into a small, flat clearing covered with fine gray dust and hard, marble-sized goat droppings, because every afternoon the goatherds brought their flocks there to water them. In the year of the drought, that little clearing was always packed full of noisy kids with big brown eyes and sticky hands, and their mothers—sinewy, overworked young women with protruding collarbones and cracked, callused brown heels. The children ran around playing tag or hide-and-seek while the women talked, shooed flies, and awaited their turns to fill up their jars with drinking water to bring home to their napping men and wet babies. There were days when we had to wait from sunup until late afternoon just to fill a small clay jar with precious, cool water.

10   Sometimes, amid the long wait and the heat and the flies and the smell of goat dung, tempers flared, and the younger women, anxious about their babies, argued over whose turn it was to fill up her jar. And sometimes the arguments escalated into full-blown, knockdown-dragout fights; the women would grab each other by the hair and curse and scream and spit and call each other names that made my ears tingle. We little brown boys who went with our mothers to fetch water loved these fights, because we got to see the women's legs and their colored panties as they grappled and rolled around in the dust. Once in a while, we got lucky and saw much more, because some of the women wore nothing at all under their long dresses. God, how I used to look forward to those fights. I remember the rush, the excitement, the sun dancing on the dust clouds as a dress ripped and a young white breast was revealed, then quickly hidden. In my calendar, that year of drought will always be one of the best years of my childhood, because it was then, in a dusty clearing by a trickling mountain spring, I got my first glimpses of the wonders, the mysteries, and the promises hidden beneath the folds of a woman's dress. Fish and oranges from heaven . . . you can get over that.

11   But, in another way, the year of the drought was also one of the worst of my life, because that was the year that Abu Raja, the retired cook who used to entertain us kids by cracking walnuts on his forehead, decided it was time Magdaluna got its own telephone. Every civilized village needed a telephone, he said, and Magdaluna was not going to get anywhere until it had one. A telephone would link us with the outside world. At the time, I was too young to understand the debate, but a few men—like Shukri, the retired Turkish-army drill sergeant, and Abu Hanna the vineyard keeper—did all they could to talk Abu Raja out of having a telephone brought to the village. But they were outshouted and ignored and finally shunned by the other villagers for resisting progress and trying to keep a good thing from coming to Magdaluna.

12   One warm day in early fall, many of the villagers were out in their fields repairing walls or gathering wood for the winter when the shout went out that the telephone-company truck had arrived at Abu Raja's *dikkan,* or country store. There were no roads in these days, only footpaths and dry streambeds, so it took the telephone-company truck almost a day to work its way up the rocky terrain from Sidon—about the same time it took to walk. When the truck came into view, Abu George, who had a huge voice and, before the telephone, was Magdaluna's only long-distance communication system, bellowed the news from his front porch. Everybody dropped what they were doing and ran to Abu Raja's house to see what was happening. Some of the more dignified villagers, however, like Abu Habeeb and Abu Nazim, who had been to big cities

like Beirut and Damascus and had seen things like telephones and telegraphs, did not run the way the rest did; they walked with their canes hanging from the crooks of their arms, as if on a Sunday afternoon stroll.

13   It did not take long for the whole village to assemble at Abu Raja's *dikkan.* Some of the rich villagers, like the widow Farha and the gendarme Abu Nadeem, walked right into the store and stood at the elbows of the two important-looking men from the telephone company, who proceeded with utmost gravity, like priests at Communion, to wire up the telephone. The poorer villagers stood outside and listened carefully to the details relayed to them by the not-so-poor people who stood in the doorway and could see inside.

14   "The bald man is cutting the blue wire," someone said.

15   "He is sticking the wire into the hole in the bottom of the black box," someone else added.

16   "The telephone man with the mustache is connecting two pieces of wire. Now he is twisting the ends together," a third voice chimed in.

17   "Because I was small and unaware that I should have stood outside with the other poor folk to give the rich people inside more room (they seemed to need more of it than poor people did), I wriggled my way through the dense forest of legs to get a first-hand look at the action. I felt like the barefoot Moses, sandals in hand, staring at the burning bush on Mount Sinai. Breathless, I watched as the men in blue, their shirt pockets adorned with fancy lettering in a foreign language, put together a black machine that supposedly would make it possible to talk with uncles, aunts, and cousins who lived more than two days' ride away.

18   It was shortly after sunset when the man with the mustache announced that the telephone was ready to use. He explained that all Abu Raja had to do was lift the receiver, turn the crank on his black box a few times, and wait for an operator to take his call. Abu Raja, who had once lived and worked in Sidon, was impatient with the telephone man for assuming that he was ignorant. He grabbed the receiver and turned the crank forcefully, as if trying to start a Model T Ford. Everybody was impressed that he knew what to do. He even called the operator by her first name: "Centralist." Within moments, Abu Raja was talking with this brother, a concierge in Beirut. He didn't even have to raise his voice or shout to be heard.

19   If I hadn't seen it with my own two eyes and heard it with my own two ears, I would not have believed it—and my friend Kameel didn't. He was away that day watching his father's goats, and when he came back to the village that evening, his cousin Habeeb and I told him about the telephone and how Abu Raja had used it to speak with his brother in Beirut. After he heard our report, Kameel made the sign of the cross, kissed his thumbnail, and warned us that lying was a bad sin and would surely land us in purgatory. Kameel believed in Jesus and Mary, and wanted to be a priest when he grew up. He always crossed himself when Habeeb, who was irreverent, and I, who was Presbyterian, were around, even when we were not bearing bad news.

20   And the telephone, as it turned out, was bad news. With its coming, the face of the village began to change. One of the first effects was the shifting of the village's center. Before the telephone's arrival, the men of the village used to gather regularly at the house of Im Kaleem, a short, middle-aged widow with jet-black hair and a raspy voice

that could be heard all over the village, even when she was only whispering. She was a devout Catholic and also the village *shlikki*—whore. The men met at her house to argue about politics and drink coffee and play cards or backgammon. Im Kaleem was not a true prostitute, however, because she did not charge for her services—not even for the coffee and tea (and, occasionally, the strong liquor called arrack) that she served the men. She did not need the money; her son, who was overseas in Africa, sent her money regularly. (I knew this because my father used to read her son's letters to her and take down her replies, as Im Kaleem could not read or write.) Im Kaleem was no slut either—unlike some women in the village—because she loved all the men she entertained, and they loved her, every one of them. In a way, she was married to all the men in the village. Everybody knew it—the wives knew it; the itinerant Catholic priest knew it; the Presbyterian minister knew it—but nobody objected. Actually, I suspect the women (my mother included) did not mind their husbands' visits to Im Kaleem. Oh, they wrung their hands and complained to one another about their men's unfaithfulness, but secretly they were relieved, because Im Kaleem took some of the pressure off them and kept the men out of their hair while they attended to their endless chores. Im Kaleem was also a kind of confessor and troubleshooter, talking sense to those men who were having family problems, especially the younger ones.

21 Before the telephone came to Magdaluna, Im Kaleem's house was bustling at just about any time of the day, especially at night, when its windows were brightly lit with three large oil lamps, and the loud voices of the men talking, laughing, and arguing could be heard in the street below—a reassuring, homey sound. Her house was an island of comfort, an oasis for the weary village men, exhausted from having so little to do.

22 But it wasn't long before many of those men—the younger ones especially—started spending more of their days and evenings at Abu Raja's *dikkan*. There, they would eat and drink and talk and play checkers and backgammon, and then lean their chairs back against the wall—the signal that they were ready to toss back and forth, like a ball, the latest rumors going around the village. And they were always looking up from their games and drinks and talk to glance at the phone in the corner, as if expecting it to ring any minute and bring news that would change their lives and deliver them from their aimless existence. In the meantime, they smoked cheap, hand-rolled cigarettes, dug dirt out from under their fingernails with big pocketknives, and drank lukewarm sodas that they called Kacula, Seffen-Ub, and Bebsi. Sometimes, especially when it was hot, the days dragged on so slowly that the men turned on Abu Saeed, a confirmed bachelor who practically lived in Abu Raja's *dikkan,* and teased him for going around barefoot and unshaven since the Virgin had appeared to him behind the olive press.

23 The telephone was also bad news for me personally. It took away my lucrative business—a source of much-needed income. Before the telephone came to Magdaluna, I used to hang around Im Kaleem's courtyard and play marbles with the other kids, waiting for some man to call down from a window and ask me to run to the store for cigarettes or arrack, or to deliver a message to his wife, such as what he wanted for supper. There was always something in it for me: a ten- or even a twenty-five-piaster piece. On a good day, I ran nine or ten of those errands, which assured a steady supply of marbles that I usually lost to Sami or his cousin Hani, the basket weaver's boy. But

as the days went by, fewer and fewer men came to Im Kaleem's, and more and more congregated at Abu Raja's to wait by the telephone. In the evenings, no light fell from her window onto the street below, and the laughter and noise of the men trailed off and finally stopped. Only Shukri, the retired Turkish-army drill sergeant, remained faithful to Im Kaleem after all the other men had deserted her; he was still seen going into or leaving her house from time to time. Early that winter, Im Kaleem's hair suddenly turned gray, and she got sick and old. Her legs started giving her trouble, making it hard for her to walk. By spring she hardly left her house anymore.

24   At Abu Raja's *dikkan,* the calls did eventually come, as expected, and men and women started leaving the village the way a hailstorm begins: first one, then two, then bunches. The army took them. Jobs in the cities lured them. And ships and airplanes carried them to such faraway places as Australia and Brazil and New Zealand. My friend Kameel, his cousin Habeeb, and their cousins and my cousins all went away to become ditch diggers and mechanics and butcher-shop boys and deli owners who wore dirty aprons sixteen hours a day, all looking for a better life than the one they had left behind. Within a year, only the sick, the old, and the maimed were left in the village. Magdaluna became a skeleton of its former self, desolate and forsaken, like the tombs, a place to get away from.

25   Finally, the telephone took my family away, too. My father got a call from an old army buddy who told him that an oil company in southern Lebanon was hiring interpreters and instructors. My father applied for a job and got it, and we moved to Sidon, where I went to a Presbyterian missionary school and graduated in 1962. Three years later, having won a scholarship, I left Lebanon for the United States. Like the others who left Magdaluna before me, I am still looking for that better life.

POST-READING QUESTIONS

CONTENT

1. By what means do Accawi and his village mark time? To what extent is this method effective for them?

2. What is the pace of life in pre-telephone Magdaluna? How does this pace reflect the villagers' attitude toward their lives and their village?

3. What reasons do the villagers give both for and against having a telephone in the village? Which side eventually wins?

4. How do people communicate before the telephone? After? What effect does the phone have on the village and its inhabitants in terms of their treatment of each other?

5. What types of entertainment and business activities did the villagers participate in before the telephone? How did the telephone change their means of work and play?

STYLE AND STRUCTURE

6. How does the first part of the essay differ from the second part? What organizational strategies does Accawi use in organizing his essay?

7. Does Accawi argue a particular point in his essay? Restate his main idea in your own words.

8. How does Accawi illustrate life before and after the telephone? To what extent are his descriptions effective?

9. What is Accawi's tone? In what ways, if any, does the tone change over the course of the essay?

10. Who is Accawi's audience? To what extent are the inhabitants of Magdaluna his audience? How can you tell? Explain and give examples from the text.

11. What role does humor play in Accawi's essay? What about his essay, if anything, is funny?

12. What does Accawi's comparison of the telephone installation process to Communion say about the village's attitude toward the telephone? Does this attitude change throughout the rest of the essay? Explain.

CRITICAL THINKING AND ANALYSIS

DISCUSSION QUESTIONS

13. How often do you think the effects of technology, such as in Magdaluna, are negative? Positive? Discuss at least three innovations that you think have significantly affected people's lives over the past twenty years.

14. Once an innovation has been introduced into society, how much control do you think people have over its effects upon their lives? Just because a cell phone is invented, for instance, how difficult is it for people not to use it? Explain.

15. Accawi describes how the men's behavior, particularly toward Im Kaleem, changed with the arrival of the telephone. What do you think the relationship between technological advancement and civility is? Examine a few specific devices such as cell phones or email in order to answer this question.

WRITING ASSIGNMENTS

16. Accawi writes that the telephone "was bad news for me personally," and that he left Lebanon for the United States but is still "looking for that better life." What do you think determines a "better life"? Write a brief essay in which you define what a "better life" means in the twenty-first century United States.

17. According to Accawi, people in Magdaluna "lived and loved and toiled and died without ever needing to know what year it was, or even the time of day." Do you think Americans put too much emphasis on time? Write three to five paragraphs arguing that Americans do or do not place too much importance upon time. Be sure to use your own experiences and observations in order to illustrate your ideas.

18. What does Accawi's last sentence imply about the effects of technology? Do you agree with this implication? In a few paragraphs, use your own experiences and observations to illustrate your ideas in responding to this question.

VOCABULARY DEVELOPMENT

19. Accawi uses specific incidents in order to mark time. What events are most meaningful to you? How would you describe these events in your life? Make a list of significant occurrences in your life and then choose a creative, specific name for each one so that someone reading your list could see the importance of the event upon your life.

GROUP ACTIVITIES

20. Think about what aspect of technology frustrates you the most and, for one day, live without that aspect (if you can). For instance, if you dislike seeing people "channel surf" using the remote control for the television, do not use the remote control for one day. Instead, get up to change the channel manually. Is the frustration of technology worth the benefit? Keep notes of your experience and bring your results to class.

21. Make a list of all the positive effects of one aspect of technology and a list of all the negative effects. Then, choose a side and debate with a classmate whether or not that aspect of technology has more benefits or drawbacks. Hold your debate in front of other students and ask them to decide who is more convincing.

My First Flame

John Seabrook

John Seabrook is a staff writer for *The New Yorker* and has written two books: *Deeper: Adventures on the Net* and *Nobrow: The Culture of Marketing, The Marketing of Culture*. In this essay, published in *The New Yorker* in 1994, Seabrook explores both the benefits and the "dark side" of the Internet when he receives his first "flame," and he examines the role of "netiquette" and the power of language online. Seabrook's essay raises questions of whether personal freedom should be sacrificed for the good of online society as a whole.

Pre-reading Questions

Freewrite for five to ten minutes in response to the following questions:
Have you been "flamed" before? What were the circumstances surrounding your flame, and how did it make you feel? What is your attitude about flaming in general?

Vocabulary Preview

Vocabulary Words:
- medium
- candor
- involuntarily
- inhibitions
- volley
- musings
- hypothesis
- repositories
- assailant
- hierarchy
- incantations

Find the words above in Seabrook's essay and write down their definitions using only the context of the essay. *Do not use a dictionary at this time.* Then, after defining each term, do use a dictionary and check your definitions. How close were you to finding the correct meaning of each word? Write a few sentences explaining which words you defined most accurately and why.

1   I got flamed for the first time a couple of months ago. To flame, according to "Que's Computer User's Dictionary," is "to lose one's self-control and write a message that uses derogatory, obscene, or inappropriate language." Flaming is a form of speech that is unique to online communication, and it is one of the aspects of life on the Internet that its promoters don't advertise, just as railroad companies around the turn of the century didn't advertise the hardships of the Great Plains to the pioneers whom they were hoping to transport out there. My flame arrived on a windy Friday morning. I got to work at nine, removed my coat, plugged in my PowerBook, and, as usual, could not resist immediately checking my e-mail. I saw I had a message from a technology writer who does a column about personal computers for a major newspaper, and whom I knew by name only. I had recently published a piece about Bill Gates, the chairman of Microsoft, about whom this person has also written, and as I opened his

e-mail to me it was with the pleasant expectation of getting feedback from a colleague. Instead, I got:

> Crave THIS, asshole:
>
> Listen, you toadying dipshit scumbag . . . remove your head from your rectum long enough to look around and notice that real reporters don't fawn over their subjects, pretend that their subjects are making some sort of special contact with them, or, worse, curry favor by TELLING their subjects how great the ass-licking profile is going to turn out and then brag in print about doing it.
>
> Forward this to Mom. Copy Tina and tell her the mag is fast turning to compost. One good worm deserves another.

2   I rocked back in my chair and said out loud, "Whoa, I got flamed." I knew something bad had just happened to me, and I was waiting to find out what it would feel like. I felt cold. People whose bodies have been badly burned begin to shiver, and the flame seemed to put a chill in the center of my chest which I could feel spreading slowly outward. My shoulders began to shake. I got up and walked quickly to the soda machines for no good reason, then hurried back to my desk. There was the flame on my screen, the sound of it not dying away; it was flaming me all over again in the subjective eternity that is time in the online world. The insults, being premeditated, were more forceful than insults spoken in the heat of the moment, and the technology greased the words—the toads, scum, shit, rectums, assholes, compost, and worms—with a kind of immediacy that allowed them to slide easily into my brain.

3   Like many newcomers to the "Net"—which is what people call the global web that connects more than thirty thousand online networks—I had assumed, without really articulating the thought, that while talking to other people through my computer I was going to be sheltered by the same customs and laws that shelter me when I'm talking on the telephone or listening to the radio or watching TV. Now, for the first time, I understood the novelty and power of the technology I was dealing with. No one had ever said something like this to me before, and no one *could* have said this to me before: In any other medium, these words would be, literally, unspeakable. The guy couldn't have said this to me on the phone, because I would have hung up and not answered if the phone rang again, and he couldn't have said it to my face, because I wouldn't have let him finish. If this had happened to me in the street, I could have used my status as a physically large male to threaten the person, but in the online world my size didn't matter. I suppose the guy could have written me a nasty letter: He probably wouldn't have used the word "rectum," though, and he probably wouldn't have mailed the letter; he would have thought twice while he was addressing the envelope. But the nature of e-mail is that you don't think twice. You write and send.

4   When I got on the Net, it seemed to me like a place where all the good things about e-mail had been codified into an ideology. The first thing I fell for about the medium was the candor and the lack of cant it makes possible. Also, although the spoken word can be richer and warmer than the written word, the written word can carry precision

and subtlety, and, especially online, has the power of anonymity. Crucial aspects of your identity—age, sex, race, education, all of which would be revealed involuntarily in a face-to-face meeting and in most telephone conversations—do not come through the computer unless you choose to reveal them. Many people use handles for themselves instead of their real names, and a lot of people develop personae that go along with those handles. (When they get tired of a particular persona, they invent a new handle and begin again.) On the Net, a bright twelve-year-old in a blighted neighborhood can exchange ideas with an Ivy League professor, and a businesswoman who is too intimidated by her male colleagues to speak up in a face-to-face meeting can say what she thinks. On the Net, people are judged primarily not by who they are but by what they write.

5   My flame marked the end of my honeymoon with online communication. It made me see clearly that the lack of social barriers is also what is appalling about the Net. The same anonymity that allows the twelve-year-old access to the professor allows a pedophile access to the twelve-year-old. The same lack of inhibitions that allows a woman to speak up in online meetings allows a man to ask the woman whether she's wearing any underwear. The same safe distance that allows you to unburden yourself of your true feelings allowed this guy to call me a toadying dipshit scumbag. A toadying dipshit scumbag! I sent e-mail to the people at CompuServe, which was the network that carried my flame to me, to ask whether their subscribers were allowed to talk to each other this way.

> To: John Seabrook
> Fr: Dawn
> Customer Service Representative
> Since CompuServe Mail messages are private communications, CompuServe is unable to regulate their content. We are aware of an occasional problem with unwanted mail and are investigating ways to control such occurrences. If you receive unwanted mail again, please notify us of the details so that we can continue to track this problem.

6   If the Net as a civilization does mature to the point where it produces a central book of wisdom, like the Bible or the Koran, the following true story might make a good parable. In 1982, a group of forty people associated with a research institute in La Jolla established a small, private online network for themselves. For about six months, the participants were caught up in the rapture of the new medium, until one day a member of the group began provoking the others with anonymous online taunts. Before long, the community was so absorbed in an attempt to identify the bad apple that constructive discourse ceased. The group posted many messages imploring whoever was doing this to stop, but the person didn't, and the community was destroyed. Stewart Brand, who is a founder of the WELL, an online service based in San Francisco, and who told me this story, said, "And not only did this break up the online community—it permanently affected the trust that those people had for each other in the face-to-face world, because they were never able to figure out who did it. To this day, they don't know which one of them it was."

7   What would Emily Post[1] advise me to do? Flame the dipshit scumbag right back? I did spend most of that Friday in front of the screen composing the most vile insults I could dream up—words I have never spoken to another human being, and would never speak in any other medium, but which I found easy to type into the computer. But I didn't send these messages, partly because I had no way of knowing for sure whether the person whose name was on the flame had actually sent it, and since this person was a respected author, with a reputation to consider, I thought someone might be electronically impersonating him, a practice that is known online as "spoofing." I managed to restrain myself from sending my reply until I got home and asked my wife to look at it. She had the good sense to be horrified, and suggested sending the message "Do you know where I could get a good bozo filter?" But I wasn't sure I had the stomach for a flame war, so I settled on a simple, somewhat lame acknowledgment of the flame:

> Thanks for your advice on writing and reporting. The great thing about the Internet is that a person like me can get useful knowledge from experts, and for free.

8   In a few days, I received a reply from the writer, asking when my new column, "Pudlicker to the Celebrated," was going to start.

9   I was in a quandary that many newcomers to the Net face. Newbies sometimes get flamed just because they are new, or because they use a commercial online service provider, like America Online or CompuServe, which shows up in their electronic addresses, just as Italian immigrants were jeered at because they had vowels at the ends of their names. Some people are so horrified by their first flame that they turn into "lurkers": They read other people's messages in the public spaces but are too timid to post themselves. (You see lots of evidence of the fear of getting flamed; for example, long posts that end, "Sorry so lengthy, please don't flame," and messages studded with smiley faces—:)—and grin signs— <g> —which remind you of the way that dogs have to go through elaborate displays of cringing around each other to avoid starting a fight.) For other newbies, getting flamed puts the taste of blood in their mouths, and they discover that they like it. They flame back, and then a flame war begins: People volley escalating rounds of insults across the wires. Now that there are an estimated twenty-three million users connected to the Internet—ten million of which have come online in the last nine months, in what amounts to a massive cultural upheaval, as though a whole generation of immigrants to the New World had come over all in one day—the "netiquette" that prevailed in its early days is breaking down. And many of the new users are not the government officials, researchers, and academics for whom the Net was designed; they're lawyers, journalists, teenagers, scam artists, lonely hearts, people in the pornography business, and the faddists who were buying CB radios in 1975.

10   On Saturday evening, some friends came over for dinner, and I told them about my flame. They asked to see it, so I went down the hall to print out a copy. But when I opened the electronic file where I store my e-mail I noticed that the title of my reply had turned into gibberish—where there had been letters there were little boxes and

---

[1]**Emily Post** (1873–1960): Her handbook *Etiquette: The Blue Book of Social Usage* (1922) made her the authority on manners for half a century.—ED.

strange symbols—and that the dates for when the message was created and modified said "8/4/72" and "1/9/4." It occurred to me then to wonder briefly whether the person who flamed me had also sent some sort of virus into my computer, but I was cooking and didn't really have time to think about it, and when our guests left it was late, and I turned the computer off and went to bed. Just before six the following morning, however, I awoke abruptly and sat up in bed with a sudden understanding of what the last line in the flame—"One good worm deserves another"—might mean. A worm, in computerese, is one of the many varieties of viruses that infect computers. "One good worm deserves another": This guy had sent me a worm!

11   I got out of bed and went down the hall, turned on my computer, opened my e-mail file, and saw with a shock that the corruption had spread to the title and dates of the message stored next to my reply. The reply itself was still corrupted, but the gibberish and weird dates had mutated slightly. I tried to delete the two corrupted messages, but the computer told me it couldn't read them. The icy feeling inside my chest was back. I copied the whole file onto a floppy disk, removed the disk from my computer, dragged the original file into the electronic trash can, emptied the trash, and then sat there regarding my computer with suspicion and fear. I had the odd sensation that my computer was my brain, and my brain was ruined, and I was standing over it looking down at the wreckage. In my excitement over the new medium, I had not considered that in going online I was placing my work and my most private musings only inches from a roaring highway of data (only the short distance, that is, between the hard disk and the internal modem of my computer), and, like most highways, it didn't care about me. After thinking about this for a while, I noticed I was sitting in the dark, so I got up and pulled the chain on the floor lamp, and the bulb blew out. I thought, Wait a second, if my computer is connected to the outlet, is it possible that the worm could have gone into the plug and through the wall circuit and come out in the light bulb?

12   The worm had entered my mind.

13   I waited for my computer to die. Even though I had removed the two corrupted messages, I was worried that the worm might have infected my hard disk. At my most paranoid, I imagined that I had received a "logic bomb," which is a virus that hides in your computer until a timing mechanism triggers it. (A few years ago, a rumor went around the Net that a lot of computers had been infected with a logic bomb that was set to go off on Bill Gate's birthday, October 28th, but the rumor turned out to be false.) I felt creepy sitting in front of my computer, as though I weren't sure whether it was my friend anymore. Every time my software did something peculiar that I couldn't remember its having done before, my heart turned over a little. I'd think, It's starting.

14   When I tried to explain this feeling to a noncomputer-using friend of mine, she said, "Yeah, it's like when someone breaks into your car," but actually it was more like someone had broken into my head. I sent e-mail to my computer-literate friend Craig Canine, a writer and farmer who lives in Iowa, asking what he knew about worms, and he e-mailed me back:

> Coincidentally, I just gave our goats their worm medicine. It's called Valbazen, and it seems to work pretty well for ruminants—I'm not sure about computers, though. What does this worm do? Should I be communicating

with you—might your e-mail be a carrier? Jesus, I've got my book on my hard disk. If your worm zaps it, I'll kill you first, then go after the evil perp, (then plead insanity, with cause).

15   I was a pariah.

16   On the Wednesday following my flaming, I took my floppy disk to work to show it to Dan Henderson, who set up the network here at the magazine. Every office where computers are networked together has a guy like Dan around, who is usually the only person who really understands the system, and is terrifically overworked, because in addition to doing his job he has to deal with all the people like me, who are mystified by their computers. Shelley said that poets are the unacknowledged legislators of the world; system administrators are the unacknowledged legislators of the Net. Sysadmins are really the only authority figures that exist on the Net. In small electronic communities, the sysadmin often owns the equipment that the community runs on—a personal computer, a modem, and a telephone line are all you need to run your own bulletin board—and therefore he has absolute power over what goes on in the community. If a sysadmin wants to read someone's mail, he reads it. If he wants to execute someone, electronically speaking—by kicking that person off the network—he doesn't need to hold a trial. A benevolent sysadmin can make the network a utopia, and a malevolent sysadmin can quickly turn it into a police state.

17   I sent Dan a QuickMail, which is the brand of interoffice e-mail we use, and told him that I thought my computer might have been infected with some sort of worm. I asked if he had time to see me, expecting that maybe he'd get to me before the end of the week. I was surprised when Dan appeared in my doorway within ten minutes.

18   "You QuickMailed me," he said. I noticed he was looking at me strangely.

19   "Yes ..."

20   "You sent me QuickMail."

21   I was slow getting his drift. "So?"

22   Then I got it. "Wait. You mean you think I infected *The New Yorker's* network?" Dan was just looking at me, his eyebrows up around his hairline. "But I took the worm off my hard disk and put it on here," I said defensively, holding up the floppy disk.

23   Dan has that intense energy you often see in guys who are really into computers; the speed at which he talks and moves always makes me think of the clatter of fingers over the keyboard. He sat down at my computer with a couple of different kinds of software that looks for worms and viruses. After about ten minutes of probing my hard disk, he announced that he couldn't find any evidence of infection. He checked the floppy and found nothing there, either. The gibberish and weird dates had gone away.

24   Dan explained that I could not have received a worm via e-mail, because worms are programs; most e-mail carries only text. A file containing a program can be sent over e-mail, but in order for it to infect your computer you'd almost certainly have to open the file and run the program. I could see he thought I was somewhat insane. This was not technical thinking. It was literary thinking I was applying to machines in a desperate hope to make sense of something I didn't understand.

25   Was it possible that my worm was just some weird software glitch I had never seen before, and that it just happened to choose my reply to the flame to make its first ap-

pearance, and that the line "One good worm deserves another" was just a coincidence? After thinking about this for a couple of days, I came up with a little experiment. My hypothesis was that perhaps the worm could have burrowed into the program I was using to set up a reply to the original message, and my experiment was to perform the reply operation again, in order to see if the worm would come back.

26   The next morning, my new reply and the message stored next to it were corrupted again. I tried to print out the gibberish, but again the machine couldn't read the characters, so I copied them down. I also got my wife's camera and took a picture of my computer screen. Then I called Dan at home.

27   "Dan? This is John. Dan, my worm is back. I'm looking at it now."

28   Dan was polite about it, but he made a sound that suggested he did not consider himself my sysadmin right now, at ten o'clock on a Saturday morning, and said, "Could we talk about this on Monday?"

29   I wanted to talk about my flame with someone else who had been flamed, but I didn't know anyone in my real-world life who had been. Then it occurred to me that I could use the Net. This is one of the great things about the Net: The spaces are organized around topics, so it's easy to find people who think like you and who share your interests. People who gather on the Net to discuss a specific topic are called newsgroups, and each newsgroup has its own "site." In a literal sense a site is just a small amount of storage space in a computer somewhere in the world, which you can reach by typing its address, but it feels like an actual room. So, for example, if you think you might be a pagan, but you're still in the closet, you can go to the newsgroup "alt.pagan" for enlightenment. When you arrive there, the best thing to do first is to read the FAQ, the list of Frequently Asked Questions. FAQ files are more than the prosaic things they sound like; they are the repositories of the useful knowledge that has been exchanged and meaningful events that have occurred in that particular site since it was established. The table of contents for the alt.pagan FAQ reads:

    1. What is this group for?
    2. What is paganism/ a pagan?
    2b. What is Paganism? How is it different from paganism?
    3. What are different types of paganism?
    4. What is Witchcraft/Wicca?
    4b. Why do some of you use the word Witch? Wiccan?
    5. What are some different traditions in the Craft?
    6. Are pagans Witches?
    7. Are you Satanists?
    8. What kinds of people are pagans?
    9. What holidays do you celebrate?
    9b. How do I pronounce . . . ? What does this name mean?
    10. What god(s) do you believe in?
    11. Can one be both a Christian and pagan?

12. What were the Burning Times?

13. How many pagans/Witches are there today?

14. Why isn't it soc.religion.paganism instead of alt.pagan?

15. Is brutal honesty or polite conversation the preferred tone of conversation around here?

16. What are the related newsgroups?

17. Are there any electronic mailing lists on this subject?

18. I'm not a pagan; should I post here?

19. How does one/do I become a pagan?

20. What books/magazines should I read?

21. How do I find pagans/Witches/covens/teachers in my area?

22. What's a coven really like?

23. How do I form a coven?

24. What does Dianic mean?

25. Aren't women-only circles discriminatory?

26. Can/will you cast me a love spell/curse my enemies?

27. Is it okay if I . . . ? Will I still be a pagan if I . . . ?

28. I am a pagan and I think I am being discriminated against because of my religion. What should I do?

29. What one thing would most pagans probably want the world to know about them?

30   Then you can scroll through a list of hundreds of discussion topics and see what people are talking about. Some are:

14. European paganism (16 msgs)

15. Statement (6 msgs)

16. College Pagan Groups

17. PAGAN FEDERATION GIG: Thanks (3 msgs)

18. Broom Closet Pagans Hurt Us All (3 msgs)

19. Pagan funerals? (27 msgs)

20. NIGGER JOKES (18 msgs)

21. Necromancy (2 msgs)

22. Another campus Pagan group (4 msgs)

23. When the Revolution comes was Re: New Forest Service . . . (6 msgs)

24. Looking for invocations to the following . . . (4 msgs)

25. New Community Pagan Group? Need help.

31   I suppose you could choose not to double-click on NIGGER JOKES, but it's harder than you think. This is the biggest drawback of the way newsgroups are set up: A really interesting post that enriches your understanding of a subject is next to a post that is ap-

propriate only for the space above the urinal. There's nothing to stop someone in alt.misanthropy or alt.tasteless from coming into rec.pets.cats and posting a graphic account of what it's like to behead a cat or drink its blood, and although you can bozo-filter that person after his first post, so that you never have to read a message from him again, the horrible words tend to stay in your memory for a long time.

32   NIGGER JOKES turns out to be a collection of racist jokes and limericks about killing African Americans, which was posted on April 5th. The name and address on the jokes is that of a student at the University of Michigan. The post has been "spammed," as they say on the Net, which means that the student has spread it around to many different newsgroups, thus ensuring himself an audience of hundreds of thousands, and maybe millions, since the jokes are still making their way through the Net. (Some employees of Fortune 500 companies have recently reported finding the jokes on their office networks.)

33   When someone posts a message that offends the other participants in a newsgroup, the group metes out the only punishment at its disposal, which is to flame the offender, and in this case the student who posted the jokes has been getting flames by the thousand. Also, in typical Net fashion, there has been much soul-searching in the newsgroups about the character of the Net itself:

> The Last Viking<paalde@stud.cs.uit.no>
> We don't have to go around being racists like those fascists in the real world! PEACE ON THE NET!!!!

> Michael Halleen <halleen@MCS.COM>
> As offensive as this is, I do not believe this should put this person "under investigation." . . . He should get hate mail, censure (not censors), and universal condemnation. There should be an open debate and discussion, but leave his right to speak alone. He may use the net for other constructive purposes and taking it away may hurt him, and he needs help.

> Richard Darsie<darsie@eecs.ucdavis.edu>
> Get a grip, man. Free speech is *not* and never has been an *absolute* right. There's gotta be some limits. . . . This person abused his First Amendment rights and should face some consequences for it. Can't have rights without responsibilities.

34   An investigation at the University of Michigan recently concluded that the student whose name was on the posts hadn't made them; someone had spoofed him. The wrongly accused and now flame-broiled student has used a university-owned computer to log on to his account, and someone had tampered with the software in that computer so that it captured his password. This person had then logged on in the student's name and posted the jokes. The day after the jokes went up, another student, who had used the same computer to log on, discovered that his identity had been used to send a message to the Islamic Circle, a campus organization, calling its members "God-forsaken terrorists."

35   I went to alt.flame, thinking this might be the site where people talk about flaming, but it turned out to be a place where people go to flame each other. I saw that an intrepid writer from *Wired* Magazine, Amy Bruckman, had posted that she was writing an article about flaming and was getting flamed for doing it.

> Insert finger in appropriate orafice and shove off.

> Sod off bitch, we don't need your glamour here. . . .

> WHAT?!? Do you think I wanted to be publicated in your low-life-scum magazine??? . . . BTW, what kind of name is Bruckman? Are you kind of a German refugees' daughter from the 2nd world war? Kraut? a sauceage woman? Anyway go to hell.

I decided not to post in alt.flame myself.

36   I considered posting a query about my worm in the newsgroup comp.virus, and I lurked around there for a while, but I didn't post, because I was worried that my assailant might hear that I was posting queries about him in public spaces—it's difficult to keep secrets on the Net—and devise some even more elaborate torture to inflict on my computer, or begin spoofing me in some diabolical fashion. I had already seen how the Net could be used to hurt someone's reputation. One day, as I was wandering around inside the Electronic Frontier Foundation discussion space, which is one of the most interesting newsgroups on the Net, I came upon a subject line that said, "Ralph Berkeley made homosexual advances toward me." Ralph Berkeley (I'm not using his real name) is a regular participant in discussions of Net policy, who appears, on the evidence of his posts, to be an articulate and thoughtful man, and often takes the position that completely unrestricted free speech on the net might not be such a good idea—a position that causes him to receive his share of flames. However, this post upped the ante a bit:

> Ralph Berkeley made homosexual advances toward me when I visited him at his office approximately two weeks ago. As I went there just to chat with him and he's not my employer or anything I don't think I have any grounds for any legal action or anything like that. But I must say that prior to that event I had a lot of respect for him (not necessarily his opinions, but the even-handed way in which he stated them). I am really disappointed.

37   This brought forth even more furious bursts of thinking and feeling over the nature of the Net:

> Dik T. Winter<dik@cwi.nl>
> I think Ralph Berkeley has enough grounds for a suit on defamation of character. Ralph, I urge you, *do* sue. I do not agree with you but please, *do* sue.

> Jim Thomas <tkOjut1@mp.cs.niu.edu>
> No. Although we all assume the original post was homophobic sleaze, a suit is even more offensive. Such a suit itself constitutes "fag bashing," because it continues the stigmatizing of gays by suggesting that homosexuality is abnormal or pathological.

38   Then, in the best spirit of the Net, Dr. Berkeley posted this reply:

> Thanks to readers whose responses showed such good sense. Of course
> it's false.
>   Ralph

39   Everywhere I went in the newsgroups, I found flames, and fear of flames. In the
absence of rules, there is a natural tendency toward anarchy on the Net anyway, and in
some stretches I'd come upon sites that were in complete chaos, where people had been
flaming each other nonstop, absolutely scorching everything around them, and driving
all the civilized people away. Sometimes I'd arrive at a dead site long after a flame war
broke out; it was like walking through what was once a forest after a wildfire. Sometimes I came upon voices that were just howling at the world; you could feel the rage
and savagery pouring out through people's fingers and into the Net. Of course, you can
hear this sound on the streets of New York City, but less often than you hear it on the
Net, and in the city it lasts only as long as the person who is making it has breath for it
and is heard only by the people within earshot. On the Net, it can be heard by millions
and reverberate for a long time.

40   Sometimes I returned from these trips on the Net feeling lonely, cold, and de-
pressed. I would see the Net less from the point of view of the acrobat and more from
the point of view of the fish. Ironically, the Net seemed most alive to me when I was
off it and found myself using a word I had picked up in my travels. The Net is a hotbed
of language, because on the Net language has to accomplish everything; the whole
world is made of words, and people are constantly forced to coin new ones. And, because typing takes more effort than speaking, people are always inventing acronyms or
abbreviations—"lol" for "laughed out loud," "f2f" for "face to face," "BTW" for "by
the way," "RTFM" for "Read the Fucking Manual," which is a message people often
send back to you when you ask them for technical help. There's something wonderful
about all this, but it's also sad to go to a chat group and see the "lol"s scrolling by on
the screen, sometimes with no other words attached to them, just people typing "lol" to
each other. How much of the pleasure of laughter can you get sitting alone with your
computer, typing "lol"?

41   I sent a copy of my flame to someone I know only as Jennifer, a woman I met on
the Net and feel I know in a strange way, although in fact I know hardly anything about
her. She replied:

> I must say that I was shocked to read about your experience. . . . The mag-
> nitude of your assailant's tirade rends my heart. I have been thinking about
> those graphic words, unbidden, for the last two days.

42   Here was another good thing about the Net—that a woman I didn't even know
would be so concerned for me. I wrote to Jennifer that the net seemed to me in some
ways a cold place, and she replied:

> You are right about the coldness of the net. There is an air of preestablished
> hierarchy there—if you're new to the net, or even to a particular group on the
> net, you don't belong a priori. As a woman, I have encountered an additional

barrier; the net is heavily male and women who want to play with the big boys either have to be ultra tough-talking—one of the boys—or else play off as coy, charming, "little-ol' ME?"-feminine. (Even geeks have fantasy lives, I suppose.) Or use a male/neutral alias with no one the wiser.

So part of the boy's club, I imagine, is the smallness, the selectivity—the geek elite, if you will. For more than a decade these guys had their own secret tin-can-on-a-string way to communicate and socialize, as obscure as ham radio but no pesky FCC requirements and much, much cooler. . . . But then the Internet—their cool secret—started to get press. . . . Imagine these geeks, suddenly afraid that their magic treehouse was about to be boarded by American pop culture. It was worse than having your favorite obscure, underground album suddenly appear on the Billboard charts.

43   As my assailant had suggested, I also forwarded a copy of the flame to my mother, whom I had got wired for e-mail. She replied:

I deleted that thing you sent me immediately. What a terrible man. He must have been drunk. . . .

44   One day at work, I asked Dan Henderson if he knew of someone I could go to for the final word on my worm—the top worm man in the country, as it were—and he gave me the e-mail address of John Norstad, at Northwestern University. Norstad is the author of Disinfectant, a popular brand of virus-protection software for the Macintosh, and probably knows as much as anyone in the world about the viruses and worms that affect Macs. I sent him an e-mail saying I would be coming out to Chicago in a couple of weeks on business and wondered if I could have him examine my PowerBook. Norstad promptly e-mailed me back to say that he was in the midst of fighting a new virus that had just broken out in Italy, and didn't have time to think about my problem now, but would be happy to see me when I came to Chicago.

45   We arranged, through e-mail, to meet at the Palmer House, where I was staying. Because my only contact with Norstad had been online, I had no clue what sort of man to expect, and as I waited for him in my room I tried to imagine what he would be like. I realized that I was envisioning Norstad not as a Western doctor but as a kind of tribal medicine man. Whether the corrupted messages in my computer were the result of a real worm or were caused by a software glitch, all my troubles seemed to be related to the general wizardry of software—the mysterious incantations of ones and zeros being whispered inside my computer. I felt as if someone had put a spell on my computer, and I was bringing it to John Norstad to have him heal it.

46   Norstad turned out to be about forty-five, not tall, with a beard that had some gray in it, glasses, and a shy, polite manner. He wore a flannel jacket over a loose gray shirt, and gray pants. He was carrying a PowerBook loaded with the dominant strains of all the nastiest viruses known to the Macintosh world; the viruses were safely corralled on his hard disk with Disinfectant, which he distributes free on the Net to anyone who wants it. Norstad set his PowerBook next to my PowerBook and showed me his collection of infected programs. He moved his cursor over and pointed it at an icon, double-clicked on it, and said, "Now, if I didn't have any protection this little guy would start

erasing my hard drive right . . . now. But because we do—there, see . . . Disinfectant caught it." It was awesome.

47   I asked Norstad about the Italian virus he had been fighting when I first e-mailed him, and he said that it had appeared in an item of software posted on a bulletin board in late February. Because the software was copyrighted, and had been posted on the board illegally, there was some suspicion that the virus writer was trying to teach the pirates a lesson about copyright infringement. Norstad opened the e-mail log in his PowerBook and showed me the hundreds of messages he had sent and received between February 28th, when he received e-mail from three people in Italy which said that a new virus was erasing people's hard disks, and March 3rd, when he and his colleagues produced vaccines. Upon hearing about the Italian outbreak, Norstad had immediately sent e-mail to a group of colleagues called the Zoo Keepers, a sort of online volunteer fire squad, to alert them to the existence of the new virus. The Zoo Keepers are a virtual community that live all over the globe—Australia, Germany, the United States—and could exist only because of the Net. Norstad received a copy of the virus from Italy, made copies, and sent the copies out over the Net to the Zoo Keepers. Keeping in touch over the Net, the scientists reverse-engineered the virus and a number of effective vaccines for it. Norstad then updated Disinfectant—version 3.3 became 3.4—and posted it around the Net, where people could download it for free. All this took fifty-six hours.

48   I asked whether virus writers were often motivated by politics, and Norstad said no, they were mostly relatively harmless hackers, at least in the Mac world. In the world of IBM-compatible machines, which is much larger than the Mac world, there are many more viruses, and they tend to be deadlier. They are the stuff of legend. Norstad told me of an account he had once heard from a Bulgarian virus expert, about software engineers commissioned by the Communist government to crack the security seals on Western software. When the regime fell, the story goes, the unemployed engineers were said to have whiled away their empty hours writing viruses for IBM compatibles.

49   I asked, "Is it possible that a terrorist could take down a large part of a country's computer systems with a virus?"

50   "It's possible. Of course, the problem with a virus that virulent is, How do they keep it from infecting their own system?"

51   I told Norstad the story of my worm, and asked whether it was possible for a technically sophisticated person such as I believed my assailant to be to send a worm through e-mail.

52   Norstad said it was not possible. "I will say that the kind of symptoms you describe could be a software problem."

53   "Like what?" I asked.

54   "Who knows?" Norstad said. "It's software. It's weird stuff. People are always writing and calling me because they think they have some kind of virus, and in almost every case it's a software problem, not a virus—but these people are fearful and need my help. For example, quite a few people have written me to say a shrieking death's head appears occasionally in the top of their screens. You know what it is? If you have Apple's Remote Access program, hold down the option key, and hit the shift key three times, your computer makes this funny trilling sound and an object appears in the corner

of your screen that could, if you were sufficiently paranoid, look like a death's head. It's not a virus. It's just a weird software thing."

55   While Norstad was talking, I brought my flame up onto the screen and asked him to look at it. He leaned toward me and silently read through the litany of insults. When he had finished, he sat back and sighed and didn't speak for a couple of seconds. Then he said, "I'm just so sorry when something like this happens." He lowered his head and shook it sadly. "Gee, that's terrible."

56   I said, "I have to admit it was upsetting. I've been thinking about it a lot. I ask myself, Do I recognize the right of this person to flame me? Yes, I do. Do I celebrate his right to flame me? I'm not sure. Do I recognize the right of this person to send me a worm? Definitely not. But at what point does a flame become a worm? I mean, can a virus be a form of free speech? In other words, could a combination of words be so virulent and nasty that it could do a sort of property damage to your head?"

57   I was rambling, and I could actually feel tears coming into my eyes, so I stopped there. But Norstad seemed to understand what I was talking about, and I felt better after I had told him. I realized that I would probably never know for sure whether my worm was real or just a software glitch. We chatted for a while longer, and then he said, "Don't get discouraged. The Net is a fundamentally wonderful place. Most of this work I do could be done only on the Net. Look at the work we did on the Italian virus, working with colleagues all over the world to reverse-engineer it. Can you imagine trying to do this by fax? Phone? Fed Ex? It would not be possible." He unplugged his Power-Book and began packing it up. "Of course," he said "the Net allows people to spread viruses much more easily than before."

58   "But that's the thing about the Net," I said. "Each of the good things about it seems to have an evil twin."

59   "Yes, but you could say that about all new technology," Norstad said. "There is always going to be a dark side to it. That is why it's so important to be decent on the Net, because the dark side is always right there."

POST-READING QUESTIONS

CONTENT QUESTIONS

1. Why, according to Seabrook, are the words of his flame "literally unspeakable"? How does the Net give people freedom to say things to each other that no other medium permits? Explain.

2. What does Seabrook say are benefits of anonymity online? Drawbacks?

3. What is another benefit of the Internet in terms of organization? Does Seabrook say that this benefit has a downside? What is it?

4. How does Seabrook react to his "first flame"? Why does he react this way? How reasonable do you think his reaction is? Explain.

5. What examples of kindness or consideration does Seabrook find online? Of rudeness or incivility? Which type of behavior in Seabrook's essay seems more common online? Give examples.

6. What types of online communication does Seabrook mention in his essay? Of these, what are the benefits and drawbacks of each? Does one form of communication seem better than another? Why?

STYLE AND STRUCTURE

7. Examine the examples Seabrook offers throughout his essay. What organizational strategy does he employ? What benefits does Seabrook derive from organizing his essay this way?

8. What is Seabrook's main idea? Where is this main idea stated? How is its location significant?

9. What types of examples does Seabrook employ? How do Seabrook's examples help support his thesis?

10. What is Seabrook's tone? To what extent does his tone change throughout his essay? Is his tone effective? Explain.

11. Who is Seabrook addressing? How can you tell? Choose words or expressions that you think best reveal Seabrook's intended audience.

12. How does Seabrook establish his credibility on the subject of flaming? Does his mention of derogatory terms within the context of his essay help or hurt his credibility? Explain.

CRITICAL THINKING AND ANALYSIS

DISCUSSION QUESTIONS

13. What are the implications of the type of extreme free speech that the Internet makes possible? Do flames improve or worsen communication? Use examples from the text and your own observations and experiences in order to illustrate your response.

14. Consider the "customs and laws" that Seabrook relied upon to protect him from insults online. Why did those conventions fail him? What new rules of conduct can you suggest that might improve online civility?

WRITING ASSIGNMENTS

15. Seabrook writes, "On the Net, people are judged primarily not by who they are but by what they write." Do you agree? (If you haven't visited a chat room, try it for this assignment.) In a few paragraphs, explain how you think people are judged and give examples.

16. To what extent do you think people should address the issue of flaming? Can or should people do anything to temper or prohibit flames? Explain in a well-developed paragraph.

17. Seabrook writes that the Internet lacks "social barriers" that often limit conversations in day to day life. Write a few paragraphs discussing what some of

these barriers are and explaining how the Internet does or does not help eliminate them.

18. Seabrook's online friend "Jennifer" writes that the Internet was begun by the
"geek elite" who are comprised largely of males. Write a brief essay in which
you argue that the gender gap online is greater or less significant than in day to
day life. Be sure to offer examples from Seabrook's essay as well as from your
own experience and observations.

19. Seabrook receives many types of electronic messages while researching his
flame, each message coming according to its sender's mood and timeline. In a
few paragraphs, argue whether or not online communication encourages or
discourages civility. Cite the text and your own experiences in responding to
this question.

VOCABULARY DEVELOPMENT

20. Make a list of the acronyms and abbreviations Seabrook uses in his essay and
write down what these terms stand for. Then, write three to five sentences explaining how the presence of these terms shows that Seabrook is targeting a
particular audience.

GROUP ACTIVITIES

21. In small groups, do an online search for "flames." What does your search produce? Follow a few links, taking notes, and report back to the class what you
learned about searching for flames online.

22. In your group, assign each member a type of chat room to visit—sports, romance, cooking, etc.—and be what Seabrook calls a "lurker," someone who
reads the comments but does not participate. In what chat room do people treat
each other with the most, or least, kindness? Take notes about your chat room
experiences and share them with your group. Then, as a group, write a paragraph drawing a conclusion about which types of chat rooms demand the
highest, or lowest, standards of behavior.

Argument Pair: Should the Internet be Regulated?

The Internet: A Clear and Present Danger? Cathleen A. Cleaver

Cyberspace: If You Don't Love It, Leave It, Esther Dyson

Since its popularity growth in the early 1990s, the Internet has become increasingly controversial. Should advertisers have free reign on sites where people visit? How safe is people's privacy if they choose to chat or shop online? But perhaps the greatest controversy lies in the issue of whether or not the Internet should be regulated. Cathleen Cleaver claims that children are at risk of happening upon graphic, even violent, sexual images, while Esther Dyson argues that Internet users have great control of where they visit and what they see. How easy these images are to chance upon, and how harmful they can be, sit at the center of this controversy.

Writing Assignments for *The Internet: A Clear and Present Danger?* and *Cyberspace: If You Don't Love It, Leave It*

1. Esther Dyson writes that Internet regulation is both unnecessary and unwise, while Cathleen Cleaver claims that the Internet presents a "clear and present danger" to its users and, thus, should be regulated. Citing these writers and others in this chapter, argue whether or not you think the Internet should be regulated. Be sure to define what you mean by regulation, and use your own observations in order to support your views.

2. Cathleen Cleaver argues for government regulation of the Internet because she claims that "any child, can get graphic and often violent sexual images" with "a few clicks of a mouse," while Esther Dyson argues for "self-rule" because she states that "cyberspace is a voluntary destination . . . people can choose where to go and what to see." Who is right? Write a well-developed paragraph based on your own readings and online experiences in which you argue that people do or do not have easy access to undesired, unpleasant images.

The Internet: A Clear and Present Danger?

Cathleen A. Cleaver

Cathleen A. Cleaver is director of legal studies at the Family Research Council, a Washington-based research and educational organization. As part of a College of Communication Great Debate, she gave this speech at Boston University on October 29, 1997. In her argument, Cleaver identifies dangers that online pornography presents to users, particularly children, and she raises the question of whether Internet regulation is in the best interest of the public.

Pre-reading Questions

Freewrite for five to ten minutes in response to the following questions:
In your mind, what about the Internet presents "danger"? Who do you think is at risk of being harmed in some way by the negative aspects of the Internet? Who do you think is responsible for seeing that online users, particularly children, are protected from online risks?

Vocabulary Preview

Vocabulary Words:
- proprietary
- apocalyptic
- depravity
- implicit
- exploit
- sanction
- abundant
- voyeurism
- mitigating
- inalienable

Look up the words above and, as you read, write a few sentences explaining how you think five of these words are particularly appropriate within the context of Cleaver's essay.

- Someone breaks through your firewall and steals proprietary information from your computer systems. You find out and contact a lawyer who says, "Man, you shouldn't have had your stuff online." The thief becomes a millionaire using your ideas, and you go broke, if laws against copyright violation don't protect material on the Internet.

- You visit the Antiques Anonymous Web site and decide to pay their hefty subscription fee for a year's worth of exclusive estate sale previews in their private online monthly magazine. They never deliver and, in fact, never intended to—they don't even have a magazine. You have no recourse, if laws against fraud don't apply to online transactions.

- Bob Guccione decides to branch out into the lucrative child porn market and creates a Teen Hustler Web site featuring nude adolescents and preteens. You find out and complain, but nothing can be done, if child pornography distribution laws don't apply to computer transmissions.

- A major computer software vendor who dominates the market develops his popular office software so that it works only with his browser. You're a small browser manufacturer who is completely squeezed out of the market, but you have to find a new line of work, if antitrust laws don't apply online.

- Finally, a pedophile e-mails your son, misrepresenting himself as a twelve-year-old named Jenny. They develop an online relationship and one day arrange to meet after school, where he intends to rape your son. Thankfully, you learn in advance about the meeting and go there yourself, where you find a forty-year-old man instead of Jenny. You flee to the police, who'll tell you there's nothing they can do, if child-stalking laws don't apply to the Internet.

THE ISSUE

1   The awesome advances in interactive telecommunication that we've witnessed in just the last few years have changed the way in which many Americans communicate and interact. No one can doubt that the Internet is a technological revolution of enormous proportion, with outstanding possibilities for human advancement.

2   As lead speaker for the affirmative, I'm asked to argue that the Internet poses a "clear and present danger," but the Internet, as a whole, isn't dangerous. In fact, it continues to be a positive and highly beneficial tool, which will undoubtedly improve education, information exchange, and commerce in years to come. In other words, the Internet will enrich many aspects of our daily life. Thus, instead of defending this rather apocalyptic view of the Internet, I'll attempt to explain why some industry and government regulation of certain aspects of the Internet is necessary— or, stated another way, why people who used the Internet should not be exempt from many of the laws and regulations that govern their conduct elsewhere. My opening illustrations were meant to give examples of some illegal conduct which should not become legal simply because someone uses the Internet. In looking at whether Internet regulation is a good idea, I believe we should consider whether regulation is in the public interest. In order to do that, we have to ask the question: Who is the public? More specifically, does the "public" whose interests we care about tonight include children?

CHILDREN AND THE INTERNET

3   Dave Barry describes the Internet as a "worldwide network of university, government, business, and private computer systems, run by a thirteen-year-old named Jason." This description draws a smile precisely because we acknowledge the highly advanced computer literacy of our children. Most children demonstrate computer proficiency that far surpasses that of their parents, and many parents know only what their children have taught them about the Internet, which gives new relevance to Wordsworth's insight: "The child is father of the man." In fact, one could go so far as to say that the Internet is as accessible to many children as it is inaccessible to many adults. This technological evolution is new in many ways, not the least of which is its accessibility to children, wholly independent of their parents.

4   When considering what's in the public interest, we must consider the whole public, including children, as individual participants in this new medium.

PORNOGRAPHY AND THE INTERNET

5   This new medium is unique in another way. It provides, through a single avenue, the full spectrum of pornographic depictions, from the more familiar convenience store

fare to pornography of such violence and depravity that it surpasses the worst excesses of the normal human imagination. Sites displaying this material are easily accessible, making pornography far more freely available via the Internet than from any other communications medium in the United States. Pornography is the third largest sector of sales on the Internet, generating $1 billion annually. There are an estimated seventy-two-thousand pornographic sites on the World Wide Web alone, with approximately thirty-nine new explicit sex sites every day. Indeed, the *Washington Post* has called the Internet the largest pornography store in the history of mankind.

6   There is little restriction of pornography-related activity in cyberspace. While there are some porn-related laws, the specter of those laws does not loom large in cyberspace. There's an implicit license there that exists nowhere else with regard to pornography—an environment where people are free to exploit others for profit and be virtually untroubled by legal deterrent. Indeed, if we consider cyberspace to be a little world of its own, it's the type of world for which groups like the ACLU have long fought but, so far, fought in vain.

7   I believe it will not remain this way, but until it changes, we should take the opportunity to see what this world looks like, if for no other reason than to reassure ourselves that our decades-old decisions to control pornography were good ones.

8   With a few clicks of the mouse, anyone, any child, can get graphic and often violent sexual images—the kind of stuff it used to be difficult to find without exceptional effort and some significant personal risk. Anyone with a computer and a modem can set up public sites featuring the perversion of their choice, whether it's mutilation of female genitals, eroticized urination and defecation, bestiality, or sites featuring depictions of incest. These pictures can be sold for profit, they can be sent to harass others, or posted to shock people. Anyone can describe the fantasy rape and murder of a specific person and display it for all to read. Anyone can meet children in chat rooms or via e-mail and send them pornography and find out where they live. An adult who signs onto an AOL chat room as a thirteen-year-old girl is hit on thirty times within the first half hour.

9   All this can be done from the seclusion of the home, with the feeling of near anonymity and with the comfort of knowing that there's little risk of legal sanction.

10   The phenomenon of this kind of pornography finding such a welcome home in this new medium presents abundant opportunities for social commentary. What does Internet pornography tell us about human sexuality? Photographs, videos, and virtual games that depict rape and dehumanization of women in sexual scenes send powerful messages about human dignity and equality. Much of the pornography freely available without restriction on the Internet celebrates unhealthy and antisocial kinds of sexual activity, such as sadomasochism, abuse, and degradation. Of course, by its very nature, pornography encourages voyeurism.

11   Beyond the troubling social aspects of unrestricted porn, we face the reality that children are accessing it and that predators are accessing children. We have got to start considering what kind of society we'll have when the next generation learns about human sexuality from what the Internet teaches. What does unrestricted Internet pornog-

raphy teach children about relationships, about the equality of women? What does it teach little girls about themselves and their worth?

12   Opponents of restrictions are fond of saying that it's up to the parents to deal with the issue of children's exposure. Well, of course it is, but placing the burden solely on parents is illogical and ineffective. It's far easier for a distributor of pornography to control his material than it is for parents, who must, with the help of software, search for and find the pornographic sites, which change daily, and then attempt to block them. Any pornographer who wants to can easily subvert these efforts, and a recent Internet posting from a teenager wanting to know how to disable the filtering software on his computer received several effective answers. Moreover, it goes without saying that the most sophisticated software can only be effective where it's installed, and children will have access to many computers that don't have filtering software, such as those in libraries, schools, and at neighbors' houses.

INTERNET TRANSACTIONS SHOULD NOT BE EXEMPT

13   Opponents of legal restrictions often argue simply that the laws just cannot apply in this new medium, but the argument that old laws can't apply to changing technology just doesn't hold. We saw this argument last in the early '80s with the advent of the videotape. Then, certain groups tried to argue that, since you can't view videotapes without a VCR, you can't make the sale of child porn videos illegal, because, after all, they're just plastic boxes with magnetic tape inside. Technological change mandates legal change only insofar as it affects the justification for a law. It just doesn't make sense that the government may take steps to restrict illegal material in *every* medium— video, television, radio, the private telephone, *and* print—but that it may do *nothing* where people distribute the material by the Internet. While old laws might need redefinition, the old principles generally stand firm.

14   The question of enforcement usually is raised here, and it often comes in the form of: "How are you going to stop people from doing it?" Well, no law stops people from doing things—a red light at an intersection doesn't force you to stop but tells you that you should stop and that there could be legal consequences if you don't. Not everyone who runs a red light is caught, but that doesn't mean the law is futile. The same concept holds true for Internet laws. Government efforts to temper harmful conduct online will never be perfect, but that doesn't mean they shouldn't undertake the effort at all.

15   There's clearly a role for industry to play here. Search engines don't have to run ads for porn sites or prioritize search results to highlight porn. One new search engine even has *sex* as the default search term. Internet service providers can do something about unsolicited e-mail with hotlinks to porn, and they can and should carefully monitor any chat rooms designed for kids.

16   Some charge that industry standards or regulations that restrict explicit pornography will hinder the development of Internet technology. But that is to say that its advancement *depends upon* unrestricted exhibition of this material, and this cannot be true. The Internet does not belong to pornographers, and it's clearly in the public interest to see that they don't usurp this great new technology. We don't live in a

perfect society, and the Internet is merely a reflection of the larger social community. Without some mitigating influences, the strong will exploit the weak, whether a Bill Gates or a child predator.

CONCLUSION: TECHNOLOGY MUST SERVE MAN

17 To argue that the strength of the Internet is chaos or that our liberty depends upon chaos is to misunderstand not only the Internet but also the fundamental nature of our liberty. It's an illusion to claim social or moral neutrality in the application of technology, even if its development may be neutral. It can be a valuable resource only when placed at the service of humanity and when it promotes our integral development for the benefit of all.

18 Guiding principles simply cannot be inferred from mere technical efficiency or from the usefulness accruing to some at the expense of others. Technology by its very nature requires unconditional respect for the fundamental interests of society.

19 Internet technology must be at the service of humanity and of our inalienable rights. It must respect the prerogatives of a civil society, among which is the protection of children.

POST-READING QUESTIONS

CONTENT

1. What questions does Cleaver say we should consider in deciding whether Internet regulation is in the public interest?
2. Why does Cleaver identify children specifically as being part of "the new medium" of online communication?
3. How does Cleaver say the Internet has changed access to pornography?
4. In what way(s) does online pornography present greater risks to people than traditionally distributed pornography?
5. What steps does Cleaver say the technology industry can take in regulating online pornography?
6. What does Cleaver mean when she says that "It's an illusion to claim social or moral neutrality in the application of technology"? How is this statement relevant to her argument?

STYLE AND STRUCTURE

7. What is Cleaver's purpose in writing this essay? Restate her main idea in your own words.
8. Cleaver states that "placing the burden on parents [of limiting children's exposure to online pornography] is illogical and ineffective." What examples does she offer to support this view?
9. What function do Cleaver's opening anecdotes serve? To what extent would her essay be more effective if she simply plunged into her main argument and omitted the anecdotes?

10. Who is Cleaver's audience? To what extent are you part of her audience? Choose words and expressions that reveal her target population.

11. Cleaver cites several arguments opposing Internet regulation. How does she counter those arguments, and what is the effect of including those arguments in her essay?

CRITICAL THINKING AND ANALYSIS

DISCUSSION QUESTIONS

12. Cleaver argues against depictions of "rape and the dehumanization of women in sexual scenes." How do you think she would react to online displays of loving, homosexual partners? Base your response on how much support Cleaver provides for your conjecture in the text.

13. In her last paragraph, Cleaver states that Internet technology "must respect the prerogatives of a civil society, among which is the protection of children." Based on your reading of the essay, what can you infer a "civil" society is? Do you agree with her idea? Explain.

WRITING ASSIGNMENTS

14. Cleaver writes that most children "demonstrate computer proficiency that far surpasses that of their parents." Why do you think this is true? Write a few paragraphs explaining why children often have greater technological expertise, or if you disagree that children have greater computer proficiency, then write a few paragraphs arguing against this idea.

15. According to Cleaver, "placing the burden [of Internet regulation] solely on parents is illogical and ineffective." Write a few paragraphs in which you explain how great a role parents should play in protecting their children from online pornography. Be sure to use your own online experiences in order to illustrate your ideas.

16. Cleaver writes that "While old laws might need redefinition, the old principles stand firm." Do you agree? Write a short essay (three to five paragraphs) in which you argue that the Internet does or does not require new guiding principles all its own. Be sure to define the "old principles" Cleaver mentions when making your argument, and cite both the essay and your own experience to illustrate your ideas.

VOCABULARY DEVELOPMENT

17. Several of the words in the Vocabulary Preview have strong connotative meanings as well as denotative meanings. Choose at least five words from the Preview and write a sentence or two about each, explaining what the connotation of each word is.

GROUP ACTIVITIES

18. How accessible is pornography to the innocent seeker? In small groups, perform Internet searches for seemingly "safe" terms such as "child," "girl," "friend," and any others you can think of. What results do you get? (You do not need to follow any links that appear to lead to unsafe or unethical places; just write down the names of such places.) Report your findings to the class and compare them with other groups in order to determine how easily available online pornography is.

19. Discuss what forms Internet regulation should take, if it is implemented at all. Present your results to the class in an open forum setting.

Cyberspace: If You Don't Love It, Leave It

Esther Dyson

Esther Dyson has written articles for *New York Times* and *Wired* magazine, and she is chairwoman of the Electronic Frontier Foundation, which fights against the Communications Decency Act. In this essay, originally published in *The New York Times,* Dyson argues that Internet regulation is both unnecessary and impractical, and she offers suggestions for dealing with questionable material in cyberspace.

Pre-reading Questions

Freewrite for five to ten minutes in response to the following questions:
How often do your Internet searches provide the information you seek? What do you think determines what kind of material you are exposed to online? How helpful do you think Internet filters, or other types of regulation, are?

Vocabulary Preview

Vocabulary Words:
- psyche
- conceivable
- constituency
- procure
- alluring
- akin
- consensual
- decibel
- terrestrial
- fanfare

Define the words above and then, as you read, write a few sentences identifying the words you find to be most or least effective in helping Dyson communicate her point.

1   Something in the American psyche loves new frontiers. We hanker after wide-open spaces; we like to explore; we like to make rules instead of follow them. But in this age of political correctness and other intrusions on our national cult of independence, it's hard to find a place where you can go and be yourself without worrying about the neighbors.

2   There is such a place: cyberspace. Lost in the furor over porn on the Net is the exhilarating sense of freedom that this new frontier once promised—and still does in some quarters. Formerly a playground for computer nerds and techies, cyberspace now embraces every conceivable constituency: schoolchildren, flirtatious singles, Hungarian-Americans, accountants—along with pederasts and porn fans. Can they all get along? Or will our fear of kids surfing for cyberporn behind their bedroom doors provoke a crackdown?

3   The first order of business is to grasp what cyberspace *is*. It might help to leave behind metaphors of highways and frontiers and to think instead of real estate. Real estate, remember, is an intellectual, legal, artificial environment constructed *on top of* land. Real estate recognizes the difference between parkland and shopping mall, between red-light zone and school district, between church, state and drugstore.

4   In the same way, you could think of cyberspace as a giant and unbounded world of virtual real estate. Some property is privately owned and rented out; other property is common land; some places are suitable for children, and others are best avoided by all but the kinkiest citizens. Unfortunately, it's those places that are now capturing the popular imagination: places that offer bomb-making instructions, pornography, advice on how to procure stolen credit cards. They make cyberspace sound like a nasty place. Good citizens jump to a conclusion: better regulate it. . . .

5   Regardless of how many laws or lawsuits are launched, regulation won't work.

6   Aside from being unconstitutional, using censorship to counter indecency and other troubling "speech" fundamentally misinterprets the nature of cyberspace. Cyberspace isn't a frontier where wicked people can grab unsuspecting children, nor is it a giant television system that can beam offensive messages at unwilling viewers. In this kind of real estate, users have to *choose* where they visit, what they see, what they do. It's optional, and it's much easier to bypass a place on the Net than it is to avoid walking past an unsavory block of stores on the way to your local 7-11.

7   Put plainly, cyberspace is a voluntary destination—in reality, many destinations. You don't just get "onto the Net"; you have to go someplace in particular. That means that people can choose where to go and what to see. Yes, community standards should be enforced, but those standards should be set by cyberspace communities themselves, not by the courts or by politicians in Washington. What we need isn't Government control over all these electronic communities: We need self-rule.

8   What makes cyberspace so alluring is precisely the way in which it's *different* from shopping malls, television, highways and other terrestrial jurisdictions. But let's define the territory:

9   First, there are private e-mail conversations, akin to the conversations you have over the telephone or voice mail. These are private and consensual and require no regulation at all.

10   Second, there are information and entertainment services, where people can download anything from legal texts and lists of "great new restaurants" to game software or dirty pictures. These places are like bookstores, malls and movie houses—places where you go to buy something. The customer needs to request an item or sign up for a subscription; stuff (especially pornography) is not sent out to people who don't ask for it. Some of these services are free or included as part of a broad service like Compuserve or America Online; others charge and may bill their customers directly.

11   Third, there are "real" communities—groups of people who communicate among themselves. In real-estate terms, they're like bars or restaurants or bathhouses. Each active participant contributes to a general conversation, generally through posted messages. Other participants may simply listen or watch. Some are supervised by a moderator; others are more like bulletin boards—anyone is free to post anything. Many of these services started out unmoderated but are now imposing rules to keep out unwanted advertising, extraneous discussions or increasingly rude participants. Without a moderator, the decibel level often gets too high.

12   Ultimately, it's the rules that determine the success of such places. Some of the rules are determined by the supplier of content; some of the rules concern prices and

membership fees. The rules may be simple: "Only high-quality content about oil-industry liability and pollution legislation: $120 an hour." Or: "This forum is unmoderated, and restricted to information about copyright issues. People who insist on posting advertising or unrelated material will be asked to desist (and may eventually be barred)." Or: "Only children 8 to 12, on school-related topics and only clean words. The moderator will decide what's acceptable."

13   Cyberspace communities evolve just the way terrestrial communities do: People with like-minded interests band together. Every cyberspace community has its own character. Overall, the communities on Compuserve tend to be more techy or professional; those on America Online, affluent young singles; Prodigy, family oriented. Then there are independents like Echo, a hip, downtown New York service, or Women's Wire, targeted to women who want to avoid the male culture prevalent elsewhere on the Net. There's SurfWatch, a new program allowing access only to locations deemed suitable for children. On the Internet itself, there are lots of passionate noncommerical discussion groups on topics ranging from Hungarian politics (Hungary-Online) to copyright law.

14   And yes, there are also porn-oriented services, where people share dirty pictures and communicate with one another about all kinds of practices, often anonymously. Whether these services encourage the fantasies they depict is subject to debate—the same debate that has raged about pornography in other media. But the point is that no one is forcing this stuff on anybody.

15   What's unique about cyberspace is that it liberates us from the tyranny of government, where everyone lives by the rule of the majority. In a democracy, minority groups and minority preferences tend to get squeezed out, whether they are minorities of race and culture or minorities of individual taste. Cyberspace allows communities of any size and kind to flourish; in cyberspace, communities are chosen by the users, not forced on them by accidents of geography. This freedom gives the rules that preside in cyberspace a moral authority that rules in terrestrial environments don't have. Most people are stuck in the country of their birth, but if you don't like the rules of a cyberspace community, you can just sign off. Love it or leave it. Likewise, if parents don't like the rules of a given cyberspace community, they can restrict their children's access to it.

16   What's likely to happen in cyberspace is the formation of new communities, free of the constraints that cause conflict on earth. Instead of a global village, which is a nice dream but impossible to manage, we'll have invented another world of self-contained communities that cater to their own members' inclinations without interfering with anyone else's. The possibility of a real market-style evolution of governance is at hand. In cyberspace, we'll be able to test and evolve rules governing what needs to be governed—intellectual property, content and access control, rules about privacy and free speech. Some communities will allow anyone in; others will restrict access to members who qualify on one basis or another. Those communities that prove self-sustaining will prosper (and perhaps grow and split into subsets with ever-more-particular interests and identities). Those that can't survive—either because people lose interest or get scared off—will simply wither away.

17   In the near future, explorers in cyberspace will need to get better at defining and identifying their communities. They will need to put in place—and accept—their own

local governments, just as the owners of expensive real estate often prefer to have their own security guards rather than call in the police. But they will rarely need help from any terrestrial government.

18   Of course, terrestrial governments may not agree. What to do, for instance, about pornography? The answer is labeling—not banning—questionable material. In order to avoid censorship and lower the political temperature, it makes sense for cyberspace participants themselves to agree on a scheme for questionable items, so that people or automatic filters can avoid them. In other words, posting pornography in "alt.sex.bestiality" would be O.K.; it's easy enough for software manufacturers to build an automatic filter that would prevent you—or your child—from ever seeing that item on a menu. (It's as if all the items were wrapped, with labels on the wrapper.) Someone who posted the same material under the title "Kid-Fun" could be sued for mislabeling.

19   Without a lot of fanfare, private enterprises and local groups are already producing a variety of labeling and ranking services, along with kid-oriented sites like Kidlink, EdWeb and Kids' Space. People differ in their tastes and values and can find services or reviewers on the Net that suit them in the same way they select books and magazines. Or they can wander freely if they prefer, making up their own itinerary.

20   In the end, our society needs to grow up. Growing up means understanding that there are no perfect answers, no all-purpose solutions, no government-sanctioned safe havens. We haven't created a perfect society on earth and we won't have one in cyberspace either. But at least we can have individual choice—and individual responsibility.

POST-READING QUESTIONS

CONTENT

1. How does Dyson define cyberspace? Why does she say defining this term is important?

2. What aspects of cyberspace does Dyson claim are receiving most of the online-oriented attention?

3. What reasons does Dyson give for why regulating the Internet will not work? Do you agree? Explain.

4. How does Dyson define the territory of cyberspace? Why do you think she categorizes cyberspace in this way? Is the categorization helpful? Explain.

5. What does Dyson say is unique about cyberspace? Do you agree with her? Why or why not?

6. What does Dyson say people who do not like cyberspace should do? What do you think?

7. What suggestion does Dyson have for dealing with questionable material? How effective do you think this suggestion is?

STYLE AND STRUCTURE

8. What is Dyson's main idea? Restate her point in your own words.

9. Who is Dyson's audience? How great a proportion do you think parents make up of Dyson's audience? Why? Choose words and examples that best target Dyson's intended population.

10. What examples does Dyson use to make her point? Are these examples enough? Explain, offering examples of your own in order to clarify your point.

11. How effective are Dyson's analogies of real estate and territories in defining cyberspace?

12. Is Dyson convincing? What about her argument is or is not convincing? Explain and cite the text for support.

CRITICAL THINKING AND ANALYSIS

DISCUSSION QUESTIONS

13. Is Dyson against regulation of any kind? Using the text to support your views, discuss whether or not Dyson approves of any kind of online regulation.

14. Dyson writes that "In a democracy, minority groups and minority preferences tend to get squeezed out. . . . Cyberspace allows communities of any size and kind to flourish . . ." What do you think? How powerful is the majority presence of the "real" world online? Do minority groups have equal voices? What determines how loud an online community's voice is?

WRITING ASSIGNMENTS

15. Dyson claims that "[Internet] users have to *choose* where they visit, what they see, what they do." Is this statement accurate? And if so, is it a viable defense against regulation? Do Internet surfers ever go places accidentally? Write two to three paragraphs either agreeing or disagreeing with Dyson's statement, and be sure to use your own experiences to illustrate your ideas.

16. How effective do you think what Dyson calls "terrestrial government" regulation could be? Write a few paragraphs or a short essay in which you argue either for or against Internet regulation by the terrestrial governments Dyson mentions. Be sure to cite this essay and others in this chapter, and use your own online experiences for support.

17. Dyson claims that parents who do not like what their children find online should restrict their children's access to the Internet. Write a few paragraphs or brief essay in which you explain what parents' role should be in limiting online exposure for their children.

VOCABULARY DEVELOPMENT

18. How do words help create tone? Scan Dyson's essay in order to determine her tone and then choose at least five words that you think best reflect her attitude in the essay. Write a few sentences explaining how the words you choose best communicate Dyson's tone.

GROUP ACTIVITIES

19. In small groups, perform an online search for anything your group decides. Follow two or three links in order to learn more about your chosen topic. Was every link you followed relevant to your search? As a group, discuss whether or not all sites are helpful and decide whether or not Dyson's claim that people choose the information they access online is accurate.

20. Dyson claims that terrestrial governments are unnecessary in cyberspace because online communities establish their own working rules. As a group, form your own fictitious cyberspace community and make your own rules. Present your guidelines to the class in order to get feedback on whether or not your rules are feasible for your community.

SYNTHESIS QUESTIONS

1. Russell Baker employs humor to explore the many ways machines frustrate us, but John Seabrook explores whether or not technology can solve some of our interpersonal conflicts by making us respond to each other based upon what we write, not what we look like. Write a well-developed paragraph or essay in which you explore the pros and cons of some aspect of technology and conclude whether or not the advantages are worth the disadvantages. Be sure to cite at least three essays from this chapter and draw on your own personal experience in order to illustrate your ideas.

2. John Seabrook writes of the comfort he receives online from a woman he's never met. However, Cathleen Cleaver, Esther Dyson, and even Seabrook himself all make mention of impolite or vulgar images and discussions that take place online every day. What kind of influence do you think the Internet has on people's ability to communicate? Write at least three well-developed paragraphs in which you argue that the Internet has a positive, negative, or mixed influence upon the way people communicate. Cite essays from this chapter and your own experience in order to clarify your ideas.

3. John Seabrook and Cathleen Cleaver both raise the issue of free speech as it pertains to the Internet. At the same time, these writers also reveal that information debasing or discriminating against groups of people is easily available to anyone with Internet access. Consider Seabrook's final quotation of Internet expert John Norstadt that "it's important to be decent on the Net because the dark side is always right there." Write an essay in which you argue where individual civility could solve the problems these authors cite and where the law, in the form of Internet regulation, should step in. Cite from these authors and any others you find in your research in order to illustrate your ideas clearly.

4. Several writers address the idea that the Internet presents "danger" to its users while also providing numerous benefits. Using the writers in the chapter and others you consult, write an essay discussing whether the benefits outweigh the risks of using the Internet.

5. In Anne Taylor Fleming's article, *Anywhere But Here: More Connected But More Alone,* she writes that the cell phone has led to "complete strangers spewing out intimacies or fighting right in front of us, needful of the validation of our attention," and John Seabrook offers numerous examples of people who "yell" at each other online. Write an essay or paragraph in which you argue whether or not people today need "validation" of others' attention. Cite from these essays as well as others in the chapter and from research in order to illustrate your ideas.

6. Anwar Accawi recounts the excitement that accompanied the arrival of his town's first telephone, while John Seabrook quotes Dave Norstadt who claims that new technology always has "a dark side." What do you think? Write a well-developed paragraph or essay in which you argue that some forms of technology have no "dark side" or no positive side. Be sure to quote both of these writers and cite your own experiences in order to illustrate your ideas.

7. Anwar Accawi writes that even as technology entered his boyhood village of Magdaluna, it did not bring the "better life" that many of his community sought. Similarly, Anne Taylor Fleming writes that technology causes us to "[disconnect] from the pleasures at hand" in order to "avoid the specter of loneliness" caused by technological advances. Write a well-developed paragraph or short essay in which you define the relationship between interpersonal relationships and technology. Do aspects of technology cause us to be ultimately more lonely, or can we stay in better touch with each other as a result of email and cell phones? Cite several readings from this chapter as well as your own observations in order to support your views.

8. Cathleen Cleaver writes that people can post obscene messages and images from "the seclusion of the home," and John Seabrook writes that "The same anonymity that allows the twelve-year-old access to the professor allows a pedophile access to the twelve-year-old." Write at least three well-developed paragraphs in which you argue whether or not anonymity plays a significant role determining people's online civility. Be sure to cite from these essays and others in this chapter in order to illustrate your views.

9. Russell Baker writes of inanimate objects whose "goal . . . is to resist man and ultimately to defeat him," while John Seabrook writes that when he thought his computer was "infected," he "waited for [it] to die." Why do these writers attribute human characteristics to machines? Write an essay in which you explain why people endow inanimate objects with human qualities. Be sure to cite both essays and others in order to support your ideas.

Reprinted with special permission of King Features Syndicate.

"The quality of service is related to the quality of life of those who provide the service. A stressed, overburdened, fatigued, harassed or underpaid employee is not likely to provide the best service."

— P.M. Forni
Speaking of Manners (Interview)

"Every action done in company ought to be with some sign of respect to those that are present."

— George Washington

> **"**The civility crisis is a permanent condition of humanity. There's always a civility crisis.**"**
>
> **— Mark Caldwell**
> *A Short History of Rudeness: Manners, Morals and Misbehavior in Modern America*

> **"**Manners are the new status accessory, pricier than a Rolex, more portable than a Day-Timer, and shinier than hand-made shoes. Polished graces can get you where you're going faster than a speeding BMW.**"**
>
> **— Marjabelle Young Stewart**
> *professional etiquette trainer*

> **"**Patterns of incivility tend to 'cascade downward' and self-perpetuate . . . That means bosses are more likely to target subordinate employees who, in turn, exhibit disrespectful behavior toward lower-level employees.**"**
>
> **— Alison Kurdock**
> *How Rude!? Companies Take on the Fight Against Workplace Incivility*

Chapter 6: Civility in the Workplace

Readings:

Argument Pair:

Websites:

www.pathfinder.com

Fortune magazine offers full-text articles online through this Pathfinder (Time Warner) site. You can search through the archives or the table of contents for relevant, timely articles.

www.inform.umd.edu/EdRes/ Topic/WomensStudies/ GenderIssues/ SexualHarassment/

This site provides access to commentary on a multitude of issues related to sexual harassment.

Introduction

Chances are, if you're reading this chapter introduction, you are on your way to earning a college degree, probably on your way to prepare yourself for a career after you've finished your education or to advance in the career you already have. If so, then you know that certain types of behavior—professionalism, responsibility, diligence— are definitely advantages in the workplace, and, thus, advantages to getting hired and promoted. Once you have achieved your goal and landed that job, however, can you relax and let the qualities you've fostered in order to be employable lie dormant? Probably not. In fact, when you find yourself in your first, or next, big career position, you will need to exercise even more of the employer-desired traits than you did in seeking a job. The pressure will have only just started.

This chapter examines the role people's actions play in different work environments, from corporate offices to the street beats of Philadelphia police officers. The readings reveal how, regardless of salary structure or job description, certain standards of behavior exist in any job, and these standards exist for both employer and employee, despite people's attempts to change the rules for themselves. "Civility in the Workplace" raises questions concerning the legality, or illegality, of what may simply be uncivil behavior. When, for instance, does requesting an employee to stay late at work become not just a favor but a form of unfairness? And when does protecting a neighborhood from "bad guys" start looking like extortion? And at what point does a lack of concern for others become against the law? These issues among others sit at the center of Chapter 6.

"Desk Rage" Takes Toll in Workplace

Lisa Girion

Citing incivility at work as one cause of low productivity, *Los Angeles Times* staff writer Lisa Girion explores the issue of people's behavior at work, citing the experience of several long-term employees. Girion reveals many causes for people's work-related stress, and she presents numerous negative effects of stressful conditions at work. Finally, Girion examines the seemingly causal relationship between incivility and low productivity at work.

Pre-reading Questions

Freewrite for five to ten minutes in response to the following questions:
On a scale of one to ten, how stressful is your job now or a job you have held in the past? What are the primary causes of workplace stress for you? How does your stress usually show itself? What, if anything, can you or your employer do to decrease the amount of stress you feel at work?

Vocabulary Preview

Vocabulary Words:	• cubicles	• commissioned	• spate
	• respondents	• anecdotal	• linearly
	• instilled	• prompted	• perceived
	• exacerbates	• grist	

As always, look up the words above and write a few related sentences using at least five of the words.

1 As a human-resources executive responsible for hundreds of insurance company employees, Maggie Jennings saw her share of office temper tantrums—arguments between co-workers, pen-throwing managers and even a guy who kicked in his computer screen.

2 Jennings' experience is not unique. Two new studies involving thousands of people suggest a significant portion of the U.S. work force is suffering everything from uncomfortable and distracting incivilities to stress-induced attacks on trash cans, keyboards and even co-workers—all expressions of what one survey called "desk rage."

3 After 30 years in the field and weary of struggling to bridge the gulf between employee needs and corporate demands, Jennings, a 52-year-old Long Island, N.Y., resident, jumped at an early retirement offer last spring.

4 "Once in awhile, out of sheer frustration, I'd just go to the ladies' room and close the cubicle and cry," said Jennings, who channeled her frustration by launching a gripe site called thisjobstinks.com. "After awhile, I realized there was little I could do. I hated my job and used to mutter in my head, 'This job stinks.'"

5   Nearly a third of 1,305 workers who responded to a telephone survey about desk rage admitted to yelling at someone in the office, and 65 percent said workplace stress is at least occasionally a problem for them. Work stress had driven 23 percent of the respondents to tears, and 34 percent blamed their jobs for a loss of sleep.

6   While workplace stress is nothing new, many experts and workers said several economic and social trends have intensified it, or at least heightened sensitivity to it. Layoffs have instilled a lingering sense of job insecurity in many workers, while making it more difficult to meet productivity demands that have risen dramatically.

7   At the same time, an increasingly fluid and diverse work force that includes more women, more dual-career couples and more generations exacerbates on-the-job tensions. And there's a growing sense that workplace innovations, from cellphones to e-mail, are really high-tech leashes that make it impossible to ever really escape.

8   "There seems to be a real underlying tension in the workplace today that I don't remember existing 10 or 15 years ago," said Sean Hutchinson, president of Integra Realty Resources Inc., a New York-based real-estate advisory and appraisal firm that commissioned a desk-rage survey in response to anecdotal reports from clients across the country.

9   "With the booming economy and people having to work long hours with tight deadlines, and in some cases limited resources, and a tight labor market, it's a difficult time for people," Hutchinson said. "It's really putting people in a pressure cooker."

10   While workplace stress occasionally erupts into highly publicized incidents of violence and death—at an estimated cost to business of $4.2 billion a year—more ordinary expressions of job frustration also contribute to the toll on employers and employees. Nearly 20 percent of the desk-rage survey respondents said stress had caused them to quit a job, and 12 percent said it had prompted them to call in sick.

11   A separate study to be published in the quarterly journal Organizational Dynamics found that workers who had been treated rudely had a variety of reactions that were bad for business. Half said they lost work time worrying about the rude behavior directed toward them.

12   A third admitted to intentionally reducing their commitment to the company. Nearly a quarter said they stopped doing their best work, and 12 percent quit their jobs.

13   "The breadth of the impact of (rudeness) was surprising for us," said Christine M. Pearson of the Kenan-Flagler Business School at the University of North Carolina, one of three researchers who interviewed and surveyed nearly 1,500 people on workplace incivility.

14   If workplace stress is bad for business, coping with it is big business. It has become an industry employing legions of organizational psychologists, security agents and researchers. And it is grist for a spate of recent books that suggest it is indeed a jungle out there, including "Anger and Conflict in the Work Place," "Managing Workplace Negativity" and "Violence at Work: How to Safeguard Your Firm."

15   "We're leading these nonstop lives, and we're continuing to accelerate the pace," said business consultant Leslie Charles, author of "Why Is Everyone So Cranky?" (Hyperion, 1999). "We're surrounded by noise and distractions. And we're so preoccupied with what we're doing and what's next that we have an inability to process what's just happened or what's bugging us. We're overwhelmed, overworked, overscheduled and overspent."

16   To keep up, many people resort to multitasking, an attempt to handle many jobs at once, which usually only adds to their aggravation, said Jerry Rubenstein, a professor of counselor education at the University of Rochester in New York.

17   "The brain tends to like to function linearly. What we're doing is creating overload situations," Rubenstein said. "Most people in the workplace are functioning in the yellow zone, which means 'Pay attention,' and it doesn't take much to take them into the red zone, which is 'Danger.'"

18   Awareness of workplace stress and its adverse effects is growing, said Paul E. Spector, a professor of industrial and organizational psychology at the University of South Florida who has been studying desk-kicking and other counterproductive work behavior for 25 years.

19   On anonymous questionnaires, a wide variety of employees have confessed a great deal to Spector and his associates. Two-thirds admit to having "tried to look busy while doing nothing," and 23 percent say they have "started an argument with a co-worker." A little more than 6 percent of workers admit to having purposely damaged work equipment or property, and 28.4 percent say they have purposely worked slowly when things needed to get done.

20   Employers need to look at such behavior as an expression of need, said Jeff Krause, manager of consultation services for Minnesota-based CIGNA Behavioral Health.

21   Krause supervises a team of eight psychologists who offer behavioral advice by telephone for managers at 650 client companies with 1.5 million employees. Krause said the calls range from helping a manager approach an employee about a bad-breath problem affecting other workers to "I've got an employee who's locked herself in her car. What do I do?"

22   Although such employee-assistance programs began in the 1960s to prevent perceived personal problems from affecting an employee's job performance, Krause said, today's employers are more likely to view such troubles as at least partially work-based.

23   "If desk rage had been coming up as a term 15 years ago, the assumption we would have made is, there is something going on in that person's home and they are bringing it to work," he said. "Now, while what we are seeing is an increase in stresses at work and home, work is seen as the culprit, and we have to look at that."

24   Jennings, the former human-resources executive, now works part time as a consultant, and work rage is still keeping her busy. She was recently called in to counsel a supervisor who had thrown a book across the room while she was talking to an employee.

25   "I think they just can't control it anymore," Jennings said.

26   "They reach a point where they explode."

POST-READING QUESTIONS

CONTENT

1. What are some examples of work-related stress that Girion lists in her article? Which ones seem most or least serious? Why?

2. What does Girion say are some causes of on-the-job stress? What do you think?

3. What are some effects of work-related stress, according to Girion?

4. What is "desk rage"? Who suffers from it?

5. What role does Girion say technology plays in causing people's job-related stress?

6. How does Girion say that people try to keep up with their tasks at work? Is this a good strategy, according to her article?

STYLE AND STRUCTURE

7. Does Girion have an argument? If so, what is it?

8. What are some of Girion's sub-points? How are they related to her main idea?

9. What examples does Girion use to illustrate her main idea? Which examples are most effective? Why?

10. What about this article reveals that it was published first in a newspaper, as opposed to a book or other more formal publication?

11. Who is Girion's audience? Cite examples from the text to illustrate your point.

12. Is Girion convincing? Why or why not?

CRITICAL THINKING AND ANALYSIS

DISCUSSION QUESTIONS

13. Girion writes that "While workplace stress is nothing new, . . . several economic and social trends have intensified it . . ." What trends do you think have caused an increase in work-related stress?

14. What kinds of stress have you encountered at work? What, if anything, could you have done to control this stress?

WRITING ASSIGNMENTS

15. Drawing from Girion's essay and your own work experience, write a few well-developed paragraphs in which you argue that workplace stress is or is not worsening.

16. Girion names several factors that contribute to people's stress at work. Write a paragraph or short essay in which you argue that one factor—competition, for instance—causes more stress at work than others. Be sure to cite the article and your own experiences and observations in order to illustrate your ideas.

17. What is the worst display of "desk rage" or workplace incivility that you have ever seen? Write a well-developed paragraph describing the events leading up to the "desk rage" incident and the incident itself.

VOCABULARY DEVELOPMENT

18. Girion claims that "desk rage" is not new, but she uses many terms, such as e-mail, that have only become commonly used over the past ten or fifteen years. Make a list of all the terms Girion uses that reveal the time Girion wrote this article.

GROUP ACTIVITIES

19. As a group, discuss the types of factors that contribute to workplace stress, ranking them according to which factors are most and least significant. Of these, which are the easiest to control? Share your results with the class.

20. Compare three or four of the different types of "rage" present in society: air rage, road rage, online flaming, desk rage. What are the causes of these types of rage? Effects? What do these types of rage have in common? Then, write a "coping" plan to help people address their rage in the different areas you discuss.

The Reasonable Woman Standard

Ellen Goodman

Educated at Radcliffe College, Ellen Goodman worked as a reporter for *Newsweek* and the *Detroit Free Press* before writing for the *Boston Globe.* Since 1972, her column has been widely syndicated. In this selection, Goodman claims that the standard for what must be considered offensive behavior in the workplace should be determined according to how a "reasonable woman" would react, just as much of law is based upon what a "reasonable man" thinks or feels.

Pre-reading Questions

Freewrite for five to ten minutes in response to the following questions:
What is your experience with gender relations at work? Have you ever encountered sexual harassment in any form? What happened? How do you think sexual harassment can be avoided in the workplace?

Vocabulary Preview

Vocabulary Words:	• volatile	• murky	• hackles
	• harassment	• coercive	• empathy
	• oxymoron		

Look up the words above and rank them in order of which words carry the greatest emotional punch. Then, after you've read the essay, write a paragraph explaining how the emotional impact of these words helps Goodman make her case.

---

1   Since the volatile mix of sex and harassment exploded under the Capitol dome, it hasn't just been senators scurrying for cover. The case of the professor and judge has left a gender gap that looks more like a crater.[1]

2   We have discovered that men and women see this issue differently. Stop the presses. Sweetheart, get me rewrite.

3   On the "Today" show, Bryant Gumbel asks something about a man's right to have a pinup on the wall and Katie Couric says what she thinks of that. On the normally sober "MacNeil/Lehrer" hour the usual panel of legal experts doesn't break down between left and right but between male and female.

---

[1] Goodman is alluding to the charges that Professor Anita Hill, of the University of Oklahoma law school, made during the Senate hearings before confirmation of Justice Clarence Thomas to a seat on the Supreme Court. The hearings were televised nationally, and several senators on the Judiciary Committee were widely regarded as having treated Hill very badly. [Editors' note].

4   On a hundred radio talk shows, women are sharing experiences and men are asking for proof. In ten thousand offices, the order of the day is the nervous joke. One boss asks his secretary if he can still say "good morning," or is that sexual harassment. Heh, heh. The women aren't laughing.

5   Okay boys and girls, back to your corners. Can we talk? Can we hear?

6   The good news is that women have stopped rolling their eyes at each other and started speaking out. The bad news is that we may each assume the other gender not only doesn't understand but can't understand. "They don't get it" becomes "they can't get it."

7   Let's start with the fact that sexual harassment is a concept as new as date rape. Date rape, that should-be oxymoron, assumes a different perspective on the part of the man and the woman. His date, her rape. Sexual harassment comes with some of the same assumptions. What he labels sexual, she labels harassment.

8   This produces what many men tend to darkly call a "murky" area of the law. Murky however is a step in the right direction. When everything was clear, it was clearly biased. The old single standard was [a] male standard. The only options a working woman had were to grin, bear it, or quit.

9   Sexual harassment rules are based on the point of view of the victim, nearly always a woman. The rules ask, not just whether she has been physically assaulted, but whether the environment in which she works is intimidating or coercive. Whether she feels harassed. It says that her feelings matter.

10   This, of course, raises all sorts of hackles about women's *feelings,* women's *sensitivity.* How can you judge the sensitivity level of every single woman you work with? What's a poor man to do?

11   But the law isn't psychiatry. It doesn't adapt to individual sensitivity levels. There is a standard emerging by which the courts can judge these cases and by which people can judge them as well. It's called "the reasonable woman standard." How would a reasonable woman interpret this? How would a reasonable woman behave?

12   This is not an entirely new idea, although perhaps the law's belief in the reasonableness of women is. There has long been a "reasonable man" in the law not to mention a "reasonable pilot," a "reasonable innkeeper," a "reasonable train operator."

13   Now the law is admitting that a reasonable woman may see these situations differently than a man. That truth—available in your senator's mailbag—is also apparent in research. We tend to see sexualized situations from our own gender's perspective. Kim Lane Scheppele, a political science and law professor at the University of Michigan, summarizes the miscues this way: "Men see the sex first and miss the coercion. Women see the coercion and miss the sex."

14   Does that mean that we are genetically doomed to our double vision? Scheppele is quick to say no. Our justice system rests on the belief that one person can get in another's head, walk in her shoes, see things from another perspective. And so does our hope for change.

15   If a jury of car drivers can understand how a "reasonable pilot" would see one situation, a jury of men can see how a reasonable woman would see another event. The crucial ingredient is empathy.

16   Check it out in the office tomorrow. He's coming on, she's backing off, he keeps coming. Read the body language. There's a *Playboy* calendar on the wall and a PMS joke in the boardroom and the boss is just being friendly. How would a reasonable woman feel?

17   At this moment, when the air is crackling with hostility and consciousness-raising has the hair sticking up on the back of many necks, guess what? Men can "get it." Reasonable men.

POST-READING QUESTIONS

CONTENT

1. Whom does Goodman say sexual harassment affects? How does she communicate the widespread nature of her topic?
2. What does Goodman mean when she calls date-rape a "should-be oxymoron"?
3. How do men and women view sexual harassment, according to Goodman? Do you agree? Explain.
4. Upon whose point of view are sexual harassment rules based?
5. By what standard does Goodman argue a woman's feelings should be measured? Describe this standard.
6. What role does empathy play in determining whether or not a situation contains elements of harassment?

STYLE AND STRUCTURE

7. How does Goodman introduce her topic? Is this means effective? Explain.
8. What is Goodman's tone? What expressions does she use that best reveal her tone?
9. Who is Goodman's audience? Does she equally target men and women? How can you tell?
10. What is Goodman's purpose in writing this essay? Restate her main idea in your own words.
11. Goodman makes reference to specific sexual harassment incidents without mentioning the names of the people involved. What is the effect of her doing this? Why does she not simply mention names?
12. Is Goodman convincing in her argument? Why or why not?

CRITICAL THINKING AND ANALYSIS

DISCUSSION QUESTIONS

13. What, to you, comprises sexual harassment? How prevalent is it today? Do you think sexual harassment is becoming more or less common? Why?
14. Compared to other on-the-job conflicts such as discrimination, how serious do you think sexual harassment is? Why?

15. What role does basic civility, or common courtesy, play in sexual harassment? Must the law solve the harassment conflict, or can good manners solve the problem? Explain.

WRITING ASSIGNMENTS

16. Goodman writes that "men and women see [sexual harassment] differently." Do you think, then, that according to her views, men can be victims of sexual harassment? Write a few paragraphs in response to this question, and cite the essay for support.

17. Goodman claims that sexually harassed women in the workplace once had only three options: "grin, bear it, or quit." What do you think? Write a brief essay in which you explain what women's options in response to sexual harassment are today. Cite this essay and your own experience for support, and feel free to consult other readings as well.

18. Goodman writes that "Our justice system rests on the belief that one person can get in another's head . . ." What do you think? Write a well-developed paragraph or essay in which you argue that people can or cannot see another person's point of view. Do your best to limit your topic to a discussion of the workplace, and cite the essay for support.

VOCABULARY DEVELOPMENT

19. Make a list of words that have neutral meanings but possibly offensive undertones. For example, the word "chick" can mean a baby bird, or it can refer to a woman. What, if anything, do these words have in common? How much of a difference would omitting these words from people's vocabulary make in avoiding sexual harassment? Explain.

GROUP ACTIVITIES

20. Write two sexual harassment policies, one directed at men, and one directed at women. What do your policies have in common? How are they different? Share your results with other groups in order to decide what elements best make a sexual harassment policy.

21. Brainstorm a list of possible sexual harassment grievances. Then, draw a chart or graph plotting which offenses your group finds most and least offensive. Present your findings to the class in order to learn how on-target you are.

How Cops Go Bad
Brutality, Racism, Cover-ups, Lies: A Guilty Police Officer Tells How the Process Works

Michael Kramer

Originally appearing in *Time* magazine in 1998, Michael Kramer's article details the behavior of one group of police officers in Philadelphia and seeks to explain how agents of the law often cross the line between law enforcers and law breakers. Kramer outlines how the pressure to "get the job done" along with high crime rates and low compensation combine to push police to take the law into their own hands, and several officers claim that their uncivil treatment of those they arrest is necessary to do their job.

Pre-reading Questions

Freewrite for five to ten minutes in response to the following questions:
How far do you think law enforcement officials should go in order to protect innocent people? Should law enforcement break laws, even if that is the only way they can arrest a guilty person? Should police or other public servants use the same type of behavior for all types of crime?

Vocabulary Preview

Vocabulary Words:			
	• aberrations	• adjunct	• vociferously
	• systemic	• humane	• contraband
	• hinder	• incriminating	• fabricated
	• unwittingly	• embellished	• laconic
	• predicament	• vengeful	• credible

Look up at least ten of the words above and write a few sentences explaining how they are or are not effective in helping Kramer communicate his point.

---

1   It was around 8 o'clock in the evening of Feb. 24, 1991, and Arthur Colbert was lost. Most of the rest of the world was focused on the Persian Gulf, where the ground war had begun only hours earlier, but Colbert had a woman on his mind. His date for the night lived in a Philadelphia neighborhood known for its crime and poverty, and Colbert couldn't find her house. Then he got lucky—or so he thought. A police wagon was idling down the block, and Colbert got out of his dark blue 1985 Toyota Camry to ask directions. Inside the police van were two uniformed cops, a lean, square-jawed officer with longish yellow hair—known and feared on the streets as Blondie—and a short, dark-haired officer named Tommy Ryan. As Colbert recalls it today, "I was in the wrong place at the wrong time. I probably would have been safer in Kuwait."

2   For both Colbert and the Philadelphia police department, a nightmare was about to begin. Before it was over, it would expose a pattern of corruption that would bring down nine Philadelphia cops, implicate scores of others and eventually lead to the freeing of 160 wrongfully convicted prisoners, all victims of a web of misdeeds masquerading as heroic police work.

3   The Colbert incident was neither as dramatic nor as horrendous as the recent brutalization of Abner Louima at the hands of New York City police. Cases like that grab national headlines, but they are aberrations. More systematic and infinitely harder to root out is a more common form of corruption: too many cops in too many places who routinely flout the laws they are sworn to uphold, cops who come to view the law itself as a maze of misguided rules that hinder their ability to "get the job done." Cops like Blondie. Cops who have created a world governed by an unwritten code of police conduct, a shadow set of rules that guide them as they go about the gritty daily business of tracking and then trapping bad guys. The shadow rules bear little resemblance to official police procedures, but in the real world of urban policing, they prevail.

4   This is a look into that world, a sort of parallel universe in which protecting "us" from "them" can cost "us" dearly, as Colbert—college student, aspiring FBI agent and a man free of any criminal history—was about to discover that Friday night. Unwittingly, Colbert walked into a fiefdom commanded by a rogue cop so intimidating that he had cowed an entire neighborhood, and so clever that he had won 14 perfect job ratings in 14 years.

5   As Colbert, 24, approached the wagon that night, Blondie and Ryan emerged to greet him. "What are you doing here, nigger?" Colbert recalls one of the cops saying. As Colbert explained his predicament, the officers patted him down and searched his car. "What are you doing?" asked Colbert, who knew the law. "What's your probable cause to search me?" Neither officer responded. "I remember thinking that I was indeed in a bad neighborhood," Colbert says. "The cops have it rough in the real world. They never know if you're a bad guy, so I figured I could take a little abuse."

6   When the search turned up nothing, Ryan and Blondie directed Colbert to his date's home on the next block. Within minutes, as Colbert and the woman were driving off, the same cops appeared again. After telling the woman to "get lost," they handcuffed Colbert and told him he resembled a drug dealer named Hakim. Procedure dictated that Colbert be booked at the 39th-district police headquarters, about a mile away. But Colbert wasn't in the land of official procedure; he was in the hands of Blondie. So, instead, he was taken to 1518 Ontario Street, a run-down three-story home and sometime crack house that served as a sort of hidden adjunct to precinct headquarters. Once inside the building, Colbert was put in a chair in the middle of a 9-ft. by 12-ft. back room on the first floor. Still in cuffs, he was beaten with fists, nightsticks and then a long-handled black flashlight. "We were trying to get him to admit he was Hakim," says Blondie, who agreed to talk to TIME over several days at a federal prison far from Philadelphia, where he is currently serving 13 years for violating the civil rights of Colbert and dozens of others and for stealing money during searches and arrests.

7   In the 39th district, Blondie was notorious for a version of Russian roulette he used with those he arrested—evidence or no evidence. Colbert fit the bill. Blondie cocked the hammer on what he now says was an empty pistol. "If you don't tell us what we want to know, I'm going to blow your head off," he said. Colbert wouldn't budge.

Even today, Blondie—who fears for his life in prison if his real name is disclosed—defends the tactic. "I viewed it as kind of a humane alternative," he says. "It was less hurtful than beating, and it usually got us the information we wanted." But not this time. Still convinced they had Hakim, the officers took Colbert to the station house, where, in a detention room, they roughed him up some more. "We thought the change of venue might work," says Blondie. It didn't. Colbert wasn't Hakim and wouldn't say he was. So, with Colbert's house keys in hand, Ryan and Blondie then traveled outside their jurisdiction to search Colbert's apartment in the close-in suburb of Cheltenham. When nothing incriminating was found, the cops returned to headquarters and released Colbert—after six hours of terror. "Let us catch you around here again," Colbert recalls Blondie's saying, "and we'll kill you."

8   The cops made a tiny mistake that evening, a small error of the sort that brings down empires: they failed to return Colbert's driver's license. (Ryan had thrown it away.) Colbert was about to move to Detroit, where he is now employed as a social worker, and he needed his Pennsylvania license to apply for one in Michigan. So, frightened and trembling, Colbert returned to the 39th headquarters the next day. "Here was a black guy complaining about two white cops to a white lieutenant," recalls John Gallagher, the duty supervisor that day. "It took some balls for him to come in."

9   This was not untrod territory for Gallagher, who comes as close as anyone to being the hero of the piece. "Over time," he says, "I've heard more than a few civilian complaints against cops. Most are grossly embellished, and some are just outright lies." But Colbert's detailed reconstruction impressed Gallagher. "I had watched a psychiatrist say on a TV program that if you put disturbed people in a pink-colored room, it calms them down," he says, "and I'd just had the detention room painted pink. There was no way Colbert could have known that unless he'd been there." The tale was "just too awful," says Gallagher. "Folks get whacked around a lot. You get used to hearing about that. But what happened to Colbert was far over the line." Colbert didn't know the names of his assailants, and there was no record of his arrest or appearance at the station house, but it didn't take long for Gallagher to figure it out: Ryan and Blondie. Yet even with Colbert's testimony, it took time—and luck—to bust Blondie and his confederates. There was, after all, no paper trail.

10   What helped was another police beating, 3,000 miles away. Seven days after Colbert's encounter, the nation's attention shifted from Kuwait to Los Angeles, where Rodney King had been beaten senseless by a gang of vengeful cops. As weeks passed and police everywhere pondered the King horror, the Philadelphia department's internal investigation was leading commanders to a logical conclusion; this was no time for a cover-up. So they released photos of Ryan and Blondie, who had been suspended during the probe, to local newspapers. A flood tide followed. Complaints about the cops' behavior inundated the department and the press. The pattern of abuse was clear, and the stories from the neighborhood spurred on the investigation that would eventually result in the jailing of Blondie and four associates. The five pleaded guilty without a trial. The government urged leniency—the cops had confessed to more crimes than anyone suspected, and implicated more than 50 fellow officers in the process—but the judge was unsympathetic. "You've squashed the Bill of Rights in the mud," he said before sending the men to stiff prison terms.

11   As the first to admit wrongdoing, Ryan received only 10 months in jail, and is now free. The others, all of whom were sentenced last year, are currently in federal prisons. Three have spoken freely with TIME but refuse to be identified by name. "We need to keep low profiles," explains Blondie dryly. "Being known as a former cop to our fellow inmates is not exactly conducive to our life-styles, or to just our continued living."

12   In appearance, Blondie, who's now 42, fits no one's image of a bad cop; to the contrary, he bears a startling resemblance to a slim, hard muscled Robert Redford. The son of a Philadelphia bartender and a clerk for the Internal Revenue Service, he coasted through Archbishop Ryan High School but never thought about college. "I didn't like school," he explains, "except for the girls and parties." He tried to become a fireman but failed the test. "The math was too hard," he says. "The police exam was easier; that's how I became a cop."

13   Blondie took the oath in early 1977. The department he joined had a long history of corruption. A common joke had it that Philadelphia's kids could play cops and robbers at the same time. This was especially true in the 1970s. The mayor was former police commissioner Frank Rizzo, who had promised to "make Attila the Hun look like a faggot" if he won election. "The way to treat criminals," Rizzo explained, is "spacco il capa" (bust their heads). Rizzo was as good as his word. A study for the U.S. Justice Department found that while individual Philadelphia police officers made no more arrests than New York City cops, during Rizzo's eight years as mayor they were 37 times more likely to shoot unarmed citizens fleeing the site of nonviolent crimes.

14   Blondie spent 14 weeks at the police academy. "It was mostly firearms training, first aid and war stories," he says. "They taught a bit about things like probable cause—just to say they had taught it—but the message was clear: What you really do as a cop you learn on the street from the veterans, and you could be sure, as they said, that it was nothing like what you learned at the academy." It wasn't. Three weeks into his new career, and teamed with a veteran officer, Blondie made his first arrest; he nabbed a rape suspect. "Nothing fit," Blondie recalls now. "The clothes description over the radio wasn't like what our guy had on, and he wasn't sweating. He said he was just standing outside his own home, which turned out to be true. But the victim ID'd him, so we took him anyway. She was so hysterical; she would have identified anyone." When Blondie vociferously questioned the arrest, he was told to "shut up, listen and learn." He then watched as the original description was altered to fit the suspect, who was held for eight months until the victim recanted her identification. "The pressure is to produce, to show activity, to get the collars," says Blondie today. "It's all about numbers, like the body count in Vietnam. The rest of the system determines if you got the right guy or not."

15   Blondie learned a lot, very quickly. Beating a suspect into a confession? O.K. Stealing from a bad guy? Fine. But he also learned that even the shadow world had its rules. "The first is, keep it in the ghetto. In the good areas, you don't go stopping people without cause," he says. "Second, you don't take money to let a criminal enterprise continue. And third, you don't frame an innocent person." Blondie says he and his crew never "planted stuff" on an innocent person. If he were that kind of cop, he insists, "then we would have put drugs on Colbert, and I wouldn't be talking to you from behind bars right now. We could have created a his-word-vs.-our-word thing, and we

would have got off." But aside from the lines you don't cross, says Blondie, "how you get a bad guy, if he really is a bad guy, is pretty much your own business. Your job is to get him. Period."

16   How you get him is to disregard the law. "Basically, the first thing you really learn as a cop is how to lie," says Blondie. For many officers, their first taste of shading the truth involves car stops. "Now, say you see some guy driving who you think is wrong," says Blondie ("wrong" in his lexicon invariably means a black youth in a late-model car). "You stop him on no basis that could stand up in court. So you lie if you have to. You say he ran a stop sign or didn't signal or had a broken taillight that you break after you've determined he's bad. That makes the initial stop legal." Then, Blondie continues, "you search the car, which you generally have no probable cause to do." The cop who finds something—guns or drugs—has two alternatives: "Lie, and testify that the guy gave you permission to search." Or say the contraband wasn't in the trunk at all, but rather in plain view. "Why sweat it?" asks Blondie. "Sure, you've fabricated the probable cause and done an illegal search, but the guy is bad, right? We do what we have to do."

17   "There's far more of this type of thing than anyone could be comfortable with," says Robert McGuire, who was New York City's police commissioner for six years. "Do cops perjure themselves routinely on warrants and arrests, where the probable cause is made up after the fact so the arrest stands up in court? Sure they do." But it isn't necessary, says McGuire: "It's possible to follow the rules and get the job done. In most communities, the bad actors are well known to both residents and the police, which means if you can't get the bad guys the first time then you can get them the next time, because there's always a next time." But most officers don't make that calculation. "Prosecutors and judges know a lot of testimony by cops is false," says Alan Dershowitz, the Harvard law professor and criminal defense attorney who has popularized the term testilying. "But they only know it generically, rather than in any particular case. So in a battle of conflicting testimony, cops are given the benefit of the doubt."

18   For those who watch cops for a living, the opening scene in the movie L.A. Confidential, with a veteran cop counseling a rookie, is disturbingly on point. "As the film puts it," says Dershowitz, "if you're not willing to break the law to do the work you're charged with doing, then you shouldn't be a cop—or at least not a detective."

19   Blondie was transferred to the 39th District in 1984. At its north end, the 39th is home to Philadelphia's elite. Large, expensive houses with well-manicured lawns are owned by business tycoons and politicians. But closer to downtown is an area of about 1 sq. mi. that is still home to the predatory crime common in America's inner cities. "It's the kind of place where if you saw a big TV satellite dish, you knew something was wrong because just about everyone there was on welfare," says the sergeant known as Schoolboy, who was Blondie's nominal boss in "Five Squad," the detachment of plainclothes officers given the task of ridding the streets of drugs, or at least confining them to Philadelphia's poorest neighborhood.

20   In most large police forces, a small percentage of aggressive cops do the dirty work. The rest simply punch their time cards, respond only when called and wait for their pensions. "Many cops go their whole careers without making an arrest," says Joseph McNamara, a former police chief of San Jose, Calif. "The small number of ag-

gressive officers every department has, and needs, are the ones we rely on to clean things up." It isn't hard to spot the ready-to-rumble officers. In Philadelphia's 39th, it became known quickly that Blondie was such a cop—a man who could do you in even if you had done no wrong. Other officers might cruise through the area and have debris or even rocks thrown at them. When Blondie drove by with his cohort, silence fell on the bleak streets. "Cross those guys, and they'd whack you upside the head," says Cory Brown, who now lives in the house where Arthur Colbert was beaten in 1991. "We had our times, Blondie and me," says Brown. "He busted me for having a gun, and I was lucky to get off with probation." No hard feelings, says Brown. "I didn't have no permit for the gun." More important, says Brown, "you got to say that Blondie and them kept a lot of the worst of the stuff around here down, no matter how they went about it."

21   Far away in that federal prison, Blondie doesn't remember Brown, but he takes his point. "You've got to show who's boss on a daily basis," he says in the deadpan, laconic manner that became legend in the 39th. "That wasn't and isn't the kind of area where you walk a beat and make nice with the residents." But many of the residents were (and are) "nice," and they were the ones who screamed loudest for the police to crack down on the crime wave. "The bosses would come back from community meetings with a string of complaints, and we were told to get on it—just get it done," says Blondie. Police supervisors, he says, had other pressures too: "Above the rank of captain, you get promoted mostly by who you know on the force and in politics. And the politicians scream as loud as the residents. Can you tell me when you ever heard a politician say he'd get tough on the cops for violating the civil rights of drug dealers?"

22   Five Squad was a coveted assignment. The officers kept their own hours—although there was always a designated eight-hour shift. "That was so we could make arrests at the end of our tour and get overtime doing the paperwork," says Blondie. In a typical year, he and his fellow Five Squad officers made $60,000 or higher, more than double their salary.

23   The way "it's supposed to work is something like this," says Blondie. "You're supposed to go to a crack house and make a buy, or have someone make it for you via a 'controlled buy.' To do that, you've got to strip the guy beforehand to make sure there is no other money on him. Then you give him some money and he makes the buy, and you strip him afterward to make sure he has no more money." Do it like that, he says, and the buy and subsequent arrest are legal. "But it's a pain for several reasons," he says. "First, you risk having your agent exposed. Second, who's gonna sell to a white guy standing in line at a crack house? So you get some piper [crack addict] or some whore to make the buy. Or you just pinch someone coming out of the house and find out who's in the place, whether they're armed, and where the dope is. Then you go in. It's illegal that way, but then you go and get a warrant later [and falsify the report], saying you made the buy yourself." Or, adds Schoolboy, "you drop a dime, which means you call in a 'shots fired' alarm to 911. Sometimes you even fire your own gun. Then you wait for the shots-fired call to come over the radio, and you respond to your own call. It's all made up, but it makes the raid legal." It's so routine," says Blondie, "that sometimes we'd laugh and say, 'Gee, which story should we use today? How about No. 23?' You get punch drunk in this business."

24   Chinaman, a Blondie confederate, even rationalizes theft: "We didn't use our badges as camouflage just to rob anyone we met who we felt like robbing. We took

from drug dealers. The way I look at it, that money wasn't theirs anyway, and we needed it more than they did, or than the city did, which was who we were supposed to turn it in to." Like most addictions, the thievery grew gradually. It began, says Blondie, as "nothing more than reimbursement. Over time, as we got greedy, it became a kind of tax on the bad guys, a spoils-of-war kind of thing. But that's different than a scum-of-the-earth activity like taking a bribe to let a drug operation continue." That may be a distinction without a difference, but not to Blondie. He's proud that once when he was offered $1,000 a week to let a drug operation flourish, he reported the bribe attempt and the dealer was convicted. Yet over time, according to the charges to which they pleaded guilty, Blondie and his fellow officers stole $100,000.

25   In Philadelphia, as in most big-city police departments, there is little or no money for informants. Yet cops on the street routinely pay $10 or $20 for information. "It adds up," says Blondie, who estimates that each of the officers in Five Squad was shelling out as much as $50 a week for tips. "I'd have more chance of being elected Governor than I would trying to get money out of the department for informants," says Blondie. "The bosses' view is that we had the best jobs. We wore soft clothes, worked our own hours and made tons of overtime. The brass viewed paying informants out of our own pocket as just a cost of doing business." That cost, adds Schoolboy, was often seen as too high. "So when we hit a place, we'd take some money to reimburse our informant payments," he says. "After a while," he recalls, "with so much dough sitting around, you just take more, and then you begin to get used to it." But not too used to it. "Unless you're completely nuts," says Chinaman, "you're careful. If you find 10 grand, say, you take only three or four. You can't raid a drug house and come back and not turn in some money. That'd be a sure tip-off."

26   Most of the time, the squad's knowledge of crack-house operations was the product of tipster information. "And you have to protect those informants," says Blondie. "It's really your No. 1 obligation. You have defense attorneys demanding that you identify them. But if you give up an informant, chances are he's dead by nightfall." At the "end of the day," says Schoolboy, "given how we lied on the probable cause, I'd say that almost all of our [2,233] arrests were bad. On the other hand, if we did everything by the book, crime would be up. Stealing the money was bad. No excuse for that, and none for the beatings either, especially when you have someone in cuffs. But frankly, I'm proud of the arrests. It may sound crazy, but what we did was kind of noble, I think. I mean, cops everywhere keep being told they're in a war. You're told to win it. You're never told to win it by the book, because those telling you to win it know it can't be won that way."

27   Of the 2,000 or so bad arrests made by Five Squad over the six years between 1984 and 1991, only 160 have been reversed. "And each one has been like pulling teeth," says Bradley Bridge, the Philadelphia public defender reviewing the files. An assistant district attorney, speaking not for attribution, sounds like Blondie as he defends the foot dragging: "It's pretty much true that all of those arrested were indeed bad guys, and no one is real eager to let them out on technicalities." The other reason for going slow is financial. To date, Philadelphia has paid out almost $5 million in wrongful-arrest settlements stemming from Five Squad's activities (Colbert settled for only $25,000). "There's simply no real appetite for going full blast on this stuff," says the district attorney.

28   From the time Colbert was terrorized in February 1991, it took prosecutors four years just to indict Blondie & Co. for their illegal activities, and it was more than another

year before they were sentenced to prison on April 15, 1996. "No matter the substance of complaints against cops," says McGuire, "if it's only the victim's word
against the cop's, it's a hard road to travel, and it always takes too much time." For
the city and federal prosecutors considering Colbert's complaint, getting Ryan to "rat
out" proved easy. "If Ryan had held fast, they couldn't have got us," says Blondie.
"He was always a weak sister." The pressure on Ryan was great. He "faced the
prospect of being convicted by the credible testimony of a completely innocent citizen," as the government said in its sentencing memorandum. Ryan caved, and the
FBI fitted him with a wire in October and November 1994. Blondie, no fool, had
grown wary of Ryan, and he made no incriminating statements on tape. But he knew
the Colbert incident would topple him, and when he was approached by the FBI directly, Blondie caved too. "I miscalculated," he says ruefully. "The other stuff was
just our word against the druggies', but I hoped to win points by cooperating. I
thought maybe I could get away with a light term or maybe even probation—13 years
never seemed possible."

29   To win such points, Blondie had to finger his fellow officers. "A real cop would
eat his gun before squealing" on other cops, says Blondie, but he did just that. As the
driving force behind the corruption that brought down Five Squad, Blondie freely rat-
ted on Chinaman and two others, and reluctantly on his sergeant, Schoolboy, as well.
Impressed with the cooperation of Blondie and his confederates, the government
urged leniency. In the future, the prosecutors argued, "other officers . . . may take
their cue from the sentencings of cooperators." Unswayed, Federal Judge Robert
Gawthrop slammed the cops with the maximum mandated by the federal sentencing
guidelines—and Blondie with even more. The result has been exactly what the government feared: only four other officers have fallen. "They took the cue all right," says
a senior FBI official. "No one's talking. And even if they do, the history of these kinds
of scandals is that cops go right back to acting as they always have when the dust settles, because the pressure they most feel is the pressure to produce results, the constant
demand to get the job done."

30   McGuire believes the pressure inevitably forces cops to make up some of their
own rules. "Most of the kind of stuff [Blondie and the others] did was in the vast gray
area that represents the real nuances of police work," he says. "We've all faced these
things; we all have our own personal lines."

31   And Blondie, now in the second year of his 13-year sentence? He remains a
stranger to remorse: "We didn't invent the system, or the ways to scam it to do the job.
We inherited it. We were its custodians. Now others are."

POST-READING QUESTIONS

CONTENT

1. How was Arthur Colbert treated by Blondie and Ryan, and how is this treatment significant?
2. What does Kramer say is a "common form of corruption" in police forces?
   Why does he claim this type of corruption exists?

3. What "mistake" caused Blondie and Ryan to be caught? Why were they not caught and convicted immediately?

4. What reasons does Blondie give for taking the law into his own hands? To what extent do you think he is justified in his actions?

5. What kind of pressure do new police officers face from their peers? How does this pressure affect their actions? Should it?

6. How did the residents of "Philadelphia's poorest neighborhood" react to the way Blondie treated them?

7. How do Blondie and his colleagues rationalize their theft? Do you agree that they were justified in stealing? Explain.

8. How do the convicted police officers feel about each other? What in their language reflects their attitudes toward each other?

9. How do the convicted officers feel about the way they did their jobs? Are they remorseful?

STYLE AND STRUCTURE

10. Does Kramer have an argument? What is it?

11. What examples does Kramer offer to support his points? To what extent are his examples effective?

12. Who is Kramer's audience? What can you tell about how sympathetic his readers are toward the police? Toward those who dealt with the police?

13. What is Kramer's tone? Does he sympathize with the convicted police officers? With their victims? How can you tell?

14. What effect do Kramer's narrative passages—describing Colbert's encounter with Blondie, and Blondie's early years as a police officer—have on your reading of the essay? Would Kramer be more effective if he simply summarized these examples instead of offering detail? Explain.

CRITICAL THINKING AND ANALYSIS

DISCUSSION QUESTIONS

15. Kramer quotes Blondie who says that "You've got to show who's boss on a daily basis." Do you think it is possible to be an effective police officer without being uncivil? Cite the article and your own observations and experiences in order to respond to this question.

16. How much effort do you think the Philadelphia courts should put into overturning convictions brought about by Blondie and his associates' "bad" arrests?

WRITING ASSIGNMENTS

17. Blondie and his colleagues discuss how they treated people differently, depending upon a number of factors. Write a few paragraphs summarizing how

certain people warranted certain treatment by the police in Kramer's article, and then argue whether or not you think the police's "flexible" behavior standard was positive or negative.

18. At what point, if ever, does the greater good—arresting "bad guys," for instance—outweigh the downside of law enforcement, such as rule-breaking? Be sure to cite the essay and your own experiences in order to illustrate your responses.

19. At what point, if ever, do people deserve incivility? Write a well-developed paragraph or essay in which you explain how some people deserve the same or less civil treatment than others. Be sure to specify your criteria for deserving civility, and cite Kramer's essay for support.

VOCABULARY DEVELOPMENT

20. Kramer describes unpleasant, even violent, aspects of life in his essay. Choose ten words that you think best communicate the tone of Kramer's essay, and explain what about these words you find particularly powerful.

GROUP ACTIVITIES

21. Watch any of the "real life" television shows that focus on police officers and the people they arrest. Based on these shows, how do law enforcement officials treat their charges? As a group, see which of Kramer's points about law enforcement are true. Present your findings to the class in an open forum session.

22. Make a list of characteristics that you think the ideal police officer has, ranking them according to which qualities are most important. Why did you make the choices you made? Discuss your results with other groups in an effort reach a class-wide consensus.

How Five Thrive by Striving to Serve

These savvy owners have beaten the odds—as you can too—by giving their customers outstanding care

John Manners and Suzanne Opton

Citing small business owners whose businesses are rapidly expanding and whose customers are wholly satisfied, John Manners and Suzanne Opton write about how taking simple steps to please their customers has resulted in huge successes. Manners and Opton focus on aspects of business that, according to one small business owner, "are no real secrets" to their success, just common courtesy and basic responsibility. Published originally in 1994, this essay first appeared in *Money Guide.*

Pre-reading Questions

Freewrite for five to ten minutes in response to the following questions:
What stores or businesses do you frequent? What makes you return to these places? What businesses, if any, have you stopped patronizing? Why?

Vocabulary Preview

Vocabulary Words:
- paraphernalia
- meticulous
- expertise
- niche
- refinements

- apparatus
- amphibious
- fledgling
- leery
- intricate

- exposure
- commission
- franchise
- testimonials

As always, look up the words above and, as you read, write a few sentences explaining which ones you find most or least persuasive in the article.

1   All of them looked like long shots in the beginning—prime candidates to join the 52% of small businesses that fail in their first four years. Pat Whitaker, recently divorced, was setting up her own interior design firm partly so she could adjust her hours to accommodate her two children's schedules. Jim Horowitz was taking over a small rural airport where business was so slow that 12 previous operators had bailed out in 15 years. Bill Parker was trying to establish a bicycle repair business with little equipment, no shop and practically no cash. Claudia Post was launching a same-day courier service in a city that already had seven of them. And Sean Nguyen, a Vietnamese refugee with limited English and little formal education, was starting a business testing high-tech printed circuit boards and assembling computer paraphernalia in his basement.

2   Yet each of these unlikely prospects has succeeded—some spectacularly—by offering customers superior service. Whether meeting impossible deadlines, doing meticulous work or just keeping in close touch with clients, they've all delivered a level of care and attention that wasn't available elsewhere. "There are no real secrets," says Whitaker. "It's the stuff everybody tells you about—calling customers back, going out of your way to

make sure they're satisfied, helping them to save money. People talk about these things, but not many do them consistently. We did." And so too, in various ways, did the other four owners profiled in the following pages. That's what they have in common—along with the satisfied customers whose repeat business helps to keep them growing.

DESIGNING WOMAN

3 Don't call Pat Whitaker an interior decorator. True, she named her St. Louis firm Interior Space Inc., and decorating is often associated with women. But Whitaker's field—the design of massive corporate offices—is not heavily populated with businesses run by women. In fact, the word decorating doesn't even appear in her company's brochures. Instead, ISI calls itself "an architectural firm specializing in the planning and design of the corporate work environment." And indeed, laying out 300,000 square feet of office space is a long way from picking curtains and wallpaper—about as far as ISI's $2.6 million 1992 revenues are from those of the typical decorating firm.

4 Whitaker, 48, set up her own business in 1977—she now employs 50 people—after working a year for a department store's interior design department. As a divorced mother of a four- and a nine-year-old, she wanted more flexible hours and the opportunity to set her own direction. Shunning work in private homes, she spent two years remodeling medical offices. But her business really took off when she was hired in 1979 to do a 200,000-square-foot office building. "I saw pretty quickly that there was a lot more money in larger jobs," she says, "but I knew they weren't going to come to me. So I decided to go to them." She joined the trade association for corporate facilities managers and got to know the people in St. Louis responsible for remodeling large workplaces. "Big companies have design work going on all the time," she says. "If they know us, then when a project comes up, they tell us."

5 In 1981, Whitaker connected with executives at Southwestern Bell as the company prepared for its independence from soon-to-be-broken-up AT&T. Over the next seven years, the burgeoning Baby Bell handed her 251 projects at various buildings—a level of repeat business that doesn't come just from habit. Whitaker's firm delivers. "We try to provide truly outstanding service," she says. "We want to make the facilities manager who hired us look good." For example, ISI's lighting design for Union Electric saved the utility $75,000 on fixtures. Advice to Missouri Blue Cross/Blue Shield kept the insurer from remodeling a building it would soon outgrow, and another timely nudge saved the company $300,000 by getting a furniture order in ahead of a price increase.

6 Giving customers such superior service takes imagination and expertise, and to provide that, Whitaker recruits top people and keeps them happy. "Paying good salaries is essential, of course," she says, "but recognition is important too. When one of our projects gets written up in the paper, we make sure the people quoted are really the people in charge of the project, not just me." In addition, ISI provides health and dental insurance, a 401(k) savings plan and—in deference to Whitaker's own experience—part-time work schedules for parents.

7 Lately, ISI has begun branching out. The firm is designing the restaurant, bar, luxury boxes, offices and locker rooms for the 664,000-square-foot Kiel Center arena that will open in St. Louis late next year. The job didn't come through ISI's usual channels, though. The client was a local nonprofit group, Civic Progress. Says Whitaker candidly: "One of the main reasons we got the contract is that we're a woman-owned business. Now that's an angle we haven't really exploited. We'll have to work on it."

A SMOOTH TAKEOFF

8   When Jim Horowitz took over the Oxford County Regional Airport in rural Maine 4 1/2 years ago, he knew it would be tough getting the operation off the ground. The county-owned airport—which included a refueling station, a repair shop and an on-again, off-again flight school—had seen 11 new operators since its first one in 1974. None had made enough money to stick around for very long. But Horowitz, 42, who had worked at marinas much of his life and had managed a small Arizona resort, had recently learned to fly, and he wanted to give it a try. "The salvage value of the plane, tools and parts I bought along with the airport lease would have equaled the $27,000 I paid," he explains. "Besides, small airports are often run by guys who have built on their skills as pilots or mechanics, not as businessmen. I didn't have their skills, but I did know how to run a business."

9   One of his first acts as owner of the company, which he renamed Oxford Aviation, was to telephone the owner of a plane that had been sitting in the hangar for a year waiting for repairs and repainting. Horowitz asked for two more months to finish the job. He then boned up on aircraft refinishing and hired an experienced painter. Before the first job was completed, another order came in, and then two more. Horowitz saw a niche. He knew that boat owners would often pay a premium for top-quality work. He figured the same would be true of plane owners looking for an alternative to barnyard paint shops competing solely on price. "I decided we were going to paint planes better than anyone else," he says. "Superior service, not low cost, would be our selling point." He instituted a painstaking 18-step refinishing process that included stripping off old paint with chemical solvents rather than taking the common shortcut of using abrasives. "Grit blasting can damage a plane's metal skin," Horowitz explains. With these refinements, Oxford was able to charge as much as $8,000 to repaint a single-engine plane—10% to 20% more than competitors. But its work was so good that by 1991, when the company got a favorable write-up in the magazine Light Plane Maintenance, Oxford was already working through a backlog of jobs obtained by word of mouth.

10   Today, revenues have grown to $900,000, and Oxford's staff numbers 30 in a custom-designed 16,000-square-foot hangar that conforms to the most stringent environmental and health regulations. Supplied-air respirators draw in clean outside air for workers' breathing apparatus. Wall sockets are protected against sparking—at a cost of $600 apiece. And a $10,000 drain funnels used stripper into huge vats for reuse. Customers are impressed: "Their facility is probably one of the best in the world, if not the best," says Gordon Collins, president of Aerofab Inc., the maker of Lake amphibious planes. The Sanford Maine manufacturer sends all its aircraft to Oxford for painting because, says Collins, "the company delivers superb quality while being very reliable at staying on schedule." Says Horowitz, who's now planning an addition that will cover 20,000 square feet: "We can't afford not to do a first-class job. Word travels fast. It would take only a few bad jobs to ruin our reputation. We'll work overtime to stay on schedule. We'll sacrifice profit now and then, but we'll never sacrifice service."

THE LONE REPAIRMAN

11   Bill Parker has found a niche. His bicycle repair service is the only one of its kind in fitness-mad Portland, Ore.: It caters principally to owners of elite $1,500-plus racing machines and offers free pickup and delivery, 24-hour turnaround and service at your home

or office. Trouble is, Parker's niche is so secure it has him in a bind. His two-year-old Mobile Bicycle Services already attracts more business than he can handle alone, yet he's not ready to expand. His initial capital spending ($5,000 for custom tools) is behind him. And with $10,000 in revenue in the first half of 1993, MBS is solidly in the black. But like many fledgling sole proprietors, Parker, a soon-to-be-divorced 44-year-old, feels his business income isn't steady enough for him to give up his day job—or rather, his night job: driving 18-wheelers for Safeway from 4 p.m. to midnight for $36,000 a year. Besides, he needs to work only eight more years to earn an $1,800-a-month pension.

12   One solution would be to hire some help, but Parker is leery. "I had an assistant come in several hours a week last summer, but he had developed bad habits from working in bike shops," says Parker. "I had to have him redo a couple of jobs because he didn't take care of little things like greasing the nuts and bolts and stretching the cables—stuff you've got to do in custom bike work." Those little things are Parker's stock in trade. They're why people who care about their bikes keep coming back. "A bike shop can do most of the jobs Bill does," says Art Peterson, a steady customer and a former racer, "and they'll charge about the same price [for example, $105 for a complete annual overhaul]. But their standards aren't as high as Bill's." Parker himself, as a customer, had similar gripes with bike shops, and that's what got him working on bikes in the first place. He began taking in friends' bikes—"entry-level stuff, old-style 10-speeds"—then gradually moved on to more intricate projects. From the start, he worked out of his van, driving it to local bike races where he did on-the-spot repairs for competitors. That exposure helped generate a steady flow of work that turned into a torrent last spring and summer.

13   "Between Safeway and the business, I was working 18 hours a day, he says. "If I could do bikes full time, it wouldn't be a problem, but I don't want to walk away from all my employee benefits." Still, he's drawn to the idea of giving the bike business a real try. "I think about it all the time," he confesses. "There was so much work last summer, it made me wonder if maybe I shouldn't just go for it."

STREET SMART

14   Claudia Post's decision to start a same-day courier service in Philadelphia three years ago was a matter of expediency. She'd just been fired. And after six years at other courier outfits, the divorced mother of two boys, 10 and 15, felt ready to go out on her own. She credits her last boss with the inspiration. "When he fired me," she says, "I thought, 'If he can run a company like this, I know I can do it.'" And do it better. "I wanted to build the Ben & Jerry's of courier services," she says, "to be socially conscious and good to employees." Post, 46, believes achieving that goal has a lot to do with the success of Diamond Courier Service, which employs about 130 mostly part-time people and will gross about $3 million this year. "Claudia and all of us on her staff treat our couriers with respect," explains sales director Tony Briscella, "so the couriers are motivated to give better service." Diamond's 50 bike and foot messengers, for example, not only get the standard commission of 50% of each job's fee, but unlike most couriers, they're also guaranteed the federal minimum wage of $4.25 an hour when work is slow.

15   There are other perks too. "They take care of us," says biker Felix Alvarado, citing cases of Gatorade laid out in hot weather and bonus pay—an extra 10% of the fee— couriers get when it rains. "Bikers can make about the same money elsewhere," says operations manager Bill Trimbur, "but here they're treated better." Customers feel

coddled, too. "Diamond always calls to tell you where things stand," says Sally Hobin, facilities manager of the law firm Cohen Shapiro. "If couriers get held up in traffic, they let the attorneys know—even after hours. That's very important." Adds Neil Weiner, vice president for the printer National Compugraphics: "Diamond's couriers get here fastest, and they deliver 95% on time. They're just more responsive than anybody else."

16   Testimonials like these, passed via Philadelphia's business grapevine, have kept Diamond's phones busy with as many as 700 calls in a day, ordering jobs that average nearly $20 each. And Post has already begun expanding: In 1992 she established Diamond Legal (revenues: $160,000 annually), which handles court filings, document searches and the like for the Philadelphia lawyers her couriers already serve. This year, she bought the local franchise of the national airfreight company Adcom Express. "This is an incredible life," she says. "I'm excited every day. I tell my sons, 'I wish that in whatever you wind up doing, you're as happy as I am.'"

RAGS TO RICHES

17   Horatio Alger himself might have called Sean Nguyen's story farfetched: Five years after arriving in Minneapolis a penniless, 17-year-old refugee, Sean sets up a company in his rented home's basement to help his father and brother earn money. Seven years later, in 1993, the firm and two spin-offs employ 175 people and generate $14 million in annual sales. Yet unlike Alger's fables, Sean's success story is true. It began in 1980, when he and his father and brother helped fellow refugees build a crude sailboat in the Vietnamese jungle and launch it toward Thailand. The Nguyens left behind Sean's mother, a younger brother and two sisters, fearing what might happen to them en route. Sure enough, pirates raided the boat seven times on its four-day voyage. All women among the 39 people aboard were raped, and everything of value was stolen, including the motor. Fortunately, winds blew the boat toward Thailand, but then came eight months in squalid refugee camps before the three could immigrate to Minneapolis, where a cousin who had escaped earlier arranged passage through a church organization.

18   Living with 12 other refugees in a two-room apartment, Sean felt fortunate to land a minimum-wage job assembling printed circuit boards at a company called Multi-Tech Systems. An adept worker, he soon began taking boards home for his father, brother and friends to inspect and test overnight. "No matter how much we gave him," says Del Palacheck, Multi-Tech's production manager, "he brought it back in the morning complete." In 1986, Sean gave his enterprise a name—Nguyen Electronics Inc. Revenues that year were $50,000. They quadrupled the next year, then doubled and nearly doubled again to $700,000 in 1989. NEI had by then moved to bigger quarters, and Sean's landlord—Bob LaRoque, a Sisseton Whapton Sioux Indian—offered him some advice: Quit your job at Multi-Tech and devote all your time to NEI. Sean not only took the advice but hired LaRoque to handle sales.

19   In the fast-moving electronics business, service means speed. And Sean credits his workers, 90% of them Asian immigrants, for NEI's ability to turn work around quickly. "They want to work to send money back home," he says. "We pay steady wages [starting at $5.50 an hour, about average for board assembly work], with lots of overtime and full family health coverage. They are comfortable here." And perhaps for that rea-

20
son, they work fast. "If our competitors need two weeks for a job," he says, "we can maybe do it in one—sometimes even 24 hours."

Customers' testimonials bear him out: "We need to turn on a dime in this business," says Bill Foster, vice president of operations at the computer maker Tricord Systems, "and NEI's ability to jump through hoops for us is unparalleled." Last year, with sales topping $4 million, NEI spawned a subsidiary, VidTech Microsystems, which makes graphic accelerator boards—devices that speed up a computer's visual display. About 6,000 have been shipped to date, and VidTech is expected to contribute half its parent's gross receipts this year.

21
A second subsidiary, Tertronics, named for its president, Sean's wife Terri, has begun programming memory chips and floppy disks. Terri emigrated from Vietnam too, fleeing by boat with her family and arriving in Minneapolis in 1980 when she was 15. Now she and Sean are trying to get used to a more comfortable life. They've recently moved with their two young children into a new six-bedroom house overlooking a golf course. Sean has taken up the game for relaxation, but his approach is what you might expect. "He tries hard," says Terri. "When he has free time for an hour, he practices." And the results? He's already shooting in the low 90s.

POST-READING QUESTIONS

CONTENT

1. What do Manners and Opton claim the five businesses have in common? To what do the writers attribute the success of each company?

2. In a sentence or two, describe each business owner. What do these people have in common?

3. In what ways does designer Pat Whitaker try to beat the competition? To what extent is she successful?

4. What about Jim Horowitz's business made him successful? Bill Parker?

5. What did Claudia Post say she wanted to emphasize in her courier business? Did her emphasis prove to be a good idea? Explain.

6. How is Sean Nguyen's success story different from the others featured in this article? How is it similar?

STYLE AND STRUCTURE

7. Does this essay have an argument? What is it? Rewrite Manners' and Opton's main point in your own words.

8. How do the examples that Manners and Opton include support their main idea?

9. What can you tell about the original audience for this magazine? Cite passages that you think best reveal the writers' intended audience.

10. How helpful do you think Manners' and Opton's sub-headings are in making their article easy to read? Why?

11. Are the writers persuasive? Why or why not?

CRITICAL THINKING AND ANALYSIS

DISCUSSION QUESTIONS

12. Of the five business owners spotlighted in the article, which one has the plan that you think would be easiest to implement? Most difficult? Why?

13. What do you think the success of the five companies described in the article says about Americans? What, if anything, do people value? Be sure to use examples from the text as well as from your own life in order to support your claims.

WRITING ASSIGNMENTS

14. How important is customer service today? Write a few well-developed paragraphs explaining how important customer service is in various aspects of society. Cite the article and your own experiences and observations in order to illustrate your ideas.

15. Manners and Opton write that all five business owners "looked like long shots in the beginning," yet they succeeded tremendously. Write a paragraph or short essay in which you describe a situation where your success was a "long shot" and explain what you did to become successful.

16. Manners and Opton quote business owners and customers who explain what is important to them: timeliness, value for money, courtesy, among other attributes. What do you think is most vital for success at work. Write a few paragraphs in which you argue that one characteristic is most important for success in the workplace. Be sure to cite the article and your own experiences and observations in order to illustrate your ideas.

VOCABULARY DEVELOPMENT

17. Choose one paragraph of Manners' and Opton's essay to rewrite for a different, non-business-oriented audience. What types of terms do you need to change? Discuss the changes you make, and read your results to other classmates, asking them to guess your intended audience.

GROUP ACTIVITIES

18. Choose a business, and as a group, write a customer service policy for that business. (Your company may real or fictitious.) What guidelines are most important to you? Share your policy with other groups and revise yours according to what you learn from others.

19. Divide your group into two factions: employees and customers. Then, using the customer service policy you designed above, have one member of the "customers" complain to one of the "employees." Make sure the "employee" follows the customer service guidelines in addressing the concerns of the "customer," and then discuss how difficult following such guidelines is. Share your results with the class.

Argument Pair: Are the Benefits of Affirmative Action Worth Its Drawbacks?

Reverse Racism, or How the Pot Got to Call the Kettle Black, Stanley Fish

With Liberty and Justice for All, Ward Connerly

In an effort to correct past wrongs, affirmative action—programs by which traditionally underrepresented populations are given preference—was enacted with the goal of creating racial parity. While writer Stanley Fish, among others, argues that even now the playing field is not level and, thus, we should continue to offer Affirmative Action, Ward Connerly counters that receiving preference for any reason is outdated and unfair. How equally represented different racial groups are in academic institutions and in the workplace, as well as whether or not "equal" representation equates with "fair" representation are among the questions this issue raises.

Writing Assignments Based on *Reverse Racism, or How the Pot Got to Call the Kettle Black* and *With Liberty and Justice for All:*

1. The Golden Rule states that people should "Do unto others as you would have them do unto you," but Stanley Fish argues that we should do more for some people through Affirmative Action. How much good would following the Golden Rule do? Write a few paragraphs in which you explore the idea that the law—in this case Affirmative Action policies—would be unnecessary if people simply followed the Golden Rule. Be sure to cite both essays and your own experience in order to illustrate your ideas.

2. Stanley Fish writes about an African American man who claims that "You walk down the street with a suit and tie and it doesn't matter. Someone will make determinations about you, determinations that affect the quality of your life," implying that race can harm him, but Ward Connerly claims that Affirmative Action cannot correct the past wrongs of this country. How effective do you think Affirmative Action programs are? Write a few well-developed paragraphs in which you argue that Affirmative Action does or does not help people. Be sure to cite both Fish and Connerly, and draw from your own experiences as well.

Reverse Racism, or How the Pot Got to Call the Kettle Black

Stanley Fish

Stanley Fish earned degrees from the University of Pennsylvania and Yale University, and he has been professor of English at the University of California at Berkeley and the Johns Hopkins University. He also served as English Department Chair at Duke University, as well as teaching law courses there. Identifying himself as a white male, Stanley Fish differentiates between racial inequity designed to persecute people and racial inequity designed to level the playing field between the races, and he argues that while some progress has been made from the days of racial segregation, more steps must be taken if parity among the races is to be achieved.

Pre-reading Questions

Freewrite for five to ten minutes in response to the following questions:
What does the term "reverse racism" call to mind for you? Why? What has your experience been with Affirmative Action or other equal opportunity programs? To what extent does this experience support the idea that "reverse racism" exists?

Vocabulary Preview

Vocabulary Words:
- stigmatized
- plight
- redress
- travesty
- cogent

- criteria
- correlation
- admixture
- taint
- socioeconomic

- miniscule
- disenfranchise
- entitlements
- inequities

Look up the words above and, after you've finished reading the essay, write a brief paragraph explaining how at least five of the words contribute to the tone of the article.

1   I take my text from George Bush, who, in an address to the United Nations on September 23, 1991, said this of the UN resolution equating Zionism with racism: "Zionism . . . is the idea that led to the creation of a home for the Jewish people. . . . And to equate Zionism with the intolerable sin of racism is to twist history and forget the terrible plight of Jews in World War II and indeed throughout history." What happened in the Second World War was that 6 million Jews were exterminated by people who regarded them as racially inferior and a danger to Aryan purity. What happened after the Second World War was that the survivors of that Holocaust established a Jewish state—that is, a state centered on Jewish history, Jewish values, and Jewish traditions: in short, a Jewocentric state. What President Bush objected to was the logical sleight of hand by which these two actions were declared equivalent because they were both expressions of racial exclusiveness. Ignored, as Bush said, was the *historical* difference between them—the difference between a program of genocide and the determination of those who escaped it to establish a community in which they would be the makers, not the victims, of the laws.

2   Only if racism is thought of as something that occurs principally in the mind, a falling-away from proper notions of universal equality, can the desire of a victimized and terrorized people to band together be declared morally identical to the actions of their would-be executioners. Only when the actions of the two groups are detached from the historical conditions of their emergence and given a purely abstract description can they be made interchangeable. Bush was saying to the United Nations, "Look,

the Nazis' conviction of racial superiority generated a policy of systematic genocide; the Jews' experience of centuries of persecution in almost every country on earth generated a desire for a homeland of their own. If you manage somehow to convince yourself that these are the same, it is you, not the Zionists, who are morally confused, and the reason you are morally confused is that you have forgotten history."

A KEY DISTINCTION

3   What I want to say, following Bush's reasoning, is that a similar forgetting of history has in recent years allowed some people to argue, and argue persuasively, that affirmative action is reverse racism. The very phrase "reverse racism" contains the argument in exactly the form to which Bush objected: In this country whites once set themselves apart from blacks and claimed privileges for themselves while denying them to others. Now, on the basis of race, blacks are claiming special status and reserving for themselves privileges they deny to others. Isn't one as bad as the other? The answer is no. One can see why by imagining that it is not 1993 but 1955, and that we are in a town in the South with two more or less distinct communities, one white and one black. No doubt each community would have a ready store of dismissive epithets, ridiculing stories, self-serving folk myths, and expressions of plain hatred, all directed at the other community, and all based in racial hostility. Yet to regard their respective racisms—if that is the word—as equivalent would be bizarre, for the hostility of one group stems not from any wrong done to it but from its wish to protect its ability to deprive citizens of their voting rights, to limit access to educational institutions, to prevent entry into the economy except at the lowest and most menial levels, and to force members of the stigmatized group to ride in the back of the bus. The hostility of the other group is the result of these actions, and whereas hostility and racial anger are unhappy facts wherever they are found, a distinction must surely be made between the ideological hostility of the oppressors and the experience-based hostility of those who have been oppressed.

4   Not to make that distinction is, adapting George Bush's words, to twist history and forget the terrible plight of African Americans in the more than two hundred years of this country's existence. Moreover, to equate the efforts to remedy that plight with the actions that produced it is to twist history even further. Those efforts, designed to redress the imbalances caused by long-standing discrimination, are called affirmative action; to argue that affirmative action, which gives preferential treatment to disadvantaged minorities as part of a plan to achieve social equality, is no different from the policies that created the disadvantages in the first place is a travesty of reasoning. "Reverse racism" is a cogent description of affirmative action only if one considers the cancer of racism to be morally and medically indistinguishable from the therapy we apply to it. A cancer is an invasion of the body's equilibrium, and so is chemotherapy; but we do not decline to fight the disease because the medicine we employ is also disruptive of nominal functioning. Strong illness, strong remedy: The formula is as appropriate to the health of the body politic as it is to that of the body proper.

5   At this point someone will always say, "But two wrongs don't make a right; if it was wrong to treat blacks unfairly, it is wrong to give blacks preference and thereby treat whites unfairly." This objection is just another version of the forgetting and

rewriting of history. The work is done by the adverb "unfairly," which suggests two more or less equal parties, one of whom has been unjustly penalized by an incompetent umpire. But blacks have not simply been treated unfairly; they have been subjected first to decades of slavery, and then to decades of second-class citizenship, widespread legalized discrimination, economic persecution, educational deprivation, and cultural stigmatization. They have been bought, sold, killed, beaten, raped, excluded, exploited, shamed, and scorned for a very long time. The word "unfair" is hardly an adequate description of their experience, and the belated gift of "fairness" in the form of a resolution no longer to discriminate against them legally is hardly an adequate remedy for the deep disadvantages that the prior discrimination has produced. When the deck is stacked against you in more ways than you can even count, it is small consolation to hear that you are now free to enter the game and take your chances.

A TILTED FIELD

6   The same insincerity and hollowness of promise infect another formula that is popular with the anti-affirmative-action crowd: the formula of the level playing field. Here the argument usually takes the form of saying "It is undemocratic to give one class of citizens advantages at the expense of other citizens; the truly democratic way is to have a level playing field to which everyone has access and where everyone has a fair and equal chance to succeed on the basis of his or her merit." Fine words—but they conceal the facts of the situation as it has been given to us by history: The playing field is already tilted in favor of those by whom and for whom it was constructed in the first place. If mastery of the requirements for entry depends upon immersion in the cultural experiences of the mainstream majority, if the skills that make for success are nurtured by institutions and cultural practices from which the disadvantaged minority has been systematically excluded, if the language and the ways of comporting oneself that identify a player as "one of us" are alien to the lives minorities are forced to live, then words like "fair" and "equal" are cruel jokes, for what they promote and celebrate is an institutionalized unfairness and a perpetuated inequality. The playing field is already tilted, and the resistance to altering it by the mechanisms of affirmative action is in fact a determination to make sure that the present imbalances persist as long as possible.

7   One way of tilting the field is the Scholastic Aptitude Test. This test figures prominently in Dinesh D'Souza's book *Illiberal Education* (1991), in which one finds many examples of white or Asian students denied admission to colleges and universities even though their SAT scores were higher than the scores of others—often African Americans—who were admitted to the same institution. This, D'Souza says, is evidence that as a result of affirmative-action policies colleges and universities tend "to depreciate the importance of merit criteria in admissions." D'Souza's assumption— and it is one that many would share—is that the test does in fact measure *merit,* with merit understood as a quality objectively determined in the same way that body temperature can be objectively determined.

8   In fact, however, the test is nothing of the kind. Statistical studies have suggested that test scores reflect income and socioeconomic status. It has been demonstrated again and again that scores vary in relation to cultural background; the test's questions assume a certain uniformity in education experience and lifestyle and penalize those who, for whatever reason, have had a different experience and lived different kinds of

lives. In short, what is being measured by the SAT is not absolutes like native ability and merit but accidents like birth, social position, access to libraries, and the opportunity to take vacations or to take SAT prep courses.

9   Furthermore, as David Owen notes in *None of the Above: Behind the Myth of Scholastic Aptitude* (1985), the "correlation between SAT scores and college grades . . . is lower than the correlation between weight and height; in other words you would have a better chance of predicting a person's height by looking at his weight than you would of predicting his freshman grades by looking only at his SAT scores." Everywhere you look in the SAT story, the claims of fairness, objectivity, and neutrality fall away, to be replaced by suspicions of specialized measures and unfair advantages.

10   Against this background a point that in isolation might have a questionable force takes on a special and even explanatory resonance: The principal deviser of the test was an out-and-out racist. In 1923 Carl Campbell Brigham published a book called *A Study of American Intelligence,* in which, as Owen notes, he declared, among other things, that we faced in America "a possibility of racial admixture . . . infinitely worse than that faced by any European country today, for we are incorporating the Negro into our racial stock, while all of Europe is comparatively free of this taint." Brigham had earlier analyzed the Army Mental Tests using classifications drawn from another racist text, Madison Grant's *The Passing of the Great Race,* which divided American society into four distinct racial strains, with Nordic, blue-eyed, blond people at the pinnacle and the American Negro at the bottom. Nevertheless, in 1925 Brigham became a director of testing for the College Board, and developed the SAT. So here is the great SAT test, devised by a racist in order to confirm racist assumptions, measuring not native ability but cultural advantage, an uncertain indicator of performance, an indicator of very little except what money and social privilege can buy. And it is in the name of this mechanism that we are asked to reject affirmative action and reaffirm "the importance of merit criteria in admissions."

THE REALITY OF DISCRIMINATION

11   Nevertheless, there is at least one more card to play against affirmative action, and it is a strong one. Granted that the playing field is not level and that access to it is reserved for an already advantaged elite, the disadvantages suffered by others are less racial—at least in 1993—than socioeconomic. Therefore shouldn't, as D'Souza urges, "universities . . . retain their policies of preferential treatment, but alter their criteria of application from race to socioeconomic disadvantage," and thus avoid the unfairness of current policies that reward middle-class or affluent blacks at the expense of poor whites? One answer to this question is given by D'Souza himself when he acknowledges that the overlap between minority groups and the poor is very large—a point underscored by the former Secretary of Education Lamar Alexander, who said, in response to a question about funds targeted for black students, "Ninety-eight percent of race-specific scholarships do not involve constitutional problems." He meant, I take it, that 98 percent of race-specific scholarships were also scholarships to the economically disadvantaged.

12   Still, the other 2 percent—nonpoor, middle-class, economically favored blacks—are receiving special attention on the basis of disadvantages they do not experience. What about them? The force of the question depends on the assumption that in this day

and age race could not possibly be a serious disadvantage to those who are otherwise well positioned in the society. But the lie was given dramatically to this assumption in a 1991 broadcast of the ABC program "PrimeTime Live." In a stunning fifteen-minute segment reporters and a camera crew followed two young men of equal education, cultural sophistication, level of apparent affluence, and so forth around St. Louis, a city where neither was known. The two differed in only a single respect: one was white, the other black. But that small difference turned out to mean everything. In a series of encounters with shoe salesmen, record-store employees, rental agents, landlords, employment agencies, taxicab drivers, and ordinary citizens, the black member of the pair was either ignored or given a special and suspicious attention. He was asked to pay more for the same goods or come up with a larger down payment for the same car, was turned away as a prospective tenant, was rejected as a prospective taxicab fare, was treated with contempt and irritation by clerks and bureaucrats, and in every way possible was made to feel inferior and unwanted.

13   The inescapable conclusion was that alike though they may have been in almost all respects, one of these young men, because he was black, would lead a significantly lesser life than his white counterpart: He would be housed less well and at greater expense; he would pay more for services and products when and if he was given the opportunity to buy them; he would have difficulty establishing credit; the first emotions he would inspire on the part of many people he met would be distrust and fear; his abilities would be discounted even before he had a chance to display them; and, above all, the treatment he received from minute to minute would chip away at his self-esteem and self-confidence with consequences that most of us could not even imagine. As the young man in question said at the conclusion of the broadcast, "You walk down the street with a suit and tie and it doesn't matter. Someone will make determinations about you, determinations that affect the quality of your life."

14   Of course, the same determinations are being made quite early on by kindergarten teachers, grade school principals, high school guidance counselors, and the like, with results that cut across socioeconomic lines and place young black men and women in the ranks of the disadvantaged no matter what the bank accounts of their parents happen to show. Racism is a cultural fact, and although its effects may to some extent be diminished by socioeconomic variables, those effects will still be sufficiently great to warrant the nation's attention and thus the continuation of affirmative-action policies. This is true even of the field thought to be dominated by blacks and often cited as evidence of the equal opportunities society now affords them. I refer, of course, to professional athletics. But national self-congratulation on this score might pause in the face of a few facts: A minuscule number of African Americans ever receive a paycheck from a professional team. Even though nearly sixteen hundred daily newspapers report on the exploits of black athletes, they employ only seven full-time black sports columnists. Despite repeated pledges and resolutions, major-league teams have managed to put only a handful of blacks and Hispanics in executive positions.

WHY ME?

15   When all is said and done, however, one objection to affirmative action is unanswerable on its own terms, and that is the objection of the individual who says, "Why me?

Sure discrimination has persisted for many years, and I acknowledge that the damage done has not been removed by changes in the law. But why me? I didn't own slaves; I didn't vote to keep people on the back of the bus; I didn't turn water hoses on civil-rights marchers. Why, then, should I be the one who doesn't get the job or who doesn't get the scholarship or who gets bumped back to the waiting list?"

16   I sympathize with this feeling, if only because in a small way I have had the experience that produces it. I was recently nominated for an administrative post at a large university. Early signs were encouraging, but after an interval I received official notice that I would not be included at the next level of consideration, and subsequently I was told unofficially that at some point a decision had been made to look only in the direction of women and minorities. Although I was disappointed, I did not conclude that the situation was "unfair," because the policy was obviously not directed at me—at no point in the proceedings did someone say, "Let's find a way to rule out Stanley Fish." Nor was it directed even at persons of my race and sex—the policy was not intended to disenfranchise white males. Rather, the policy was driven by other considerations, and it was only as a by-product of those considerations—not as the main goal—that white males like me were rejected. Given that the institution in question has a high percentage of minority students, a very low percentage of minority faculty, and an even lower percentage of minority administrators, it made perfect sense to focus on women and minority candidates, and within that sense, not as the result of prejudice, my whiteness and maleness became disqualifications.

17   I can hear the objection in advance: "What's the difference? Unfair is unfair: you didn't get the job; you didn't even get on the short list." The difference is not in the outcome but in the ways of thinking that led up to the outcome. It is the difference between an unfairness that befalls one as the unintended effect of a policy rationally conceived and an unfairness that is pursued as an end in itself. It is the difference between the awful unfairness of Nazi extermination camps and the unfairness to Palestinian Arabs that arose from, but was not the chief purpose of, the founding of a Jewish state.

THE NEW BIGOTRY

18   The point is not a difficult one, but it is difficult to see when the unfairness scenarios are presented as simple contrasts between two decontextualized persons who emerge from nowhere to contend for a job or a place in a freshman class. Here is student A; he has a board score of 1,300. And here is student B; her board score is only 1,200, yet she is admitted and A is rejected. Is that fair? Given the minimal information provided, the answer is of course no. But if we expand our horizons and consider fairness in relation to the cultural and institutional histories that have brought the two students to this point, histories that weigh on them even if they are not the histories' authors, then both the question and the answer suddenly grow more complicated.

19   The sleight-of-hand logic that first abstracts events from history and then assesses them from behind a veil of willed ignorance gains some of its plausibility from another key word in the anti-affirmative-action lexicon. That word is "individual," as in "The American way is to focus on the rights of individuals rather than groups." Now, "individual" and "individualism" have been honorable words in the American political

vocabulary, and they have often been well employed in the fight against various tyrannies. But like any other word or concept, individualism can be perverted to serve ends the opposite of those it originally served, and this is what has happened when in the name of individual rights, millions of individuals are enjoined from redressing historically documented wrongs. How is this managed? Largely in the same way that the invocation of fairness is used to legitimize an institutionalized inequality. First one says, in the most solemn of tones, that the protection of individual rights is the chief obligation of society. Then one defines individuals as souls sent into the world with equal entitlements as guaranteed either by their Creator or by the Constitution. Then one pretends that nothing has happened to them since they stepped onto the world's stage. And then one says of these carefully denatured souls that they will all be treated in the same way, irrespective of any of the differences that history has produced. Bizarre as it may seem, individualism in this argument turns out to mean that everyone is or should be the same. This dismissal of individual difference in the name of the individual would be funny were its consequences not so serious: It is the mechanism by which imbalances and inequities suffered by millions of people through no fault of their own can be sanitized and even celebrated as the natural workings of unfettered democracy.

20   "Individualism," "fairness," "merit"—these three words are continually misappropriated by bigots who have learned that they need not put on a white hood or bar access to the ballot box in order to secure their ends. Rather, they need only clothe themselves in a vocabulary plucked from its historical context and made into the justification for attitudes and policies they would not acknowledge if frankly named.

POST-READING QUESTIONS

CONTENT

1. How does Fish differentiate between Zionism and racism? Why does he claim that these terms get confused?

2. What role does Fish say history plays in determining whether or not Affirmative Action is a form of racism? What do you think?

3. How does Fish differentiate between the "hostility of the oppressors" and the "hostility of those who have been oppressed"? What examples does he give?

4. How does Fish define Affirmative Action?

5. Why does Fish say the word "unfair" is inadequate to describe the way African-Americans have been treated at the hands of white Americans?

6. Why does Fish say that the idea of a level playing field is inappropriate when talking about Affirmative Action? Do you agree? Explain.

7. What reasons does Fish give in support of the idea that the Scholastic Aptitude Test (SAT) is an inaccurate way to measure merit?

8. How does Fish counter the argument that some beneficiaries of preferential treatment do not need it as much as some people that Affirmative Action excludes? What do you think of this argument?

9. How does Fish counter the argument that Affirmative Action is "unfair" to those, like Fish himself, who are qualified for positions but do not get them due to preferential policies? What do you think?

10. In what way does Fish say the idea of "individualism" has been distorted by opponents of Affirmative Action?

STYLE AND STRUCTURE

11. What is Fish's main argument? What sub-arguments does he make in order to support his main idea?

12. How is Fish's title significant? What does it imply?

13. What examples do you find most effective/ineffective in helping Fish illustrate his ideas? Why?

14. How effective is the metaphor of using chemotherapy to fight cancer?

15. How does Fish establish credibility with his audience? Should he do more? Explain.

CRITICAL THINKING

DISCUSSION QUESTIONS

16. How often, if ever, do you think Affirmative Action is warranted? Use your own experiences in order to illustrate your ideas.

17. Fish writes that he accepted his failure to be hired for a job because he did not take the hiring committee's decision personally. How many people do you think react like Fish? How many people do take such an experience personally? What causes some people to react one way and others not to react that way? Explain and give examples.

18. What relationship do fairness and civility have? Can you practice one without the other? Explain.

WRITING ASSIGNMENTS

19. How fair is Affirmative Action? Citing Fish's essay and your own experiences, write a few paragraphs explaining how preferential treatment of certain groups either is or is not fair.

20. Write a well-developed paragraph or an essay in which you define the terms "racism" and "reverse racism." Be sure to cite examples from your own experiences and observations, as well as from Fish's essay, in order to clarify your definition.

21. Fish claims that people against Affirmative Action and other similar policies "clothe themselves in a vocabulary plucked from its historical context and made into the justification for attitudes and policies they would not acknowledge if frankly named." Is he right? Write a few paragraphs explaining how people do or do not disguise their motives using misleading language.

VOCABULARY DEVELOPMENT

22. Choose at least three words from Fish's essay, either from the Vocabulary Preview or from the rest of the essay—and define each word as many times as you can, changing the context of the word in order to match the definition. For instance, define the word "fairness" according to how an advocate of Affirmative Action would define it, and then give the word meaning according to how an opponent of Affirmative Action would.

GROUP ACTIVITIES

23. Write a letter to a job applicant who has just missed being hired due to Affirmative Action policies. Assume that the person you write to is in favor of Affirmative Action. Share your letter with other groups in order to test your skills of audience awareness.

24. Follow the instructions for the exercise above, but this time assume the applicant is against Affirmative Action. How does your letter change? In which letter are you more honest? Discuss your paragraph with the class in an open forum setting.

With Liberty and Justice for All

Ward Connerly

A Regent of the University of California and Director of the American Civil Rights Institute, Connerly has long opposed Affirmative Action which, he claims, was "meant to be temporary." In "With Liberty and Justice for All," he argues for a "colorless" society through the abolition of preferential hiring and admission policies fostered by Affirmative Action.

Pre-reading Questions

Freewrite for five to ten minutes in response to the following questions:
What is your understanding of the purpose of Affirmative Action? Who that you have seen has benefited from Affirmative Action? Who, if anyone, has been harmed? What do you think determines whether or not Affirmative Action assists people or hurts them? Explain.

Vocabulary Preview

Vocabulary Words:
- perfunctory
- warranty
- relegated
- protrusion
- entrenched
- immunity
- rationale
- constituency
- matrix
- corrosive
- egalitarian
- divisive
- enclaves

Look up the words above and, as you read, write a few sentences explaining why at least five of the words are particularly powerful within the context of Connerly's essay.

1   I pledge allegiance to the flag of the United States of America, and to the republic for which it stands, one nation, under God indivisible, with liberty and justice for all.

2   Thirty-one words tightly compressed into one sentence, a sentence that is more universally known and more often repeated in America than any other.

3   There is hardly a day that passes that I do not cite that pledge—in public or in private—at least half a dozen times. How many hundreds of times has each of us cited those words? Do we reflect on the meaning of the words embodied in that sentence, or is it like so many other things we say during the course of our days, giving little thought or commitment to what is meant? "Have a nice day!" "Good to see you again!" Perfunctory words of life.

4   But, this pledge is no ordinary sentence. It is a definition of American democracy, and a constant reaffirmation of our dedication to the fundamental principles of that democracy.

5   You flatter and honor me today by this opportunity to share what I believe is the significance of that pledge, to discuss the meaning of American citizenship, America's passion for fairness, matters relating to that delicate subject of race, and why I believe

the time is at hand for us to pursue a new course with regard to what we call "Affirmative Action."

6   When we become citizens of this nation, at birth or otherwise, we get a warranty. That warranty is supposed to be honored by every government franchise in every village and hamlet of this nation. It is not transferable, and it is good for the life of the vehicle.

7   We are guaranteed the right to vote, the right to due process, the right to be free, not to be enslaved, as long as we conduct ourselves in accordance with the laws of our nation, and the right to equal treatment under the law, regardless of our race, color, sex, religion, or national origin. These are rights which attach to us as individuals, not as members of a group.

8   This warranty has not always been honored for some of us. Because of the color of our skin or the place from whence we came, some of us were denied the right to vote, we were enslaved, we were denied due process, and the equal treatment granted to others was not ours to enjoy.

9   In my lifetime, I can give testimony to America's meaner instincts and their consequences upon my life. To reflect upon this nation's past, with my racial background, it is oh so tempting to mock that pledge to devalue the warranty and to be embittered by those who would urge me to forget the past. One need only invoke a few memories to become enraged and to feel entitled to all of the preferences that can be presented:

- Rosa Parks relegated to the back of the bus

- Drinking fountains for "whites only"

- Restrooms for "men," "women," "colored"

- George Wallace standing in the schoolhouse door saying "segregation now, segregation forever"

- Images of black people being hosed in the streets simply because they demanded that the warranty be honored

- And my thirty-year-old uncle being called "boy" by a ten-year-old white kid.

10   Because we were treated like animals, there are some who say "America owes us."

11   But, the past is a ghost that can destroy our future. It is dangerous to dwell upon it. To focus on America's mistakes is to disregard its virtues.

12   This nation has a passion for fairness. That passion is evidence in our constitution, in the bill of rights, in executive orders, in court decisions but, most of all, it courses through the arteries of our culture.

13   "Do unto others as you would have them do unto you" is centerpiece of virtually all of our religious faiths.

14   That great American pastime—baseball—is a reminder of the intensity of our passion for fairness as we exhort the crowd "to kill the umpire" if he makes what we consider an unfair call.

15   As we drive home at the end of the day, our hands gripping the steering wheel, our bumper kissing the one ahead, when to our right, a vehicle speeds along the curb and merges ahead of us the moment when an opening appears, our passion for fairness sur-

faces. The protrusion of one of our fingers signals our belief that one of the rules of fairness has been violated.

16   In every sport I can think of—baseball, basketball, football, tennis—one is expected to play between the white lines. To do otherwise is unfair and carries a penalty.

17   Our passion for fairness seeps out of every pore of our existence. Great leaders understand that passion. In his early days, when members of his own church were urging him to "cool it," Dr. Martin Luther King Jr. appealed to America's sense of fairness and morality.

18   It was Dr. King's appeal to fairness that resonated throughout the land and inspired Americans of all races and colors to travel to the deep south, and to put their lives on the line in defense of what they considered the right thing, the fair thing to do.

19   Affirmative Action has its roots in that passion for fairness. When President Lyndon Johnson explained Affirmative Action to the nation, it is significant that he said, you can't bring a man to the starting line who has been hobbled by chains and expect him to run the race competitively.

20   Fairness suggested that the nation pursue Affirmative Action to compensate black Americans for the wrong that had been done. Affirmative Action was a technique for jump starting the process of integrating black Americans into the fabric of American society, for changing the culture of America from an exclusive society into an inclusive one.

21   I believe Affirmative Action was meant to be temporary. It was meant to be a stronger dose of equal opportunity for individuals, and the prescription was intended to expire when the body politic had developed sufficient immunity to the virus of prejudice and discrimination. It was not meant to be a system of preferences that would harm innocent people. The rationale for Affirmative Action thirty years ago was a moral one.

22   Three decades later, Affirmative Action is permanent and firmly entrenched as a matter of public policy. It has its own constituency that is prepared to defend its continuation at any cost, not because of any moral imperative, but because it has become the battleground for a political and economic war that has racial self-interest as its centerpiece.

23   Affirmative Action, as most of us originally understood the term, enjoyed the support of a majority of Americans. Many Americans still support this concept as long as it does not involve preferences. Preferences, on the other hand, were wrong at the outset and are wrong today.

24   Affirmative Action has become a system of racial preferences in my state. Jobs are solicited with explicit acknowledgment that we want a woman or an African-American or an Hispanic for this position. Contracts are set aside for certain groups, with the taxpayers paying what amounts to an Affirmative Action tax. This is the result of contractors who set up shell minority and women owned businesses to front for white-owned businesses in order to benefit from the minority set-asides.

25   Wealthy sons and daughters of "underrepresented minorities" receive extra points on their admissions applications to the university, based solely on their race, while higher-achieving Asians and Whites from lower income families are turned away from the university. Families are forced to mortgage their homes to send their children out of state to an institution comparable to Berkeley and UCLA.

26   A racial matrix is used at most of our campuses which establishes a racial pecking order that distributes extra points on the basis of one's racial background.

27   When the nation began its use of Affirmative Action decades ago, America's racial landscape was rather clear. There was the dominant white majority and the oppressed black minority. Today, we have several dozen racial and ethnic categories in California.

28   There is no dominant majority and there is no oppressed minority. Within a few years, the group which will numerically be the largest is Hispanic. Our racial tensions are no longer just Black and White. They are Black and Korean. Black and Hispanic. White and Hispanic. Russian and Hispanic. Every conceivable racial conflict is present and lurking somewhere beneath the surface, in California. How, then, do we decide who among us should receive a preference?

29   A direct product of our diversity is the emergence of a whole new set of racial configurations and problems which defy the old racial order. Yet, Affirmative Action operates as if the old order was still in place, as if our racial dilemma was still Black against White.

30   The end of Affirmative Action will be difficult for black Americans. It is our nature not to be trusting of the good will of Whites. It is instinctive for us to harbor the belief that our rights will only be as secure as the amount of ammunition issued to the federal troops to protect us. Well, it is time to let the troops go home and to place our faith in the American system of democracy, in America's passion for fairness.

31   It is time for black Americans to enter the arena of democracy instead of seeing ourselves as spectators. This is our land, not Africa. The blood and sweat of black Americans can be found in the pot of democracy in just as great a quantity as that of others. It is time for black Americans to proudly accept America as their land, the land of opportunity.

32   To black Americans, I say look through the windshield at America's opportunity, not through the rear view mirror at this nations mistakes. Resist the temptation to believe that our nation owes us a debt. Let us take the initiative to say that the debt has been paid and the books are closed, and the Republican party should say, come home to your party, you have been gone too long.

33   A significant phenomenon in my in my state is the growing political influence of Hispanics. As the emerging numerical majority, many Hispanics see Affirmative Action as their passport to college, jobs and contracts. Many see Affirmative Action as a tool that has benefitted black Americans and they now believe it is their turn to be the preferred minority. They see it as the express lane to a better life. I urge them not to pursue this strategy. It is corrosive and dangerous.

34   I am often asked why is it that California, one of the most multiracial states in the nation is the first to begin the process of dismantling Affirmative Action. The answer is twofold: First, because California is a window of the future. We often experience events before other states. Second, it is precisely because of our diversity that we know how destructive Affirmative Action can be of fundamental democratic values of self-reliance, individualism and equal opportunity for all.

35   California is as close as any society on the face of the earth to being that promised land where racism is considered repulsive and has no place. But, this promised land can become a battle zone if we allow the continued tribalization of California.

36   We can point with pride to the fact that the mayor of one of America's favorite cities—San Francisco—is a black man: Willie Brown. The mayor of one of the largest cities in the nation, Los Angeles, for years was a black man—Tom Bradley. Our two

United States senators are women. The mayor of our state capital is Hispanic, Joe Serna. Although, I as a Republican don't always agree with the political judgment of my fellow Californians, I believe no one can dispute their egalitarian impulses.

37   As one looks at California state government, for example, the conclusion is inescapable: equal opportunity is now in-bred. The cabinet of Governor Wilson is nearly equally divided among men and women, and it only takes a casual meeting with any of them to confirm that raw talent, and not Affirmative Action, is the basis of that fact.

38   I am terrified at the prospect of what can become of us if we maintain our existing preferences policies. In police departments, in fire departments, in middle class homes throughout California, there is a growing perception that if I am white, I and my kids will not have an equal opportunity to succeed. No matter where it comes from, if anyone among us believes the warranty is not being honored, we have a duty to investigate the legitimacy of their complaint and to make it right if their complaint is proven to be valid.

39   Throughout this debate, you will hear about blacks being stopped in white neighborhoods, white women clutching their purses as black men approach, about the difficulty of black men getting a taxi in urban centers late at night, about the glass ceiling, about the lack of role models, about the percentage of black males in prison, and about the shortage of women in the Congress. All of these complaints warrant our attention, but none of them, no matter how true, justifies a suspension of that warranty that I talked about.

40   There are those who say that racism and sexism are not dead in America, and they are correct. But, racism and sexism in our society do not justify our government giving a preference to Jose over Chang because Susan's father discriminated against Willie's father fifty years ago. Not in America.

41   If you are a student of history, you know that every now and then, the opportunity to alter the course of human events presents itself. Such is now the occasion for the people of this nation.

42   Every now and then, the challenge confronts us to step out from among the crowd to perform extraordinary acts. Such is the moment for the Republican party.

43   The challenge is to end the corrosive system of racial preferences that has evolved in our nation, a system that has the potential to fatally damage the most fundamental values of our democracy, and to do so in a way that does not unleash the meaner instincts of some and the fears of others.

44   The opportunity is to resume that noble journey of building an inclusive family of Americans in which men and women of all races and colors can work and play in harmony, with mutual respect, and expecting nothing more than an equal opportunity to compete and from that competition we can build that more perfect union of which our forefathers dreamed.

45   The vehicle for this journey is the California Civil Rights Initiative. This initiative is simple and direct. No government agency shall discriminate against anyone on the basis of race, sex, or national origin, and no government agency shall give anyone preferential treatment for any of those reasons.

46   Two days ago, I appeared on a talk show with congresswoman Maxine Waters. She argued that the California Civil Rights Initiative will create divisiveness. That may be true, but we are not the ones creating the divisiveness. Those who cling to the notion that preferences must continue are the ones responsible for dividing our society.

47   Ask the student who works hard for four years to earn a 4.0 grade point average only to be denied admission to Berkeley or UCLA in favor of someone with a 3.0, merely because UC wants racial diversity, whether she thinks we are being divisive.

48   Ask the poor Vietnamese student who is turned away from Berkeley or Irvine, despite his high grades, in favor of a wealthy under represented minority whether he thinks we are being divisive. Ask him whether he is satisfied with the explanation that we are getting "too many Asians" at those campuses.

49   Ask the daughter of a third generation Chinese-American family whether she thinks we are being divisive when we say that it is unfair for applicants who are in this country illegally to get a preference over her.

50   Ask the parents of James Cook, only one of two California students admitted to Johns Hopkins University in 1994, only to be denied admission to UC San Diego medical school because he is white, whether they think we are being divisive. Ask them and thousands of other middle class families who are forced to take out $80,000 to $100,000 second mortgages on their homes, to send their kids out of state to college because racial preferences prevent them from being able to attend UC, whether they think we are being divisive.

51   Ask the high-achieving black or Chicano student who works hard and gains entry to college solely on the basis of his merit but must endure the nagging question of whether he was admitted because of Affirmative Action whether he thinks we are being divisive. Ask him whether he thinks it is fair that his accomplishments are devalued.

52   Do we not believe it was divisive when those from an earlier period said that "slavery is immoral and should be ended?" Was it not divisive when our nation's people fought among themselves over this very issue? Was it not divisive when we sent troops into Montgomery and Selma Alabama to protect the rights of people like Rosa Parks and James Meredith to ensure their right to sit wherever they wanted on the bus and to attend a college that wasn't segregated?

53   Yes, those were divisive times. But, the seeds of division are planted not by those of us who seek to eliminate racial and ethnic preferences, they are planted by those who believe that our skin color and gender and how we spell our last name should entitle us to the harvest of diversity—college admission, government employment and contracts.

54   My friend and ally throughout this experience has been governor Pete Wilson. When I first brought the fact that the University of California was engaged in an offensive system of racial preferences, the governor unhesitatingly said, "let's fix it." When our opponents accuse us of being divisive, the governor is correct when he says that sometimes the only way to resolve issues in a democracy is through the ballot box. That is why this initiative is so important.

55   I find it interesting that a nation which claims to have the heart to solve an ethnic war in Bosnia shouldn't have the stomach to prevent one here at home.

56   If there is any lesson that we can learn from the rest of the world, it is the fact that America's experiment with democracy will fail if we divide our people into racial enclaves and allocate jobs, contracts and college educations on the basis of group identity.

57   We often hear about the "angry white male." If anyone is discriminated against because of his or her color, they have a right to be angry. And, we should all share that anger, not belittle or rationalize it by citing glass ceiling statistics. As individuals, none of our rights are secure when the fruits of our society are allocated on the basis of group allotments.

58   Yogi Berra once said, when you reach a fork in the road, take it. Well, try as we might, we can't take his advice. We must make a conscious choice.

59   We can continue down the path of numerical parity, racial preferences, and a continuing preoccupation with the concept of race. We can continue perpetuating the outdated premise on which racial preferences are based: that blacks, women and other minorities are incapable of competing without a handicap.

60   Or, we can return to the fundamentals of our democracy: the supremacy of the individual, equal opportunity for the individual, and zero tolerance for discrimination.

61   As a Republican, I want my party to be known not just as the party that eliminated the deficit and concerned itself with the fiscal health of our nation. I want us to be remembered as the party that stood fast in support of the proposition that racial preferences are a social deficit that has to be eliminated, that true equality of opportunity cannot be compromised, that the next generation should not have to inherit the task of solving the horrible problems that Affirmative Action is creating.

62   I am not worried about the Skinheads, the Ku Klux Klan, and the Aryan Nation. In our time, we have discredited them and their brand of racism. Now, we must fight those who, in their own way, peddle a form of racism and bigotry that is just as destructive of democratic principles as the bigots of yesteryear.

63   You know, it pains me to say that within the past year, I have experienced more hate from my fellow black Americans than I have seen in the previous 55 1/2 years of my life. For example, a black state senator, Diane Watson, recently said that I want to be white, that I consider myself colorless, that I have no racial pride—all because my wife is white and because I oppose racial discrimination and racial preferences.

64   The one thing that I have learned from this experience is that bigots come in all shapes and colors. Despite their physical differences, they have one thing in common; they all reside in the same intellectual sewer.

65   The senator is right about several things. First, I do want to be colorless in the eyes of my government. I thought that was a goal to which we all subscribed. Second, I am lacking in racial pride. I have self-pride. I am proud to be an American. I am proud to be a Rotarian. I am proud of my family. I am proud to own my own business. But, I am racially indifferent, not racially proud.

66   Those who proclaim pride in their color or race trouble me, unless they have earned that color laying on the beach or in front of a sun lamp. To any of you who want to travel down that road of racial pride, leave me out of the vehicle. But, I urge you to be attentive for those signs which read, "slippery road ahead."

67   And so, my friends, we find ourselves poised at this moment in the life of a great people, trying to define the character of our nation.

68   Throughout America, we are restructuring our institutions. Our nation is desperately trying to embrace policies which place greater reliance on the rights and responsibilities of individuals. The debate about Affirmative Action must be seen in that context.

69   This issue will define the political parties in our nation for generations to come. The challenge for Republicans will be to convince all Americans that preferences are not in the national best interest, that a preference for some, means a loss of liberty and the pursuit of happiness for others.

70   We have to convince black Americans, a group which has become addicted to the drug of a powerful central government that their rights can be no more secure than

anyone else's when we empower government to make decisions about people's lives on the basis of a government melanometer which measures melanin levels. None of our rights are secure in a game of racial self-interest.

71   I will never abandon my faith that America can become Ronald Reagan's "shining city on the hill" a society in which a person's gender or race or ethnic background are irrelevant in the transactions of their government.

72   Let us not mourn the death of Affirmative Action. Instead, let us proclaim our belief that the spirit of equal opportunity, which Affirmative Action engendered, has become a permanent feature of America's social, economic and political landscape. Let us have faith in our own sense of fair play.

73   On February 27, 1860, in his Cooper Institute address, President Lincoln urged his party to hold fast to their beliefs. He said: "Neither let us be slandered from our duty by false accusations against us, nor frightened from it by menaces of destruction to the government nor of dungeons to ourselves. Let us have faith that right makes might, and in that faith let us to the end dare to do our duty as we understand it."

74   Why do I take the position I have? Because it is my duty as an American citizen.

75   I am often asked if I would do it over again, knowing what I know now about the loss of privacy, the personal insults and the occasional negative stories. My response is: "in a heart beat." This is the price of citizenship in a democracy. This is the fee which democracy exacts from each of us. If you don't have the courage of your convictions, then you forfeit the best that a democracy has to offer.

76   Please indulge me in this moment of personal pride, as a citizen, who has no political aspirations, who derives no economic benefit from this effort, in sharing with you the fact that I have taken the best blows that the opposition has been able to deliver, and I am still in the ring and on my feet.

77   Is it too presumptuous of me to say that one person can indeed make a difference? Is it too naive of me to consider my experience as a reassurance that democracy works, that the Republic for which it stands is a value worthy of our aspirations and dedication? Is it wrong for me to think that the pledge of allegiance obligates me to believe and act upon my belief that the pursuit of liberty and justice for all is a duty for all of us?

78   I hope you will agree with me that those propositions are not presumptuous and naive. Thank you for inviting me.

POST-READING QUESTIONS

CONTENT

1. Why does Connerly say the "Pledge of Allegiance" is important? What, for him, does it define?

2. What are we guaranteed, according to Connerly, under the "warranty" issued to us at birth in the United States? To what extent has this warranty been honored for all Americans?

3. Upon what assumption is Affirmative Action based, according to the essay?

4. What examples of racial inequity does Connerly offer?

5. What role does fairness play, according to Connerly, in American culture?

6. Does Connerly think Affirmative Action should never have been implemented? Cite the text for support.

7. What does Connerly identify as one key defect in contemporary Affirmative Action policies?

8. Why does Connerly say he's "not worried about the Skinheads, the Ku Klux Klan, and the Aryan Brotherhood"?

9. What does Connerly mean when he say that "a preference for some, means a loss of liberty and the pursuit of happiness for others"? Do you agree?

STYLE AND STRUCTURE

10. How does Connerly establish credibility on the subject of Affirmative Action? To what extent do you think he presents himself as knowledgeable on the subject? Explain.

11. What effect do Connerly's use of the pronouns "we," "our," and "my" have on your reading of the essay? To what extent do they cause you to feel more or less included in his message?

12. What function does the "Pledge of Allegiance" at the start of the essay serve?

13. What clues does Connerly give that reveal his piece to be a speech originally?

14. What arguments does Connerly offer against Affirmative Action? Is his support convincing? Explain.

15. What is Connerly's primary argument? Upon what assumptions is it based? Restate his main idea in your own words.

16. Who is Connerly's audience? What proportion of his audience do white Americans comprise? Black Americans? How do Connerly's language and examples reveal his audience?

CRITICAL THINKING AND ANALYSIS

DISCUSSION QUESTIONS

17. To what extent does Connerly, an African-American man, break or fit stereotypes in arguing against Affirmative Action? Upon what do you base your conclusions?

18. Connerly cites people who feel that, because they were discriminated against, "America owes [them]." What do you think? To what extent can contemporary policies make right the wrongs of the past?

19. Connerly refers to the "angry white man" and to Hispanic people in terms of those affected by Affirmative Action. To what extent do you think the conflicts of Affirmative Action are limited to specific gender and racial groups? Be sure to share your own experiences in responding to this question.

WRITING ASSIGNMENTS

20. Connerly writes that the time for Affirmative Action in California has passed because there exists "no dominant majority" and that Affirmative Action policies operate under the "old order . . . black against white." What about states that do have dominant majorities? Write a few paragraphs in which you argue whether or not Affirmative Action should continue under any circumstances. Be sure to identify the circumstances, if any, under which you think Affirmative Action should operate, and cite Connerly's speech for support.

21. Connerly criticizes Affirmative Action as being intrinsically "unfair" to many Americans, yet he claims that the California Civil Rights Initiative will be "divisive." How, then, can both fairness and unity be achieved? Write a few well-developed paragraphs in which you provide your own suggestions for fostering racial equality.

22. Connerly claims that "democracy exacts [a fee] from each of us." Is he right? Write a few paragraphs in which you explain how Americans pay "a fee" for democracy. Try to keep your argument within the context of Affirmative Action, and cite the text for support.

VOCABULARY DEVELOPMENT

23. Using only single-word examples from Connerly's essay, characterize Connerly. What words best reveal details about the author and his biases?

GROUP ACTIVITIES

24. Choose three to five statements from Connerly's essay with which you strongly agree and three to five more statements with which you strongly disagree. Then, discuss all your statements as a group, noting the statements that more than one person chose and analyzing why certain statements evoked powerful responses. Broaden your discussion to include other groups, as well.

25. Using Connerly's essay (and Stanley Fish's, if you like), hold a debate among the entire class on the merits versus the drawbacks of Affirmative Action. Which side is stronger? Which side seems to be more emotional in its pleas? Why? Write a short paragraph analyzing the debate when you have finished.

SYNTHESIS QUESTIONS

1. Ellen Goodman writes that in terms of sexual harassment, women may "assume the other gender not only doesn't understand but can't understand." Write an essay in which you explain how important understanding your employer or employee is in order to work well with him/her. Cite these essays and your own work-related experiences in order to illustrate your ideas.

2. Michael Kramer quotes Robert McGuire, former New York City police chief, who states that on-the-job pressure forces police officers to "make up some of their own rules," and Ward Connerly lists numerous examples of unfairness suffered by African-Americans. At what point, if ever, should people change the rules to benefit themselves? Write an essay in which you argue that, when under pressure or when suffering, people do or do not have the right to change rules to make their lives easier. Be sure to cite from these readings and others, as well as from your own experiences, in order to illustrate your ideas.

3. Michael Kramer quotes former New York City police commissioner Robert McGuire who states that "we all have our own personal lines" between right and wrong, but Ellen Goodman claims that in order to decide fairness in a situation we must "get in another's head." How do you make decisions? Write a few paragraphs in explaining what factors—your own values and other people's opinions, among others—determine how you act in different situations.

4. Lisa Girion quotes business consultant Leslie Charles who claims that many employees are "overwhelmed, overworked, overscheduled and overspent," while John Manners and Suzanne Opton write of business owners who have "succeeded . . . by offering customers superior service." Who is more important, the employee or the customer? Assuming the position of a business owner, write a letter to your investors, arguing that either your employees or your customers are your first priority. Be sure to cite Girion's essay as well as Manners' and Opton's in order to make your ideas clear.

5. At what point, if any, can civility be a drawback? John Manners and Suzanne Opton write about successful business owner Pat Whitaker, who tries to "provide truly outstanding service" to her clients, but former police officer Blondie in Michael Kramer's article claims that being an effective cop involves showing area residents, "who's boss on a daily basis," even to the point of using violence. Write a few well-developed paragraphs or a short essay in which you argue that civility is or is not an effective way of doing one's job. Be sure to cite at least two articles from this chapter, and you may use personal examples to clarify your points.

6. Ward Connerly writes that fairness is important in American culture while Ellen Goodman writes that, in order for sexual harassment at work to stop, "The crucial ingredient is empathy." What qualities do you think are most necessary for employees and employers to get along? Write a few paragraphs in which you explain what personal characteristics or behavior guidelines are necessary for people to maintain fruitful working relationships. Cite at least two essays from this chapter, and use examples from your own experiences as well.

Chapter 7

Civility Toward the Environment

"A city person encountering nature hardly recognizes it, has not patience for its cycles, and disregards animals and plants unless they roar and exfoliate in spectacular aberrations."

— **Maxine Hong Kingston**
A City Person Encountering Nature

"The circle is the way to see. The circle is the way to live, always keeping in mind the seven generations to come, always asking: how will my deeds affect the lives of my children's children's children?"

— **Joseph Bruchac**
The Circle is the Way to See

> **"**With the collapse of Marxism, environmentalism has become the new refuge of socialist thinking.**"**
>
> **— Rush Limbaugh III**
> *The Environmental Mindset*

> **"**Properly speaking, global thinking is not possible. Those who have 'thought globally' . . . have done so by means of simplifications too extreme and oppressive to merit the name of thought. Global thinkers have been, and will be, dangerous people.**"**
>
> **— Wendell Berry**
> *Out of Your Car, Off Your Horse*

> **"**There are those who never once have even considered animals' rights: those who have been taught that animals actually want to be used and abused by us, as small children 'love' to be frightened, or women 'love' to be mutilated and raped . . . .**"**
>
> **Alice Walker**

Introduction

For decades people have debated the question: if a tree falls in the forest with no one around, does that tree make noise? The answers to this question vary widely, depending upon how necessary people believe human witnesses to be in determining the fact of the tree's fall. Similarly, Chapter 7 asks: Is civility only civility when people are present? Or, if no one is around to be offended, can someone be guilty of incivility?

Several writers included in this chapter offer a resounding "Yes!" to these questions, just as others claim that disrupting nature is no sin if the end result serves humans. Writers in this chapter further consider whether we should bother to show consideration to sites that may never host another visitor, even if we found such a spot pristine. Questions such as these present a multi-faceted debate with no clear answers. Chapter 7 examines how civility is defined in terms of the environment and raises the question of just when civility toward nature oversteps its bounds and harms humans.

Saving Nature, But Only For Man

Charles Krauthammer

Continually exploring the relationship between people and the environment, Charles Krauthammer writes a conservative column for *The Washington Post.* In *Saving Nature, But Only For Man,* Krauthammer argues that, while conservation is a worthy practice, its ends must be primarily for the benefit of humanity.

Pre-reading Questions

Freewrite for five to ten minutes in response to the following questions:
What do you think the primary benefits of nature are? How do you classify these benefits: as entertainment to be enjoyed, natural resources to be used, a ward to be protected? Why?

Vocabulary Preview

Vocabulary Words:
- aversion
- axiom
- ozone
- speculative
- parched
- anthropocentric
- chronic
- idolatry
- benignity
- aesthetic

Look up each word above in the dictionary and find the sentences where they appear in the text. Then, rewrite the sentences from which they came, substituting their definitions (groups of words) for the words themselves. What effects do your substitutions have on the readability of the essay?

1   Environmental sensitivity is now as required an attitude in polite society as is, say, belief in democracy or aversion to polyester. But now that everyone from Ted Turner to George Bush, Dow to Exxon has professed love for Mother Earth, how are we to choose among the dozens of conflicting proposals, restrictions, projects, regulations and laws advanced in the name of the environment? Clearly not everything with an environmental claim is worth doing. How to choose?

2   There is a simple way. First, distinguish between environmental luxuries and environmental necessities. Luxuries are those things it would be nice to have if costless. Necessities are those things we must have regardless. Then apply a rule. Call it the fundamental axiom of sane environmentalism: Combatting ecological change that directly threatens the health and safety of people is an environmental necessity. All else is luxury.

3   For example: preserving the atmosphere—stopping ozone depletion and the greenhouse effect—is an environmental necessity. In April scientists reported that ozone damage is far worse than previously thought. Ozone depletion not only causes skin cancer and eye cataracts, it also destroys plankton, the beginning of the food chain atop which we humans sit.

4   The reality of the greenhouse effect is more speculative, though its possible consequences are far deadlier: melting ice caps, flooded coastlines, disrupted climate,
parched plains and, ultimately, empty breadbaskets. The American Midwest feeds the
world. Are we prepared to see Iowa acquire New Mexico's desert climate? And Siberia
acquire Iowa's?

5   Ozone depletion and the greenhouse effect are human disasters. They happen to
occur in the environment. But they are urgent because they directly threaten man. A
sane environmentalism, the only kind of environmentalism that will win universal public support, begins by unashamedly declaring that nature is here to serve man. A sane
environmentalism is entirely anthropocentric: it enjoins man to preserve nature, but on
the grounds of self-preservation.

6   A sane environmentalism does not sentimentalize the earth. It does not ask people
to sacrifice in the name of other creatures. After all, it is hard enough to ask people to
sacrifice in the name of other humans. (Think of the chronic public resistance to foreign aid and welfare.) Ask hardworking voters to sacrifice in the name of the snail
darter, and, if they are feeling polite, they will give you a shrug.

7   Of course, this anthropocentrism runs against the grain of a contemporary environmentalism that indulges in earth worship to the point of idolatry. One scientific
theory—Gaia theory—actually claims that Earth is a living organism. This kind of environmentalism likes to consider itself spiritual. It is nothing more than sentimental. It
takes, for example, a highly selective view of the benignity of nature. My nature worship stops with the April twister that came through Kansas or the May cyclone that
killed more than 125,000 Bengalis and left 10 million (!) homeless.

8   A nonsentimental environmentalism is one founded on Protagoras' maxim that
"Man is the measure of all things." Such a principle helps us through the thicket of environmental argument. Take the current debate raging over oil drilling in a corner of the
Alaska National Wildlife Refuge. Environmentalists, mobilizing against a bill working
its way through the U.S. Congress to permit such exploration, argue that Americans
should be conserving energy instead of drilling for it. This is a false either/or proposition. The U.S. does need a sizeable energy tax to reduce consumption. But it needs
more production too. Government estimates indicate a nearly fifty-fifty chance that under the ANWR lies one of the five largest oil fields ever discovered in America.

9   The U.S. has just come through a war fought in part over oil. Energy dependence
costs Americans not just dollars but lives. It is a bizarre sentimentalism that would
deny oil that is peacefully attainable because it risks disrupting the calving grounds of
Arctic caribou.

10   I like the caribou as much as the next man. And I would be rather sorry if their
mating patterns are disturbed. But you can't have everything. And if the choice is between the welfare of caribou and reducing an oil dependency that gets people killed in
wars, I choose man over caribou every time.

11   Similarly the spotted owl in Oregon. I am no enemy of the owl. If it could be preserved at no or little cost, I would agree: the variety of nature is a good, a high aesthetic
good. But it is no more than that. And sometimes aesthetic goods have to be sacrificed
to the more fundamental ones. If the cost of preserving the spotted owl is the loss of
livelihood for 30,000 logging families, I choose family over owl.

12   The important distinction is between those environmental goods that are fundamental and those that are merely aesthetic. Nature is our ward. It is not our master. It is
to be respected and even cultivated. But it is man's world. And when man has to
choose between his well-being and that of nature, nature will have to accommodate.

13   Man should accommodate only when his fate and that of nature are inextricably
bound up. The most urgent accommodation must be made when the very integrity of
man's habitat—e.g., atmospheric ozone—is threatened. When the threat to man is of
a lesser order (say, the pollutants from coal- and oil-fired generators that cause death
from disease but not fatal damage to the ecosystem), a more modulated accommodation that balances economic against health concerns is in order. But in either case the
principle is the same: protect the environment—because it is man's environment.

14   The sentimental environmentalists will call this saving nature with a totally wrong
frame of mind. Exactly. A sane—a humanistic—environmentalism does it not for
nature's sake but for our own.

POST-READING QUESTIONS

CONTENT

1. How does Krauthammer say we should decide what to do to save the environment?

2. How does Krauthammer differentiate between environmental "luxuries" and
    "necessities"? What do you think?

3. Why does Krauthammer say that ozone depletion and the greenhouse effect
    are "disasters"? Do you agree?

4. How does Krauthammer define "sane environmentalism"? What examples
    does he give to characterize it?

5. Why does Krauthammer say he does not believe in the "Gaia worship" type of
    enviromentalism?

6. Why does Krauthammer say he would choose oil drilling and supporting log-
    gers over saving caribou and spotted owls, respectively? What do you think?

STYLE AND STRUCTURE

7. What is Krauthammer's basic argument? Restate his main idea in your own
    words.

8. What examples does Krauthammer give to support his main idea? Which, if
    any, is most convincing? Why?

9. Who is Krauthammer's audience? How can you tell? Cite the text for support.

10. How does Krauthammer counter the argument that drilling for oil in Alaska
    might disrupt the mating patterns of caribou?

11. What is Krauthammer's tone? Choose quotes from the text that you think best
    reveal his tone.

12. When was this essay written? Cite the text for proof of its original publication
    date.

CRITICAL THINKING AND ANALYSIS

DISCUSSION QUESTIONS

13. To what extent do you agree or disagree with Krauthammer's assertion that "not everything with an environmental claim is worth doing"? Cite your own experiences as well as the text in responding to this question.

14. How accurate is Krauthammer's statement "Environmental sensitivity is now as required an attitude in polite society as is, say, belief in democracy . . ."? Explain.

WRITING ASSIGNMENTS

15. Write at least one well-developed paragraph in which you differentiate between environmental "luxuries" and "necessities." Be sure to offer a definition of each, and use multiple examples to illustrate your ideas.

16. Krauthammer claims that some environmental disasters are "urgent because they directly threaten man." Can disasters that do NOT threaten humans be considered "urgent"? Write a few paragraphs in which you argue that environmental disasters are or are not significant, or urgent, only if they threaten people. Be sure to cite Krauthammer and your own observations in order to illustrate your ideas.

17. How true is Krauthammer's claim that "Nature is our ward. It is not our master"? Write a short essay in which you discuss which of these two statements is the most accurate. Cite the text and your own examples for support.

VOCABULARY DEVELOPMENT

18. Choose one of the words from the Vocabulary Preview and, based on its definition, let the concept of that word serve as the focus for a short paragraph. How difficult is focusing your writing on a single word? Why? Write a few sentences explaining the ease or difficulty with which you were able to write your word-oriented paragraph.

GROUP ACTIVITIES

19. As a group, sketch your own pyramid of life forms, indicating what species are, to you, most and least important. What determines how you rank the life forms? Compare your pyramid with other groups.

20. Make two lists: one of environmental "luxuries" and one of "necessities." Then, present your lists to the class in an effort to create a class-wide policy for determining what types of environmental activities are most important. What factors determine how important an environmental act is?

Am I Blue?

Alice Walker

Probably best known for her National Book Award winning novel *The Color Purple,* Alice Walker is also an accomplished poet and essayist. In *Am I Blue?* Walker poses the question of what makes us human, or not, and in doing so offers a poignant message for the just treatment of animals.

Pre-reading Questions

Freewrite for five to ten minutes in response to the following questions:
What distinction, if any, do you make between "animals" and "humans"? Do you think these two groups possess more similarities or differences? Why? Describe some of your experiences with animals in order to respond to these questions.

Vocabulary Preview

Vocabulary Words:
- cropping
- flanks
- relished
- whinny

- enormity
- euphemism
- ambled
- mutual

- crazed
- integrity

Look up the words in the list above and use them in a paragraph of your own on any aspect of animal-related issues. Pay attention to which words are most, or least, difficult to use and why.

---

1   For about three years my companion and I rented a small house in the country that stood on the edge of a large meadow that appeared to run from the end of our deck straight into the mountains. The mountains, however, were quite far away, and between us and them there was, in fact, a town. It was one of the many pleasant aspects of the house that you never really were aware of this.

2   It was a house of many windows, low, wide, nearly floor to ceiling in the living room, which faced the meadow, and it was from one of these that I first saw our closest neighbor, a large white horse, cropping grass, flipping its mane, and ambling about—not over the entire meadow, which stretched well out of sight of the house, but over the five or so fenced-in acres that were next to the twenty-odd that we had rented. I soon learned that the horse, whose name was Blue, belonged to a man who lived in another town, but was boarded by our neighbors next door. Occasionally, one of the children, usually a stocky teen-ager, but sometimes a much younger girl or boy, could be seen riding Blue. They would appear in the meadow, climb up on his back, ride furiously for ten or fifteen minutes, then get off, slap Blue on the flanks, and not be seen again for a month or more.

3   There were many apple trees in our yard, and one by the fence that Blue could almost reach. We were soon in the habit of feeding him apples, which he relished, especially because by the middle of summer the meadow grasses—so green and succulent

since January—had dried out from lack of rain, and Blue stumbled about munching the dried stalks half-heartedly. Sometimes he would stand very still just by the apple tree, and when one of us came out he would whinny, snort loudly, or stamp the ground. This meant, of course: I want an apple.

4　　It was quite wonderful to pick a few apples, or collect those that had fallen to the ground overnight, and patiently hold them, one by one up to his large, toothy mouth. I remained as thrilled as a child by his flexible dark lips, huge, cubelike teeth that crunched the apples, core and all, with such finality, and his high, broad-breasted *enormity;* beside which, I felt small indeed. When I was a child, I used to ride horses, and was especially friendly with one named Nan until the day I was riding and my brother deliberately spooked her and I was thrown, head first, against the trunk of a tree. When I came to, I was in bed and my mother was bending worriedly over me; we silently agreed that perhaps horseback riding was not the safest sport for me. Since then I have walked, and prefer walking to horseback riding—but I had forgotten the depth of feeling one could see in horses' eyes.

5　　I was therefore unprepared for the expression in Blue's. Blue was lonely. Blue was horribly lonely and bored. I was not shocked that this should be the case; five acres to tramp by yourself, endlessly, even in the most beautiful of meadows—and his was—cannot provide many interesting events, and once rainy season turned to dry that was about it. No, I was shocked that I had forgotten that human animals and nonhuman animals can communicate quite well; if we are brought up around animals as children we take this for granted. By the time we are adults we no longer remember. However, the animals have not changed. They are in fact *completed* creations (at least they seem to be, so much more than we) who are not likely *to* change; it is their nature to express themselves. What else are they going to express? And they do. And, generally speaking, they are ignored.

6　　After giving Blue the apples, I would wander back to the house, aware that he was observing me. Were more apples not forthcoming then? Was that to be his sole entertainment for the day? My partner's small son had decided he wanted to learn how to piece a quilt; we worked in silence on our respective squares as I thought . . .

7　　Well, about slavery: about white children, who were raised by black people, who knew their first all-accepting love from black women, and then, when they were twelve or so, were told they must "forget" the deep levels of communication between themselves and "mammy" that they knew. Later they would be able to relate quite calmly, "My old mammy was sold to another good family." "My old mammy was _____." Fill in the blank. Many more years later a white woman would say: "I can't understand these Negroes, these blacks. What do they want? They're so different from us."

8　　And about the Indians, considered to be "like animals" by the "settlers" (a very benign euphemism for what they actually were), who did not understand their description as a compliment.

9　　And about the thousands of American men who marry Japanese, Korean, Filipina, and other non-English-speaking women and of how happy they report they are, *"blissfully,"* until their brides learn to speak English, at which point the marriages tend to fall apart. What then did the men see, when they looked into the eyes of the women they married, before they could speak English? Apparently only their own reflections.

10 I thought of society's impatience with the young. "Why are they playing the music so loud?" Perhaps the children have listened to much of the music of oppressed people their parents danced to before they were born, with its passionate but soft cries for acceptance and love, and they have wondered why their parents failed to hear.

11 I do not know how long Blue has inhabited his five beautiful, boring acres before we moved into our house; a year after we had arrived—and had also traveled to other valleys, other cities, other worlds—he was still there.

12 But then, in our second year at the house, something happened in Blue's life. One morning, looking out the window at the fog that lay like a ribbon over the meadow, I saw another horse, a brown one, at the other end of Blue's field. Blue appeared to be afraid of it, and for several days made no attempt to go near. We went away for a week. When we returned, Blue had decided to make friends and the two horses ambled or galloped along together, and Blue did not come nearly as often to the fence underneath the apple tree.

13 When he did, bringing his new friend with him, there was a different look in his eyes. A look of independence, of self-possession, of inalienable *horse*ness. His friend eventually became pregnant. For months and months there was, it seemed to me, a mutual feeling between me and the horses of justice, of peace. I fed apples to them both. The look in Blue's eyes was one of unabashed "this is *it*ness."

14 It did not, however, last forever. One day, after a visit to the city, I went out to give Blue some apples. He stood waiting, or so I thought, though not beneath the tree. When I shook the tree and jumped back from the shower of apples, he made no move. I carried some over to him. He managed to half-crunch one. The rest he let fall to the ground. I dreaded looking into his eyes—because I had of course noticed that Brown, his partner, had gone—but I did look. If I had been born into slavery, and my partner had been sold or killed, my eyes would have looked like that. The children next door explained that Blue's partner had been "put with him" (the same expression that old people used, I had noticed, when speaking of an ancestor during slavery who had been impregnated by her owner) so that they could mate and she conceive. Since that was accomplished, she had been taken back by her owner, who lived somewhere else.

15 Will she be back? I asked

16 They didn't know.

17 Blue was like a crazed person. Blue *was,* to me, a crazed person. He galloped furiously, as if he were being ridden, around and around his five beautiful acres. He whinnied until he couldn't. He tore at the ground with his hooves. He butted himself against his single shade tree. He looked always and always toward the road down which his partner had gone. And then, occasionally, when he came up for apples, or I took apples to him, he looked at me. It was a look so piercing, so full of grief, a look so *human* I almost laughed (I felt too sad to cry) to think there are people who do not know that animals suffer. People like me who have forgotten, and daily forget, all that animals try to tell us. "Everything you do to us will happen to you; we are your teachers, as you are ours. We are one lesson" is essentially it, I think. There are those who never once have even considered animals' rights: those who have been taught that animals actually want to be used and abused by us, as small children "love" to be frightened, or women "love" to be mutilated and raped. . . . They are the great-grandchildren of those who honestly thought, because someone taught them this: "Women can't think," and

"nigger's can't faint." But most disturbing of all, in Blue's large brown eyes was a new look, more painful than the look of despair: the look of disgust with human beings, with life; the look of hatred. And it was odd what the look of hatred did. It gave him, for the first time, the look of a beast. And what that meant was that he had put up a barrier within to protect himself from further violence; all the apples in the world wouldn't change that fact.

18   And so Blue remained, a beautiful part of our landscape, very peaceful to look at from the window, white against the grass. Once a friend came to visit and said, looking out on the soothing view: "And it *would* have to be a *white* horse; the very image of freedom." And I thought, yes, the animals are forced to become for us merely "images" of what they once so beautifully expressed. And we are used to drinking milk from containers showing "contented" cows, whose real lives we want to hear nothing about, eating eggs and drumsticks from "happy" hens, and munching hamburgers advertised by bulls of integrity who seem to command their fate.

19   As we talked of freedom and justice one day for all, we sat down to steaks. I am eating misery, I thought, as I took the first bite. And spit it out.

POST-READING QUESTIONS

CONTENT

1. What is the setting for Walker's essay? In what ways is the setting important?
2. Why does Walker say she was "unprepared for the expression in Blue's [eyes]"? What expression does she mean?
3. Why does Walker mention non-English-speaking brides? How does this relate to Blue?
4. What does Walker mean when she writes of Blue and Brown that "there was . . . a mutual feeling . . . of justice, of peace"?
5. What other "lessons" of mistreatment and misunderstanding does Walker outline? What is her purpose in doing so?

STYLE AND STRUCTURE

6. What is Walker's main idea? Restate her primary argument in your own words.
7. Aside from echoing a once-popular song, what function does the title serve?
8. Why does Walker spend the first four paragraphs, more than one quarter of the essay, describing Blue and his setting?
9. What is Walker's tone? Cite the text to reveal her tone.
10. Who is Walker's audience? To what extent do African Americans and white Americans comprise her audience?
11. What function does Walker's discussion of slavery serve? Is it effective? Explain.
12. What other examples of people's poor treatment at the hands of others does Walker give?

CRITICAL THINKING AND ANALYSIS

DISCUSSION QUESTIONS

13. What role does communication play in people's evaluation of others (animals included)? What types of communication, if any, are most significant in developing relationships?

14. Walker writes that after Brown left, Blue developed "the look of a beast." What does she mean? Why does one horse's expression matter, according to Walker? Explain, citing the text for support.

WRITING ASSIGNMENTS

15. Walker claims that "There are those who never once have even considered animals' rights . . ." Write a few well-developed paragraphs in which you outline animals' rights. You may cite Walker if you wish, or you may develop your policy completely based upon your own experiences. Just be sure to offer a clear explanation of why you feel animals deserve the rights you outline.

16. What is the correlation between kindness to animals and kindness to people? Write at least one well-developed paragraph in which you argue that kindness to animals is or is not a sign of inherent civility. Cite your own observations and experiences for support.

17. Walker writes that "animals are forced to become for us merely 'images' of what they once so beautifully expressed." Write a brief essay based upon your observation of animal portrayal in advertising and the media in which you agree or disagree with Walker's assertion that animals are just "images."

VOCABULARY DEVELOPMENT

18. Walker communicates several emotions as she writes of her encounter with Blue. Identify at least two of these emotions, and then scan her essay to find at least five words or expressions that best represent each emotion. Then, write a few sentences explaining why the expressions you choose are powerful for you.

GROUP ACTIVITIES

19. Rank life forms on a linear graph, starting with one-celled organisms at one end and placing humans at the other end. At what point, if any, do life forms begin to deserve a lesser standard of treatment than humans? Upon what criteria do you base your decision?

20. Search online for animal rights groups such as PETA, and make notes as to what their primary arguments are for animal rights and protection. Then, share your results with the class and discuss whether or not you are convinced by what you learn online.

The Great American Desert

Edward Abbey

Known for his passionate love of the American Southwest, Edward Abbey wrote several novels and the semi-autobiographical *Desert Solitaire* in which he recounts his experience as a park ranger in the Utah and Arizona canyon wilderness. Abbey often practically rants against people who fail to respect nature, and his suggestions for preserving the wilderness often seem extreme.

Pre-reading Questions

Freewrite for five to ten minutes in response to the following questions:
Have you ever been to a desert before? What is your experience? How is the desert often portrayed on television or in the movies? Do these descriptions make you want to visit the desert? Explain. Where, if anywhere, is a place that you love to the point of irrationally wanting to protect?

Vocabulary Preview

Vocabulary Words:	• incarnation	• formidable	• mummified
	• acerbity	• indolent	• circumambulate
	• labyrinthine	• melancholy	• quagmires
	• prospect	• ubiquitous	

Look up the words above and, as you read, write a few sentences discussing how these words do, or do not, help Abbey communicate his tone.

1   In my case it was love at first sight. This desert, all deserts, any desert. No matter where my head and feet may go, my heart and my entrails stay behind, here on the clean, true, comfortable rock, under the black sun of God's forsaken country. When I take on my next incarnation, my bones will remain bleaching nicely in a stone gulch under the rim of some faraway plateau, way out there in the back of beyond. An unrequited and excessive love, inhuman no doubt but painful anyhow, especially when I see my desert under attack. "The one death I cannot bear," said the Sonoran-Arizonan poet Richard Shelton. The kind of love that makes a man selfish, possessive, irritable. If you're thinking of a visit, my natural reaction is like a rattlesnake's—to warn you off. What I want to say goes something like this.

2   Survival Hint #1: Stay out of there. Don't go. Stay home and read a good book, this one for example. The Great American Desert is an awful place. People get hurt, get sick, get lost out there. Even if you survive, which is not certain, you will have a miserable time. The desert is for movies and God-intoxicated mystics, not for family recreation.

3   Let me enumerate the hazards. First the Walapai tiger, also known as conenose kissing bug. *Triatoma protracta* is a true bug, black as sin, and it flies through the night quiet as an assassin. It does not attack directly like a mosquito or deerfly, but alights at

a discreet distance, undetected, and creeps upon you, its hairy little feet making not the slightest noise. The kissing bug is fond of warmth like Dracula requires mammalian blood for sustenance. When it reaches you the bug crawls onto your skin so gently, so softly that unless your senses are hyperacute you feel nothing. Selecting a tender point, the bug slips its conical proboscis into your flesh, injecting a poisonous anesthetic. If you are asleep you will feel nothing. If you happened to be awake you may notice the faintest of pinpricks, hardly more that a brief ticklish sensation, which you will probably disregard. But the bug is already at work. Having numbed the nerves near the point of entry the bug proceeds (with a sign of satisfaction, no doubt) to withdraw blood. When its belly is filled, it pulls out, backs off, and waddles away, so drunk and gorged it cannot fly.

4   At about this time the victim awakes, scratching at a furious itch. If you recognize the symptoms at once, you can sometimes find the bug in your vicinity and destroy it. But revenge will be your only satisfaction. Your night is ruined. If you are of average sensitivity to a kissing bug's poison, your entire body breaks out in hives, skin aflame from head to toe. Some people become seriously ill, in many cases requiring hospitalization. Others recover fully after five or six hours except for a hard and itchy swelling, which may endure for a week.

5   After the kissing bug, you should beware of rattlesnakes; we have half a dozen species, all offensive and dangerous, plus centipedes, millipedes, tarantulas, black widows, brown recluses, Gila monsters, the deadly poisonous coral snakes, and giant hairy desert scorpions. Plus an immense variety of near-infinite number of ants, midges, gnats, bloodsucking flies, and blood-guzzling mosquitoes. (You might think the desert would be spared at least mosquitoes? Not so. Peer in any water hole by day: swarming with mosquito larvae. Venture out on a summer's eve: The air vibrates with their mournful keening.) Finally, where the desert meets the sea, as on the coasts of Sonora and Baja California, we have the usual assortment of obnoxious marine life: sandflies, ghost crabs, stingrays, electric jellyfish, spiny sea urchins, man-eating sharks, and other creatures so distasteful one prefers not even to name them.

6   It has been said, and truly, that everything in the desert either stings, stabs, stinks, or sticks. You will find the flora here as venomous, hooked, barbed, thorny, prickly, needled, saw-toothed, hairy, stickered, mean, bitter, sharp, wiry, and fierce as the animals. Something about the desert inclines all living things to harshness and acerbity. The soft evolve out. Except for sleek and oily growths like the poison ivy—oh yes, indeed—that flourish in sinister profusion on the dank walls above the quicksand down in those corridors of gloom and labyrinthine monotony that men call canyons.

7   We come now to the third major hazard, which is sunshine. Too much of a good thing can be fatal. Sunstroke, heatstroke, and dehydration are common misfortunes in the bright American Southwest. If you can avoid the insects, reptiles, and arachnids, the cactus and the ivy, the smog of the southwestern cities, and the lung fungus of the desert valleys (carried by dust in the air), you cannot escape the desert sun. Too much exposure to it eventually causes, quite literally, not merely sunburn but skin cancer.

8   Much sun, little rain also means an arid climate. Compared with the high humidity of more hospitable regions, the dry heat of the desert seems at first not terribly uncomfortable—sometimes even pleasant. But that sensation of comfort is false, a deception, and therefore all the more dangerous, for it induces overexertion and an insufficient

consumption of water even when water is available. This leads to various internal complications, some immediate—sunstroke, for example—and some not apparent until much later. Mild but prolonged dehydration, continued over a span of months or years, leads to the crystallization of mineral solutions in the urinary tract, that is, to what urologists call urinary calculi or kidney stones. A disability common in all the world's arid regions. Kidney stones, in case you haven't met one, come in many shapes and sizes, from pellets smooth as BB shot to highly irregular calcifications resembling asteroids, Vietcong shrapnel, and crown-of-thorns starfish. Some of these objects may be "passed" naturally; others can be removed only by means of the Davis stone basket or by surgery. Me—I was lucky; I passed mine with only a groan, my forehead pressed against the walls of the pissoir in the rear of a Tucson bar that I cannot recommend.

9   You may be getting the impression by now that the desert is not the most suitable of environments for human habitation. Correct. Of all the Earth's climatic zones, excepting only the Antarctic, the deserts are the least inhabited, the least "developed," for reasons that should now be clear.

10   You may wish to ask, Yes, okay, but among North American deserts which is the *worst?* A good question—and I am happy to attempt to answer.

11   Geographers generally divide the North American desert—what was once termed "the Great American Desert"—into four distinct regions or subdeserts. These are the Sonoran Desert, which comprises southern Arizona, Baja California, and the state of Sonora in Mexico; the Chihuahuan Desert, which includes west Texas, southern New Mexico, and the states of Chihuahua and Coahuila in Mexico; the Mojave Desert, which includes southeastern California and small portions of Nevada, Utah, and Arizona; and the Great Basin Desert, which includes most of Utah and Nevada, northern Arizona, northwestern New Mexico, and much of Idaho and eastern Oregon.

12   Privately, I prefer my own categories. Up north in Utah somewhere in the canyon country—places like Zeke's Hole, Death Hollow, Pucker Pass, Buckskin Gulch, Nausea Crick, Wolf Hole, Mollies's Nipple, Dirty Devil River, Horse Canyon, Horseshoe Canyon, Lost Horse Canyon, Horsethief Canyon, and Horseshit Canyon, to name only the more classic places. Down in Arizona and Sonora there's the cactus country; if you have nothing better to do, you might take a look at High Tanks, Salome Creek, Tortilla Flat, Esperero ("Hoper") Canyon, Holy Joe Peak, Depression Canyon, Painted Cave, Hell Hole Canyon, Hell's Half Acre, Iceberg Canyon, Tiburon (Shark) Island, Pinacate Peak, Infernal Valley, Sykes Crater, Montezuma's Head, Gu Oidak, Kuakatch, Pisinimo, and Baboquivari Mountain, for example.

13   Then there's The Canyon. *The* Canyon. The Grand. That's one world. And North Rim—that's another. And Death Valley, still another, where I lived one winter near Furnace Creek and climbed the Funeral Mountains, tasted Badwater, looked into the Devil's Hole, hollered up Echo Canyon, searched for and never did find Seldom Seen Slim. Looked for *satori* near Vana, Nevada, and found a ghost town named Bonnie Claire. Never made it to Winnemucca. Drove through the Smoke Creek Desert and down through Big Pine and Lone Pine and home across the Panamints to Death Valley again—home sweet home that winter.

14   And which of these deserts is the worst? I find it hard to judge. They're all bad—not half bad but all bad. In the Sonoran Desert, Phoenix will get you if the sun, snakes,

bugs, and arthropods don't. In the Mojave Desert, it's Las Vegas, more sickening by far than the Glauber's salt in the Death Valley sinkholes. Go to Chihuahua and you're liable to get busted in El Paso and sandbagged in Ciudad Juárez—where all old whores go to die. Up north in the Great Basin Desert, on the Plateau Province, in the canyon country, your heart will break, seeing the strip mines open up and the power plants rise where only cowboys and Indians and J. Wesley Powell ever roamed before.

15   Nevertheless, all is not lost; much remains, and I welcome the prospect of an army of lug-soled hiker's boots on the desert trails. To save what wilderness is left in the American Southwest—and in the American Southwest only the wilderness is worth saving—we are going to need all the recruits we can get. All the hands, heads, bodies, time, money, effort we can find. Presumably—and the Sierra Club, the Wilderness Society, the Friends of the Earth, The Audubon Society, the Defenders of Wildlife operate on this theory—those who learn to love what is spare, roughly wild, undeveloped, and unbroken will be willing to fight for it, will help resist the strip miners, highway builders, land developers, weapons testers, power producers, tree chainers, clear cutters, oil drillers, dam beavers, subdividers—the list goes on and on—before that zinc-hearted, termite-brained, squint-eyed, nearsighted, greedy crew succeeds in completely californicating what still survives of the Great American Desert.

16   So much for the Good Cause. Now what about desert hiking itself, you may ask. I'm glad you asked that question. I firmly believe that one should never—I repeated *never*—go out into that formidable wasteland of cactus, heat, serpents, rock, scrub, and thorn without careful planning, thorough and cautious preparation, and complete—never mind the expense!—*complete* equipment. My motto is: Be Prepared.

17   That is my belief and that is my motto. My practice, however, is a little different. I tend to go off in a more or less random direction myself, half-baked, half-assed, half-cocked, and half-ripped. Why? Well, because I have an indolent and melancholy nature and don't care to be bothered getting all those *things* together—all that bloody *gear*—maps, compass, binoculars, poncho, pup tent, shoes, first-aid kit, rope, flashlight, inspirational poetry, water, food—and because anyhow I approach nature with a certain surly ill-will, daring Her to make trouble. Later when I'm deep into Natural Bridges Natural Moneymint or Zion National Parkinglot or say General Shithead National Forest Land of Many Abuses why then, of course, when it's a bit late, then I may wish I had packed that something extra, matches perhaps, to mention one useful item, or maybe a spoon to eat my gruel with.

18   If I hike with another person it's usually the same; most of my friends have indolent and melancholy natures too. A cursed lot, all of them. I think of my comrade John De Puy, for example, sloping along for mile after mile like a goddamned camel—indefatigable—with those J.C. Penney hightops on his feet and that plastic pack on his back he got with five books of Green Stamps and nothing inside it but a sketchbook, some homemade jerky, and a few cans of green chiles. Or Douglas Peacock, ex–Green Beret, just the opposite. Built like a buffalo, he loads a ninety-pound canvas pannier on his back at trailhead, loaded with guns, ammunition, bayonet, pitons and carabiners, cameras, field books, a 150-foot rope, geologist's sledge, rock samples, assay kit, field glasses, two gallons of water in steel canteens, jungle boots, a case of C-rations, rope hammock, pharmaceuticals in a pig-iron box, raincoat, overcoat,

two-man mountain tent, Dutch oven, hibachi, shovel, ax, inflatable boat, and near the top of the load and distributed through side and back pockets, easily accessible, a case of beer. Not because he enjoys or needs all that weight—he may never get to the bottom of that cargo on a ten-day outing—but simply because Douglas uses his pack-bag for general storage both at home and on the trail and prefers not to have to re-arrange everything from time to time merely for the purposes of a hike. Thus my friends De Puy and Peacock; you may wish to avoid such extremes.

19   A few tips on desert etiquette:

1. Carry a cooking stove, if you must cook. Do not burn desert wood, which is rare and beautiful and required ages for its creation (an ironwood tree lives for over 1,000 years and juniper almost as long).

2. If you must, out of need, build a fire, then for God's sake allow it to burn itself out before you leave—do not bury it, as Boy Scouts and Campfire Girls do, under a heap of mud or sand. Scatter the ashes; replace any rocks you may have used in constructing a fireplace; do all you can to obliterate the evidence that you camped here. (The Search & Rescue Team may be looking for you.)

3. Do not bury garbage—the wildlife will only dig it up again. Burn what will burn and pack out the rest. The same goes for toilet paper: Don't bury it, *burn it.*

4. Do not bathe in desert pools, natural tanks, *tinajas,* potholes. Drink what water you need, take what you need, and leave the rest for the next hiker and more important for the bees, birds, and animals—bighorn sheep, coyotes, lions, foxes, badgers, deer, wild pigs, wild horses—whose *lives* depend on that water.

5. Always remove and destroy survey stakes, flagging, advertising signboards, mining claim markers, animal traps, poisoned bait, seismic exploration geo-phones, and other such artifacts of industrialism. The men who put those things there are up to no good and it is our duty to confound them. Keep America Beautiful. Grow a Beard. Take a Bath. Burn a Billboard.

20   Anyway—why go into the desert? Really, why do it? That sun, roaring at you all day long. The fetid, tepid, vapid little water holes slowly evaporating under a scum of grease, full of cannibal beetles, spotted toads, horsehair worms, liver flukes, and down at the bottom, inevitably, the pale cadaver of a ten-inch centipede. Those pink rat-tlesnakes down in The Canyon, those diamondback monsters thick as a truck driver's wrist that lurk in shady places along the trail, those unpleasant solpugids and unneces-sary Jerusalem crickets that scurry on dirty claws across your face at night. Why? The rain that comes down like lead shot and wrecks the trail, those sudden rockfalls of ob-scure origin that crash like thunder ten feet behind you in the heart of the dead-still af-ternoon. The ubiquitous buzzard, so patient—but only so patient. The sullen and hostile Indians, all on welfare. The ragweed, the tumbleweed, the Jimson weed, the snake-weed. The scorpion in your shoe at dawn. The dreary wind that blows all spring, the psychedelic Joshua trees waving their arms at you on moonlight nights. Sand in the soup du jour. Halazone tablets in your canteen. The barren hills that always go up, which is bad, or down, which is worse. Those canyons like catacombs with quicksand lapping at your crotch. Hollow, mummified horses with forelegs casually crossed, dead

for ten years, leaning against the corner of a barbed-wire fence. Packhorses at night, iron-shod, clattering over the slickrock through your camp. The last tin of tuna, two flat tires, not enough water and a forty-mile trek to Tule Well. An osprey on a cardón cactus, snatching the head off a living fish—always the best part first. The hawk sailing by at 200 feet, a squirming snake in its talons. Salt in the drinking water. Salt, selenium, arsenic, radon, and radium in the water, in the gravel, in your bones. Water so hard it bends light, drills holes in rock and chokes up your radiator. Why go there? Those places with the hardcase names: Starvation Creek, Poverty Knoll, Hungry Valley, Bitter Springs, Last Chance Canyon, Dungeon Canyon, Whipsaw Flat, Dead Horse Point, Scorpion Flat, Dead Man Draw, Stinking Spring, Camino del Diablo, Jornado del Muetro . . . Death Valley.

21   Well then, why indeed go walking into the desert, that grim ground, that bleak and lonesome land where, as Genghis Khan said of India, "the heat is bad and the water makes men sick"?

22   Why the desert, when you could be strolling along the golden beaches of California? Camping by a stream of pure Rocky Mountain spring water in colorful Colorado? Loafing through a laurel slick in the misty hills of North Carolina? Or getting your head mashed in the greasy alley behind the Elysium Bar and Grill in Hoboken, New Jersey? Why the desert, given a world of such splendor and variety?

23   A friend and I took a walk around the base of a mountain up beyond Coconino County, Arizona. This was a mountain we'd been planning to circumambulate for years. Finally we put on our walking shoes and did it. About halfway around this mountain, on the third or fourth day, we paused for a while—two days—by the side of a stream, which the Navajos call Nasja because of the amber color of the water. (Caused perhaps by juniper roots—the water seems safe enough to drink.) On our second day there I walked down the stream, alone, to look at the canyon beyond. I entered the canyon and followed it for half the afternoon, for three or four miles, maybe, until it became a gorge so deep, narrow and dark, full of water and the inevitable quagmires of quicksand, that I turned around and looked for a way out. A route other than the way I'd come, which was crooked and uncomfortable and buried—I wanted to see what was up on top of this world. I found a sort of chimney flue on the east wall, which looked plausible, and sweated and cursed my way up through that until I reached a point where I could walk upright, like a human being. Another 300 feet of scrambling brought me to the rim of the canyon. No one, I felt certain, had ever before departed Nasja Canyon by that route.

24   But someone had. Near the summit I found an arrow sign, three feet long, formed of stones and pointing off into the north toward those same old purple vistas, so grand, immense, and mysterious, of more canyons, more mesas and plateaus, more mountains, more cloud-dappled sun-spangled leagues of desert sand and desert rock, under the same old wide and aching sky.

25   The arrow pointed into the north. But what was it pointing *at?* I looked at the sign closely and saw that those dark, desert-varnished stones had been in place for a long, long time; they rested in compacted dust. They must have been there for a century at least. I followed the direction indicated and came promptly to the rim of another canyon and a drop-off straight down of a good 500 feet. Not that way, surely. Across this canyon was nothing of any unusual interest that I could see—only the familiar sun-blasted sandstone, a few scrubby clumps of blackbrush and prickly pear, a few acres of

nothing where only a lizard could gaze, surrounded by a few square miles of more nothingness interesting chiefly to horned toads. I returned to the arrow and checked again, this time with field glasses, looking away for as far as my aided eyes could see toward the north, for ten, twenty, forty miles into the distance. I studied the scene with care, looking for an ancient Indian ruin, or significant cairn, perhaps an abandoned mine, a hidden treasure of some inconceivable wealth, the mother of all mother lodes. . . .

26   But there was nothing out there. Nothing at all. Nothing but the desert. Nothing but the silent world.

27   *That's why.*

POST-READING QUESTIONS

CONTENT

1. What is Abbey's first reaction to people who want to visit the desert? Why?

2. List some of the names of different desert locales and explain how they are or are not appropriate for the desert as Abbey describes it.

3. Based on your reading of Abbey's essay, what can you conclude that he values? That he hates? Cite the text in order to support your response.

4. What rules of etiquette does Abbey offer? In what ways might these rules be considered tools of civility? In what ways might they not be considered tools of civility? Explain your response using examples from the text and from your own experiences and observations.

5. For whom is Abbey most concerned in the desert? Where do people rank on his list of what matters?

6. What does Abbey mean when he writes that "Nothing at all. Nothing but the desert" is his rationale for loving the desert?

STRUCTURE AND ANALYSIS

7. What is Abbey's main idea in writing this essay? Rewrite his main idea in your own words.

8. Who is Abbey's audience? How does Abbey feel about his audience? How can you tell? Cite the text in order to support your response.

9. Is Abbey a credible source? Does he know what he is talking about? Choose several words and phrases that illustrate his tone. How effective is his tone in communicating his main idea?

10. Abbey writes that he loves the desert, but he offers almost exclusively negative descriptions of desert plant and animal life. In what ways, if at all, do the "love" and the negative comments work together to communicate a single idea? What is that idea? Use the text to illustrate your ideas.

11. What examples, if any, make you most want to visit the desert? What examples make you least want to go? Cite the text for support.

12. Is Abbey persuasive? Why or why not? Explain.

CRITICAL THINKING AND ANALYSIS

DISCUSSION QUESTIONS

13. What kind of a person is Abbey? Do you think his passion for his subject outweighs his overly zealous means to protect it? Explain and cite the text for support.

14. How do you react to Abbey? Do his descriptions make you want to visit the desert, or do they make you want to stay away? Why?

WRITING ASSIGNMENTS

15. Using Abbey's essay as a reference, write a well-developed paragraph or short essay in which you argue whether or not the desert is a place worth visiting. Be sure to cite the essay for support, and use your own experiences with the desert, however limited, in order to illustrate your ideas.

16. In a few well-developed paragraphs, write a description of a place that you love but that other people might not. Make sure your reader can tell both that you love this place but that others may not.

17. Abbey offers several etiquette rules for visiting the desert. Write at least a paragraph in which you analyze his rules, explaining what principle underlies all his rules and explaining why following such rules is or is not important.

VOCABULARY DEVELOPMENT

18. Mimic Abbey for one paragraph, using your own subject matter in place of his. Keep the sentence structure consistent with Abbey's—substituting an adjective for an adjective, a verb for a verb, etc. How does your tone compare to Abbey's?

GROUP ACTIVITIES

19. Write a letter to someone in the same tone that Abbey adopts, and discourage that person from doing something that you love. Share your writing with other groups in order to determine if you are persuasive.

20. Choose an activity that you love but that you want fewer people to do, as Abbey does, and write "a few tips on . . . etiquette" for your desired activity. How serious are your rules? Whose rights do they respect? Share your rules with the class in an open-forum setting.

Unchopping A Tree

W. S. Merwin

Known and acclaimed for his poetry and for his Pulitzer Prize-winning collection *The Carrier of Ladders,* W.S. Merwin describes an impossible process in *Unchopping A Tree,* offering commentary for each step while starkly revealing the futility of the act.

Pre-reading Questions

Freewrite for five to ten minutes in response to the following questions:
Have you every chopped down a tree? If so, how much effort did it involve? If not, how much effort do you imagine it would involve? What feelings, if any, do you have about deforestation? What do you know about it?

Vocabulary Preview

Vocabulary Words:
- arduous
- mutilated
- simulate
- scaffolding
- panoply
- involuntary
- fixative
- adhesives
- translucent
- subcutaneous
- sustaining

Read each word within the context of Merwin's essay and write definitions, making sure to note any secondary, especially emotional, meanings. Then, look up all of the words and use five of them in sentences related to the topic of the environment.

1   Start with the leaves, the small twigs, and the nests that have been shaken, ripped, or broken off by the fall; these must be gathered and attached once again to their respective places. It is not arduous work, unless major limbs have been smashed or mutilated. If the fall was carefully and correctly planned, the chances of anything of the kind happening will have been reduced. Again, much depends upon the size, age, shape, and species of the tree. Still, you will be lucky if you can get through this stage without having to use machinery. Even in the best of circumstances it is a labor that will make you wish often that you had won the favor of the universe of ants, the empire of mice, or at least a local tribe of squirrels, and could enlist their labors and their talents. But no, they leave you to it. They have learned, with time. This is men's work. It goes without saying that if the tree was hollow in whole or in part, and contained old nests of bird or mammal or insect, or hoards of nuts or such structures as wasps or bees build for their survival, the contents will have to be repaired where necessary, and reassembled, insofar as possible, in their original order, including the shells of nuts already opened. With spiders' webs you must simply do the best you can. We do not have the spider's weaving equipment, nor any substitute for the leaf's living bond with its point of attachment and nourishment. It is even harder to simulate the latter when the leaves have once become dry—as they are bound to do, for this is not the

labor of a moment. Also it hardly needs saying that this is the time for repairing any neighboring trees or bushes or other growth that may have been damaged by the fall. The same rules apply. Where neighboring trees were of the same species it is difficult not to waste time conveying a detached leaf back to the wrong tree. Practice, practice. Put your hope in that.

2   Now the tackle must be put into place, or the scaffolding, depending on the surroundings and the dimensions of the tree. It is ticklish work. Almost always it involves, in itself, further damage to the area, which will have to be corrected later. But as you've heard, it can't be helped. And care now is likely to save you considerable trouble later. Be careful to grind nothing into the ground.

3   At last the time comes for the erecting of the trunk. By now it will scarcely be necessary to remind you of the delicacy of this huge skeleton. Every motion of the tackle, every slight upward heave of the trunk, the branches, their elaborately re-assembled panoply of leaves (now dead) will draw from you an involuntary gasp. You will watch for a leaf or a twig to be snapped off yet again. You will listen for the nuts to shift in the hollow limb and you will hear whether they are indeed falling into place or are spilling in disorder—in which case, or in the event of anything else of the kind—operations will have to cease, of course, while you correct the matter. The raising itself is no small enterprise, from the moment when the chains tighten around the old bandages until the bole hangs vertical above the stump, splinter above splinter. Now the final straightening of the splinters themselves can take place (the preliminary work is best done while the wood is still green and soft, but at times when the splinters are not badly twisted most of the straightening is left until now, when the torn ends are face to face with each other). When the splinters are perfectly complementary the appropriate fixative is applied. Again we have no duplicate of the original substance. Ours is extremely strong, but it is rigid. It is limited to surfaces, and there is no play in it. However the core is not the part of the trunk that conducted life from the roots up into the branches and back again. It was relatively inert. The fixative for this part is not the same as the one for the outer layers and the bark, and if either of these is involved in the splintered section they must receive applications of the appropriate adhesives. Apart from being incorrect and probably ineffective, the core fixative would leave a scar on the bark.

4   When all is ready the splintered trunk is lowered onto the splinters of the stump. This, one might say, is only the skeleton of the resurrection. Now the chips must be gathered, and the sawdust, and returned to their former positions. The fixative for the wood layers will be applied to chips and sawdust consisting only of wood. Chips and sawdust consisting of several substances will receive applications of the correct adhesives. It is as well, where possible, to shelter the materials from the elements while working. Weathering makes it harder to identify the smaller fragments. Bark sawdust in particular the earth lays claim to very quickly. You must find your own ways of coping with this problem. There is a certain beauty, you will notice at moments, in the pattern of the chips as they are fitted back into place. You will wonder to what extent it should be described as natural, to what extent man-made. It will lead you on to speculations about the parentage of beauty itself, to which you will return.

5   The adhesive for the chips is translucent, and not so rigid as that for the splinters. That for the bark and its subcutaneous layers is transparent and runs into the fibers on either side, partially dissolving them into each other. It does not set the sap flowing

again but it does pay a kind of tribute to the preoccupations of the ancient thorough-fares. You could not roll an egg over the joints but some of the mine-shafts would still be passable, no doubt. For the first exploring insect who raises its head in the tight echoless passages. The day comes when it is all restored, even to the moss (now dead) over the wound. You will sleep badly, thinking of the removal of the scaffolding that must begin the next morning. How you will hope for sun and a still day!

6   The removal of the scaffolding or tackle is not so dangerous, perhaps, to the sur-roundings, as its installation, but it presents problems. It should be taken from the spot piece by piece as it is detached, and stored at a distance. You have come to accept it there, around the tree. The sky begins to look naked as the chains and struts one by one vacate their positions. Finally the moment arrives when the last sustaining piece is re-moved and the tree stands again on its own. It is as though its weight for a moment stood on your heart. You listen for a thud of settlement, a warning creak deep in the intricate joinery. You cannot believe it will hold. How like something dreamed it is, standing there all by itself. How long will it stand there now? The first breeze that touches its dead leaves all seems to flow into your mouth. You are afraid the motion of the clouds will be enough to push it over. What more can you do? What more can you do?

7   But there is nothing more you can do.

8   Others are waiting.

9   Everything is going to have to be put back.

POST-READING QUESTIONS

CONTENT

1. What steps does Merwin say people should take in undertaking the process he describes?
2. Which steps, if any, involve the most effort? Why?
3. What role does scaffolding play in the "unchopping" process? Why do you think Merwin includes it?
4. What challenges do the "unchoppers" face in restoring the tree? Which ones seem most, or least, difficult to conquer?
5. How effective does Merwin lead you to believe this process will be?

STYLE AND STRUCTURE

6. What is Merwin's point? Restate his main idea in your own words.
7. Why doesn't Merwin just come out and say his point? What effect do his de-scriptions have on you?
8. Who is Merwin's audience? How does the use of the second-person "you" ref-erences affect you as you read?
9. What is Merwin's tone? Cite the text in order to illustrate his tone.
10. What examples best support Merwin's main idea? Describe a few examples and explain why they are particularly effective.

11. Why is knowing the level of effort involved in the "unchopping" process important?

12. Is Merwin persuasive? What role do logic and emotion play in determining whether or not he is convincing? Explain.

CRITICAL THINKING AND ANALYSIS

DISCUSSION QUESTIONS

13. Upon what assumption does Merwin base his argument? How can you tell?

14. What is your gut reaction, if any, to Merwin's essay? Why?

WRITING ASSIGNMENTS

15. Write a paragraph in which you assume the position of a logger, and describe in detail your feelings as you chop down a tree. (If you do not know all the steps involved, just do the best you can.)

16. Merwin writes that "care now is likely to save you considerable trouble later" as he describes the process of "unchopping" a tree. To what else could his statement apply? On the topic of your choice, write a few paragraphs in which you explain how "care now" pays off later. Be sure to cite examples from your own experiences and observations in order to illustrate your ideas.

17. Choose any topic and argue obliquely, making your point without an explicit thesis statement. Write at least three paragraphs, and use examples from your experiences and any readings that assist you in making your point.

VOCABULARY DEVELOPMENT

18. Merwin has a definite bias in his attitude toward his subject. Choose at least five words that you think best communicate his slant on this topic and write a few sentences explaining how his diction is or is not effective in helping him to convey his point.

19. Using Merwin's essay as a guide, choose at least three of the most prominent steps involved in felling a tree, and find at least three different ways of describing those steps. Which descriptions seem the most emotionally loaded? Why? Write a few sentences describing the emotional impact certain language can have.

GROUP ACTIVITIES

20. Using Merwin's essay as a guide, write a paragraph in which you describe the steps involved in any controversial process. How emotional is your subject? How emotional is your tone? Share your paragraph with the class in order to compare each group's language use.

21. Rewrite Merwin's process using neutral language or language that favors the logger. Then, discuss how difficult changing the tone of a piece can be.

Argument Pair: Does Nature Need Saving?

A Logger's Lament, Leila Kysar

The End of Nature, Bill McKibben

Seemingly every time people publicly discuss the environment, the same question arises: what is more important—saving the environment, or making use of it as a natural resource? Often the responses to this question are extreme, requiring people either to abandon completely their use of a wilderness area or to ruin it completely for human consumption. Thus, another question arises: can nature be "used" and "preserved" simultaneously? Leila Kysar argues that public consumption of our forests is necessary both for our economy and for our lifestyle, but Bill McKibben warns that with every tree we fell, we irrevocably alter nature for the worse.

Writing Assignments Based on *A Logger's Lament,* and *The End of Nature:*

1. Leila Kysar argues that the United States has more protected forest land than is likely for anyone to see in a lifetime, while Bill McKibben argues that just one chain saw down the valley from him "drive[s] away the feeling that you are in another, separate, timeless, wild sphere." How important is completely "unspoiled" land? Write a well-developed paragraph or short essay in which you argue that more land should or should not be preserved and why. Use quotes from both essays in order to clarify your points.

2. Bill McKibben writes that motorboats and chain saws disrupt his communion with nature, while Leila Kysar, daughter and wife of loggers, claims that loggers' economic well-being is threatened by environmentalists. Who has the more compelling case? Write a few paragraphs comparing these two writers' arguments in order to conclude who makes the more selfless claim. Be sure to cite both writers for support.

A Logger's Lament

Leila Kysar

Writing for the *My Turn* section of *Newsweek,* Leila Kysar represents the voice of loggers, who have made up her family for at least two generations. Kysar argues that preserving old-growth forests and growing trees for profit are simultaneously possible, but only if people recognize the economic realities faced by tree growers.

Pre-reading Questions

Freewrite for five to ten minutes in response to the following questions:

How important is forest conservation to you? Upon what do you base your response? Make a list of all the wood-oriented products you use on a regular basis. How important are these products to you?

Vocabulary Preview

Vocabulary Words:
- species
- siege
- denude
- acreage
- commercial
- beleaguered
- recessions
- regenerates
- terrorist
- environmentalist

Use each of the words above in a short paragraph on some environmentally related topic. Then, look up each of the words and revise your paragraph, if necessary, to correct diction.

1   My father was a logger. My husband is a logger. My sons will not be loggers. Loggers are an endangered species, but the environmental groups, which so righteously protect endangered species in the animal kingdom, have no concern for their fellow human beings under siege. Loggers are a much misunderstood people, pictured as brutal rapists of our planet, out to denude it of trees and, as a result, of wildlife.

2   It is time to set the record straight. Loggers take great pride in the old-growth trees, the dinosaurs of the forests, and would be sorry to see them all cut. There are in the national forests in Washington and Oregon (not to mention other states) approximately 8.5 million acres of forested land, mostly old growth set aside, never to be used for timber production. In order to see it all, a man would have to spend every weekend and holiday for sixty years looking at timber at a rate of more than one-thousand acres per day. This does not include acreage to be set aside for spotted-owl protection.

3   In addition to this huge amount of forested land never to be logged, the State of Washington Forest Practices Act, established in 1973, specifies that all land that is clear-cut of trees must be replanted unless converted to some other use. As a tree farmer generally plants more trees per acre than he removes, more trees are being planted than are being cut. In the last twenty years in Clark County, Washington, alone, the Department of Natural Resources has overseen the planting of at least 15,000 acres of previously unforested private lands.

4   The term *logger* applies to the person harvesting trees. A tree farmer is the one who owns the land and determines what is to be done with it. To a tree farmer, clear-cutting is no more than the final harvest of that generation of trees. The next spring, he reforests the land. To the public, clear-cutting is a bad word. Does the public cry shame when a wheat farmer harvests his crop and leaves a field of stubble in place of the beautiful wheat?

5   In the Pacific Northwest, in five years, the newly planted trees will grow taller than the farmer's head; in ten years, more than fifteen feet tall; and in twenty to thirty years, the trees will be ready for the first commercial harvest. The farmer then thins the trees to make room for better growth. In forty to fifty years, he will be ready to clear-cut his

farm and replant again. Contrary to public opinion, it does *not* take three hundred to four hundred years to grow a Douglas fir tree to harvestable age.

6   Tree farming keeps us in wood products. We build with wood, write on paper, and even use the unmentionable in the bathroom. But in order to keep this flow of wood products available, we need to keep it economically feasible to grow trees. If we restrict the tree-farming practices because we do not like clear-cuts or because some animal might (and probably might not) become extinct, or we restrict markets for the timber by banning log exports or overtax the farmer, we are creating a situation where the farmer will no longer grow trees. If he cannot make money, he will not tree-farm. He will sell his tree farm so that it can grow houses. The *land* that grows trees is the natural resource; the *trees* are just a crop.

7   Legislation is constantly being introduced to take away the private-property rights of tree farmers. They are beleaguered by the public, who believe that any forest belongs to the public. Who, after all, buys the land and pays the taxes? Who invests money in property that will yield them an income only once every twenty to thirty years? Would John Q. Public picnic in a farmer's wheat field?

8   The tree farmer must have a diversified market. When there is a building slump in this country, it is vital to the industry to have an export market. Earlier recessions were devastating to tree farmers until markets were developed overseas. Some trees have little market value in the United States. The logs China and Korea bought in the late 1980s could not be sold here to cover the cost of delivery.

9   As to the wildlife becoming extinct, that is a joke that is not very funny. Animals thrive better in clear-cuts than in old-growth timber. Look at the Mount St. Helens blast area. Nature created an immense clearing and now deer, elk, and other wildlife are returning in numbers. Why? Because there is more food growing in an open area than under the tall trees. And as for the spotted owl, surely the 8.5 million acres set aside is enough to maintain quite a respectable owl population. Numerous recent observations show that the owl lives in second-growth timber as well as in old growth. In the Wenatchie National Forest there are more than two hundred fifty examples of spotted owls living in other than old-growth timber. The owl is a tool of the environmentalist groups to get what they want: the complete eradication of the species *Logger.*

BEAUTIFUL NEW TREES

10   Consider the scenic value of a preserved old-growth forest versus a managed stand of timber. In Glacier National Park, Montana, for example, which is totally untouched, one sees the old trees, the dead and dying trees, the windfalls crisscrossing the forest. In a managed forest, one sees the older stands with the forest floor cleared of the dead windfalls, leaving a more parklike setting. In the younger stands, one sees the beautiful new trees with their brilliant greens thrusting their tops to the sky and, in the clear cuts, before the new trees obscure the view, one sees the huckleberry bushes with their luscious-tasting berries, the bright pink of fireweed and deer and elk feeding. True environmentalists husband the land; they do not let the crops stagnate and rot. Tree farming regenerates the trees *and* utilizes the product.

11   A tree farmer from Sweden (where they are fined if they do *not* tree-farm their forests) asked me recently why we do not just explain these facts to the environmental groups so that they will work *with* us instead of *against* us. Well, do you know the difference between a terrorist and an environmentalist? It is easier to reason with the terrorist.

POST-READING QUESTIONS

CONTENT

1. What does Kysar offer as her reason for writing this essay?

2. What myths does Kysar seek to dispel in writing her argument? To what extent do you think she succeeds?

3. In what way does Kysar differentiate between the land and trees? Why do you think this distinction is important?

4. What does Kysar say is necessary to "keep this flow of wood products available"?

5. How does Kysar counter the argument that clear-cutting may lead to animal extinction?

6. What benefits does Kysar say tree farming has for the land?

STYLE AND STRUCTURE

7. What is Kysar's guiding idea? State her main point in your own words.

8. How apt is Kysar's comparison of tree farming to wheat farming? How effective is it?

9. Who is Kysar writing for? What conclusions can you draw about her audience? Cite the text for support.

10. What is Kysar's tone? To what extent does her tone help or hurt her argument? Explain.

11. How does Kysar establish credibility on her subject? How convinced are you that she is a credible source of information on logging and preservation?

12. What examples do you find most convincing in Kysar's essay? Why?

13. Why does Kysar end her essay with the "joke" about terrorists and environmentalists?

CRITICAL THINKING AND ANALYSIS

DISCUSSION QUESTIONS

14. What is your gut feeling about how important forest preservation is? Did Kysar sway your views? Explain.

15. Kysar claims that clear-cut forests have more "scenic value" than old-growth forests. What do you think? Explain, citing your experiences for support.

WRITING ASSIGNMENTS

16. Kysar claims that "the environmental groups, which so righteously protect endangered species . . . have no concern for their fellow human beings under siege." How much should environmentalists care about people? Write a few paragraphs in which you argue that environmentalist causes—ones that seek to preserve animal or plant life—are inherently civil or uncivil because of their effects upon human beings. Cite Kysar and your own experiences in order to illustrate your ideas.

17. In a well-developed paragraph, write your own timber policy, stating how much clear-cutting should occur in a given forest. Cite the essay and your own experiences and observations for support.

18. Kysar mentions financial concerns related to tree farmers. How much do you think money matters to Kysar? Examining the text closely, write a one-paragraph analysis of Kysar's essay, arguing that money is or is not a major factor in her support for loggers.

VOCABULARY DEVELOPMENT

19. How does Kysar use language to conjure up certain emotions? Choose at least two paragraphs from Kysar's essay and identify descriptive terms in each. Then, write a few sentences explaining how her language in those paragraphs is particularly effective in communicating her message.

GROUP ACTIVITIES

20. As a group, use the Internet to learn about clear-cutting. Draw a conclusion about the extent to which you think clear-cutting should be allowed, and write a paragraphs expressing these views. Then, present your findings to the class in an open forum setting.

21. Divide the class into two groups and hold a debate on the issue of clear-cutting. Feel free to cite other readings from this chapter or do research on your own prior to engaging in debate.

The End of Nature

Bill McKibben

A staff writer and editor for *The New Yorker,* Bill McKibben also avidly hikes and camps and has written several books about environmental issues. In *The End of Nature,* the title essay from one such book, McKibben explores some of the man-made consequences that the environment faces, and he argues that, should we fail to alter our treatment of nature, severe consequences will follow.

Pre-reading Questions

Freewrite for five to ten minutes in response to the following questions:
How concerned are you about the environment? What, if anything, causes you more worry than others? How much, if at all, do you feel that preserving nature is within your power? Explain.

Vocabulary Preview

Vocabulary Words:	• timeless	• extinct	• mergansers
	• felling	• elemental	• loon

Look up the words above, writing a sentence or two about each one in order to explain how it is appropriate in an essay about nature.

1   Almost every day, I hike up the hill out my back door. Within a hundred yards the woods swallows me up, and there is nothing to remind me of human society— no trash, no stumps, no fence, not even a real path. Looking out from the high places, you can't see road or house; it is a world apart from man. But once in a while someone will be cutting wood farther down the valley, and the snarl of a chain saw will fill the woods. It is harder on those days to get caught up in the timeless meaning of the forest, for man is nearby. The sound of the chain saw doesn't blot out all the noises of the forest or drive the animals away, but it does drive away the feeling that you are in another, separate, timeless, wild sphere.

2   Now that we have changed the most basic forces around us, the noise of that chain saw will always be in the woods. We have changed the atmosphere, and that will change the weather. The temperature and rainfall are no longer to be entirely the work of some separate, uncivilizable force, but instead in part a product of our habits, our economies, our ways of life. Even in the most remote wilderness, where the strictest laws forbid the felling of a single tree, the sound of that saw will be clear, and a walk in the woods will be changed—tainted—by its whine. The world outdoors will mean much the same thing as the world indoors, the hill the same thing as the house.

3   An idea, a relationship, can go extinct, just like an animal or a plant. The idea in this case is "nature," the separate and wild province, the world apart from man to which

he adapted, under whose rules he was born and died. In the past, we spoiled and polluted parts of that nature, inflicted environmental "damage." But that was like stabbing a man with toothpicks: though it hurt, annoyed, degraded, it did not touch vital organs, block the path of the lymph or blood. We never thought that we had wrecked nature. Deep down we never really thought we could: it was too big and too old; its forces—the wind, the rain, the sun—were too strong, too elemental.

4   But, quite by accident, it turned out that the carbon dioxide and other gases we were producing in our pursuit of a better life—in pursuit of warm houses and eternal economic growth and of agriculture so productive it would free most of us from farming—*could* alter the power of the sun, could increase its heat. And that increase *could* change the patterns of moisture and dryness, breed storms in new places, breed deserts. Those things may or may not have yet begun to happen, but it is too late to altogether prevent them from happening. We have produced the carbon dioxide—we are ending nature.

5   We have not ended rainfall or sunlight; in fact, rainfall and sunlight may become more important forces in our lives. It is too early to tell exactly how much harder the wind will blow, how much hotter the sun will shine. That is for the future. But the *meaning* of the wind, the sun, the rain—of nature—has already changed. Yes, the wind still blows—but no longer from some other sphere, some inhuman place.

6   In the summer, my wife and I bike down to the lake nearly every afternoon for a swim. It is a dogleg Adirondack lake, with three beaver lodges, a blue heron, some otter, a family of mergansers, the occasional loon. A few summer houses cluster at one end, but mostly it is surrounded by wild state land. During the week we swim across and back, a trip of maybe forty minutes—plenty of time to forget everything but the feel of the water around your body and the rippling, muscular joy of a hard kick and the pull of your arms.

7   But on the weekends, more and more often, someone will bring a boat out for water-skiing, and make pass after pass up and down the lake. And then the whole experience changes, changes entirely. Instead of being able to forget everything but yourself, and even yourself except for the muscles and the skin, you must be alert, looking up every dozen strokes to see where the boat is, thinking about what you will do if it comes near. It is not so much the danger—few swimmers, I imagine, ever die by Evinrude. It's not even so much the blue smoke that hangs low over the water. It's that the motorboat gets into your mind. You're forced to think, not feel—to think of human society and of people. The lake is utterly different on these days, just as the planet is utterly different now.

POST-READING QUESTIONS

CONTENT

1. What effects does McKibben say that the introduction of the chain saw into the forest has on the experience of nature? Are we supposed to take his examples literally? Explain.

2. In what ways does McKibben say that "nature" is in danger of becoming extinct? Be specific in your response.

3. Why does McKibben say people in the past did not take their harm to nature seriously?

4. What, according to McKibben, is responsible for "ending nature"? What are the results of this cause?

5. What does McKibben mean when he says that "the motorboat gets in your mind"? What do you think?

STYLE AND STRUCTURE

6. What is McKibben's primary argument? Restate his main idea in your own words.

7. What examples of civilization invading nature does McKibben give? Which of these are most convincing? Explain.

8. Who is McKibben's audience? How can you tell? Cite the text to reveal McKibben's target readers.

9. How does McKibben establish credibility on his subject? What about his writing makes you believe him, or not?

10. Is McKibben convincing? Explain.

CRITICAL THINKING AND ANALYSIS

DISCUSSION QUESTIONS

11. What ideas, other than "nature," do you think have become extinct, as McKibben writes? Explain.

12. McKibben states that the noise of a chain saw "does drive away the feeling that you are in another, separate, timeless, wild sphere." To what extent do you agree or disagree that a small amount of mechanized intervention can ruin a "natural" experience?

WRITING ASSIGNMENTS

13. McKibben writes that the "*meaning* of the wind, the sun, the rain—of nature—has already changed." Write a brief essay in which you define the term "nature." You may cite McKibben and others from this chapter, or you may base your definition entirely upon your own observations.

14. In what ways do you think the planet is "utterly different now" from how it was ten or fifteen years ago? Write a well-developed paragraph in which you argue that the world is or is not dramatically different from past years. Be sure to cite the text and your own observations in order to illustrate your ideas.

15. McKibben writes of the enjoyment he and his wife receive from swimming across a nearby lake, but he says that when people bring boats to the lake, it is "utterly different," implying that the difference is negative. Is McKibben denying others the pleasures he wants for himself? Write a few paragraphs

analyzing McKibben's essay and arguing whether or not he is truly concerned about the environment or simply unwilling to share his pleasure in nature.

VOCABULARY DEVELOPMENT

16. Choose any topic and mimic McKibben's style for one paragraph, substituting nouns for nouns, verbs for verbs, and modifiers for modifiers. Then, answer the following questions: How readable is your paragraph? What about McKibben's style makes it easy or difficult to read?

GROUP ACTIVITIES

17. Using the Internet, search for "nature" or "environment." Since these are broad terms, you will have many results. Follow at least three links, taking notes on what you find. Then, as a group write a paragraph concluding how nature is defined online.

18. Discuss places you have visited, and make notes of the changes those places have undergone over the years. Then, decide whether or not those changes are positive or negative. Share your results with the class in an open-forum setting.

SYNTHESIS QUESTIONS

1. Both Alice Walker and Edward Abbey express strong views toward elements of the environment. Using their essays in this text as a basis for argument, write a few paragraphs or an essay in which you contrast these two writers in order to determine what you think their most significant similarity or difference is. Would they be on the same side in a fight to save the environment? Would they think so? Be sure to cite the texts in order to illustrate your arguments clearly and specifically.

2. Civility experts have concluded that people who show civility toward the environment are more likely to act politely in other situations. What do you think? Write a well-developed paragraph or essay in which you discuss the correlation between treating the earth with respect and treating your fellow humans with respect. Quote from at least three readings in this chapter in order to clarify and support your views.

3. Edward Abbey writes that "nothing at all" is what matters to him in the desert, and Bill McKibben claims that the "meaning" of nature has changed. Citing at least three writers from this chapter, write your own definition of "wilderness," making sure your attitude toward wilderness is clear in your definition.

4. Alice Walker writes that it is in animals' nature "to express themselves," but that "they are ignored." Edward Abbey, however, warns us to stay away from the desert—and its animals—in order to preserve it. Are the desert animals, or other animals in the wild, best "ignored" in the sense that Walker writes about? Write a few paragraphs in which you argue how much contact people should have with animals, for the animals' own good. Make sure you qualify the con-

ditions under which people communicate with animals—whether they are in the wild or in captivity, for example—and cite these two writers and your own experiences for support.

5. Charles Krauthammer writes that the "aesthetic good" of nature must be sacrificed to more fundamental goods, while Bill McKibben writes that the "idea" of nature has become extinct as a result of humans using nature for their pleasure. Who is right? Write a well-developed paragraph in which you decide whether or not we should preserve nature or use nature as a natural resource. Be sure to cite both writers and your own observations in order to illustrate your ideas.

6. In his essay, "Unchopping a Tree," W.S. Merwin writes that in replacing parts of the tree to their original places, "There is a certain beauty. . . . You will wonder to what extent it should be described as natural, to what extent man-made." Leila Kysar, on the other hand, argues that clear-cut forests have higher levels of aesthetic value since they have been "cleared" of old, dead trees. Which is more beautiful, the natural or the man-made forest? Write at least three well-developed paragraphs in which you argue that one type of forest is more aesthetically pleasing than another. Be sure to define your idea of beauty, and cite at least three writers from this chapter to clarify your ideas.

7. Edward Abbey offers etiquette tips for visiting the desert. Do other "natural" places require rules as well? Write a brief essay in which you outline "etiquette tips" for visiting some unspoiled place, explaining why such rules are important to follow. Be sure to cite at least three writers from this chapter in explaining your views.

8. How much do we value nature? Write a few paragraphs or an essay in which you discuss how important the wilderness is to people today. Cite at least three writers from this chapter, and feel free to interview people, in order to support your position.

9. Alice Walker and W.S. Merwin describe an animal and a tree, respectively, that are seemingly unalterably harmed by humans. Should these two entities—animals and plants—receive the same consideration under the law? Write a few paragraphs in which you explain whether or not all living creatures deserve the same type of treatment, and why. Be sure to use examples from at least three writers from this chapter as well as illustrations from your life.

DOONESBURY © 2001 G.B. Trudeau. Reprinted with permission of UNIVERSAL PRESS SYNDICATE. All rights reserved.

> **"**Ultimately, history will not judge [Michael] Jordan's greatness by his vicious slam dunks or clever ad campaigns. Rather it will judge him as a father and a son, and as a man, a Black man—one of the best we've ever had.**"**
>
> **— Nelson George**
> *Rare Jordan*

> **"**We need to make heroes out of people who have shown the courage not to be rich, like my young friend who left Wall Street to become an English teacher, simply because he loves books more than he loves money.**"**
>
> **— Elizabeth Austin**

"... the figure of the serial killer—defined, roughly, as one who commits serial individual murders, usually of strangers, over a period of time, to achieve sexual gratification and/or a sensation of power over others—is ubiquitous, and by now, wondering why that should be the case seems almost beside the point."

— Terrence Rafferty

"The hero ... overcomes the ordinary and attains greatness by serving some great good."

— George Roche

"We hear about constitutional rights, free speech, and the free press. Every time I hear these words I say to myself, "That man is a Red, that man is a Communist. You never hear a real American talk like that."

— Frank Hague
New York World-Telegram, 1938

Chapter 8: Civility in Our Heroes

Readings:

Argument Pair:

Websites

www.theory.org.uk/
　ctr-role.htm

This site offers full text articles on many different types of role models, both traditional and nontraditional.

www.sikids.com/

The youth-oriented version of *Sports Illustrated*, the Website for *Sports Illustrated for Kids* offers articles generally praising good role models in sports and criticizing those showing poor sportsmanship.

Introduction

We love to be thrilled—by the athlete who slams the basketball through the hoop over the heads of his opponents with unbridled ferocity, by the steamy sexpot who titillates our senses as she giggles her way toward her ends, or by the wealthy financier who uses his millions to succeed in business and, sometimes, in love. Excitement fuels our fantasies, and we eagerly follow the exploits of exciting people in order to learn how the "rich and famous" live.

We also love winners, people who are the best at what they do time and time again. But is just being a thriller or a winner enough to make someone a hero? The recent popularity of such violent figures as "Unabomber" Ted Kaczynski and serial killer and cannibal Jeffrey Dahmer attests to our fascination with the macabre, even if we claim to be disturbed by such dark figures. Further, flamboyant athletes and slick politicians have caught our attention even as we "tsk tsk" their actions. The idea of heroism seems to be clouded, if not lost, in a haze of famous figures.

Chapter 8, "Civility in Our Heroes," seeks to identify individuals who are genuine heroes, as well as those who simply entertain us. Further, writers in this chapter raise questions of what we value in others, as well as what we will tolerate from those we admire in order to determine just what Americans deem necessary for heroism.

Why Homer's My Hero

The All-American family shouldn't have to wear Gucci to feel good

Elizabeth Austin

Elizabeth Austin is a Chicago writer who focuses often on health and behavior issues. Claiming that "average" people with "average" incomes are no longer available in entertainment as American role models, Austin questions the role money plays in determining who our heroes are and seeks to explain the reasons for our changing values in "Why Homer's My Hero."

Pre-reading Questions

Freewrite for five to ten minutes in response to the following questions: Who in contemporary society, if anyone, do you admire? What about this person, specifically, do you find admirable? Why? How closely do you pattern your life after people you see on television or in the movies? Explain.

Vocabulary Preview

Vocabulary Words:
- flaunt
- conscientious
- nemesis
- spartan
- sumptuous
- conundrum
- frugal
- sardonic
- jaundiced
- inundated
- ingenuity
- squander

Look up the words above and use them in sentences of varying structure and length. Then, write a brief analysis of your sentences: which words were easiest, and most difficult, to put into context? Why?

---

1 WHO WANTS TO BE A MILLIONAIRE? You do. We all do. Don't we? So what's wrong with that? This country's on an unprecedented economic roll. Why not flaunt it? And if I don't like the glorification of wealth, why don't I just roll up the newspaper, turn off the television, and ignore it?

2 I try. Really, I try.

3 I roll my eyes in moral superiority when I read about nouveau riche mummies and daddies draping their tots in $400 cashmere coats by designer Sonia Rykiel. I shudder at the furnishings and upkeep costs of those sprawling new McMansions cropping up down the block. I have long, earnest talks with my two young daughters about integrity, about privilege, about following your heart instead of filling your wallet.

4 But sometimes in the middle of the night, I lie awake doing endless math problems: Three years until college, minus the home equity loan, divided by my failing desktop computer, added to our looming IRS bill, multiplied by the broken air conditioner on the minivan. In those dark hours, when those grim equations encircle my pillow, I come up with only one response—I've been a stupid, irresponsible fool. What's

wrong with me? Why didn't I invest in the market in 1982? How are my children going to get through college without a debt load that will follow them into middle age? Why didn't I ever get a real job, with stock options? If I'm so smart, why am I not rich?

5   These financial nightstalkers visit my friends, too. By day, they're bright, hardworking, talented people, with nice homes, reliable cars, and generally happy families. But when, insomniac, they hear the downstairs clock strike two and three, they feel like they're the only chumps in America who don't have a comfortable million or two stashed away in a high-yield mutual fund. Half-envyingly, I read about young, earnest foreign service officers who are being plucked from the financial obscurity of the State Department by golden claws of Goldman Sachs. I feel a bittersweet pang when my seven-year-old eagerly describes her planned career as a marine archaeologist; when she's a little older, will she find more romance in day-trading? I hope she'll have the courage to pursue a life and career that offers satisfactions beyond a fat paycheck. But I don't know. It's so easy for her to turn on the television, or pick up a magazine and lose herself in those seductively portrayed trappings of wealth that make our home seem scruffy by comparison. Maybe some day she'll look at me and see one of life's also-rans, a mere scribe who lacked the ambition to sashay downtown and commandeer one of those six-figure public relations gigs.

MOM, DAD, AND MONEY MAGAZINE

6   Take financial advisor Suze Orman's breathtaking title: The Courage to Be Rich. What does that make the rest of us? Cowards? (In case you missed it, Orman reveals that "money is attracted to people who are strong and powerful, respectful of it, and open to receiving it." Thanks. That explains a lot.) Would-be financial heroes can receive Orman's gospel courtesy of our high-minded friends at PBS, which has starred the financial guru in two hour-long specials. Stay tuned for next season's BBC import: "Upstairs, Further Upstairs."

7   Our thinking has become so distorted that being comfortably middle-class now feels like the next step to actual poverty. In one recent survey on "Money and the American Family," the AARP found that one in three adults believes a family of four with an income under $50,000 is poor—and one in five considered an annual income of $200,000 as the bare minimum required for wealth.

8   We don't want all this dough for ourselves, of course. It's the kids we're thinking about. Leaf through the ads in Money magazine and you'll find a whole nursery full of dimpled youngsters. The little sweetheart dancing in her socks on Daddy's big shoes is fronting for Chase Vista Funds, while the youngster out sailing his toy boat works for American Century Investment Management. A sleepy newborn touts Barclays Global Investors. An intent little fisherman helps the Northern Fund trawl for new customers. (The only discordant adult note in this lullabye is struck by the handsome couple who've hit the sheets for E*Trade. Their post-coital bliss is captioned: "Imagine rolling over and saying, 'That was better than investing.'")

9   The ads shamelessly target worried, conscientious parents. And boy, do they have our number. One ad, for MetLife Financial Service, shows a father joyously lifting his little son high up in the air, while the caption muses: "I want to make sure they never have to carry me." A similar note is sounded by the TV commercial for Scudder Invest-

ments: "What if your kid gets into Harvard? What if your mother needs long-term care? What if they happen at the same time?" The worst-case scenario is illustrated by one grim little ad for Conseco Life Insurance that asks: "How do you plan on providing for your family after you pass away?" The grave of the improvident parent is marked by a tombstone reading "Your ad here."

10   But let's be honest. We're not planning to hand all of our millions (real or coveted) straight to the kids. We're bullish on the way we define the necessities of life. In 1982, the average new home sold for $84,000, according to the National Association of Home Builders. Last year, the average sale price was $196,000. Much of that increase was due to inflation—of the house. In 1982, the average buyer got 1,710 square feet; last year, the average size of a new home was 2,225 square feet. And 17 percent of the 1.31 million new homes built last year boasted 3,000 square feet or more.

11   We're simply unwilling to make do with the charming bungalows and modest Cape Cods our parents once cherished. As proof, look at the growing number of teardowns— unpretentious to moderately swanky homes in desirable older communities that have been demolished to make room for oversized manses whose most prominent architectural feature is the gaping maw of a four-car garage. The NAHB estimates that 100,000 of these so-called replacement homes went up nationwide last year. In Hinsdale, an elegant, 120-year-old Chicago suburb, almost 17 percent of its vintage housing stock has been knocked down over the past decade and a half. In the Seattle area, the bumper crop of mansionless technomillionaires led to a reported 4,000 teardowns last year alone. Delta Airlines chair Gerald Grinstein paid $8 million for Bill Gates' old house, a 60-year-old estate on the shores of Lake Washington—then promptly bulldozed it to the ground for a new $3 million structure.

MR. BLANDINGS

12   It's not surprising that an $8 million house is no longer enough to satisfy the housing needs of the super-rich. We've spent the last 20 years being told that the best isn't nearly good enough. Look at the way Hollywood sequels insist on giving all their characters an upgrade to first class. In the 1948 classic, Mr. Blandings Builds His Dream House, Cary Grant played a Manhattan ad man making a very comfortable $15,000 a year. Carried away by the sylvan charm of the Connecticut countryside, he ends up sinking $38,000 into a nice, roomy, Colonial-flavored home. The "Blandings house" (which was actually constructed for the film) proved so pretty and so practical that the architectural plans were sold publicly, and 70-some copies of the three-bedroom house were built across the country. But when Hollywood revisited the Blandings saga with The Money Pit in 1986, our hero was suddenly a hotshot entertainment lawyer, and the house was a huge mansion on Long Island's North Shore.

13   Or consider the more recent bracket shift imposed on another favorite film, The Shop Around the Corner. In director Ernst Lubitsch's hands, it was the story of two Budapest shop clerks living in furnished rooms, workplace rivals who unwittingly become anonymous pen pals and slowly discover that they're soulmates. At the movie's end, star Jimmy Stewart gets a promotion to store manager—and the hand of pretty coworker Margaret Sullivan. He doesn't win the Hungarian lottery, or find out she's an heir to the Hapsburgs; he just winds up with a few extra coins and a

smart, spunky, angel-faced little wife. Back in 1940, that was enough to qualify as a happy ending.

14   But in the 1998 update, You've Got Mail, director Nora Ephron transforms the two high-minded clerks into Meg Ryan, owner of a small children's bookstore on the Upper West Side, and Tom Hanks, heir to a huge chain of megabookstores. They're hardly colleagues. In fact, he eventually succeeds in driving her out of business. But don't worry. Thanks apparently to some supremely benevolent ATM, Meg manages to keep her chic, sunny apartment and maintain her Starbucks habit. And when her endearing erstwhile nemesis comes courting, there's never any doubt that she'll yield. After all, he's rich and stylish, and magnificence is the only Aristotelian virtue the movies really appreciate. (Justice, courage, and temperance aren't nearly so photogenic.) Since Hanks has a nice fat checkbook in the pocket of his Armani pants, he is, by definition, lovable. So as the music swells and the closing credits roll, it's clear they'll soon be joyously inking a prenup. The financial bliss doesn't stop there. Jean Stapleton, the elderly bookkeeper who's left unemployed by the bookshop's demise, has no worries; she bought Intel at six. So You've Got Mail provides lots of happy endings—millions of 'em.

15   On the small screen, producers like to shower their characters with all the trappings of affluence, even when the gap between their wages and their lifestyles is wide enough to spark an IRS audit. In "Friends," a personal shopper and her sous-chef roommate manage to maintain a funky, charmingly decorated two-bedroom apartment in downtown New York. And the young marrieds in "Mad About You"—a mid-level publicist and a documentary filmmaker—have snagged a spacious flat filled with genuine Stickley furniture. When we're shown life among the lowly (those with, say, less than $150,000 annually) they're appalling, whether they're the fictional characters in "Roseanne" or "Married with Children" or the real-life working-class people who grace the stages of Jerry Springer and Queen Latifah's talk shows.

16   It's instructive to spend an evening tuned to Nick at Nite, a cable channel dedicated to reruns of 1960s sitcoms. In watching a marathon presentation of "The Andy Griffith Show," I was struck by the show's warmhearted depiction of everyday life. Andy Taylor, the town sheriff, lives in a little house with his son and maiden aunt; he doesn't even own a lawnmower. His best friends are a barber shop owner, a car mechanic, and his own deputy, and his girlfriend is an underpaid schoolteacher. By today's standards, they're barely middle-class. Yet Andy is a strong, proud, dignified, and well-respected man.

17   Or take the "Dick Van Dyke Show." Rob Petrie is a college-educated man with a good job as head writer for a hit comedy show. But he lives in an ordinary suburban home, and Laura is clearly keeping house on a comfortable but limited budget. In Watching TV: Four Decades of American Television, Harry Castleman and Walter J. Podrazik note that the show presented "a world not very different from the one most [white middle-class] viewers faced. Rob and Laura lived in a real middle-class town in which real people commuted to and from jobs." Even now, I hear echoes of my own household concerns in the script—as when a tearful Laura confronts spendthrift Rob about his insistence on picking up the check every time they go out with friends. "Don't you want our son to go to college?" she wails. Thank God Laura never had to leaf through the ads in Money magazine; she'd have had a nervous breakdown.

18   OK. It's true that the "Dick Van Dyke Show" was not a documentary—just as most Depression-era moviegoers did not share in Carole Lombard's perplexing struggle to find the right butler. The point is that we once had a wider, more realistic array of aspirational models, both in the media and in real life.

AARON SPELLING AND THE BIG BACK END

19   For this, I partly blame color television. In black and white, a spartan interior can look elegant, while a cluttered room seems comfy and cozy. In living color, however, spare is drab, and homey is tacky. The economics of television also play a major role. When producers such as Aaron Spelling dazzle viewers with sumptuous sets and extravagant costumes, they're actually making a sharp business decision. If you distract the audience with high-priced eye candy, they may not notice the flatness of the script. And while that $8,000 designer dress or $15,000 Florentine brocade sofa may boost a show's initial cost, neither is likely to demand back-end participation when the series moves into international syndication.

20   The media landscape has changed in other ways, as well. Back when Preston Sturges sent Joel McCrea slumming through Sullivan's Travels, the reading public got a wide-angle view of the world through general-interest publications such as *Life* and *Collier's*. Now, magazines are niche-marketed, and the upscale readers of *Money* simply aren't interested in hearing how the other 80 percent lives. It's hard to imagine advertisers vying for space on the pages of *Limited Aspirations Monthly*.

21   In fairness, we can't blame the media alone for the perpetual ratcheting-up of our desires. Movies and television are only magic mirrors that reflect and refocus our own visions. As David Brooks explains in Bobos in Paradise: The New Upper Class and How They Got There, the rise of the educated class boosted the stakes in the status game. The Bobos (bourgeois bohemians) define themselves by their rarefied consumption. The '50s-era host who offered a choice of "red" or "white" has been replaced by an amateur sommelier who delights in dazzling his guests with an array of cabernets, syrahs, barberas, and pinots both noir and gris. These high-end consumers would be mortally offended by any suggestion that they've gone over the top. And since they've become the nation's tastemakers, the rest of us nod wistfully and wish we had extensive wine cellars too.

22   The conundrum is how to cover the wealthy and celebrated without celebrating wealth itself, how to keep us informed about life at the top of the economic food chain without setting up a feedback loop of unlimited envy. A glitzy little story is fun once in a while, like sprinkles on an ice cream cone. But a steady diet of them leaves us fretful and discontented, forever dissatisfied with our own portion of abundance. We find ourselves nodding in agreement with the young mother, quoted in the Post's Style section, who complains: "Being frugal is not what everyone talks about when you go out. It's what did you buy, how much did you pay, and do they have any left?"

23   Another major factor in our perverted view of the American Dream is the worldly success of the journalists who write all these articles. Reporters used to be working-class stiffs who would have snorted at the thought of paying someone $65 an hour to clean out your closets. (Imagine Mike Royko heading down to Pottery Barn to pick up an extra lingerie chest.) Now, a New York Times reporter with two years' experience pulls down a minimum of $1,360 week, according to Newspaper Guild figures.

24   As journalists have moved up the economic food-chain, they've lost their knee-jerk identification with the values and realities of working-class life. Instead of casting a sardonic glance through the window that divides the wealthy from the rest of us, many reporters now leave damp noseprints on the glass ceiling. Take, for example, the Post's appreciation of the late philanthropist Paul Mellon. By any measure, Mellon was a most admirable billionaire. (You've got to love a guy who tells a high-school graduating class: "What this country needs is a good five-cent reverie.") But to underscore Mellon's lack of affectation, his appreciator solemnly intones: "His jet wasn't new."

25   Warmer-hearted writers try to give the un-rich the sympathy they deserve. One 1996 newspaper story still burns in my memory. In *The New York Times'* award-winning series, "The Downsizing of America," we read the tragic tale of a middle-aged man who lost his high-powered job. He was left with only a $300,000 savings account, a $130,000 severance check, an aging Mercedes, and a roomy ranch house with a pool in the San Fernando Valley. The author solemnly detailed how the emotionally wounded former exec was trying to make ends meet on his wife's $30,000 salary, plus the $25,000 or so he earned in temporary jobs. Their daughters, who lived at home, made about $40,000 between them, but didn't contribute to the household expenses.

26   Now look. I've been there. My dad and my husband have both lost good jobs to recession and downsizing. I know first hand how wounding un- or underemployment can be to a man whose self-esteem rests on his ability to provide for his family. But when I read the Times story, I see a family of four living on a combined income of roughly $95,000, plus almost half a million in savings. An American Tragedy? Please.

UP—AND UP AND UP

27   It's hard to find any hint that regular middle-class life might be pleasant, honorable, or desirable. Part of this, I think, stems from all those baby boomers who used to stand around college quads and denounce middle-class morality and bourgeois standards. Now, seeing them in middle age, we realize they were quite sincere in rejecting the middle class; they all really wanted to be rich.

28   Maybe I have an unusual take on this. I'm an unabashed fan of the bourgeoisie. Both my parents grew up in working-class families in Mayberry-sized towns. While I have a wholehearted respect for my grandparents' thrift and their lifelong work ethic, I also know how dowdy, constricting, and culturally barren their world could be. I have absolutely no romantic notions about real life in the exit lane. Yet having watched my grandparents lead long, productive, satisfying lives without ever making a single purchase at Crate and Barrel, I'm sure that you don't need a multimillion dollar bank account to bring up successful, happy children and lead a contented, honorable life. Whenever I cast a jaundiced eye on my serviceable but uninspiring dining room rug, or gaze speculatively at our ripe-for-renovation bathroom, I can hear my grandmother's voice scolding gently in my ear, "Much wants more."

29   Look. I don't want to be rich. I am plumb delighted to live in a pretty nice house in a pretty nice suburb. And I don't want to lead a simpler life; I've worked too hard to amass this modest level of complexity, thank you very much. I just want to carry

on in my little niche without feeling like America's biggest idiot every time I take an unwilling glance at my svelte bank account. And I'd like to hear a few voices talking about what's right with the choices I've made. Because there are a lot of people who have made the same choices, and it's shameful that so many of us are staying awake at night wishing we could revise our lives. Even worse, our children are inundated by media messages whispering that anyone who isn't rich is a loser—and that includes Mom and Dad.

30   It's darkly ironic that our rejection of homespun virtues and our worship of the new affluence are pushing some poor souls to the brink of poverty. Some months ago, the New Yorker ran a sad little story by a young writer named Meghan Daum. In it, she confessed that she'd based her college choices on the alma maters of the privileged brides featured on the Times wedding pages: "Columbia rather than NYU, Wisconsin rather than Texas, Yale rather than Harvard, Vassar rather than Smith." After graduating (from Vassar) she spent seven years in New York pursuing her vision of life as an urban sophisticate—a vision distilled over a couple decades of scrutinizing style sections, fashion magazines, movie sets, and similar avatars of affluence.

31   Wryly, Daum explained how she managed to spend herself into $75,000 of debt by indulging in such stylish necessities as fresh flowers, Starbucks coffee, and pricey white wine—all easily affordable items, if you happen to be a bookstore owner named Meg Ryan or a waitress on "Friends." Admittedly, Daum's tale of self-inflicted financial woe gave some readers a severe case of the yips. But I think there's something desperately wrong when a smart, pretty, funny, talented young woman feels compelled to court financial ruin in the name of stylish living.

32   It's time to demand a more attractive group of role models and a more attainable definition of style and success, that reflect an authentic American mix of taste and ingenuity. We don't need *The New York Times'* helpful articles explaining how to train our butlers, or fire our personal trainers. What we desperately require are some fresh new thoughts on how to leaven our overworked daily lives with some healthy doses of affordable elegance and achievable chic. We need to make heroes out of people who have shown the courage not to be rich, like my young friend who left Wall Street to become an English teacher, simply because he loves books more than he loves money.

33   We need a few national cheerleaders for ordinary life. Whenever I feel overwhelmed with my nagging financial anxieties, I pull out my worn copy of Jean Kerr's *Please Don't Eat the Daisies,* a collection of warm-hearted, witty essays about middle-class suburban family life. Published the year before I was born, it describes the challenges and pleasures of my life in a way that I can't find anywhere in the current media. If a glance through the real estate section leaves me dissatisfied with my four-bedroom, 1.5 bath, 1,600 square-foot fixer-upper, I can restore my sense of perspective with Kerr's law of real estate: "All the houses you can afford to buy are depressing."

34   I realize that our reach has always exceeded our grasp. The principle that anyone can become a millionaire is a basic part of the American character; we prefer not to notice that, while everybody theoretically can make a fortune, most of us don't. Nevertheless, I think there's something terribly amiss when the former pinnacle of the American

dream is redefined as the minimum standard. We need to celebrate the entire journey, not just a destination that most of us will never reach.

35   Right now, the only place I see anything vaguely resembling my own life is on "The Simpsons." Sure, Homer's an idiot and Bart's a brat. But in the Simpsons' Springfield, I see people who go to work, go to church, go to the grocery, attend school plays, take occasional family vacations to Disney World, and generally enjoy the discreet charms of middle-class existence. I love Marge's heartfelt belief that money can't buy happiness, and little Lisa's marrow-deep distrust of corporate America. Even though Homer is always cooking up some harebrained get-rich-quick scheme, he's never particularly distressed when they don't pan out. You never hear Marge complain about the millions her husband and children have managed to accumulate and squander within the limits of a 22-minute TV episode. Despite their wacky adventures, they're a mostly happy, mostly contented, middle-class family much like my own—except, of course, that we exist in three dimensions.

36   We need more shows like "The Simpsons" (preferably starring characters that don't have primary-colored skins.) We need to hear what's right about middle-class life. Because markets fall. Businesses falter. Booms go bust. And when adversity comes, as it inevitably will, we'll need a value system that doesn't blame the victim for lacking the courage to be rich. We shouldn't kick ourselves for failing to amass the $30 million that one of my friends says you need to be "bulletproof." When those canny marketers at Scudder Investments ask what we'll do if we find ourselves facing college tuition payments and nursing home bills, we need to answer boldly: "We'll think of something. We'll have faith. We'll all work together, and we'll get by."

37   Oh, how incredibly middle class.

POST-READING QUESTIONS

CONTENT

1. What does Austin identify as a primary goal of Americans today? How does she feel about this goal?

2. Why, according to Austin, do people claim they want wealth?

3. Why does Austin say people really do want wealth?

4. What role does the entertainment industry play in causing people to want more money?

5. What examples does Austin give to show how entertainment has changed to emphasize the importance of wealth?

6. Why, according to Austin, do entertainment producers emphasize material aspects of their shows?

7. What effect does "a steady diet" of "glitzy" entertainment have on viewers? What do you think?

8. Why does Austin say we need to live affordably, and be happy about it?

9. What television show does Austin say offers realistic lifestyles? What do you think?

STYLE AND STRUCTURE

10. What is Austin's point? Restate her main idea in your own words.

11. What sub-arguments does Austin include in her essay? Which of these do you think is most crucial to the development of her main idea?

12. What examples does Austin use to illustrate her main ideas? To what extent are they effective?

13. What conclusions can you draw about Austin's target audience? Are you part of her audience? How can you tell?

14. What role does humor play in helping Austin communicate her ideas? Cite some passages you find particularly indicative of her humor.

15. Is Austin convincing? Why or why not?

CRITICAL THINKING AND ANALYSIS

DISCUSSION QUESTIONS

16. What qualities in general do you think people most admire in others? How closely are these traits linked to money? Explain.

17. How accurate is Austin's statement that "we once had a wider, more realistic array of aspirational models, both in the media and in real life"? Give examples from contemporary entertainment and your own lives.

WRITING ASSIGNMENTS

18. Austin claims that "Movies and television are only magic mirrors that reflect and refocus our own visions." What do you think? Write a well-developed paragraph or short essay in which you explain whether the media causes people to value materialistic ideals or whether the media simply reflects what people already value. Be sure to cite Austin's essay and your own observations in order to illustrate your ideas.

19. Austin writes that "It's hard to find any hint that regular middle-class life might be pleasant, honorable, or desirable." Do you agree? Write a few paragraphs in which you agree or disagree with Austin's claim that evidence of a pleasing middle-class life is hard to come by, citing contemporary entertainment and trends for support.

20. Do you think Americans have become more materialistic? Austin writes that "there's something terribly amiss when the former pinnacle of the American dream is redefined as the minimum standard." Write at least one well-developed paragraph in which you argue that Americans are or are not becoming more materialistic. Cite Austin's essay and your own experiences for support.

VOCABULARY DEVELOPMENT

21. What words contribute most effectively to Austin's tone? Skim her article and choose at least seven words *not* on the Vocabulary Preview list that you think

best reveal Austin's attitude toward her subject. Then, write a few sentences explaining why you chose the words you chose.

GROUP ACTIVITIES

22. Make a list of all the characters you admire on television or in the movies. Then, write down the characteristics that make these people admirable to you. What role does money play in terms of how you feel about them? Discuss the effects of income on these characters' style, humor, and appeal.

23. First, write down individually what qualities you think a contemporary "hero" or "role model" has. Then, share your results with the group. Where, if anywhere, do finances come in? Can a person be someone we want to emulate even if he/she is poor? Explain and share your results with the class.

Heroine Worship: The Age of the Female Icon

Holly Brubach

Holly Brubach is the style editor for the *New York Times Sunday Magazine,* in which this article first appeared in 1996, and she has authored *Girlfriend: Men, Women, and Drag* and *A Dedicated Follower of Fashion.* Claiming that women today have so many varied role models that emulating just one is "arbitrary and limiting," Brubach argues that such women provide heroines after which young girls can model themselves, as well as casting "a longer shadow" upon the world.

Pre-reading Questions

Freewrite for five to ten minutes in response to the following questions:
Who, if anyone, are some famous women you admire? What about these women is admirable? Are the qualities that make women "heroic" the same as the qualities that make men "heroic"? Explain.

Vocabulary Preview

Vocabulary Words:
- pantheon
- contemporaneous
- ubiquitous
- eminently
- inculcated
- encompass
- proliferation
- voyeurs
- relinquish
- allegorical

Look up each of the words above and, choosing at least five of the words, write a few sentences on women role models in the 21st century. Which words are easiest to employ? Write a sentence or two explaining why some words are easier than others to use in your own writing.

1 It's the 90's, and the pantheon we've built to house the women in our minds is getting crowded. Elizabeth Taylor, Eleanor Roosevelt, Oprah Winfrey, Alanis Morissette, Indira Ghandi, Claudia Schiffer, Coco Chanel, Doris Day, Aretha Franklin, Jackie Onassis, Rosa Parks—they're all there, the dead and the living side by side, contemporaneous in our imaginations. On television and in the movies, in advertising and magazines, their images are scattered across the landscape of our everyday lives. Their presence is sometimes decorative, sometimes uplifting, occasionally infuriating. The criteria for appointment to this ad hoc hall of fame that takes up so much space in our thoughts and in our culture may at first glance appear to be utterly random. In fact, irrespective of their achievements, most of these women have been apotheosized primarily on the basis of their ability to appeal to our fantasies.

2 An icon is a human sound bite, an individual reduced to a name, a face and an idea: Dale Evans, the compassionate cowgirl. In some cases, just the name and an idea suffice. Few people would recognize Helen Keller in a photograph, but her name has

become synonymous with being blind and deaf to such an extent that she has inspired an entire category of jokes. Greta Garbo has gone down in collective memory as an exalted enigma with a slogan about being alone. Asking a man if that's a gun in his pocket is all it takes to invoke Mae West. Catherine Deneuve's face, pictured on a stamp, is the emblem of France. Virginia Woolf has her own T-shirt. Naomi Campbell has her own doll. Celebrity being the engine that drives our culture, these women have been taken up by the media and made famous, packaged as commodities and marketed to a public eager for novelty and easily bored. . . .

3   Our icons are by no means exclusively female, but the male ones are perhaps less ubiquitous and more accessible. The pedestals we put them on are lower; the service they are called on to perform is somewhat different.

4   Like women, men presumably look to icons for tips that they can take away and apply to their lives. The men who are elevated to the status of icons are the ones who are eminently cool, whose moves the average guy can steal. They do not prompt a fit of introspection (much less of self-recrimination), as female icons often do in women. What a male icon inspires in other men is not so much the desire to *be* him as the desire to be accepted by him—to be buddies, to shoot pool together, to go drinking. I have all this on good authority from a man of my acquaintance who insists that, though regular guys may envy, say, Robert Redford for his ability to knock women dead, what they're thinking as they watch him in a movie is not "Hey, I wonder if I have what it takes to do that, too," but "I wonder if Redford would like to hang out with me."

5   Whereas women may look at an icon like Raquel Welch, whose appeal is clearly to the male half of humanity, and ask themselves, "If that's what's required to appeal to a man, have I got it, or can I get it?"(The thought of hanging out with Welch—going shopping together or talking about boyfriends—would, I think it's safe to say, never cross most women's minds.)

6   An entire industry, called fashion, has grown up around the business of convincing women that they need to remake themselves in someone else's image: makeup and clothes and other products are presented not as alterations but as improvements. The notion of appearance and personality as a project to be undertaken is inculcated early on. A man may choose to ignore certain male icons; a woman has no such luxury where the great majority of female icons are concerned. She must come to terms with them, defining herself in relation to them—emulating some, rejecting others. In certain cases, a single icon may exist for her as both an example and a reproach.

7   Our male icons are simply the latest entries in a tradition of long standing, broad enough in any given era to encompass any number of prominent men. But the current array of female icons is a rare phenomenon, the outgrowth of aspirations many of which date back no more than 100 years.

8   What were the images of women that informed the life of a girl growing up 200 years ago? It's hard for us to imagine the world before it was wallpapered with ads, before it was inundated with all the visual "information" that comes our way in the course of an average day and competes with real people and events for our attention. There were no magazines, no photographs. In church, a girl would have seen renderings of the

Virgin Mary and the saints. She may have encountered portraits of royalty, whose station, unless she'd been born an aristocrat, must have seemed even more unattainable
than that of the saints. There were picturesque genre paintings depicting peasants and
chambermaids, to be seen at the public salons, if anyone thought to bring a girl to
them. But the most ambitious artists concentrated on pagan goddesses and mythological women, who, being Olympian, inhabited a plane so lofty that they were presumably immune to quotidian concerns. History and fiction, for the girl who had access to
them, contained tales of women whose lives had been somewhat more enterprising
and action-packed than those of the women she saw around her, but her knowledge of
most women's exploits in her own time would have been limited to hearsay: a woman
had written a novel, a woman had played hostess to one of the greatest philosophers of
the age and discussed ideas with him, a woman had disguised herself as a man and
gone to war. Most likely, a girl would have modeled herself on a female relative, or on
a woman in her community. The great beauty who set the standard by which others
were measured would have been the one in their midst—the prettiest girl in town,
whose fame was local.

9   Nineteenth-century icons like Sarah Bernhardt and George Sand would have imparted no more in the way of inspiration; their careers were predicated on their talents,
which had been bestowed by God. It was Florence Nightingale who finally provided an
example that was practicable, one to which well-born girls could aspire, and hundreds
of women followed her into nursing.

10   Today, the images of women confronting a girl growing up in our culture are far
more diverse, though not all of them can be interpreted as signs of progress. A woman
who in former times might have served as the model for some painter's rendering of
one or another pagan goddess is now deployed to sell us cars and soap. The great
beauty has been chosen from an international field of contenders. At the movies, we
see the stories of fictional women brought to life by real actresses whose own lives
have become the stuff of fiction. In the news, we read about women running countries,
directing corporations and venturing into outer space.

11   The conditions that in our century have made possible this proliferation of female icons were of course brought on by the convergence of advances in women's
rights and the growth of the media into an industry. As women accomplished the unprecedented, the press took them up and made them famous, trafficking in their accomplishments, their opinions, their fates. If, compared with the male icons of our
time, our female icons seem to loom larger in our culture and to cast a longer shadow,
perhaps it's because in so many cases their stories have had the urgency of history in
the making.

12   When it comes to looking at women, we're all voyeurs, men and women alike.
Does our urge to study the contours of their flesh and the changes in their faces stem
from some primal longing to be reunited with the body that gave us life? Women have
been the immemorial repository of male fantasies—a lonesome role that many are
nonetheless loath to relinquish, given the power it confers and the oblique satisfaction
it brings. The curiosity and desire inherent in the so-called male gaze, deplored for the
way it has objectified women in art and in films, are matched on women's part by the

need to assess our own potential to be found beautiful and by the pleasure in putting ourselves in the position of the woman being admired.

13　　Our contemporary images of women are descended from a centuries-old tradition and, inevitably, they are seen in its light. Women have often been universalized, made allegorical. The figure who represents Liberty, or Justice, to say nothing of Lust or Wrath, is a woman, not a man—a tradition that persists: there is no Mr. America. The unidentified woman in innumerable paintings—landscapes, genre scenes, mythological scenes—transcends her circumstances and becomes Woman. It's the particular that is customarily celebrated in men, and the general in woman. Even our collective notions of beauty reflect this: a man's idiosyncrasies enhance his looks; a woman's detract from hers.

14　　"I'm every woman, it's all in me," Chaka Khan sings, and the chords in the bass modulate optimistically upward, in a surge of possibility. Not all that long ago, the notion that any woman could be every women would have been dismissed as blatantly absurd, but to our minds it makes evident sense, in keeping with the logic that we can be anything we want to be—the cardinal rule of the human-potential movement and an assumption that in America today is so widely accepted and dearly held that it might as well be written into the Constitution. Our icons are at this point sufficiently plentiful that to model ourselves on only one of them would seem arbitrary and limiting, when in fact we can take charge in the manner of Katherine Hepburn, strut in the way we learned by watching Tina Turner, flirt in the tradition of Rita Hayworth, grow old with dignity in the style of Georgia O'Keeffe. In the spirit of post-modernism, we piece our selves together, assembling the examples of several women in a single personality—a process that makes for some unprecedented combinations, like Madonna: the siren who lifts weights and becomes a mother. We contemplate the women who have been singled out in our culture and the permutations of femininity they represent. About to move on to the next century, we call on various aspects of them as we reconfigure our lives, deciding which aspects of our selves we want to take with us and which aspects we want to leave behind

POST-READING QUESTIONS

CONTENT

1. What, according to Brubach, do the women she lists in the first paragraph have in common? In what ways, if any, is this quality worthy of admiration?
2. How does Brubach define "icon"?
3. How are male and female icons different? Why is this difference significant?
4. What were the images of women 200 years ago? What impact did these images have on young girls?
5. Why do female icons seem to have a greater, longer lasting impact than male icons, according to Brubach? What do you think?
6. What about women's attitudes shows that progress has been made in terms of how we view and react to female icons?

STYLE AND STRUCTURE

7. What is Brubach's point? Restate her main idea in your own words.

8. What examples does Brubach offer in order to support her main idea? Of these, which do you find most effective? Explain.

9. Who is Brubach's audience? What about her language and examples reveals this audience?

10. What is Brubach's tone? Cite the text for examples that express her tone.

11. Is Brubach convincing? Why or why not?

CRITICAL THINKING AND ANALYSIS

DISCUSSION QUESTIONS

12. How accurate is Brubach when she writes that "What a male icon inspires in other men is . . . the desire to be accepted by him . . . Whereas women may look at an icon . . . and ask themselves, "If that's what's required to appeal to a man, have I got it, or can I get it?" To what extent do you think her statements do or do not reflect the differences in men's and women's attitudes toward their icons?

13. Brubach writes that in the past girls modeled themselves "on a female relative, or on a woman in her community," whereas today, "[women] can be anything [they] want to be . . ." How does the relationship between a girl and her role model today differ from the relationship between a girl and her role model 200 years ago?

WRITING ASSIGNMENTS

14. Brubach claims that women today can "[assemble] the examples of several women in a single personality . . ." How often do you think women do this? Write at least one well-developed paragraph in which you discuss whether or not women do "piece together" parts from different female role models. You may use famous women as your examples, or you may draw from people in your own life.

15. Brubach writes that "An icon is a human sound bite, an individual reduced to a name, a face, and an idea: . . ." What makes a woman an icon? Write a few paragraphs or short essay in which you define the criteria for a woman to be considered such a symbol. Cite Brubach's essay and your own observations in order to illustrate your ideas.

16. Brubach claims that "the images of women confronting a girl growing up in our culture are far more diverse, though not all of them can be interpreted as signs of progress." Write a few paragraphs or a short essay in which you argue the extent to which contemporary images of women do or do not mark signs of progress for women. Cite the text and your own experiences for support.

VOCABULARY DEVELOPMENT

17. Choose one paragraph from Brubach's essay and rewrite it from the point of view of a man. What words or expressions do you need to change in order to reveal your new persona? Share your results with your classmates for feedback.

GROUP ACTIVITIES

18. As a group, perform an online search for at least one prominent woman of your choice. What characteristics are emphasized on the websites you visit? What conclusions can you draw about what people value in their female heroines? Share your results with other groups.

19. Hold a debate with the entire class where you argue that male and female heroes do or do not share similar qualities for greatness. Cite Brubach's essay and contemporary examples in order to strengthen your points.

Bad Sports

Mariah Burton

Author of *The Unburdened Heart: Five Keys to Forgiveness and Freedom,* Mariah Burton Nelson is a freelance writer living in Arlington, Virginia. Claiming that the hero worship of professional athletes praises, even demands, abuse against women, Nelson argues that such violence will end only when people hold the perpetrators accountable for their actions, regardless of their standing within the sports world.

Pre-reading Questions

Freewrite for five to ten minutes in response to the following questions:
In general, what do you think of the way professional athletes behave? How often do you think they are good role models? What is people's attitude toward the character strengths and weaknesses of famous athletes?

Vocabulary Preview

Vocabulary Words:
- stipulation
- alleged
- inextricably
- condoned
- barred
- boisterous
- raunchy
- cliquish
- masculinity
- reveres

Look up each of the words above and use all the words in as few sentences as possible. (Make sure your sentences make sense.) How effective are your sentences compared to how they would be if you only used one vocabulary word per sentence? Explain.

1   O. J. Simpson is not alone.

2   The baseball star Darryl Strawberry has admitted beating his wife and pointing a gun in her face.

3   John Daly, the golfer was arrested at his home for allegedly hurling his wife against a wall, pulling her hair and trashing the house. He pleaded guilty to a misdemeanor harassment charge and was placed on two years' probation with the stipulation that he complete a domestic violence treatment program.

4   The basketball star Moses Malone was accused by his wife of physical and verbal brutality, including death threats. He insisted he never hit her or threatened to kill her but admitted having "moved her out of the way."

5   Wimp Sanderson resigned as the men's basketball coach at the University of Alabama in 1992 after his secretary, Nancy Watts, filed a sex discrimination complaint against him. Ms. Watts, with whom he had had a longtime affair, alleged that he hit her as part of a continuing pattern of physical and sexual abuse, and was awarded $275,000

in a settlement. Mr. Sanderson claimed in court documents that Ms. Watts got her black eye by colliding with his outstretched hand.

6   Juanita Leonard testified in divorce court in 1991 that her husband, Sugar Ray Leonard, often punched her, threw her around and harassed her "physically and mentally in front of the children." He threatened to kill himself with a gun, she said. He threw lamps and broke mirrors.

7   The boxer denied none of this. At a press conference, he admitted having struck his wife with his fists. Yet he justified the behavior by saying that he and Juanita "fought, argued" and "grabbed each other," but that it "was in our house, between us."

8   Spectators also get into the spirit of things. Boston Celtics fans have hung banners saying they like to beat rival teams almost as much as they like to "beat our wives."

9   "I'm going to go home and beat my wife," Coach Joe Paterno of Penn State once said at a press conference after his football team lost to the University of Texas. Later he defended the statement as "just part of the sports culture, locker room talk, harmless, a joke that did not mean anything."

10   What is this "harmless" sports culture?

11   Whether hockey fights, football tackles or baseball brawls, intentionally hurtful acts are portrayed as natural—for men. Society's concept of violence is inextricably interwoven with its concept of expected, condoned male behavior. Boys are given boxing gloves as toys; girls and women who try to join wrestling or football teams are often ridiculed, sexually harassed or simply barred from taking part.

12   Most of the women whom male players see are not coaches or other athletes. They are the short-skirted cheerleaders and the university "hostesses" who escort them around campus during the recruiting process. The locker room is not a place to brag about your wife's or girlfriend's accomplishments. It is a place where men discuss women's bodies in graphic sexual terms, where they boast about "scoring" and joke about beating women.

13   In *The Hundred Yard Lie,* Rick Telander, a reporter for *Sports Illustrated,* writes that he has heard so much degrading talk of women in the locker room he's sure that "the macho attitudes promoted by coaches contribute (perhaps unwittingly) to the athlete's problems in relating to women."

14   Sexist comments can get men fired in some circles. But in sports, a world where sexism is a badge of honor, it is a common ground, a familiar language.

15   Timothy Jon Curry, an Ohio State sociologist who employed researchers to record locker-room conversations over several months, found that talk of women as objects took the form of loud performances for other men. Talk about ongoing relationships with women, on the other hand, took place only in hushed tones, often behind rows of lockers, and was subject to ridicule. "This ridicule tells the athlete that he is getting too close to femaleness, because he is taking relatedness seriously," he writes. "'Real men' do not do that."

16   A former college football star who spoke to me only on the condition that he not be named said of Mr. Curry's research: "That's right on target. We never talked about respecting women." This man, who later signed with the Philadelphia Eagles, recalls college teammates making crude boasts about sexual conquests. His college teammates hosted

"pig parties." The man who brought the ugliest date would win a trophy. This football star says he learned to respect women from his mother and three athletic sisters, and did not attend the parties. But he would laugh at his teammates' jokes, which he now regrets.

17 "I remember the first time they showed the trophy, in the locker room," he says. "I was a 17-year-old freshman in a room full of upperclassmen. It was boisterous, raunchy, there was screaming and yelling. I laughed along. Men are extremely cliquish. I didn't want to be left out."

18 When quarterback Timm Rosenbach of the Phoenix Cardinals quit pro football after the 1992 season, he told Ira Berkow of *The New York Times:* "I thought I was turning into some kind of animal. You go through a week getting yourself up for a game by hating the other team, the other players. You're so mean and hateful, you want to kill somebody. Football's so aggressive. Things get done by force. And then you come home, you're supposed to turn it off? 'Oh, here's your lovin' daddy.' It's not that easy. It was like I was an idiot. I felt programmed. I had become a machine."

19 O.J. Simpson, who pleaded not guilty to charges of murdering his former wife and her friend, was programmed. He was, like all of us, a product of a culture that allows more than two million women each year to be beaten by husbands or boyfriends. About 1,400 women a year die at the hands of these "lovers." He was also part of a football culture that taught him to equate masculinity with violence.

20 Our society reveres athletes regardless of their behavior off the field. Even after he pleaded no contest to beating his wife on New Year's Day 1989, Mr. Simpson continued to work for Hertz and NBC, and to be described by fans and in the media as a "great guy" and an "American hero." When he was chased by police cars along the Los Angeles freeways, commuters stopped their cars to wave to him and chant, "Go, O.J., go!" They acted as if nothing—not wife-beating, not alleged murder—mattered, as if star athletes should be able to do exactly as they please.

21 Which is what they will continue to do until we stop glorifying them and stop training them to hate women.

[1994]

POST-READING QUESTIONS

CONTENT

1. What kinds of crimes or other bad acts are the athletes Burton lists accused of? How significant are these types of behavior?
2. What does Burton say the causes of these types of behavior are? What do you think?
3. How does Burton say people rationalize athletes' poor behavior?
4. What role do "macho attitudes" play in contributing to athletes' illegal or unkind actions?
5. Who are the primary victims of professional athletes' actions? What does this say about the athletes who commit such uncivil acts?

6. How does Burton say men are "trained" by their peers to act uncivilly?

STYLE AND STRUCTURE

7. Does Burton have a point? What is it?

8. What examples does Burton use in order to support her main idea? Of these, which are most effective? Explain.

9. Who is Burton's audience? To what extent are athletes the target readers? Women? Cite the text for support.

10. What is Burton's tone? Choose several examples from the text that reveal her tone.

11. Is Burton convincing? Explain.

CRITICAL THINKING AND ANALYSIS

DISCUSSION QUESTIONS

12. Many of Burton's examples come from the early 1990s. Do you think that the violence and abuse she writes about are more or less common from professional athletes now? Explain.

13. What reasons, aside from the ones Burton cites, can you think of for the many instances of uncivil behavior from professional athletes?

WRITING ASSIGNMENTS

14. Burton writes that "Society's concept of violence is inextricably interwoven with its concept of expected, condoned male behavior." What do you think? Write a few paragraphs or short essay in which you argue that society does or does not encourage men to behave violently. Cite Burton's essay and your own observations in order to illustrate your ideas.

15. According to Burton, "Our society reveres athletes regardless of their behavior off the field." Is this true? Write at least two well-developed paragraphs in which you argue that American culture does or does not revere athletes despite uncivil behavior. Be sure to use examples from Burton's essay and your own experiences in order to support your points.

16. Is uncivil behavior one-sided? In a few paragraphs or short essay, discuss the extent to which women, women athletes in particular, are guilty of uncivil behavior. Use examples from your own experiences and observations and from contemporary news stories in order to clarify your ideas.

17. Burton writes of an athlete who laughs at unkind, sexist jokes because he "didn't want to be left out." How necessary is a macho, often women-hating attitude to be successful in sports? Write a few paragraphs explaining whether or not athletes can be respected if they choose not to indulge in unkind, sexist behavior. Cite Burton's essay and current sports events for support.

VOCABULARY DEVELOPMENT

18. How emotionally loaded is Burton's language? Substitute less emotionally charged synonyms for the Vocabulary Preview words in their sentences in the text. What is the result of the substitutions? Write a few sentences explaining how your changes affected the meaning of the text.

GROUP ACTIVITIES

19. As a group, perform an online search for one of the athletes named in Burton's essay. Follow at least three links, keeping notes on how the athletes are represented on the Internet. How much is made of the athletes' uncivil acts? Write a few sentences discussing how large a part of his history uncivil, even violent, behavior comprises.

20. Brainstorm a list of athletes who are known for their civil, even kind, behavior. How long is your list? Discuss whether or not the athletes on your list are as respected as some who have committed illegal or uncivil acts. What role does incivility play in an athlete's popularity?

See No Evil

Terrence Rafferty

Critic-at-large for *GQ* magazine, in which this article was first published, Terrence Rafferty also contributes frequently to other publications. Citing the popularity of John Harris's novel *Hannibal* as indicative of our culture's fascination with serial killers, Rafferty claims that society vaults such murderers into the limelight, making them a kind of celebrity. Rafferty questions the values of a citizenry that eagerly follows the moves of convicted killers.

Pre-reading Questions

Freewrite for five to ten minutes in response to the following questions:
What does the term "serial killer" call to mind for you? What names, if any, do you associate with this term? What characteristics do you attribute to serial killers? Are any of these traits admirable? How do you account for the popularity of movies and books that feature serial killers?

Vocabulary Preview

Vocabulary Words:

• allure	• ubiquitous	• aestheticism
• archetype	• psychopath	• misogyny
• scabrous	• antagonist	• preternaturally
• grisly	• astute	• enigmatic
• genre	• banally	• audacity
• sanguinary	• nihilism	• intrepid

Look up at least ten of the words above and use them in a paragraph about some aspect of crime: committing it, solving it, or viewing it, for instance. How many of the words easily fit into your paragraph? Why? Write a few sentences explaining how some words are or are not easy to use in writing.

1 There's something about a serial killer: a certain je ne sais quoi, a weird allure. Or so it seems, on the evidence of Thomas Harris's novel *Hannibal,* which spent the entire summer—the most competitive season for popular fiction—perched atop every best-seller list, gazing down imperiously on its defeated rivals. In a sense, the book's commercial success is no surprise: Harris, the Stanley Kubrick of suspense novelists, hadn't published a book since *The Silence of the Lambs,* in 1988, and in the intervening eleven years that novel, which began the story of the odd symbiotic relationship between an earnest young FBI trainee named Clarice Starling and the homicidal psychiatrist Hannibal "the Cannibal" Lecter, had time to find millions of appalled/fascinated readers. (As did Harris's even scarier 1981 thriller, *Red Dragon,* in

which Lecter appears as a minor character.) And Anthony Hopkins's mesmeric performance as Lecter in Jonathan Demme's film *The Silence of the Lambs* (1991) helped elevate the demented shrink to the level of pop-culture myth—a horror archetype as seductive, and perhaps as unkillable, as Dracula. So, of course, everybody rushed out to buy *Hannibal.* My wife and I both read it the week it came out; a friend of ours read it from cover to cover—it's 484 pages long—the day it came out. My dog, in a perverse sort of homage to the title character, tried to eat it, with some kibble and a nice bowl of filtered water. What is surprising is how easily Harris's large public has swallowed this willfully outrageous piece of fiction, which is only incidentally the kind of brooding police procedural we'd all expected. *Hannibal* is, at its dark heart, a scabrous comic fable, of which the alarming Dr. Lecter is not merely the protagonist but the moral center. This is the serial-killer story to end all serial-killer stories. And maybe it's about time.

2   It has to be said that in the decade since *The Silence of the Lambs* was published, the mass audience's tolerance for the grisly details of serial killers' crimes, and the even grislier details of their psyches, has increased exponentially, to the point where these statistically rather rare predators are wildly overrepresented in our entertainment and "news" media and, for that matter, in serious literature. With this genre, the line between the popular and the serious is piano-wire thin: Basically, if the sociopath tells his story in the first person and is not caught by the police (see Bret Easton Ellis's *American Psycho* and Joyce Carol Oates's *Zombie*), it's art; otherwise, it's just good, clean sanguinary fun. (In the high-literary mode, that is, the artist himself—or herself—assumes the heroic task, more plausibly performed by detectives and profilers in genre fiction, of entering the mind of the killer.) At both the high and the low end of culture, the figure of the serial killer—defined, roughly, as one who commits several individual murders, usually of strangers, over a period of time, to achieve sexual gratification and/or a sensation of power over others—is ubiquitous, and by now, wondering why that should be the case seems almost beside the point.

3   The fact is, although not one in a million of us will ever encounter a serial killer, probably a majority of American-pop-culture consumers would be able to construct a plausible FBI-style profile of one. This is an infallible measure of how powerful a phenomenon is in the popular imagination: the huge disproportion between the extent of our knowledge of a subject and its practical value. Our collective fascination with this sort of violent criminal is undoubtedly a symptom of some unwholesome condition, but the specific diagnosis is probably best left to the social scientists, who can use the work. (And it'll keep them off the streets.) Maybe it's just human nature to be curious about evil. Maybe, in our relative prosperity, we simply need ever more extreme vicarious thrills from our entertainment. Maybe our interest in serial killers indicates an endemic sexual anxiety in the culture (as a similar obsession did in Weimar Germany, according to Maria Tatar's stimulating 1995 book, *Lustmord*). Or maybe the sociopath's distinctive qualities—the ruthlessness, the predatory cunning, the will to power—are ones we're all too familiar with in our daily lives, either in ourselves or in others.

4   The more you think about this, the more cynical you're likely to become. Here's another reflection: The serial killer—unlike the spree killer and the mass murderer, those squirrelly guys who go berserk for an afternoon and then end their own lives—

actually has a career, which, as long as he remains unapprehended, he has to be considered pretty good at. (Interesting work, too: traveling, interacting with the public, meeting demanding production quotas, figuring out ingenious ways to get around the government's pesky regulations.) Some serial murder buffs undoubtedly feel a kind of sneaking admiration for the daredevil exploits of, say, Ted Bundy, who is one of the few real-life examples of the charming, intelligent sociopath we encounter so frequently in crime fiction and movies.

5   Bundy was a good-looking guy (Mark Harmon played him in the 1986 TV miniseries *The Deliberate Stranger*) who had a B.A. in psychology and was attending law school at the time of his first arrest; who had worked at various times as a volunteer at a suicide-prevention center, as an assistant to the director of the Seattle Crime Prevention Commission and as an assistant to the chairman of the Washington State Republican Party; and who managed to escape from two jails before he was captured, convicted and ultimately executed in Florida. According to the former FBI profiler John Douglas (who became famous as the model for Harris's behavioral-science guru Jack Crawford and has since written several books about his experiences), "Bundy was full of charm, and attracted an ever-increasing following of groupies for the widely covered trial. This is not an uncommon phenomenon." Bundy, more presentable and more articulate than the average homicidal sexual deviant, was a perfect fit for a couple of attractive pop archetypes—the Jekyll-and-Hyde myth and the criminal-genius myth—and so became (and remains) a superstar, the Elvis of serial murder.

6   There's a ton of literature on Bundy, much of it compellingly novelistic. The crime reporter Ann Rule, who worked with Bundy on the suicide hot line, wrote a classic book, *The Stranger Beside Me,* about her friendship with this man who she didn't want to believe was a murderer, a narrative structure it shares with three of the greatest works of serial-killer fiction: Marie Belloc Lowndes's novel *The Lodger* (1913), Alfred Hitchcock's film *Shadow of a Doubt* (1943) and Michael Powell's film *Peeping Tom* (1960). In each of these stories, a woman is drawn to a man who proves to be a killer. *The Lodger's* Ellen Bunting finds it impossible, despite an abundance of clues, to admit to herself that the "gentleman" upstairs is the self-styled "Avenger" who has been terrorizing, and titillating, London with a series of Jack the Ripper-like murders. In *Shadow of a Doubt,* a smart small-town girl discovers that her namesake and favorite relative, urbane Uncle Charlie, is the Merry Widow Murderer and the object of a nationwide manhunt. And in *Peeping Tom,* a sweet young woman named Helen develops an attachment to her shy neighbor, Mark, a psychopath who kills women while he films their reactions. (His father, it seems, was a scientist who subjected little Mark to sadistic filmed experiments: "He was interested in the reactions of the nervous system to fear . . . especially fear in children.") Like Rule's Bundy, all these characters are seen at some point in the narrative, and through the eyes of a kindly female observer, as sympathetic: Each of these stories is therefore, to some degree, a macabre variant on a familiar motif of romantic narrative—a woman's rueful recognition that an attractive guy can have, well, sort of a dark side.

7   And that realization generates, in turn, the suspicion of a more disturbing possibility: Is the violent, evil aspect of the man's personality really separable from the qualities the heroine—and we, the readers or viewers whose surrogate she is—finds appealing about him? Are we all, on some level, Ted Bundy's groupies? As a topic for reflection

on the collective unconscious of the culture, this is distinctly in the don't-go-there category. Beyond this point, one might say, are monsters. (Robert K. Ressler, who was John Douglas's mentor and who is credited with having coined the term "serial killer," called his two volumes of memoirs *I Have Lived in the Monster* and *Whoever Fights Monsters.*) Thanks in large part to Thomas Harris, the psychological-profiler type of investigator has become the antagonist of choice for the serial killer of popular fiction: the mythic figure who allows us both to acknowledge and to distance ourselves from the killer inside us—to go toward the frightening source of our fascination with violence but without risking the annihilating shock of full self-recognition. Still, the purest example of the profiler archetype is *Red Dragon's* Will Graham, who's tormented by his freakish, near psychic ability to penetrate the diseased thought processes of sociopaths. The fact that this talent is involuntary—not learned, but innate—is, of course, unsettling, since it implies the psychological identification of the investigator with the killer (who, not coincidentally, places mirrors in the eye sockets, and other orifices, of his victims). But Graham, like later, similarly endowed psychic detectives, such as the protagonists of the TV series *Profiler* and *Millennium,* uses his terrible knowledge for social good, which affords both him and us the comfort of attributing a positive value to darker impulses.

8   Will Graham, significantly, does not appear in the two novels Harris has written since *Red Dragon,* while Lecter has become steadily more prominent. Starling, who replaces Graham as the investigator in *The Silence of the Lambs,* seems to be refreshingly normal, blessedly unburdened by any special insight into the sociopathic mind; and even more surprisingly, the profiler role has been reassigned to the evil Dr. Lecter, whose scarily astute understanding of psychology helps Starling track down a serial killer known as Buffalo Bill. (In his 1995 book *The Riverman,* the Washington police detective Robert Keppel reveals that in the mid-'80s he attempted to use Ted Bundy, then on death row, in the same way, to develop a profile of the so-called Green River Killer.) As John Douglas has written, "We have yet to come across in real life anyone quite as perversely brilliant and resourceful as the warped psychiatrist Dr. Lecter." Not even Bundy, who was no genius but merely an uncommonly bold and relentless predator of above-average intelligence. (And, as the courtroom groupies presumably did not know, he was also a dedicated necrophiliac.) Although most of us probably didn't notice it at the time, in *The Silence of the Lambs,* Harris began to loosen Lecter's connections to "real life," to let him start drifting upward into the thinner air of literary myth. The Lecter of that book is clearly not motivated—as virtually every other serial killer known to man has been—by sexual pathology. He's a disinterested, philosophical murderer, who terminates the lives of people who offend him: many of them psychiatric patients of his who, in his discerning professional judgment, are so viciously and banally disordered that they simply don't deserve to exist. A character in *Hannibal* reports, "He told me once that, whenever it was 'feasible,' he preferred to eat the rude." In the area of artistic consumption, his taste is more refined—exquisite, actually—but his connoisseurship and his homicidal impulses are essentially of a piece: Both express a rigorous nihilism that is also a form of aestheticism.

9   In a way, Lecter is a direct descendant of *Shadow of a Doubt's* elegant Uncle Charlie, who tells his adoring niece, "The whole world's a joke to me," and later, after she

has discovered the awful truth about him, expands on this theme with uncommon bluntness: "How do you know what the world is like? Do you know the world is a foul sty? Do you know that if you ripped the fronts off houses you'd find swine? The world's a hell! What does it matter what happens in it?" (It's worth noting that swine—actual swine—figure prominently in *Hannibal.*) Yet even Uncle Charlie is, by virtue of his misogyny and his barely suppressed rage, quite a bit more real than the preternaturally cool Lecter. Nothing disturbs his inhuman sangfroid, except Clarice Starling: She is beautiful (i.e., she satisfies his rather lofty aesthetic criterion), and more important, she's the only person alive who's capable of surprising him. "With all his knowledge,"

10 we read in *Hannibal,* "he could never entirely predict her."

One of the reasons for the enormous popularity of both the novel *The Silence of the Lambs* and its extraordinarily faithful film adaptation is that Harris managed to graft a fair amount of romantic tension—completely unexpected and pretty unsettling in the context—onto the conventional thrill-of-the-chase tensions of the suspense genre. The erotic subtext of the relationship between Lecter, the killer-profiler, and Starling, who begins as his potential victim, becomes his student and ends as the object of (at least) his intellectual desire, is hard to miss, though it's developed delicately enough to avoid seeming, you know, rude. Harris left the precise nature of that peculiar bond tactfully and tantalizingly unresolved at the end of *The Silence of the Lambs,* and most readers and viewers, I'd guess, didn't mind; they probably preferred the enigmatic suggestiveness of the story to any more explicit thematic closure. But there's closure to burn in *Hannibal,* and Harris's audacity in pushing the implications of his previous novel to their logical conclusion is breathtaking. There's no Buffalo Bill figure here, no fiend to be hunted down by an intrepid profiler. The novel's plot, more intricate and less linear than those of Harris's earlier books, concerns Starling's disillusionment with the FBI and Lecter's attempt to elude the revenge of one of his surviving victims, a grotesquely disfigured, filthy-rich pedophile named Mason Verger. Although Starling and Lecter don't actually meet until near the end—sort of like in *Sleepless in Seattle*—they're on the run, we realize, from the same malign forces: from human natures so profoundly corrupted by money and envy and ambition that the world seems exactly what the likes of Lecter and Uncle Charlie always knew it was, a foul sty, a hell. In this context, even Hannibal the Cannibal can turn out to be a knight in shining armor.

11 This, to say the least, puts a somewhat disturbing spin on the issue of our culture's attraction to the serial killer. Lecter is, of course, a pure abstraction, and *Hannibal* is basically a comedy, albeit a remarkably mordant and twisted one. (Come to think of it, the two Starling-and-Lecter books constitute an unprecedentedly dark variety of screwball farce: The hero and the heroine "meet cute," don't trust each other at first; are kept apart by means of very elaborate narrative contrivances and finally . . .) If Hannibal Lecter were more like a real serial killer—a lethal but pathetic sexual misfit on the order of Bundy or Gacy or Dahmer—obviously Harris would be unable to represent him as a hero; but he would also be unable to reveal so much about the kind of culture that can produce our mass obsession with human predators. Harris's capper for *Hannibal,* his equivalent of "And they lived happily ever after," is "We can only learn so much and live." By which I think he means that we've become so cynical that we are now too

thoroughly acquainted with the night—the permanent moral night of the absolute nihilist. It's Hannibal's world, and the rest of us are merely avid profilers. We've learned to see the world through his cold eyes.

POST-READING QUESTIONS

CONTENT

1. What reasons does Rafferty give for the popularity of the novel *Hannibal?*
2. What is one effect of people's increased "tolerance for the grisly details of serial killers' crimes," according to Rafferty?
3. What is the definition of a "serial killer"?
4. Why, according to Rafferty, are people fascinated by serial killers?
5. How does Rafferty account for Ted Bundy's popularity?
6. How are accounts of serial killers similar to fiction about serial killers? Why is this similarity significant?
7. In what ways is the role of "profiler" important to readers of serial-killer fiction?
8. What role does romance play in tales about serial killers?

STYLE AND STRUCTURE

9. Does Rafferty have an argument? What is it?
10. How does Rafferty use the novel *Hannibal* to illustrate his main idea? Is he effective?
11. Who is Rafferty's audience? What conclusions can you draw about the types of people who read Rafferty's essay?
12. What is Rafferty's tone? Cite the text for examples of his tone.
13. What role does humor play in Rafferty's essay? Cite the text for support.

CRITICAL THINKING AND ANALYSIS

DISCUSSION QUESTIONS

14. Do you agree with Rafferty's statement that "There's something about a serial killer: . . . a weird allure"? Using examples from contemporary news stories and entertainment, respond to this question.
15. How accurate is Rafferty's speculation that "Maybe it's just human nature to be curious about evil"? Explain and give examples.

WRITING ASSIGNMENTS

16. Rafferty claims that "the mass audience's tolerance for the grisly details for serial killers' crimes, and the even grislier details of their psyches, has increased

exponentially . . ." What do you think? Write a well-developed paragraph or essay in which you argue that people are or are not more accustomed to gruesome details, either in the news or in fiction than they were in the past. Cite modern forms of entertainment as well as modern news stories in order to illustrate your ideas.

17. Rafferty raises the question of whether or not "the violent, evil aspect of the man's personality [is] really separable from the qualities the heroine . . . finds appealing about him." Write a few paragraphs or short essay in which you argue that the evil aspects of serial killers are or are not what people find compelling about him. Be sure to cite Rafferty's essay as well as your own observations in order to illustrate your ideas.

18. In quoting from *Hannibal,* Rafferty says that "we've become so cynical that we are now too thoroughly acquainted with the night . . ." Are we jaded? Write at least two well-developed paragraphs in which you argue whether or not people have become overly numb to details of "dark" tales. Cite your own experiences and observations for support.

19. Does our interest in serial killers necessarily imply an admiration for them? Write a short essay in which you discuss whether or not you think people can be fascinated by killers or other negative celebrities without admiring them. Cite Rafferty's essay and your own experiences in order to illustrate your ideas.

VOCABULARY DEVELOPMENT

20. Using at least seven words from Rafferty's essay (they can be from the Vocabulary Preview list, but they do not have to be), write a short paragraph describing a serial killer. What do you notice about the types of words Rafferty has chosen, as opposed to the ones you might ordinarily choose to describe a murderer? Share your results with your classmates.

GROUP ACTIVITIES

21. Choose a serial killer from the nation's headlines—Ted Bundy, Jeffrey Dahmer, Carey Staynor, among others—and perform an online search for information about the one you choose. What is the attitude of people who have posted information about the serial killer of your choice? What does this say about what people value? Share your results with the class in an open-forum setting.

22. Watch any movie or read a description from any book that features a serial killer and make a list of characteristics that you think best modify the murderer. Then, discuss which of these qualities, if any, are admirable in order to determine why people are fascinated with serial killers. Share your results with the class.

Argument Pair: What Defines a "Hero" Today?

Larger Than Life, Phil Sudo

A World Without Heroes, George Roche

Do we need heroes? Or if we do need them, does that mean we will have them? George Roche and Phil Sudo address the topic of heroism, addressing these questions within the context of famous, possibly heroic people, past and present. While Sudo contends that "anyone" can be a hero, Roche despairs in the view that heroes are all but a memory in American culture.

Writing Assignments Based on *Larger Than Life* and *A World Without Heroes*

1. George Roche writes that "If we cannot agree that dragons are evil, we will have no dragon-fighters," indicating that society determines whether or not we have heroes, while Phil Sudo quotes Martin Luther King, Jr. who claims that "If a man hasn't found something he will die for, he isn't fit to live," implying that the burden of heroism lies with the individual. Who is right? Write at least three paragraphs or a short essay in which you decide whether society or the individuals within society are more responsible for ensuring the presence of heroes. Be sure to cite both essays and your own experiences in order to illustrate your ideas.

2. Phil Sudo claims that "there is the potential to become heroes ourselves," but George Roche claims that most people "can not think of half-a dozen" people who can be considered heroes. How difficult to find is heroism? Write a few paragraphs or short essay in which you argue that heroism is or is not rare in society. Be sure to define "heroism" and cite both essays and your own life and observations for support.

Larger Than Life

Phil Sudo

Searching through past cultures and countries, Phil Sudo explains how people in history rose to the level of hero. While, he claims, such individuals are extraordinary, they also need not be limited solely to the past. Instead, Sudo argues that anyone has the potential to act as a hero.

Pre-reading Questions

Freewrite for five to ten minutes in response to the following questions:
What does the term "hero" mean to you? Who are people whom you consider to be heroic in some way? Why? Is your list of heroic people longer, or shorter, than it was ten years ago? Why?

Vocabulary Preview

Vocabulary Words:
- mythical
- embodied
- epics
- forge
- samurai
- bestow
- debased
- thwarting
- reap
- transcends

Write definitions for each word above without using a dictionary. Then, look up each word in order to learn its formal definition. How close were your definitions to the original meanings? Write a few sentences explaining how accurate you were and why.

COURAGE AND LOYALTY

1   The word "hero" comes from the Greek word *heros,* meaning to protect or to serve. Originally, the term applied only to mythical figures—gods or semidivine beings, such as Hercules and Perseus, who excelled in battle and embodied such values as courage and loyalty. The ancient Greeks developed an entire tradition of literature around such heroes; in classic epics like the *Iliad* and the *Odyssey,* Homer spun tales of the brave Odysseus and other warriors, whose adventures were first passed down orally, then later through the written word.

2   The notion of heroes was not unique to the West. Other early societies, such as China and India, developed similar traditions, around heroes such as Kuan Ti and epics like the *Mahabharata.*

3   Over time, historians began to look upon real people as heroes—Simón Bolívar, Sun Yat-sen, George Washington—larger-than life individuals who founded countries or dedicated their lives to liberation. These were the rare men and women who embodied, as one historian wrote, "the perfect expression of the ideal of a group, in whom all human virtues unite."

4   Learning the tales of these greats helps forge values and a cultural identity. When you read the story of George Washington cutting down a cherry tree and saying, "I cannot tell a lie," you learn the value of honesty in American society. In Japan, when schoolchildren read the tale of the *47 Ronin,* a band of samurai who stick together through years of hardship to avenge their master's death, they learn the value of loyalty and group togetherness. . . .

5   In this country, some educators believe our heroes are too one-sided. U.S. history books, they say, are filled with the accomplishments of white European males to the exclusion of women and minorities.

6   In fact, many Americans today are beginning to question the very definition of a "hero." These days, we bestow the honor mainly on sports figures, movie stars, musicians, and comedians. "The word 'hero' is a debased word," says Michael Lesy, a professor at Hampshire College in Amherst, Mass., and author of the . . . book *Rescues.* It has become confused with "celebrity," "role model," and "idol," he says. . . .

WHAT MAKES A HERO?

7   But if there is argument over what constitutes a "hero," few among us fail to admire heroic acts. Thwarting a robbery, rescuing a drowning man, pulling a child from a burning house—these are all unquestionable acts of heroism. And while the brave souls who perform them may never become famous or reap rewards, they are certainly heroes.

8   In fact, the one trait of heroes that transcends all cultural boundaries, Lesy says, is the willingness to risk one's life for the good of others. "It's not an American trait, it's not Japanese, it's not Iraqi, it's the bottom-line of the human species," he says.

9   Consider the words of Nelson Mandela: "I have cherished the idea of a democratic and free society. It is an ideal which I hope to live for and to achieve. But if needs be, it is an ideal for which I am prepared to die."

10   And these words from slain civil rights leader Martin Luther King, Jr.: "If a man hasn't found something he will die for, he isn't fit to live."

POTENTIAL WITHIN US ALL

11   We hail these men as heroes because their courage gives us strength, their ideals give us vision, and their spirit enlarges our own. But keep in mind that, extraordinary as these heroes may seem, they are still human beings like you and me. And as such, they demonstrate that within all of us, there is the potential to become heroes ourselves.

12   Look around you, at your friends, your family, your school. Is there someone among them that you'd call a hero? Probably so.

13   Now take a look in the mirror. What do you see?

14   What do you *want* to see?

POST-READING QUESTIONS

CONTENT

1.   Where does the word "hero" come from? How is its origin significant?
2.   What countries, according to Sudo, have heroes? Who are the people that become heroes? Why?
3.   What function does learning about heroes serve?
4.   What terms has "hero" become confused with?
5.   What is the one trait that "transcends all cultural boundaries" in terms of determining heroism? Do you agree?

STYLE AND STRUCTURE

6.   What is Sudo's primary argument? Restate his main idea in your own words.
7.   What examples of his main idea does Sudo provide? Of these, which are most compelling? Explain.
8.   Who is Sudo writing for? Cite the text to identify his audience.
9.   What purpose does beginning the essay with the definition of "hero" serve?

10. Is Sudo convincing? Why or why not?

CRITICAL THINKING AND ANALYSIS

DISCUSSION QUESTIONS

11. Sudo writes that "In this country, some educators believe our heroes are too one-sided." What do you think? Has the idea that only white males are identified as heroes been revised over the past few years? Explain and give examples.

12. Can "anyone" become a hero, as Sudo asserts? Explain, taking care to define heroism and offering examples from your life and observations for support.

WRITING ASSIGNMENTS

13. Sudo writes that the term "hero" has become confused with terms such as "celebrity" and "role model." Write at least one well-developed paragraph in which you compare and contrast "hero" with one of the two terms listed above. Be sure to offer specific examples of each term in order to illustrate your ideas.

14. What, for you, defines a hero? Write a few paragraphs or short essay in which you define the term "hero." You may want to start with a dictionary definition, but be sure to cite examples from your own experiences and observations in order to illustrate your ideas.

15. Sudo writes, "These days, we bestow the honor mainly on sports figures, movie stars, musicians, and comedians." How accurate is he? Write a few paragraphs in which you argue that Americans do or do not primarily revere such figures as Sudo mentions. Cite Sudo's essay and examples from contemporary culture in order to support your argument.

VOCABULARY DEVELOPMENT

16. Write a brief paragraph describing someone you consider to be a hero, but only allow yourself to use the term "hero" once. What other expressions do you come up with? Share your results with classmates in order to broaden your vocabulary on this topic.

GROUP ACTIVITIES

17. Choose a controversial figure such as former President Clinton, Malcolm X, or Princess Diana and hold a class-wide debate over whether this figure can be considered a "hero." You may want to do some research prior to attending class in order to learn more about the person you are debating.

18. Create a visual representation of a "hero" using materials you normally bring with you for school. For instance, if you think a "hero" is a learned person, use one of your books to signify education. Present your interpretation of a hero to the class and explain its significance.

A World Without Heroes

George Roche

George Roche has served as president of Hillsdale College in Michigan, but he is also a re-spected historian. The following essay comes from Roche's book *A World Without Heroes* and poses the question of whether or not such selfless individuals as we've known to be he-roes in the past are still present among us.

Pre-reading Questions

Freewrite for five to ten minutes in response to the following questions:
Do you think that becoming a hero is more or less difficult today than it has been in the past? What, to you, determines who becomes a hero? Can a person be a hero in secret? Explain.

Vocabulary Preview

Vocabulary Words:
- rebukes
- pervasive
- ennobled
- replenishes
- bereft
- purveyors
- viable
- repudiation
- tangible
- inundated
- cynic

Look up each of the words above and then use them in sentences of your own, varying the length and structure of each sentence you write. Then, write a few sentences analyzing how difficult or easy using certain words is.

1   "It is an unhappy country that has no heroes," says Andrea Sarti, puzzlingly, in Bertolt Brecht's 1939 play, "Galileo." Odder still is the fictional Galileo's reproach: "It is an unhappy country that needs heroes." What are we—dwellers in a world without heroes—to make of this? . . .

THE LESSONS OF HEROES

2   Who are our heroes, and how can they make us happier? Heroes are a fading mem-ory in our times, but we still can recall a little about them. We know, at least, that what sets the hero apart is some extraordinary achievement. Whatever this feat, it is such as to be recognized at once by everyone as a good thing; and somehow, the achieving of it seems larger than life. The hero, furthermore, overcomes the ordi-nary and attains greatness by serving some great good. His example very nearly re-bukes us, telling us that we fail, not by aiming too high in life, but by aiming far too low. Moreover, it tells us we are mistaken in supposing that happiness is a right or

an end in itself. The hero seeks not happiness, but goodness, and his fulfillment lies in achieving it. In truth, the question is less about heroes than about the framework of belief in which they can, and cannot, flourish. In the end, it concerns what we ourselves believe in and what we ask of life. What the hero gives us is a completely fresh, unfailed way of looking at life and, perhaps, the answer to our pervasive, mysterious unhappiness. Heroes, by their example, remind us that to pursue happiness for its own sake is the surest way to lose it.

3   Modern experience certainly bears this out. If nothing else, then, the hero yanks us out of the old rut and bids us to reexamine our values and goals. At the same time, he shows us by his own example that higher purposes in life, far from being an illusion, are the key to our richest potentials. Already, this is much more than the how-to books can promise.

4   Real heroism requires courage. It entails peril or pain. The dictionary says heroes are "distinguished by valor or enterprise in danger or fortitude in suffering." Plainly, heroism also has a selfless quality. The hero's deed is ennobled not by courage alone, but by the call to duty or by service to others. In this, it gains a larger symbolic value that can inspire and bind a whole nation. The hero acts for what is common and precious to all, and thereby replenishes the strength of our shared convictions.

5   Our debt to heroes is no metaphor, but the very substance of a free society. Our duty to one another and to moral law is exemplified by the hero's selflessness, but we have not kept our end of the bargain. The very words we need to think about when we discuss heroes—valor, magnanimity, fortitude, gallantry—rust from disuse.

6   If I were to depart from this theoretical discussion of heroes for a moment and ask you to name a dozen who are living today who generally are recognized as heroes, who would you name? It ought to be an easy list to make, but, on the contrary, most people cannot think of half-a-dozen who fulfill the requirements I have outlined. Rock stars, movie idols, sports figures, and political celebrities, as well as the occasional ordinary person who acts bravely in an emergency, are the substitutes for absent heroes and are thus a symptom of a paralyzing moral division in America.

7   If our knight-errant rode out and slew a dragon, half the editorials the next day would brand him "insensitive," if not an outright warmonger, and they would remind us that dragons are on the endangered species list. If we can not agree that dragons are evil, we will have no dragon-fighters. Unhappy is the country that loses its moral bearings. Unhappy the many, bereft of spiritual leadership, who are doomed to cling to the self as the only reality in an unfathomable existence. Small wonder that we fling ourselves on the treadmills of sensation and turn for our redemption to the purveyors of clinically tested, guilt-free selves. . . .

8   The heroes we recognize all affirm, by their very deeds, the larger spiritual dimension to life. Materialist conceptions may purport to tell us what we are, but cannot touch our souls because, in the last analysis, they can not tell us what we should be. There is no "should" in the materialist cosmos, nor can it produce heroes. In Brecht's play, Galileo says that "it is an unhappy country that needs

heroes." He is telling mankind, "it is your own reason and determination which control your destiny.". . .

9   Galileo's is an ancient faith, man's second oldest, as old as Eden, but reanimated by the seemingly invincible science of the 19th century: "ye shall be as gods." It is the vision of man without God, of man at the center of being, autonomous, free of external controls and in command of his own destiny. It is the promise of a new man and of a new world given purpose and plan by man, the new Creator. . . .

10   By its own view and the Christian alike, "good" is the one thing the vision and its works cannot be. The natural universe, according to the vision, is all there is, and there is no good or evil in it, only natural events. What, then, makes a priest or an artist or a teacher or even a politician choose his vocation when he knows he can receive greater material rewards doing something else? What, then, drives men and women to suffer and die for their family, their country, their beliefs? Don't these acts suggest that man may have a spiritual side, if not a pervasively spiritual nature?

11   A great many experts will tell you that the materialist vision is stone dead today, an empty husk. The purely scientific explanation of man is no longer viable in popular or intellectual circles. Even the atheists and agnostics among us admit they believe that "something" out there in the cosmos is bigger than all of us. The clearest expression of this sentiment is to be found in the enormously successful "Star Wars" films. There is a Force in the universe. It is all-powerful, it is mystical, it can only be tapped by those who have enough faith to believe in it. So far as it goes, this is not a bad message, but it is a limited one and it can not be regarded as an adequate repudiation of the materialistic view. . . .

12   This is why we need heroes so desperately. By deed and symbol, they replenish our spiritual strength. They are tangible proof that man does not live by reason alone— that he has a moral conscience which is divinely inspired, that he freely may choose virtue over sin, heroism over cowardice or resignation.

THE DOMINANCE OF THE ANTIHERO

13   However, another kind of image has become dominant in the 20th century; it is that of the antihero. While you may have trouble thinking of genuine heroes, you will probably have no trouble recalling names in this case. In literature and in the movie industry, the antihero is a common phenomenon and, more often than not, he is a smash hit. Modern Western culture has been inundated with the antihero in various shades. He is generally an iconoclastic, angry young man who cynically writes off religion (except for some vague thing such as the Force) as a tool of the Establishment. For him, God can not be an authority because he is against *all* authority, and he owes no responsibility or allegiance to anyone except himself or those under his immediate protection. He may exhibit many heroic qualities like bravery and self-sacrifice, but he does not recognize purpose in human life. He is a complete cynic.

14   Quite conversely, the genuine hero tells us that life *can* be what it *should* be; that bravery and self-sacrifice occur because there are beliefs and responsibilities which warrant bravery and self-sacrifice. The hero tells us there is indeed purpose in human life.

CONTENT

1. What does Roche say sets heroes apart from us? Do you agree?

2. What function does the hero serve, aside from assisting others?

3. Why does Roche say "we have not kept our end of the bargain" in terms of heroes? What do you think?

4. What does Roche mean when he writes that "The heroes we recognize all affirm, by their very deeds, the larger spiritual dimension to life"?

5. Why, according to Roche, do priests, artists, teachers, and politicians choose their vocations? Do you agree?

6. Why does Roche say "we need heroes so desperately"?

7. How does Roche describe an "antihero"? Who are people you consider to be antiheroes? Explain.

STYLE AND STRUCTURE

8. What is Roche's main idea? Restate his primary argument in your own words.

9. What purpose does Roche's example of the "knight-errant" serve? Would a contemporary example be more effective? Explain.

10. What examples does Roche offer in order to support his views? What other illustrations do you think might strengthen his ideas? Explain.

11. Who is Roche's audience? How do his examples reveal this audience?

12. Is Roche convincing? Explain.

DISCUSSION QUESTIONS

13. Of the qualities Roche mentions in his opening paragraphs, which do you think are most essential to heroism? What other characteristics might you add? Explain.

14. To what do you attribute the popularity of the antihero? Using examples from contemporary culture, explain why the antihero has become so popular.

WRITING ASSIGNMENTS

15. Roche claims that "Heroes are a fading memory in our times . . ." What do you think? Write a few paragraphs in which you argue that heroes are or are not present in contemporary American culture. Be sure to cite Roche's essay and your own observations for support.

16. What is the difference between seeking "happiness" and "goodness"? Why is seeking one heroic and the other not? Write a well-developed paragraph in

which you explain why heroism demands pursuit of "goodness" rather than "happiness." Be sure to define each term and cite Roche's essay and your own observations for support.

17. Roche claims that "By deed and symbol, [heroes] replenish our spiritual strength." Write a few paragraphs in which you explain why "replenishing spiritual strength" is or is not important for people. Be sure to explain what "replenishing spiritual strength" means, and then cite examples from your own life and from Roche's essay in order to clarify your ideas.

VOCABULARY DEVELOPMENT

18. Brainstorm a list of words that you think share some characteristics with the term "hero." (You should come up with at least five.) Then, look up the words on your list. How close in meaning were your words to "hero"? Explain in a few sentences.

GROUP ACTIVITIES

19. Brainstorm a list of American heroes, past and present. Then, rank the members of your list from most to least heroic. What determines who is ranked higher or lower? Present your list to the class in an open forum setting.

20. As a group, decide upon someone from contemporary culture—real or fictional—to be a hero. Then, without using this person's name, write a paragraph describing this person's heroic qualities. Read your paragraph to other groups in order for them to try to guess your hero. Discuss why this person is "heroic" for you.

SYNTHESIS QUESTIONS

1. What role does civility play in determining whether or not someone is a hero? Write a few paragraphs or essay in which you explain how important civil behavior is in "heroic" actions. Cite at least three essays from this chapter as well as examples from contemporary culture in order to illustrate your ideas.

2. George Roche writes that "we are mistaken in supposing that happiness is a right or an end in itself" while Mariah Burton Nelson points out that many athletes are forgiven their off-court foibles because they are successful in their sports. Is winning enough for heroism? Can someone who "loses" be a hero? Write a few paragraphs in which you discuss the role success plays in heroism. Be sure to cite both essays and your own experiences in order to clarify your points.

3. Mariah Burton Nelson claims that athletes like O.J. Simpson are revered "regardless of their behavior off the field," but athletes like Cal Ripken, Jr. are respected for their civility. Who is more likely to be viewed a hero: the athlete who breaks

the rules, or the athlete who upholds them? Write an essay in which you discuss how great a role athletes' off-the-court behavior plays in their standing as a hero. Be sure to use examples from both essays and from contemporary sports for support.

4. Mariah Burton Nelson writes that we accept sexist behavior from athletes because it is "a badge of honor" in the sports world, and Terrence Rafferty states that much serial killer fiction is "a macabre variant on a familiar motif . . . that an attractive guy can have, well, sort of a dark side." Even Superman is weakened by the presence of Kryptonite. Can our heroes have weaknesses? Write at least three paragraphs discussing the role that frailty plays in our heroes. Be sure to cite examples from Nelson and Rafferty, as well as from any others from this chapter or from your own experiences, in order to support your views.

5. Terrence Rafferty discusses how the "hero" in serial killer fiction, the "psychological-profiler type of investigator . . . allows us both to acknowledge and to distance ourselves from the killer inside us" while Elizabeth Austin writes that "the only place I see anything vaguely resembling my own life is on [the animated television program] 'The Simpsons.'" Does a hero need to be someone we relate to? Write a few paragraphs or short essay in which you explain how heroes do or do not need to be people with whom we identify. Cite Rafferty and Austin as well as examples from contemporary culture, in order to illustrate your ideas.

6. Elizabeth Austin writes that in entertainment, wealth is a prerequisite for happiness and admiration, while George Roche claims that "some extraordinary achievement" is what sets heroes apart from the rest of us. What do Americans value in their heroes? Write an essay, or a few well-developed paragraphs, in which you define what traits Americans most value in their heroes. Be sure to cite Austin and Roche and use examples from popular entertainment sources in order to support your views.

7. Holly Brubach claims that "in the news, we read about women running countries, directing corporations and venturing into space," just as Mariah Burton Nelson calls our attention to "famous" athletes who are given chance after chance. How important is the media in determining whether or not someone is a hero? Write a few paragraphs or short essay in which you argue that people can or cannot be heroes without fame. Be sure to cite Brubach and Nelson, and give examples from your own observations in order to illustrate your ideas.

8. Holly Brubach claims that "When it comes to looking at women, we're all voyeurs, men and women alike," but Mariah Burton Nelson claims that male athletes, regardless of their comportment away from their sports, are admired. Who is more likely to be idolized, men or women? Write at least two well-developed paragraphs in which you argue whether men or women are more easily elevated to hero status. Cite Brubach's and Nelson's essays, and use examples from contemporary culture for support.

9. Are the standards for "real life" heroes different from those of fictional heroes? Choose at least one person from "real life" you consider heroic and one person from fantasy. Then, explain how the qualities for heroism in these two people are or are not similar, and what accounts for the similarities or differences in the standards for heroism. Feel free to cite any essays from this chapter or any examples from your own experiences or observations in order to illustrate your ideas.

10. In "Why Homer's My Hero," Elizabeth Austin observes that many people value "stylish necessities," making few material personal sacrifices, even if keeping their pricey lifestyle means going into debt. Citing at least two readings from this chapter, write an essay or paragraph in which you explain how much someone needs to sacrifice in order to be considered a "hero."

"I appreciate this. It's been so long
since anyone really *listened*."

MARMADUKE reprinted by permission of United Feature Syndicate, Inc.

"... the founding fathers created a nation in reaction against the British empire's class distinctions and stuffy monarchical order. Informality—and, by extension, incivility—became a quintessential American ideal."

— **Phil Bacharach**

"We've had the legacy of the Sixties that manners are bad because they're artificial, and we should behave naturally."

— **Judith Martin**

> **"**The hardest job kids face today is learning good manners without seeing any.**"**
>
> — **Fred Astaire**

> **"**If someone tells you he is going to make a 'realistic decision,' you immediately understand that he has resolved to do something bad.**"**
>
> — **Mary McCarthy**

> **"**A lot of people mistake a short memory for a clear conscience.**"**
>
> — **Doug Larson**

Introduction

So many of the rituals our parents and grandparents followed seem quaintly archaic and irrelevant in the 21st century: women rarely feel compelled to wear hats for formality, "business casual" dominates many corporate settings, and fast food has eliminated the need to know which fork goes where. But in the midst of all this behavioral relaxation, have we lost something? Though etiquette for etiquette's sake can seem forced and artificial, its goal has been to make others feel comfortable, and the motivation for kindness and consideration still exists. However, as we let down our guard and wear jeans to church or address our elders by their first names, we have to ask if we are retaining our civility.

How necessary are the rules and guidelines of formal etiquette in ensuring fairness and an absence of hurt? Writers in Chapter 9 seek to examine a history of civil, and downright cruel, behavior in an effort to explain how significant the tenets of earlier generations are. Whether we become our mothers and fathers, whether those practicing unkind behavior should be punished or rehabilitated, and whether hurtful habits perpetuated in the name of fun should be curtailed: these are some of the issues raised and addressed in Chapter 9.

Crimes Against Humanity

Ward Churchill

The coordinator of the American Indian Movement for the state of Colorado, Ward Churchill is the author of several books on Native Americans including *Fantasies of the Master Race: Literature, Cinema, and the Colonization of American Indians.* Comparing American treatment of Native Americans to Nazi treatment of Jewish people, Ward Churchill argues that the seemingly "harmless" practice of naming sports teams after Native American people and customs is insulting and cruel.

Pre-reading Questions

Freewrite for five to ten minutes in response to the following questions:
What does the title "Crimes Against Humanity" call to mind for you? How do you define a crime against humanity? Does such a crime have to be physical, such as genocide or torture, or can it be mental or emotional? Explain.

Vocabulary Preview

Vocabulary Words:		
• virulently	• moniker	• indigenous
• dubious	• articulated	• endemic
• lexicon	• decimated	• salient
• epithet	• eradication	

Look up the words above and use them in sentences of varying length, style, and structure. Which words are most easy or difficult to use? Write a few sentences explaining why some words are more difficult to use than others.

1 During the past couple of seasons, there has been an increasing wave of controversy regarding the names of professional sports teams like the Atlanta "Braves," Cleveland "Indians," Washington "Redskins," and Kansas City "Chiefs." The issue extends to the names of college teams like Florida State University "Seminoles," University of Illinois "Fighting Illini," and so on, right on down to high school outfits like the Lamar (Colorado) "Savages." Also involved have been team adoption of "mascots," replete with feathers, buckskins, beads, spears and "warpaint" (some fans have opted to adorn themselves in the same fashion), and nifty little "pep" gestures like the "Indian Chant" and "Tomahawk Chop."

2 A substantial number of American Indians have protested that use of native names, images and symbols as sports team mascots and the like is, by definition, a virulently racist practice. Given the historical relationship between Indians and non-Indians during what has been called the "Conquest of America," American Indian Movement leader (and American Indian Anti-Defamation Council founder) Russell Means has

compared the practice to comtemporary Germans naming their soccer teams the "Jews," "Hebrews," and "Yids," while adorning their uniforms with grotesque caricatures of Jewish faces taken from the Nazis' anti-Semitic propaganda of the 1930s. Numerous demonstrations have occurred in conjunction with games—most notably during the November 15, 1992 match-up between the Chiefs and Redskins in Kansas City—by angry Indians and their supporters.

3   In response, a number of players—especially African Americans and other minority athletes—have been trotted out by professional team owners like Ted Turner, as well as university and public school officials, to announce that they mean not to insult but to honor native people. They have been joined by the television networks and most major newspapers, all of which have editorialized that Indian discomfort with the situation is "no big deal," insisting that the whole thing is just "good, clean fun." The country needs more such fun, they've argued, and "a few disgruntled Native Americans" have no right to undermine the nation's enjoyment of its leisure time by complaining. This is especially the case, some have argued, "in hard times like these." It has even been contended that Indian outrage at being systematically degraded—rather than the degradation itself—creates "a serious barrier to the sort of intergroup communication so necessary in a multicultural society such as ours."

4   Okay, let's communicate. We are frankly dubious that those advancing such positions really believe their own rhetoric, but, just for the sake of argument, let's accept the premise that they are sincere. If what they say is true, then isn't it time we spread such "inoffensiveness" and "good cheer" around among *all* groups so that *everybody* can participate *equally* in fostering the round of national laughs they call for? Sure it is—the country can't have too much fun or "intergroup involvement"—so the more, the merrier. Simple consistency demands that anyone who thinks the Tomahawk Chop is a swell pastime must be just as hearty in their endorsement of the following ideas—by the logic used to defend the defamation of American Indians—[to] help us all really start yukking it up.

5   First, as a counterpart to the Redskins, we need an NFL team called "Niggers" to honor Afro-Americans. Half-time festivities for fans might include a simulated stewing of the opposing coach in a large pot while players and cheerleaders dance around it, garbed in leopard skins and wearing fake bones in their noses. This concept obviously goes along with the kind of gaiety attending the Chop, but also with the actions of the Kansas City Chiefs, whose team members—prominently including black team members—lately appeared on a poster looking "fierce" and "savage" by way of wearing Indian regalia. Just a bit of harmless "morale boosting," says the Chief's front office. You bet.

6   So that the newly-formed Niggers sports club won't end up too out of sync while expressing the "spirit" and "identity" of Afro-Americans in the above fashion, a baseball franchise—let's call this one "Sambos"—should be formed. How about a basketball team called the "Spear-chuckers"? A hockey team called the "Jungle Bunnies"? Maybe the "essence" of these teams could be depicted by images of tiny black faces adorned with huge pairs of lips. The players could appear on TV every week or so gnawing on chicken legs and spitting watermelon seeds at one another. Catchy, eh? Well, there's "nothing to be upset about," according to those who love wearing "war

bonnets" to the Super Bowl or having "Chief Illiniwik" dance around the sports arenas of Urbana, Illinois.

7   And why stop there? There are plenty of other groups to include. "Hispanics"? They can be "represented" by the Galveston "Greasers" and San Diego "Spics," at least until the Wisconsin "Wetbacks" and Baltimore "Beaners" get off the ground. Asian Americans? How about the "Slopes," "Dinks," "Gooks," and "Zipperheads"? Owners of the latter teams might get their logo ideas from editorial page cartoons printed in the nation's newspapers during World War II: slant-eyes, buck teeth, big glasses, but nothing racially insulting or derogatory, according to the editors and artists involved at the time. Indeed, this Second World War—vintage stuff can be seen as just another barrel of laughs, at least by what current editors say are their "local standards" concerning American Indians.

8   Let's see. Who's been left out? Teams like the Kansas City "Kikes," Hanover "Honkies," San Leandro "Shylocks," Daytona "Dagos," and Pittsburgh "Polacks" will fill a certain social void among white folk. Have a religious belief? Let's all go for the gusto and gear up the Milwaukee "Mackerel Snappers" and Hollywood "Holy Rollers." The Fighting Irish of Notre Dame can be rechristened the "Drunken Irish" or "Papist Pigs." Issues of gender and sexual preference can be addressed through creation of teams like the St. Louis "Sluts," Boston "Bimbos," Detroit "Dykes," and the Fresno "Fags." How about the Gainesville "Gimps" and Richmond "Retards," so the physically and mentally impaired won't be excluded from our fun and games?

9   Now don't go getting "overly sensitive" out there. None of this is demeaning or insulting, at least not when it's being done to Indians. Just ask the folks who are doing it, or their apologists like Andy Rooney in the national media. They'll tell you—as in fact they *have* been telling you—that there's been no harm done, regardless of what their victims think, feel, or say. The situation is exactly the same as when those with precisely the same mentality used to insist that Step 'n' Fetchit was okay, or Rochester on the Jack Benny Show, or Amos and Andy, Charlie Chan, the Frito Bandito, or any of the other cutesy symbols making up the lexicon of American racism. Have we communicated yet?

10   Let's get just a little bit real here. The notion of "fun" embodied in rituals like the Tomahawk Chop must be understood for what it is. There's not a single non-Indian example used above which can be considered socially acceptable in even the most marginal sense. The reasons are obvious enough. So why is it any different where American Indians are concerned? One can only conclude that, in contrast to the other groups at issue, Indians are (falsely) perceived as being too few, and therefore too weak, to defend themselves effectively against racist and otherwise offensive behavior.

11   Fortunately, there are some glimmers of hope. A few teams and their fans have gotten the message and have responded appropriately. Stanford University, which opted to drop the name "Indians" from Stanford, has experienced no resulting dropoff in attendance. Meanwhile, the local newspaper in Portland, Oregon, recently decided its long-standing editorial policy prohibiting use of racial epithets should include derogatory team names. The Redskins, for instance, are now referred to as "the Washington team," and will continue to be described in this way until the franchise adopts an inoffensive moniker (newspaper sales in Portland have suffered no decline as a result).

12   Such examples are to be applauded and encouraged. They stand as figurative beacons in the night, proving beyond all doubt that it is quite possible to indulge in the pleasure of athletics without accepting blatant racism into the bargain.

13   On October 16, 1946, a man named Julius Streicher mounted the steps of a gallows. Moments later he was dead, the sentence of an international tribunal composed of representatives of the United States, France, Great Britain, and the Soviet Union having been imposed. Streicher's body was then cremated, and—so horrendous were his crimes thought to have been—his ashes dumped into an unspecified German river so that "no one should ever know a particular place to go for reasons of mourning his memory."

14   Julius Streicher had been convicted at Nuremberg, Germany, of what were termed "Crimes Against Humanity." The lead prosecutor in his case—Justice Robert Jackson of the United States Supreme Court—had not argued that the defendant had killed anyone, nor that he had personally committed any especially violent act. Nor was it contended that Streicher had held any particularly important position in the German government during the period in which the so-called Third Reich had exterminated some 6,000,000 Jews, as well as several million Gypsies, Poles, Slavs, homosexuals, and other untermenschen (subhumans).

15   The sole offense for which the accused was ordered put to death was in having served as publisher/editor of a Bavarian tabloid entitled *Der Sturmer* during the early-to-mid 1930s, years before the Nazi genocide actually began. In this capacity, he had penned a long series of virulently anti-Semitic editorials and "news" stories, usually accompanied by cartoons and other images graphically depicting Jews in extraordinarily derogatory fashion. This, the prosecution asserted, had done much to "dehumanize" the targets of his distortion in the mind of the German public. In turn, such dehumanization had made it possible—or at least easier—for average Germans to later indulge in the outright liquidation of Jewish "vermin." The tribunal agreed, holding that Streicher was therefore complicit in genocide and deserving of death by hanging.

16   During his remarks to the Nuremberg tribunal, Justice Jackson observed that, in implementing its sentences, the participating powers were morally and legally binding themselves to adhere forever to the same standards of conduct that were being applied to Streicher and the other Nazi leaders. In the alternative, he said, the victorious allies would have committed "pure murder" at Nuremberg—no different in substance from that carried out by those they presumed to judge—rather than establishing the "permanent benchmark for justice" which was intended.

17   Yet in the United States of Robert Jackson, the indigenous American Indian population had already been reduced, in a process which is ongoing to this day, from perhaps 12.5 million in the year 1500 to fewer than 250,000 by the beginning of the 20th century. This was accomplished, according to official sources, "largely through the cruelty of [Euro-American] settlers," and an informal but clear governmental policy which had made it an articulated goal to "exterminate these red vermin," or at least whole segments of them.

18   Bounties had been placed on the scalps of Indians—any Indians—in places as diverse as Georgia, Kentucky, Texas, the Dakotas, Oregon, and California, and had been maintained until resident Indian populations were decimated or disappeared altogether.

Entire peoples such as the Cherokee had been reduced to half their size through a policy of forced removal from their homelands east of the Mississippi River to what were then considered less preferable areas in the West.

19   Others, such as the Navajo, suffered the same fate while under military guard for years on end. The United States Army had also perpetrated a long series of wholesale massacres of Indians at places like Horseshoe Bend, Bear River, Sand Creek, the Washita River, the Marias River, Camp Robinson, and Wounded Knee.

20   Through it all, hundreds of popular novels—each competing with the next to make Indians appear more grotesque, menacing, and inhuman—were sold in the tens of millions of copies in the U.S. Plainly, the Euro-American public was being conditioned to see Indians in such a way as to allow their eradication to continue. And continue it did until the Manifest Destiny[1] of the U.S.—a direct precursor to what Hitler would subsequently call Lebensraumpolitik (the politics of living space)—was consummated.

21   By 1900, the national project of "clearing" Native Americans from their land and replacing them with "superior" Anglo-American settlers was complete; the indigenous population had been reduced by as much as 98 percent while approximately 97.5 percent of their original territory had "passed" to the invaders. The survivors had been concentrated, out of sight and mind of the public, on scattered "reservations," all of them under the self-assigned "plenary" (full) power of the federal government. There was, of course, no Nuremberg-style tribunal passing judgment on those who had fostered such circumstances in North America. No U.S. official or private citizen was ever imprisoned—never mind hanged—for implementing or propagandizing what had been done. Nor had the process of genocide afflicting Indians been completed. Instead, it merely changed form.

22   Between the 1880s and the 1980s, nearly half of all Native American children were coercively transferred from their own families, communities, and cultures to those of the conquering society. This was done through compulsory attendance at remote boarding schools, often hundreds of miles from their homes, where native children were kept for years on end while being systematically "deculturated" (indoctrinated to think and act in the manner of Euro Americans rather than as Indians). It was also accomplished through a pervasive foster home and adoption program—including "blind" adoptions, where children would be permanently denied information as to who they were/are and where they'd come from—placing native youths in non-Indian homes.

23   The express purpose of all this was to facilitate a U.S. governmental policy to bring about the "assimilation" (dissolution) of indigenous societies. In other words, Indian cultures as such were to be caused to disappear. Such policy objectives are directly contrary to the United Nations 1948 Convention on Punishment and Prevention of the Crime of Genocide, an element of international law arising from the Nuremberg proceedings. The forced "transfer of the children" of a targeted "racial, ethnical, or religious group" is explicitly prohibited as a genocidal activity under the Convention's second article.

24   Article II of the Genocide Convention also expressly prohibits involuntary sterilization as a means of "preventing births among" a targeted population. Yet, in 1975, it was conceded by the U.S. government that its Indian Health Service (IHS), then a subpart of the

---

[1] MAINIFEST DESTINY: A 19th century belief that the White people had the duty and right to control and develop the entire North American Continent.

Bureau of Indian Affairs (BIA), was even then conducting a secret program of involuntary sterilization that had affected approximately 40 percent of all Indian women. The program was allegedly discontinued, and the IHS was transferred to the Public Health Service, but no one was punished. In 1990, it came out that the IHS was inoculating Inuit children in Alaska with Hepatitis-B vaccine. The vaccine had already been banned by the World Health Organization as having a demonstrated correlation with the HIV-Syndrome which is itself correlated to AIDS. As this is written, a "field test" of Hepatitis-A vaccine, also HIV-correlated, is being conducted on Indian reservations in the northern plains region.

25   The Genocide Convention makes it a "crime against humanity" to create conditions leading to the destruction of an identifiable human group, as such. Yet the BIA has utilized the government's plenary prerogatives to negotiate mineral leases "on behalf of" Indian peoples, paying a fraction of standard royalty rates. The result has been "super profits" for a number of preferred U.S. corporations. Meanwhile, Indians, whose reservations ironically turned out to be in some of the most mineral-rich areas of North America, which makes us, the nominally wealthiest segment of the continent's population, live in dire poverty.

26   By the government's own data in the mid-1980s, Indians received the lowest annual and lifetime per capita incomes of any aggregate population group in the United States. Concomitantly, we suffer the highest rate of infant mortality, death by exposure and malnutrition, disease, and the like. Under such circumstances, alcoholism and other escapist forms of substance abuse are endemic in the Indian community, a situation which leads both to a general physical debilitation of the population and a catastrophic accident rate. Teen suicide among Indians is several times the national average.

27   The average life expectancy of a reservation-based Native American man is barely 45 years; women can expect to live less than three years longer.

28   Such itemizations could be continued at great length, including matters like the radioactive contamination of large portions of contemporary Indian Country, the forced relocation of traditional Navajos, and so on. But the point should be made: Genocide, as defined in international law, is a continuing fact of day-to-day life (and death) for North America's native peoples. Yet there has been—and is—only the barest flicker of public concern about, or even consciousness of, this reality. Absent any serious expression of public outrage, no one is punished and the process continues.

29   A salient reason for public acquiescence before the ongoing holocaust in Native North America has been a continuation of the popular legacy, often through more effective media. Since 1925 Hollywood has released more than 2,000 films, many of them rerun frequently on television, portraying Indians as strange, perverted, ridiculous, and often dangerous things of the past. Moreover, we are habitually presented to mass audiences one-dimensionally, devoid of recognizable human motivations and emotions; Indians thus serve as props, little more. We have thus been thoroughly and systematically dehumanized.

30   Nor is this the extent of it. Everywhere, we are used as logos, as mascots, as jokes: "Big Chief" writing tablets, "Red Man" chewing tobacco, "Winnebago" campers, "Navajo" and "Cherokee" and "Pontiac" and "Cadillac" pickups and automobiles. There are the Cleveland "Indians," the Kansas City "Chiefs," the Atlanta "Braves," and the Washington "Redskins" professional sports teams—not to mention those in thousands of colleges, high schools and elementary schools across the country—each with their own degrading caricatures and parodies of Indians and/or things Indian. Pop fiction

continues in the same vein, including an unending stream of New Age manuals purporting to expose the inner works of indigenous spirituality in everything from pseudo-philosophical to do-it-yourself styles. Blond yuppies from Beverly Hills amble about the country claiming to be reincarnated 17th century Cheyenne Ushamans ready to perform previously secret ceremonies.

31   In effect, a concerted, sustained, and in some ways accelerating effort has gone into making Indians unreal. It is thus of obvious importance that the American public begin to think about the implications of such things the next time they witness a gaggle of face-painted and war-bonneted buffoons doing the "Tomahawk Chop" at a baseball or football game. It is necessary that they think about the implications of the grade-school teacher adorning their child in turkey feathers to commemorate Thanksgiving. Think about the significance of John Wayne or Charlton Heston killing a dozen "savages" with a single bullet the next time a western comes on TV. Think about why Land-o-Lakes finds it appropriate to market its butter with the stereotyped image of an "Indian princess" on the wrapper. Think about what it means when non-Indian academics profess—as they often do—to "know more about Indians than Indians do themselves." Think about the significance of charlatans like Carlos Castaneda and Jamake Highwater and Mary Summer Rain and Lynn Andrews churning out "Indian" best-sellers, one after the other, while Indians typically can't get into print.

32   Think about the real situation of American Indians. Think about Julius Streicher. Remember Justice Jackson's admonition. Understand that the treatment of Indians in American popular culture is not "cute" or "amusing" or just "good, clean fun."

33   Know that it causes real pain and real suffering to real people. Know that it threatens our very survival. And know that this is just as much a crime against humanity as anything the Nazis ever did. It is likely that the indigenous people of the United States will never demand that those guilty of such criminal activity be punished for their deeds. But the least we have the right to expect—indeed, to demand—is that such practices finally be brought to a halt.   [1993]

POST-READING QUESTIONS

CONTENT

1. What does Churchill identify as a controversial issue surrounding sports teams? To what has this issue been compared in world history?

2. What does Churchill suggest sports teams do, in order to be consistent in their use of Native American images as mascots and include other racial and ethnic groups? How serious is he?

3. Why does Churchill say that Native Americans are singled out as a racial group in terms of having sports teams named after them? What do you think?

4. What examples of hope does Churchill present?

5. For what offense was Julius Streicher hanged? Did his punishment fit the crime? Explain.

6. What is the U.N. Genocide Convention? Why is it important within the context of this essay?

7. How does Churchill say Justice Jackson differentiated between executing Nazi war criminals and the Nazi's execution of Jewish people?

8. In what ways, according to Churchill, have Native Americans been mistreated?

STYLE AND STRUCTURE

9. Does Churchill have a point? Restate his main idea in your own words.

10. What function does the example of Julius Streicher serve?

11. What is Churchill's tone? Cite the text in order to reveal his tone.

12. What role, if any, does humor play in Churchill's essay? How much true humor exists in it?

13. Who is Churchill's audience? To what extent do you identify with what he says? Explain.

14. What examples of his main idea does Churchill provide? Which is most compelling? Why?

15. Is Churchill persuasive? Explain.

CRITICAL THINKING AND ANALYSIS

DISCUSSION QUESTIONS

16. Churchill describes in great detail a number of fictitious sports teams that would "spread such 'inoffensiveness' and 'good cheer' around among *all* groups . . ." How do these teams compare in terms of offensiveness to the sports teams already claiming Native American mascots and themes? Are they more offensive? Less? Explain.

17. Based upon Churchill's essay, discuss ways in which Native Americans have been treated similarly to, or differently from, Jewish people under Nazi rule. How apt is Churchill's comparison?

WRITING ASSIGNMENTS

18. Churchill quotes people who claim that naming sports teams and mascots after racial and/or ethnic groups is not "demeaning or insulting, at least not when it's being done to Indians." Is he right? Consider the examples Churchill offers and your own observations, and write a few paragraphs arguing that naming sports teams after Native Americans is or is not offensive. If you choose to argue against Churchill, be sure to counter the arguments he offers in his essay with points and examples of your own.

19. What is a "crime against humanity"? Write at least one well-developed paragraph in which you define "crimes against humanity." You may start with Churchill's definition, or you may use one of your own. Just be certain to use examples from your own knowledge and experiences in order to illustrate your ideas.

20. Are all forms of discrimination equally harmful? Write an essay in which you explain how some forms of prejudiced acts are more or less offensive than

others, and why. Be sure to cite Churchill's essay and your own observations in order to illustrate your ideas.

21. Churchill writes this essay in 1993, at which time he claims that "a 'field test' of Hepatitis-A vaccine . . . is being conducted on Indian reservations . . ." Have Americans' treatment of Native Americans improved at all? Write a few paragraphs or essay in which you discuss whether or not Native Americans are being treated better than they were in the past (you can decide how far in the past you want to go). You may need to do some research in order to learn about this topic and offer intelligent, specific examples for support.

22. Churchill writes of his facetious examples of team names that "not a single non-Indian example used above . . . can be considered socially acceptable in even the most marginal sense." Does our awareness of the minority groups that Churchill identifies indicate an increased sensitivity on the part of Americans? Write a few paragraphs or short essay in which you argue that Americans are or are not becoming more sensitive toward minority groups. Cite Churchill's essay and your own experiences in order to illustrate your ideas.

VOCABULARY DEVELOPMENT

23. Using at least six of the words from the Vocabulary Preview, write a paragraph summarizing your views on the issue of sports teams being named for Native Americans.

GROUP ACTIVITIES

24. As a group, perform an online search for information about Native Americans. You may search for information about them as a whole, or you may search for individual tribes. What do you learn? Share your results with the class.

25. Are any other contemporary mascots offensive? Discuss what makes a mascot or team symbol hurtful to others, using any contemporary examples that come to mind.

The Good Marriage

Judith S. Wallerstein and Sandra Blakeslee

Judith S. Wallerstein is a senior lecturer at the School of Social Welfare at the University of California at Berkeley, and Sandra Blakeslee is an award-winning science writer for the *New York Times.* Together, they have written *Second Chances: Men, Women, and Children a Decade After Divorce* and *The Good Marriage: How and Why Love Lasts,* from which this selection comes. Starting by examining the cultural changes that have affected marriage, Wallerstein and Blakeslee address and then answer the question: What makes a good marriage?

Pre-reading Questions

Freewrite for five to ten minutes in response to the following questions:
Of all the people you know who are or have been married, what percentage of people are still married? What percentage of people are happily married? How can you tell? What do you think makes a difference between whether or not people are happy in a marriage or not? Explain.

Vocabulary Preview

Vocabulary Words:
- optimism
- passe
- irrevocable
- centripetal
- centrifugal
- vicissitudes
- conjugal
- milieu
- presentiments
- beleaguered

Look up the words above, paying attention to how they are used in the essay. Then, substitute the definitions of the words for the words themselves. What is the overall effect on the readability of the essay? Explain this effect in a few sentences.

1   We have been so preoccupied with divorce and crisis in the American family that we have failed to notice the good marriages that are all around us and from which we can learn. In today's world it's easy to become overwhelmed by problems that seem to have no solution. But we *can* shape our lives at home, including our relationships with our children and marriage itself. The home is the one place where we have the potential to create a world that is to our own liking; it is the last place where we should feel despair. As never before in history, men and women today are free to design the kind of marriage they want, with their own rules and expectations.

2   Fortunately, many young people have not yet become cynical and are still able to speak directly from the heart. After spending some wonderful hours talking to college students about their views of marriage, I received the next day a letter from Randolph Johnson, a twenty-one-old senior at the University of California in Santa Cruz. He wrote: "What I want in a wife is someone whom I know so well that she is a part of who I am and I of her. Someone to fill all that I am not but aspire to be. My wife is

someone not just to share a life with but to build a life with. This is what marriage is to me, the sharing of two lives to complete each other. It is true that people change, but if people can change together then they need not grow apart."

3   Randolph speaks for a new generation that is still capable of optimism about love and marriage and "the sharing of two lives to complete each other." He also speaks for a society that is tired to death of the war on marriage, escalating divorce rates, and the search for new partners in middle age. All of us want a different world for our children. When we're honest, we want it for ourselves.

4   It is absurd, in fact, to suggest that the need for enduring love and intimacy in marriage is passé. The men and women I've seen in twenty-five years of studying divorce begin actively searching for a new relationship even before the divorce is final. In every study in which Americans are asked what they value most in assessing the quality of their lives, marriage comes first—ahead of friends, jobs, and money. In our fast-paced world men and women need each other more, not less. We want and need erotic love, sympathetic love, passionate love, tender, nurturing love all of our adult lives. We desire friendship, compassion, encouragement, a sense of being understood and appreciated, not only for what we do but for what we try to do and fail at. We want a relationship in which we can test our half-baked ideas without shame or pretense and give voice to our deepest fears. We want a partner who sees us as unique and irreplaceable.

5   In the past twenty years, marriage in America has undergone a profound, irrevocable transformation, driven by changes in women's roles and the heightened expectations of both men and women. Without realizing it, we have crossed a marital Rubicon. For the first time in our history, the decision to stay married is purely voluntary. Anyone can choose to leave at any time—and everyone knows it, including the children. There used to be only two legal routes out of marriage—adultery and abandonment. Today one partner simply has to say, for whatever reason, "I want out." Divorce is as simple as a trip to the nearest courthouse.

6   Each year two million adults and a million children in this country are newly affected by divorce. One in two American marriages ends in divorce, and one in three children can expect to experience their parents' divorce. This situation has powerful ripple effects that touch us all. The sense that relationships are unstable affects the family next door, the people down the block, the other children in the classroom. Feelings of intense anxiety about marriage permeate the consciousness of all young men and women on the threshold of adulthood. At every wedding the guests wonder, privately, will this marriage last? The bride and groom themselves may question why they should marry, since it's likely to break up.

7   To understand how our social fabric has been transformed, think of marriage as an institution acted upon by centripetal forces pulling inward and centrifugal forces pulling outward. In times past the centripetal forces—law, tradition, religion, parental influence—exceeded those that could pull a marriage apart, such as infidelity, abuse, financial disaster, failed expectations, or the lure of the frontier. Nowadays the balance has changed. The weakened centripetal forces can no longer exceed those that tug marriages apart.

8   In today's marriages, in which people work long hours, travel extensively, and juggle careers with family, more forces tug at the relationship than ever before. Modern marriages are battered by the demands of her workplace as well as his, by changing

community values, by anxiety about making ends meet each month, by geographical moves, by unemployment and recession, by the vicissitudes of child care, and by a host of other issues.

9 Marriage counselors like to tell their clients that there are at least six people in every marital bed—the couple and both sets of parents. I'm here to say that a crazy quilt of conflicting personal values and shifting social attitudes is also in that bed. The confusion over roles and the indifference of the community to long-term conjugal relationships are there, as are the legacies of a self-absorbed, me-first, feminist-do-or-die, male-backlash society. The ease of divorce and changing attitudes about the permanence of marriage have themselves become centrifugal forces.

10 Our great unacknowledged fear is that these potent outside forces will overwhelm the human commitment that marriage demands and that marriage as a lasting institution will cease for most people. We are left with a crushing anxiety about the future of marriage and about the men and women within it.

11 My study of divorce has inevitably led me to think deeply about marriage. Just as people who work with the dying worry about death, those of us who work with troubled marriages are constantly forced to look at our own relationships. So I have carefully taken note of my marriage and those of my three grown children. As our fiftieth wedding anniversary approaches, I have thought long and hard about what my husband and I have done to protect our marriage. Why have we been able to love each other for so many years? Did we begin differently from those who divorced? Did we handle crises differently? Or were we just lucky? What have I learned that I can pass on to my children and my grandchildren?

12 I certainly have not been happy all through each year of my marriage. There have been good times and bad, angry and joyful moments, times of ecstasy and times of quiet contentment. But I would never trade my husband, Robert, for another man. I would not swap my marriage for any other. This does not mean that I find other men unattractive, but there is all the difference in the world between a passing fancy and a life plan. For me, there has always been only one life plan, the one I have lived with my husband. But why is this so? What makes some marriages work while others fail?

13 An acquaintance of mine—a highly regarded psychologist who has done extensive marriage counseling—called me when she became engaged. She said, "I want to spend several hours with you, drawing on your experience. My fiancé is several years older than I am and has been though one divorce. He's afraid of another failure. I'm thirty-eight years old and have for many years been frightened of marriage. What wisdom do you have for me based on your own marriage, which has always looked so ideal to me, and also based on your many years of work with divorce? Help me anticipate what lies ahead for Jim and me, so I can be prepared." Her request intrigued me. What wisdom did she seek? She did not want shortcuts or hints but a realistic vision that could guide their efforts in building a successful marriage.

14 Not long after her call I decided to design a qualitative study of fifty couples who had built lasting, happy marriages, couples who had confronted the same obstacles, crises, and temptations as everyone else and had overcome them. As I began setting up the study, I drew up a list of questions that would guide my inquiry. Are the people in

good marriages different from the men and women whose marriages fall apart? Are there common ideas, ways of dealing with the inevitable crises? What can we learn about selecting a partner, about sex, the stresses of the workplace, infidelity, the arrival of a baby or of adolescence, coping with midlife, aging, and retirement? What is happy in a marriage when people are in their twenties, thirties, forties, or fifties, or when they reach retirement? What are the central themes of each life stage? What makes men happy? What makes women happy? What does each spouse value in one another? What do they regard as the glue of their marriage?

15   A good marriage is a process of continual change as it reflects new issues, deals with problems that arise, and uses the resources available at each stage of life. All long-lasting marriages change, if simply because we all change as we grow older. People's needs, expectations, and wishes change during the life cycle; biological aging is intertwined with psychological change in every domain, including work, health, sex, parenting, and friends. The social milieu and external circumstances change as well. Thus the individuals change, the marriage changes, and the world outside changes—and not necessarily in sync with one another. As one woman said, "John and I have had at least six different marriages."

16   Many men and women are still becoming adults as they work on the first chapter of their lives together—getting to know each other sexually, emotionally, and psychologically. This time of absorbing exploration is critically important for defining the couple's core relationship. Sadly, many couples find they cannot navigate this difficult first leg of the course. But if they do succeed, they will have a sturdy foundation for the structure of their marriage.

17   The birth of a child entirely revamps the internal landscape of marriage. Becoming a father or mother is a major step in the life course, a step that requires inner psychological growth as well as changes in every part of the marital relationship and the extended family. It is also usually a time when one or both partners have made career commitments; the tough road of the workplace stretches ahead, and its stresses are high.

18   For many people the years when the children are growing up is the busiest time of their lives. A central issue is balancing the demands of work and of home. Children's needs for parental time and attention multiply along with the continuing demands of the workplace and often of school. Many couples cannot find enough time to be together even to exchange greetings, let alone make love.

19   The course of marriage changes again when children become adolescents, when parents dealing with midlife issues and presentiments of aging are suddenly faced with sexually active youngsters. The growing dependency, illness, or death of the spouses' own aging parents adds further turbulence to this period. When the children leave home, the couple must find each other again and rebuild their relationship. This new stage provides an opportunity to re-create the marriage in a different mold, perhaps with time to travel and play together. If a husband and wife have not succeeded in building a good marriage by now, they may find themselves merely sharing a household.

20   A later part of the journey is retirement, when issues of dependency and illness, as well as the opportunity to pursue new hobbies and interests and the continuing need for sexuality, take center stage. Once again, the marriage is redefined, as the

couples face life's final chapters and inevitably consider the loss of the partner and their own deaths.

21   All through adulthood our internal lives change as we create new images of ourselves and call up old images from the past. At each stage we draw on different memories and wishes, pulling them out like cards from a deck held close to the heart. The birth of a child draws on the memories and unconscious images of each parent's own infancy and childhood. That child's adolescence evokes the memories and conflicts of one's own teen years. Parents, watching their teenagers assert their independence, remember their own risk-taking behavior and realize that they were often saved from disaster by the skin of their teeth. And as old age approaches, every person draws on the experiences of prior losses in the family.

22   We have for many years told our children that marriage requires hard and continuing work, but since we could not tell them where or how to begin this work, we soon lost their attention. How could we tell them what we did not know?

23   What then are the secrets? How do a man and woman who meet as strangers create a relationship that will satisfy them both throughout their lives?

24   First, the answer to the question I started with—what do people define as happy in their marriage?—turned out to be straightforward. For everyone, happiness in marriage meant feeling respected and cherished. Without exception, these couples mentioned the importance of liking and respecting each other and the pleasure and comfort they took in each other's company. Some spoke of the passionate love that began their relationship, but for a surprising number love grew in the rich soil of the marriage, nourished by emotional and physical intimacy, appreciation, and fond memories. Some spoke of feeling well cared for, others of feeling safe, and still others of friendship and trust. Many talked about the family they had created together. But all felt that they were central to their partner's world and believed that creating the marriage and the family was the major commitment of their adult life. For most, marriage and children were the achievements in which they took the greatest pride.

25   For these couples, respect was based on integrity; a partner was admired and loved for his or her honesty, compassion, generosity of spirit, decency, loyalty to the family, and fairness. An important aspect of respect was admiration of the partner as a sensitive, conscientious parent. The value these couples placed on the partner's moral qualities was an unexpected finding. It helps explain why many divorcing people speak so vehemently of losing respect for their former partner. The love that people feel in a good marriage goes with the conviction that the person is worthy of being loved.

26   These people were realists. No one denied that there were serious differences—conflict, anger, even some infidelity—along the way. No one envisioned marriage as a rose garden, but all viewed its satisfaction as far outweighing the frustrations over the long haul. Most regarded frustrations, big and small, as an inevitable aspect of life that would follow them no matter whom they married. Everyone had occasional fantasies about the roads not taken, but their commitment to the marriage withstood the impulse to break out.

27   Above all, they shared the view that their partner was special in some important regard and that the marriage enhanced each of them as individuals. They felt that the fit between their own needs and their partner's responses was unique and probably irreplaceable. In this they considered themselves very lucky, not entitled.

28   Their marriages had benefited from the new emphasis in our society on equality in relationships between men and women. However they divided up the chores of the household and of raising the children, the couples agreed that men and women had equal rights and responsibilities within the family. Women have taken many casualties in the long fight to achieve equality, and many good men have felt beleaguered, confused, and angry about this contest. But important goals have been achieved: marriages today allow for greater flexibility and greater choice. Relationships are more mature on both sides and more mutually respectful. A couple's sex life can be freer and more pleasurable. Today's men and women meet on a playing field that is more level than ever before.

29   Unlike many unhappy families, these couples provide no evidence for the popular notion that there is a "his" marriage and a "her" marriage. On the contrary, the men and women were very much in accord. I did not see significant differences between husbands and wives in their goals for the marriage, in their capacity for love and friendship, and in their interest in sex, in their desire to have children, or in their love and commitment to the children. They fully shared the credit for the success of the marriage and the family. Both men and women said, "Everything we have we did together."

30   Although some men were inhibited in their expression of feelings at the beginning of the marriage, as compared with their wives, I did not find much difference between the sexes in their ability to express emotions over the course of their relationship. Both spoke easily of their love for their partner. In response to my questioning, both men and women cried when they contemplated losing the other.

31   The children were central, both as individuals and as symbols of a shared vision, giving pleasure and sometimes unexpected meaning to the parents' lives and to the marriage. As the couples reported to me in detail, the children reflected their love and pride. And this powerful bond did not diminish when the children left home.

32   As I compared the happily married couples with the thousands of divorcing couples I have seen in the past twenty-five years, it was clear that these men and women had early on created a firm basis for their relationship and had continued to build it together. Many of the couples that divorced failed to lay such a foundation and did not understand the need to reinforce it over the years. Many marriages broke because the structure was too weak to hold in the face of life's vicissitudes. The happy couples regarded their marriage as a work in progress that needed continued attention lest it fall into disrepair. Even in retirement they did not take each other for granted. Far too many divorcing couples fail to understand that a marriage does not just spring into being after the ceremony. Neither the legal nor the religious ceremony makes the marriage. *People* do, throughout their lives.

33   As I write these final paragraphs, my thoughts turn to my grandmother and to Nikki, my youngest grandchild. My grandmother, who brought her three young children to the new land in the hold of a ship and raised them by herself, knew exactly what she wanted for me. When I was growing up, she used to sing Yiddish folk songs about

love and marriage, about mysterious suitors from distant lands. Whom will you marry? the songs asked. Her hopes for me were built on her own tears. My future happy marriage and my unborn healthy children made her sacrifice worthwhile.

34   Nikki has just turned four. She has recently demoted her twenty or so stuffed bears, puppies, kittens, even her beloved tiger, to the foot of her bed. They who were her special joy hardly have her attention now. She has entered a new phase. I am to address her as "Princess" when I call. (The great advantage of grandmothers, I have discovered, is that they follow instructions, whereas mothers issue instructions.) She is Princess Jasmine, and she awaits Aladdin. She is practicing at being a grown-up young lady, preparing for the future with all the energy and devotion that she brought to caring for her animals. No one works harder or with greater purpose than a child at play.

35   What do I want for Nikki? The roads that were so clear to my grandmother have become harder to follow. They fork often and sometimes lead to a dead end. Some directions, however, are still visible. I, too, want my granddaughter to be strong and brave and virtuous. I want her to love and be loved passionately and gently and proudly by a man worth loving. I want her to experience the joys and terrors of raising children. But far beyond what my grandmother envisioned for me, I want Nikki to have the choices in life that I and many others had to fight for, real choices that the community will respect and support. And I want her to know how to choose wisely and understand how to make it all work. I hope that Nikki finds the Aladdin that she has started to look for. If he comes flying into her life on a magic carpet, so much the better.

POST-READING QUESTIONS

CONTENT

1. Why do Wallerstein and Blakeslee say people have forgotten to pay attention to good marriages? What signs of hope for lasting marriages do the authors offer?
2. What has caused marriage to undergo a "profound, irrevocable transformation," according to Wallerstein and Blakeslee?
3. What are some factors that work against a marriage lasting? Which of these seems, to you, most significant? Explain.
4. Wallerstein and Blakeslee ask numerous questions regarding the nature of good marriages. What answers do they give to questions such as "What [is] the glue of the marriage?"?
5. What stages mark major changes in a marriage?
6. How do the writers define happiness in a marriage?
7. What are some other factors necessary to happy marriages?

STYLE AND STRUCTURE

8. Do the writers have a single point? What is it?
9. What is the purpose of the questions the writers use throughout their essay?

10. What examples do the writers offer to clarify and strengthen their ideas?

11. What is the writers' attitude toward marriage? How can you tell?

12. Who is the writers' audience? Cite the text for evidence of the target readers.

13. Are the writers convincing? Explain.

CRITICAL THINKING AND ANALYSIS

DISCUSSION QUESTIONS

14. Wallerstein and Blakeslee write that "For everyone, happiness in marriage meant feeling respected and cherished." What do you think is most important in a lasting marriage? Explain and give examples.

15. The authors write, "For the first time in our history, the decision to stay married is purely voluntary." What are some effects of this situation? Discuss whether you think more benefits or drawbacks have resulted from the ease of getting divorced.

WRITING ASSIGNMENTS

16. Wallerstein and Blakeslee mention many factors that contribute to happy marriages, among these: respect, pleasure, comfort, passion, friendship, and trust. What do you think is most important in making a marriage last? Write at least one well-developed paragraph in which you explain what factor is most responsible for ensuring a lasting marriage. Cite the text and your own experiences for support.

17. The authors write ". . . think of marriage as an institution acted upon by centripetal forces pulling inward and centrifugal forces pulling outward." In a few well-developed paragraphs, identify some of the forces pulling inward and outward, and argue which ones are stronger. Cite the essay and your own observations in order to clarify and strengthen your ideas.

18. What role does civility play in a lasting marriage? Write a few paragraphs or short essay in which you explain the importance of civility in a good marriage. Cite Wallerstein and Blakeslee and your own experiences for support.

19. The writers claim that getting a divorce "is as simple as a trip to the nearest courthouse." Do you think the ability to get an easy divorce is generally positive or negative? Write a few paragraphs explaining whether or not you think the ease of divorce is beneficial or detrimental to marriage. Use examples from Wallerstein and Blakeslee and your own life in order to illustrate your ideas.

VOCABULARY DEVELOPMENT

20. Choose at least one paragraph from Wallerstein's and Blakeslee's essay, and rewrite it from the point of view of someone who is divorced. What changes do you make? Do your changes take the form of word switches, or example changes? Explain the nature of your revisions in a few sentences.

GROUP ACTIVITIES

21. Before coming to class, watch any contemporary television programs that address the concept of marriage. Then, try to find re-runs of marriage-oriented television programs from twenty to forty years ago, and compare the depictions of marriage. What has changed? What has stayed the same? Share your results with your group and then discuss them with the class in an open forum setting.

22. As a group, make two lists: one of the characteristics of a happy marriage, and one of the qualities of a "tolerable" union. How are the lists similar? Different? Share your lists with other groups for comparison.

The Unspeakable Pleasure
A Study of Human Cruelty

Leonard Sax

Leonard Sax, M.D., Ph.D. is a physician and psychologist practicing in Montgomery County, Maryland. In "The Unspeakable Pleasure," Sax begins with the Littleton, Colorado massacre of April 1999 and chronicles various examples of human cruelty throughout history, claiming that the seemingly shocking brutality of murderers Eric Harris and Dylan Klebold was nothing new to the human race. Rather, Sax, contends, not only are people accustomed to witnessing physical suffering, but we enjoy it.

Pre-reading Questions

Freewrite for five to ten minutes in response to the following questions:
How much do you think people enjoy seeing others suffer physically? Are some kinds of suffering more entertaining to watch than others? Explain. To what extent do you think people are fascinated with cruelty? Why?

Vocabulary Preview

Vocabulary Words:	• cursory	• zealous	• avail
	• bestial	• magnanimous	• manifestation
	• naivete	• subjection	• juxtaposed
	• solitary	• notoriety	• vignettes
	• pious		

Look up the words above and then rank them according to which words are most, or least, powerful. Then, write a few sentences explaining why you ranked the words the way you did.

LITTLETON, COLORADO, APRIL 20, 1999, AROUND 11:20 A.M.

1   Eric Harris and Dylan Klebold enter the library of Columbine High School. Armed with a double-barreled shotgun, a pump shotgun and two semi-automatic rifles, they open fire on their classmates. As students scream and dive for cover, the two killers stroll around the library, looking for targets. One of the gunmen spots 17-year-old Kacey Ruegsegger crouching under a table. "Peekaboo," he says, stooping to fire a bullet into her neck. He laughs as she crumples to the floor, bleeding.

2   "They were shooting everywhere. . . . They wanted to kill everything in sight," recalled senior Nick Foss, who managed to escape the shooters by punching through a ceiling panel and shimmying down a ventilation shaft. "They were, like, orgasmic," said 19-year-old Nicholas Schumann, who heard the shooters' laughter while hiding in a room under the library.

KAUNAS, LITHUANIA, JUNE 27, 1941, AROUND 11 A.M.

3   From the report of a German army officer:

4   While I was traveling through the town, I went past a gasoline station which was surrounded by a dense crowd of people. There was a large number of women in the crowd and they had lifted up their children or stood them on chairs or boxes so that they could see better. At first I thought this must be a victory celebration or some type of sporting event because of the cheering, clapping, and laughter that kept breaking out. However, when I inquired what was happening, I was told that the "Death-Dealer of Kovno" was at work. . . . I became witness to probably the most frightful event that I had seen during the course of two world wars.

5   A blond man of medium height, aged about twenty-five, stood leaning on a wooden club, resting. At his feet lay about fifteen to twenty dead or dying people. Water flowed continuously from a hose washing blood away into the drainage gully. Just a few steps behind this man some twenty men, guarded by armed civilians, stood waiting for their cruel execution in silent submission. In response to a cursory wave the next man stepped forward silently and was then beaten to death with the wooden club in the most bestial manner, each blow accompanied by enthusiastic shouts from the audience.

6   The report of the photographer who was present:

7   Within three-quarters of an hour he had beaten to death the entire group of 45 to 50 people in this way . . . After the entire group had been beaten to death, the young man put the club to one side, fetched an accordion and went and stood on the mountain of corpses and played the Lithuanian national anthem. . . . The behavior of the civilians present (women and children) was unbelievable. After each man had been killed they began to clap. . . . In the front row there were women with children in their arms who stayed there right until the end of the whole proceedings.

THE UNSPEAKABLE PLEASURE OF CRUELTY

8   There is an important difference between the killing spree of the Lithuanians on June 27, 1941, and the killing spree of Dylan Klebold and Eric Harris on April 20, 1999. The Lithuanians were acting in accordance with the directives of their newly arrived German occupiers; Klebold and Harris were breaking the law. The Lithuanians were interested in killing only Jews; Klebold and Harris had a laundry list of hatreds that included athletes, Christians, blacks, and Hispanics. According to some witnesses, Harris and Klebold fired at anything that moved.

9   But the two killing sprees share something that has not received as much attention as it should. In both cases the executioners were having a good time. Eyewitnesses to both events commented on the laughter that accompanied the killing. These people were enjoying themselves. They were having a ball.

A SHORT HISTORY OF CRUELTY

10   The taste for cruelty—for getting a kick out of watching other people suffer and die—is not new. There have always been individuals who took pleasure in killing other human beings. There have even been cultures in which the taste for murder could be indulged with a good conscience. As Friedrich Nietzsche observed, in modern times we are not

able "to imagine, vividly, the degree to which cruelty was the basis for all the great festival pleasures of more primitive peoples. It was an ingredient mixed into almost every one of their pleasures. And they showed their thirst for cruelty with complete naivete, without the slightest feeling of guilt."

11   Nietzsche may have been thinking of imperial Rome, which had a well-deserved reputation for institutionalized cruelty. When Caligula was named emperor in a.d. 37, the centerpiece of his inauguration was the public slaughter of 160,000 slaves and criminals. Watching people die was a staple of popular entertainment in imperial Rome. Any citizen could go to the Coliseum and watch gladiators fight to the death, or enjoy the spectacle of condemned criminals being torn apart by wild beasts.

12   Emperor Nero—who ruled from a.d. 54 to 68—had a particular fondness for first-hand murder. His favorite pastime was to wait in disguise on the backstreets of Rome for an opportune moment to assault a solitary pedestrian, stab the unfortunate man repeatedly, and then throw the corpse into the sewer. On one occasion a victim fought back with ferocious strength, thrashing Nero almost to the point of death. After that, the emperor made sure to have a squad of armed men close at hand in the event that things went awry.

13   The advent of Christianity did not eliminate the taste for cruelty. Will Durrant, surveying the whole history of official torture during the Middle Ages in Europe, concluded that "the worst tortures were practiced not upon murderers by barons but upon pious heretics by Christian monks." Brother Robert was a Dominican monk and a zealous Inquisitor. On a single day in the year 1239, Robert ordered 180 prisoners under his authority to be burned at the stake. Pope Gregory, alarmed, removed Robert from office. The Dominican monks were so bloodthirsty during the Inquisition that they were nicknamed, as a pun, Domini canes: the hunting dogs of God.

14   It might be argued that the Inquisitors were cruel only because of their passion for their cause. They believed that they were doing God's will, or so they said. Surveying the whole history of human cruelty, however, one finds cruel men in every time and place. I suspect that men who chose to be Inquisitors did so because they knew—perhaps only subconsciously—that as Inquisitors they would be able to satisfy their appetite for cruelty.

CHOOSING CRUELTY

15   Appamattox, Virginia, April 9, 1865. Lee has just surrendered to Grant; the Civil War is over. The men of the Union Army have good reason to be enraged toward the defeated Confederates. They have seen their Union Army comrades wounded and killed by the rebels. A decision has to be made: What shall be done with the men of the Confederacy? If Brother Robert had been the commanding general at Appomattox, he might well have ordered—in the words of another papal officer six hundred years earlier—"Kill them all." But General Grant ordered that the defeated soldiers be fed and permitted a safe passage home with their horses and gear, so that they would be able to finish the spring planting in time to ensure a good harvest for the fall. Confederate officers were even allowed to keep their sidearms.

16   Maj. Holman Melcher of the 20th Maine Regiment was impressed by Grant's decision. Melcher wrote to his brother that "a feeling of indignation would rise within me

when I would think of all the bloodshed and mourning these [Confederate soldiers] had caused. But it is honorable to be magnanimous to a conquered foe. And as civilized men and gentlemen, we strive to keep such feelings in subjection."

17   Melcher understood that cruelty is a choice, as magnanimity is a choice. Following Grant's example, he chose magnanimity—although he and other Union Army soldiers had much more justification to kill the Confederates than the Lithuanians had for killing their Jewish neighbors, or than Klebold and Harris had for killing their fellow students.

18   The discovery, after the Second World War, that millions of civilians had been murdered in concentration camps constituted "the final and utter condemnation of the Nazi Party . . . such a disgrace to the German people that their names must be erased from the list of civilized nations." The Nazis had made a choice opposite to that made by General Grant and Major Melcher: They had chosen cruelty instead of magnanimity. As C.S. Lewis observed shortly after the war's end:

> What was the sense in saying the enemy were in the wrong unless Right is a real thing which the Nazis at bottom knew as well as we did and ought to have practiced? If they had no notion of what we mean by Right, then, though we might still have had to fight them, we could no more have blamed them for that than for the colour of their hair.

19   Lewis rejected any idea that the Nazis were "programmed" or "conditioned" to behave as they did. He insisted that the Nazis knew good from evil as well as anybody did, but they had chosen to do evil.

20   The Nazis who tortured and killed their victims could have chosen to do otherwise. After the war, many Nazis defended their actions by claiming that they themselves would have been shot if they had refused to kill. The postwar German government carried on investigations of these claims for over forty years after the war, and not a single case showed that a German soldier was severely punished, let alone shot, for refusing to take part in the persecution or murder of the Jews. There were, on the other hand, a great many cases in which German soldiers and officers were excused from duty or transferred to other duties when they objected that they could not do what they were being asked to do. One soldier recalled, "As a result of considerable psychological pressures, there were numerous men who were no longer capable of conducting executions and who thus had to be replaced by other men. On the other hand, there were others who could not get enough of them and often reported to these executions voluntarily."

'TOTAL DEPRAVITY'

21   Soon after the massacre in Littleton, Colorado, fifteen memorial crosses were erected on a hill near Columbine High School: thirteen for the victims and two for the killers. The fact that Eric Harris and Dylan Klebold were included in the memorial made it seem as though the gunmen themselves were somehow victims: victims of high school bullies (according to one theory), victims of poor parenting (another theory), or victims of abnormal brain blood flow. From a historical perspective, what has been most remarkable about the aftermath of Columbine is the general reluctance to place the blame directly on the ones who did the shooting. Yet the killers certainly wanted all the blame—and all the notoriety and all the attention—for themselves. "Do not blame others for our actions," Harris wrote in the suicide note he left behind.

22   The inclusion of the two gunmen among the victims did not attract much comment. But could anyone ever imagine putting up a memorial to the Nazis killed in the Second World War at, say, the Holocaust Museum in Washington, D.C.? The father of the one of the Columbine victims finally tore down the crosses set up for Klebold and Harris. But the search for the "real" cause of the killing spree continues in the media. Few are willing to let the responsibility rest on the two young men who pulled the triggers.

23   This search for the "root causes of teen violence" would have been incomprehensible to people living a hundred or a thousand years ago: not because they didn't have violent teenagers—they did—but because they had a fundamentally different concept of human nature.

24   Until quite recently, people were not thought to be "naturally" good. The natural tendency of human nature was thought to be inclined toward evil. In Judaism this tendency is called the yetzer ha-ra, the Evil Urge. In Roman Catholicism this idea takes several forms, one of which is the doctrine of Original Sin: an innate stain on the soul of every human being, inherited from Adam's sin in the Garden of Eden. Calvinist theology teaches the doctrine of "total depravity," according to which all human beings, in the final analysis, are at heart totally evil, unless they avail themselves of God's saving grace.

25   I mention these doctrines only as a reminder that until the twentieth century, the mainstream of Western moral thought conceived of human nature as basically evil, but redeemable (Rousseau and his intellectual heirs are the notable exceptions to this rule). Evil actions by an individual were interpreted as a manifestation of "raw" human nature breaking through.

26   No longer. In the aftermath of Littleton, there was—and continues to be—endless debate over why "brainy kids from seemingly stable, affluent homes becoming killing machines without a hint of remorse?" (Note Newsweek's choice of the words killing machine. A machine cannot make moral choices.) "We all [began] chattering at once," mused Time reporter Lance Morrow. "American society in the late 90's is a busy chat room set up for just this kind of thing . . . with noisy experts on tap, interrupting one another from different quadrants of the screen. We round up the usual suspects—in the current case, our cretinous popular culture; the Internet, with its rancid cul-de-sacs; violent movies; idiot television; vicious rap; ubiquitous sex."

27   There has been a momentous shift in perspective in just the past fifty years. Today the unspoken assumption is that people are naturally good. If someone does something evil, there must be some external explanation for it, or so we believe nowadays: Perhaps the criminal was abused or neglected by his parents; maybe he watched too much violent television or played too many violent video games. The implication is that if only these boys had not been conditioned by the wrong influences, they might never have committed their crimes. The killers are thereby absolved of responsibility for their actions, at least partially.

28   What happened to bring about such a shift in perspective, in such a comparably short time? One man, more than any other, is responsible for this transformation. Although his name was a household word in the United States in the 1950s, few now remember him or read his books. But his beliefs, for better or worse, have come to influence every aspect of debate on topics as diverse as crime, child development, education, and discipline in the

home. His name was Burrhus Frederick Skinner. B.F. Skinner (1904–1990) was a professor of psychology who disagreed with the central premise of Western morality: namely, that every person is responsible for his own actions. Skinner was convinced that people could not, and should not, be held responsible for their own actions. He wrote: In what we may call the prescientific view, a person's behavior is at least to some extent his own achievement. . . . he is to be given credit for his successes and blamed for his failures. In the scientific view . . . a person's behavior is determined by a genetic endowment traceable to the evolutionary history of the species and by the environmental circumstances to which as an individual he has been exposed. (Note Skinner's cleverness is referring to the whole tradition of Western moral thought as "the prescientific view.")

29   Why are some people cruel? Because they have been rewarded in the past for being cruel, Skinner would answer. Why are some people kind? Because they have been rewarded in the past for being kind. Moral choice does not exist, according to Skinner. "Conditioning shapes behavior as a sculptor shapes a lump of clay," he wrote. "We could solve many of the problems of delinquency and crime if we could change the early environment of offenders," he confidently predicted. Skinner was immensely influential in his heyday, the late 1940s and '50s. After the Second World War, there was a widespread belief that traditional Western culture had failed. After all, no society had been more "cultured" than German society. And yet some German concentration camp guards had taken pleasure in torturing the inmates; German camp commandants had made lampshades out of the inmates' skins. Being "cultured" was not, apparently, any protection against the lure of cruelty. According to Skinner's theories, the Germans must have been "conditioned" to torture and kill. People were ready to believe that the right kind of conditioning could prevent a repetition of the Holocaust.

30   Everything depended on early childhood, Skinner believed. The business of child raising was therefore much too important to be left to parents: It should be taken over by the state, and run by professionals such as himself. "Wonderful things can be done in the first years of life," he imagined, if only children could be raised in central state-run institutions. In our current state of ignorance, children are left "to people [i.e., parents] whose mistakes range all the way from child abuse to overprotection and the lavishing of affection on the wrong behavior. . . . That is all changed when children are, from the very first, part of larger community." Skinner considered communist China to be "closer to the solutions I have been talking about, but a Communist revolution in America is hard to imagine." More's the pity.

THE THEORY DIES, THE MYTH SURVIVES

31   Skinner's theories about the power of "conditioning" turned out to be a dismal failure. By the mid-1960s, psychologists had recognized that Skinner had grossly overestimated the power of conditioning, even in laboratory animals. His theories were completely unable to account for whole realms of human behavior, such as language acquisition. (Skinner's predictions about how and why children learn to talk turned out to be wildly inaccurate.) His refusal to explore or even consider individual differences within species made it impossible for him or his students to study even the few important questions that could be raised within his theoretical framework: for instance: why

do some people enjoy gambling and others don't? (To put it in Skinner's language: Why is gambling a positive reinforcer for some people and not for others?) He could argue that people who gamble as adults are people who were rewarded for gambling when they were children, but that seems unlikely.

32   Skinner's theories of conditioning are still regarded as useful in explaining simple behaviors, such as a pigeon pecking at a key for food. But his ideas are now recognized as being of little value in understanding most of the issues of interest to psychologists today, such as: how children learn; why marriages break apart; why some people get addicted to drugs and other people don't; and so on.

THE MEDICALIZATION OF BEHAVIOR

33   Skinner's theories may have failed as science, but they have been tremendously successful as myth. They still influence public thinking and debate to a much greater extent than is generally recognized. In popular novels such as Aldous Huxley's Brave New World and Anthony Burgess' *A Clockwork Orange,* writers assumed the correctness of Skinner's theories regarding the power of conditioning and then imagined what the social consequences of Skinnerian conditioning might be. Amplified in the popular culture not only by books such as these, but also by endless TV shows and B-movies in which a character is "conditioned" or "brainwashed" to perform some bizarre act, Skinner's beliefs gave rise to a whole generation that accepts the notion that people do whatever they are "conditioned" to do. Major Melcher's insight at Appomattox—that humans can and must choose which of their impulses to act on—was neglected. The idea that a person is responsible for his actions has been blunted, replaced by Skinner's idea that a person just does what he has been conditioned to do. You can't hold someone responsible for his conditioning, Skinner argued. Hence, the responsibility for a crime should not be laid on the criminal but on the society that conditioned him to behave as he did.

34   In the past twenty years, Skinner's ideas have acquired a medical gloss. Whereas Skinner might have said that conditioning is destiny, today's popular science writers implicitly believe that neurobiology is destiny. Behavior is determined—so the modern science writer believes—by a mix of Skinnerian conditioning and neurophysiology. Skinner's key belief—that moral choice is an illusion—has been accepted hook, line, and sinker, without ever being carefully examined.

JUDGMENT AT LITTLETON

35   The week after Littleton, Newsweek ran an article titled "Why the Young Kill." Its writers claimed to know "the bottom line: you need a particular environment imposed on a particular biology to turn a child into a killer." Note that the killer himself no longer has any choice in the matter, according to Newsweek. His biology and his environment determine what he will become. The article juxtaposed interviews with a variety of brain scientists alongside vignettes of teenage killers. "The early environment programs the nervous system to make an individual more or less reactive to stress," one scientist explained. "[Parental] neglect impairs the development of the brain's cortex, which controls feelings of belonging and development." Colorful "brain scans" were

included in the article to show how the brains of "violent" teens "show several abnormalities compared with a normal brain." The article quoted approvingly from books with titles such as The Biology of Violence and Change Your Brain/Change Your Life. The word evil was never mentioned.

36   The scientific foundation for this way of thinking about human behavior is practically nonexistent. A few studies do suggest subtle differences in brain blood flow between murderers and nonmurderers. But the differences are small and have not yet been replicated by subsequent studies. Even if it were the case—which it is not—that all murderers have a different pattern of brain blood flow than nonmurderers have, that would by no means prove that the difference in blood flow was the cause of the violent behavior. On the contrary, it would be much more likely that the different blood flow was the result of the violent mode of thought.

37   THE HOT POTATO OF BLAME

The blame for "the real causes of teen violence" has been tossed around like a hot potato. When it was discovered that Klebold and Harris had downloaded plans for their pipe bombs from the Internet, the Internet was blamed. But "defenders of the Net rightfully note that criticizing the reach of the increasingly pervasive Web is like blaming paper for bad poetry." Thomas Jipping, writing in the July 1999 issue of The World & I, argued that the killers at Littleton may have acted as they did because they listened to the wrong kind of music. Reporters have learned that Klebold and Harris enjoyed playing the violent video game Doom. Should such video games be outlawed? "I'm less worried about [violent video games]," responded Bob Settles, a man who creates such games, "than the danger of having a gun in the household." Aha! The hot potato had been tossed to the gun industry. Charlton Heston, president of the National Rifle Association, was quick to take the offensive. "If there had been even one armed guard in the school," Heston said on morning TV after the shootings, "he could have saved a lot of lives and perhaps ended the whole thing instantly." (Heston was later informed that there was an armed guard at the school. The guard, sheriff's deputy Neil Gardner, had exchanged fire with Klebold and Harris in the first-floor hallway as the gunmen were exiting the cafeteria and heading up the stairs to the library. Gardner failed to hit either of the killers.)

38   These arguments fail to recognize one essential fact about human nature. Cruelty is not an invention of the 1990s. The Lithuanians in Kaunas in June 1941 were no less brutal than Eric Harris and Dylan Klebold were in Colorado in April 1999. The favorite scapegoats for the massacre at Littleton—violent video games, violent television, Marilyn Manson's music—did not exist in 1941, but the killers in Lithuania appear to have enjoyed their killing spree at least as much as Klebold and Harris did.

39   Cruelty is nothing new. The capacity to take pleasure in another person's suffering is a dark side of the human soul that has been with us as long as there have been human beings. Those who want to blame the massacre at Littleton entirely on modern gizmos—video games, shock rock, or the Internet—should go back to the library and read some history. They might start with Nero.

'OUR SENSE OF FUN AND OUR HIGH SPIRITS'

41 The German army during the Second World War—like all armies—needed entertainment. Oberwachtmeister Thoma was a professional musician who was drafted in 1943 to provide live entertainment for German soldiers occupying Poland. Thoma formed an ensemble with twelve other musicians, also drafted. He called his ensemble "The Twelve Toppers and the Little Hat."

42 The group's only responsibility was to make music. They had no military obligations. Nevertheless, in their spare time—when they weren't making music—the men found that they enjoyed killing Jews.

43 They volunteered to participate in the mass slaughters of Jews from nearby vil-
44 lages. Oberwachtmeister Thoma even made a poster to commemorate his group's participation in the massacre of Jews from the Polish village of Stanislav. In English it reads:

"Even the war can't take away our sense of fun and high spirits."

This says it all. This is Paradise.

POST-READING QUESTIONS

CONTENT

1. What do Sax's opening anecdotes have in common with each other? How are they different?

2. To what does Sax's title refer?

3. In what way was Nero cruel?

4. Who, according to Sax, were some of the most cruel humans in history? What reasons does Sax offer for their enthusiasm for torturing others? What do you think?

5. How did General Grant treat the conquered Confederate soldiers? What does this example say about the nature of cruelty?

6. How does Sax say people's view of human nature has changed? Who is responsible for this shift in perspective?

7. What role does Sax say blame plays in explaining the causes of cruelty, particularly in the Littleton, Colorado massacre? What does it fail to consider?

STYLE AND STRUCTURE

8. What is Sax's overall argument? Rewrite his main idea in your own words.

9. What does Sax's title mean?

10. How does Sax counter the argument that people are "conditioned" to act certain ways? Is he convincing?

11. What examples does Sax use to illustrate his ideas? Of these, which do you find most persuasive? Why?

12. Who is Sax writing for? How can you tell if you are part of his intended audience? Cite the text for support.

13. What is Sax's tone? What role, if any, does humor play in Sax's essay?

CRITICAL THINKING AND ANALYSIS

DISCUSSION QUESTIONS

14. Sax writes "Until quite recently, people were not thought to be "naturally" good. The natural tendency of human nature was thought to be inclined toward evil." What do you think? How "good" are people born? What factors determine whether or not someone grows to be kind or cruel? Explain and give examples.

15. Sax claims that "Today . . . If someone does something evil, there must be some external explanation for it . . ." Is he right? To what extent do we try to explain away people's unkind, or cruel, deeds? Explain.

WRITING ASSIGNMENTS

16. Sax quotes Major Homan Melcher who, according to Sax, "understood that cruelty is a choice." What do you think? Write at least two well-developed paragraphs in which you argue the extent to which people do or do not choose to be cruel. Be sure to cite Sax and your own experiences and observations in order to support your views.

17. Sax cites numerous examples of physical cruelty from groups of humans toward others, each highlighting the extensive bodily suffering of some people at the hands of others. But can other types of unkindness be as damaging as physical torture? At what point does unkindness become cruelty? Write a few paragraphs in which you explain the point at which incivility becomes cruelty. Be sure to define both "incivility" and "cruelty," and offer examples from Sax's essay and your own life in order to illustrate your ideas.

18. Since the time of Nero and others known for their cruel behavior, people have developed very advanced weapons, some that require no person-to-person contact, such as bombs. What role, if any, does technology play in cruelty? Write a few paragraphs or short essay in which you explain how technology does or does not play a role in determining how cruel people are to each other. Be sure to cite Sax and contemporary news stories for support.

VOCABULARY DEVELOPMENT

19. How does Sax create his tone? Write a short paragraph explaining how specific words or examples (at least five) contribute to Sax's tone.

GROUP ACTIVITIES

20. As a group, perform an online search for some aspect of the Littleton, Colorado massacre. You may search for information on the killers, the victims, the weapons, or anything else as long as it is somehow tied to Columbine High School's tragedy. How is this massacre recorded online? Write a brief paragraph based on what you learn online, explaining the overall attitude people display toward the tragedy and what this attitude says about humans. Compare your paragraphs with other groups'.

21. How popular is cruelty? Bring in popular magazines targeting different audiences and skim them to see how often cruelty appears as a topic or as a part of humor. What conclusions can you draw about the popularity of cruelty? Discuss your findings in an open forum setting.

Argument Pair: Are Teens' Manners Worse Than They Used to Be?

Enfants Not-So-Terribles, Alex Beam

Etiquette is Lost on a Generation of Teens

Regardless of the year, older generations seem to view younger ones as marking the latest sign that the world as they know it is ending. Writers from the *Los Angeles Times* address this concept of changing times in *Etiquette is Lost on a Generation of Teens,* claiming that, while hope exists for a civil future, contemporary youth have a long way to go toward enacting such civility. Alex Beam, however, presents hope for the notion that you can't judge the young by their birth dates alone, and he offers examples of youth growing up to be polite.

Writing Assignments Based Upon *"Enfants Not-So-Terribles"* and *"Etiquette is Lost on a Generation of Teens"*:

1. Alex Beam writes that youth enrolled in Judith Re's etiquette courses express "inevitable groans" during a lesson, while business etiquette expert Peter Post says that people are concerned about incivility and "want to do something about it." How proactive are today's youth? Write a few paragraphs or short essay in which you argue that youth today are or are not willing to act in order to make a difference. Cite at least one of the texts as well as your own experiences for support.

2. The writers of *Etiquette is Lost on a Generation of Teens* offer up Britney Spears as an example of a contemporary teen at the time this was written, and Alex Beam characterizes students in Judith Re's etiquette class as "nose-fingering, suburban ducklings." Are youth unfairly stereotyped? Write a well-developed paragraph describing how you think "typical" contemporary youth are portrayed, and then write a few paragraphs either defending or attacking this portrayal. Cite the essays and your own observations for support.

Enfants Not-So-Terribles

Alex Beam

After watching his soccer-playing eight-year-old son participate in flower arranging and dance lessons, Alex Beam concludes that etiquette maven Judith Re just might have hit on something. While many of the lessons on social graces can appear forced, Beam lauds Re for her efforts to teach civility to children.

Pre-reading Questions

Freewrite for five to ten minutes in response to the following questions:
How important do you think good manners are for children? Who should teach kids good manners? At what age do you think children should be taught formal manners, if ever? Explain.

Vocabulary Preview

Vocabulary Words:
- urchins
- savvy
- surly
- farrago
- gastronomically
- repast
- imparts
- Lilliputian
- laconic
- regales

Look up the words above and, as you read, rewrite the sentences of at least five words, substituting synonyms for the words Beam chose. What effect do your substitutions have on the nature of the sentences? Write a few sentences explaining how your revisions change the nature of Beam's sentences.

1   "**L**adies and gentlemen."

2   Huh? You mean us?

3   Sullenly separated for one sunny Saturday from their Game Boys and Topsy Styling Tools, the assembled children survey Judith Re, self-proclaimed directrice of the Academie for Instruction in the Social Graces, with understandable suspicion. After all, during her day-long course on "Social Savvy" at Boston's Ritz-Carlton Hotel, the elegantly attired Ms. Judith intends to succeed where all parents have failed: teaching manners to children.

4   But not to worry, dear reader. Ms. Judith knows what she is about. (The surname is Portuguese, by way of Holyoke, Massachusetts. The whole French thing is kind of a pose.) She learned her own Old World manners at her parents' dinner table, and during visits to European relatives. Several years ago, while watching a pair of ill-mannered urchins ruin their parent's restaurant meal, Re realized: "In busy, two-career families, nobody's at home long enough to teach their children manners." So for the past eight years, shuttling among Boston, New York, Cleveland and Los Angeles, Ms. Judith has been doing it for them.

5   Can Ms. Judith turn nose-fingering, suburban ducklings into socially savvy swans? I enrolled my eight-year-old son Christopher, who blew off the group's early-morning tour in favor of a pressing soccer commitment. Sweaty and a tad surly, he caught up with his class of two other boys and six girls just in time for . . . flower arranging. Naturellement.

I. LES FLEURS

6   Yes, flower arranging. The Ritz has laid out nine bulb-shaped vases and a panoply of freesia, iris and Queen Anne's lace for the children to, uh, dispose of as they see fit.

After 15 minutes, Ms. Judith sidles up to the long table and comments on her pupils' creations.

7   Generally speaking, the girls have fashioned harmonious combinations—something tells me they've done this before—and the boys have jammed the stalks in helter-skelter. Future Florists of America they're not. "Each one of these reflects your personalities," Ms. Judith coos, tactfully ignoring the psychological farrago revealed in the tangled underbrush. Commenting on one boy's design that pays homage to Phyllis Diller's hairdresser, Ms. J. says: "That looks like something from the jungle." She knows the child will take this as a compliment, and he does.

II. LA TABLE

8   Shortly before noon, the children buckle down to some serious etiquette training. The Ritz has laid out ten place settings, complete with silver, china plates and fan-folded linen napkins, around a table for them. Ms. Judith identifies the various utensils, endures the inevitable groans at the mention of the salad fork ("SAL-ud? We're having SAL-ud?"), and then summons the children to the table.

9   Gastronomically speaking, the lunch surges over the top. The hotel's award-winning kitchen has prepared a shrimp hors d'oeuvre ("SHREY-imp! Yuck!"), a chicken breast cooked in Champagne and caviar sauce—a far cry from the children's habitual McFare. Towards the end of the repast, the wait staff presents a palate-clearing papaya sorbet. This passes muster with the finicky McKids, because it tastes like ice cream, sort of.

10   Undaunted by the sotto voce complaining and one basso profundo belch, Ms. Judith cheerily imparts useful knowledge: always look the server in the eye; use the "power finger" (in her world, the index finger; in their world, the Bird) when cutting and when spearing with the fork. If you must burp, "sometimes you can do it with your lips close together," although leaving the room is preferable. When finished with your meal, leave your silverware in a 4:30 position (facing down and to the right) so the servers will know you are done. Against all odds, some of this is actually sinking in.

III. LE SMALL TALK; LE MACAULAY CULKIN

11   Small talk is hard to explain to boys and girls under 12 years old, because their conversation is by definition quite Lilliputian: Beavis's latest mot; correct use of the Creepy Crawlers oven; will the red Power Ranger ever return? Ms. Judith likens chat to volleyball: the point is to keep the bladder in the air. "Steer away from politics and religion," she says. "Don't talk about what it was like when the Berlin Wall came down." (Little chance of that, don't you think?) "Ladies and gentlemen, just because you're young doesn't mean you don't have anything to say for yourselves."

12   Well, yes and no. As an acceptable subject for conversation, Ms. Judith suggests table mishaps. My ordinarily laconic son tells his mess mates how his mother's hair once caught fire in a Prague restaurant. (Funny, I don't remember visiting Prague. . . .) Dizzy with success, he regales his friends with stories of his father being fed dog biscuits as a child. Polite tittering ensues.

13   A brief etiquette module features introductions and greetings, and the correct formulas for introducing important people, e.g. your parents, to less important people, e.g.

your friends. This won't be a problem should you meet with the President, Ms. Judith explains, because he has his own staff of professional introducers. One boy poses a stumper: what if Macaulay Culkin visited your home? Isn't he more important than your parents? Absolutely not, Ms. Judith replies. Clearly, no one believes her.

IV. LES PATISSES; LE TELEPHONE; LE FITNESS CLUB

14   While digesting their four-star chow, Ms. Judith's wards are force-fed a potpourri of new information. Minions wheel in a cart piled high with delicate pastry shells, fresh strawberries and melted chocolate. Then the Ritz's pastry chef Paw Mikkelsen shows the children how to decorate "Boston Swans." They watch in rapt attention, as if this might show up on the Groton admissions test.

15   Then it's on to telephone etiquette, taught at dummy phone consoles separated by a screen. "Joshua, what do you do if you get a crank call?" Ms. Judith asks the class cut-up who, Christopher tells me, has been showing off some salty language in the men's room. True to form, Joshua answers: "If you know who it is, you crank call them back." Mais, bien sur, Mme. La Directrice!

16   When his turn comes, Christopher fields a call from Alexis, a tall, willowy, 11-year-old fox hailing from one of the region's most desirable zip codes. "Is Christopher Beam in?" she asks. "No," he replies, "Christopher is in the shower." I upbraid him later, sharing my own life experience. Whatsa matter wif you! You think the foxes call every day?

17   In the late afternoon, Ms. Judith has scheduled a strategic visit to the hotel's health club, to let the children work off excess energy on the Stairmaster before changing into evening attire for the Grand Finale. . . .

V. LA DANSE

18   "Sometimes the ladies and gentlemen can be a bit . . . nervous before a dance," Ms. Judith says, standing in front of a trembling Joshua, who is about to pay dearly for his earlier imitation of Sir Toby Belch.

19   Earlier, Ms. J. told me that "her" children wax most inventive when dreaming up excuses not to participate in the dance lesson. Young girls evoke the scourge of flesh-eating bacteria; old athletic injuries tend to flare up in 10-year-old boys. A touch of the vapors; that flushed feeling—could it be Lyme disease? Any ailment can break out when the children march into a small banquet room after dinner, and spy the waiting tape deck and the miniature parquet dance floor, and grasp the full horror of the Dancing Lesson.

20   But Christopher's group is—dare I say it—well-behaved? Yes, the boys cringe in a corner, slurping their ice cream sundaes, hoping against hope that the dreaded music will never begin. But when Ms. Judith calls them forward, they face their fate like men.

21   The Fearless Leader seizes Joshua, claps his right hand around her waist, and snatches his left hand in hers. Waiting for "Blue Danube" to swell its banks, she calls out: "Get ready, here it comes." Then the gentle thunder of Strauss rolls through the room, and the "ladies and gentlemen" stumble back and forth in graceless, triple time. They don't protest, they don't chafe; there is even an undercurrent of small talk audible in the room: "Where were you when the Berlin Wall came down?" (Well, not quite.)

22   Needless to say, I am amazed. The wild horses have been broken; the domestica-
tion process has begun. A few minutes later, their parents swoop in to fetch the children back to exurbia, where—in spite of their underage selves—the lessons of the
"power finger," proper phone conversation, and of the dance floor, will never be entirely expunged.

23   Now, when grasping for squishy bags of ketchup at fast-food emporia, Christopher
always says, "Please." The last time he capsized his brother's Super Size Diet Coke in
an effort to steal some McChow, I thought I heard him say, "Excuse me." The specter
of Ms. Judith hangs over us, like a friendly—and exquisitely mannered—ghost.

POST-READING QUESTIONS

CONTENT

1. What is the subject of Beam's article? What is the setting?
2. What areas does Judith Re focus on during her instruction? Of these, which
   seem helpful? Irrelevant? Explain.
3. What is the kids' reaction to the lessons they are being taught?
4. How seriously are the children taking their lessons? How can you tell?
5. How effective are the lessons? Cite the text for support.

STYLE AND STRUCTURE

6. Does Beam have an argument? Restate his main idea in your own words.
7. What examples does Beam use to support his main idea?
8. What is Beam's tone? How seriously is he taking this topic? Cite the text for
   support.
9. Who is Beam's audience? How can you tell?
10. Is Beam convincing? Explain.

CRITICAL THINKING AND ANALYSIS

DISCUSSION QUESTIONS

11. What types of manners, if any, do you think are most important for kids to
    learn? Upon what do you base your conclusions?
12. Who do you think should undertake to teach kids manners? What do you think
    of such institutions as Judith Re's "Academie"? Explain.

WRITING ASSIGNMENTS

13. Etiquette expert Judith Re claims, "In busy, two-career families, nobody's at
    home long enough to teach their children manners." What is the solution?
    Write a few paragraphs in which you explain how children should learn how
    to act properly. Cite Beam's essay and your own experiences for support.

14. Beam makes reference to the types of lessons his son learns: from flower arranging and dancing to how to introduce people to each other. What lesson is most important for children to learn? Write at least one paragraph in which you argue that one particular lesson in civility is the most important for children to be taught. Cite the text and your own life for support.

VOCABULARY DEVELOPMENT

15. What is the children's attitude toward the lessons they are learning? Choose at least one paragraph from Beam's essay and rewrite it from the point of view of one of the students. What kinds of language and content changes do you need to make? Discuss your changes with your classmates.

GROUP ACTIVITIES

16. As a group, write out guidelines for your own etiquette workshop for children. Outline one lesson in particular—table manners, for instance—and then present your workshop to the class. You may want to consult an etiquette book in order to learn all the details of the formal lesson you teach.

17. As a group, perform an online search for "etiquette." Follow at least three links, taking notes on the sites you visit. What options do you have for learning about etiquette? Share your results with the class.

Etiquette Is Lost on a Generation of Teens

Citing a lack of positive role models and the breakdown of the family as causes for teen incivility, the writers of this article explore just how to help teens improve their manners. Further, etiquette experts offer hope for teens, but only if they are given the behavioral guidance necessary for success.

Pre-reading Questions

Freewrite for five to ten minutes in response to the following questions:
How good or bad are manners in your generation compared to those of your parents' generation? Your grandparents? What accounts for the differences? The similarities?

Vocabulary Preview

Vocabulary Words:
- Etonian
- comportment
- weaned

- fallout
- protocol
- extracurricular

- travesty
- savvy
- superfluous

Look up the words above and use them in a short paragraph on the topic of manners. Work on varying the sentences you use in order to practice different styles and structures.

---

1 So Prince William has a little crush on Britney Spears. Brilliant.

2 So Britney might actually hook up with the future king of England. Awesome.

3 So let's imagine Wills and Brit on their first dinner date. Gross.

4 If Spears has the manners of the generation she sings and swivels to, then we're all in trouble. Just consider the meeting between the pop teen queen and the Etonian-mannered future monarch. One can vividly imagine Britney showing up to dinner in bare midriff, high-fiving Prince Charles, requesting her Dover sole be super-sized, reapplying lip gloss between courses and asking for a shot of Jaegermeister for the road.

5 To be fair, Spears might have the private comportment of Audrey Hepburn and the manners of Emily Post (befitting her Southern roots). But as a teen, Spears is the poster girl for a generation weaned on MTV, Jerry Springer, Adam Sandler, the Internet and mall food. A generation that has all but forgotten to address adults with respect, write thank-you notes for gifts received, greet people with a handshake and say "please" and "thank you."

6 It may be harsh to saddle the entire teen population with bad-manners rap, but one needs only to see and hear the Class of 2000 to know it is a generation moving even further away—dangerously so—from decency, respect and basic rules of social conduct.

7 "We have a generation coming up now that does not know the first thing about why we have manners in our society," said Noe, who answers etiquette questions for the Web site Etiquette Hell (http:www.thinds.com/jmh/ehell). "It's not the chil-

dren's fault; it's the parents'. They think their children have common sense and know right from wrong. But does that child know a thank-you card needs to be written when a gift is received? Or that you hug your Aunt Gracie even though you can't stand her perfume? That kind of training begins at home. It's polite. It endears us to one another.

8   Noe, who lives in Dallas and says she was "raised with a Bible in one hand and Emily Post in the other," believes that today's ill-mannered teens are a product of a generation that didn't place importance on manners.

9   "What I'm seeing more and more of in children is actually a fallout of the free-wheeling '60s, the 'me' generation; do it if it feels good," she said. "They basically threw Emily Post out the window."

10   Noe isn't the only etiquette expert to point a finger—rude as that may be—at parents for the lack of teen manners we see today.

11   "The parents of today aren't confident teachers of social skills," said Joan K. Hopper, an etiquette and protocol consultant in West Hartford, Conn., who teaches children how to manage social situations.

12   It was rude teen behavior that helped get Hopper into the etiquette business. She remembers about six years ago when she and her husband, while dining at a New Haven, Conn., restaurant, saw a group of well-dressed teens celebrating their prom.

13   "All of a sudden, I noticed what deplorable manners they had at the table," Hopper said. "All their physical beauty, at that point, was completely wiped out."

14   Hopper, who has taught etiquette the last five years, says parents need to emphasize manners just as much as grades and extracurricular activities such as sports and music. Even more important is resurrecting the family dinner table.

15   "The biggest travesty of this generation is that families don't dine together," she said. "Dining together not only fosters good table manners but good social skills. There's an awareness of others that comes from sitting down together."

16   Author and etiquette expert Judith Re agrees.

17   "The role models we used to have years ago no longer exist," said Re, who teaches etiquette at the Judith Re Academie in Fairfield, Conn. "We no longer have the mother or father at home with the child. We don't have the family meal. Many of the social-savvy tools we have were learned at the dinner table. Now it's islands and stools."

18   While Re believes teens are not taught social graces, she also believes that their generation is getting a bad rap.

19   "I listen to some of these parents and they say, "Oh, they're a teenager, what do you expect?" And I think to myself, they might be a teenager, but they're also a human being. A human being that age still needs to be taught. A parent, or society in general, should never stop teaching simply because someone has reached their teenage years. Teenagers are our future."

20   Re has great hope in reversing the tide of ill-mannered teens.

21   "I absolutely have hope," she said. "But' it's going to be a bit harder for them because of the structure of the state we're in now."

22   That state is one in which the impersonal Internet rules; where "please" and "thank you" may be deemed superfluous; where manners aren't seen as tools to get ahead and negotiate a successful life.

23   And nothing could be more wrong, said Peter Post, co-author of *"The Etiquette Advantage in Business: Personal Skills for Professional Success."*

24   "It's not enough to have the job skills—you have to have the interpersonal skills, too," said Post, the great-grandson of Emily Post. "What etiquette does for us is to produce an opportunity to have better interpersonal relationships. The problem is that most people don't have the confidence in their ability to make correct choices. So they get stuck; they get nervous, apprehensive and antsy."

25   Post said we're seing a generation of young business people who are suffering for ignoring manners. The young business barons-to-be may know all about economics, but when they sit down to the dinner table with the president of the company they don't know what to do, he said.

26   "Etiquette is a way to become comfortable with that," he said.

27   But Post, like his etiquette advice peers, believes the tide is shifting. Society, he says, is recognizing a need for better manners in teens.

28   "People are perceiving that there does seem to be an increased amount of rudeness and uncivil behavior in teens today. I don't have the numbers. I'm not interested in that," he said. "But I am interested in people caring about it. They are concerned with it and want to do something about it. Without that desire to do something about it, nothing can be done."

29   "I do see a great hope," said Hopper, adding that some schools are addressing the issue of manners and etiquette training. "The awareness has come back. There is a societal awareness. The other way just didn't work. Consideration for human kindness really does work."

POST-READING QUESTIONS

CONTENT

1. What anecdote does the author use to open the essay? Why does she choose those particular subjects for her example?
2. How does the writer characterize Britney Spears' generation? Is this a fair assessment? Explain.
3. What purpose, according to etiquette expert Noe, do manners serve?
4. Who is to blame for teens' lack of etiquette, according to the article?
5. Why is a family's dining together important, according to the article?
6. What role, if any, do manners play in business success?

STYLE AND STRUCTURE

7. What is the writer's primary argument? Restate the main idea in your own words.
8. What function does the opening example serve?
9. Who is the audience for this article? How can you tell?

10. What is the writer's purpose of offering hope for teens' manners, which seems to argue against the main idea?

11. How convincing is this article? Explain.

CRITICAL THINKING AND ANALYSIS

DISCUSSION QUESTIONS

12. The writer claims that teens are moving "dangerously" away from manners. What about a lack of manners can be considered "dangerous"? Explain and give examples.

13. In terms of behavior and etiquette, how are teens portrayed in entertainment? Is this portrayal accurate? Explain.

WRITING ASSIGNMENTS

14. Etiquette expert Judith Re claims that "The role models we used to have years ago no longer exist." Write at least one well-developed paragraph in which you discuss the effect role models have on teens' learning good manners. Cite the text and your own experiences for support.

15. Judith Re claims to have hope for teens' future, but she states that "it's going to be a bit harder for them because of the structure of the state we're in now." What does she mean? In a few paragraphs or short essay, identify factors that you think comprise the "structure of the state we're in now," and explain how these factors make learning manners difficult. Cite the text and your own observations in order to clarify and strengthen your position.

16. Joan K. Hopper, an etiquette consultant, claims that "Consideration for human kindness really does work." Is she right? Citing examples from contemporary entertainment and media, write a few paragraphs in which you argue that being kind does or does not help people succeed.

VOCABULARY DEVELOPMENT

17. How would a teenager address this topic? Rewrite a few paragraphs of this article, but adopt the point of view of a teen. What kinds of language and examples do you need to change? Share your results with your classmates.

GROUP ACTIVITIES

18. As a group, visit the web site "Etiquette Hell." How relevant are the etiquette tips offered there? Based upon your experience at this web site, write a brief paragraph explaining how important you think etiquette is.

19. Brainstorm a list of manners that you think are important, and then rank those items. What is your rationale for placing some items ahead of others? Share your results with the class.

SYNTHESIS QUESTIONS

1. Leonard Sax writes in *The Unspeakable Pleasure* that "cruelty is a choice, as magnanimity is a choice." Must cruelty be chosen, or can it just happen? Write a few paragraphs or essay in which you argue that cruelty is or is not a choice. Cite at least two readings from this chapter, and use your own examples in order to illustrate your ideas.

2. Leonard Sax writes that "cruelty is not new," and Ward Churchill recounts examples from WWII. Even if cruelty is not new, are its practitioners younger? Write at least three well-developed paragraphs in which you discuss whether or not American youth are more cruel than they used to be. You may narrow your own scope of time in which to argue your case; just cite from at least two readings from this chapter and from contemporary news stories in order to support your argument.

3. Alex Beam describes etiquette courses attended by children whose parents "have failed" to teach them manners. In *Etiquette is Lost on a Generation of Teens,* etiquette experts claim that parents and "society in general" need to be responsible for teaching teens manners. How important is parental guidance in terms of teaching kids how to behave? Write at least one well-developed paragraph in which you discuss the importance, or lack of importance, of parental guidance in teaching children acceptable behavior. Cite at least three articles from this chapter and draw from your own experiences for support.

4. Etiquette expert Noe, in *Etiquette is Lost on a Generation of Teens* claims that parents do not teach their children etiquette because "They think their children have common sense and know right from wrong," yet Alex Beam writes that the Academie for Instruction in the Social Graces teaches such skills as flower arranging. What lessons are most important for children to be taught? Write a few paragraphs recommending the rules you think most important for youth to learn. Be sure to cite at least two essays from this chapter as well as your own observations for support.

5. Judith S. Wallerstein and Sandra Blakeslee write in *The Good Marriage* that "marriage in America has undergone a profound, irrevocable transformation, driven by changes in women's roles . . ." yet Alex Beam tells of parents determined to educate their children in traditional polite behavior. How much do you think people's roles have changed over the past generation or two? Write a few paragraphs or short essay in which you discuss how either women's or men's roles have changed over your lifetime and your parents' lifetime. Be sure, throughout your description, to make clear how the changes you cite are significant, and cite at least one text from this chapter and your own experiences for support.

6. In *The Good Marriage,* Judith S. Wallerstein and Sandra Blakeslee write that for marriages to last, they must be regarded as "work in progress that needed continued attention," but the writers of *Etiquette is Lost on a Generation of Teens* claim that young business people today "don't know what to do" in

terms of treating people politely. What do young adults value today? Write at least three well-developed paragraphs explaining what values are important to young adults, citing at least two essays and your own experiences in order to strengthen and clarify your ideas.

7. Leonard Sax writes of killers from different points in history who were "enjoying themselves. They were having a ball," and Ward Churchill writes in *Crimes Against Humanity* that people view the naming of sports teams after Native Americans as "good clean fun." How much do people enjoy incivility? Write a few paragraphs or short essay in which you discuss the role that you think pleasure plays in unkindness. Cite at least two essays from this chapter, and draw from your own experiences as well.

8. Are there some rules more important for teens and children to follow than for adults? Write a few paragraphs arguing that manners should or should not be the same for all people, regardless of age or position. Cite at least two readings from this chapter and draw from your own experiences to support your views.

"Those who have mastered etiquette, who are entirely, impeccably right, would seem to arrive at a point of exquisite dullness."

— Dorothy Parker
Mrs. Post Enlarges on Etiquette

"There's a point to civility, of course, and I know this because I lived for many years in a land untouched by etiquette in any form—not New York, New York, as you may imagine, but Long Island, New York, where one is considered remiss for failing to give the finger to any motorist one happens to pass."

— Barbara Ehrenreich

"Humanitarianism is the expression of stupidity and cowardice."

— Adolf Hitler
Mein Kampf

"Today it is fashionable to talk about the poor. Unfortunately it is not fashionable to talk with them."

— Mother Teresa

THE FAMILY CIRCUS.   By Bil Keane

9-12
©2000 Bil Keane, Inc.
Dist. by King Features Synd.

"When you have scoops of different flavors, you're s'posed to let 'em take turns being eaten."

Reprinted with special permission of King Features Syndicate.

"In the case of the politically correct, the prohibition of certain words, phrases and ideas is advanced in the cause of building a brave new world free of racism and hate, but this vision of harmony clashes with the very ideals of diversity and inclusion that the multicultural movement holds dear, and it's purchased at the cost of freedom of expression and freedom of speech."

— Michiko Kakutani

"Give me your tired, your poor, your huddled masses yearning to breathe free, the wretched refuse of your teeming shore, send these, the homeless, tempest-tossed, to me: I lift my lamp beside the golden door."

— Emma Larzarus

Websites:

www.zpg.org/
  Website for zero population growth organization.

www.ora.com/people/staff/sierra/flum/index.htm
  Michael Sierra's indexed collection of news items focusing on how the political correctness movement has pervaded society.

Introduction

With the emphasis on becoming more civil, people fall easily into the habit of criticizing those who seem unkind or uncivil, or those who seem focused on what they need for themselves. But at some level can this self-absorption actually be considered civil behavior? If, for instance, we tend to our own needs and place no demands upon others, then are we not indirectly considering others by allowing them to be free of worry for us? Or, conversely, can showing concern for others have negative effects?

Chapter 10 examines the possibility that civility can, indeed, go too far. Though aid organizations hasten to feed the hungry in underdeveloped countries, they—through their concern—are contributing to the problem of overpopulation. This is not the only example of how a basic concern for others, the base for civility, can run amok. From artificially chipper telephone representatives of large corporations to U.S.-Mexico border residents who harbor illegal immigrants, these people push into prominence the question of whether or not civility can cause more harm than good.

"Border Samaritans" Risk the Law to Offer Aid; Humanitarian Crisis Prompts More Arizona Residents to Feed, Shelter Illegal Immigrants

Tim Vanderpool

A freelance writer based in Tucson, Tim Vanderpool has written much on the subject of immigration. In this selection, Vanderpool explores the plight of illegal Mexican immigrants and their temporary benefactors, Arizona residents living near the border who provide food, shelter, and medical aid to ailing travelers. The conflict, Vanderpool points out, arises when such good Samaritans are faced with stiff penalties for assisting the illegal immigrants; seemingly good intentions lead to unhappy endings, for both those in need of help and those providing it.

Pre-reading Questions

Freewrite for five to ten minutes in response to the following questions:
How do you define a "good Samaritan"? In your mind, can a good Samaritan be someone who breaks the law? At what point, if any, can helping someone become harmful? Explain.

Vocabulary Preview

Vocabulary Words:

- compassionate
- badlands
- vigilantes
- humanitarian
- reminiscent
- Samaritans
- rural
- ascertain
- revitalized
- ominous

Look up each of the words above and use at least seven of them in a paragraph on the topic of assisting illegal immigrants.

---

1   In vast deserts along the US-Mexico border, illegal immigration wears a very human face—both that of the travelers and of compassionate residents, who straddle a precarious line between performing good deeds and breaking the law.

2   The suffering of immigrants—56 men, women, and children have died of heat exhaustion in the arid badlands since October—has prompted growing numbers of Americans to offer help. Their actions stand in sharp contrast with anti-immigrant vigilantes making headlines earlier this year.

3   While many northbound travelers are given food, water, and temporary shelter by people quietly acting on their own, the humanitarian crisis has also sparked several new assistance groups throughout the Southwest, reminiscent of the much-publicized Sanctuary Movement in the 1980s.

4   But these borderland Samaritans face a difficult choice: Punishment for harboring or transporting undocumented immigrants can mean up to 10 years in jail and fines of more than $250,000.

5   "We would caution anyone about what it could be worth to their personal freedom," says Cathy Colbert of the US Attorney's office in Arizona.

6   Jan Weller trod that fine line on a cold night last March, when she discovered three travelers shivering outside her gate in rural southeastern Arizona.

7   "They were wet and cold."

8   "At first my husband said, 'Don't you dare bring them in,'" she says.

9   "But I was standing out there with them, and they were wet and cold. Then I looked back at our house and saw smoke coming out our chimney, and thought, 'I know I can help these people. I can't solve their problems, but I can help them right now.'"

10   More immigrants were waiting on the road, and Ms. Weller eventually found 22 unexpected visitors—including a 10-year-old boy—gathered around her wood-burning stove.

11   By sunrise, Border Patrol agents had picked up the group for return to Mexico.

12   Weller says she wasn't worried about landing in jail. "The way I look at it, if you are just trying to help, and not trying to break the law, it's OK to give them food or whatever until the authorities come."

13   That's the way the Border Patrol looks at it, too, says David Aguilar, chief of the Border Patrol's Tuscon sector.

14   "First, people should call the appropriate law-enforcement entities." If that occurs, Mr. Aguilar says, "We certainly do not discourage [citizens] from helping any individual in distress."

15   But enforcing the law while not condemning innocent good deeds can be a tricky balancing act for the government.

16   "Clearly, in a situation where there's humanitarian need, any reasonable person would respond with assistance," says Russ Bergeron, a spokesman for the US Immigration and Naturalization Service. At the same time, "It is a felony to harbor undocumented aliens," he says. "If you are caught harboring them, you might very well be in violation of the law."

17   And some groups are deliberately probing those legal boundaries.

18   Based 45 minutes north of Mexico in tiny Bisbee, Ariz., Citizens for Border Solutions is consulting attorneys to ascertain just how far it can go in offering food, shelter, and medical assistance. The group is planning workshops, and has begun networking with like-minded organizations in neighboring states, says member Roy Goodman.

19   "We're also trying to get information to people coming across that, 'Hey, when you cross the border, you're not just going to go a couple of miles where there's going to be a highway or a town,'" he says. "That's why people are dying—even people with infants are going willy-nilly into the wilderness."

20   The budding network has also revitalized many veterans of the Sanctuary Movement, including the Rev. John Fife.

21   In 1986, the minister of Tuscon's Southside Presbyterian Church was among eight activists convicted on various immigrant-smuggling charges, stemming from an underground railroad the group operated for refugees from civil-war-torn Central America.

OFFERING SANCTUARY

22   Mr. Fife served five years' probation for his efforts. Today, the minister says a new assistance movement is "just beginning to be organized. . . . Faith communities are meeting to address the whole set of moral issues along the border.

23   "We're going to be public about everything we do, because it's part of the obligation to change immoral and disastrous immigration policies."

24   He considers it among the "best traditions along the borderlands. People in this region have always responded to human need with compassion."

25   Meanwhile, more ominous echoes of the Sanctuary days also rumble through the region. The government earned much bad press by infiltrating the earlier organization and aggressively prosecuting its members.

26   Modern-day activists likewise report many rumors of plain-clothed "agent provocateurs" among their ranks.

27   This makes people "very cautious" about discussing their assistance, says Mr. Goodman.

28   Mr. Bergeron of the INS doesn't deny that his agency uses informants along the border, but says he's "obviously not going to comment on specific activities."

29   The resulting suspicions are causing some to rethink offering help—and has even driven a wedge between friends.

30   Bisbee architect Todd Bogatay discovered that on the day before Easter, when a band of immigrants arrived at his doorstep.

31   "I was planning to feed them, put them up overnight, and let them go on their way," Mr. Bogotay says.

32   But a pal who was visiting him buckled out of fear, and called the Border Patrol as the travelers slept.

33   "As it turned out, I felt like I was leading lambs to the slaughter when we turned them over to the Border Patrol. It was very upsetting," Bogatay says. "They were young kids with bright eyes and bushy tails, and I didn't see why I had to do that. It kind of broke our friendship right there."

34   Weller's experience ended on a more uplifting note. "They were very courteous, very nice and appreciative," she says.

35   "They were even concerned about getting mud on the floor. The little boy had a plastic-covered picture of Jesus, and he tried to give it to me, to thank me for helping him. I told him to keep it, that he needed the help."

36   Her husband eventually softened his stance, and their young daughter also joined the gathering.

37   "It just moved all of us," Weller says. "We were so thankful for what we had, and we felt so sorry for these people."

POST-READING QUESTIONS

CONTENT

1. What conflict do Arizona border residents face? How, according to Vanderpool, are many of these residents addressing this conflict?

2. What is the penalty for harboring illegal immigrants? How fair do you think this penalty is?

3. How are US Immigration representatives represented in Vanderpool's article? To what extent are they sympathetic or critical of border residents' actions?

4. What are some consequences faced by Arizona residents who help illegal immigrants?

5. How do the immigrants respond to the assistance from Arizona residents?

STYLE AND STRUCTURE

6. Does Vanderpool have an argument? What is it?

7. What examples does Vanderpool use to illustrate his ideas? Of these, which are most compelling? Explain.

8. What is Vanderpool's tone? To what extent do Vanderpool's language and examples reveal his attitude toward helping illegal immigrants?

9. Who is Vanderpool's audience? Do you think residents of border states such as Arizona and California would react the same way to Vanderpool's article as residents of non-border states? Explain.

10. What about Vanderpool's article, if anything, reveals that it was written for a newspaper, as opposed to a collection of literary essays?

CRITICAL THINKING AND ANALYSIS

DISCUSSION QUESTIONS

11. How difficult would helping illegal immigrants be for you? What determines your willingness, or unwillingness, to help illegal immigrants?

12. Do you think that people who help illegal immigrants should be punished? To what extent? Why?

WRITING ASSIGNMENTS

13. In addressing the topic of aiding illegal immigrants, at what point should the Golden Rule—"Do Unto Others as You Would Have Them Do Unto You"—not count? Write at least three well-developed paragraphs in which you explain at what point people do not have to, or should not, help others. Keep your views within the context of the illegal immigrant issue, and be sure to cite Vanderpool and your own knowledge for support.

14. Vanderpool writes of "compassionate residents, who straddle a precarious line between performing good deeds and breaking the law." At what point, if any, can being a good Samaritan be harmful? Write a few paragraphs in which you discuss whether or not kindness can ever be harmful. You may use examples from Vanderpool, if you wish, but you may also cite illustrations from issues other than illegal immigration in order to clarify and strengthen your ideas.

15. Do you think US residents should help illegal immigrants? Consult other sources as well as Vanderpool in order to learn more about your subject, and then write a few paragraphs or short essay in which you argue that US residents should or should not offer assistance to illegal immigrants.

VOCABULARY DEVELOPMENT

16. Choose at least three examples of text that you think best reveals Vanderpool's tone. Then, rewrite those passages, but from the point of view of someone whose attitude toward helping illegal immigrants is the opposite of Vanderpool's. Is changing the language enough? Write a few sentences explaining what you had to do to make your revisions convincing.

GROUP ACTIVITIES

17. As a group, visit your library or perform an online search in order to learn more about US immigration policies and penalties. Then, discuss the extent to which you think such policies are fair. Take notes as you search and discuss and share your results with the class.

18. Write your own immigration policy for your state, country, or any other boundary-determined location of your choosing. What criteria must immigrants meet in order to be able to legally immigrate to your location? Share your results with the class in an attempt to create a class-wide policy.

The Weak Shall Inherit the Gym

Rick Reilly

Author of *Sports Illustrated*'s column *The Life of Reilly,* Rick Reilly addresses, with varying degrees of humor, issues that often seem at once trivial and significant. Such is the case in *The Weak Shall Inherit the Gym,* where Reilly argues that abolishing Dodgeball in schools, rather than making youth more sensitive, will only take away one of the few opportunities left for students to express their aggressions with impunity.

Pre-reading Questions

Freewrite for five to ten minutes in response to the following questions:
To what extent have you or someone you know ever been the last one chosen in a pick-up sports game? How damaging do you think this experience is for the one who is chosen last? How do you recommend students deal with feelings of weakness or inadequacy on the sports field at school?

Vocabulary Preview

Vocabulary Words:
- exhibit
- womb
- commune
- demeaning
- deemed
- gruesome
- capitalistic
- accrued

Look up the words above and write a few sentences, based on the words and the title of the essay, explaining what you think the tone of the article will be. After you've read the essay, review your sentences; have you changed your mind?

---

1   Not to alarm you, but America is going softer than left-out butter. Exhibit 9,137: Schools have started banning dodgeball.

2   I kid you not. Dodgeball has been outlawed by some school districts in New York, Texas, Utah and Virginia. Many more are thinking about it, like Cecil County, Md., where the school board wants to ban any game with "human targets." Personally, I wish all these people would go suck their Birkenstocks.

3   Human targets? What's tag? What's a snowball fight? What's a close play at second? Neil Williams, a physical education professor at Eastern Connecticut State, says dodgeball has to go because it "encourages the best to pick on the weak." Noooo! You mean there's weak in the world? There's strong? Of course there is, and dodgeball is one of the first opportunities in life to figure out which one you are and how you're going to deal with it.

4   We had a bully, Big Joe, in our seventh grade. Must have weighed 225 pounds, used to take your underwear while you were in the shower and parade around the locker room twirling it on his finger. We also had a kid named Melvin, who was so thin

we could've faxed him from class to class. I'll never forget the dodgeball game in which Big Joe had a ball in each hand and one sandwiched between his knees, firing at our side like a human tennis-ball machine, when, all of a sudden, he got plunked right in his 7-Eleven-sized butt. Joe whirled around to see who'd done it and saw that it was none other than Melvin, all 83 pounds of him, most of it smile.

5   Some of these New Age whiners say dodgeball is inappropriate in these times of horrifying school shootings. Are you kidding? Dodgeball is one of the few times in life when you get to let out your aggressions, no questions asked. We don't need less dodgeball in schools, we need more!

6   I know what all these NPR-listening, Starbucks-guzzling parents want. They want their Ambers and their Alexanders to grow up in a cozy womb of noncompetition, where everybody shares tofu and Little Red Riding Hood and the big, bad wolf set up a commune. Then their kids will stumble out into the bright light of the real world and find out that, yes, there's weak and there's strong and teams and sides and winning and losing. You'll recognize those kids. They'll be the ones filling up chalupas. Very noncompetitive.

7   But Williams and his fellow wusses aren't stopping at dodgeball. In their Physical Education Hall of Shame they've also included duck-duck-goose and musical chairs. Seriously. So, if we give them dodgeball, you can look for these games to be banned next: Tag. Referring to any child as it is demeaning and hurtful. Instead of the child hollering, "You're it!" we recommend, "You're special!"

8   Red Rover. Inappropriate labeling of children as animals. Also, the use of the word red evokes Communist undertones.

9   Sardines. Unfairly leaves one child alone at the end as the loser—a term psychologists have deemed unacceptable.

10   Hide-and-seek. No child need hide or be sought. The modern child runs free in search of himself.

11   Baseball. Involves wrong-headed notions of stealing, errors and gruesome hit-and-run. Players should always be safe, never out.

12   Hopscotch. Sounds vaguely alcoholic, not to mention demeaning to our friends of Scottish ancestry.

13   Marbles. Winning others' marbles is overly capitalistic.

14   Marco Polo. Mocks the blind.

15   Capture the flag. Mimics war.

16   Kick the can. Unfair to the can.

17   If we let these PC twinkies have their way, we'll be left with: Duck-duck-duck. Teacher spends the entire hour patting each child softly on the head.

18   Upsy down. The entire class takes turns fluffing the gym teacher's pillow before her nap.

19   Swedish baseball. Players are allowed free passage to first, second or third, where they receive a relaxing two-minute massage from opposing players.

20   Smear the mirror. Students take turns using whipped cream to smear parts of their reflection they don't like, e.g., the fat they have accrued from never doing a damn thing in gym class. Dodgeball is one of the few times in life when you get to let out your aggressions, no questions asked.

POST-READING QUESTIONS

CONTENT

1. What causes Reilly to write that "America is going softer than left-out butter"?
2. What reason do educators give for banning certain games in school?
3. What does Reilly say parents of modern children want for their children in terms of dealing with other students?
4. What objections does Reilly have to banning certain games in school?
5. List at least three games Reilly postulates will be banned next.

STYLE AND STRUCTURE

6. What is Reilly's main point? Restate his primary argument in your own words.
7. What points does Reilly make in support of his main idea? Of these, which do you find most convincing? Explain.
8. Who is Reilly's audience? How can you tell?
9. How seriously does Reilly take his subject? Cite the text in order to illustrate his tone.
10. Is Reilly convincing? Explain.

CRITICAL THINKING AND ANALYSIS

DISCUSSION QUESTIONS

11. How much should educators consider kids' feelings when it comes to sports-based games? Explain.
12. How harmful, if at all, can games like dodgeball be to kids? Explain and give examples.

WRITING ASSIGNMENTS

13. Reilly claims that, "Of course [there are weak and strong in the world], and dodgeball is one of the first opportunities in life to figure out which one you are and how you're going to deal with it." At what point should people be exposed to situations where they will discover how weak or strong they are? Explain and give examples from your own life for support.
14. Reilly cites people who claim that "dodgeball is inappropriate in these times of horrifying school shootings." What do you think? Explain and give examples.
15. How do you think schools should address the problem of students being singled out, as in duck-duck-goose or musical chairs? Explain.

VOCABULARY DEVELOPMENT

16. What about Reilly's language makes his tone distinctive? Choose a topic that interests you and write a paragraph imitating Reilly's voice. What kinds of

language and sentence structures do you have to use? Share your results with your classmates.

GROUP ACTIVITIES

17. Before coming to class, poll five to ten people on campus to learn what their feelings about Reilly's issue is. Share your results with the class, along with any explanations or observations people offered as you polled them.

18. As a small group, adopt the point of view of a concerned parent writing on the issue of whether or not dodgeball should be banned, and revise two or three of Reilly's paragraphs in order to reflect this change in point of view. What types of changes do you have to make in order for your writing to be persuasive? Share your results with other groups.

The Civility Glut

Barbara Ehrenreich

Columnist for *The Progressive*, Barbara Ehrenreich is also the author of *The Worst Years of Our Lives: Irreverent Notes of the Middle Class, Fear of Falling: The Inner Life of the Middle Class*, and *Nickel and Dimed: On (Not) Getting by in Boom-time America*. In *The Civility Glut* Ehrenreich claims that, while civility does have a purpose, it can also be divisive and hurtful; hence, we need to check both our intentions and our actions in practicing etiquette.

Pre-reading Questions

Freewrite for five to ten minutes in response to the following questions:
What expressions of civility do you find most meaningful? Why? Do you think people have gone too far in their desire for courtesy? Do you think people can be too polite? Explain.

Vocabulary Preview

Vocabulary Words:
- mavens
- peremptorily
- omnipotent
- deity
- impertinent
- requisite
- hierarchy
- sycophancy
- locution

Look up the words above in a dictionary, and then consult a thesaurus for synonyms. Choose sentences from the text using at least five words from the list above, and substitute synonyms for those words. What is the overall effect of your substitutions? Write a few sentences explaining whether or not your substitutions have a significant effect on the original meaning or tone of the sentences.

1   The professional chin-strokers and morality-mavens keep telling us America could use a little more civility. To which I say—with all due respect, of course—heck no, what we've got here is a civility glut.

2   Take your morning news on CNN, where the expert of the moment—some former deputy assistant secretary of such-and-such—is being hauled away after his ninety-second interview.

3   "Thank you," says the anchorperson.

4   "Thank you," insists the former deputy assistant secretary.

5   "Appreciate it," the anchorperson retaliates.

6   Who knows where this frenzy of competitive gratitude would take us if the former deputy assistant secretary were not peremptorily replaced with a Geico commercial?

7   Here's my personal favorite: I call some corporate bureaucracy and, whether out of loneliness or confusion, opt for "0"—the chance to speak to an actual human. "Kelly" or "Tracey" wants to know my account number, which I willingly share.

8   "Great!" says Kelly.

9   Next she wants to know my zip code, and it turns out to be "perfect!"

10   Or suppose I'm calling a publishing company and get an administrative assistant with a pricey British accent. When I tell her my phone number, she declares that it's "brilliant!"

11   I should be flattered, of course, to be associated with such an admirable collection of numbers. But unless these ladies are mathematicians who have speedily determined that my zip code is a perfect square and my account number is the exact distance in light years between here and the nearest ongoing supernova, then I see no reason to comment on them. My zip code is OK at best, my account number a little stodgy, and nothing you say, Kelly, can make me swell with pride when I recite them.

12   Or consider the standard, all-purpose sign-off, "Have a nice day!" There were grumblings when this one took hold—sometime in the '70s, I think—and you still see a surly bumper sticker now and then warning, "Don't tell me what kind of a day to have!" No one, however, is complaining about the recent escalation to "Have a great day" or "Have a really great day."

13   You might think it would be enough to commend a departing companion to the care of an omnipotent deity, as in "good-bye," which is shorthand for "god be with you." But compared to the competition, "goodbye" has come to sound dismissive or even impertinent. It has no future. In fact, the day will come when one of the tearful lovers will cry out to the other, as they are torn from each others' arms by rival clan members, "Have a really great day, Romeo!"

14   There's a point to civility, of course, and I know this because I lived for many years in a land untouched by etiquette in any form—not New York, New York, as you may imagine, but Long Island, New York, where one is considered remiss for failing to give the finger to any motorist one happens to pass. Having moved to a small, Southern town, I've learned to appreciate the old-fashioned habit of lubricating all business transactions with a few leisurely observations about the weather and the upcoming game. I am even glad, in a way, when strangers randomly encountered on the phone express pleasure when learning of my mother's maiden name and otherwise seem to approve of my presence on Earth.

15   But civility is also about class, and hence about forms of exclusion and oppression that are, at bottom, extremely impolite. Much of our current idea of etiquette was invented a little over 400 years ago in the royal courts of Europe, largely for the purpose of foiling any would-be intruders from the merchant class. It wasn't a foolproof system, since social climbers could always master the upper class's politesse, which included, at the beginning, such easy-to-learn rules as: Don't relieve yourself at the dinner table; don't blow your nose into your napkin. To outwit the merely middle class, the upper crust kept elaborating the rules and multiplying the requisite statements of deference—and the middle class kept scrambling to keep up.

16   There's nothing aristocratic, though, about today's civility glut. Kelly at Citibank isn't angling for an invitation to my next black-tie event; she's been trained, like a majority of American service workers, to exude a "positive attitude," and she's being taped to make sure there are no lapses in perkiness. Wal-Mart, the nation's largest private employer, uses videotapes to instruct its employees in the art of "aggressive hospitality"—meaning the in-your-face, what-can-I-do-for-you smile. Even CNN's unctuous Bill Hemmer and Leon Harris dwell in a corporate hierarchy (Time-Warner-CNN-AOL, etc.), where it is difficult to succeed without sycophancy.

17   Hence the edge of hostility that overlays so many examples of corporate-mandated civility, as in competitive thanking and the escalation of sign-off directives. Or take the cruel new locution "I sure don't!"—delivered in a tone of blithe cheer even when the question was whether she might have any seats available on the last flight out of the doomed volcanic island.

18   It isn't easy being perky all day to people you don't know and probably wouldn't like if you did. In fact, as Arlie Hochschild wrote in The Managed Heart: Commercialization of Human Feeling (University of California, 1983), the effort can be decidedly stressful. At Wal-Mart, the really considerate floor clerks are the ones who ignore you, for your own sake as well as theirs. They know that "aggressive hospitality" sounds like "aggressive hostility" for a reason: One of its functions is to put potential shoplifters on notice that they're being watched.

19   Real civility is not forced. It thrives among equals and proceeds from a deep-down sense of well-being. To nurture it, we'd need better pay all around (and especially in the underpaid service industry), a more leisurely pace of work, and corporate hierarchies that reward performance over brown-nosing.

20   There's a difference, after all, between civility and servility.

POST-READING QUESTIONS

CONTENT

1. Why does Ehrenreich argue that we have a "civility glut?" What do you think?

2. How does Ehrenreich feel about the customer service representatives she speaks with who commend her for giving them such personal information as her account number and zip code?

3. What is Ehrenreich's attitude toward civility? How can you tell?

4. What else, aside from politeness, is civility about? How, according to Ehrenreich, are these aspects of civility impolite?

5. What does Ehrenreich claim the bases of today's civility are? How does she feel about them?

6. What does Ehrenreich say we need to do if we want "to nurture" civility?

STYLE AND STRUCTURE

7. What is Ehrenreich's primary argument? Restate her main idea in your own words.

8. What examples does Ehrenreich use to illustrate her main idea? Of these, which do you find most compelling? Explain.

9. What is Ehrenreich's tone? Cite the text in order to reveal her attitude toward her subject.

10. Who is Ehrenreich's audience? To what extent are you part of her audience? Explain.

11. Is Ehrenreich persuasive? Explain.

CRITICAL THINKING AND ANALYSIS

DISCUSSION QUESTIONS

12. How much do you appreciate, or dislike, the "perkiness" expressed by some customer service representatives on the telephone?

13. Have you ever been in a situation where someone's manners have made you feel uncomfortable? Describe the situation and explain why you felt the way you did.

WRITING ASSIGNMENTS

14. Ehrenreich writes that "civility is also about class, and hence about forms of exclusion and oppression. . . ." What do you think? Write at least one well-developed paragraph in which you discuss the ways that civility can "exclude" or "oppress" people. Cite the text and your own experiences for support.

15. Ehrenreich writes of her appreciation for "lubricating all business transactions with a few leisurely observations about the weather and the upcoming game." How effective is civility in facilitating business, or personal, transactions? Write a few paragraphs or short essay in which you discuss whether or not civility eases or impedes relationships. Be sure to cite Ehrenreich and your own experiences and observations to support your ideas.

16. Ehrenreich claims that "Real civility is not forced." What do you think? Write a few paragraphs or short essay in which you argue that civility is or is not forced. Cite examples from Ehrenreich's essay and your own life in order to illustrate your views.

VOCABULARY DEVELOPMENT

17. What about Ehrenreich's writing helps to communicate her tone? Invent another example that Ehrenreich might use in her essay, and write a paragraph or two describing this example in your best imitation of Ehrenreich's tone. How successful are you at mimicking her? Discuss your results with classmates.

GROUP ACTIVITIES

18. Choose an area where customer service is important: telemarketing, food serving, retail shopping, for instance. Then, draw a spectrum showing the range of behavior from "very uncivil" to "very polite." What sort of examples do you choose to illustrate such a range? Consider such issues as whether or not insincere civility is more or less polite than outright rudeness.

19. How great a role does civility play in determining a company's success? Brainstorm a list of businesses that display a wide range of civility: the night-shift clerk at a self-serve gas station versus a food server at an expensive restaurant. How do people's actions vary? Discuss how significant you think civility is for business success and share your conclusions with the class.

Who Will Heed the Warnings on the Population Bomb?

Patt Morrison

A staff writer for the *Los Angeles Times,* Patt Morrison is a member of two Pulitzer-winning teams that covered the Los Angeles riots, among many other accolades including five Emmys and the publication of her book, *Rio LA, Tales from the Los Angeles River.* Starting from the premise that nearly all of the world's contemporary problems stem from overpopulation, Morrison cites the wasteful tendencies of Americans as causing part of the problem, but she also targets worldwide aid programs that support countries such as Egypt that would have long been starving if not for outside subsistence.

Pre-reading Questions

Freewrite for five to ten minutes in response to the following questions:
What are your top three daily irritations or frustrations? What do you think is the cause of such situations? What relationship between a crowded living environment—your home, your neighborhood, your city—and your daily frustrations exist? What might possible solutions be? Explain.

Vocabulary Preview

Vocabulary Words:	• arguably	• outstrip	• upshot
	• predator	• mortality	• divisive
	• ailment	• collectively	
	• paradox	• subsistence	

Look up the words above and use all the words in no more than three sentences. How does the forced style of writing—where you are told what to include in a sentence—compare to your normal style? Explain in a few sentences.

1   Consider, if you can stand it, almost every public crisis that blips on the radar, and follow each back to its source.

2   Every lane of roadway too crowded, forests leveled for housing timber or grazing land, not enough clean water, not enough clean air, not enough open space—not enough of anything, except us. People. Just too damn many of us, 6 billion strong, a billion more than what we were just a dozen years ago.

3   We are arguably the most successful species in history. We have our brains to make tools—tools of steel, tools of antibiotics—to defeat almost every natural predator.

4   If our own numbers are the problem, then policymakers the world over are simply nibbling at the edges, treating the symptoms, not the ailment, the crises that overpopulation creates, not overpopulation itself. Yet the paradox is that reproduction is both the

first and the ultimate right; no one in this country—nor in most others—can tell anyone else how many children they can have.

5   In his 20s, Robert Gillespie was a soils science expert studying in Egypt, and everywhere were hungry kids and sick kids, yet no matter how he cut the numbers, he realized "the population was doubling every 23 years. {As for} agricultural production, it was very obvious population was quickly going to outstrip food production. And that's what's happened. If it weren't for huge international aid programs, no doubt Egypt would be starving tomorrow."

6   So he switched from soils to a different sort of cultivation, working for nearly 40 years with organizations that sent him to Taiwan, Bangladesh, Iran and Turkey to set up family planning programs.

7   In that time, he became a founding member of Zero Population Growth, has become president of Pasadena-based Population Communication—and has seen world population double.

8   "The Information Age has taught us that labor is not the power, that the brain is the power. {The} places where people are ending up with five or six kids—most of sub-Saharan Africa for example, where it's gone on for the last 5,000 years—is where governments spend 12% or less of budgets on health and education services combined. As poverty increases, the reinforcement for large families increases: 'We need more children to substitute for the ones gone through infant mortality.' Individually that sounds like a great idea for a family, but collectively that is suicide."

9   Just as he learned that agriculture alone could not cure hunger, Gillespie knows that birth control devices alone will not solve overpopulation. States in India have raised the legal age for marriage. Educating women lowers birthrates.

10   The father of population policy—and a controversial one he is, too—was English economist Thomas Malthus. Malthus decreed that population always tends to outgrow subsistence, the upshot of which is that nature will enforce its own limits with disease and famine. "He never conceived," says Gillespie, "that the technology would have as much influence, that urbanization would have as much influence. People say, 'Malthus was wrong.' Malthus was right. It's just that the bubble has gotten bigger, and it will go and go and go, and ultimately the population will stabilize by increasing the death rate or lowering the birthrate."

11   The most divisive issue in population battles is immigration control. Gillespie's is one of the few population groups that concerns itself with the matter. Gillespie has, like fellow ZPG co-founders Paul and Anne Ehrlich, split with that group over the issue of "not addressing immigration as an important component of population growth," and the assessment that "we are allowing in more people than we can afford."

12   It drives him nuts to be "with people who want immigration reform for the wrong reasons. They are racist. They just think Hispanics are stupid and lazy and will rape and pillage, when the fact is they're the hardest working population we have."

13   It also drives him nuts that people have already made up their minds. "Latino activists or the Heritage Foundation, they won't look at the facts. I just send literature to both sides and say, 'These are the facts.'"

14   If you're congratulating yourself on being a Responsible American with just one or two kids, don't.

15   The paradox is that one American consumes as much as 60 Bengalis, as much as three Japanese, twice as much as a German. We are wasteful and heedless children, gobbling down fossil fuel and other goods willy-nilly. Like children, we keep depending on technology to haul us to safety in the last reel.

16   We are the most gluttonous country in the world, with no discipline economically or politically. That's going to go on until there's a major crisis such as gas and oil running out. If that were to happen today, more people would be starving in New York City than Bangladesh, because in Bangladesh people live closer to their level of subsistence.

17   We live in an artificial world, and nobody is addressing the future as it relates to finite resources. And all resources are finite except population.

POST-READING QUESTIONS

CONTENT

1. What, by implication, does Morrison claim to be the source of "almost every public policy crisis"? Do you agree?
2. What is the paradox of overpopulation, according to Morrison?
3. Who is Robert Gillespie, and what are his accomplishments?
4. What does Morrison claim reinforces the need for large families in countries where people already have many children? How is this ironic?
5. Who was Thomas Malthus, and what is his philosophy on population growth?
6. What, according to Morrison, is "the most divisive issue in population battles"? Why do you think this issue is so controversial?

STYLE AND STRUCTURE

7. What is the effect of Morrison's title?
8. What is Morrison's primary argument? Restate her main idea in your own words.
9. What examples does Morrison use to illustrate her points? Of these, which example do you find most compelling? Explain.
10. What is Morrison's attitude toward her subject? Cite the text for examples of her tone.
11. Who is Morrison's audience? What about her language and examples reveals this target reader?
12. Is Morrison convincing, or is she unnecessarily dramatic? Explain.

CRITICAL THINKING AND ANALYSIS

DISCUSSION QUESTIONS

13. How great a problem do you think overpopulation is? Upon what do you base your conclusions? Explain.

14. What suggestions, if any, do you have for solving the overpopulation dilemma, either locally, nationally, or worldwide?

WRITING ASSIGNMENTS

15. Morrison writes that "reproduction is both the first and the ultimate right . . ." Do you agree? Write a few paragraphs or short essay arguing that reproduction should or should not be "the ultimate right" of individuals. Cite Morrison and your own observations for support.

16. Morrison cites immigration as the "most divisive issue in population battles." What is your attitude toward immigration to the United States? Write a few paragraphs or short essay in which you explain why immigration to the United States should or should not be more limited. Feel free to consult outside references in order to learn more about this topic before responding, and be sure to cite from Morrison and your own experiences for support.

17. Morrison writes that Americans are "wasteful and heedless children" in terms of the consumptions of natural resources. What do you think? Write at least one well-developed paragraph in which you explain how Americans are or are not wasteful. Use examples from Morrison's essay and your own life in order to illustrate your ideas.

VOCABULARY DEVELOPMENT

18. How strongly does Morrison feel about the topic of overpopulation? Skim her essay and identify words and phrases that best reveal her tone. Write a few sentences explaining how her vocabulary does or does not effectively communicate her attitude toward her subject.

GROUP ACTIVITIES

19. As a group, perform an online search for one of Robert Gillespie's organizations: Zero Population Growth or Population Communication. What do you learn? Does what you learn alter your opinions surrounding overpopulation in any way? Explain.

20. As a class, debate the issue of overpopulation, one side arguing that the number of earth's inhabitants is everyone's responsibility and one side arguing that some people should bear the responsibility more than others. Feel free to research your topic before coming to class in order to be more knowledgeable on your issue.

Argument Pair: How Sensitive Should We Be in Our Use of Language?

Why We Need Bias-Free Language, Rosalie Maggio

The Word Police, Michiko Kakutani

"Sticks and stones can break my bones, but words will never hurt me." Many of us grow up learning this rhyme as a means to dealing with hurtful comments directed our way, but for how many of us does this saying really help? The issue of political correctness, or general sensitivity to others via language, has raised much speculation throughout American society. While, as Rosalie Maggio quotes Sanford Berman in her essay, biased language can "powerfully harm people," Michiko Kakutani claims that "the methods and fervor of the self-appointed language police can lead to a rigid orthodoxy." The extent to which people should consider others through language, thus, remains unresolved.

Writing Assignments Based On *Why We Need Bias-Free Language* and *The Word Police*

1. Rosalie Maggio quotes Sanford Berman who claims that biased language can "powerfully harm people," but Michiko Kakutani writes, " the utopian world envisioned by the language police would be bought at the expense of the ideals of individualism and democracy articulated in 'The Gettysburg Address.'" Which price—the harm of individuals or the loss of democracy—is higher to pay? Write a few paragraphs or short essay citing both Maggio and Kakutani in which you argue that one side of the bias-free language argument would result in larger consequences throughout society. Use your own experiences for support as well.

2. Rosalie Maggio writes that "The textbook on American government that consistently uses male pronouns for the president . . . reflects the fact that all our presidents have so far been men. But it also shapes a society in which the idea of a female president somehow 'doesn't sound right.'" Michiki Kakutani, however, queries whether or not "making such [politically correct] changes [in the English language will] remove the prejudice in people's minds." How closely linked are language and bias? Write a few paragraphs or short essay in which you discuss the extent to which language and bias are connected. Be sure to cite both Maggio's and Kakutani's essays as well as your own observations in order to illustrate your ideas.

Why We Need Bias-Free Language

Rosalie Maggio

Author of *The Nonsexist Word Finder* (1987), *How to Say It: Words, Phrases, Sentences, and Paragraphs for Every Situation* (1990), and *The Music Box* (1990) and editor of several college textbooks, Rosalie Maggio argues that as the United States continues to grow and become increasingly diverse, the need for explicit, accurate language becomes more acute. Further, the connection between language and law, says Maggio, makes clear, unbiased language essential, and only through such language can we hope for fair representation and recognition between different parties.

Pre-reading Questions

Freewrite for five to ten minutes in response to the following questions:
Have you ever been hurt or offended by someone's insensitive or inaccurate remarks about you? Describe the circumstances surrounding this incident. What role, if any, do you think political correctness would have played in helping make your situation less hurtful? Explain.

Vocabulary Preview

Vocabulary Words:
- contrary
- facilitated
- impoverishment
- grist
- ethnocentrism
- germane
- entity
- obscures
- generic
- subjective
- relinquish

Look up the words above and use them in sentences of varying length, structure, and style. Which words were easier or more difficult to use? Write a few sentences explaining which words were easiest to use and why.

1   Language both reflects and shapes society. The textbook on American government that consistently uses male pronouns for the president, even when not referring to a specific individual (e.g., "a president may cast his veto"), reflects the fact that all our presidents have so far been men. But it also shapes a society in which the idea of a female president somehow "doesn't sound right."

2   Culture shapes language and then language shapes culture. "Contrary to the assumption that language merely reflects social patterns such as sex-role stereotypes, research in linguistics and social psychology has shown that these are in fact facilitated and reinforced by language" (Marlis Hellinger, in *Language and Power,* ed., Cheris Kramarae et al.).

3   Biased language can also, says Sanford Berman, "powerfully harm people, as amply demonstrated by bigots' and tyrants' deliberate attempts to linguistically dehumanize and demean groups they intend to exploit, oppress, or exterminate. Calling Asians 'gooks' made it easier to kill them. Calling blacks 'niggers' made it simpler to enslave and brutalize them. Calling Native Americans 'primitives' and 'savages' made it okay to conquer and despoil them. And to talk of 'fishermen,' 'councilmen,' and 'longshoremen' is to clearly exclude and discourage women from those pursuits, to diminish and degrade them."

4   The question is asked: Isn't it silly to get upset about language when there are so many more important issues that need our attention?

5   First, it's to be hoped that there are enough of us working on issues large and small that the work will all get done—someday. Second, the interconnections between the way we think, speak, and act are beyond dispute. Language goes hand-in-hand with social change—both shaping it and reflecting it. Sexual harassment was not a term anyone used twenty years ago; today we have laws against it. How could we have the law without the language; how could we have the language without the law? In fact, the judicial system is a good argument for the importance of "mere words"; the legal profession devotes great energy to the precise interpretation of words—often with far-reaching and significant consequences.

6   On August 21, 1990, in the midst of the Iraqi offensive, front-page headlines told the big story: President Bush had used the word *hostages* for the first time. Up to that time, *detainee* had been used. The difference between two very similar words was of possible life-and-death proportions. In another situation—also said to be life-and-death by some people—the difference between *fetal tissue* and *unborn baby* (in referring to the very same thing) is arguably the most debated issue in the country. So, yes, words have power and deserve our attention.

7   Some people are like George Crabbe's friend: "Habit with him was all the test of truth, / it must be right: I've done it from my youth." They have come of age using *handicapped, black-and-white, leper, mankind,* and pseudogeneric *he;* these terms must therefore be correct. And yet if there's one thing consistent about language it is that language is constantly changing; when the *Random House Dictionary of the English Language: 2nd Edition* was published in 1988, it contained 50,000 new entries, most of them words that had come into use since 1966. There were also 75,000 new definitions. (Incidentally, *RHD-II* asks its readers to "use gender-neutral terms wherever possible" and it never uses *mankind* in definitions where *people* is meant, nor does it ever refer to anyone of unknown gender as *he.*) However, few supporters of bias-free language are asking for changes; it is rather a matter of choice—which of the many acceptable words available to us will we use?

8   A high school student who felt that nonsexist language did demand some changes said, "But you don't understand! You're trying to change the English language, which has been around a lot longer than women have!"

9   One reviewer of the first edition commented, "There's no fun in limiting how you say a thing." Perhaps not. Yet few people complain about looking up a point of grammar or usage or checking the dictionary for a correct spelling. Most writers are very fussy about finding the precise best word, the exact rhythmic vehicle for their ideas. Whether or not these limits "spoil their fun" is an individual judgment. However, most of us accept that saying or writing the first thing that comes to mind is not often the way we want to be remembered. So if we have to think a little, if we have to search for the unbiased word, the inclusive phrase, it is not any more effort than we expend on proper grammar, spelling, and style.

10   Other people fear "losing" words, as though there weren't more where those came from. We are limited only by our imaginations; vague, inaccurate, and disrespectful words can be thrown overboard with no loss to society and no impoverishment of the language.

11   Others are tired of having to "watch what they say." But what they perhaps mean is that they're tired of being sensitive to others' requests. From childhood onward, we

all learn to "watch what we say": we don't swear around our parents; we don't bring up certain topics around certain people; we speak differently to friend, boss, cleric, English teacher, lover, radio interviewer, child. Most of us are actually quite skilled at picking and choosing the appropriate words; it seems odd that we are too "tired" to call people what they want to be called.

12   The greatest objection to bias-free language is that it will lead us to absurdities. Critics have posited something utterly ridiculous, cleverly demonstrated how silly it is, and then accounted themselves victorious in the battle against linguistic massacre. For example: "So I suppose now we're going to say: He/she ain't heavy, Father/Sister; he/she's my brother/sister." "I suppose next it will be the 'ottoperson'." Cases have been built up against the mythic "woperson," "personipulate," and "personhole cover" (none of which has ever been advocated by any reputable sociolinguist). No grist appears too ridiculous for these mills. And, yes, they grind exceedingly small. Using a particular to condemn a universal is a fault in logic. But then ridicule, it is said, is the first and last argument of fools.

13   One of the most rewarding—and, for many people, the most unexpected—side effects of breaking away from traditional, biased language is a dramatic improvement in writing style. By replacing fuzzy, overgeneralized, cliché-ridden words with explicit, active words and by giving concrete examples and anecdotes instead of one-word-fits-all descriptions you can express yourself more dynamically, convincingly, and memorably.

14   "If those who have studied the art of writing are in accord on any one point, it is on this: the surest way to arouse and hold the attention of the reader is by being specific, definite, and concrete" (Strunk and White, *The Elements of Style*). Writers who talk about *brotherhood* or *spinsters* or *right-hand men* miss a chance to spark their writing with fresh descriptions; they leave their readers as uninspired as they are. Unthinking writing is also less informative. Why use the unrevealing *adman* when we could choose instead a precise, descriptive, inclusive word like *advertising executive, copywriter, account executive, ad writer,* or *media buyer?*

15   The word *manmade,* which seems so indispensable to us, doesn't actually say very much. Does it mean artificial? handmade? synthetic? fabricated? machine-made? custom-made? simulated? plastic? imitation? contrived?

16   Communication is—or ought to be—a two-way street. A speaker who uses *man* to mean *human being* while the audience hears it as *adult male* is an example of communication gone awry.

17   Bias-free language is logical, accurate, and realistic. Biased language is not. How logical is it to speak of the "discovery" of America, a land already inhabited by millions of people? Where is the accuracy in writing "Dear Sir" to a woman? Where is the realism in the full-page automobile advertisement that says in bold letters, "A good driver is the product of his environment," when more women than men influence car-buying decisions? Or how successful is the ad for a dot-matrix printer that says, "In 3,000 years, man's need to present his ideas hasn't changed. But his tools have," when many of these printers are bought and used by women, who also have ideas they need to present? And when we use stereotypes to talk about people ("isn't that just like a welfare mother/Indian/girl/old man"), our speech and writing will be inaccurate and unrealistic most of the time.

DEFINITION OF TERMS

Bias/Bias-Free

18   Biased language communicates inaccurately about what it means to be male or female; black or white; young or old; straight, gay, or bi; rich or poor; from one ethnic group or another; disabled or temporarily able-bodied; or to hold to a particular belief system. It reflects the same bias found in racism, sexism, ageism, handicappism, classism, ethnocentrism, anti-Semitism, homophobia, and other forms of discrimination.

19   Bias occurs in the language in several ways.

1. Leaving out individuals or groups. "Employees are welcome to bring their wives and children" leaves out those employees who might want to bring husbands, friends, or same-sex partners. "We are all immigrants in this country" leaves out Native Americans, who were here well before the first immigrants.

2. Making unwarranted assumptions. To address a sales letter about a new diaper to the mother assumes that the father won't be diapering the baby. To write "Anyone can use this fire safety ladder" assumes that all members of the household are able-bodied.

3. Calling individuals and groups by names or labels that they do not choose for themselves (e.g., *Gypsy, office girl, Eskimo, pygmy, Bushman, the elderly, colored man*) or terms that are derogatory (*fairy, libber, savage, bum, old goat*).

4. Stereotypical treatment that implies that all lesbians/Chinese/women/people with disabilities/teenagers are alike.

5. Unequal treatment of various groups in the same material.

6. Unnecessary mention of membership in a particular group. In a land of supposedly equal opportunity, of what importance is a person's race, sex, age, sexual orientation, disability, or creed? As soon as we mention one of these characteristics—without a good reason for doing so—we enter an area mined by potential linguistic disasters. Although there may be instances in which a person's sex, for example, is germane ("A recent study showed that female patients do not object to being cared for by male nurses"), most of the time it is not. Nor is mentioning a person's race, sexual orientation, disability, age, or belief system usually germane.

20   Bias can be overt or subtle. Jean Gaddy Wilson (in Brooks and Pinson, *Working with Words*) says, "Following one simple rule of writing or speaking will eliminate most biases. Ask yourself: Would you say the same thing about an affluent, white man?"

Inclusive/Exclusive

21   Inclusive language includes everyone; exclusive language excludes some people. The following quotation is inclusive: "The greatest revolution of our generation is the discovery that human beings, by changing the inner attitudes of their minds, can change the outer aspects of their lives" (William James). It is clear that James is speaking of all of us.

22   Examples of sex-exclusive writing fill most quotation books: "Man is the measure of all things" (Protagoras). "The People, though we think of a great entity when we use

the word, means nothing more than so many millions of individual men" (James Bryce). "Man is nature's sole mistake" (W.S. Gilbert).

Sexist/Nonsexist

23 Sexist language promotes and maintains attitudes that stereotype people according to gender while assuming that the male is the norm—the significant gender. Nonsexist language treats all people equally and either does not refer to a person's sex at all when it is irrelevant or refers to men and women in symmetrical ways.

24 "A society in which women are taught anything but the management of a family, the care of men, and the creation of the future generation is a society which is on the way out" (L. Ron Hubbard). "Behind every successful man is a woman—with nothing to wear" (L. Grant Glickman). "Nothing makes a man and wife feel closer, these days, than a joint tax return" (Gil Stern). These quotations display various characteristics of sexist writing: (1) stereotyping the entire sex by what might be appropriate for some of it; (2) assuming male superiority; (3) using unparallel terms (*man and wife* should be either *wife and husband/husband and wife* or *woman and man/man and woman*).

25 The following quotations clearly refer to all people: "It's really hard to be roommates with people if your suitcases are much better than theirs" (J. D. Salinger). "If people don't want to come out to the ball park, nobody's going to stop them" (Yogi Berra). "If men and women of capacity refuse to take part in politics and government, they condemn themselves, as well as the people, to the punishment of living under bad government" (Senator Sam J. Ervin). "I studied the lives of great men and famous women, and I found that the men and women who got to the top were those who did the jobs they had in hand, with everything they had of energy and enthusiasm and hard work" (Harry S. Truman).

Gender-Free/Gender-Fair/Gender-Specific

26 Gender-free terms do not indicate sex and can be used for either women/girls or men/boys (e.g., *teacher, bureaucrat, employee, hiker, operations manager, child, clerk, sales rep, hospital patient, student, grandparent, chief executive officer*).

27 Writing or speech that is gender-fair involves the symmetrical use of gender-specific words (e.g., *Ms. Leinwohl/Mr. Kelly, councilwoman/councilman, young man/young woman*) and promotes fairness to both sexes in the larger context. To ensure gender-fairness, ask yourself often: Would I write the same thing in the same way about a person of the opposite sex? Would I mind if this were said of me?

28 If you are describing the behavior of children on the playground, to be gender-fair you will refer to girls and boys an approximately equal number of times, and you will carefully observe what the children do, and not just assume that only the boys will climb to the top of the jungle gym and that only the girls will play quiet games.

29 Researchers studying the same baby described its cries as "anger" when they were told it was a boy and as "fear" when they were told it was a girl (cited in Cheris Kramarae, *The Voices and Words of Women and Men*). We are all victims of our unconscious and most deeply held biases.

30 Gender-specific words (for example, *alderwoman, businessman, altar girl*) are neither good nor bad in themselves. However, they need to be used gender-fairly; terms for women and terms for men should be used an approximately equal number of times

in contexts that do not discriminate against either of them. One problem with gender-specific words is that they identify and even emphasize a person's sex when it is not necessary (and is sometimes even objectionable) to do so. Another problem is that they are so seldom used gender-fairly.

31   Although gender-free terms are generally preferable, sometimes gender-neutral language obscures the reality of women's or men's oppression. *Battered spouse* implies that men and women are equally battered; this is far from true. *Parent* is too often taken to mean *mother* and obscures the fact that more and more fathers are very much involved in parenting; it is better here to use the gender-specific *fathers and mothers* or *mothers and fathers* than the gender-neutral *parents*.

Generic/Pseudogeneric

32   A generic is an all-purpose word that includes everybody (e.g., *workers, people, voters, civilians, elementary school students*). Generic pronouns include: *we, you, they*.

33   A pseudogeneric is a word that is used as though it included all people, but that in reality does not. *Mankind, forefathers, brotherhood,* and *alumni* are not generic because they leave out women. When used about Americans, *immigrants* leaves out all those who were here long before the first immigrants. "What a Christian thing to do!" uses *Christian* as a pseudogeneric for *kind* or *good-hearted* and leaves out all kind, good-hearted people who are not Christians.

34   Although some speakers and writers say that when they use *man* or *mankind* they mean everybody, their listeners and readers do not perceive the word that way and these terms are thus pseudogenerics. The pronoun *he* when used to mean *he and she* is another pseudogeneric.

35   Certain generic nouns are often assumed to refer only to men, for example, *politicians, physicians, lawyers, voters, legislators, clergy, farmers, colonists, immigrants, slaves, pioneers, settlers, members of the armed forces, judges, taxpayers*. References to "settlers, their wives, and children," or "those clergy permitted to have wives" are pseudogeneric.

36   In historical context it is particularly damaging for young people to read about settlers and explorers and pioneers as though they were all white men. Our language should describe the accomplishments of the human race in terms of all those who contributed to them.

SEX AND GENDER

37   An understanding of the difference between sex and gender is critical to the use of bias-free language.

38   Sex is biological: people with male genitals are male, and people with female genitals are female.

39   Gender is cultural: our notions of "masculine" tells us how we can expect men to behave and our notions of "feminine" tell us how we expect women to behave. Words like *womanly/manly, tomboy/sissy, unfeminine/unmasculine* have nothing to do with the person's sex; they are culturally acquired, subjective concepts about character traits and expected behaviors that vary from one place to another, from one individual to another.

40   It is biologically impossible for a woman to be a sperm donor. It may be culturally unusual for a man to be a secretary, but it is not biologically impossible. To say "the secretary . . . she" assumes all secretaries are women and is sexist because this issue is gender, not sex. Gender describes an individual's personal, legal, and social status without reference to genetic sex; gender is a subjective cultural attitude. Sex is an objective biological fact. Gender varies according to the culture. Sex is a constant.

41   The difference between sex and gender is important because much sexist language arises from cultural determinations of what a woman or man "ought" to be. Once a society decides, for example, that to be a man means to hide one's emotions, bring home a paycheck, and be able to discuss football standings while to be a woman means to be soft-spoken, love shopping, babies, and recipes, and "never have anything to wear," much of the population becomes a contradiction in terms—unmanly men and unwomanly women. Crying, nagging, gossiping, and shrieking are assumed to be women's lot; rough-housing, drinking beer, telling dirty jokes, and being unable to find one's socks and keys are laid at men's collective door. Lists of stereotypes appear silly because very few people fit them. The best way to ensure unbiased writing and speaking is to describe people as individuals, not as members of a set.

Gender Role Words

42   Certain sex-linked words depend for their meanings on cultural stereotypes: *feminine/masculine, manly/womanly, boyish/girlish, husbandly/wifely, fatherly/motherly, unfeminine/unmasculine, unmanly/unwomanly,* etc. What a person understands by these words will vary from culture to culture and even within a culture. Because the words depend for their meanings on interpretations of stereotypical behavior or characteristics, they may be grossly inaccurate when applied to individuals. Somewhere, sometime, men and women have said, thought, or done everything the other sex has said, thought, or done except for a very few sex-linked biological activities (e.g., only women can give birth or nurse a baby, only a man can donate sperm or impregnate a woman). To describe a woman as unwomanly is a contradiction in terms; if a woman is doing it, saying it, wearing it, thinking it, it must be—by definition—womanly.

43   F. Scott Fitzgerald did not use "feminine" to describe the unforgettable Daisy in *The Great Gatsby.* He wrote instead, "She laughed again, as if she said something very witty, and held my hand for a moment, looking up into my face, promising that there was no one in the world she so much wanted to see. That was a way she had." Daisy's charm did not belong to Woman; it was uniquely hers. Replacing vague sex-linked descriptors with thoughtful words that describe an individual instead of a member of a set can lead to language that touches people's minds and hearts.

NAMING

44   Naming is power, which is why the issue of naming is one of the most important in bias-free language.

Self-Definition

45   People decide what they want to be called. The correct names for individuals and groups are always those by which they refer to themselves. This "tradition" is not always

unchallenged. Haig Bosmajian (*The Language of Oppression*) says, "It isn't strange that those persons who insist on defining themselves, who insist on this elemental privilege of self-naming, self-definition, and self-identity encounter vigorous resistance. Predictably, the resistance usually comes from the oppressor or would-be oppressor and is a result of the fact that he or she does not want to relinquish the power which comes from the ability to define others."

46   Dr. Ian Hancock uses the term *exonym* for a name applied to a group by outsiders. For example, Romani peoples object to being called by the exonym *Gypsies.* They do not call themselves Gypsies. Among the many other exonyms are: the elderly, colored people, homosexuals, pagans, adolescents, Eskimos, pygmies, savages. The test for an exonym is whether people describe themselves as "redmen," "illegal aliens," "holy rollers," etc., or whether only outsiders describe them that way.

47   There is a very small but visible element today demanding that gay men "give back" the word *gay*—a good example of denying people the right to name themselves. A late-night radio caller said several times that gay men had "stolen" this word from "our" language. It was not clear what language gay men spoke.

48   A woman nicknamed "Betty" early in life has always preferred her full name, "Elizabeth." On her fortieth birthday, she reverted to Elizabeth. An acquaintance who heard about the change said sharply, "I'll call her Betty if I like!"

49   We can call them Betty if we like, but it's arrogant, insensitive, and uninformed: the only rule we have in this area says we call people what they want to be called.

"Insider/Outsider" Rule

50   A related rule says that insiders may describe themselves in ways that outsiders may not. "Crip" appears in the *Disability Rag;* this does not mean that the word is available to anyone who wants to use it. "Big Fag" is printed on a gay man's T-shirt. He may use that expression; a non-gay may not so label him. One junior-high student yells to another, "Hey, nigger!" This would be highly offensive and inflammatory if the speaker were not African American. A group of women talk about "going out with the girls," but a co-worker should not refer to them as "girls." When questioned about just such a situation, Miss Manners replied that "people are allowed more leeway in what they call themselves than in what they call others."

"People First" Rule

51   Haim Ginott taught us that labels are disabling; intuitively most of us recognize this and resist being labeled. The disability movement originated the "people first" rule, which says we don't call someone a "diabetic" but rather a "person with diabetes." Saying someone is "an AIDS victim" reduces the person to a disease, a label, a statistic; use instead "a person with/who has/living with AIDS." The 1990 Americans with Disabilities Act is a good example of correct wording. Name the person as a person first, and let qualifiers (age, sex, disability, race) follow, but (and this is crucial) only if they are relevant. Readers of a magazine aimed at an older audience were asked what they wanted to be called (elderly? senior citizens? seniors? golden agers?). They rejected all the terms; one said, "How about 'people'?" When high

school students rejected labels like kids, teens, teenagers, youth, adolescents, and juveniles, and were asked in exasperation just what they would like to be called, they said, "Could we just be people?"

Women as Separate People

52   One of the most sexist maneuvers in the language has been the identification of women by their connections to husband, son, or father—often even after he is dead. Women are commonly identified as someone's widow while men are never referred to as anyone's widower. Marie Marvingt, a French-woman who lived around the turn of the century, was an inventor, adventurer, stunt woman, superathlete, aviator, and all-around scholar. She chose to be affianced to neither man (as a wife) nor God (as a religious), but it was not long before an uneasy male press found her a fit partner. She is still known today by the revealing label "the Fiancée of Danger." If a connection is relevant, make it mutual. Instead of "Freida, his wife of seventeen years," write "Freida and Eric, married for seventeen years."

53   It is difficult for some people to watch women doing unconventional things with their names. For years the etiquette books were able to tell us precisely how to address a single woman, a married woman, a divorced woman, or a widowed woman (there was no similar etiquette on men because they have always been just men and we never had a code to signal their marital status). But now some women are Ms. and some are Mrs., some are married but keeping their birth names, others are hyphenating their last name with their husband's, and still others have constructed new names for themselves. Some women—including African American women who were denied this right earlier in our history—take great pride in using their husband's name. All these forms are correct. The same rule of self-definition applies here: call the woman what she wants to be called.

POST-READING QUESTIONS

CONTENT

1. What role, according to Maggio, does language play in society and culture?

2. Summarize the reasons Maggio offers against having bias-free language. How persuasive are these reasons?

3. What are at least three ways Maggio claims bias occurs in language? What main idea connects all these ways? Explain.

4. What are "gender-free," "gender-fair," and "gender-specific" terms? Can these terms be broadened to include language that is biased in terms of race, religion, or disability? Explain and give examples.

5. What does Maggio mean by "generic" words? By "pseudogeneric" words? How can pseudogeneric words be harmful?

6. Why do you think Maggio considers "naming" to be so important? Cite at least three examples from the text.

STYLE AND STRUCTURE

7. What is Maggio's primary argument? Restate her main idea in your own words.

8. What are some sub-arguments that Maggio makes in order to better establish her main idea? Of these, which do you think are most significant in terms of helping Maggio be convincing?

9. What kinds of examples does Maggio use in order to illustrate her ideas? Of these, which do you find most convincing?

10. What is Maggio's tone? In what ways, if any, does her tone contribute to her persuasiveness?

11. Who is Maggio's audience? How much are you a part of her audience?

12. Is Maggio convincing overall? Explain.

CRITICAL THINKING AND ANALYSIS

DISCUSSION QUESTIONS

13. How important do you think political correctness is? For whom, if anyone, is it most important? Why?

14. What steps can people take in order to ensure that their language is sensitive and accurate? How realistic is it to think that people will employ these steps? Explain.

WRITING ASSIGNMENTS

15. Maggio writes that "Culture shapes language and then language shapes culture." What do you think? Write a few paragraphs or short essay in which you explain how language and culture do or do not "shape" each other. Be sure to define what you mean by "shaping" and use examples both from Maggio's essay and from your own experiences in order to illustrate your ideas.

16. Maggio writes that "Naming is power . . . ." What do you think? Write a few paragraphs or short essay illustrating how the act of naming is also an act of power. You may focus on the use of positive or derogatory names in your writing; just be sure to cite Maggio and your own experiences for strength and clarity.

17. Maggio refers to Haim Ginott who, she claims, "taught us that labels are disabling." Is this right? Write at least two well-developed paragraphs in which you argue that labels are, or do not necessarily have to be, disabling. Cite Maggio and your own life for support.

VOCABULARY DEVELOPMENT

18. Maggio writes, "Certain sex-linked words depend for their meaning on cultural stereotypes: . . ." Choose at least three of such expressions (you may refer to Maggio's list in her essay, if you wish), define each expression and

explain its connection to sexual stereotypes. For instance, if you choose the word "boyish," write what that word means for you, and then explain how that meaning is somehow linked to a stereotype.

GROUP ACTIVITIES

19. Choose a topic that lends itself to some sort of bias, such as sports, beauty, hair loss, or giving birth. Then, write a paragraph on this topic exaggerating the "correctness" of your language, singling no one out in terms of gender, race, religion, or any other means of distinguishing people. Next, revise the paragraph in order to be more readable, without exaggeration. How difficult is using correct language? Share your conclusions with the class.

20. As a group, skim a number of publications targeting different audiences: a newspaper, a fashion magazine, or a sports magazine, for instance. Examine the language in each publication and then write a paragraph explaining how the language you found either was or was not biased in some way. Share your results with the class.

The Word Police

Michiko Kakutani

A staff writer for *The New York Times,* Michiko Kakutani writes that while people should of course strive for sensitivity and accuracy in their language, they should also be realistic in what they hope to accomplish. Simply changing the labeling of situations and people, according to Kakutani, can have harmful effects, minimizing the plight of those whose misfortune has been euphemized, or even censoring ideas in the name of fairness.

Pre-writing Questions

Freewrite for five to ten minutes in response to the following questions:
What is your opinion of the political correctness movement? Do you think political correctness can be overused? How so? What examples of politically correct language can you think of that are particularly effective or ineffective?

Vocabulary Preview

Vocabulary Words:
- puritanical
- zeal
- talismanic
- orthodoxy
- parody
- meticulous
- hierarchical
- rhetorically
- connotations
- semantics
- euphemism
- androgynous

Look up the words above, paying attention to how they are used in Kakutani's text as you read. Then, after reading the essay, substitute synonyms for each word above (you may consult a thesaurus if you wish, but you do not need to). What effect do your substitutions have on the overall meaning of the sentences you revise? Explain the effects of your revisions in a few sentences.

---

1   This month's inaugural festivities, with their celebration, in Maya Angelou's words, of "humankind"—"the Asian, the Hispanic, the Jew/The African, the Native American, the Sioux,/The Catholic, the Muslim, the French, the Greek/The Irish, the Rabbi, the Priest, the Sheik,/The Gay, the Straight, the Preacher,/The privileged, the homeless, the Teacher"—constituted a kind of official embrace of multiculturalism and a new politics of inclusion.

2   The mood of political correctness, however, has already made firm inroads into popular culture. Washington boasts a store called Politically Correct that sells pro-whale, anti-meat, ban-the-bomb T-shirts, bumper stickers and buttons, as well as a local cable television show called "Politically Correct Cooking" that features interviews in the kitchen with representatives from groups like People for the Ethical Treatment of Animals.

3   The Coppertone suntan lotion people are planning to give their longtime cover girl, Little Miss (Ms?) Coppertone, a male equivalent, Little Mr. Coppertone. And even Su-

perman (Super-person?) is rumored to be returning this spring, reincarnated as four ethically diverse clones: an African-American, an Asian, a Caucasian and a Latino.

4   Nowhere is this P.C. mood more striking than in the increasingly noisy debate over language that has moved from university campuses to the country at large—a development that both underscores Americans' puritanical zeal for reform and their unwavering faith in the talismanic power of words.

5   Certainly no decent person can quarrel with the underlying impulse behind political correctness: a vision of a more just, inclusive society in which racism, sexism and prejudice of all sorts have been erased. But the methods and fervor of the self-appointed language police can lead to a rigid orthodoxy—and unintentional self-parody—opening the movement to the scorn of conservative opponents and the mockery of cartoonists and late-night television hosts.

6   It's hard to imagine women earning points for political correctness by saying "ovarimony" instead of "testimony"—as one participant at the recent Modern Language Association convention was overheard to suggest. It's equally hard to imagine people wanting to flaunt their lack of prejudice by giving up such words and phrases as "bull market," "kaiser roll," "Lazy Susan," and "charley horse."

7   Several books on a bias-free language have already appeared, and the 1991 edition of the Random House Webster's College Dictionary boasts an appendix titled "Avoiding Sexist Language." The dictionary also includes such linguistic mutations as "womyn" (women, "used as an alternative spelling to avoid the suggestion of sexism perceived in the sequence m-e-n") and "waitron" (a gender-blind term for waiter or waitress).

8   Many of these dictionaries and guides not only warn the reader against offensive racial and sexual slurs, but also try to establish and enforce a whole new set of usage rules. Take, for instance, "The Bias-Free Word Finder, a Dictionary of Nondiscriminatory Language" by Rosalie Maggio (Beacon Press)—a volume often indistinguishable, in its meticulous solemnity, from the tongue-in-cheek "Official Politically Correct Dictionary and Handbook" put out last year by Henry Beard and Christopher Cerf (Villard Books). Ms. Maggio's book supplies the reader intent on using kinder, gentler language with writing guidelines as well as a detailed listing of more than 5,000 "biased words and phrases."

9   Whom are these guidelines for? Somehow one has a tough time picturing them replacing "Fowler's Modern English Usage" in the classroom, or being adopted by the average man (sorry, individual) in the street.

10 The "pseudogeneric 'he,'" we learn from Ms. Maggio, is to be avoided like the plague, as is the use of the word "man" to refer to humanity. "Fellow," "king," "lord" and "master" are bad because they're "male-oriented words," and "king," "lord" and "master" are especially bad because they're also "hierarchical, dominator society terms." The politically correct lion becomes the "monarch of the jungle," new-age children play "someone on top of the heap," and the "Mona Lisa" goes down in history as Leonardo's "acme of perfection."

11 As for the word "black," Ms. Maggio says it should be excised from terms with a negative spin: she recommends substituting words like "mouse" for "black eye," "ostracize" for "blackball," "payola" for "blackmail" and "outcast" for "black sheep."

Clearly, some of these substitutions work better than others: somehow the "sinister humor" of Kurt Vonnegut or "Saturday Night Live" doesn't quite make it; nor does the "denouncing" of the Hollywood 10.

12   For the dedicated user of politically correct language, all these rules can make for some messy moral dilemmas. Whereas "battered wife" is a gender-biased term, the gender-free term "battered spouse," Ms. Maggio notes, incorrectly implies "that men and women are equally battered."

13   On one hand, say Francine Wattman Frank and Paula A. Treichler in their book "Language, Gender, and Professional Writing" (Modern Language Association), "he or she" is an appropriate construction for talking about an individual (like a jockey, say) who belongs to a profession that's predominantly male—it's a way of emphasizing "that such occupations are not barred to women or that women's concerns need to be kept in mind." On the other hand, they add, using masculine pronouns rhetorically can underscore ongoing male dominance in those fields, implying the need for change.

14   And what about the speech codes adopted by some universities in recent years? Although they were designed to prohibit students from uttering sexist and racist slurs, they would extend, by logic, to blacks who want to use the word "nigger" to strip the term of its racist connotations, or homosexuals who want to use the word "queer" to reclaim it from bigots.

15   In her book, Ms. Maggio recommends applying bias-free usage retroactively: she suggests paraphrasing politically incorrect quotations, or replacing "the sexist words or phrases with the ellipsis dots and/or bracketed substitutes," or using "sic" "to show that the sexist words come from the original quotation and to call attention to the fact that they are incorrect."

16   Which leads the skeptical reader of "The Bias-Free Word Finder" to wonder whether "All the King's Men" should be retitled "All the Ruler's People"; "Pet Cemetery," "Animal Companion Graves"; "Birdman of Alcatraz," "Bird-person of Alcatraz," and "The Iceman Cometh," "The Ice Route Driver Cometh"?

17   Will making such changes remove the prejudice in people's minds? Should we really spend time trying to come up with non-male-based alternatives to "Midas touch," "Achilles' heel," and "Montezuma's revenge"? Will tossing out Santa Claus—whom Ms. Maggio accuses of reinforcing "the cultural male-as-norm system"—in favor of Belfana, his Italian female alter ego, truly help banish sexism? Can the avoidance of "violent expressions and metaphors" like "kill two birds with one stone," "sock it to em" or "kick an idea around" actually promote a more harmonious world?

18   The point isn't that the excesses of the word police are comical. The point is that their intolerance (in the name of tolerance) has disturbing implications. In the first place, getting upset by phrases like "bullish on America" or "the City of Brotherly Love" tends to distract attention from the real problems of prejudice and injustice that exist in society at large, turning them into mere questions of semantics. Indeed, the emphasis currently put on politically correct usage has uncanny parallels with the academic movement of deconstruction—a method of textual analysis that focuses on language and linguistic pyrotechnics—which has become firmly established on university campuses.

19   In both cases, attention is focused on surfaces, on words and metaphors; in both cases, signs and symbols are accorded more importance than content. Hence, the attempt by some radical advocates to remove "The Adventures of Huckleberry Finn" from curriculums on the grounds that Twain's use of the word "nigger" makes the book a racist text—never mind the fact that this American classic (written in 1884) depicts the spiritual kinship achieved between a white boy and a runaway slave, never mind the fact that the "nigger" Jim emerges as the novel's most honorable, decent character.

20   Ironically enough, the P.C. movement's obsession with language is accompanied by a strange Orwellian willingness to warp the meaning of words by placing them under a high-powered ideological lens. For instance, the "Dictionary of Cautionary Words and Phrases"—a pamphlet issued by the University of Missouri's Multicultural Management Program to help turn "today's journalists into tomorrow's multicultural newsroom managers"—warns that using the word "articulate" to describe members of a minority group can suggest the opposite, "that 'those people' are not considered well educated, articulate and the like."

21   The pamphlet patronizes minority groups, by cautioning the reader against using the words "lazy" and "burly" to describe any member of such groups; and it issues a similar warning against using words like "gorgeous" and "petite" to describe women.

22   As euphemism proliferates with the rise of political correctness, there is a spread of the sort of sloppy, abstract language that Orwell said is "designed to make lies sound truthful and murder respectable, and to give an appearance of solidity to pure wind." "Fat" becomes "big boned" or "differently sized"; "stupid" becomes "exceptional"; "stoned" becomes "chemically inconvenienced."

23   Wait a minute here! Aren't such phrases eerily reminiscent of the euphemisms coined by the Government during Vietnam and Watergate? Remember how the military used to speak of "pacification," or how President Richard M. Nixon's press secretary, Ronald L. Zeigler, tried to get away with calling a lie an "inoperative statement"?

24   Calling the homeless "the underhoused" doesn't give them a place to live; calling the poor "the economically marginalized" doesn't help them pay the bills. Rather, by playing down their plight, such language might even make it easier to shrug off the seriousness of their situation.

25   Instead of allowing free discussion and debate to occur, many gung-ho advocates of politically correct language seem to think that the simple suppression of a word or concept will magically make the problem disappear. In the "Bias-Free Word Finder," Ms. Maggio entreats the reader not to perpetuate the negative stereotype of Eve. "Be extremely cautious in referring to the biblical Eve," she writes; "this story has profoundly contributed to negative attitudes toward women throughout history, largely because of misogynistic and patriarchal interpretations that labeled her evil, inferior, and seductive."

26   The story of Bluebeard, the rake (whoops!—the libertine) who killed his seven wives, she says, is also to be avoided, as is the biblical story of Jezebel. Of Jesus Christ, Ms. Maggio writes: "There have been few individuals in history as completely androgynous as Christ, and it does his message a disservice to overinsist on his maleness." She doesn't give the reader any hints on how this might be accomplished; presumably, one is supposed to avoid describing him as the Son of God.

27   Of course, the P.C. police aren't the only ones who want to proscribe what people should say or give them guidelines for how they may use an idea; Jesse Helms and his supporters are up to exactly the same thing when they propose to patrol the boundaries of the permissible in art. In each case, the would-be censor aspires to suppress what he or she finds distasteful—all, of course, in the name of the public good.

28   In the case of the politically correct, the prohibition of certain words, phrases and ideas is advanced in the cause of building a brave new world free of racism and hate, but this vision of harmony clashes with the very ideals of diversity and inclusion that the multi-cultural movement holds dear, and it's purchased at the cost of freedom of expression and freedom of speech.

29   In fact, the utopian world envisioned by the language police would be bought at the expense of the ideals of individualism and democracy articulated in "The Gettysburg Address": "Fourscore and seven years ago our fathers brought forth on this continent a new nation, conceived in liberty and dedicated to the proposition that all men are created equal."

30   Of course, the P.C. police have already found Lindoln's words hopelessly "phallocentric." No doubt they would rewrite the passage: "Fourscore and seven years ago our foremothers and forefathers brought forth on this continent a new nation, formulated with liberty, and dedicated to the proposition that all humankind is created equal."

POST-READING QUESTIONS

CONTENT

1. What does Kakutani say "the methods and fervor of the self-appointed language police" can lead to? What do you think?

2. To what does Kakutani compare "The Bias-Free Word Finder"? What does this comparison say about the nature of the text in question?

3. What are some examples of political correctness that Kakutani criticizes?

4. What does Kakutani say is "the point" of the "word police excesses"?

5. What is one negative effect of creating politically correct euphemisms with which to describe people, according to Kakutani?

6. To whom does Kakutani compare the "word police" in their efforts to eliminate certain kinds of language? How is this comparison significant?

STYLE AND STRUCTURE

7. What does Kakutani's attitude toward the political correctness movement seem to be in her first four paragraphs? How does this introduction help or detract from her main idea?

8. What is Kakutani's primary argument? Restate her main idea in your own words.

9. What examples does Kakutani offer to support her ideas? Of these, which do you find most compelling? Why?

10. Who is Kakutani's audience? To what extent are you part of her audience?

11. What is Kakutani's tone? Cite the text for examples of her tone.

12. Is Kakutani convincing? Explain.

CRITICAL THINKING AND ANALYSIS

DISCUSSION QUESTIONS

13. Can the issue of political correctness be taken too far? Explain.

14. To what extent do you think that political correctness should be applied retroactively? Should these applications include all areas of life, including, for instance, art that depicts slavery or other discriminatory institutions? Explain.

WRITING ASSIGNMENTS

15. Kakutani writes, "The mood of political correctness . . . has already made firm inroads into popular culture." To what extent is this true? Write at least one well-developed paragraph in which you explain whether or not the political correctness movement has effected changes in society. Cite Kakutani and your own observations for support.

16. Kakutani writes of speech codes on university campuses that prohibit racist or otherwise derogatory language. Are you in favor of such codes? Write a few paragraphs or short essay in which you argue that certain language should or should not be prohibited on campus. Cite Kakutani and your own experiences in order to illustrate your ideas.

17. Kakutani claims that "by playing down [the homeless's] plight [through euphemistic politically correct language], such language might even make it easier to shrug off the seriousness of their situation." Is she right? Write a few paragraphs discussing how certain language can or cannot make issues seem more or less important than they really are. Use examples from Kakutani's essay as well as from your own life in order to strengthen and clarify your ideas.

VOCABULARY DEVELOPMENT

18. What words or expressions best communicate Kakutani's tone? Choose at least five such words or expressions and explain why, to you, they best reveal Kakutani's tone in her essay.

GROUP ACTIVITIES

19. Choose an article from a publication that traditionally targets a specific audience, such as *The Gentleman's Quarterly, Glamour,* or *Essence.* Then, revise one paragraph from that article, eliminating any language that you feel is not politically correct. What effect do your revisions have on the meaning and tone of the paragraph? Share your results with the class.

20. Make a list of words or expressions that somehow identify people according to a characteristic other than their humanity ("AIDS victim" and "wife" are two examples). Then, substitute your own words—either real or invented—for the words on the list. What substitutions sound most reasonable? Why? Share your results with the class in an effort to determine what types of language changes are most likely to occur and continue.

SYNTHESIS QUESTIONS

1. Rick Reilly not-so-subtly pokes fun at educators and parents who he thinks go overboard in trying to be sensitive to their children's feelings, and Barbara Ehrenreich explains how overt attempts at friendliness actually make consumers feel uncomfortable. Can people be too polite? Write a few paragraphs or short essay in which you argue whether or not it is possible for people to be "too polite." Cite Reilly's and Ehrenreich's essays and your own experiences for support.

2. Tim Vanderpool writes of people penalized for helping illegal immigrants, and Barbara Ehrenreich criticizes companies that require their employees to be "perky all day to people [they] don't know and probably wouldn't like if [they] did." Can employing civility ever be wrong? Write at least one well-developed paragraph in which you argue whether or not being civil can be the wrong way to act. Cite Vanderpool and Ehrenreich and other writers from this chapter for support, as well as drawing from your own observations.

3. Patt Morrison writes of major problems caused by overpopulation: "Every lane of roadway too crowded, forests leveled for housing timber or grazing land, not enough clean water, not enough clean air, not enough open space. . . . Just too damn many [people]." But Tim Vanderpool writes of "compassionate [border] residents, who straddle a precarious line between performing good deeds and breaking the law." At what point, if any, should compassion for needy people stop? Write a few paragraphs or an essay in which you argue that helping less fortunate people, or countries, should or should not have limits. Be sure to cite Morrison and Vanderpool and your own observations for support.

4. Tim Vanderpool cites penalties of $250,000 and up to 10 years of jail time for citizens who harbor or aid illegal immigrants, but Patt Morrison claims that "If it weren't for huge international aid programs, no doubt Egypt would be starving tomorrow." How tough should penalties, or restrictions, for assisting others be? Write a few paragraphs or short essay in which you argue that good Samaritans should or should not be restricted or punished in their efforts to aid others. Cite these writers and draw from your own experiences and observations in order to strengthen your argument.

5. Barbara Ehrenreich writes of the "civility glut" that has arisen from companies' monitoring their employees "to make sure there are no lapses in positive attitude," while Patt Morrison bemoans the fact that humans have worsened the

problem of overpopulation by using "our brains to make tools . . . to defeat almost every natural predator." Choose an issue of any scale where civility plays a role—food service in a restaurant or world hunger, for instance—and write a letter to an audience of your choice recommending levels of concern for others. For example, recommend that food servers should only be polite when they feel like it, to ensure sincerity, or that international aid groups should only feed the hungry who are the victims of natural disasters. Just be sure to narrow the scope of your argument, and cite at least three writers from this chapter for support. You may also want to consult outside sources in order to learn more about your chosen issue.

6. Rick Reilly mocks school activists who, he feels, go too far in fostering political correctness on the playground while Michiko Kakutani writes of the "comical" revisions in language that bias-free wording would effect. At what point does civility become ridiculous? Choose an issue in which civility plays a role—making small talk, table manners, driving etiquette, to name a few—and argue in a short essay for the proper place for civility to be discontinued. For example, if you think that any instance of "artificial" politeness should be eliminated, then give examples illustrating the differences between "real" and "artificial" civility. Or, if you think that civility is always appropriate, offer numerous examples of how civility is never out of place. (You may have a more difficult time making a "reasonable" argument for such an absolute stance.) Be sure to cite at least three readings from this chapter as well as your own experiences for support.

7. Barbara Ehrenreich writes, "civility is also about class, and hence about forms of exclusion and oppression," while Rosalie Maggio claims that linguistically demeaning people through biased language helps bigots and tyrants, as Sanford Berman states, "to exploit, oppress, or exterminate" those they wish to dominate. How exclusive, or even oppressive, can civility be? Write a few paragraphs or short essay in which you explain whether or not civility can cause people to be excluded or treated negatively. Be sure to cite both Ehrenreich and Maggio and your own life for support.

8. Michiko Kakutani writes that "many gung-ho advocates of politically correct language seem to think that simple suppression of a word or concept will magically make the problem [of discrimination] disappear," but Barbara Ehrenreich raises the question of what happens when people display friendliness with an "edge of hostility." Does civility make a difference in how a situation is resolved? If so, at what point? Write a few paragraphs or short essay in which you discuss the point at which civility can make a difference in the outcome of a situation. Be sure to describe the situation fully, and then explain what about civility's presence causes the situation to take the course it does.

Credits

"Etiquette On a Generation of Teens," © 2000, *Los Angeles Times.*

Firstenberg, Jean Picker. "On Heroes and the Media." American Film, 1987.

Fish, Stanley. "Reverse Racism or How the Pot Got to Call the Kettle Black," *The Atlantic Monthly,* Nov. 1993.

"Profits by the Gross." Reprinted by permission of Forbes Magazine © 2001 Forbes Inc.

"Anywhere But Here" by Anne Taylor Fleming, © 1999 *Los Angeles Times.*

From ALL I REALLY NEED TO KNOW I LEARNED IN KINDERGARTEN by Robert L. Fulghum, copyright © 1986, 1988 by Robert L. Fulghum. Used by permission of Villard Books, a division of Random House, Inc.

"Desk Rage Takes Toll in Work Place" by Lisa Girion, © 2000, *Los Angeles Times.*

Goodman, Ellen. "The Reasonable Woman Standard." *Boston Globe.*

Grimsley, Kirstin Downey. "Service with a Forced Smile," © 1998, *The Washington Post.* Reprinted with permission.

Gould, Stephen Jay. "Nonmoral Nature." With permission from *Natural History* (February, 1982). Copyright © the American Museum of Natural History (1982).

Horowitz, Craig. "Law and Disorder: How the Juvenile Justice System is Letting Kids Get Away with Murder," *New York Magazine*: January 10, 1994.

"How Cops Go Bad," Time 12/15/97, © 1997 Time Inc. Reprinted by permission.

Jarrett, Joyce M. "Freedom," reprinted by permission of author.

Johnson, Julie. "Along for the Ride: Reality Journalism and the Right to Privacy," The Harvard International Journal of Press/Politics, 4:3 (Summer, 1999), pp. 106–112. © 1999 by the President and Fellows of Harvard College and the Massachusetts Institute of Technology.

Kakutani, M. "The Word Police" (1/31/93), © *The New York Times*

Kysar, Leila. " A Logger's Lament," reprinted by permission of the author.

From BIRD BY BIRD by Anne Lamott, copyright © 1994 by Anne Lamott. Used by permission of Pantheon Books, a division of Random House, Inc.

Lawrence, B. "Four Letter Words Can Hurt You" (10/27/73), © *The New York Times.*

Loh, Sandra Tsing. "The Return of Doris Day." Reprinted by permission of International Creative Management, Inc. Copyright ©1995 by Sandra Tsing Loh.

"Kelley's Shows . . ." by Brian Lowry, © 1999, *Los Angeles Times.*

The Dictionary of Bias-Free Usage: A Guide to Nondiscriminatory Language, Rosalie Maggio. Copyright © 1991 by Oryx Press. Reproduced by permission of Greenwood Publishing Group, Inc., Westport, CT.

Manners, John and Susan Opton. *Money* magazine, © 1993 Time Inc. All rights reserved.

"Marilyn Monroe," *Time* 6/14/99. © 1999 Time Inc. Reprinted by permission.

Marks, John. "The American Uncivil Wars." Copyright 1996 U.S. News & World Report, L.P. Reprinted with permission.

McCormick, Patrick. "Out of the Closet and Into Your Livingroom." Reprinted with permission from *U.S. Catholic* magazine, Claretian Publications, www. uscatholic.org. 800-328-6515.

"Larger Than Life" by Phil Sudo in SCHOLASTIC UPDATE, November 1990. Copyright © 1990 by Scholastic Inc. Reprinted by permission.

Vanderpool, Tim. "Border 'Samaritans' Risk the Law to Offer Aid; Humanitarian Crisis Prompts More Arizona Residents to Feed, Shelter Illegal Immigrants," published in The Christian Science Monitor, Aug. 4, 2000.

"Am I Blue?" from LIVING BY THE WORD: SELECTED WRITINGS 1973–1987, copyright © 1986 by Alice Walker, reprinted by permission of Harcourt, Inc.

From THE GOOD MARRIAGE by Judith S. Wallerstein and Sandra Blakeslee. Copyright © 1995 by Judith S. Wallerstein and Sandra Blakeslee. Reprinted by permission of Houghton Mifflin Company. All rights reserved.

Index